W9-ACU-146

$23.25

Fences
&
Retaining Walls

by

William McElroy

Craftsman Book Company

6058 Corte del Cedro, P.O. Box 6500, Carlsbad, CA 92008

Acknowledgements

The author thanks *Wolcott's Inc.*, 15124-6 Downey Avenue, Paramount, California 90723 for permission to include copies of their business forms in the Contractor's Law chapter of this book.

Library of Congress Cataloging-in-Publication Data

McElroy, William.
   Fences & retaining walls / by William McElroy.
     p.   cm.
   Includes index.
   ISBN 0-934041-53-9
   1. Fences—Design and construction. 2. Walls—Design and
construction. 3. Retaining walls—Design and construction.
4. Gates—Design and construction. 5. Construction industry-
-Management. I. Title. II. Title: Fences and retaining walls.
   TH4965.M38   1990
   717—dc20   90-2211
                                         CIP

Contents

one

Fence and Wall Specialties

*I*t's hard to imagine a world without fences. We need them to keep some things in and other things out. We need them to preserve our privacy. A world without fences? Not likely. And that's why fence building is good business for construction contractors. Nearly every significant new construction project includes a fence or wall. If you're qualified to build fences and retaining walls, there will be work to bid on nearly every job. That can help build a nice extra profit into every project you handle.

This book is written for professional fence and retaining wall builders. Maybe you're already a licensed contractor. Maybe you're working in the trade on the payroll of a contractor. Maybe you're building your first fence. Or maybe you're a student who wants to learn fence and wall building. It doesn't matter, this manual has the information you need.

Established contractors will learn the fine points of fence building — including suggestions on dealing with customers, employees and the I.R.S. After reading this book, you'll probably want to pass it along to a friend, apprentice, or new employee.

If you're new to fence building, you should have no trouble following my explanations. I'll take it step by step and include all the pictures you could want. That should make it easier to learn the essentials of fence building.

If you're an apprentice studying for your license, this book is for you. I wrote it with the California C-13 Fence Contractor's license exam in mind. Between the covers of this manual you'll find answers to nearly all the questions on the exam. The business chapters will help you set up your own contracting business and keep you from making expensive mistakes.

For the homeowner building a first fence, I've provided simplified designs and construction techniques. The section on fence and retaining wall problems can help you avoid mistakes others have made. You'll also learn to fix existing fences and walls. I've included a glossary of terms, so when you talk to suppliers and contractors, you'll be speaking their language.

Teachers can use this book as a course manual. It covers everything from setting up a business, selling and preparing legal contracts, to building fences and walls. Throughout this manual I've tried to use plain conversational English that's easy for students to follow.

All readers will benefit from the chapter on safety.

You'll learn about all kinds of fences, gates, retaining walls, sea walls, and railings. We'll cover the most familiar types and styles of fences and walls, and several uncommon types. I'll describe all the common construction methods and dozens of materials. You'll see what kinds of equipment you need to build each type of fence. And I've included a section on estimating costs and man-hours.

With all this in mind, let's start with:

The History of Fences

The first true fences were probably barriers to animals. For protection, primitive people probably used piles of rocks or logs to protect their possessions and families from other tribes. Rocks were laid in horizontal courses and held in place with mud. The first mortars were dried mud or earth. Even at this early time, fence building must have become a skill to be learned and passed from generation to generation.

Early tribes were nomad hunters who traveled from place to place. Fences didn't have to be any more than temporary. As time passed, people learned to grow crops and domesticate animals. At this point, they needed more permanent ways to mark off their fields and corral their livestock. They made fences from rocks or trees cleared from their planting fields. They made corrals by suspending vines and rope between logs and trees — the forerunner of the barbed wire fence.

In areas of the world where trees and rocks aren't readily available, people had to make fences out of soil. Ordinary dirt mixed with water can be molded into a building block. But dry blocks of dirt erode very easily in the rain. Some earth materials hold up better when wet. Clay from river banks, ponds, and mines, for example, was used to make more durable adobe block. Then someone discovered that heating clay fire-hardened and waterproofed the blocks.

Centuries later we learned to draw heated metal through a small hole, turning it into wire. That's a fine material to fence in animals and fence out trespassers.

People are very adaptable. In their search for homes near food, entertainment, work and riches, they sometimes built homes on the edges of mountains, oceans, and rivers. But nature is an unpredictable adversary. Mountains fall, oceans rise, and rivers flood. That's why man invented retaining walls, sea walls, and dikes. Cement made all that possible. Mix cement with sand, gravel and water. Then form and cure the mix to hold back that mountain, ocean, or river.

Even though people are independent by nature, they need each other. They formed groups that developed into towns and cities. As people moved closer together, the urge to maintain privacy increased. An industry matured and prospered — the fence building industry.

Modern Fence Building

To compete effectively as a fence builder, you need a wholesale materials supplier who will sell to you at a discount. You'll also need a vehicle and certain tools. You need to know how to construct a sound, legal wall and how to make money doing it. That's what this manual is going to teach.

Later in this chapter, I'll tell you how much it costs to set up a fence contracting business and what you'll need to know. For now, let's begin with a discussion of the various types of fence contracting specialties and the equipment you'll need for each.

Block Walls

Block walls are very common in the southwestern United States because the materials are readily available there. The principal materials are adobe or cement blocks, steel reinforcing bars

Figure 1-1
Residential block wall

(rebar), mortar and lumber. Figure 1-1 shows a typical block wall in a residential development. Here's an equipment list — what you'll need to get started in block wall construction:

- vehicle, 3/4 to 1 ton truck
- transit for laying out wall (optional)
- motor-driven cement mixer
- chisels for cutting block
- circular saw for cutting forming lumber
- trowels for spreading mortar
- rebar cutter
- crowbar
- sledge hammer
- claw hammer
- chalk line
- cord and line blocks
- mortarboard
- assortment of screwdrivers and wrenches
- levels, 18 inch and 6 foot
- wire cutters to tie rebar
- drill and assortment of masonry bits
- protective clothing and glasses

It will cost you about $20,000 to buy everything on the list. I'm assuming your supplier will deliver materials to the job site and will provide a forklift. I'm also assuming that you'll subcontract the trenching work to someone with a backhoe. You'll also need a cement contractor to lay the foundation.

Sometimes you won't be able to get a concrete truck close to the job site. Then you'll have to pump cement through a large hose (about 4 inches in diameter) from the truck to the wall location. Pumping also works very well when pouring into narrow, formed-out foundations or wall cavities.

Most transit mix concrete trucks hold about 9 cubic yards of concrete. You'll be charged by the cubic yard, of course. But if you order less than 9 yards, you'll probably have to pay a surcharge for the short load. Still, I order transit mix concrete for any job that needs more than 3 cubic yards at once. Less than that and you're probably better off mixing it yourself on site.

Brick Walls

These require about the same equipment as block walls. You'll be working with more but smaller building units. Brick work is popular nationwide, but more common in the Northeast.

Figure 1-2
Design detail using brick

Brick is also used extensively in the Southeast where Georgia clay abounds. Once again, the cost of basic equipment needed by a brick contractor would be about $20,000. Figure 1-2 is an attractive brick wall with some interesting design detail.

Rock Walls

These fall into two categories, natural rock and manmade rock. Natural rock walls are common in rural areas where rock is the waste product when land is cleared. Rock wall builders don't need any special tools except a tractor, a wagon to cart the rock, and a strong back. When rock walls are laid in mortar, mortar mixing equipment is needed. You'll usually have to lay a foundation and will need a cement contractor. Figure 1-3 shows a wall of natural rock.

Manmade rock veneer is popular with some architectural styles. It's usually applied over wood frame or concrete block walls. The contractor who frames the wall or lays the block may also apply the veneer. The tools required for applying veneer are the same as for building block walls.

Poured Concrete Walls

These are reasonably inexpensive compared with other types of walls. They're very strong and can be used in most areas. You'll need forms, usually made of wood, fiberglass, or sheet metal. They come in sections that you can assemble and remove easily. You'll need a concrete pumping service to pump concrete from the truck to the forms. You'll also need a source for rebar to reinforce the concrete.

For some jobs it's cheaper to use prefab wall sections. If this is your choice, you'll need a crane or hoist to place these sections in position. The other equipment and tools are about the same as for wall building, with the addition of the forms. Forms for a job can cost anywhere from a few hundred to a few thousand dollars. Figure 1-4 shows a poured concrete wall that's part of a storm channel.

Wire Mesh Fences

This is an easy type of fence contracting to get into. Wire mesh fencing is common in rural and semi-rural areas where ranchers have to enclose animals and fowl rather than restrict access to people. These are the materials you'll need to build wire fences:

◆ a truck, 1/2 ton, 8-foot bed or larger

◆ a hand truck for moving rolls of mesh

◆ gas-powered post hole digger

◆ a block and tackle or stretcher

◆ wire cutters

Figure 1-3
Clear the land and build a wall

Figure 1-4
Poured concrete storm channel

Figure 1-5
Barbed wire discourages climbing

♦ wheelbarrow

♦ gas-powered cement mixer

♦ long tape measure, 100 feet minimum

♦ level, 6 foot

♦ transit for layout and leveling long sections

♦ string line and batten

♦ shovel, pick, hoe and manual post hole digger

♦ assortment of screwdrivers and wrenches

This setup will cost about $15,000. Unless there's a high demand for wire mesh fencing, I suggest you handle barbed wire and chain link fencing as well as wire mesh.

Barbed Wire Fences

In rural areas ranchers use barbed wire to contain cattle on rangeland. It's also used to mark off fields, though any hunter can climb through it. Sometimes you'll find barbed wire along the top of chain link fences to discourage people from climbing over. See Figure 1-5.

The equipment is the same as you'd need for wire mesh fence contracting. The wire stretcher is a different design, and you'll need a hammer or two. The cost to get started is the same.

Chain Link Fences

You'll find chain link fences mostly in urban commercial areas. They're very effective for keeping intruders out of storage areas, off factory grounds, and out of streams and lakes. They may be used inside factories to fence off equipment or inventory. These fences are usually 8 to 10 feet high. Lower chain link fences, in the 4 to 6 foot range, are used to define residential lots.

Chain link is very versatile. It's used to pen animals, form baseball fields, surround swimming pools, tennis courts, and parking lots. You'll need about the same equipment as for wire mesh fencing. For work inside industrial buildings you'll need some concrete drilling equipment, since most warehouse floors are poured concrete. Your truck should have a rack for carrying 20-foot sections of pipe. Cost of equipment will be about $15,000.

Wood Fences

Here is where style takes over. There are about as many types of wood fences as there are sizes of

Figure 1-6
Decorative metal fencing

lumber. The equipment is similar for all kinds of wood fences. You'll need:

- a truck, 1/2 ton, 8-foot bed or larger
- gas-powered post hole digger
- power saws and hand saws
- electrical generator for working in isolated areas
- assortment of screwdrivers and wrenches
- string line and batten
- shovel, axe, pick, hoe, and manual post hole digger
- hammers, claw and sledge
- drill and bits
- transit (optional)
- levels, 6 foot and 2 foot
- gas-powered cement mixer
- wheelbarrow
- assortment of woodworking chisels

Once again, your cost for equipment is about $15,000. You can build these fences from scratch, or buy and install prefab fencing. You'll usually buy materials, but on some rural jobs you might use timber cut on the site. For this type of work you'll need a chain saw, log splitter, and possibly a bulldozer. The chain saw and log splitter will cost about $1,500. You can rent the dozer.

Constructed Metal Fences

These fences include those made from ornamental iron or pipe. Ornamental iron is very popular with homeowners, and most of this work will be residential. Figure 1-6 shows some typical ornamental iron fencing.

Metal security fences and gates are common in commercial buildings. Pipe fences usually restrain animals, mainly horses and cattle. They're also used as safety railings where there's danger of people falling: balconies and scenic lookouts along highways. A third type of metal fencing is highway guardrail.

What do you need in the way of equipment and tools?

Figure 1-7
Combine wall materials for function and beauty

- a truck, 1 ton or better
- a gas or gas-powered electric welder and tips
- gas-powered post hole digger
- metal cutting saws
- drills for wood, concrete, and metal
- gas-powered cement mixer
- assortment of screwdrivers and wrenches
- hammer and mallet
- shovel, pick, hoe, and manual hole digger
- transit (optional)
- string line
- levels, 2 foot and 6 foot
- metal grinder or drill attachment
- paint and brushes for touch-up

Equipment and tools will cost about $20,000. If you're doing highway work, you may also need a bulldozer.

Plastic and Glass Fences

These are usually combined with one of the other types of fences. For instance, Figure 1-7 shows fiberglass panels installed on top of a block wall. This offers extra privacy without blocking so much sunlight. Clear plastic and glass fences are windscreens used to surround patios and swimming pools without reducing the view. Many homes built on high ground use glass or plastic fences.

Indoor plastic screens are common in banks and savings offices. One- to 2-inch-thick clear Plexiglas is designed to be bulletproof and is used to screen teller booths. These screens are very expensive. Bulletproof glass is usually sold by the square inch. You'll need a good supplier of shatterproof glass, Plexiglas, or *Lexan*. Lexan is a highly shatterproof polycarbonate material. Many stores now use it for their display windows. It's also used for windows on boats because of its high resistance to wind and waves.

Besides the basic equipment kit for wood or block walls, you'll need the following:

- glass cutters
- saber saw to cut plastic sheet
- a torch to fire-edge the plastic

- hacksaw to cut aluminum channel
- metal, glass and wood drills and bits
- vertical rack in truck for carrying sheets of material
- cleaners for removing adhesive paper and glue
- suction cup glass transporters

These items will cost you about $350.

Fire-edging removes burrs and rounds the cut edges of plastics. You use a low heat torch to just slightly soften the plastic. Fire-edging helps prevent cracking. You should also fire the edges of all mounting holes you drill.

Glass and plastic screen is usually mounted in aluminum channel. Use either a rubber gasket or caulking, or use epoxy to hold the material in the channels.

Siding and Stucco

You can use any kind of siding material to build fences: aluminum, steel, vinyl or stucco. First you build a conventional wall frame from 2 x 4 or 2 x 6 lumber. Then you use the siding material as a facing. The equipment and tools you need are basic saws, drills, and hand tools.

Landscape Fencing

You can use trees and other plants, or combine these with most other types of walls and fences, to form barriers. You have to know what plants work best in your climate. A trip to a local nursery, or the library, will help here. Cost for tools and equipment is usually very low.

Later chapters cover each of these fence and wall specialties in detail. For now I'll cover things that are common to all types of fence and wall construction.

Retaining Walls

These walls are used to keep soil or falling rock from intruding on occupied area. They're also built to reduce wind and noise in some places. Many retaining walls are built under government contracts. If you plan to bid on public works jobs, you'll probably find plenty of retaining wall work available in your area.

Equipment needed to build retaining walls tends to be more expensive. You don't need many hand tools, but for most work you'll probably need a bulldozer and a dump truck. The investment would probably be more than $100,000. You're generally better off renting these unless you intend to specialize in this type of work.

In most cities and counties, retaining walls have to be approved by the building department. The inspector wants to be sure the wall is strong enough to support the load. Except for small retaining walls, the building department isn't going to determine what's safe and what isn't. Instead, they rely on the opinion of the civil engineer *you* hire to prepare the plans. The engineer's stamp on the plans certifies that the wall meets accepted engineering standards. That's important. Dirt's cheap. But lives aren't. You can't afford to have your wall collapse.

Once the wall is finished, the slope above the wall should be landscaped to help hold the soil in place. You should be ready to suggest landscaping materials that will hold your manmade hills together.

Sea Walls

If you're near the ocean, a lake or river, you'll probably have the opportunity to bid on these walls intended to prevent damage from rising water. Sea walls are made from rock, dirt, cement, wood piles, sheet metal, asphalt, or old tires. Figure your minimum startup costs at $20,000.

Every Job Begins With a Sale

There won't be much work to do until you start selling jobs. Selling is an important part of the business. Consider two questions: Can you afford to hire a full-time salesperson? If not, can you afford to spend time selling jobs rather than building or supervising a crew?

My advice is to let the builders build and the salespeople sell. Unless you've got a special talent for making sales, find someone who likes meeting the public and knows (or is willing to learn) something about fence building and retaining walls. Many people can learn to be good salespeople and enjoy selling. Favor someone who can make a sketch of what they're trying to sell. Some training in drafting or architecture is an advantage.

Your salesperson (or salespeople) should work on commission, earning more when they close more jobs. Commissions range from 5 to 15 percent of the contract price, often with a weekly draw. In Chapter 14, I suggest sales techniques that can keep your company busy and prosperous.

Fence Maintenance Contracting

This is a good starter or add-on business. As a starter business, it's a way to get established while you learn the ins and outs of the fence contracting business. You need to be a good handyman, proficient in the use of hand tools.

Some fence maintenance contractors offer fence maintenance contracts to customers with existing fences and walls. You offer to come by on a regular basis to inspect and repair any minor damage. You'll oil hinges, tighten screws and bolts, and renail loose boards. You can also offer limited emergency service. You'd do this on a per-call basis when severe damage has occurred. This could be necessary after a wind storm, or when someone has run their car through a fence. Your service would include periodic painting or waterproofing of customers' fences.

Your startup cost for this type of service is small: a few basic hand tools, a small inventory of materials, and a pickup truck or van. Who do you sell to? Mostly business and local governments, but many homeowners will also hire you. They either can't or don't want to bother doing it themselves. There is a market for this. I took hundreds of pictures of fences for this book. Close to 90 percent of those fences needed repair. Start by looking for work in older neighborhoods.

On fence repair jobs, I recommend that you charge by the hour and add the cost of materials. Charging a fixed fee for this kind of work is usually a mistake. You'll often find hidden damage. Chapter 9 has more information on fence repairs and maintenance.

Design and Architecture

Anyone who's making a living in the fence business should see the difference between a fence that adds beauty to a home or neighborhood and a fence that's an eyesore. In many cases, you're going to be the designer, the person who recommends the fence material and design. I've seen too many fences and walls that just didn't complement the property. Don't make that mistake.

I've seen many others that fell apart way too soon due to poor design. The designer didn't consider how the fence would be used and problems that came with the site. Don't make that mistake either. The chapters that follow will help you select designs and materials to make attractive, well-engineered walls and fences.

Drafting and Layout

When you prepare plans for a fence or wall, your focus should be on technical accuracy. You have to take the ideas and sketches of the designer and turn them into working blueprints that show in detail how all parts fit together. A year or two of drafting experience and familiarity with fence building are essential.

Fence Rentals

Fence rental is good business in areas where many commercial or industrial buildings are under construction. Construction contractors rent fences to protect their equipment and tools on a job site. Insurance companies and local governments like fenced construction sites because fencing helps keep kids off the site at night and on weekends.

Farmers and ranchers use temporary fence to hold livestock during roundup. Businesses use it when they have to secure inventory outside temporarily.

Most rental fences are chain link. You install them the same way you do permanent chain link fences, but you usually don't cement the posts into the ground. If you cement them in, you're going to have a lot of fun when it's time to return the fence to the rental yard.

Here's how to charge for rental fencing:

1) Charge from a third to a seventh of your cost for the materials — the mesh, posts, and gates. This is based on the expectation that you can rent the same materials at least seven times, and perhaps as many as 20 times.

2) Charge your regular rate for delivery and installation. Add a charge for removal.

In the Los Angeles area, at the time of this writing, temporary fences rent for from $250 to $450 for 100 linear feet of 6-foot-high fence with one gate. The variation in price depends on soil conditions and how level the site is. Some companies charge the same whether you rent the fence for a week or a year.

If this sideline interests you, check with some of your local competitors for prices. Use them as a guide to see whether you can make money renting fences.

Fence-Building Equipment Rentals

If you're in the fence building business, consider renting your unused equipment. Other contractors, subcontractors, and property owners may need a good source of specialized equipment. Require a deposit, good identification, and a rental contract from your customers. In some states your customers will need special operator licenses to use heavy equipment such as backhoes or bulldozers.

Here are some examples of the equipment that's usually in demand:

♦ backhoe

♦ bulldozer

♦ power post hole diggers

♦ outdoor heaters

♦ cement mixers

♦ trucks

♦ tractors

♦ stretchers

♦ electrical generators

♦ airless sprayers

♦ power washers

♦ specialized small hand and power tools

The daily rental rate for most smaller pieces of equipment is usually about 5 percent of the purchase price. That means you can recover the purchase price once equipment is rented about 20 times. But some equipment may only rent out a few times a year. So it may take several years to earn a decent payback. Some operators of rental businesses give discounts for weekly and monthly rental terms. For example, a cable puller may rent for $15 for one day, $45 for a week, and only $90 for a month.

Insurance will be very important if you rent fence building equipment. You should be protected from loss due to equipment damage, liability, and theft. To be competitive in this business, you'll probably need to invest several hundred thousand dollars in equipment. After the initial payback, you'll keep from 40 to 60 percent of each rental dollar after expenses. It's a good business if you can afford to get into it.

Material Sales

Here is another good money-maker for fence contractors. Sell materials to other fence contractors. You're probably stocking both raw materials and some hardware. Offer delivery to the site and off-loading service. Many lumberyards carry some fencing materials, but as you'll see in later chapters, a lot of materials are unique to fence building.

You can supply just one line, wood fencing for example. Or you can be a full line supplier, offering block, brick, metal, wood, glass, plastics, etc. To be competitive as a fence material dealer, you need to make a substantial investment — several hundred thousand to a few million dollars. It's easier to accumulate capital like that if several people pool their resources and form a corporation. I'll tell you more about that in Chapter 12.

You might consider prefab fencing as a business. Some fence material dealers assemble and sell prefabricated metal, concrete or wood fence sections. You need a few good designs, a materials supplier, a building, and tools. You'll also need a way to deliver the completed sections to your dealers' or customers' locations. Unless you install the equipment, you won't need a contractor's license.

Many companies already offer prefab fencing. Check out their designs and prices to be sure you can either build a better product or build the same product at a lower cost.

As you can see, the fencing and retaining wall business offers a wide range of opportunities through specialties or branch businesses. Most states now require that contractors be licensed. And all companies that have employees need to know something about labor laws. I'll cover those subjects next.

Get Your License

All states that require contractors to be licensed have contractor license schools. Some only teach the test, some only teach the basics of construction, some may teach both. Before you invest several weeks or months and hundreds of dollars in a course, find out exactly what they offer. Ask about these things:

♦ Do they pre-test you to find out if you even qualify to become a licensed contractor? Many don't. All they want to do is sell you a manual.

♦ Do they tell you in advance just how much money the school and the license will cost? If they don't, you could be in for a shock later.

♦ Do they teach you the trade using hands-on experience? Not many do. Most assume you already know how to build a fence or wall.

♦ Will they help you find that first job after you get your license?

♦ Will they guarantee success in passing your test? Some will refund your money if you don't pass after you take the test twice.

How Much Does a Contractor's License Cost?

The schools that teach only the test charge an average of $200 to $550. You get an average of 15 hours class time over a few weeks, several manuals, and sample tests to take. Most schools will allow you to retake the course if you fail the state exam. Most will even refund part of your fee if you fail the state exam three times in a row. Make sure your contract covers restrictions and refunds.

Schools that teach a trade average $2,000 to $4,000. Plan on spending your evenings and weekends for at least six months, studying and building. There are a few full-time schools that will teach you what you need to know in three to four weeks.

Check these schools out carefully before you sign a contract. Your state consumer affairs office or contractor's license board can tell you if a school is legitimate.

The license itself can cost anywhere from a few dollars to several hundred dollars, depending on the state. California charges $150 for the first classification, and $50 for each additional classification or specialty.

Some states will require both a license and a *contractor's license bond*. If you default on a job, abandoning it before the work is finished, the state can revoke your license and the bond proceeds are available to compensate the owner. You may also have to show proof that you have enough *working capital* to support a contracting business. Working capital is money available to pay for labor and materials. The minimum in most license states is $2,500.

Many county and local governments will require that you post a bond when you bid on work under a government contract. Usually both a bid bond and a completion bond are required. The bid bond is submitted with the bid. It guarantees that you'll sign a contract to do the work if your bid is accepted. The completion bond guarantees that you'll complete work identified in the contract. Bid and completion bonds are written by insurance companies specializing in this type of work.

Most cities require contractors doing business in their city to have a business license. The license is usually a set amount plus a tiny fraction of your estimated gross receipts in the city for the coming year.

Proof of the Pudding

Can you prove you know your trade? With your application for a license, many states now require that you submit proof of prior experience working for a licensed contractor. For example, California now requires a *Certificate in Support of Experience Qualifications*. See Figure 1-8.

You may substitute college-level education or union apprenticeship for construction experience. You can also substitute building your own home or owning an apartment or condo complex in which you do all your own maintenance. However, these substitutions are sometimes prorated. Building your own home is only worth three months' experience toward the four year requirement in California. On the other hand, apartment and condo complex owners generally get full credit for their years of ownership.

Of course, every state can set its own requirements for a fence contracting license. Check out the requirements before you invest a lot of time and money on something you may not qualify for. Even if you feel qualified, the license board may not agree.

The Contractor's License Application

Where do you apply for your contractor's license? Look in your telephone directory under the name of your state. If there isn't a listing for a contractor's license board, call your state department of consumer affairs. If there's a license requirement, get a copy of the license law and ask for an application. Figure 1-9 shows a typical application form. Notice the type of questions on the form. This is California's six page form. I've only included the first two pages here.

Your contractor's license doesn't give you any special privileges except the right to bid jobs and get paid the contract price for the work you've done. In fact, it creates special duties owed to your employees, your customers and the license board.

Now if you do the wrong thing, you can be fined or lose your license.

You'll also be subject to regulation by the labor board, federal, state and local taxing agencies, and by OSHA (Occupational Safety and Health Administration). They all have rules you must know and follow.

Fines and penalties for misconduct as a contractor can cost you dearly. We'll cover some of the contractor regulations on sales and safety in later chapters. Here are some of the rules about what you can't do as a licensed contractor.

You're subject to disciplinary action if you:

- lie or misrepresent material facts on your application for a contractor's license.

- help an unlicensed person evade the provisions of contractor's law. This includes things like falsely verifying experience so that another person can get a contractor's license.

- lend or sell your contractor's license to another person.

- deliberately withhold pay from employees, subcontractors, and suppliers for their services. If you accept a customer's payment of less than $1,000 and don't use the money to pay for services received, you're probably guilty of a misdemeanor. If the amount exceeds $1,000, you may have committed a felony.

- start work on a job without first getting the required building permits. Your contractor's license may be suspended or revoked for doing so.

- contract for construction work that isn't covered by the valid license classification you hold. The exception is when the prime contract requires the contractor to do closely-related work. For example, you're permitted to paint a fence after you install it. But you can't add a wing to the customer's house that attaches to a fence.

CERTIFICATE IN SUPPORT OF EXPERIENCE QUALIFICATIONS

IMPORTANT! **READ THE INFORMATION ON THE REVERSE SIDE OF THIS FORM BEFORE COMPLETING THE CERTIFICATE.**

I, _____ , certify that I have personally known _____
name of certifier — print   name of applicant — print

and that I have direct knowledge of his/her experience which I have listed below.

EMPLOYER'S NAME	DESCRIBE IN DETAIL THE TYPE OF WORK PERFORMED BY THE APPLICANT (TRADES AND DUTIES)

From   To
__/__/__ __/__/__ Full-time ☐
    Part-time ☐
    (If part-time, do not total as full-time)
Total ____ Yr. ____ Mo.	

LEVEL APPLICANT WORKED AT:

☐ JOURNEYMAN

☐ FOREMAN

☐ SUPERVISOR

☐ CONTRACTOR

☐ OWNER/BUILDER

☐ OTHER _____
            specify

(SEE REVERSE SIDE FOR DEFINITIONS OF ABOVE LEVELS)

Did the applicant demonstrate a level of knowledge and skill expected of a journeyman or better in the craft(s) or trade(s) listed above?

☐ YES   ☐ NO

Check the box that identifies your business relationship to the applicant:

☐ employer   ☐ fellow employee   ☐ journeyman   ☐ union representative   ☐ architect

☐ engineer   ☐ building inspector   ☐ other, specify relationship _____

FOR UNION REPRESENTATIVE ONLY—USE TO CERTIFY COMPLETION OF APPRENTICESHIP PROGRAM

NAME OF UNION _____ UNION NO. _____ CITY _____

INITIATION DATE _____   DATE OF COMPLETION _____
          month   year   month   year

On _____ at _____ , I certify under penalty of perjury
        date   city/county   state

under the laws of the State of California that the foregoing is true and correct.

_____   Number: _____   State: _____
SIGNATURE of the Certifier   If you are a licensed/registered contractor,
                                enter your license/registration number and state.

_____   _____   _____   _____
Address of Certifier: Number and Street   City   State   ZIP Code

( )_____   ( )_____
Home—Telephone Number   Business—Telephone Number

Figure 1-8
Certificate in Support of Experience Qualifications form

To Persons Requested to Certify to Applicant's Experience:

The applicant must detail four full years of experience within the past 10 years, in the classification s/he is applying for, at the level of a Journeyman, Foreman, Supervisor, or Contractor (see definitions below). The applicant must also submit certificates to support this experience. The certificates must be completed by a qualified and responsible person, that is, by an employer, fellow employee, journeyman, union representative, building inspector, architect, or engineer who has DIRECT KNOWLEDGE of the applicant's experience.

DIRECT KNOWLEDGE is knowledge of the truth in regard to a particular fact, which is original, and does not depend on information or hearsay.

The applicant is requesting that you complete this form to certify as to your DIRECT KNOWLEDGE of his/her experience. As a qualified and responsible person you must certify that the applicant demonstrated a level of knowledge and skill expected of a journeyman or better in the classification for which application is being made.

JOURNEYMAN is an experienced worker in the trade who is fully qualified as opposed to a trainee, and is able to perform the trade without supervision; or one who has completed an apprenticeship program. (Board Rule 825.)

FOREMAN/SUPERVISOR is a person who has the knowledge and skill of a journeyman and also directly supervises the physical construction.

CONTRACTOR is (a) a currently licensed California contractor
        (b) a former licensed California contractor
        (c) personnel of record on a California license
        (d) out of state contractor (if a license is required in the state in which you are contracting)

A Contractor is a person who has the skills necessary to manage the daily activities of a construction business, including field supervision.

OWNER/BUILDER is a person who has the knowledge and skills of a Journeyman and performs work on his/her property.

Your cooperation is earnestly solicited so that the Contractors State License Board can determine whether this applicant has had the experience necessary to become a capable and qualified contractor.

IMPORTANT: YOU MAY BE REQUESTED TO PROVIDE DOCUMENTATION TO VERIFY ALL EXPERIENCE TO WHICH YOU ARE ATTESTING. FOR YOUR RECORDS, IT IS SUGGESTED THAT YOU KEEP A COPY OF THE CERTIFICATE(S) YOU HAVE COMPLETED.

SECTION 7114.1 OF THE BUSINESS AND PROFESSIONS CODE PROVIDES THAT: ANY LICENSEE WHOSE SIGNATURE APPEARS ON A FALSIFIED CERTIFICATE IN SUPPORT OF EXAMINEE'S EXPERIENCE QUALIFICATIONS, OR OTHERWISE CERTIFYING TO FALSE OR MISLEADING EXPERIENCE CLAIMS BY AN APPLICANT, WHICH HAVE BEEN SUBMITTED TO OBTAIN A CONTRACTOR'S LICENSE SHALL BE SUBJECT TO DISCIPLINARY ACTION.

SECTION 115 OF THE PENAL CODE PROVIDES THAT: EVERY PERSON WHO KNOWINGLY PROCURES OR OFFERS ANY FALSE OR FORGED INSTRUMENT TO BE FILED, REGISTERED, OR RECORDED IN ANY PUBLIC OFFICE, WITHIN THIS STATE, WHICH INSTRUMENT, IF GENUINE, MIGHT BE FILED, OR REGISTERED, OR RECORDED UNDER ANY LAW OF THIS STATE OR OF THE UNITED STATES, IS GUILTY OF A FELONY.

DO NOT SEND THIS FORM TO THE CONTRACTORS STATE LICENSE BOARD. RETURN IT TO THE APPLICANT SO THAT S/HE MAY ATTACH IT TO HIS/HER APPLICATION.

When filed with an application, this certificate becomes the property of the Contractors State License Board and is kept as a matter of record.

Figure 1-8 (cont'd)
Certificate In Support of Experience Qualifications form

STATE OF CALIFORNIA—STATE AND CONSUMER SERVICES AGENCY

DEPARTMENT OF
Consumer Affairs

CONTRACTORS STATE LICENSE BOARD
3132 Bradshaw Road, Sacramento, California
Mailing Address: P.O. Box 26000, Sacramento, California 95826

APPLICATION FOR ORIGINAL CONTRACTOR'S LICENSE

APPLICATION FEE $150 for a single classification
$50 for each additional classification*

Pursuant to Section 7138 of the Business and Professions Code, all fees paid in connection with the application are NOT refundable once the application is filed.
* You can only apply for additional classification(s) on this form if you are NOT required to take the examination for any of the classifications you are applying for.

Attach a money order, personal, certified or cashier's check payable to the Registrar of Contractors. **DO NOT SEND CASH.**
There will be a $10.00 service charge for each dishonored check.

FOR OFFICE USE ONLY

APP. FEE NO:

I.L. FEE NO.

GRANTED DATE

LICENSE NO.

TYPE OR PRINT LEGIBLY IN INK

1. FULL NAME OF BUSINESS (A CORPORATION MUST USE CORPORATE NAME AS REGISTERED WITH SECRETARY OF STATE)

2. BUSINESS MAILING ADDRESS | CITY | STATE | ZIP CODE | AREA CODE/TELEPHONE NO. ( )

3. CLASSIFICATION CODE(S) APPLYING FOR (see information sheet)

4. DESCRIBE TYPE OF CONSTRUCTION YOU INTEND TO CONDUCT

5. CONDUCTING BUSINESS AS: ☐ INDIVIDUAL ☐ PARTNERSHIP ☐ CORPORATION | **FOR OFFICE USE ONLY** —

6. LIST ALL PERSONNEL: If an individual, list OWNER; If a Partnership, list all PARTNERS; If a Corporation, list all OFFICERS, this list must include the PRESIDENT SECRETARY and TREASURER; List RESPONSIBLE MANAGING EMPLOYEE, if such person is to qualify. Show **FULL LEGAL NAMES, NO INITIALS;** if your legal name contains initials only, so state. **P.O. BOXES/GENERAL DELIVERY/AND RT,** are **NOT ACCEPTABLE** for residential addresses, **SHOW NAME OF ROAD OR DISTRICT AND NEAREST CROSS STREETS.** All items of information requested, except social security and driver's license numbers are mandatory. These numbers are requested for identification purposes only.

(A) NAME Last | First | Middle | Date of Birth-mo/day/yr | Social Security No. | Driver's License No.

RESIDENCE ADDRESS: Number/Street | City | State | ZIP Code | Residence Telephone ( ) | **DO NOT USE** %

TITLE OR POSITION (check one)
☐ Owner ☐ Gen. Partner ☐ Ltd. Partner ☐ Qual. Partner ☐ RME | ☐ Corporate Officer ☐ RMO/Corporate Officer } (INDICATE CORPORATE TITLE)

(B) NAME Last | First | Middle | Date of Birth-mo/day/yr | Social Security No. | Driver's License No.

RESIDENCE ADDRESS: Number/Street | City | State | ZIP Code | Residence Telephone ( ) | **DO NOT USE** %

TITLE OR POSITION (check one)
☐ Owner ☐ Gen. Partner ☐ Ltd. Partner ☐ Qual. Partner ☐ RME | ☐ Corporate Officer ☐ RMO/Corporate Officer } (INDICATE CORPORATE TITLE)

(C) NAME Last | First | Middle | Date of Birth-mo/day/yr | Social Security No. | Driver's License No.

RESIDENCE ADDRESS: Number/Street | City | State | ZIP Code | Residence Telephone ( ) | **DO NOT USE** %

TITLE OR POSITION (check one)
☐ Owner ☐ Gen. Partner ☐ Ltd. Partner ☐ Qual. Partner ☐ RME | ☐ Corporate Officer ☐ RMO/Corporate Officer } (INDICATE CORPORATE TITLE)

(D) NAME Last | First | Middle | Date of Birth-mo/day/yr | Social Security No. | Driver's License No.

RESIDENCE ADDRESS: Number/Street | City | State | ZIP Code | Residence Telephone ( ) | **DO NOT USE** %

TITLE OR POSITION (check one)
☐ Owner ☐ Gen. Partner ☐ Ltd. Partner ☐ Qual. Partner ☐ RME | ☐ Corporate Officer ☐ RMO/Corporate Officer } (INDICATE CORPORATE TITLE)

ADDITIONAL PERSONNEL MUST BE LISTED ON A SEPARATE SHEET OF PAPER GIVING THE INFORMATION REQUESTED ABOVE. EACH ADDITIONAL PERSON MUST ALSO SIGN AND DATE A CERTIFICATION AS IN SECTION 7.

7. **IMPORTANT**: The following certification must be **dated** and each person listed in section 6 must **sign**.

On _____ date _____ at _____ city/county _____ State _____ , I certify under penalty of perjury under the laws of the State of California that all statements, answers and representations in this application, including all supplementary statements attached hereto, are true and accurate, and that I have reviewed the entire contents of this application. I hereby apply for a license under the provisions of Division 3, Chapter 9 of the Business and Professions Code.

(A) _____ SIGNATURE _____ TITLE | (C) _____ SIGNATURE _____ TITLE
(B) _____ SIGNATURE _____ TITLE | (D) _____ SIGNATURE _____ TITLE

Figure 1-9
Contractor's License Application form

ALL OF THE FOLLOWING QUESTIONS PERTAIN TO EACH MEMBER OF THE PERSONNEL. EACH QUESTION MUST BE ANSWERED. AFFIRMATIVE ANSWERS ON QUESTIONS 8, 9, 10, 11 and 12 MUST BE SUPPORTED BY A DETAILED STATEMENT.

8. Are there now any unpaid past due bills or claims for labor, materials, or services as a result of any construction contract or work undertaken by you or any organization in which you were a member? Yes ☐   No ☐

9. Are there now any outstanding citations issued by the Contractors State License Board, liens, suits, or judgments of record or pending as a result of any construction contract or work undertaken by you or any organization in which you were a member? Yes ☐   No ☐

10. Are there now any judgments or admitted claims against any bond or cash deposit required by Division 3, Chapter 9 of the Business and Professions Code? Yes ☐   No ☐

    (For the purpose of questions 8, 9 and 10 an obligation is not satisfied by the bar of the statute of limitations.)

    If you answered "yes" to questions 8, 9, and/or 10 attach a detailed statement identifying the transaction (i.e., past-due bills, claims, suits, judgments of record or pending, or liens of record) and including the names and addresses of the parties involved. Indicate on the statement whether or not the obligation was discharged in bankruptcy.

11. Have you ever been convicted of any offenses in this State, or elsewhere, other than traffic violations? Yes ☐   No ☐

    If so, attach a detailed statement including the crime for which there was a conviction, the approximate date, the location, the sentence served, if any, and parole, if any.

12. Have you, or any organization in which you were a member of the personnel, had a contractor's license or any professional or vocational license denied, suspended, or revoked by this or any other state? Yes ☐   No ☐

    If so, attach a detailed statement.
    (For the purpose of this question, "denied" does not mean that one has previously failed an examination and "suspended" does not mean bond suspension or lack of qualifier suspension.)

13. **APPLICANT'S STATEMENT OF FINANCIAL ABILITY AND CONDITION**

    Pursuant to Section 7067.5 of the Business and Professions Code every applicant, other than one applying for a Joint License on Form 13A-3, shall possess and shall evidence financial solvency. For purposes of Section 7067.5, financial solvency shall mean that the applicant's Operating Capital shall exceed Two Thousand Five Hundred Dollars ($2,500). Does your Operating Capital exceed $2,500? Yes ☐   No ☐

    (Operating Capital as defined by Board Rule 817--Current Assets Minus Current Liabilities)

    AN ADDITIONAL STATEMENT IS NOT NECESSARY.

14. **CERTIFICATION OF DUTIES AND RESPONSIBILITIES OF QUALIFYING INDIVIDUAL**

    Every applicant or licensee who qualifies by the appearance of a qualifying individual is required to verify that the person qualifying on behalf of an individual or firm is responsible for exercising such direct supervision and control of his/her employer's or principal's construction operation as is necessary to secure full compliance with the provisions of the Contractors License Law and the rules and regulations of the Board relating to such construction operations.

    The Registrar of Contractors has determined that direct supervision and control includes any one or any combination of the following activities: supervising construction, managing construction activities by making technical and administrative decisions, checking jobs for proper workmanship, or direct supervision on construction job sites.

    Any disciplinary action taken against this license, <u>MAY</u> result in the suspension or revocation of any additional license(s) with which you are associated.

    Will the Qualifying Individual perform one or more of the duties cited above? Yes ☐   No ☐

    IMPORTANT: Pursuant to Board Rule 823, a Responsible Managing Employee must work at least 32 hours or 80% of the total operating hours of the entity for which he/she is qualifying.

15. **CORPORATIONS ONLY**

    All corporations must be registered as a domestic or foreign corporation in good standing with the Secretary of State of the State of California pursuant to Sections 200 and 2105 of the Corporate Code.

    ENTER CORPORATE NUMBER ASSIGNED BY THE SECRETARY OF STATE: _____

    THIS CORPORATION IS: ☐ -DOMESTIC   ☐ -FOREIGN

16. If this pending application is to be qualified by a Responsible Managing Officer or Qualifying Partner, complete the following, if applicable:

    _____ owns _____ % of the voting stock/
    name of qualifier

    equity of this Corporation/Partnership. (See Sections 7068, 7068.1 and 7071.9 of the Business and Professions Code)

    IMPORTANT: Pursuant to Section 7083 of the Business and Professions Code, the Contractors State License Board must be notified within 90 days of any changes which reduce the percentage of the equity owned by the Responsible Managing Officer or Qualifying Partner.

17. PRINT NAME OF THE PERSON WHO IS TO BE THE QUALIFYING INDIVIDUAL ON THIS APPLICATION. _____

Figure 1-9 (cont'd)
Contractor's License Application form

◆ deliberately write checks for materials or services supplied by others without enough money in the bank to cover the checks.

◆ enter into a contract with an unlicensed person, not an employee, to construct a project.

◆ default on a construction contract. If you fail to complete a contract, and you don't have a valid excuse, you may be fined and jailed. The jail term can be one year.

◆ use funds collected specifically for completion of one job on another job. This is diversion of funds.

◆ disregard and violate the laws and provisions of any official authority, such as building codes, state and local codes, labor laws, safety laws, and water codes. This also includes tax and insurance laws.

◆ join with another licensed contractor to submit a joint bid or contract on a job, without first getting a *joint contractor's license*.

◆ fail to list your correct contractor's license number on contracts, bids, legally required forms, and advertising. This includes the sign on the side of your truck.

It is a misdemeanor to:

◆ advertise as a contractor unless you hold a valid license for the applicable classification. There's probably a fine for operating without a license.

◆ refuse to surrender your license to the contractor's license board when requested to do so.

◆ operate as a contractor with an expired or forged contractor's license.

◆ use or display a contractor's license that is not issued to you.

◆ violate state safety provisions.

◆ remove, deface, or destroy safety signs or notices required by state agencies.

It's a crime to falsely state the purpose of a loan when you apply for one. You can't apply to a bank for a loan to build a retaining wall on your property and then use the money for a new car. That's embezzlement.

Those are just a few of the rules for starters. If you have or will be hiring employees, there are more — lots more.

Laws Governing Employers

If you're an owner building on your own property, you don't need a contractor's license, providing you don't offer the property for sale for at least one year after you finish building. If you hire someone to help you build your project, you need Workers' Compensation insurance. See your insurance agent. Heavy penalties are usually imposed on employers who fail to buy the necessary coverage: a 10 percent penalty and all medical expenses if a person gets hurt while working for you. This applies to relatives as well as non-relatives.

Generally, buying Workers' Compensation insurance relieves you of liability for job-related injuries. The injured employee's only claim is for Workers' Compensation unless you're guilty of negligence that caused the injury.

Any time you pay a worker more than $100 in a calendar quarter (three months), you're probably an employer under state law. As an employer you have to comply with both state and federal laws that apply to employers. For example, you need a Federal Employer I.D. number, you must file a form 941 (and remit both the employer's and employee's withheld taxes) each quarter. Both your state government and the federal government have very effective ways to enforce these laws.

Like all construction contracting, fence contracting isn't the easiest job in the world. There isn't much paperwork if you're a one-man company. But most fence contractors need help carrying materials, mixing cement, laying out paths, and many other tasks. Unless you're a superman, you'll probably hire some help. Once you do, you're an employer and have to meet the requirements placed on all employers. Here are some of the things all employers need to know. Most states have laws that require the following.

♦ If you pay an employee with a check and that check bounces, you're subject to a civil penalty. If you lay off an employee and the final paycheck bounces, you're liable for up to 30 days' additional pay, or pay until you make the check good, whichever comes first.

♦ If you fire an employee for cause and refuse to give them their final pay at the time of firing, you're liable for the back pay plus an additional 30 days' pay. You also have to pay them at the place of discharge. Failure to do so is a misdemeanor and may result in disciplinary action by the license board.

♦ You may not *require* your employees to work more than 40 hours per week. You can ask them to. But they don't have to. If you discipline them for not working over 40 hours, you're subject to a fine of $50 or more, a possible jail sentence of up to 30 days, or both.

But note this carefully. The 40 hours need not be in a five day week. You can ask employees to work six out of every seven days. If you have to work seven days or more in a row, you can. But you have to notify your employees in advance and give rest days equal to one for each seven days in the month.

♦ You can *dock* employees who are late. For example, you can adopt a policy of docking late employees 30 minutes when an employee is late by 10 minutes or more. You don't have to pay for docked time.

♦ You can't include requirements in help wanted ads that would discriminate against an applicant. Federal law prohibits discrimination based on age, sex, national origin, or creed (color or religion). Of course, you may discriminate on the basis of qualification. You can also reject a candidate who can't do a job because of physical or mental limitations.

♦ You have to pay equal wages for equal work, providing there is equal skill, responsibility, and effort involved. You can't hire a man for $8.00 an hour to nail boards on a fence and then hire a woman for $5.00 an hour to do the same thing.

♦ You can't ask an applicant about their past criminal or arrest record. A private employer can't require an applicant to take a polygraph (lie detector) test. State, federal, and local government employers may.

♦ You can't demand that an applicant or employee purchase items from you. You can require the person to purchase items required for the job, but not from you. For example, you can require safety shoes. You should tell applicants this before you hire them.

♦ You can't hire an illegal alien. To knowingly hire an illegal alien to the detriment of legal residents is punishable by a fine. Examine the applicant's *green card*. This is a work permit granted by the INS (Immigration & Naturalization Service). You should also check for a passport. The green card identification number should be listed in the passport and should match the number on the card.

♦ You must provide employees with safe working conditions. Explain any job hazards and safety procedures to new employees before they start work.

♦ You can't fire or take other disciplinary action against an employee who complains to the authorities of a health or safety violation. If you fire an employee for refusing to work in an unsafe environment, you will have to reinstate them with full back pay. If you demote them, you will have to return them to the status they held before the demotion and make up the difference in pay and benefits.

♦ If an employee is injured due to unsafe working conditions, the employer must report the injury to the Department of Labor Statistics, OSHA, and their insurance company. In most states, if an employee is killed on the job because of unsafe working conditions, the employer can be fined and jailed.

- If a fellow employee causes another employee to be injured, the injured employee or their surviving family may seek damages from the employer. You're expected to watch over your help and make sure they're all working safely.

- You can't forbid or punish an employee for belonging to, or speaking out for, a political party, person, or activity.

- An employer who advertises for replacement help during a labor dispute must include in the advertisement that there is a labor dispute going on.

- If your employees go on strike, you may use family or supervisory personnel to replace the striking workers.

- All employers must get a Federal Identification Number from the Internal Revenue Service. States have the same requirement.

- You are required to withhold federal and state income taxes, Social Security contributions and disability insurance from employee wages. You also have to contribute matching Social Security funds and federal unemployment tax based on your total payroll.

    Contributions and withholding amounts change from year to year. When you register with your state and local taxing agencies, you'll be notified of current withholding rates, and the method for depositing them.

- You have to pay *nonexempt* employees at least twice during each calendar month. Nonexempt employees are the ones you pay by the hour. *Exempt* employees are usually management people, and get paid a monthly or yearly salary without regard for the number of hours they work.

- You have to pay employees in *legal tender*. You can't use merchandise, coupons, scrip, notes, stock, bonds, or other forms of payment. Legal tender means check or cash. You can ask your employees to accept items other than legal ten-

der, but employees have to accept voluntarily. New companies sometimes use notes and stock as compensation during the first few months when they're going into business.

- You must keep a list of all employees on file. The list must include the ages of all minors and the names and addresses of all employees.

- You have to keep payroll records for at least four years from the time you filed the returns that apply to them, or paid the taxes, whichever is later. See the I.R.S. Publication #334, *Tax Guide for Small Business*. You can get it free from any I.R.S. office.

- You must also keep employment application forms, even from people you didn't hire, for at least a year from the date of the application.

Collecting Sales Tax

For sales tax purposes, contractors are generally considered to be consumers and pay sales tax on their materials. When they sell material to their customer, they don't add sales tax as a separate item on the bill.

In some states, dealers who hold a seller's permit (sometimes called a resale license) don't pay sales tax on their materials. Instead, they collect the tax from retail customers and remit the tax collected to the taxing agency every few months. That's a nuisance. It's easier to pay the tax, consider it a cost of materials, and avoid filing sales tax returns monthly or quarterly.

I hope this discussion hasn't discouraged you. After a while, most of these laws will begin to make sense. Following them almost gets to be automatic. But it's never cheap or easy.

In the next several chapters, I'll tell you all about the mechanics of building fences and walls of all kinds. Later in the book, I'll explain how to get your fence and retaining wall contracting business started on the right foot and how to keep it running successfully.

two

Layout and Design

*B*efore you start to build, you need a good plan. Take a walk around town with your camera and a note pad. Try to see why fences were designed the way they were. Study the construction techniques, look for problems, and judge how well the walls and fences have withstood the test of time. You can learn a lot about fence design simply by noticing the mistakes of others.

Take pictures to use later as examples for your customers. Compile a fence and wall catalog. This "walk and shoot" routine will also give you a good idea of what your competition is doing. And as a bonus, you can use your snapshots as a selling tool. If you're selling a fence like the one in Figure 2-1, show your customer that picture, and say, "I can prevent post rail splitting, Mr. Jones. I put a metal strap around the top of each post I install. That solves the problem and makes a quality job."

Start Planning by Asking Questions

Layout and design is the part of fence and wall building that I especially enjoy. But before you can begin, you have to ask some questions:

1) What's the purpose of the fence? Is it for security, to prevent passage of children, pets, or livestock? Should it provide a windbreak, sound insulation, or a light shield?

Figure 2-1
Split rails are OK, split posts are not

2) How much money is your customer willing to spend?

3) How long do they want the fence or wall to last?

4) Does the design have to blend with an existing building or fence?

5) Will you do all the work yourself, or subcontract part of it?

A fence or wall is a major investment that your customer will live with for many years. Be sure it turns out the way they intended. You don't want to do a top-notch building job, only to find out you misunderstood your customer's intent. It might be what they *wanted*, but not what they *needed*. You're the expert. It's up to you to ask the right questions and make sure the final product is what the customer wants *and* needs.

If your customer makes a mistake, it's still your reputation that's on the line. So take the time to list everything the fence or wall is intended to do. Sometimes it will have to do several things at once, or different things at different points along its path. That brings us to more questions:

6) What *is* the path of this fence or wall? Will it surround the property, divide the property into areas, or cross only one section of the property? How high should the fence be? Does it have to block the view of late night swim parties?

7) Are there several people concerned with the location of this fence? Is a neighbor involved in the design or purchase? Might the fence or wall block someone's view? Are there restrictions by a homeowners' association that you must abide by?

8) Where will you need access gates? Does the customer want a storage area for trash containers, firewood, utility meters, gas tanks, pool supplies and pumps, a boat or recreational vehicle? Some areas require those to be out of sight from the street and neighbors.

9) Do you plan a barbecue grill, waterfall, or a tool shed? You can often incorporate them into your fence or wall design. Just be sure they're located where you want them. Once built, they'll be hard to move.

10) Exactly where are the property lines? On new properties, you can often find the metal surveying stakes at the corners of the property. In older developments, or where landscaping is heavy, these might be gone, or buried. To play it safe, order a new survey. That costs about $150 to $250.

You can either order the survey and include it in the contract with your customer, or the customer can order it himself. If you put a fence in the neighbor's yard because you didn't check the location of the property line, both you and the customer could be forced to move the fence. If you have a survey and it proves to be incorrect, then the surveyor is responsible for any costs involved.

11) Do your local building codes impose rules or restrictions on height or materials? Will your design require consultation or approval by a civil or structural engineer? Will you need a building permit? What restrictions does the utility company have about access to their meter?

12) If the fence is built on the property line, will you need legal assistance to draw the contract? This is usually a good idea if the construction cost and maintenance responsibilities are shared. It also helps solve the problem of who looks at the back side of the fence.

So far, you might not think all these questions are much fun, but they're important to a good fence or wall design.

The Finer Points of Design

When you've asked all the questions and gathered all the information you need — there's still one more thing to do. Take a hike. Walk the proposed fence line with a clipboard, your drawings, and a red pencil in hand. Mark down the spots that will give you trouble.

- Mark any obstacles like trees, boulders, a patch of tall weeds, or a stream.

- Do you have to build up or down a hill?

- Are there power lines, water lines, or other utilities to watch out for?

- Do you have to move sprinklers or remove part of an old wall?

Account for any items that will take extra effort, time, or materials. Plan for them before you get started, and you won't have any surprises later.

For instance, is your new fence or wall going to be near existing trees? Will trees be planted along the fence after it's built? Many types of trees have invasive roots that can upset fence posts or the wall foundation. Caution your customers.

I had a customer who planted palm trees right on the property line at the two rear corners of his lot. Ten years later he decided to enclose the rear yard with a wall. We had to cut down the palms to build the wall. Then the customer had to pay for new landscaping. The total cost was more than $3,000. The cost would have been much less if the trees had been planted a few feet inside the property line.

Ask your customer about long-range plans for home improvements. If they plan to build a pool or tennis court, or add to their house later on, they'll need access for heavy equipment. It's foolish to build a fence that has to be ripped out to get a dozer or backhoe into the yard.

Climate

You have to consider the weather when you design a fence or wall project.

If the ground freezes in winter, extend wall foundations below the frost line. That's the depth the ground will freeze during the coldest weather. Your local building department will explain how deep foundations have to be to get below the frost line.

How much rain do you get, and what are your soil conditions? In wet weather, nice solid ground turns into a liquid mass of jelly. Fence posts and wall foundations have to be well below the mud level. Otherwise the fence or wall will float on mud until the ground dries.

I suggest a minimum depth of 18 inches for all fence posts and wall foundations. Make them a minimum of 24 inches deep anywhere the ground freezes. In rural areas, 3 feet isn't too much.

Consider the prevailing wind direction and the expected top wind speed for the area where you're building. You may have to reinforce sections of the fence where the wind loads will be greatest, or design a fence that lets air flow through it. Select an open design if snow drifting may be a problem. Nobody wants snowdrifts to cover their (or a neighbor's) driveway.

Water

Water is funny stuff. It flows in all directions. It can flow down, sideways, and even up. And it eventually destroys all it touches. It will be one of the chief destroyers of your work. Try to anticipate what water will do to ruin your fences and walls, and plan against it.

Capillary action sucks water out of the ground into concrete and lumber. To reduce capillary action, keep the bottom of all wood fences at least 3 inches above ground level. If this isn't practical, use lumber that's resistant to water damage. I recommend cedar, redwood, treated lumber, or coated lumber.

Water trapped in a wood fence will eventually destroy that fence. Water seeps between boards. It accumulates at the bottom edge of boards and then soaks upward by capillary action. It sits on the top edge and seeps in. Chapter 8 has suggestions for painting and waterproofing fences and walls.

Warping

Warping is caused by both water and heat. In less time than you would imagine, warping can destroy a fence. Most lumber is sold as S-dry, which contains up to 19 percent water. When this water evaporates, the lumber tends to shrink. This shrinking results in splits and warping. I prefer to use kiln dried (KD) lumber when possible.

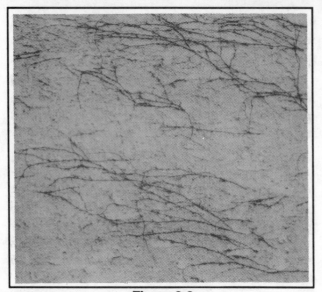

Figure 2-2
Plants can destroy a wall's surface

Wood Rot

Wood rot is a fungus that grows in wet wood and actually consumes it. You can kill this black fungus with an application of bleach. Prevention is the best cure for this problem. Leave space between pickets or boards of wood fences. This promotes drying after a rain. The space also helps prevent popped nails and warping. Use treated lumber when possible. Mound the dirt around fence posts so water drains away from them.

Landscaping

As a fence and wall expert, you should be alert for opportunities to build extra value into your jobs. For example, lawn mowing and plant care are a nuisance at the base of a fence or wall. Plan a *dead* area under or next to the fence or wall. At the base of the wall, bury polyethylene plastic sheeting or use cement, bricks, or block to keep plants and grasses out. Plants that climb or grow against the wall or fence will damage it. They do this two ways:

1) They hold water against the fence and prevent thorough drying. Rot and fungus soon develop.

2) Plants such as ivy can actually consume a fence or wall. In Figure 2-2, you can see the effects of ivy on a stucco wall. The facing

material has been eaten away where the ivy attached itself. The same thing would happen with concrete.

What if you *want* plants on your wall or fence? Include planters as part of the design. Build the planters so water doesn't drain onto the fence or wall surface. Furnish a replaceable liner for the plants.

Most plant nurseries sell inexpensive plastic planter tubs. Provide drainage through the liner by installing a drain pipe that empties away from the wall. Use half-inch PVC cold water pipe and slip-fit PVC fittings for the drain lines. You can assemble those materials quickly and easily with "purple primer" and PVC cement. Thoroughly clean and sandpaper the outside of the pipe and the inside of the fitting where they will be joined. Use primer and let it dry before you apply the cement, then, as you squeeze the parts together, give them a quarter-turn. This makes for a more secure bond. Be sure of your alignment when you put the parts together, as it sets up very fast.

If you can't arrange drainage for the planter, then fill the first few inches of the planter with stone or coarse gravel, and cover that with dirt. That will help keep the plants from being over watered.

Buy the liner before you build the planter, so you can size everything correctly. You may even want to build a watering device into the wall, such as a trickle outlet or hose bib.

Access Beyond the Wall

Does the area outside the wall belong to the owner? Does the owner have to maintain that space? For example, there may be a strip of grass between a wall and sidewalk, or between the sidewalk and the street. If the owner has to maintain it, include access to water and power for electric motors and trimmers.

Other Design Considerations

Appearance

Consider turning a plain block wall into a thing of beauty by adding decorative block layers or inserting face block. You can stylize a wood

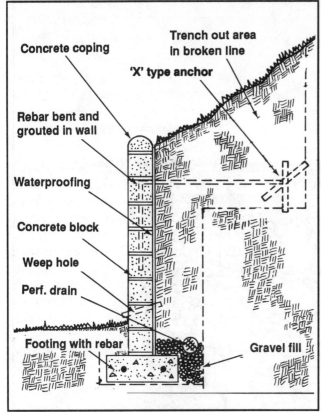

Figure 2-3
Backfilled wall detail

Labels on figure:
- Concrete coping
- Trench out area in broken line
- 'X' type anchor
- Rebar bent and grouted in wall
- Waterproofing
- Concrete block
- Weep hole
- Perf. drain
- Footing with rebar
- Gravel fill

fence by mixing pickets of different widths or with distinctive top treatments.

You can apply dozens of textures to a stucco wall with simple hand tools. You can also inlay all kinds of things to make a wall design unique. I've seen walls with bottle caps, horseshoes, broken colored glass, marbles, old farm and ranch equipment, tools, and driftwood set into the face.

Allow for Equipment

Consider the path and size of the equipment the owner will pass through gates and openings in the fence. This is especially important on ranches and farms, or if a boat or motor home will be stored on site. Allow for good traffic flow. And if an owner later buys some wide equipment, like an RV or a boat, and the fence *you* built doesn't have a gate big enough, whose fault is it? Yours, of course — just ask the owner. My point is this: It's your responsibility to alert the owner to possibilities he may not have considered.

Sunlight and Shadows

The sun comes up in the east, arches overhead and to the south, and settles in the west. In winter, fences can cast very long shadows in the mornings and afternoons. Your choice of height or material might change if your customer plans a garden, or wants to control heat entering a south-facing room.

If solar heating, cooling or shade are important, do some testing. Before you build that permanent fence or wall, buy about a dozen pieces of cheap 1 x 2 lumber, several inches longer than the proposed height of the project. Get some marking lime, too. Put the stakes in the ground at various locations along the fence line. Pound them in so their tops are at the height you plan for the fence or wall. Use the lime to mark the range of shadows thrown by the stakes. You'll soon see if a chain link fence would be better next to the garden, or if the wall needs to be higher outside the south bedroom window.

Check the effect on neighboring property, too. If the new wall will block the neighbor's sun deck, they probably won't be happy.

Design for Drainage and Soil Retention

Will you be digging into a hillside or backfilling against a wall to hold or level an area? You may need help from a civil engineer in this case. If the containment is under 4 feet high, you can design it yourself. But plan on *deadman anchors* every few feet. A deadman anchor is an anchor rod with a holding support on each end. Attach one end to the wall and bury the other end perpendicular to the wall, 6 to 10 feet away. It prevents the weight of the dirt from pushing the wall over. See Figure 2-3.

The cross bar anchors are available commercially in several designs such as stamped metal or a metal concave dish. You can make your own from two pieces of redwood 2 x 4 bolted together with the rebar or threaded rod.

This brings us to another water problem. Water that backs up behind a wall can undermine the foundation or build up enough pressure to topple the wall. Provide weep holes to keep your wall from becoming a dam.

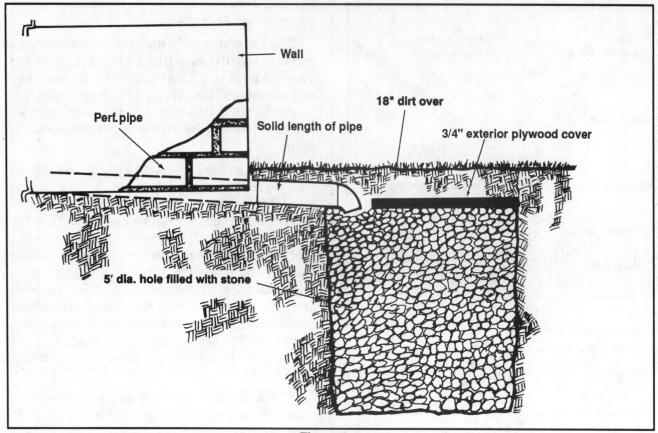

Figure 2-4
A dry well to collect drainage

Even a block wall around a level yard can create problems if most of the landscaping is near the wall. This can cause water to back up against the wall, creating puddles, flooding, and causing poor plant growth. Plan drainage holes every few feet at ground level. Figure 2-3 also shows how to design a backfilled retaining wall with proper drainage. If this isn't enough, you may have to connect to a sewer line or build a dry well like the one shown in Figure 2-4.

Slopes and Hills

Terrain is a major consideration in your design. A flat level lot poses few problems, while a hilly lot may pose many. You can use your elevation drawing here. (We'll talk about doing the drawings later in this chapter.) If you're going to step a fence on a slope, you need to calculate the length of the sections between fence posts. If the section length is too short for the degree of slope,

you'll use too much material. If it's too long, you'll wind up with very large voids under your fence. See Figure 2-5.

I've calculated some section lengths for you in Figure 2-6. You'll have to know how much the land slopes to use this chart. To find the slope, use a *story pole*, a ball of cord, a tape measure and a stake or two. Figure 2-7 shows you the proper setup.

First, you pound the story pole into the ground so that 90 inches of the pole is above ground, and plumb it to vertical.

Move the metal ring that's attached to the string up the pole and stake the other end of the string to the hillside at the point where the 90 inch mark on the string is level with the ring on the pole. You've formed a right angle between the pole and the string. Now, count the notches in the story pole from the ground up to the metal ring. Each notch represents two degrees of slope. Figure

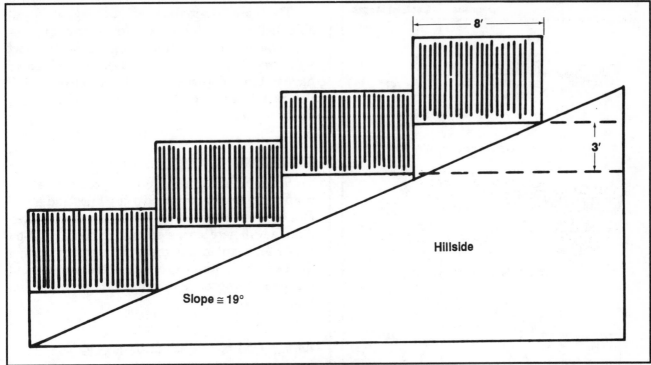

Figure 2-5
Stepping not practical on a steep slope

2-7 indicates a slope of 26 degrees. You may have to repeat these measurements at several locations along the sloped fence line and take an average.

Of course, you could just follow the lay of the land and not worry about stepping. Note the fence that climbs the mountain in the center of Figure 2-8. That's acceptable for a ranch or farm. But most residential fences should be stepped.

Crossing Water

You have two choices when the fence line crosses a stream or pond. You can end your fence at the water's edge or suspend the fence across. Here you have to consider water levels, adequate post anchors, and materials floating in the water. Will the fence obstruct boaters? Again, be sure you build a fence, not a dam.

Animal Pens

Design these to *contain* animals, not injure them. Barbed wire is fine for cattle, but not recommended for horses. A cow won't try to jump a fence; a horse will. Barbed wire can injure a horse as severely as it can injure a human.

Many animals, especially dogs, can dig under a fence. You may have to extend a fence 12 to 18 inches below ground level to discourage them. To contain birds, you'll need to design a mesh top enclosure and proper inside supports.

Artificial Light

We talked about the relationship between a fence and sunlight, but not artificial light. Light from a nearby school, industrial area, street light or traffic can be annoying. But it can be blocked by the right kind of fence. Check the fence or wall site at night. Plot these light sources and plan your fence or wall to block out unwanted light.

Maybe your customer *wants* light. You may be asked to build security or decorative lighting into a fence or wall. See Figure 2-9. In this case, you need to check the local electrical code and draw up a wiring diagram. Make this as detailed as possible. Describe the fixtures, their wattage and cost, the routing of the wiring and conduit, the circuit

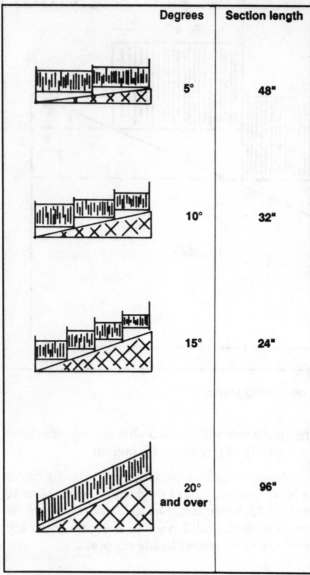

Degrees	Section length
5°	48"
10°	32"
15°	24"
20° and over	96"

Figure 2-6
Section lengths for various slope angles

breaker or fusing system, and a timer, if one is required. Chapter 10 has more information about electrical installations.

Security Systems

Your customer may require a security system like the one in Figure 2-10. If cameras or other sensors are involved, you have to take into account their location, type and protection from thieves and vandals. You also have to consider how to minimize false triggering. Describe in detail all the wiring and protection circuits.

There are "do-it-yourself" security kits available that you can install, but for maximum security, you or your customer should subcontract with a security expert. In any case, you'll probably have to build the wiring into the fence or wall. If you're not trained to do this, hire an electrician to do it for you.

Safety Barriers

Some buildings need protection from vehicle traffic. Homes located on curves, hills, and at the end of a "T" intersection are common examples. Build a wall here strong enough to take a head-on crash. You want to stop them in the front yard, not the bedroom. Built-in reflectors are a must. Put reflectors on posts on either side of driveway entrances, also.

Turning Room, Access and Visibility

Allow enough space for vehicles to maneuver through gates and driveways. Many garages and driveways are arranged in an "L" shape. It's hard to back a car out of a garage and around a wall or fence. Don't get yourself known as the dummy who built a fence so the car couldn't get out of the garage. Lay out the proposed fence path on the ground, then test your design by actually driving around it. Check for clearance and visibility. And be sure driveways are wide enough so people can get in and out of their vehicles easily.

In some places, you may need to put a separate post or bumper in front of a wall to keep people from hitting it. Make the post or bumper tall enough so drivers can see it through their rear view mirror.

Public Domain Access

According to common law, someone who passed over the land of another without objection for many years may have a *prescriptive easement*. That may give them the right to continue passing over the land. In fact, your fence may be intended to prevent anyone from getting a prescriptive easement over the owner's land. You could wind up having to remove the fence, or add a gate. If your customer plans to build a wall or fence over a path that people were formerly free to use, sug-

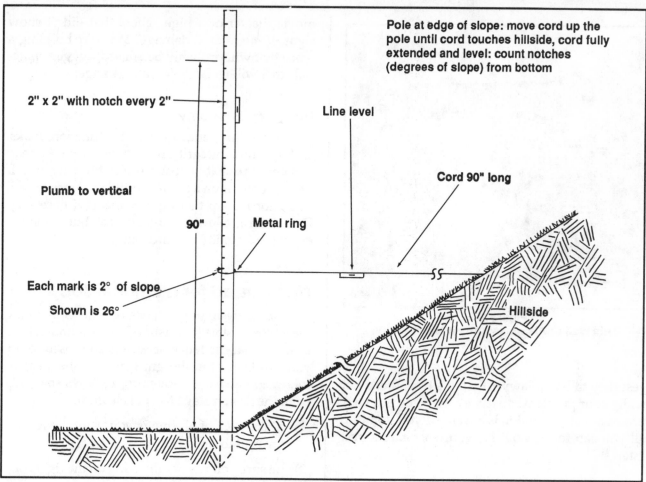

Pole at edge of slope: move cord up the pole until cord touches hillside, cord fully extended and level: count notches (degrees of slope) from bottom

2" x 2" with notch every 2"

Line level

Plumb to vertical

Cord 90" long

90"

Metal ring

Each mark is 2° of slope

Shown is 26°

Hillside

Figure 2-7
Use a story pole to measure slope

Figure 2-8
A nearly vertical fence follows land contours

Figure 2-9
A fence with built-in lighting

Figure 2-10
This wall contains security system wiring

gest they talk to a lawyer first. It's true, that's not really your problem as a fence contractor. But your professional reputation is at stake if you don't do all you can to look out for your customer's best interests.

Expect the Unexpected

Children and puppies like to climb. Fences and walls are favorite places to do it. I lost the bottom rail of one fence several times. The rail was butted to the post and toenailed in place. Kids stood on the bottom rail to see over. Sooner or later the nails would let go, and down would come the rail — and the kid. I finally solved the problem with proper blocking under the rail.

What I'm getting at is that people, including adults, will do things you don't expect — or want them to do. Take this into consideration, and make your design as structurally sound as possible. And here's another consideration: wood fences have splinters. If you're building a fence that kids are sure to climb on, suggest a block wall instead.

Many fences are subject to intentional abuse. Have you ever seen a chain link fence at a drive-in movie theater or a high school that didn't show signs of intentional damage? If you're building a fence that will probably be abused, suggest materials that will resist deliberate damage.

Design for Economy

Design any fence or wall for function, looks, and structural integrity, not for cost alone. A cheap fence will probably cost more in the long run. If the customer is on a budget, build the fence or wall in sections. Help them get financing if necessary. Design for the lowest possible cost, but not at the expense of quality or function.

Plan Ahead for a Smooth Job

Part of designing a fence or wall is planning the job from start to finish. When you understand exactly what the fence or wall is supposed to do, you can begin the design. Here are the steps to follow to make sure your project flows smoothly from the design stage to final cleanup.

1) Make a list of all things you want the fence or wall to do.

2) Be sure you're not infringing on the rights of others, or creating a nuisance for your customer (or yourself).

3) Check on all rules and restrictions.

4) Pay attention to the legal issues. Get the proper permits. Settle any questions about ownership or property lines.

5) Draw a plan and elevation view of your project. I'll tell you how a little later.

6) Make up a detailed materials list. Allow for defects and waste. Order materials in advance of the job start date.

7) Schedule material deliveries for the day before you plan to begin work.

8) Plan for securing the materials during work.

9) Review everything before you finalize the plans and spend any money.

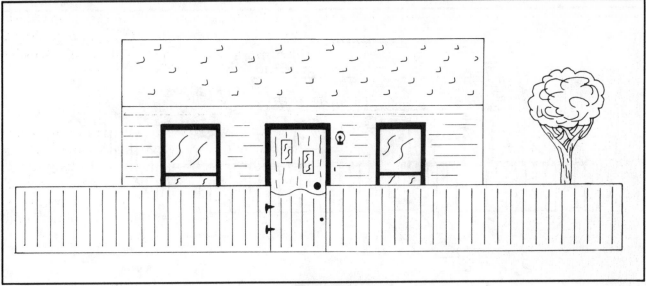

Figure 2-11
Elevation view

Drawing the Plans

When you've decided what kind of fence or wall to build and where to build it, it's time to start drawing the plans. You may need any or all of these drawings, depending on the job:

- Sketch

- Preliminary

- Plan view

- Elevation view

- Detail view

- Artist's conception

A *sketch* is the first rough draft of your ideas about what the final design will look like. The *preliminary* drawing is the cleaned-up version of your sketch. You can present this to your customer to get design approval.

You'll need a *plan* view of the property. A plan view is like a floor plan, as though you were looking down on the property from an airplane. Draw it to scale, usually 1/8 inch to a foot. Mark compass directions on the plan view. You'll need them when you consider where light and shadows will fall.

You'll also need an *elevation* view that shows what the wall or fence will look like when viewed from eye level. Include buildings, plants and trees in your elevation drawing. Figure 2-11 is an example. Notice the elevation drawing only shows the surface that faces you.

You might be able to get construction drawings for the property from either the builder or the city planning department. Those will include both plan and elevation views. You can have several copies made from the original blueprints, and use them as your worksheets.

Detail drawings are like close-ups. They show how components will go together. You'd use a detail drawing to show how to anchor a wood fence post. Because detail drawings are so important, there's a separate section on details a little later in this chapter.

Don't skip making these drawings. Your building department may require them before they issue your permit. And you can prevent expensive mistakes by making detailed drawings before you build.

The *artist's conception* is an elevation and *perspective* view of the final design, usually done with colored chalk or pencils. Perspective drawings show a fence or wall as though you were looking at it from a corner. Figure 2-12 is a perspective

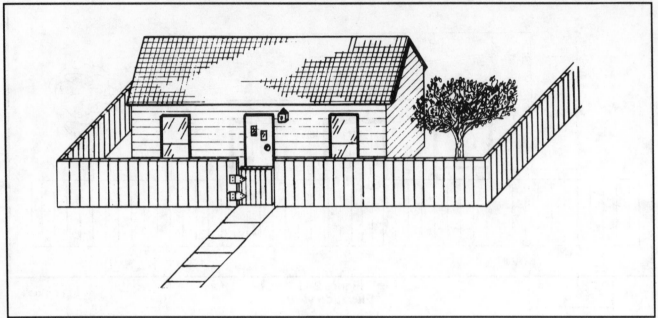

Figure 2-12
A perspective drawing

view. I'd use a drawing like this to help make the sale. It helps the owner understand exactly what you intend to build.

If You Can't Draw ...

How well can you draw? Nearly anyone who can draw a straight line can create an elevation view and plan view of a fence or wall. A perspective drawing is a little harder, of course. But if drawing scares you off, here are a few suggestions:

1) Use a drafting service or hire a freelance drafter. Most communities have freelance artists and draftsmen. Look in the Yellow Pages under "Drafting Services" or "Artists, Commercial."

2) Use *peel and stick* layouts, *rub-offs*, or templates. You can get these from stationery stores, art suppliers and book stores. Draftsmen use them to draw plans and to apply texture designs to their plans. You can buy designs that represent brick, wood, rock, and so on. The publisher of this book produced Figure 2-13 by pasting a piece of brick texture decal onto the page layout.

You can get complete peel and stick kits for around $25. One supplier is:

Plan-a-flex
Stanley Tools
600 Myrtle Street
New Britain, CT 06050

Their kit comes in a round tube about 20 inches long and has materials for a complete plan view of a property. It's a landscaping design kit, but it works well for fence and wall layout.

3) Improvise. You don't have to be a professional artist to draw a fence plan. Get a few #2 and #4 pencils and some grid paper. Do your best at sketching out your plan and elevation layout. You'll be surprised at how

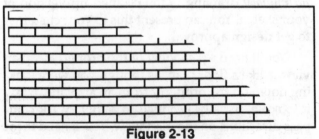

Figure 2-13
Produced from a texture decal

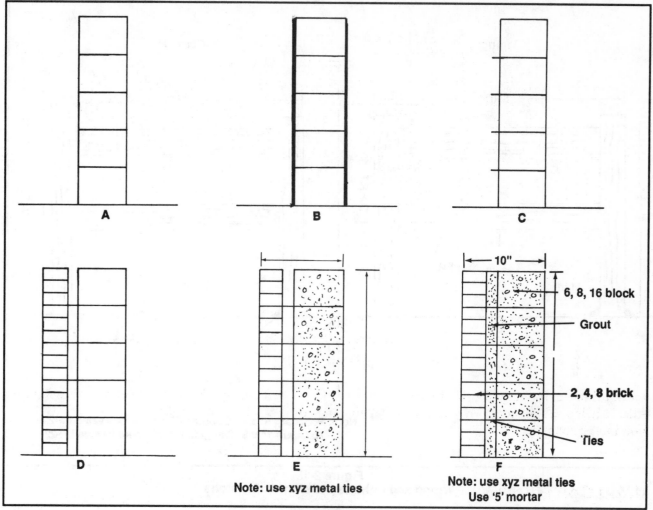

Figure 2-14
Six steps to a completed drawing

well you can draw — or what a building inspector will accept.

You can also make other low-cost drawings by tracing. Use illustrations from this book, if necessary. Copy photos or drawings and paste them to your layout. When you're done, photocopy the whole layout, and you're in business.

You'll need copies of your drawing for your customer and your crew, of course. The building or planning department at city hall will probably need at least three copies. You might have to submit one or more copies to any homeowner's association concerned with your project.

How to Do the Drawing Yourself

If you're talented enough — or brave enough — to do the drawings yourself, here's how to begin: Start drawing from the inside out. Let's say you're drawing a block wall with facing brick on the outside. First, outline the blocks lightly, then darken the lines when they're satisfactory. These steps are shown in parts A and B of Figure 2-14. Next, show the ties for the brick, and the brick, steps C and D. Then add the dimension lines and begin the notes. Finally, enter the dimensions and fill in textures and descriptions.

◆ *Profile* your drawings. That means emphasize the main objects with heavier lines to make

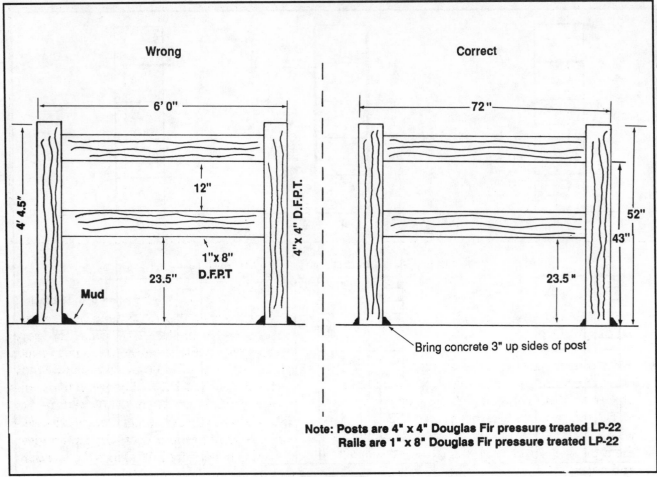

Figure 2-15
Wrong and right way to show dimensions

them stand out. You can *pouche* your drawing, also. Pouche means to shade the drawing on the back side of the vellum with a medium blue pencil so the shaded areas stand out. Don't use wax crayons or black or red pencils for the shading. Those block the copier process so the copy will come out black in the shaded areas

◆ *Pointers* should be straight lines, not wavy or curved lines. Pointers are the lines you draw between notes and bubbles and the object they relate to. End each pointer with an arrow at the object.

◆ Make your *notes* generic. Don't use brand names unless you intend to use brand name material. Say 8 x 8 x 16 standard block, not

Blockwest standard block, unless you mean to use only block from a company named Blockwest.

Call out *sizes* in whole numbers whenever possible. Avoid fractions if you can. When you can't, use fractions a builder can measure accurately with a standard tape measure. Callouts down to a thirty-second of an inch will drive your workers nuts. Use 1/16, 1/8, 1/4, 1/2, or their decimal equivalents, .0625, .125, .25, .50. Don't mix fractions and decimals on the same drawing or group of drawings.

◆ You can use *nominal sizes* in your notes, but your drawing and dimensional information must be exact and drawn to scale. For instance, your note can say, "2 x 4, #1 common, pine."

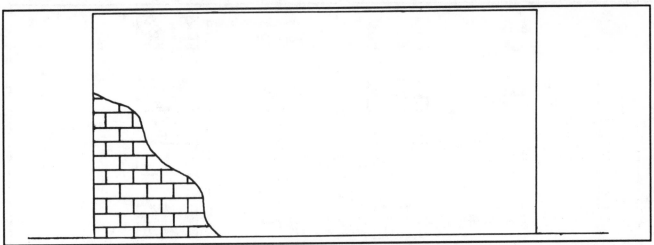

Figure 2-16
You only have to texture part of a drawing

Your scale drawing and dimensions must be 1-1/2 x 3-1/2.

♦ Write *dimensions* so they're all read from the same direction. Don't list one across the page and another up the side. Group your dimensional information together rather than scattering it all over the page. Figure 2-15 shows the right and wrong way to show dimensions and notes.

You can specify dimensions three ways:

1) Plus-or-minus tolerance: 84 inches ± 1/8 inch. This means that anything between 84-1/8 and 83-7/8 would be acceptable.

2) Minimum/maximum dimension: 84 (max). The item can be less than 84, but not more.

3) Hold means *hold* the dimension, no tolerance allowed.

♦ Don't use abbreviations and slang on your drawings. Abbreviations can mean different things to different readers. For example, to a grader, "F.G." means *finished grade*. To a pipe fitter, it means *fuel gas*. Your drawings are part of your contract with your customer. That makes them legal documents, so keep them professional. Use "mortar," not "mud."

♦ If you decide to *texture* your drawing for better detail, use the correct texture or symbolic de-

sign for the scale you're working in. The general rule is that the larger the scale, the more detailed the symbolic design is. You can make a break line across an object, and texture only part of it, like Figure 2-16. Be careful to use the correct symbols when you show texture. For instance, when you show concrete in cross section, use triangles and dots. On a plan view, use dots only. Figure 2-17 shows the standard symbols for various materials.

♦ A *cross section* is a cut view of an item. It shows what the item looks like if you cut through it and expose one of the cut sides. Figure 2-18 shows a cross section. You draw a line through the section you want to show. Beginning with "A," label the two ends of each cross section line with the same letter. Label your detail of each section with the letters you assigned, A-A, B-B, C-C, etc. You use a *break line* to show that you've drawn only part of an object. That's the wavy line on the detail A-A of Figure 2-18. The break line shows that an item continues. You don't have to show all of a 100-foot-long wall. You can just show one or two sections. It's assumed that the wall continues outward from this line to some distant point. If you want to show both ends of something, but leave out the center part, use a double break line. Figure 2-19 shows both types of break lines.

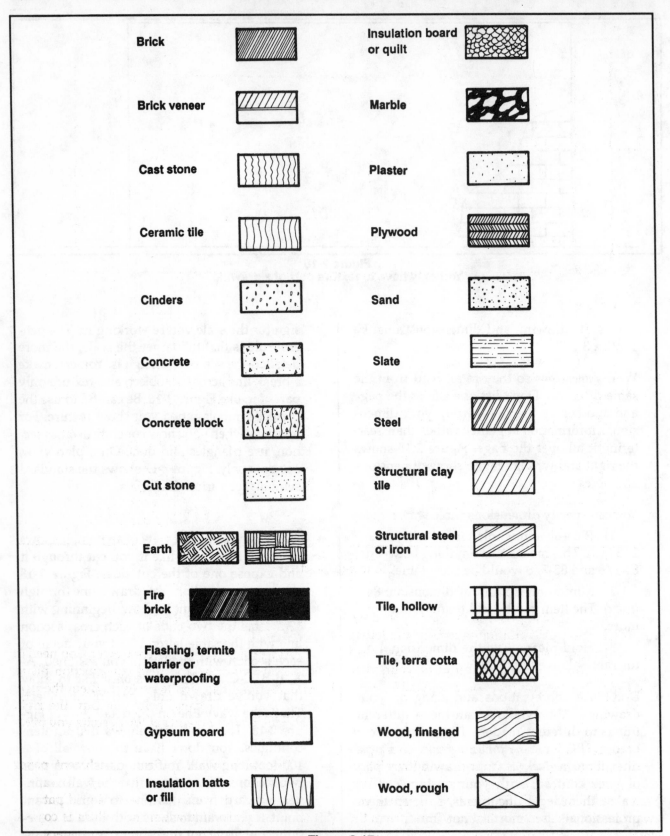

Figure 2-17
Architectural design symbols

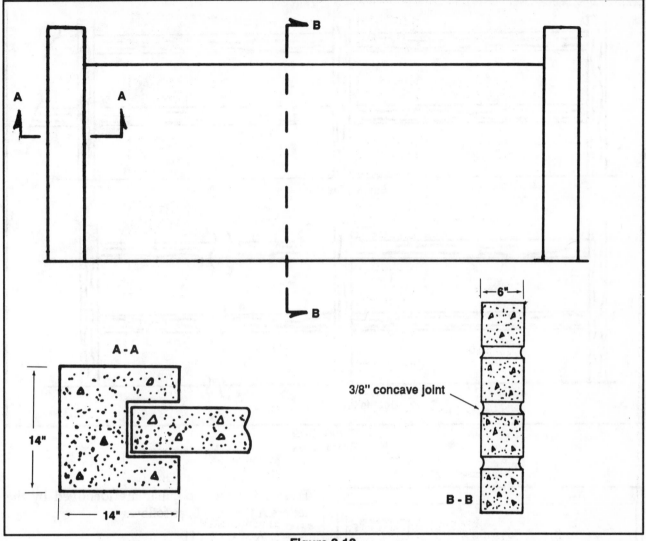

Figure 2-18
Cross section details

- Good penmanship is a must when you draw plans. Use *block printing* and keep the letters vertical and evenly spaced. If people can't read your writing, they can't build to your plan. Figure 2-20 shows five don'ts and a do.

You can buy rub-on lettering for a more professional-looking job. Or you can use a Kroy lettering machine. Their machine contains a print wheel and a tape. You spin the wheel to the letter you want and press a button. The machine prints the letter on clear or colored pressure-sensitive adhesive tape that you can stick onto your drawing.

Producing Blueprints

As a professional fence contractor, you need to know how to draw and read construction plans. And you might as well learn to do them the *right* way. Blueprints (plans) help you buy the right materials for the job and get the permits you need.

Start with *vellum,* a firm, translucent paper especially made for original drawings. You can get it either plain or with various-sized grid patterns that don't reproduce when the vellum is copied. Vellum is available at most office, stationery, and drafting supply stores. It comes in various sizes.

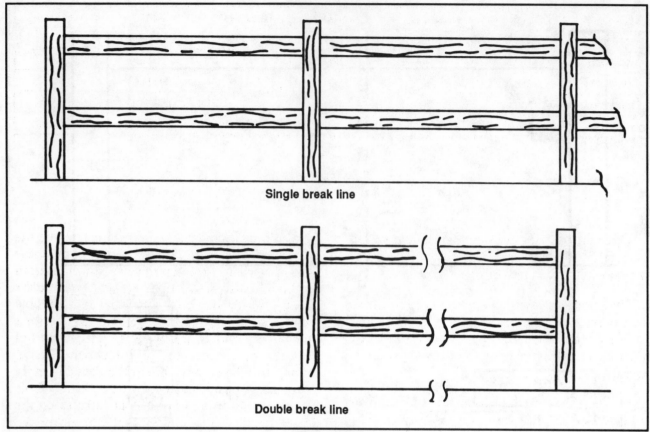

Single break line

Double break line

**Figure 2-19
Break lines**

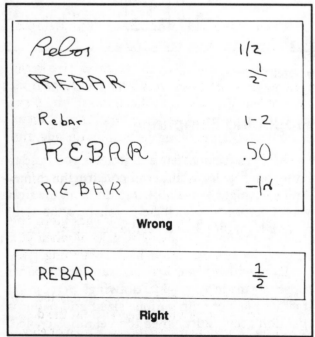

Wrong

REBAR $\frac{1}{2}$

Right

**Figure 2-20
Make your lettering easy to read**

Five of the most popular are identified by the letters A through E, as follows:

A   8-1/2 x 11

B   11 x 17

C   17 x 22

D   22 x 34

E   30 x 42

Copy machines for producing blueprints (or whiteprints) cost several thousand dollars. But there's no need to buy one. Most communities have a print or copy shop that will copy your drawings for a modest cost.

You'll need a large, flat table or a drafting table, and a T-square. You'll also need an assortment of drafting pencils, pens, rules and templates. You can get these at drafting and art supply stores. You can buy what you need to get started for about $50, not including the table.

Drawing #	Drawing type	Size	Drawn by	Drawn for	Date	Description
100000-top	Plan	D	Bill	Mrs. Jones	02/01/89	Side fence
100000-1	Detail	C	Bill		02/03/89	Top rail
100000-2	Detail	C	Bill		02/03/89	Post
100000-last	Detail	B	Jim		02/04/89	Bottom rail
100001-top	Elevation	C	Bill	Mrs. Smith	02/15/89	Rear gate

Figure 2-21
Drawing log

I recommend you use B-size vellum or larger, even for detail drawings. It's too easy to lose A-size drawings among other papers.

Once your contracting business is established, you can have vellum printed with your company name and logo. But at first, just fill in the title block in the lower right-hand corner of standard drafting paper.

I suggest a 1/8 inch to 1 foot scale for your plan and elevation drawings. Use 1/8 or 1/4 inch scale for your detail drawings. Note in the scale box the scale you're using.

Number each drawing. And keep a file log describing the drawing, the drawing size, who it was drawn for, by, and the date it was drawn. Use a log something like the one shown in Figure 2-21. *Top* in the log refers to the first or top drawing in a series. *Last* is the final or last drawing in the series. Include the size, because you'll probably file the different sizes in different cabinets or drawers. You use the names and numbers as references to retrieve the drawings.

You'll find a revision block in the upper right corner of the vellum. Use that to record drawing revisions, the date you made them, and the reason. Before you revise a drawing, make a copy of it and file the copy. Now make your changes and give the new drawing a revision letter, A, B, C, etc. The revision block is your history of changes for that drawing. You may want to add a revision column to your log. When you make a change to the drawing, put a small triangle near the change and draw a line from the triangle to the change. Write the revision letter in the triangle.

You'll see some vertical lines just above the title block. Use your T-square and extend these lines upward. Now start numbering the lines from the bottom up. These numbers are your *bubble numbers*. Every item on the drawing gets a bubble and a number. A bubble is a small circle with a number in it and an arrow pointing to the part of the drawing the number in the bubble list describes. If the item appears on the drawing more than once, you only need one entry on the bubble list. There can be any number of bubbles on the drawing with the number of that entry. Now it's easy to count how many of each item you'll need, and put the amount in the materials box. Figure 2-24 later in the chapter shows how to use bubble numbers.

When you're done you'll have a complete materials list for costing and ordering.

You can have as many as six views on a detail drawing. In most cases, you'll start with the front view. When you walk around a fence, you'll see the right side, back, and left side. If you crawl under the fence, you'll see the bottom-up side, and if you climb over it, the top-down side.

Figure 2-22 shows how to position the different views on your drawing.

You usually need the front and back view. The others are optional, but will be helpful when you want to be specific about how something goes together.

You probably don't need a materials block on the plan or elevation views. Put that on the detail drawings. What you do need on the plan or elevation views is a reference to the detail drawings. You circle the places you want to detail and then

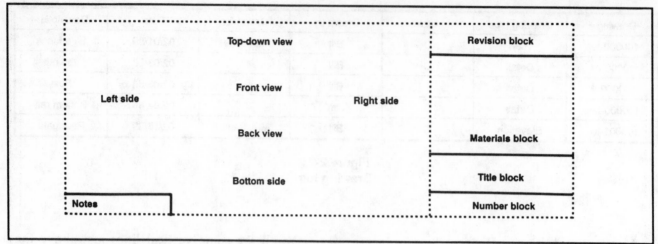

Figure 2-22
The views on a detail drawing

draw a line to a *split* bubble. A split bubble is a circle with a horizontal line drawn through it. Put the detail drawing size in the top of the bubble, and the drawing number in the bottom. You can see a split bubble in the center of Figure 2-24.

If you want to put special notes on your drawings, there's a block in the lower left corner of the vellum for this. Notes might include calling for a certain brand of paint, its stock number, federal specification, number of coats, and method of application.

Detail Drawings

Materials expand and contract, they swell and shrink, they rot and warp. You must consider all this when you design a fence or wall. That's why the plan view and elevation views aren't enough to do most jobs. You need some detail drawings.

On your elevation view, circle the areas that require construction details. Number each circle consecutively. Now, use graph paper and sketch a close-up detailed drawing of what is in each circle. Make this as accurate as possible. Draw it to scale and call out all dimensions. Include everything you'll use to construct the detail.

When you're preparing the detail drawings, you'll likely discover some problems that are much easier to correct on paper than during construction. You may find that things don't fit to-

gether as you thought they would. Maybe you'll see an easier way to join a rail to a post than you first planned.

You'll need about nine detail drawings for a typical wood fence.

1) Corner post bracing

2) Corner post lower rails

3) Corner post upper rails

4) Corner and line post to earth anchoring

5) Line post lower rails

6) Line post upper rails

7) Pickets to rail attachment

8) Picket top treatment or design

9) Post top treatment or design

You'll probably be adding a gate, so you'll make a few more detail drawings.

1) Gate top treatment or design

2) Hinge attachment and style

3) Latch attachment and style

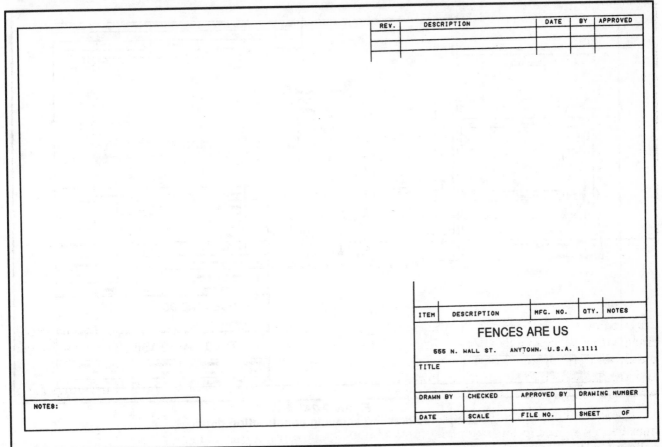

REV.	DESCRIPTION	DATE	BY	APPROVED

ITEM	DESCRIPTION	MFG. NO.	QTY.	NOTES

FENCES ARE US

555 N. WALL ST.   ANYTOWN, U.S.A. 11111

TITLE			
DRAWN BY	CHECKED	APPROVED BY	DRAWING NUMBER
DATE	SCALE	FILE NO.	SHEET OF

NOTES:

Figure 2-23
Blank drawing format reduced from B size

4) Handle type and location

5) Bracing or attachment of gate boards

6) Left and right gate post anchoring

7) Overall view with dimensions and clearances

I know that's a lot of detail drawings. But if you do them at the beginning, you'll save time and money later. It only takes a little drawing time to save hours of rebuilding time. Also, a mistake made on a piece of paper is considerably cheaper than one made on a block wall.

Use Your Computer

All the drawings that follow were produced on a relatively inexpensive personal computer system using a CAD (computer aided design) program. These programs produce very professional-looking drawings and have features that can simplify your accounting, purchasing and inventory jobs.

Figure 2-23 is a reduced view of a blank B-size vellum. You can customize this form by adding customer information, job number, or a warranty statement.

In Figure 2-24, you can see some drafting techniques I covered earlier. Notice the top down view in the upper left corner and the side (end) view to the right of the front view drawing. On the left post of the front view drawing is the "Detail A" bubble, with the corresponding enlarged detail drawing to the right of the side view.

The split bubble to the left of the side view drawing indicates that there's an A-size drawing, numbered B-23 (not shown) that shows the metal

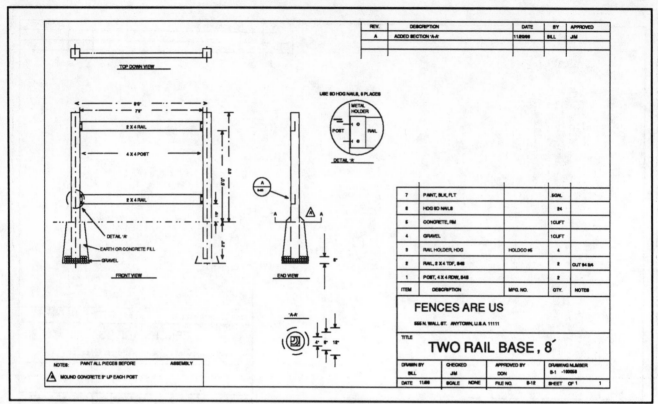

Figure 2-24
Completed drawing showing construction detail

holder and the post-to-rail construction in more detail. The triangle with the letter A inside it refers to the identical triangle in the *Notes* block, where you see the note that applies to the base of the post.

Just below the triangle next to the side view drawing, the A-A cross section is indicated, and below the side view is the top down detail of the cross section, also labeled A-A. The square in the center is the post, the solid line is the mound of concrete, and the dotted line is the bottom of the post hole. You can see the dimensions for each of these to the right of the detail drawing.

Since this part of the drawing was added after the original drawing was approved, there's a reference to it in the revision block at the upper right corner of the drawing. Always keep copies of the original, as well as any revised drawings.

Figure 2-25 is similar to the previous one, but not all the materials are shown. On this drawing, the numbers in the small circles refer to the materials list above the title block. Notice that item #1 calls out the drawing number for Figure 2-24, so

you know you need both drawings and the materials from both materials lists to complete this fence section. An "X" as a dimension indicator, like the one for the height on this drawing, means you can substitute an appropriate number. That way, you don't have to make a new drawing every time you change that dimension.

Figure 2-26 contains a *schedule* that lets you show 28 different common board fences with one drawing. To use this drawing, just insert the number you want for X and circle the board size on the schedule.

On Figure 2-27, the two-sided board and panel fence, there's an options list that also lets you use one drawing for many applications. Just check off the appropriate filler panel option.

On this drawing you'll also see an arrow and the letters EXT in the *Notes* block for Note A. That means you can continue the fence by adding duplicate sections, but you cut 1-3/4" off the top board of the first section. Notice I also used a square instead of a triangle for the B note. It's

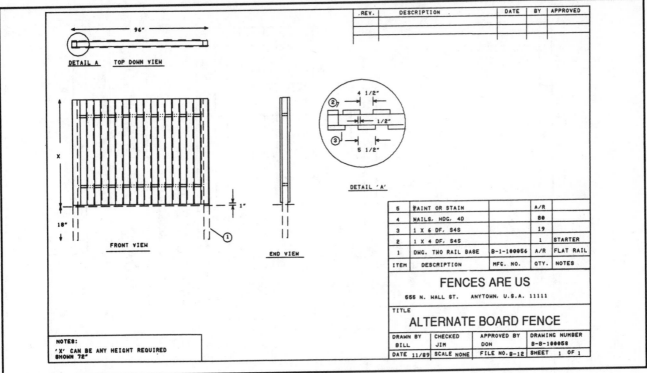

Figure 2-25
Alternate board fence detail drawing

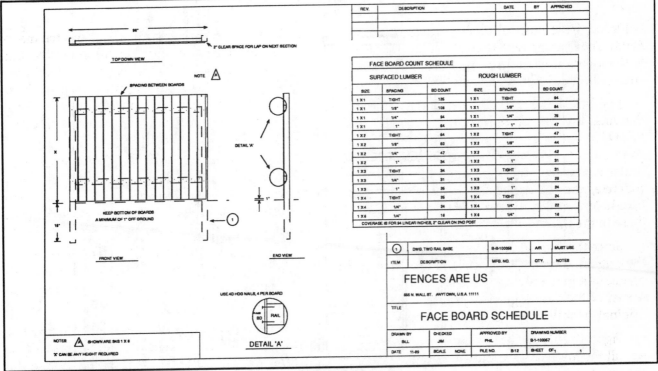

Figure 2-26
An all-purpose face board drawing

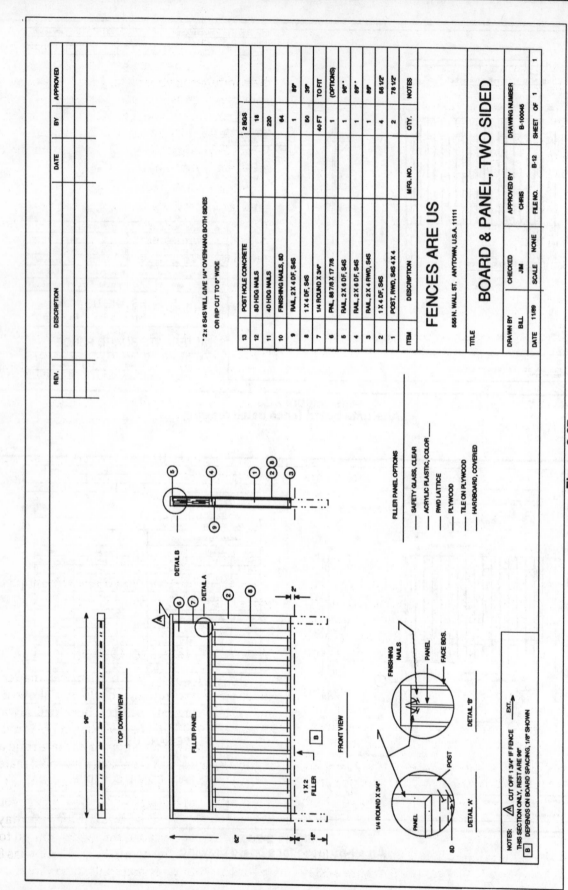

Figure 2-27
Drawing with optional choices

really not accepted practice to mix those symbols on the same drawing, but I did it here to show you that you can use a square if you want to.

On Figure 2-28, you'll see I've made a little mistake on the drawing. Look at the right side of the front view, and you'll see that it appears that the last picket won't cover the post. That's why it's important to make a scale drawing before you build the job. It's a lot easier to correct a drawing than it is to rip off all the face boards and start over because the spacing wasn't right. By the way, the spacing chart *is* correct.

This drawing has two schedules. One is the spacing chart and the other is called Table A. That table goes with detail B, and gives you dimensions for cutting your own pickets. The widths shown are for both rough sawn and surfaced lumber.

The front view in Figure 2-29 shows a letter on each of the boards. The Fabrication Instructions block refers to those letters and tells how to assemble the fence. You probably know the fastest, easiest way to build this fence, but your workers may not. Include specific instructions in your drawings when necessary. Paper is cheap, manhours are not.

Figure 2-30 combines a schedule with instructions. The schedule would be too large and confusing if it included all the options, so I've written instructions for modifying the options for each job. The numbers on the blocks are the recommended order for installation.

Figure 2-31 is a set of tables that I could have typed on standard 8-1/2 x 11 paper, but I've made it a B-size drawing for two reasons. First, its larger size makes it harder to misplace among other papers. Second, as a standard drawing, I can call it out on the materials list of other drawings, as you saw in Figure 2-25.

When I release a job to my workers, I copy this drawing and circle the brick type and grade, and the mortar type. I keep a copy of the circled drawing in the customer file for future reference.

Figure 2-32 is another drawing that takes the place of many individual ones. The two side views in the boxes are alternates to the basic double-sided wall shown in the front view. The shading emphasizes the half-size bricks.

Figures 2-33 and 2-34 demonstrate some of the other advantages of CAD programs. Figure 2-33 is an enlargement of the front and top down views of Figure 2-32. It was produced by selecting part of the original drawing, then manipulating it from the computer keyboard to make the second one. It only took a couple of minutes to do — much less time than it would take to redraw it. You can show more detail of part of a drawing, as shown in Figure 2-34, a greatly enlarged view of the starter corner in Figure 2-33.

Figure 2-35 is a handy chart that shows how CAD programs can directly scale both linear dimensions and angles. I rounded the degree of slope, but the computer can show them to 5 decimal places, an accuracy of 0.00001 degree.

List Your Materials

When you're making your detail drawings, you're also creating a detailed list for materials and tools. Once you have a list for one detail, it's easy to count all the sections that have the same detail. Then multiply the materials required for one by the number of sections. That's your materials list.

For instance, the materials list to place a post in the ground reads:

1/3 bag of gravel

1/3 bag of concrete

tar

4 x 4 redwood post, 8 feet long

Also list the tools you'll need to complete this part of the job.

When It's Time to Order

Here's a word to the wise: No matter how much material you need, always allow a little more for waste and scrap. There will always be some material that's not worth using. You'll spoil some by cutting it too short or at the wrong angle. Figure on about 5 percent extra for most materials.

When you're ready to order, plan ahead. Your suppliers won't always be ready when you are. You may have a job scheduled for Saturday that requires 10-foot lumber, but when you go to pick it up on Friday afternoon, the yard only has 8-foot in stock. Order your materials in advance.

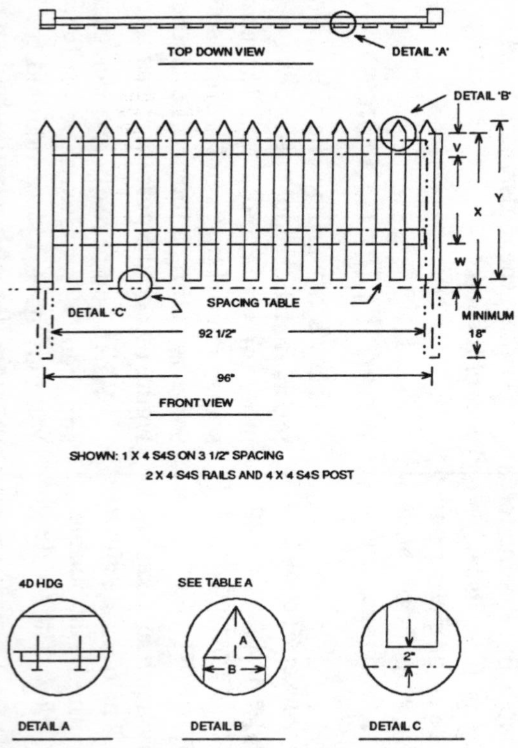

RECOMMENDED SPACING AND DISTANCES

HEIGHT	WIDTH	SPACING	BD. CNT.	V	W	X	Y
18"	1 1/2"	1 1/2	33	4"	5	16	16"
18"	2"	1 5/8	28	4	5	16	16
18"	2 1/2	1 7/8	25	4	5	16	16
24"	2"	1 5/8	28	6	7	21	22
24"	2 1/2	1 7/8	26	6	7	21	22
24"	3"	2	20	6	7	21	22
36"	2 1/2	1 7/8	26	7	9	33	34
36"	3"	2	20	7	9	33	34
36"	3 1/2	2 7/8	16	7	9	33	34
42"	3"	2	20	8	11	38	40
42"	3 1/2	2 7/8	16	8	11	38	40
42"	4"	3 15/16	13	8	11	38	40

*REQUIRES 4 40 HDG NAILS PER BOARD

TABLE 'A'

WIDTH	B 1/2 WIDTH	A =
3/4"	3/8"	5/8"
1"	1/2"	7/8"
1 1/2	3/4"	1 3/8
2"	1"	1 3/4
2 1/2	1 1/4"	2 1/8
3"	1 1/2"	2 1/2
3 1/2"	1 3/4"	2 7/8
4"	2"	3 3/8
4 1/2"	2 1/4"	3 7/8
5 1/2"	2 3/4"	4 5/8

REV.	DESCRIPTION	DATE	BY	APPROVED

ITEM	DESCRIPTION	MFG. NO.	QTY.	NOTES

FENCES ARE US
555 N. WALL ST. ANYTOWN, U.S.A. 11111

TITLE: **PICKET FENCE**

DRAWN BY	CHECKED	APPROVED BY	DRAWING NUMBER
BILL	JIM	CHRIS	B-100060
DATE 11/89	SCALE NONE	FILE NO. B-12	SHEET OF 1

TOP DOWN VIEW

DETAIL 'A'

DETAIL 'B'

DETAIL 'C'

FRONT VIEW

96"

92 1/2"

16" MINIMUM

SPACING TABLE

SHOWN: 1 X 4 S4S ON 3 1/2" SPACING
2 X 4 S4S RAILS AND 4 X 4 S4S POST

SEE TABLE A

4D HDG

DETAIL A

DETAIL B

DETAIL C

2"

NOTES: 18" USE 2 X 2 POST, 1 X 2 RAILS
24" USE 2 X 4 POST, 1 X 3 RAILS

**Figure 2-28
Picket fences**

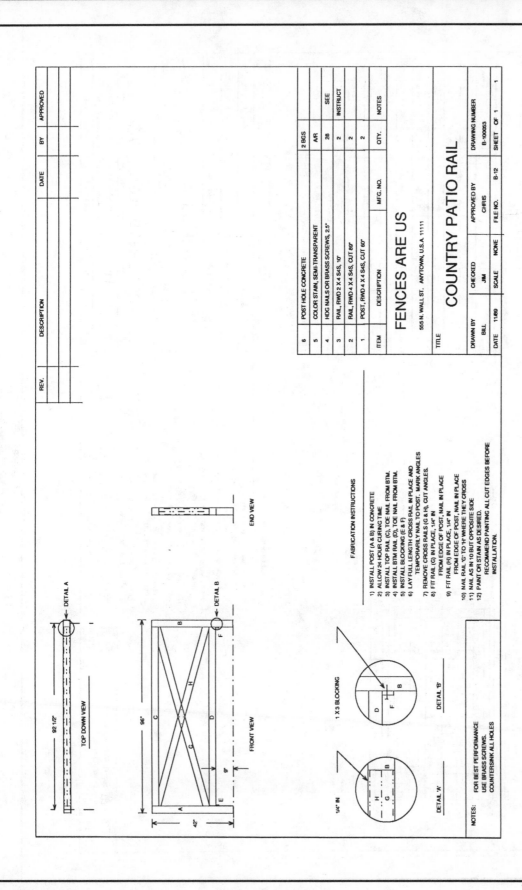

Figure 2-29
Drawing Includes assembly Instructions

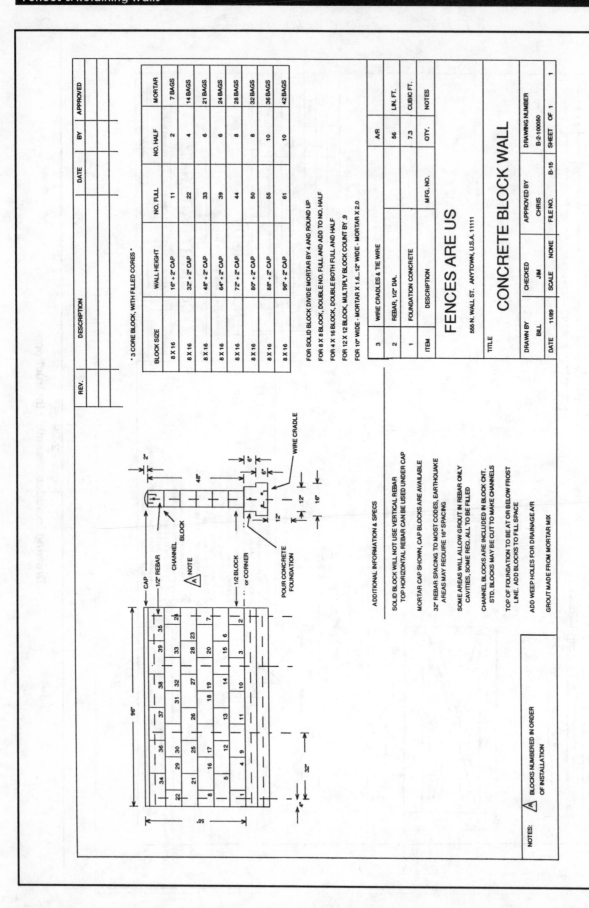

Figure 2-30
Build by the numbers

BRICK TYPE	NOMINAL SIZE INCHES			JOINT SIZE	MANUFACTURED SIZE, INCHES			COURSES VS. IN.
	WIDTH	HEIGHT	LENGTH		WIDTH	HEIGHT	LENGTH	
STANDARD	4	2 2/3	8	3/8	3 5/8	2 1/4	7 5/8	3C = 8
ENGINEER	4	3 1/5	8	3/8	3 5/8	2 15/16	7 5/8	5C = 16
ECONOMY 8	4	4	8	3/8	3 5/8	3 5/8	7 5/8	1C = 4
DOUBLE	4	5 1/3	8	3/8	3 5/8	4 15/16	7 5/8	3C = 16
ROMAN	4	2	12	3/8	3 5/8	1 5/8	11 5/8	2C = 4
NORMAN	4	2 2/3	12	3/8	3 5/8	2 1/4	11 5/8	3C = 8
NORWEGIAN	4	3 1/3	12	3/8	3 5/8	2 13/16	11 5/8	5C = 16
ECONOMY 12	4	4	12	3/8	3 5/8	3 5/8	11 5/8	1C = 4
TRIPLE	4	5 1/3	12	3/8	3 5/8	4 15/16	11 5/8	3C = 16
SCR	6	2 2/3	12	3/8	5 5/8	2 1/4	11 5/8	3C = 8
NORWEGIAN-6	6	3 1/3	12	3/8	5 5/8	2 13/16	11 5/8	5C = 16
JUMBO-6	6	4	12	3/8	5 5/8	3 5/8	11 5/8	1C = 4
JUMBO-8	8	4	12	3/8	7 5/8	3 5/8	11 5/8	1C = 4

ADDITIONAL INFORMATION & SPECS.

BRICK IS SOLD FOR MORTAR JOINT USED. FOR 1/2" JOINTS SUBTRACT 1/8" FROM MANUFACTURED SIZES

ECONOMY 8 IS ALSO KNOWN AS JUMBO CLOSURE

ECONOMY 12 IS ALSO KNOWN AS JUMBO UTILITY

BRICK SHOULD MEET ASTM C62 or C216 or C652

SOLID BRICK MAY NOT HAVE MORE THAN 25% OF CROSS AREA OPEN

NOTES:

REV.	DESCRIPTION	DATE	BY	APPROVED

BRICK GRADE AND USAGE

GRADE	USAGE
NW	USE AS BACKUP SUPPORT FOR INTERIOR MASONRY
MW	USE AS FACING BRICK IN LOCATIONS WHERE THERE IS A LOW CHANCE OF WATER PENETRATION AND FREEZING. MODERATE WEATHER USAGE ONLY. MOST CALIFORNIA BRICK IS MW BRICK
SW	SEVERE WEATHER BRICK. USE IN AREAS SUBJECT TO FREEZING, HEAVY RAIN AND WIND.

MORTAR GRADE AND USAGE

GRADE	USAGE
K	INTERIOR NON LOAD BEARING PARTITION WALLS
M	BELOW GRADE. WALKS, SEWERS, FOUNDATIONS, RETAINING WALLS, EARTH CONTACT.
N	PARAPET WALLS, CHIMNEYS, EXTERIOR WALLS
O	INTERIOR NON LOAD, NON FREEZING WALLS
S	EARTHQUAKE OR GROUND MOVEMENT AREAS AND WHERE HIGH BOND STRENGTH IS NEEDED.

ITEM	DESCRIPTION	MFG. NO.	QTY.	NOTES

FENCES ARE US

555 N. WALL ST. ANYTOWN, U.S.A. 11111

TITLE

BRICK SPECIFICATIONS

DRAWN BY	BILL	CHECKED	JIM	APPROVED BY	CHRIS	DRAWING NUMBER	SPEC-B-100000
DATE	11/89	SCALE	NONE	FILE NO.	B-1	SHEET OF 1	1

Figure 2-31

A drawing without pictures

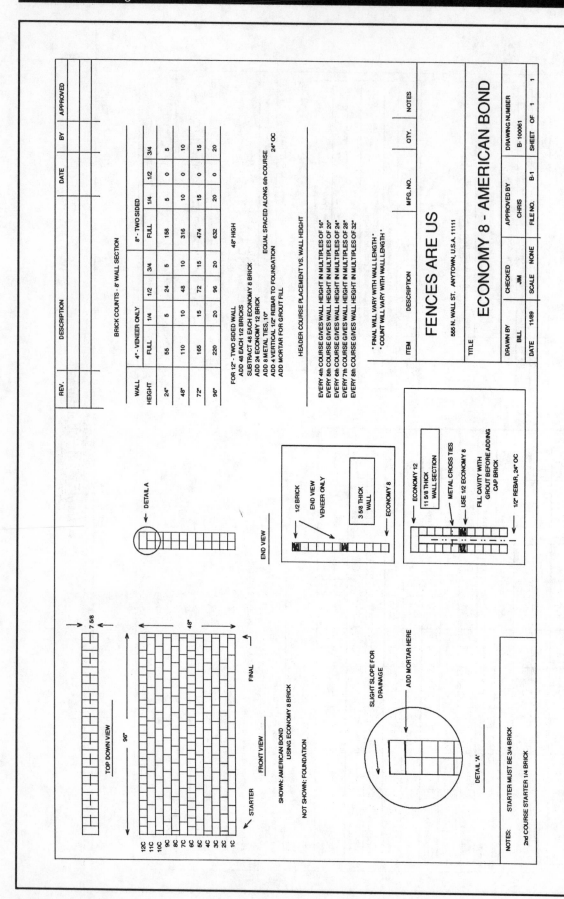

2-32

A multi-use drawing

BRICK COUNTS - 8' WALL SECTION

WALL HEIGHT	4" - VENEER ONLY				8" - TWO SIDED			
	FULL	1/4	1/2	3/4	FULL	1/4	1/2	3/4
24"	55	5	24	5	158	5	0	5
48"	110	10	48	10	316	10	0	10
72"	165	15	72	15	474	15	0	15
96"	220	20	96	20	632	20	0	20

FOR 12" - TWO SIDED WALL
ADD 48 EACH 1/2 BRICKS
SUBTRACT 48 EACH ECONOMY 8 BRICK
ADD 24 ECONOMY 12 BRICK
ADD 8 METAL TIES, 10"
ADD 4 VERTICAL 1/2" REBAR TO FOUNDATION
ADD MORTAR FOR GROUT FILL

48" HIGH
EQUAL SPACED ALONG 6th COURSE
24" OC

HEADER COURSE PLACEMENT VS. WALL HEIGHT

EVERY 4th COURSE GIVES WALL HEIGHT IN MULTIPLES OF 16"
EVERY 5th COURSE GIVES WALL HEIGHT IN MULTIPLES OF 20"
EVERY 6th COURSE GIVES WALL HEIGHT IN MULTIPLES OF 24"
EVERY 7th COURSE GIVES WALL HEIGHT IN MULTIPLES OF 28"
EVERY 8th COURSE GIVES WALL HEIGHT IN MULTIPLES OF 32"

* FINAL WILL VARY WITH WALL LENGTH *
* COUNT WILL VARY WITH WALL LENGTH *

REV.	DESCRIPTION	DATE	BY	APPROVED

ITEM	DESCRIPTION	MFG. NO.	QTY.	NOTES

FENCES ARE US
565 N. WALL ST. ANYTOWN, U.S.A. 11111

TITLE **ECONOMY 8 - AMERICAN BOND**

DRAWN BY	CHECKED	APPROVED BY	DRAWING NUMBER
BILL	JIM	CHRIS	B-100061
DATE 11/89	SCALE NONE	FILE NO. B-1	SHEET 1 OF 1

DETAIL A

END VIEW

1/2 BRICK
END VIEW
VENEER ONLY

3 5/8 THICK WALL

ECONOMY 8

ECONOMY 12
11 5/8 THICK WALL SECTION
METAL CROSS TIES
USE 1/2 ECONOMY 8
FILL CAVITY WITH GROUT BEFORE ADDING CAP BRICK
1/2" REBAR, 24" OC

7 5/8

48"

96"

TOP DOWN VIEW

12C
11C
10C
9C
8C
7C
6C
5C
4C
3C
2C
1C

STARTER

FINAL

FRONT VIEW

SHOWN: AMERICAN BOND USING ECONOMY 8 BRICK

NOT SHOWN: FOUNDATION

SLIGHT SLOPE FOR DRAINAGE

ADD MORTAR HERE

DETAIL 'A'

NOTES: STARTER MUST BE 3/4 BRICK
2nd COURSE STARTER 1/4 BRICK

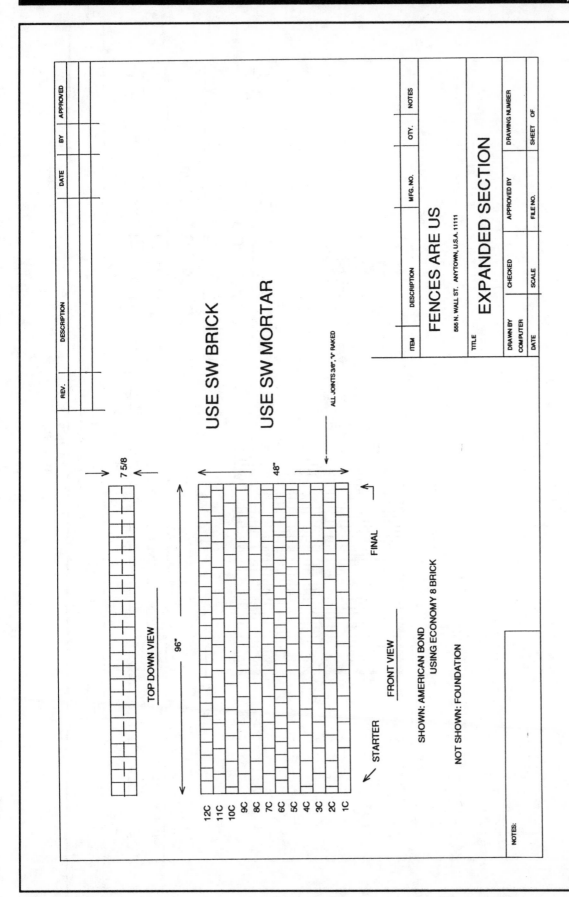

**Figure 2-33
Expanded view**

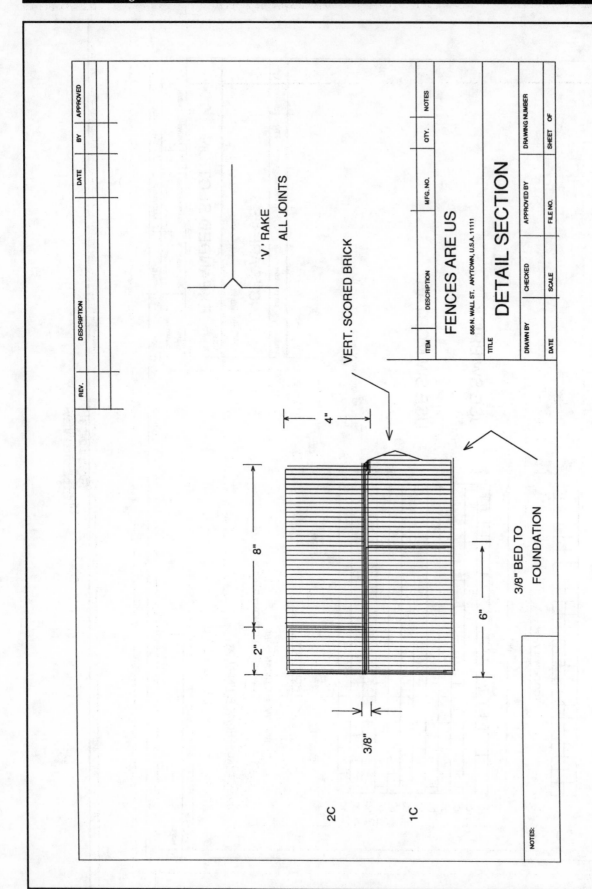

Figure 2-34
Detail section

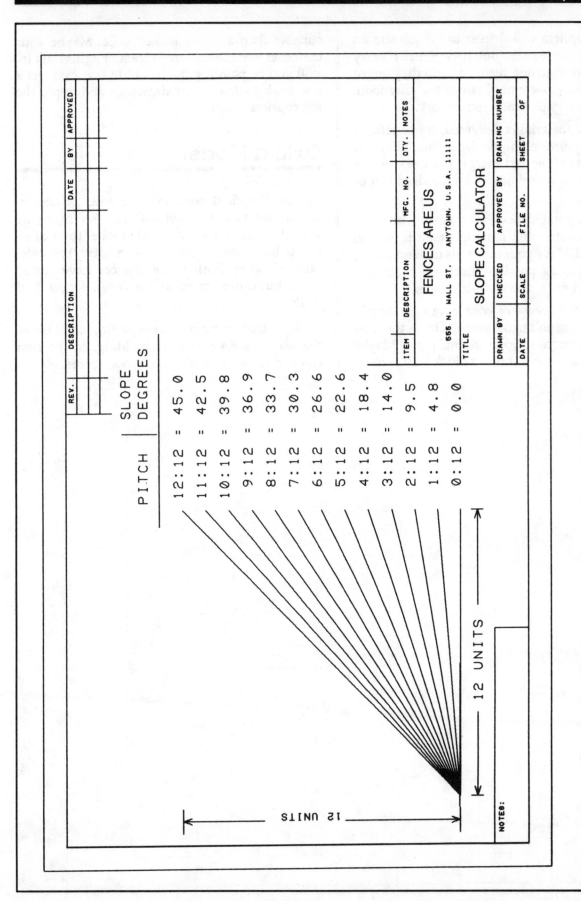

Figure 2-35
Slope calculator

Most suppliers will deliver to the job site on the day of your choice. But they usually carry loads for more than one customer, and they might not get to your job site until late in the afternoon. That's hardly a good time to start work.

When the material is delivered, try to offload it at various points along the fence line. That will save you a lot of time and energy. You'll waste a lot of both carrying a skid of block a hundred feet or so.

But be sure to balance convenience with security. Loose construction materials tend to vanish after nightfall. Have your materials delivered to as secure an area as possible. Lock up tools and equipment when you're not using them.

Make a final review of your layout for the job. Does everything still make sense? This is the time to make corrections to your original plans. Maybe after all this, it turns out that a block wall is more suitable than a wood picket fence. Maybe your customer wants an alarm system or lights built in. Will you be painting the fence? In that case, get a few *whiteprints* of your drawings and apply the appropriate colors.

Build a Model

Here's a final note on the subject of design. Sometimes a scale model will help you make the sale. Consider building a scale model from cardboard, balsa wood, or kits from a hobby or model railroad store. Both those sources have scaled trees, buildings, bushes, and even fences and walls.

Now that we've gotten the preliminaries out of the way, it's time to start building. In the next chapter, I'll tell you all about wood fences.

three

Wood Fences

When most people think of fences, they naturally think of wood fences. Wood has warmth and charm. Because it's a natural material, it blends with the landscape. It lasts a long time (if kept dry), doesn't cost a lot, is easy to work with, and is an inexhaustible resource (if our forests are managed intelligently).

One notable exception is *redwood*, which is being used faster than new forests are planted and reach maturity. That's unfortunate, because redwood is a favorite choice for fence material. It weathers nicely, isn't prone to insect infestation, and it resists rotting.

Another wood that's resistant to both decay and insects is *cypress*. It's a strong wood that's easy to work. That makes it popular for decking, shingles, and fences. The wood is hard and red. Cypress isn't easily cultivated, and the price is higher than equivalent grades of pine or fir.

Bald cypress grows in swamps in the southeastern United States, so it's hard to harvest and replant. It's one of a variety of cypress that grow around the world. Monterey cypress grows in a small region of northern California, but it's protected and not available for commercial use. Europeans use Mediterranean cypress, and Australians harvest a type grown there. The kinds of cypress grown commercially in the United States are more closely related to fir and pine trees.

After redwood, I like fences made of *cedar*. It resists decay, swelling, warping and shrinking. But it's not very resistant to insects, and it needs periodic maintenance. Cedar is easy to work with and is usually less expensive than equivalent grades of redwood or cypress. Its aromatic odor makes it a favorite for lining cabinets, closets and hope chests. Wormy cedar is popular with fence builders. As you can see in Figure 3-1, it has a character of its own that you don't find in other species.

Fir, spruce and *pine* are all common, commercially grown woods. Almost all construction lumber used today is one of these three. They're all suitable for fences, but they require care to protect them from decay and insects. You should paint or clear-coat fences made from these materials to protect them from weather. The coating should include an insecticide.

Figure 3-1
Wormy cedar

Rough nominal	Finished dry	Finished green
1 x 4	3/4 x 3-1/2	25/32 x 3-9/16
1 x 6	3/4 x 5-1/2	25/32 x 5-5/8
1 x 8	3/4 x 7-1/4	25/32 x 7-1/2
1 x 10	3/4 x 9-1/4	25/32 x 9-1/2
1 x 12	3/4 x 11-1/4	25/32 x 11-1/2
2 x 4	1-1/2 x 3-1/2	1-9/16 x 3-9/16
2 x 6	1-1/2 x 5-1/2	1-9/16 x 5-5/8
2 x 8	1-1/2 x 7-1/4	1-9/16 x 7-1/2
2 x 10	1-1/2 x 9-1/4	1-9/16 x 9-1/2
2 x 12	1-1/2 x 11-1/4	1-9/16 x 11-1/2
3 x 4 through 12	2-1/2 x width	2-9/16 x width
4 x 4 through 12	3-1/2 x width	3-9/16 x width
5 x and up lumber is 1/2" thinner in height and width than nominal		
Dry is less than 19% moisture Green is over 19%		

Figure 3-2
Nominal vs. finished lumber

Hemlock is another evergreen used for fencing. It's easy to work with, has a uniform grain pattern and is light weight. It's not resistant to insects or decay and does require a sealer and periodic maintenance. Don't confuse the tree with the herb also called hemlock. The herb is poisonous; lumber from a hemlock tree is not.

Rough Cut vs. Milled Lumber

When you buy lumber, you ask for a specific size, like a 1 x 8. This is the *nominal* or name size of the lumber before it's finished. A rough, unfinished, green 1 x 8 board may measure very nearly 1 inch by 8 inches. But a finished, dry 1 x 8 will be smaller. You won't use much rough lumber that hasn't been either air dried or kiln dried. Unseasoned lumber tends to warp and bend as it dries. It's usually full of splinters and probably varies more in width and thickness. All these things make rough, unseasoned lumber harder to work with.

Lumber manufacturers give you a better product that's dried, milled and sanded. Your material will be uniform in width and thickness, reasonably straight and fairly splinter-free. But it won't be as thick as rough cut lumber. For instance, a 2 x

4 is only 1-1/2 x 3-1/2 inches when you get it. Figure 3-2 shows you the difference between nominal and finished sizes. Milling provides a harder, more weatherproof surface. It's easier to sand and paint. Rough cut lumber is hard to paint properly.

But don't totally dismiss rough cut lumber. Some people prefer the old, rugged look and want their fences built from rough material. It blends with western, oriental, or modern styles. The dominance of the grain lets the full strength of the lumber show through. You usually finish rough cut lumber by staining rather than painting.

Moisture Content

Most wood contains a lot of water when it's first cut, up to 80 percent of its weight. The mills rack and dry the lumber so the moisture is reduced to a set percentage. Of course, it will still have *some* water in it, and the grade stamp will tell you how much.

- **S-Grn** has the highest water content. It hasn't been seasoned or dried.

- **S-Dry** is the most common grade sold. Its water content must not exceed 19 percent.

- **KD** stands for *kiln dried* and may contain no more than 12 percent water. KD lumber is your best bet if you need wood that won't warp, split or cup. It's also the most expensive since it takes extra effort and costs the most to manufacture.

Grading

The mills plane and sand the wood to various degrees and grade the finished lumber accordingly. This is called *dressed lumber*. Since boards have four sides, you can buy lumber that's milled on one, two, three, or all four sides. Figure 3-3 shows abbreviations used for the surfacing that's been done to wood. I've also included grades EV1S, CM, D&M, and T&G.

Each piece of lumber is further graded for tightness of the grain and presence of knots. Use the right grade for the job. In structural work, the building inspector might reject the job and make you do it over if you use the wrong grade. In fencing, aim for the best appearance at the lowest possible cost. If you use a grade that's *too* good, you'll spend too much. If it's not good enough, your fence won't look first rate.

If you're building wood retaining walls or balconies, strength of the lumber is important. Structural grading is divided into four categories:

1) Board lumber, 1 inch or less thick.

2) Studs, used in walls to 10 feet high.

3) Light framing, to support light loads as in homes.

4) Structural framing, to support heavy loads.

Board lumber is graded as follows:

Grade stamp	Meaning
S1E	One edge surfaced
S1S	One side surfaced
S1S1E	One side, one edge
S1S2E	One side, two edges
S2S	Two sides surfaced
S4S	Four sides surfaced
EV1S	Edge vee one side
CM	Center matched
D&M	Dressed and matched
T&G	Tongue and grooved

Figure 3-3
Grades of dressed lumber

- #1 Common is the best grade, with few, if any, knots. Use it for shelves, paneling and siding where appearance is important. You can clearcoat #1 grade boards.

- #2 Common and #3 Common have more knots and will usually be less expensive. If you're going to paint the surface, use #2 or #3 boards.

Tight, straight grain wood is the strongest. So a #3 Common with tight grain and lots of knots might be stronger than a #1 Common with wide, loose-looking grain and no knots.

Stud grade lumber doesn't have to be used for studs and all studs don't have to be cut from *stud grade* lumber. The term "stud" can also refer to any 2 x 4 or 2 x 6 that's used in a wall. Stud grade lumber is usually cut to 92-1/4 inches long and is intended for use in residential construction.

Light framing lumber is either construction, standard or utility grade. Many mills mix two or more grades together and label the result something like "standard or better." That means all the lumber is at least standard grade and some may be better. Usually, at least 25 percent will be construction grade, but this varies with requirements at the mill.

1) *Construction* is the best of the three. Use this if you're concerned about appearance.

2) *Standard* is second best

3) *Utility* is the least desirable.

Structural grades include lumber 2 x 4 and larger, as opposed to board lumber. They're used for rafters, beams, load-bearing studs, posts, trusses and joists. They are graded as:

1) Structural Select

2) Light Structural

3) Framing, #1, #2 and #3. These are the least expensive structural grades.

Grading Redwood and Cedar

Redwood and cedar have their own grading codes. You'll probably be using a lot of both. The heartwood of these trees is most resistant to rot, decay and insects. The *sapwood* or *whitewood* is no more resistant than fir or pine. You can identify the heartwood, sometimes termed "duramen," by its red color. It comes from the center, or heart, of the tree. The sapwood is cream colored and nearer the tree's bark.

1) *Clear All Heart* is the best. It's used for siding, cabinets, and paneling.

2) *Clear* is next best. It does contain some cream-colored wood. Clear is commonly used for fences and siding.

3) *Construction Heart* comes from the center and is red but has some knots and visual flaws. It's also commonly used as a fence material.

4) *Construction Common* has some heartwood and some sapwood.

5) *Merchantable* can be from either heart or sapwood. It usually has some loose knots and will be the cheapest of the grades.

You may also find *Select* and *Select Heart*. These are generally the most expensive grades, free from defects.

Cypress also has both heartwood and a sapwood. Only the heartwood is resistant to insects, rot and decay.

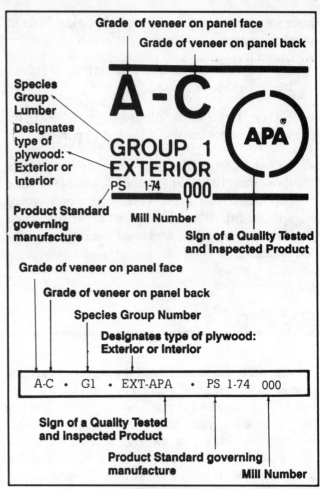

Figure 3-4
Lumber markings

Other marks you'll find on lumber are the grading association marking, the mill number, and the wood species. Figure 3-4 shows some examples.

A Word About Grading Accuracy

Moisture content grading is fairly accurate. An inexpensive, hand-held probe can measure the moisture content of lumber to a fraction of a percent. Selection grading is a little more vague. Nearly all building lumber is graded visually. That means the lumber inspector simply looks at each piece and decides what grade applies. Naturally, different inspectors can have different opinions.

If you get into a dispute about lumber grades, you can have the lumber regraded by an independent inspector. The minimum fee will usually be several hundred dollars plus travel time. You'll probably have to supply a helper and a forklift for the inspector's use. But you can get nearly any lumber regraded, if necessary.

For me, grades are just the starting place. They get me to the right pile of lumber at the yard. I'm the final judge of which pieces are best suited for the job I'm working on. Lumberyards don't like it, but nearly all will let you pick through a pile to select the pieces you want.

If your supplier is delivering the order, I still suggest you pick the load in advance. If you don't, you may end up with an assortment of good and bad lumber, or worse yet, all the stuff no one else wanted. Even properly graded lumber can be warped and split.

When you're checking the lumber, look for the defects in Figure 3-5:

◆ A *cup* — the surface is not level, there's a curvature, one side in, one side out.

◆ A *warp* or twist — the lengthwise surface varies from a true plane. Warped lumber won't sit flat on a flat surface. If any of the four corners don't touch the surface, the lumber is warped.

◆ A *wane* — there's a missing edge or corner somewhere along the length of the lumber. It usually happens when the piece is cut from the outermost area of the tree, where bark has been peeled off.

◆ A *shake* — a crack or split that follows the growth rings of the lumber.

◆ A *crack* — a split outward from the center of the tree.

Chemically-Treated Alternatives

The most durable fence lumber is redwood, cedar, or cypress heartwood. But lumber like this is expensive. A good alternative is pine, hemlock, fir, or larch that's been treated with chemicals. Treated material can last 40 years or more in the ground.

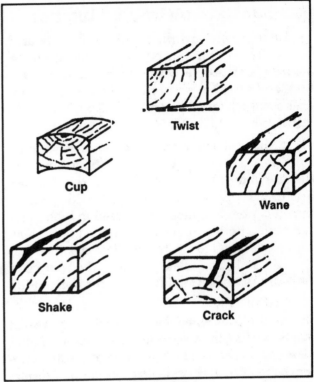

**Figure 3-5
Lumber defects**

Chemicals injected into the lumber under high pressure protect the wood fibers from insects, dry rot, decay, and sometimes even from weathering. Weathering turns the wood from its natural red or cream to a silvery gray color.

As a fence contractor, you should know the following treatment standards:

◆ LP-22 contains 0.40 pounds of preservative per cubic foot of lumber.

◆ LP-2 contains 0.25 pounds of preservative per cubic foot of lumber.

These grades are determined by the American Wood Preserver's Bureau. Wood used outdoors and in contact with the ground should be redwood, cedar, or cypress heartwood, or treated wood with the LP-22 rating. You may not choose to build your entire fence from these woods. That's perfectly acceptable. But at least use them for the posts.

Use Caution with Treated Lumber

There are a few words of caution about treated lumber. The chemicals used are harmless to plants, animals, and people when contained within the lumber. But with age and weathering, some chemicals can leach into the ground. This can kill plants growing close to the fence.

If you ever have to tear down a fence built from treated lumber, be careful about how you dispose of the old fence. *Never burn treated lumber.* The smoke will carry the chemicals with it. Chromated copper and arsenic are used in wood preservatives. Both are dangerous. Why do you think the insects won't touch it? Arsenic is absorbed into the skin and accumulates in the body. Your body can't dispose of it. Continuous exposure can result in dangerous concentrations.

Wear gloves when you work with any treated lumber. As a contractor building fences year after year, you'll be exposed to potential health problems. Don't treat them lightly. For more information, contact the lumber or chemical manufacturer. Chapter 15 has more information on using treated lumber.

Why use treated lumber at all? Because untreated lumber rots, decays, and is prime food and lodging for many insects. Ants and termites love wood. Ants everywhere make fences and walls their homes. To build their nests, they tunnel through wood, stucco, brick, block — even cement. Treated materials or insecticides will kill them before they can do too much damage.

Termites, also known as white ants, not only live in wood, they raise their young on it. No matter which name you use, these insects are highly destructive. They live all over the United States. The least susceptible areas are the cold northern states of Maine, Vermont, New Hampshire, Michigan, North Dakota, South Dakota, Minnesota, Montana, and Wyoming. The most susceptible states are the warm southern ones: East Texas, Louisiana, Mississippi, Alabama, Florida, Georgia, South Carolina, and California. The wood treatment used for killing termites is CCA, Chromated Copper Arsenate, a pesticide registered with the Environmental Protection Agency.

Kop-Coat, Inc., 1850 Koppers Bldg., 436 Seventh Avenue, Pittsburgh, Pennsylvania 15219, manufactures Wolman® *RainCoat*® Water Repellent, a product that protects lumber from splintering, checking, and twisting.

Chemical Treatments You Can Apply

What about treating posts yourself? You can, but it won't be as effective as the commercial treatments. You can brush on a preservative like creosote or tar. You can also soak the lumber in a commercial chemical bath. Neither of these provide the protection you'd get from pressure-treating the lumber.

Brushing will apply about three gallons of material to each 40-foot section of 6-foot high fence made of 1 x 6 boards. Soaking will use 12 to 13 gallons for the same length of fence. Brushing only protects the surface. Soaking only penetrates to about 1/8 inch. Pressure treatment applies 60 gallons of preservative to that same section of fence because the liquid seeps deeply into the sapwood. But brush or soak the wood if you have to. It's a lot better than no treatment at all.

Lumber Prices

Some lumberyards price fence material by the piece. Others sell by the board foot. Board foot measure is based on nominal sizes, not actual sizes. And, to make it easy, any board less than 1 inch thick is considered to be 1 inch thick. A board 12 inches wide, 12 inches long and 1 inch thick (in nominal measure) has 1 board foot of lumber. A 2 x 6 that's 12 inches long also has one board foot of lumber. A 2 x 6 that's 10 feet long has 10 board feet of lumber.

Lumberyards buy lumber in lots of 1,000 board feet, usually abbreviated *MBF*. If a thousand board feet of #3 common pine costs $350, can you figure the cost for a single 2 x 4 that's 8 feet long? Here's my answer:

1) Multiply the width by the thickness: 2 times 4 is 8

2) Divide your answer by 12. This tells you how many board feet there are in each linear foot: 8 divided by 12 is 0.6667

3) Multiply 0.6667 by the length in feet to find the board feet in the entire piece: 0.6667 times 8 is 5.3336 board feet.

4) Multiply the cost per board foot ($350 divided by 1000 is $.35) to find the cost for the piece: 5.33 times $0.35 is $1.87

Now, let's convert a cost per piece to a board foot price. Suppose 1-inch by 2-inch stake, 2 feet long, costs 28 cents. Here's how to figure the cost per board foot:

1) 2" (width) times 1" (thickness) is 2.

2) Divide by 12: 2 divided by 12 is 0.1667

3) Multiply by the length in feet: 0.1667 times 2 is 0.3333. That's the board feet per stake.

4) Divide the cost per stake ($.28) by the board feet per stake (0.3333) to get the cost per board foot: 0.28 divided by 0.3333 is 84 cents per board foot, or $840 per MBF. That's expensive lumber!

Figure 3-6 shows the board feet of lumber in various widths and lengths of lumber. If you buy posts and rails by the board foot, this table will probably make conversions much easier.

Fasteners

Now that we've selected the lumber, let's decide how we'll fasten it all together. We could use nails, screws, staples or a combination of those. We may use "L" or "T" angles, or metal supports. We could anchor the posts in dirt, asphalt, rock, or concrete. Let's look at the alternatives.

Nails

I'll start with nails. You've probably seen nail charts showing lengths of nails and identifying each in "d" or *penny* numbers. The shortest nail you'll generally use is the 2d, which is 1 inch long. From there, each penny number means an increase in length of 1/4 inch, thus 4d is 1-1/2 inches, 6d is 2 inches long, etc. The maximum nail size is 24d, or 6 inches. Anything larger than that is known as a *spike*.

Thickness	Width	Board feet				
		8'	10'	12'	14'	16'
1	1	0.67	0.83	1.00	1.17	1.33
1	2	1.33	1.67	2.00	2.33	2.67
1	3	2.00	2.50	3.00	3.50	4.00
1	4	2.67	3.33	4.00	4.67	5.33
1	6	4.00	5.00	6.00	7.00	8.00
1	8	5.33	6.67	8.00	9.33	10.67
1	10	6.67	8.33	10.00	11.67	13.33
1	12	8.00	10.00	12.00	14.00	16.00
2	2	2.67	3.33	4.00	4.67	5.33
2	3	4.00	5.00	6.00	7.00	8.00
2	4	5.33	6.67	8.00	9.33	10.67
2	6	8.00	10.00	12.00	14.00	16.00
2	8	10.67	13.33	16.00	18.67	21.33
2	10	13.33	16.67	20.00	23.33	26.67
2	12	16.00	20.00	24.00	28.00	32.00
4	4	10.67	13.33	16.00	18.67	21.33
4	6	16.00	20.00	24.00	28.00	32.00
4	8	21.33	26.67	32.00	37.33	42.67
4	10	26.67	33.33	40.00	46.67	53.33
4	12	32.00	40.00	48.00	56.00	64.00
6	6	24.00	30.00	36.00	42.00	48.00

Figure 3-6
Board feet equivalents

Selecting the Nail Length

How do you select the correct length nail for the lumber you're using? Choose a nail long enough to pass through the board being nailed and penetrate one-third of the way into the board being nailed to.

A board with a nominal thickness of 1 inch is actually 5/8 of an inch thick. A 2 x 4 is actually 1-1/2 x 3-1/2 inches thick. If you're nailing a 1 x 6 to the flat side of a 2 x 4, your nail should be 5/8 inch plus 1/2 inch, or 1-1/8 inches long. A 3d or 4d nail would be enough. You'd need a 5d or 6d nail to fasten a 1-by to the edge of the 2 x 4.

If you use a nail that's too short, the board will pull off easily. If you use a nail that's too long, you can crack the wood or penetrate all the way through and come out the other side. But doing that isn't always a mistake. Sometimes you want to *clinch* the nail for maximum holding power. To do that, you use a longer nail, whose point will come out the other side of the wood. Then you bend this point at a 90 degree angle, flattening it against the back side of the board. The nail tip should protrude a minimum of 1/4 to 3/8 inch beyond the board for proper clinching.

In our example, where we nail a 1 x 6 to the flat side of a 2 x 4, we have 5/8 inch plus 1-1/2 inch plus 3/8 inch. That's a total of 2-1/2 inches, so use an 8d nail. You can clinch with any type of nail, but there are specially-designed nails called *clinchers* available. The shank and tip are designed to make clinching easy.

The longer the nail, the thicker it is. One problem with thick nails is that they tend to split wood, especially if you're nailing within a few inches of the end edge of a board. There are two ways to avoid this problem:

1) Pre-drill the nail holes. Use a drill bit slightly smaller in diameter than the nail you're using.

2) Flatten the nail point so it cuts or punches through the wood fibers instead of spreading them. To flatten the point of a nail, place the nail, head down, on a hard surface, and strike the point with your hammer.

Choosing Nails with Holding Power

Common nails tend to pull out of fences. You start out with flat, straight lumber, and the wind, rain, sun, and cold cause the boards to cup and warp. Common nails are no match for this kind of stress.

Glue (cement) coated nails are usually amber colored. The glue is activated by the moisture in the wood, increasing the bond to the wood. The problem I've found is that the glue sticks very well to the wood but not to the nails. Eventually they'll loosen and pull out.

One solution is to use *ring shank* nails. These have pressed-in rings around the shaft or nail

shank that hold the nails in place. These are still steel nails, though, with a built-in weakness.

Choosing Nails That Don't Rust

Another problem with nails is that they rust. Most common nails are made from steel or iron. I'd love to see stainless steel nails that don't rust and stain the wood or paint.

Blued nails don't rust as easily. Their blue color comes from heating the steel until it forms an anti-rust oxide coating. Or you can buy *electro galvanized* (EG) nails. These are common nails that have a zinc coating applied with an electrical charge. They look dull compared to common nails which have a bright shine. In fact, common nails are sometimes called *bright nails*.

The EG nails are good, but they can pull out. The zinc coating is thin and will eventually fail. Hitting the head of one of these nails wipes off some of the zinc coating, leaving a bare spot that will rust.

There is a nail that meets all the requirements of holding power, rust prevention, and resistance to damage during nailing. *Hot dipped zinc galvanized nails* are my first choice for nailing fences together. Unfortunately, they're hard to find — and getting harder. Too many amateurs settle for EG or cement coated nails and some professional fence builders may not care. If you do, use hot dipped galvanized nails.

The hot dipped nails have a dull aluminum-like look. The difference is that the coating is thick and very rough. Roughness adds to the holding power once these nails are in place. The thick coating provides long-term corrosion resistance and helps them withstand hammer blows.

Aluminum nails are my second choice for fence nails. They don't rust and they hold fairly well. They cost more than steel nails, and they bend too easily if you hit off center. But I still feel they're a good choice for fences.

Screws

Screws are powerhouse holders of wood. Because of the way they twist into the wood, they're almost impossible to pull out. The holding power of screws keeps the boards in place without warping or cupping. The disadvantage is that they cost two to 20 times more than nails and take longer to install.

There are screws for sheet metal, plastic, and wood. For now, we're only concerned with wood screws. These are either common head (with a slot) or Phillips head (with an X). Use the Phillips head screws if you're installing the screws with a power screwdriver or power drill with a screwdriver bit.

For attaching fence boards, I like aluminum or zinc coated decking screws designed to secure decking lumber to joists. These have either a Phillips head or a square hole that receives a driver bit. They cost about 9 cents each, though. But since they're designed to be installed with a power driver and don't require a pilot hole, they save on labor costs. It takes 10 to 20 seconds to install a wood screw because you have to pre-drill it. It only takes 3 to 4 seconds to drive a deck screw. You have to figure out the time savings versus the extra cost. An extra 10 or 15 seconds isn't much, but when you're doing hundreds of screws, it adds up. One problem with using decking screws, however, is that they're 2-1/2 to 3 inches long, so you can only use them where they won't penetrate all the way through the lumber.

The square or "box" head is the easiest of the two to use. It stays in the bit better during installation. Screwdriver bits for your power screwdriver or drill will cost about 80 cents each.

Select a screw long enough to extend through the board you're fastening, and at least a third of the way through the rail you're fastening to. Unless you're using decking screws or screws under 1/2 inch long, you've got to pre-drill the holes before inserting the screws.

Most screws are made of steel, so they rust. You can prevent this with *cadmium plated* screws. Use brass screws if you're building a good quality redwood fence. They cost a lot, about 20 cents each as I'm writing this, but the results are worth it. Redwood has tannic acid that reacts with most other metals and creates unsightly stains.

You'll *have* to use screws to attach hinges and latches. Nails pull out too easily for use here.

Staples

The fastest way to attach boards to rails is with staples. You can drive U-shaped staples into the wood with either an electrical or pneumatic gun. It's fast and easy and does a good job. Most prefab wooden fences are stapled together. The double prongs provide twice the holding power of a nail but less than a screw.

If you haven't used staples before, I recommend you rent stapling equipment before buying. If you're serious about fence contracting, then I suggest you explore the various models available and choose the one that suits your needs. Cost is about $150 to $250, but you'll find the work goes about three times faster than when you use nails.

Post Holders and Brackets

Metal post holders, "L" and "T" brackets are handy for fence building. You don't have to bury posts in the ground where they're vulnerable to rot and insects. Instead, you create a foundation of concrete and set the post holder in the concrete before it hardens. Then, after it's hardened, you fasten the posts to the holder with nails, screws or bolts. Post holders are made of steel, so they're best for fences that will be painted.

There's another advantage to metal post holders. When the post finally fails, you can just put another post into the holder, which should still be intact. This is much easier than having to break out the concrete and start over. It's a good selling point too, when you're trying to get the job.

I always clean, prime and paint my metal hardware before I install it to prevent rusting — another selling point.

I do recommend that you use brackets when you put gates together. They make for a stronger, longer-lasting gate. Figure 3-7 illustrates one way to use "L" and "T" brackets. You can also use the 90 degree "L" to secure square corners.

Setting Fence Posts

Ready to plant a post? I'll assume you've read Chapter 2 on design and layout and know where

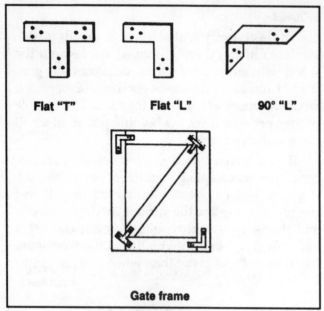

Flat "T"   Flat "L"   90° "L"

Gate frame

Figure 3-7
Use metal reinforcing brackets

the posts are going. So, now you'll dig a hole, put the post into it, backfill with dirt, and go on to the next one. Right?

Wrong!

When you do that, you make a cozy home for bugs while the post decays from contact with the wet ground. You also fail to supply a firm foundation for the fence, so a strong wind will eventually blow it over.

Let's do it right the first time.

1) Dig a hole with a diameter about three times larger than the widest dimension of your post. A power auger is the best post hole digger, especially in hard or rocky soil. If you use a small gas-powered auger, it's best to have two people hold it. If access allows, use a truck-mounted auger, especially where there are lots of rocks, or where you have to dig through asphalt in a driveway or parking lot.

You can rent or buy a manual post hole digger or *clam shell* shovel. These have two opposing handles and blades that are hinged together. You'll need one of these handy devices even if you do most of your digging with power tools. A post hole dig-

ger will help you pick up dirt remaining in the hole after you drill. The shovel costs about $25. The gas-power auger sells for about $1,300 and rents for about $45 per day. A truck-mounted auger will cost about $400 per day, including an operator. You can buy one of your own for about $30,000. I opted not to do this.

2) Widen the bottom of each hole about a third larger than the top. This wide section acts as a key, holding the post in place against vertical pull out. Use your clam shell shovel to widen the hole. Here's a tip: It's messy, but sometimes to your advantage to water the hole as you dig. The water softens the soil and makes digging easier.

3) Dig your post holes at least 18 to 24 inches deep. In very cold areas you may have to go even deeper to get below the frost line. I recommend you make the bottom of the hole at least 12 inches below the frost line.

4) Fill the bottom third of each hole with gravel for drainage. This gravel drains water away from the post and lets moisture percolate into the surrounding earth.

5) Set your post in place and prop it up plumb. Figure 3-8 shows a post that's braced plumb in one direction, but you'd use four braces to be sure it's straight in both directions. While the post is held vertical by the braces, pour concrete in the hole, filling it completely. Tamp this down and refill until you're about 2 inches above ground level. Shape the above-ground concrete so that it's 2 inches high on the post and slopes *away* from the post in all directions. This *water shield* drains water away from the post. See Figure 3-9.

6) Recheck for height and plumb and make any necessary adjustments. See Chapter 4 for a description of the various concrete mixes you can use.

7) When all the posts are in place, give the concrete five or six days to set. It takes that long for the concrete to harden and cure

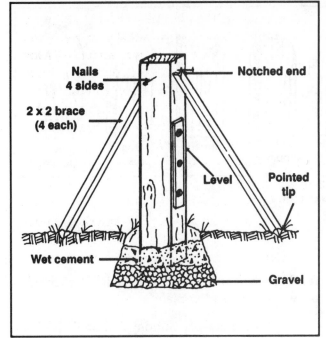

Figure 3-8
Level and brace the post

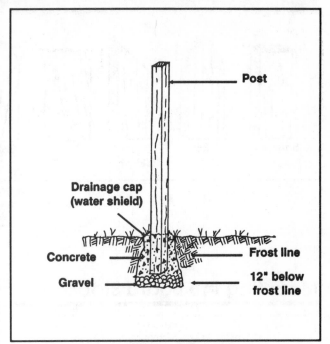

Figure 3-9
A securely anchored post

properly. If you rush it, the concrete may fracture and fail from the stress you put on it when you nail the rails and slats. The first good wind will topple the fence.

Installing the Rails

Once the curing time has passed, you're ready to install the rails.

1) If the fence isn't climbing up or down a hill and you want everything to be level, then start at an end or corner post. String a line from that post to the end or corner post at the end of that run of posts. The line should be 8 to 12 inches below the top of each post, or at the level where you want the top rail to be. Hang a string level on the cord and adjust one end until the line is level from one end to the other.

Now make a pencil mark on each post where the string line crosses that post. These marks are where the top rail will attach. Don't worry about the bottom rail yet.

2) Measure the lengths between posts and cut each top rail the appropriate length. You'll have slight variations in distance from post to post. Install the top rails either with joist hangers or by toenailing them into place. Check each rail with a level as you nail it in place.

3) Now measure down from one top rail to within 12 inches of the ground, or your selected location for the bottom rail. You could use the same measurement on every rail, but it's faster to make a *jig*. Cut a 1 x 4 or other lumber to the measurement of the distance between the two rails. Use this jig to mark the location of each bottom rail. Just put the jig against the post, flush with the bottom of the top rail, and mark the post at the bottom of the jig. The mark is where the top of the bottom rail should go.

Measure and cut your bottom rails and attach each one the same way you attached the top rails.

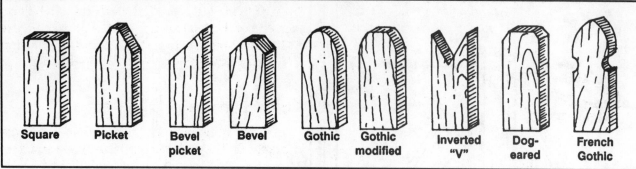

Figure 3-10
Fence board designs

Mounting the Board Stock

Now you're ready for the board stock or fencing. Start at one end and plumb and level the first board. Attach it to the rail. Continue attaching the boards until you're done. Keep your level handy and check frequently as you proceed.

Do some measuring and a little math before you start putting up the boards. Otherwise you'll get to the end of the fence and only have room for half a board, or an extra-large gap between the last few boards.

Don't butt the boards together too tight. Leave some space for expansion, about 1/8 to 1/4 of an inch. Use a spacer made from a piece of plywood or a metal strip. If you're installing a picket fence, you can make a spacer or use a picket for your spacer.

Figure 3-10 shows you several designs for the board tops. Dog-ears are probably most popular. Many lumberyards offer boards with pre-cut patterns. If you're going to cut a design into the top of your board lumber or slats, make the cuts before installing the boards.

You can cut your own design with a radial arm, table, band, or jig saw. Make a full-size drawing of your design. When you're satisfied with it, make a template from plastic, metal, cardboard, or plywood. As you drive around town, you might see a design you like. Ask the property owner if you can trace the pattern. If you offer to replace a few broken boards they may even let you take one or two to use as a template.

Here's a note of caution: Although it's frequently not done, I recommend that you keep the bottoms of board stock *above* the ground. Lumber in contact with the ground will decay and harbor insects. And it's harder to cut grass and pull weeds when a fence touches the ground. Keep the boards 2 or 3 inches above ground level. You may even want it higher. A lawn mower needs about 6 inches of clearance.

If the boards *have* to touch the earth, seal the board ends before you install them. In fact, it's a good idea to seal the board ends even if they don't touch the ground. Rain runs down the lumber and hangs at the bottom edge. Unsealed lumber will soak up this water. Eventually the wood will rot. If you're going to paint the fence, dip the ends or the entire board in paint before installation. If you're going to clear-coat the fence, or leave it unfinished, brush a clear sealer on the cut edges. Three coats will be needed to protect the wood completely. Be sure, when you're selling the job, that you tell your prospective customer you're going to do all this. It usually makes them see that they're going to get a much better fence than the low-bidder is going to give them.

If your boards will contact the ground, the best choice is to soak the ends in preservative or brush on an asphalt or creosote coating. A little extra time and effort now will result in a much more durable fence.

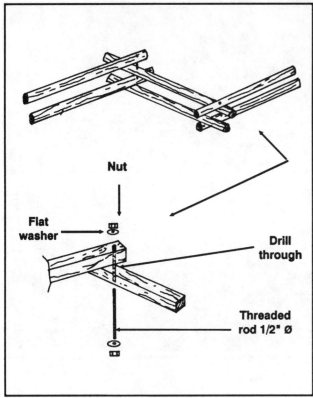

Figure 3-11
Anchor a zigzag split rail fence

Nut

Flat washer

Drill through

Threaded rod 1/2" Ø

Wood Fence Designs and Variations

Here are some of the most popular wood fence designs. There are probably hundreds of other variations, but I'll cover the most common.

Split Rail

Many years ago, when wood was plentiful, people simply cut down a tree or two, split the trunk with a few wedges, and stacked up a fence. The fence was laid out in a zigzag pattern to keep it from falling down. And so the split rail fence was born.

Today we do much the same, except that we anchor each joint with spikes or threaded rod. Spikes are just hammered into place. The threaded rod takes a little drilling.

Drill a hole that's slightly larger than the rod, through each piece of lumber. Then thread the rod

through the holes. Use a flat washer and a bolt on each end of the rod to complete the project. Figure 3-11 shows you how to do this. Each 8-foot section of this fence costs you about $15 for materials.

Picket Fences

As lots grew smaller, zigzag fences became impractical. They take up too much space. *Picket* fences are a better choice. Minimize the cost by leaving large spaces between the pickets. An 8-foot section costs about $30 for materials to build a 3-foot-high fence with the pickets spaced one picket-width apart.

Picket fences are usually more decorative than physical barriers. But they do mark boundaries and offer some wind, snow, and sun protection. And who doesn't dream of the cottage with a white picket fence in front? Figure 3-12 is a good example of this style, complete with roses and ivy.

Sapling Fences

Sapling fences are inexpensive because they're usually built in rural, wooded areas where materials are readily available. You just cut as many small trees as you'll need and nail them to the fence rails. Note Figure 3-13.

The saplings should be no more than 1 or 2 inches in diameter. These fences make good snow and weather shields and are a barrier to small children and animals. The drawback is that they don't last long and have to be replaced every few years.

Because sapling fences have their bark left on, you can't effectively paint them or treat them with preservatives. They eventually rot, and they're prone to attack by insects.

The best kinds of wood to use for sapling fences are oak, hickory, black locust, western juniper, and Osage orange. You can expect those to last for 15 years or more.

Reed Fences

The *reed* fence is a variation of the sapling fence. Most reed fences are built with bamboo, which is technically a grass. Either use the bamboo stalk whole, or split it.

Figure 3-12
The classic white picket fence

To split bamboo, use a two-handled shaver blade. These curved blades are 8-12 inches long with a handle at each end. You start splitting at one cut end of the bamboo, then pull the blade toward you, through the length of the bamboo. You want to be careful when you're using one of these.

If you're going to use whole bamboo, pre-drill the nail holes. It's very hard to drive nails into bamboo. See Figure 3-14.

Split bamboo is usually tied or woven into a screen that you attach to the fence rails. As with saplings, bamboo will have to be replaced every few years. It does offer snow, sun, and weather protection, and will contain small children and animals — if they aren't very adventuresome or aggressive. A 6 x 15 foot section of split bamboo costs you from $4.00 to $8.00, plus another $12 or so for posts and rails.

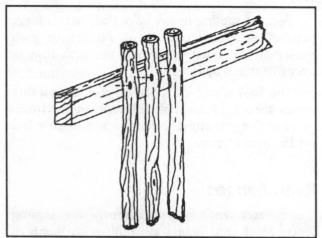

Figure 3-13
Attach saplings to fence rails

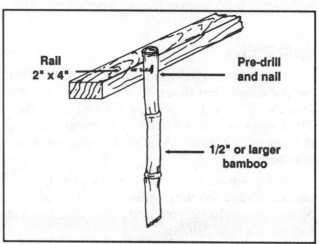

Figure 3-14
Pre-drill bamboo or reed fencing

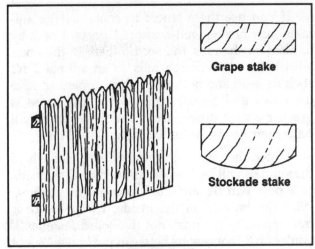

Figure 3-15
Grape stake or stockade stake fence

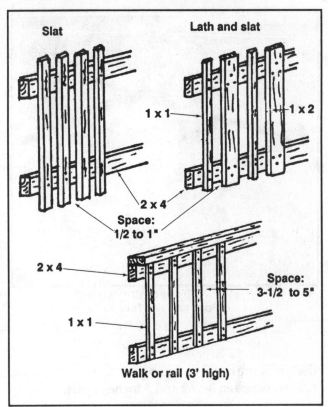

Figure 3-16
Slat fences

You can also buy *woven fencing* made from softwood slats. The wood is split into thin slats and then woven together with wire or cord. People use these for sun screens on patios and windows. You just hang them on nails or screws from a frame or rafter with the wire clips attached to their top rails. Their cost is low, about $15 for a 6 x 8 foot section.

Grape Stake Fences

Grape stake fences are made from 2 x 2 split redwood slats hung vertically from rails. These slats or stakes are usually sold only in 3 to 6 foot lengths. They're inexpensive, and because they're redwood, they last several years. Vineyards use these stakes to support grape vines.

An 8-foot section of grape stake fence 6 feet high will cost you about $50 for materials. Figure 3-15 illustrates a section of grape stake fencing. This fencing is highly resistant to decay and insects. It weathers to a nice silver gray that blends with most surroundings. Watch out for splinters here. This is split, not milled lumber.

Stockade Stake

The stockade stake you see in Figure 3-15 is cut from the branches stripped from felled pine and fir. First the bark is removed, and then the stakes are cut, leaving one side rounded. The

contractor's cost for prefabricated 8 x 6 foot stockade sections is about $35.

Slat Fences

Slat fences are 1 x 1 or 1 x 2 lumber hung vertically from rails. The slats differ from grape stakes in that they are cut, not split, lumber. The lumber can be redwood or any of the softwood varieties. Slat fences are good wind breaks if you build them with an open design — slats spaced one slat apart. The slats are cut from standard lumber and are available in lengths from 2 to 12 feet. The cost of materials for an 8-foot section of 6-foot-high slat fence is about $45. Figure 3-16 shows a slat fence.

Lath and Slat Fences

A variation of the slat fence is the *lath and slat* fence, also shown on Figure 3-16. It's the same fence except you intermix or alternate between the small and large slats. Another variation on this

Figure 3-17
Post and rail fence

If you use these fences to contain large animals, use heavy, well-anchored posts. Use 2-by lumber for the rails and secure them to the posts with bolts. Use enough rails so an animal can't stick its head and neck through the opening. Like us, cows and horses believe that the grass is greener on the other side of the fence, so they'll poke their heads through and munch all day.

Fasten the rails to the side of the posts where the animals will be. Boards fastened on the outside of a post will be subjected to constant pushing. With the boards on the inside, the pressure is transferred to the post, not the board fastener. If you're on 8-foot centers between posts, use 16 foot boards for the rails. Stagger the rails so that the joints between boards fall on alternate posts. Note Figure 3-18. Your fence will be stronger that way. Cost of materials will vary with the number of rails or boards.

Avoid using white paint on your animal containment fence, especially around horses. They chew on fences. Black tar base coatings seem to discourage this. Probably it doesn't taste so good. White fences look great, but an application of hot tar will last longer, protect the wood longer, and be easier to maintain and repair.

The post and *crossed* board fence shown in Figure 3-19 is a variation of the post and board fence.

Lumber Fencing

Use your imagination to design lumber fencing using 2 x 4s or 4 x 4s. You can combine them into various decorative combinations like the ones

design is the walk or railing fence, with the slats spaced between 3-1/2 and 5 inches apart.

Post and Rail, Post and Board

These fences are commonly used to contain animals on farms. They have a crisp, clean look, and are at home in rural or urban areas. As the name implies, you use only posts and rails. The rails can be 4 x 4, 2 x 4, 2 x 6, 2 x 8, or board lumber. You can use from one to five or more rails, and attach the rails to one or both sides of the posts. You can even run them through the posts, like in Figure 3-17.

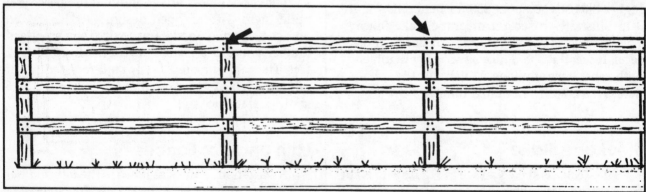

Figure 3-18
Staggered rail joints

**Figure 3-19
Crossed board fence**

in Figure 3-20. Use them for front yards, porch railings or walkways. Once you've designed the first section, duplicate the pattern as many times as you need to. Don't be afraid to doodle. You'll come up with many interesting arrangements that way.

Board Fences

The last group of wood fences is loosely termed *board fencing*. Some call it *panel* fencing. The construction is much the same as for post and slat fencing. The difference is that you use many boards and space them close together. You can use any size board lumber you want. Most people prefer 1 x 4, 1 x 6, and 1 x 8 in redwood, cedar, pine, or fir. You can vary the height from a foot or two to 16 feet, with most being 6 or 8 feet high.

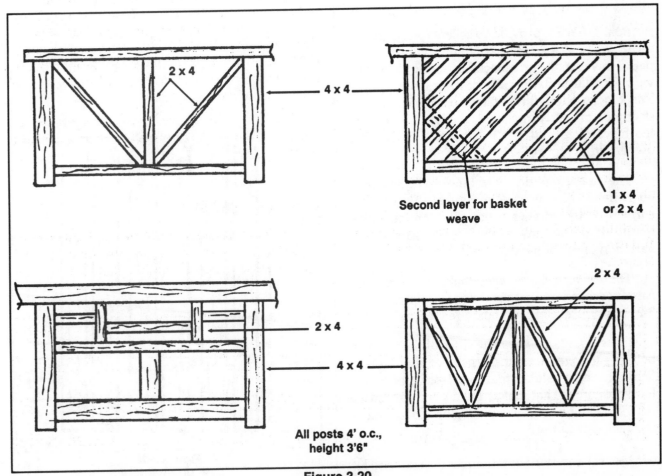

**Figure 3-20
Lumber fencing**

Figure 3-21
Some fences need help

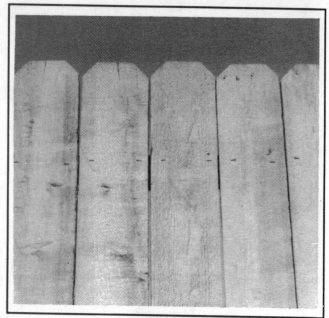

Figure 3-22
Dog-eared boards

Board fences provide excellent privacy and security. They're great for containing children and pets. However, they do block out sunlight and the view. The large flat surface of most board fences also blocks wind flow. If the fence posts aren't strong or properly anchored, the wind will blow the fence over, and you'll have to do what the owner did in Figure 3-21.

The most common board fence is the *dog-eared* board fence like the one in Figure 3-22. The top corners of the lumber droop like the ears of a hound dog. The drawing in Figure 3-23 shows a variation of the dog-eared fence.

The *common board* fence looks like the dog-eared fence except that the tops are square. Figure 3-24 is a typical common board fence.

Place boards on alternate sides of the top and bottom rail to reduce wind resistance. One advantage of the alternate board design is that both sides look the same. That makes them good for fences between neighboring yards. No one has to look at the back side of the fence.

Vertical and horizontal louver designs also let a certain amount of wind and sunlight pass through. When you look through these fences at

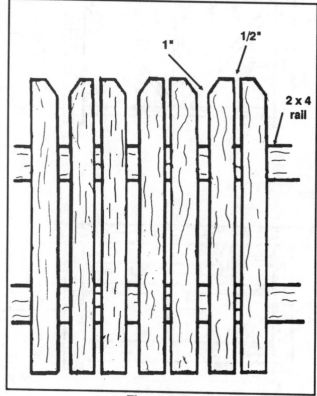

Figure 3-23
Split dog-ear fence

Figure 3-24
Common board fence

inserted. For a vertical louver fence, cut the grooves in the top and bottom rails. Fasten the louvers with a few 4d nails at their ends.

Panel Fences

You can build *panel* fences from plywood, safety glass, Plexiglas™, fiberglass, boards, or any material that you can assemble into a flat panel. You form a post and rail frame, and secure the plywood panels inside the frame. Use quarter round trim on both sides of the panel to hold it in place. An alternate method is to groove the post and rails to accept the panel. Figure 3-26 illustrates both these methods.

Horizontal Slat Fences

Finally, look at Figures 3-27 (diagonal board fence) and 3-28 (basket weave fence). The drawing in Figure 3-29 shows you two ways to build a basket weave fence.

an angle, you can see both in and out. But when you look straight on, you can't see a thing.

Figure 3-25 shows you how to build a louvered fence. Cut the posts to allow the louvers to be

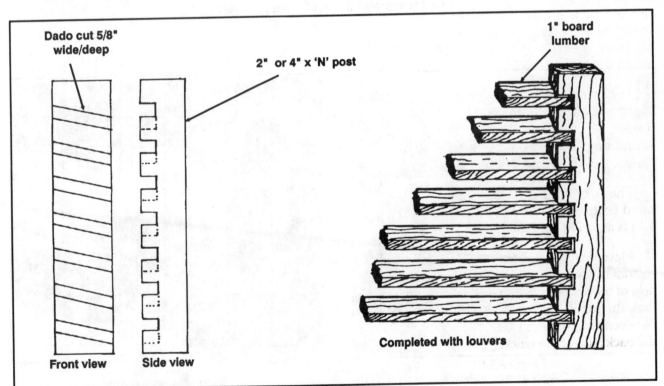

Figure 3-25
Horizontal louver fence

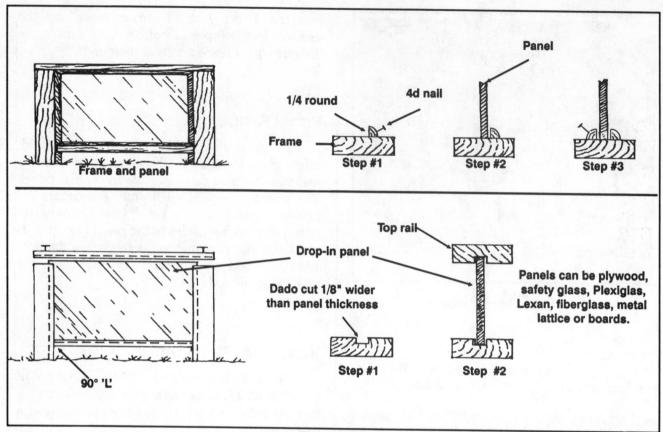

Frame and panel

Panel

1/4 round   4d nail

Frame

Step #1   Step #2   Step #3

Top rail

Drop-in panel

Dado cut 1/8" wider
than panel thickness

Panels can be plywood,
safety glass, Plexiglas,
Lexan, fiberglass, metal
lattice or boards.

Step #1   Step #2

90° 'L'

Figure 3-26
Panel fence with grooved post and rails

Figure 3-27
Diagonal board fence

Figure 3-28
Basket weave fence

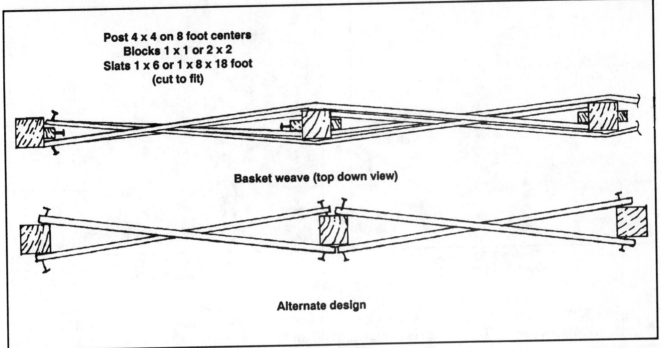

Post 4 x 4 on 8 foot centers
Blocks 1 x 1 or 2 x 2
Slats 1 x 6 or 1 x 8 x 18 foot
(cut to fit)

Basket weave (top down view)

Alternate design

Figure 3-29
Woven fence construction details

Construction Details

Before leaving this chapter, I want to offer suggestions on attaching rails to posts. This is important. If the connection between the post and rail fails, the fence will fail. Most rails are just butted to the post and toenailed into place as shown in Figure 3-30. This is a cheap and easy way, but it isn't very sturdy. Rails that are installed in grooves, slots, or holes will stay in place longer.

Figure 3-31 shows a *lap joint*. This one is especially strong if you use 3/8-inch bolts like the ones in the picture. You can use nails or screws, but they won't hold as well.

Figure 3-30
Butt joint

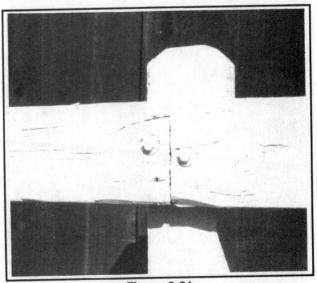

Figure 3-31
Bolted lap joint

Figure 3-32
Overlap joint

Figure 3-33
Grooved joint

Figure 3-32 is another lap joint, but this time the rails overlap each other. This design isn't much stronger than the standard lap joint, but most people think it looks sturdier and more attractive.

Figure 3-33 shows a strong connection. This *grooved joint* holds the rail in tightly. The vertical loading force on the rail is applied directly to the post. You can use grooved joints in the line posts as well as the end posts. At the corner post, you cut the groove on two sides of the post, and miter the ends of the rail. The groove should be about one-third of the way into the post or sized so the rail is recessed flush with the post. Fasten the rail in place with nails, screws, or bolts. Install fasteners at an angle from the rail into the post, at both the top and bottom of the rail.

Figure 3-34 is a log rail and post. Make the groove in the log post only half the diameter of the log rail for best support. Cut the groove in a semi-circle to fit the rail. I don't recommend a square cut groove for this application unless you square off the end of the rail. You want a tight fit for maximum strength.

Figure 3-35 shows another log rail to log post connection — one that required some help. This connection is called an *overlapping joint*. The verti-

Figure 3-34
Log rail and post

Figure 3-35
Overlapping joint that failed

Figure 3-36
Double posts give strength in two directions

cal strength is very good. The full load of the rail is applied to the post. But the horizontal strength isn't very good. That's why the owner added the chains and straps to reinforce the spikes. This is a corral, and it was just too easy for the horse to knock rails off the post.

That reminds me of a point I want to make. Know in advance what the loading will be. Is it vertical, horizontal, or both? Use a rail to post connection that satisfies the conditions. People sit on rails, they don't push against them. So they need vertical strength. Large animals push against fences, so the strength should be in the horizontal direction.

Figure 3-36 is one man's solution to both horizontal and vertical loading forces. The double posts hold the fence in the horizontal direction.

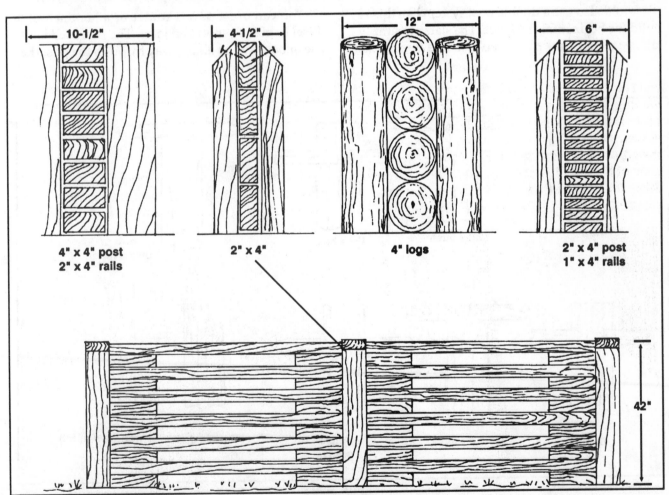

Figure 3-37
Horizontal slat construction details

**Figure 3-38
Rail enclosed in pilaster**

The bolts through both of the posts and the rail hold in the vertical direction.

You'd also use a double post system like this to build the horizontal slat fence. The slats are simply laid (stacked) into place between the two posts.

Then you nail the top slat to the posts to keep everything in place. Figure 3-37 shows construction details for horizontal slat fences. The top part of the drawing shows end views of several designs. The bottom shows how you can make interesting designs with short filler boards between the slats.

Figure 3-38 shows a brick pilaster that locks the rail in place in both directions. The pilaster could just as well be wood, block or concrete.

Figure 3-39 illustrates the most common methods for joining rails to posts. The strongest joints are the mortised and slotted joints illustrated in Figure 3-40.

To make the slotted hole, you drill holes in all four corners of the hole location. Then you insert a keyhole saw or power saber saw through one of the drill holes to cut out the larger hole.

You can use a power router or a hammer and chisel to make a mortised joint. The mortised joint doesn't always go all the way through the post the

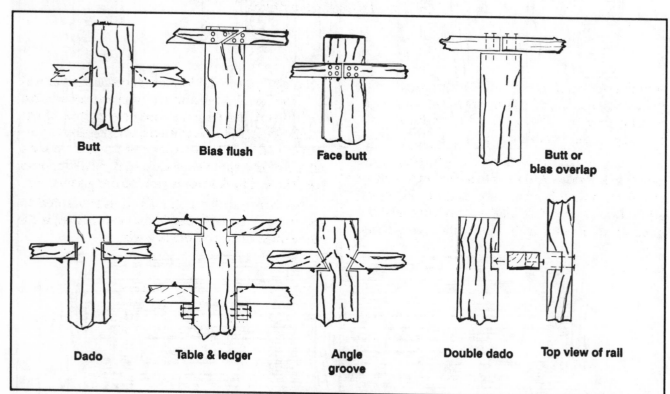

**Figure 3-39
Rail to post connections**

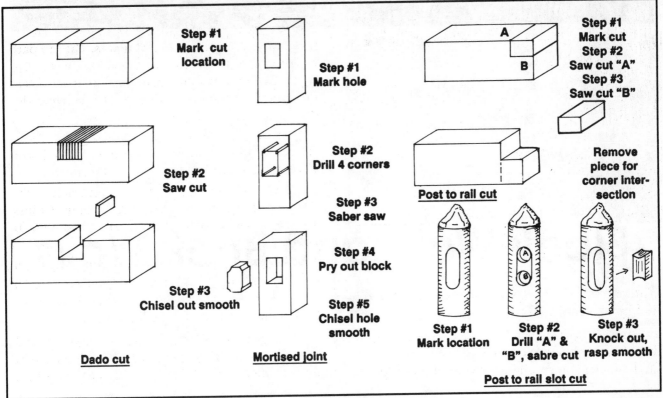

Figure 3-40
Secure rail to post connections

way the slot cut does. To make the grooved joints, (labeled "Dado cut" in the drawing) you use a circular saw to cut several closely-spaced slots, and then chisel out the wood.

If you're making posts in a shop or factory, you can *dado* the slots. A dado blade fits on a table or radial arm saw. It has two outer cutting blades and several inner chipping blades. You can make dadoes up to about 1 inch wide with a single saw pass.

When you make louver fences, both vertical and horizontal, I recommend you use a dado for the rail slots. You'll have complete control of the depth of cut, the louver angle, and the louver-to-louver spacing. Dado blades cost $35 and up for a set. *Don't attempt to use a dado blade on a hand-held saw.* The kickback force is just too dangerous.

So there you have it, all you ever wanted to know about wood fences. In the next chapter, we'll move on to brick and block walls.

four

Block Walls and Brick Walls

Most of this chapter is about concrete block. It's nearly an ideal building material. Block is relatively cheap (compared to formed concrete), it's durable, comes in a variety of colors and styles, and can be adapted to build walls of nearly any shape or size. But building with brick and block requires some knowledge and more than a little skill. That's the purpose of this chapter.

Materials

Manufacturers make block from many different materials. Most are *concrete* block. But block made from mud and straw, cinders, or clay is available and is sold under the name *adobe*.

In the 1800's, adobe block was made by hand in small wooden presses, one at a time. Today, concrete block is made by machine to precise specifications. We use block to build homes, barns, office buildings, factories and walls. If you learn the correct techniques for building block walls, you'll open up many other opportunities for your-self in construction. Concrete block is used everywhere.

Dimensions

For the rest of this chapter I'll use the term *block* to describe those blocks classified as concrete masonry. These can be either solid blocks, hollow blocks, split face blocks, decorative blocks, or accessory blocks. The basic unit size, 8 x 8 x 16 inches, is called *standard block*. Block measurements are always given with the width first, then the height, and then the length. It's important to remember that. A 4 x 8 x 16 block is *not* the same as an 8 x 4 x 16 block.

Blocks come in the following dimensions:

- Widths: 4, 6, 8, 10, and 12 inches

- Heights: 4 and 8 inches

- Lengths: 8, 12, and 16 inches

These are *nominal* measurements. Actual dimensions are 3/8 inch smaller to allow for the mortar joint. The block size plus the mortar joint equals the finished size.

Note that finished lengths are multiples of four. That way you can use an even quantity of block for walls of any length that you can divide by four. The chart in Figure 4-1 shows you how many standard blocks you need to build walls in six different lengths.

Partition blocks are 4 or 6 inches wide. You can use them to partition off an area using a minimum of floor space for the wall. Don't use partition blocks for load-bearing walls.

Configurations

Blocks are made in special shapes for special applications. *Standard* block is the style you'll use the most. These are also called *filler* or *stretcher* blocks. Both ends of the stretcher are U-shaped. Butting two stretcher blocks together forms a cavity. Most block are hollow. They have cavities called *cores*. Some blocks have two cores, others have three.

On alternating layers, or *courses*, you'll usually use *half size* blocks. They're only 7-5/8 inches long on a job where you're using standard 16-inch stretchers. These allow you to stagger the layers so the joints don't overlap each other. This makes your wall stronger.

At pilasters (posts) you can use *open end* blocks larger than those you use for the rest of the wall. You can insert a standard block into these to produce a clean-looking expansion joint. Figure 4-2 shows an open end block in use.

Rows	Height in inches	Height in feet	Wall length					
			4'	8'	12'	16'	20'	24'
1	8	0.67	3	6	9	12	15	18
2	16	1.33	6	12	18	24	30	36
3	24	2.00	9	18	27	36	45	54
4	32	2.67	12	24	36	48	60	72
5	40	3.33	15	30	45	60	75	90
6	48	4.00	18	36	54	72	90	108
7	56	4.67	21	42	63	84	105	126
8	64	5.33	24	48	72	96	120	144
9	72	6.00	27	54	81	108	135	162
10	80	6.67	30	60	90	120	150	180
11	88	7.33	33	66	99	132	165	198
12	96	8.00	36	72	108	144	180	216
13	104	8.67	39	78	117	156	195	234
14	112	9.33	42	84	126	168	210	252
15	120	10.00	45	90	135	180	225	270
16	128	10.67	48	96	144	192	240	288
17	136	11.33	51	102	153	204	255	306
18	144	12.00	54	108	162	216	270	324

Figure 4-1
Number of standard block required

Figure 4-2
Open end block to use for pilasters

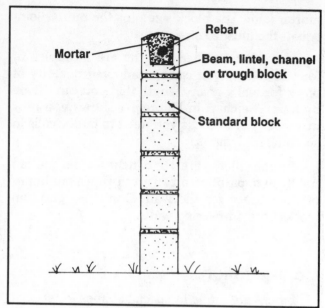

Figure 4-3
Channel block to top a wall

You can also use open end blocks at gate openings. That way you can recess the gate post into the block and anchor it with mortar or cement.

Bond beam block, or *channel* block, has a channel molded into it that accepts metal reinforcing rods. It's used on the top layer of a wall to give extra strength and stability. A higher channel block, 5 inches high, is called a *trough* block. You use trough blocks to contain water lines and power conduits, or as lintel blocks. Fill them with concrete to give a wall extra strength. Figure 4-3 shows an end view of these types of block.

Lintels or *beam* blocks are U-shaped blocks used above doorways and windows to provide extra reinforcement to support the load above them. Filling lintel block with concrete adds extra strength over the opening.

Use *sash blocks* for framing windows and doors. These have a 3/4-inch groove molded into one edge or side that serves as a holding channel for the window or door frame.

There are two types of pilaster blocks, called *alternate* pilaster and *open* pilaster. You use them in combination to form the corner or end post for a wall. Open pilasters are usually 32 inches long. You use them as the starting or base unit. The alternate pilasters are usually 16 inches long and

are set over the center of the open pilaster. Now the standard blocks butt against the alternates and over the extension on the open block. This locks the wall in place. You layer the open and alternate blocks as shown in Figure 4-4.

You use *cap* or *paving* blocks to give a wall a finished look. These are thin, flat blocks that cap a wall and keep rain from entering the wall cavities. Some styles of cap blocks have recesses, called *keys*, on the downward side. Filling the recesses with mortar helps hold the block in place. Figure 4-5 is a table of available cap block sizes.

Notice that modular cap blocks are the same width and length as standard stretchers. Standard cap blocks are wider and longer. They're used most often for capping a wall, because they cover the mortar joints and overhang the top blocks' width. This overhang gives some protection from water dripping onto the wall's surface.

The preferred way to build a block wall is to use channel block for the top layer, and fill it with rebar and concrete. Then you can either mound the concrete to form a cap on top, or use cap blocks. Cap blocks look better than mounded mortar.

If you're building a wall to filter sunlight without completely blocking the view, use *screen blocks*.

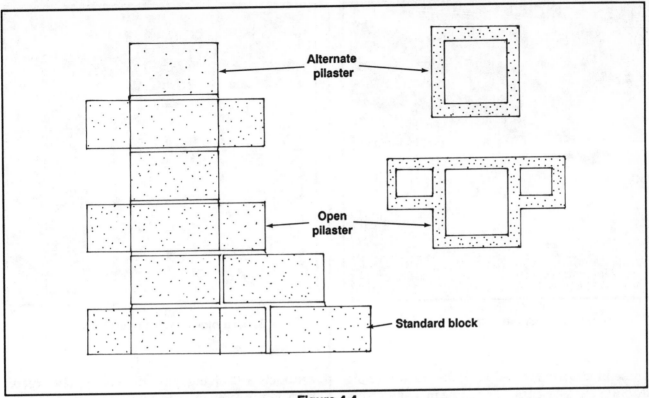

Figure 4-4
Pilaster blocks used to form column

Type block	Actual size		
	W	H	L
1M	3-5/8	2-1/4	7-5/8
2M	3-5/8	2-1/4	15-5/8
3M	5-5/8	2-1/4	7-5/8
4M	5-5/8	2-1/4	15-5/8
5M	7-5/8	2-1/4	7-5/8
6M	7-5/8	2-1/4	9-1/4
7M	7-5/8	2-1/4	11-5/8
8M	7-5/8	2-1/4	15-5/8
9M	9-1/4	2-1/4	15-5/8
10M	11-5/8	2-1/4	15-5/8
11M	15-5/8	2-1/4	15-5/8
12M	3-5/8	1-5/8	15-5/8
13M	5-5/8	1-5/8	15-5/8
14M	7-5/8	1-5/8	15-5/8

M = modular

Type block	Actual size		
	W	H	L
1S	3-3/4	2-1/4	8
2S	3-3/4	2-1/4	16-1/2
3S	5-7/8	2-1/4	8
4S	5-7/8	2-1/4	16-1/2
5S	8	2-1/4	8
6S	8	2-1/4	10
7S	8	2-1/4	12-1/4
8S	8	2-1/4	16-1/2
9S	10	2-1/4	16-1/2
10S	12-1/4	2-1/4	16-1/2
11S	3-3/4	1-5/8	16-1/2
12S	5-5/8	1-5/8	16-1/2
13S	8	1-5/8	16-1/2
14S	12-1/4	1-5/8	16-1/2

S = standard

Figure 4-5
Cap block size chart

Figure 4-6
Screen block

Figure 4-7
Scored blocks add textural interest

These blocks are molded with the cores running through the face sides. They come in many different designs and sizes. You can use them as ornamental fillers, as a decorative top layer, or to build an entire wall. Figure 4-6 is a screen block wall.

For those people who object to the cold, commercial look of the standard block wall, there are *scored* blocks. See Figure 4-7. These have vertical grooves or scores in one face to add variety to the finished wall. They're available with only one score, or with multiple grooves that give the appearance of bricks stacked on end.

If you want to build a wall with variations in its thickness or width, you can use *offset* blocks. They are one width for half the block and then another width for the second half. The width varies by about 1/2 an inch. You can use them to create designs or accents in otherwise dull-looking walls.

Split-faced block has one rough-textured side or face. The block is made oversize and then chopped or split. You use them for decoration, either as inserts in a plain wall like Figure 4-8, or you can build an entire wall using them like the one in Figure 4-9.

Notice also the 1 x 6 redwood expansion joint in Figure 4-9. Block and concrete expands and contracts with changes in temperature. The expansion joints prevent the wall from cracking or breaking apart. Place expansion joints every 16 feet in a long wall.

Stumped blocks are the same as split-faced blocks, except they're rough-textured on all sides.

Figure 4-8
Split-faced block used for decoration

Figure 4-9
A wall built entirely of split-faced block

You can use either *corner* or *bullnose* block for turning corners. Corner block has three sides faced flat and one end U-shaped. The U is really half of a cavity and butts up against the half cavity in the stretcher block. You can also get double corner blocks with all faces and edges flat. You use these for building posts or piers. Bullnose block is rounded on one corner. You use it to make a 90-degree rounded intersection between two walls. Figure 4-10 illustrates these.

At doorways and gateways you can use *jamb* block with a 2 x 4 inch cutout on one edge. The cutout is for the insertion of 2 x 4 door or gate post.

Veneer blocks are added as decoration to the face of wood frame construction. Veneer block is only 2 inches thick (nominal), and can be cemented to a wood frame, giving the appearance of a solid block wall.

Types of Block

♦ Lightweight block is used where the block doesn't have to support anything but the block itself. The compression strength of these blocks is from 700 to 1,800 PSI (pounds per square inch). These block will absorb from 7 to 16 pounds of water per cubic foot of concrete.

♦ Structural block is much denser and heavier. It has compression strengths above 1,800 PSI and up to 3,000 PSI. Because the block is so dense, it absorbs less water, usually 4 to 5 pounds per cubic foot of cement.

You can usually use two-cavity, light grade block that is 6 or more inches thick for block walls up to 9 feet high. Heights above 9 feet require structural block in most areas of the country. Check with your building inspection department before you buy block for higher walls or for retaining walls.

The color of natural block depends on the type of sand and gravel used to make the block. In the Southwest, you'll find tans, pinks, light orange, and some grays. In the Northwest, blacks and

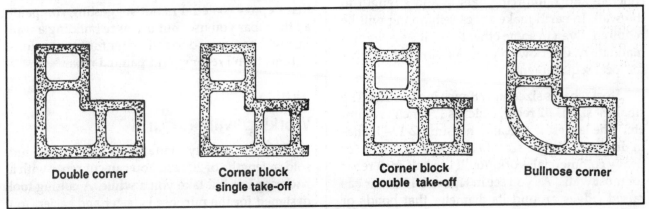

Double corner   Corner block single take-off   Corner block double take-off   Bullnose corner

Figure 4-10
Blocks to turn corners

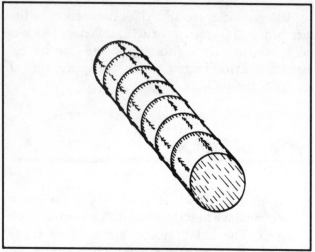

Figure 4-11
Ridges on rebar make a strong bond
with mortar or grout

reds, the natural color of the volcanic rock in that area, are common. In the Southeast you'll find tans, grays, reds, and bright whites. Gray is the most common color in the Northeast. Of course, all block can be colored with coloring agents.

Reinforcement

The following information will be of particular interest to those of you planning to qualify for your contractor's license. The test will probably cover the types and uses of rebar, mortar, concrete and cement.

The cores in concrete block can be filled with concrete and reinforcing bars to add strength to the wall. In earthquake zones reinforcing will be required. Even in some other areas, it's sometimes mandatory. Check with your building department for local requirements.

Steel rebar is sized in 1/8-inch increments. The smallest size is #2 rebar, which is 1/4 inch in diameter. The largest is #18 and measures 2-1/4 inches in diameter. Larger sizes (#14 to #18) are used for heavy commercial work. You'll use half-inch rebar for most walls. As you see in Figure 4-11, rebar has raised ridges around its diameter that bonds or locks the bar in place. Rebar is also graded by strength. Grades are #60 through #75.

Rebar is used both in the wall and in the foundation. You insert rebar vertically into the foundation when you pour it. These bars stick up through the block cores as the wall is built. When the wall is finished, you fill the cores with bars with *grout*, which is nothing more than soupy (very wet) mortar. It fills the cavity better than the dryer mortar mixture used to bond the block together. This ties the wall and foundation together. You should also put horizontal rebar in the foundation. The wall or foundation may eventually crack, but the rebar will prevent total failure. Other bars are run horizontally in bond beam blocks and the cavity is filled with concrete. Half-inch rebar satisfies code requirements for walls from 4 to 6 feet high.

The combination of block, grout, and rebar produces a wall that's highly flexible and yet very strong. The top of a 6 foot high, 4 inch thick block wall can flex up to 2 inches without causing the wall to fail. This ability to flex is what keeps the wall standing in 100 mile per hour winds and 6.0 earthquakes.

Rebar Failure

In the 1980's there were several bridge failures in the northeastern United States. The cause was traced to the rebar. In winter, bridges were salted to melt the ice. The salt dissolved in the melting ice and soaked into the concrete. When it soaked in enough to reach the rebar, it reacted with the steel and formed a gas. The gas expanded the concrete and fractured it badly, causing the bridge to fail.

The solution to this problem is to use rebar that's epoxy coated. I'm not suggesting you paint all the rebar you use. But if you're building a wall that will be exposed to salt water for long periods of time, then I recommend painted rebar.

Working with Rebar

Rebar is usually made in 60 foot lengths but sold in lengths of 20 feet. You can cut rebar with a hacksaw, but it'll take you a while. A cutting tool designed for the purpose is faster and easier. You can rent one for a few dollars a day or buy one for about $400.

You'll also need a rebar *bender*. The cost will be under $40. If you buy a cutter, the bender is usually part of it. You'll also need *tie wire* and some heavy duty wire cutters. Cutters will cost less than $20. Tie wire is steel wire used to splice pieces of rebar together.

You always have to splice rebar together. You can't just lay it next to another piece and pour on the mortar, or jam it down into the wet grout. Your local building code probably describes how bars have to be spliced. Many codes require that when you splice two lengths of rebar together, they must overlap by 40 times the diameter of the rebar itself. In other words, if you're using 1/2-inch rebar, the bars must overlap at least 20 inches. You must tie the overlapped bars at three points along the overlap. Each tie must be a minimum of three complete wraps of the tie wire.

Generally, vertical rebar is placed in every other block. Again, check your building code. Since you place the vertical rebar in the foundation *before* you install any block, it's essential you measure carefully for the location. Don't just measure from one rebar to the next. If your measurements are off by even a fraction of an inch, you'll eventually wind up with a block that won't fit over the rebar. This always adds a nice little touch to your day.

Instead, measure the path of the wall from one corner to the next. If you're using standard block, mark for rebar every 32 inches. That puts rebar in every other block. Begin measuring from the position of the first rebar. This is just slightly less than 4 inches from the edge of the first block for two-core block, and 2.6 inches from the leading edge of three-core block. You'll find more detailed information about this later in the chapter, under *Putting It All Together*.

Mortar

You use *mortar* to fasten blocks together and in place. Mortar is a mixture of sand, lime, water and portland cement. Here are a few recipes you can use:

Type S

One measure of portland cement

Three measures of washed sand

One-fourth measure of hydrated lime

Water to make a workable paste

or:

Type M

One measure of masonry cement type II

One measure of portland cement

Six measures of washed sand

Water to make a workable paste

or:

Type O

One measure of masonry cement type II

Three measures of masonry sand

Water to make a workable paste

A *measure* can be anything you want it to be as long as you use the same measure for each ingredient. The most popular measure is a *bag*, since most materials are packaged by the bag. In the recipes above, if you use bag measurements, you'll have about 3 cubic feet of mortar. That's enough to cement 30 to 50 blocks.

When you add water to your mix, be sure all the dry ingredients are well mixed first. Then add the water slowly, mixing all the while. The final mix should be uniform in color and texture, free of dry material and lumps.

To test for the proper amount of water in your mix, let the mix stand for about 10 minutes. If the consistency stays the same, the water content is fine. If it's thick and heavy, add water. If it's very loose, let it sit until it's the consistency of stiff butter.

Keep the mortar bunched together and covered. If it gets stiff, add more water. If it gets lumpy, discard it and mix a new batch. Don't add old mortar to a new mortar batch. The two batches won't mix together. Mortar is usually good for up to 2-1/2 hours after you mix it. Once it's older than that, discard it.

Parts per volume of mix of materials				
Type mortar	Portland cement	Masonry cement	Hydrated lime	Aggregate (sand)
M	1	1	None	5
M	1	None	1/4	3-1/4
N	1	None	1	5
N	None	1	None	2-1/4
O	1	None	2	6-3/4
O	None	1	None	2-1/4
S	1	None	1/4	3-1/4
S	1/2	1	None	3-1/2
Grout	1	1	1/10	3
Grout*	1	1	1/10	2

*Coarse grout using small pebbles as aggregate

Figure 4-12
Mortar mixes for masonry work

Mortar Grades

There are several grades of mortar. Each has its own special use. The grade depends on the proportion of each ingredient in the mix.

♦ Type K mortar is a low-strength mortar you use for interior partition walls.

♦ Type M mortar is very high-strength mortar, used below grade to bond block to the foundation. It's also the recommended mortar to use whenever the mortar will be in contact with the ground, such as in retaining walls.

♦ Type N mortar is used for above-grade walls that are exposed to the weather. Use it for block walls, chimneys, and exterior brick work. Type N mortar is a medium strength mortar.

♦ Type O mortar is like Type K (low strength interior) mortar except that it shouldn't be used where temperatures may drop below freezing.

♦ Type S mortar is a high-strength exterior mortar with a good deal of bond strength. Use it in high wind and earthquake-prone areas.

Figure 4-12 is a copy of Table 24-20B of the Uniform Building Code that gives the mix proportions for each type.

Some wall contractors add calcium chloride to their mortar to lower the freezing point of the mix. I don't recommend this. Even though it speeds up the cure time, it weakens the mortar. If you must use it, add it in solution and don't exceed 2 percent by weight of the portland cement you're using. Two percent is the maximum allowed under the code.

Lay the Foundation

Every block wall should start with a firm, sound foundation. The foundation is the load-carrying part of the wall. It keeps the rest of the wall upright and plumb. You make it from rebar-reinforced concrete.

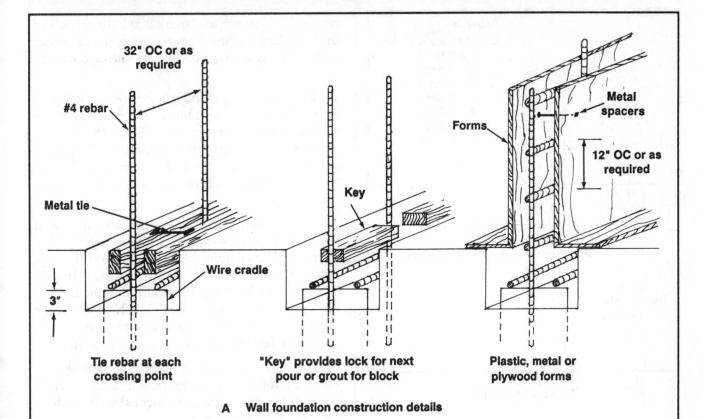

32" OC or as required

#4 rebar

Metal tie

3"

Wire cradle

Tie rebar at each crossing point

Key

"Key" provides lock for next pour or grout for block

Forms

Metal spacers

12" OC or as required

Plastic, metal or plywood forms

A   Wall foundation construction details

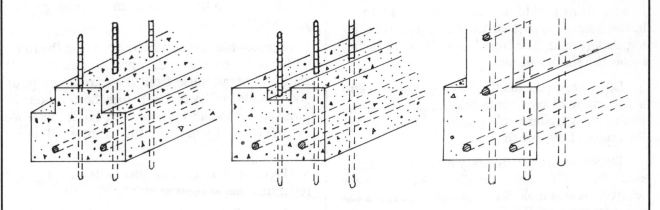

B   Foundation cross section

**Figure 4-13
Laying the foundation**

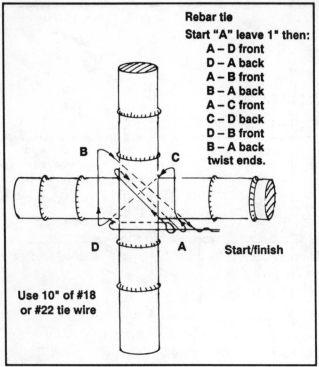

Rebar tie
Start "A" leave 1" then:
A – D front
D – A back
A – B front
B – A back
A – C front
C – D back
D – B front
B – A back
twist ends.

B   C

D   A   Start/finish

Use 10" of #18
or #22 tie wire

Figure 4-14
Tie rebar securely

In Chapter 2, I gave some rules for the depth of a foundation. You'll remember that the base of your foundation should be below the frost line. This is the depth where the ground no longer freezes during cold weather, usually 18 to 24 inches below the surface. Check with your building department. The frost line is 36 to 72 inches below the surface in some places.

Dig a trench the depth of your foundation and a minimum of two times wider than the block you're using. Later you'll position the block over the center of the trench.

Once you dig the trench, you install *cradles* or *standoffs*. You'll see these in Figure 4-13. They are wire forms that look like an inverted U with a flat top. Make the cradles from tie wire or bent rebar. They should be about 6 inches high and about 4 inches narrower than the trench. Space them about 2 feet apart, the full length of the trench, and insert them about 3 inches into the ground.

Lay two lengths of rebar on top of the cradles, each one from 2 to 6 inches in from the side of the trench. Tie the rebar to the cradles with a piece of tie wire. One or two loops will do. Now find the

center of the trench and mark it at both corners of the wall. String a line from corner center to corner center. This is your guide line for setting the vertical rebar.

If you're using standard, 2-core block, locate the position of the first block, and measure in 3.9 inches from its outer end edge. That's the position of your first vertical rebar rod. From there, mark every 32 inches for the rest of the vertical rebar. Use your corner-to-corner guide string to keep the rods in line.

Set the height of the vertical rebar at 1 inch below the top of the top course of the wall. The top course is the channel block just below the cap. Extend the rebar into the ground at least 12 inches. So a 6-foot-high finished wall with a foundation 24 inches deep will require vertical rebar 9 feet long. One foot goes in the ground, 2 feet in the foundation and 6 feet (minus 1 inch) above ground.

Next, tie a horizontal rebar to all the vertical rebar the full length of the trench. This top horizontal rebar should be 3 to 6 inches below the final height of the foundation.

You can make metal form ties like the one shown in Figure 4-13 in the field from tie wire or 16 gauge metal strips. You can also buy ready-made ties from most block suppliers. These act as spacers to keep the forms from separating when you pour the concrete.

The key blocks form indentations in the foundation so the next layer of concrete or mortar can't shift and break loose from the foundation pour. You remove the key blocks before the next pour. *Be sure you remove all key and form lumber after the concrete cures.* If you don't, the termites will move in.

Figure 4-14 illustrates how to tie two pieces of rebar together at right angles to each other.

Now call the ready-mix truck. You're ready to pour.

What kind of concrete are you going to ask for? Your supplier will know which mix is correct for your area and application, so just tell them what you're doing. If they can't help you, try a 1:2-3/4:4 mix. That means 1 part cement, 2-3/4 parts sand, and 4 parts gravel. Each measure of this mix will contain about six gallons of water.

Portland Cement

Portland cement is made from ground limestone, clay, shale, slag, and trace amounts of ore. It begins hardening when water is added. Drying tends to stop the hardening process. Each bag contains 1 cubic foot of portland cement and weights 94 pounds.

Concrete made from portland cement is graded according to mix and use. Here are the portland cement/concrete types:

- Type I is the most commonly used mix, and the one you'll probably use for wall foundations.

- Type II is best where the soil may contain sulfate. Use it for pouring foundations in warm weather. It doesn't heat up as much as the Type I while it cures (hydrates).

- Type III is quick-setting cement you'd use when you want to remove concrete forms as soon as possible. Use it also in areas where you expect low or freezing temperatures during the cure period.

- Type IV is a low-heat-generating cement. It's recommended for pouring large masses of concrete, such as for a dike or sea wall. Use this where the sulfate concentration is higher than Type II conditions.

- Type V cement is used where there are very high concentrations of sulfates in the ground.

Type IA, IIA, & IIIA are the same as Types I, II, and III, except they have an additive that generates and holds air bubbles within the concrete. These air bubbles provide expansion space in the formed mix. Water has room to expand in freezing weather. That helps keep the concrete from cracking.

One other type of portland cement you may be using is *pure white* portland cement. Unlike regular portland cement, pure white doesn't have traces of manganese and iron oxides. The oxides are what give regular cement its gray color. Use pure white concrete and washed white sand to produce a bright white mortar or cement. You'd also use white cement when you want to add color to the mortar. Colors are brighter if you use white cement and white sand. Don't buy this unless you

have to, though. It costs several times as much as regular portland cement.

Estimating Foundation Concrete

How much concrete should you order? Measure your trench. Let's say it's 40 feet long, 2 feet deep, and 1 foot wide.

$40 \times 2 \times 1 = 80$ cubic feet

Divide this by 27. (There are 27 cubic feet in a cubic yard.)

$80 \div 27 = 2.96$ cubic yards

You might get by with 3 cubic yards, but I recommend you order 3.5. The trench might vary in width and depth along its length, and there's bound to be some waste. Concrete usually costs between $60 and $80 per cubic yard when you order a full truck load. But ordering less than a truck load will increase the cost.

Some Useful Formulas

Here's how you figure out how much cement, sand, and gravel you need to mix a cubic yard of concrete or mortar. (A cubic yard is a block that's 3 feet wide, 3 feet long, and 3 feet high.)

- For a two-component mixture such as mortar, use the *Rule of 38*:

Suppose you want to make a cubic yard of 1:3 mix mortar. This means you want one part cement to three parts of sand. How much cement and sand do you need?

First add 1 and 3, the parts of your formula: $1 + 3 = 4$

Then divide 38 (the "magic number" in the rule of 38) by 4: $38 \div 4 = 9.5$

Now apply that number to your original formula:

$9.5 \times 1 = 9.5$ bags of cement

$9.5 \times 3 = 28.5$ cubic feet of sand

If you add the numbers together, it seems that you've got 38 cubic feet of material. But when you mix the fine cement particles with the coarser sand, the cement particles fill in the voids between the larger sand particles, so the total volume doesn't greatly increase. Also, the mix compacts somewhat. This mixture will actually yield one cubic yard of mortar.

◆ For a three-part mix of cement, sand, and aggregate (stone), use the *Rule of 41*. (In this formula, the aggregate must be no larger than 1 inch in diameter.)

Suppose you want a 1:2:4 mix:

$$1 + 2 + 4 = 7$$

$$41 + 7 = 5.86$$

Therefore, you'd need 5.86 cubic feet of cement, 11.72 cubic feet of sand (2 x 5.86), and 23.44 cubic feet of aggregate (4 x 5.86).

◆ Use the *Rule of 42* where the aggregate is from 1 inch to a maximum of 2-1/2 inches in diameter. In this case your 1:2:4 mix requires 6 cubic feet of cement, 12 cubic feet of sand, and 24 cubic feet of rock. (Aggregate of over 1 inch in diameter is considered rock.)

If you must know the weight of the mix, here's how to calculate it:

Material	Weight per cubic foot
Cement	94 lbs
Sand	105 lbs
Aggregate	105 lbs
Rock	100 lbs

If we use the quantities in the above example under the Rule of 42:

$$6 \times 94 = 564 \text{ lbs of cement}$$

$$12 \times 105 = 1,260 \text{ lbs of sand}$$

$$24 \times 100 = 2,400 \text{ lbs of rock}$$

Therefore, each cubic yard of this concrete would weigh 4,224 pounds, not including the water content.

How much water do you add? Water content should be based on the volume of *cement*, not the volume of *concrete*. A range of ratios for a good mix is between 3.5 and 8 gallons of water for each bag of cement. In practice, a 3.5:1 ratio is very dry and not very workable, while an 8:1 ratio is very wet and results in weak concrete. A ratio of 6 gallons of water to each bag of cement will generally work best.

If you can work with a mix that has less water, do so. Your concrete will be stronger and more resistant to weather.

A gallon of water weighs 8.8 pounds. Multiply the number of gallons by 8.8 and add it to the dry weight to find total weight of the cubic yard of concrete described above.

Each of 6 bags of cement requires 6 gallons of water: 6 x 6 = 36

$$36 \times 8.8 = 316.8 \text{ pounds}$$

Therefore a cubic yard of 1:2:4 (wet) concrete weighs 4,540.8 pounds.

$$316.8 + 4,224 = 4,540.8$$

Pour and Level the Concrete

Use a wood *float* to level your concrete foundation. A float is simply a board with a handle attached. They cost from $5 to $25 depending on material, craftsmanship, size, and manufacturer. A float may be called a *darby* or *bullfloat*, depending on the size. A float is hand-held, and usually not over 18 inches long. A darby float is also hand-held, about 45 inches long. The bullfloat is 42 to 60 inches long and has a long handle. Use a darby and bullfloat to level walks, driveways and slabs. Bullfloats cost about $80 to $90 each, but you can rent them for about $7.00 a day. Darby floats cost about $30.

If the concrete mix is a little coarse, *tamp* it before you level it. Just pound the poured concrete with the end of a 2 x 4 to compact the concrete, removing trapped air and giving a more dense mix. On a large job, use a concrete vibrator. Purchase price will be about $600, but rental is only about $30 per day.

Bleeding describes the water rising to the top of the concrete. The heavier aggregate, rock, and sand settle to the bottom as the water rises. You don't want this to happen. Tamping, vibrating and floating the concrete keep the mixture from separating until it begins to cure. When water rises to the surface, concrete on the surface gets very weak and will *craze*, *dust*, or *scale*. A crazed surface has hundreds of tiny cracks. A dusted surface is powdery. Thin flat pieces will chip off a scaling surface.

Don't try to pour a foundation deeper than about 20 inches. It won't cure right, and your finished foundation will be weak. If you have a foundation that's deeper than 20 inches, make two pours, several days apart. For instance, if your foundation is 35 inches deep, make two pours of about 17-1/2 inches each. Be sure to clean and roughen the top of the lower concrete level before pouring the second level. That helps make a better bond.

If you're using wood forms instead of the trench wall to hold the concrete until it hardens, moisten the forms before you pour. Use water, lacquer or oil. You do this so the forms can be removed easily once the concrete has set. But don't use oil as your release agent if you plan to stucco, plaster, or paint over the concrete. Use water instead. Many finishes won't stick to concrete contaminated with oil.

Cure Your Foundation

Concrete will *set up* or stiffen in just a few hours. But it takes several days for it to dry properly and harden. During that time, keep the concrete moist so hydration (hardening) can continue. There are several ways to do this:

1) Cover the exposed concrete with wet burlap.

2) Mist-spray the concrete several times a day for several days.

3) Cover the concrete with plastic.

4) Spray the concrete with a commercial sealer.

Why go to all this trouble? Because if concrete loses moisture too fast, it won't harden like it's supposed to. There may be weak or dry spots within the concrete that can eventually lead to complete failure of the foundation, and your wall. Concrete hardens slowly and doesn't reach full

strength for up to 30 days. Let a poured foundation sit for at least a week before you begin to lay block on it. A month would be better, but that's usually not practical. And if you're going to paint it, you have to let it cure for at least 12 months.

Weather and temperature play a part in the curing of the concrete. The air temperature should be from 50 to 70 degrees F. If it's too warm, the water in the concrete will evaporate too fast. In warm weather, be careful to keep the surface wet for the first six days after you pour. Cold weather will slow down curing. You might not be able to build on the concrete for up to two weeks.

Freezing temperatures will freeze the moisture in the mix and prevent proper curing. The concrete will be weak and porous. In freezing weather, cover the concrete with 10 to 12 inches of straw. Curing, or *hydration*, produces heat within the concrete. The straw will help hold in that heat and prevent freezing.

Lay the Block

Once the foundation is properly cured, it's time to lay the block. Do yourself a favor and *dry lay* the first layer, leaving 3/8 of an inch between blocks. Dry lay means to put them in place without mortar. Use 8 x 8 inch pieces of 3/8-inch plywood as spacers. This way, you'll locate your two end corner blocks properly and precisely.

Now, carefully remove all but the two end blocks. Then stretch a line from the top of each corner block and hang a *line level* on it. If the corner blocks aren't level, shim the lower one until it's the proper height. Now mix just enough mortar to *bed* the two corner blocks. *Bedding* means to cover the foundation with enough mortar to coat the entire surface under the block being installed.

Make this bed of mortar a little deeper than necessary to bring the block to the right height. Then tamp the corner block down and into place, checking it lengthwise, widthwise, and crosswise with a level. Do the same with the other corner. But be sure your line level is still level. Let the corner blocks set up for an hour or two.

Apply (butter) mortar to surface shown as XXXX 3/4" thick with a pointed mason trowel. Move block over (A), press down (B), tap (C) (B) until joints are 3/8" and block is level.

Figure 4-15
Laying the block

Now you can lay the rest of the blocks on their bed of mortar. Use your level often, and in all directions. A mistake now can cause the entire wall to be out of plumb, not to mention your profits on the job. Give the *base*, or first layer, an hour to set up and then proceed with the next layer. Use a 6 or 9 inch mason's trowel to *butter* the top of each base block with 3/4 to 1 inch of mortar. Also coat the end surface of the block you're putting on top. See Figure 4-15. When you tap the block into place, the mortar will compress to form the required 3/8-inch mortar joint. The excess will squeeze into the cavity, and outside the wall. Rake the outside to remove the excess and finish the joint, as described in the next section.

It's not hard to lay block. An experienced mason can lay two to three blocks a minute if he has a helper to supply the block and fresh mortar. If you're just starting out, it'll probably take you quite a bit longer than that. The key is to take your time and double-check the position of every block as you go. It's real discouraging to discover that some blocks two courses back have to be replaced.

Finishing the Mortar Joints

The process of finishing is called *striking off*, or *raking* the joint. There are dozens of tools available for this purpose. A joint raker with roller wheels costs about $10. Hand-held jointers cost a little less. A *sled runner* is a tool that does the same thing, but it's longer and has a handle. You use all of these to get rid of the excess mortar between the blocks, and weatherproof the joint. Raking compresses the mortar and makes its surface hard and more water resistant. The shape of the rake controls water runoff.

Figure 4-16 illustrates several joint finishes. The best ones are the concave and the V joint. Keep a bucket of water nearby when you're finishing off joints. Dip the tool in water to clean it off.

If you miss a section of a joint or have to repair an old joint, you'll do some *tuck pointing*. You tuck a small amount of mortar into the joint with a pointed trowel and then finish the repair by raking the joint as described above.

Stacking the Block

For variety, consider different stacking patterns in your *courses* of block. I'll describe several patterns in the next section on brick work. Masonry block work generally uses only two, called *stack bond* and *running bond*. Figure 4-17 shows a stack bond where the blocks are stacked directly on top of one another. This is a non-structural wall, and each column of block should contain a rebar. You can also use stack bond for open or screen blocks like the ones shown earlier in Figure 4-6.

Running bond is the most common stacking method. Note Figure 4-18. This design uses all stringer blocks, with each row offset by half a block length over the one below it. Use rebar in every other vertical block.

Top Treatments

You can use a variety of top treatments to finish off a block wall. One choice is to make a crown of concrete or mortar like the one in Figure 4-3, or use cap blocks. A row of screen block adds interest to a wall. Note Figure 4-19. You can use brick, or you can place a board on top of the wall, as in Figure 4-20.

Top treatments are both decorative and functional. The function is to keep dirt, trash, animals, insects, and water out of the wall.

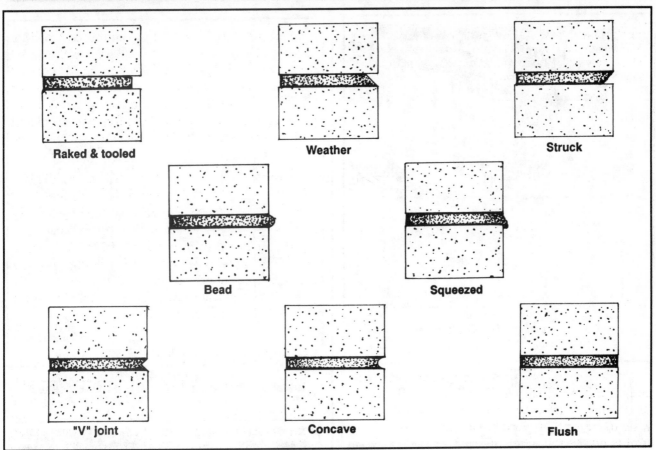

Raked & tooled   **Weather**   **Struck**

Bead   **Squeezed**

"V" joint   **Concave**   **Flush**

Figure 4-16
Joint finishes

Figure 4-17
Stack bond

Figure 4-18
Running bond

Figure 4-19
Top a plain wall with screen block

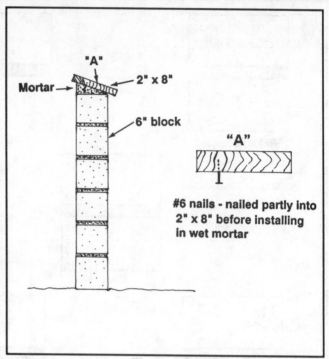

Figure 4-20
Install a board on a slant on top of a block wall

Allow for Drainage

Include a drainage system in walls that have backfill against them. Figure 4-21 shows a typical drainage system that helps keep water from flowing into and through the wall. It also helps reduce water pressure buildup, called *hydrostatic* pressure. Water weighs just over 64 pounds per cubic foot, and it's a great solvent. Given enough time, anything will dissolve in it. The combination of pressure and water's ability to dissolve concrete can eat through or topple a foundation or wall easily. Figure 4-22 shows in detail how to build a drainage system.

Water will also travel upward into a wall by capillary action. Grade the site of your wall so water flows away from it, and allow for drainage at the base. Figure 4-23 illustrates this.

Putting It All Together

Try to plan your wall so it's an even multiple of the size block you're using. Standard block with a 3/8-inch mortar joint is 16 inches long, so you

Figure 4-21
Provide drainage for a wall

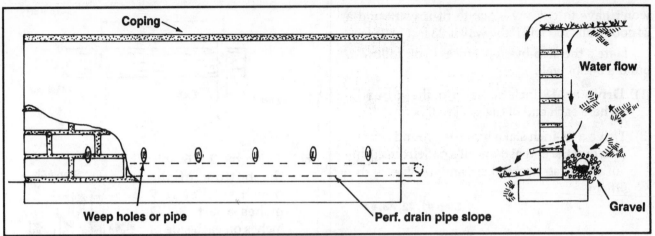

Figure 4-22
Construction details for drainage system

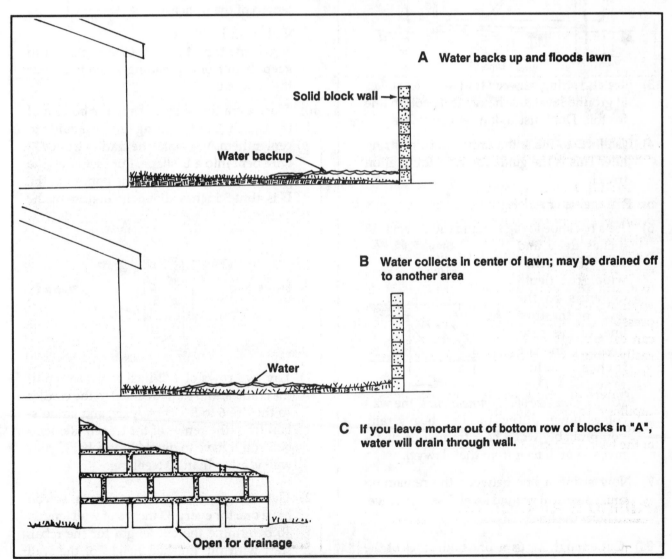

A Water backs up and floods lawn

B Water collects in center of lawn; may be drained off to another area

C If you leave mortar out of bottom row of blocks in "A", water will drain through wall.

Figure 4-23
Plan for drainage

won't have to cut any block to fit if you build a 24-foot wall. You will if the wall is 23 feet or 25 feet.

Here's the step-by-step process you follow to build a 6-foot wall:

1) Drive an 18-inch stake into the ground where each end of the wall will be.

2) Drive a 24-inch stake into the ground 5 feet beyond the end of the wall's path from each of the first two stakes, and in line with them.

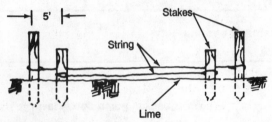

Step #1, #2, #3, #4

3) Stretch a string between the two inner stakes at ground level. Use heavy-duty cotton line for this. Don't use nylon — it stretches.

4) Use lime to mark the ground at the string line. This is the guide for your foundation trench.

5) Pull the inner stakes.

6) Use a backhoe to dig a foundation trench 18 inches deep and 16 to 20 inches wide. The depth depends on the level of the frost line. In this case, the frost line is 6 inches below grade. *Don't*

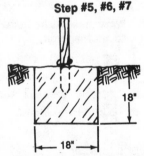

Step #5, #6, #7

skimp on the size of the foundation. If the wall comes down during the first heavy rain, you probably won't hear from your customer — you'll hear from their lawyer.

7) Now string a line between the remaining outer stakes at ground level. Use a line level to level the line.

8a) Cut enough 2 x 6s to line both sides of the trench. Nail a 24-inch stake to the 2 x 6s every 2 feet.

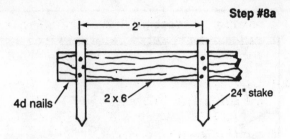

Step #8a

8b) Drive the 2 x 6s into the bottom of the trench so they're 7 inches apart, 3-1/2 inches on each side of the string line. Level the 2 x 6s along the length of the trench.

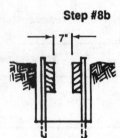

Step #8b

9) Nail a 12-inch stake across the top of the 2 x 6s every 4 feet to keep them from spreading when you pour the concrete.

10) Place a cradle every 4 feet in the bottom of the trench. Use the string line as a guide to center them. You make the cradles from #12 wire bent into a U shape. Put them into the ground upside down, so the bottom of the U is abut 3 inches above the bottom of the trench.

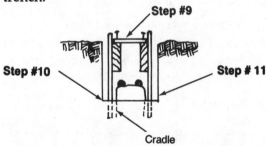

Step #9

Step #10

Step # 11

Cradle

11) Lay two rows of 1/2-inch rebar on top of the cradles, and tie-wire them to the cradles so they're 6 to 8 inches apart, and equidistant from the center of the trench. Remember, you'll have to overlap the rebar if your wall is more than 20 feet long.

12) Cut enough pieces of 1/2-inch rebar so you have one for every 32 inches of wall length. To determine the cut length for the rebar, start with the finished height of the wall and subtract 1 inch. Then add the depth of the trench, plus 12 inches. For example,

rebar for a 6-foot wall with an 18-inch foundation would be 101 inches long, 72 - 1 + 18 + 12 = 101.

13) Drive two more stakes, one at each end of the string line. These should be at least 8 feet high for a 6-foot wall. String and level a line between these stakes, 71 inches above ground.

14) Mark the location of the end of the wall in the trench. Drive a piece of rebar into the center of the trench, 4 inches in from the end mark if you're using 2-core block. (Place the rebar 2-1/2 inches from the mark if you're using 3-core block.) Plumb the rebar, and drive it into the ground so its top is even with the top string line.

Step #12, #13, #14

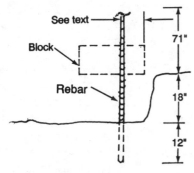

15) Measuring from the first rebar, drive a vertical rebar every 32 inches along the string lines. Measure *all* the positions from the first rebar, not from one to the next.

Step #15

16) Cut enough 1/2-inch rebar to fit the length of the trench. Tie-wire this to the vertical rebar about 3 inches below

Step #16

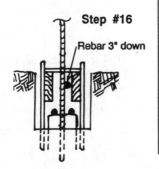

the top of the 2 x 6 forms. Re-check the vertical rebar for height and plumb.

17) Fill the bottom of the trench wall-to-wall with concrete, and to the top of the trench between the forms. Tamp the concrete with a 2 x 4 to settle it. Smooth the top with a trowel. Fill any low spots so the concrete is level with the forms.

Step #17, #18, #19

18) Let the concrete harden for several hours, then spray it lightly with water every four to five hours for three to five days. This keeps the concrete moist so it'll cure properly. If the weather is very hot, cover the concrete with a plastic tarp. In freezing weather, cover the concrete with 12 to 15 inches of straw.

19) When the concrete is cured, has turned white and is dry, remove the form lumber. This is a must to prevent termites and dry rot along the foundation.

20) Slip the corner blocks down over the vertical rebar on top of the foundation. Position the corner blocks with their U shaped sides facing each other.

Step #20

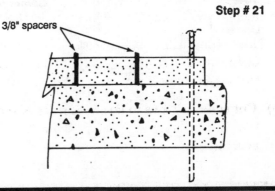

21) Dry lay the filler or stretcher blocks along the top of the foundation, without any mor-

Step # 21

tar. Use 3/8-inch plywood as spacers between the blocks. When everything is adjusted to fit properly, mark the end position of the corner blocks on the foundation with a wax crayon.

22) Remove all the blocks except the corner blocks.

23) Mix about a cubic foot of mortar.

24) Lift the corner blocks and apply a 1 to 1-1/2 inch layer of mortar over the entire width of the foundation where the corner blocks go.

Step #22, #23, #24, #25

25) Bed the corner blocks into the mortar so the mortar is about 3/4 inch thick under the blocks.

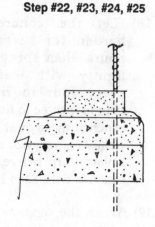

26) String a line from the outside of one corner block to the outside of the other. Use corner block line holders to hold the string in place. You can buy these small, plastic L's at the hardware store for about 60 cents each.

27) Hang a line level on the string. Tap the corner blocks down and adjust until the string is level. Mortar should be about 3/8 inch thick, up to a maximum of 1 inch thick at this point.

Step #26, #27

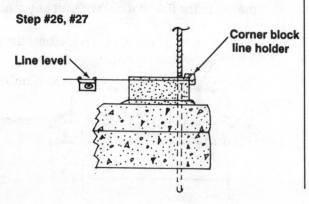

Line level

Corner block line holder

28) Use a rubber mallet to adjust the corner blocks to level in all directions. Clean up excess mortar with a trowel, then strike the joint with a U-shaped striking tool to compact the mortar and prevent water from entering the joint. Now, leave for a few hours to let the mortar set firm before you continue.

Step #28

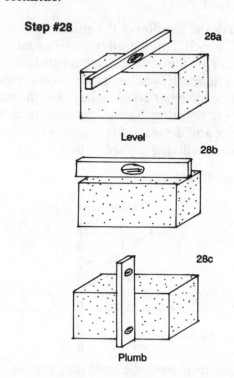

28a

Level

28b

28c

Plumb

29) Begin laying the stretcher blocks. Butter the foundation with about an inch of mortar under each block, lower the blocks over the rebar and tap in place. Be sure to butter the U end of each block where it contacts the previous one. If the mortar doesn't stick to the block, wet the block with water before you apply the mortar. Mortar joints

Step #29

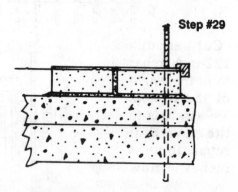

between blocks should be 3/8 inch wide. Place the blocks one at a time, checking *each one* for plumb and level *in all directions* before you go on to the next one. Be sure the blocks are in line with your string guide.

30) Let the first course of block set for a few hours before you go on. Go back to the corner where you started, and install a half-corner block. You can buy these, or cut one from a full corner block using a circular saw and masonry blade.

Step #30, #31, #32

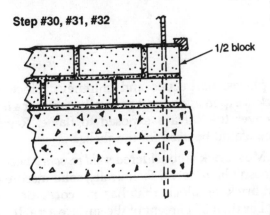

1/2 block

31) Continue laying stretcher blocks as before. You may have to cut the last corner block to fit.

32) Begin the third course with a full corner block, and continue as before.

33) Use channel block for the top course, with the U side up.

34) Lay 1/2-inch rebar in the channel the full length of the wall. The top end of the vertical rebar should be about 1 inch below the top of the channel. Tie-wire the horizontal rebar to the vertical rebar.

Step #33, #34, #35

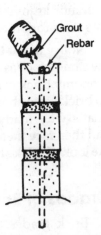

Grout
Rebar

35) Make a very wet mortar mixture to use for grout. Pour grout into each block space that contains a

vertical rebar. Then fill the channel blocks with grout.

36) Use fresh mortar to install the cap blocks over the channel blocks. Place the cap blocks so they overhang the wall by about 1/2 inch on each side.

Step #36, #37, #38

Cap block key down

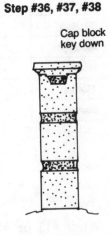

37) Remove lines, stakes, and trash, and backfill the trench with dirt. Mound the dirt about 1 to 2 inches high on the wall to allow for compacting and run-off.

38) Clean up the area and your tools, and go collect your money. You're done.

Here's a reminder: If your wall is below a slope, allow for drainage, or there will be a water buildup during rainstorms. Either install drain pipes in the first layer of block at ground level, or leave the mortar out of alternate joints in the first course of block.

Materials Summary

Forming lumber: Enough 2 x 6s for twice the length of the wall.

Rebar, horizontal: Four times the length of the wall

Rebar, vertical: Wall height + foundation depth + 12 inches times the length of the wall (in inches) divided by 32, plus one piece.

Block: Length of the wall, divided by the size of the block, times the number of courses.

Corner blocks: Two for each odd-numbered course.

Half corner blocks: Two for each even-numbered course.

Cradles: Wall length (in feet) divided by 4, plus one extra.

Brick type	Nominal size			Actual size		
	H	W	L	H	W	L
American	2-5/8	4-1/8	7-3/8	2-1/4	3-3/4	8
English	3-3/8	4-7/8	9-3/8	3	4-1/2	9
Modular	4	4	8	3-5/8	3-5/8	7-5/8
Norman	3-1/8	4-3/8	12-3/8	2-3/4	4	12
Roman	1-7/8	4-3/8	12-3/8	1-1/2	4	12
Standard	2-7/8	4-1/4	8-5/8	2-1/2	3-7/8	8-1/4

Figure 4-24
Brick sizes

Wire, #12 or #14 (to make cradles): Thirty inches for each cradle.

Tie wire: Ten inches for every intersection of rebar, and rebar to cradle.

Wood stakes, 24 inch: One for every foot of wall length, plus 2.

Wood stakes, 12 inch: One for every foot of wall length, divided by 4, plus 1 extra.

Concrete (for the foundation in the example): 1-3/4 cubic feet for each foot of wall length.

Mortar, grout: 1/5 cubic foot per block.

Brick Walls

Brick wall building is similar to concrete block wall building except for the materials you'll use. You still need a foundation, the building materials, some rebar to strengthen the wall, and mortar or cement to hold it all together. The tools are similar. The difference is in the size of the materials, the vocabulary, and the bond patterns.

Materials

Bricks are smaller than masonry blocks. They can be made from concrete, but are more likely made from clay. Clay brick is made from clay shaped into a block and then *fired* in a kiln or oven at high temperature. *Fire brick* is made from a special type of clay that resists the extreme heat in fireplaces, barbecues and chimneys. Since fire brick is expensive, you'd generally use it for a *liner*, to cover the surface exposed to flame. Regular brick would be used for the shell.

Most brick is considered *solid masonry* because it doesn't have cores. Technically, solid masonry is any brick or block that has no cores or cores smaller than 25 percent of the surface area. If over 25 percent of the surface area is open, it's considered a hollow brick.

Dimensions

The actual standard size for a common brick is 2-1/2 x 3-7/8 x 8-1/4 inches. That's height, width, and length in that order. The standard size for an economy or modular brick is 4 x 4 x 8 inches nominal. Actual size is 3-5/8 x 3-5/8 x 7-5/8 inches. Remember, nominal sizes include a 3/8-inch mortar joint on the top and side. Figure 4-24 lists sizes for other varieties of brick you may use.

Notice that it takes eight economy bricks to fill the same space as one 8 x 8 x 16 block. The average economy brick costs 45 cents, a block about $1.30. So brick costs about three times as much as block. That's why many contractors build block walls and then face them with brick veneer. That creates the look of brick at about the cost of concrete block.

Grades of Brick

Brick grades are based on water absorption rates and compressive strength, among other things. The ASTM (American Society for Testing Materials) tests for brick require conformance to the standards shown in Figure 4-25.

Type	% Water		Description	Note below
	1 Hr Test	5 Hr Test		
FTX			Structural unglazed facing tile	(1)
FTS			Sturctural unglazed facing tile	(1)
LB	28		Structural load bearing tile	
LBX	19		Structural load bearing tile	
NB	28		Structural non-load bearing	(3), (5)
MW		25	General building grade	(2)
NW		*	General building grade	(2), (3)
SW		20	General building grade	(2), (4), (6)
I		26	Hollow core brick, general construction	(2)
II		26	Hollow core brick, general construction	(2)

* No limit

(1) May be used above or below grade, in load- or non-load-bearing applications

(2) Made of clay or shale, or clay/shale mixture

(3) Exterior use where there is exposure to weather

(4) Interior use where there is no exposure to weather

(5) Can be used below grade

(6) May not be used below grade

**Figure 4-25
ASTM brick standards**

There are also sand/lime composition bricks in the SW and MW types. No water absorption rates are given for these. The S grade is structural, glazed, facing tile. The thickness of the S grade does not exceed 3/4 inch. It's basically a veneer.

In both block and brick, the N grade is for exterior use where there will be exposure to weather. The S grades are for interior use where there is no such exposure. N grade can be used below grade, S grade may not.

The compressive strength of brick is greater than that of block. Brick starts at 1,600 PSI and goes up to 20,000 PSI. That's why brick will support vertical loads much better than block. Compressive strength depends on the material used, the firing temperature and time, and the amount of water the brick absorbs. The harder and denser the brick, the less water it will absorb and the stronger it will be. Water absorption is very important in cold weather. Brick loses load-bearing capacity very quickly when water seeps in and then freezes.

Appearance

Brick comes in many styles and colors: whites, blacks, reds, purples, creams, tans, maroons, and grays. Some brick is made to look like *used brick* and may show several colors. Actual used brick is just that, brick that has been used before in another wall. Used brick that has been exposed to the weather for a long time has a unique surface glow that's very desirable in some colonial architecture.

The brick *style* refers to the surface texture that's molded into the brick. You can find them flat or smooth, or with sandmold, stipple, barks, matte-vertical, matte-horizontal, waterstruck, or rug textures.

The Bricklayer's Language

The way a brick is used determines the name used to describe that brick in the wall. These names change according to which surface appears on the face of the wall. The following descriptions apply to standard brick where there's a difference between the width and height:

◆ A *stretcher* is the same as block — the length and height show with the brick placed horizontally.

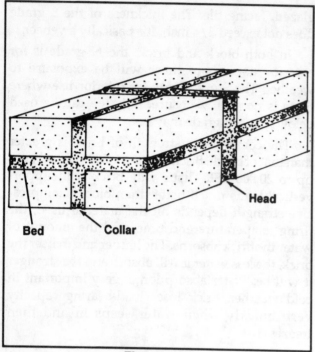

Figure 4-26
Masonry joint names

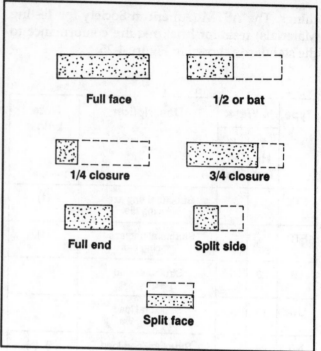

Figure 4-27
Names for cut bricks

◆ A *soldier* also shows the length and height, but the brick is laid vertically. (The bricks stand in a row like soldiers.)

◆ A *sailor* is placed upright like a soldier, with length and *width* showing. If you lay a sailor on its side, you call it a *shiner*.

◆ A *header* shows only the end of the brick. Only the height and width show, with the width horizontal.

◆ A *rowlock* or *rolock* is the same as a header, with the height as the horizontal dimension.

◆ A *wythe* is a horizontal row or layer of bricks.

◆ The vertical joint between two bricks is called a *head joint*.

◆ A *bed joint* is the horizontal joint.

◆ If you join two bricks back to back, the joint is a *collar joint*.

The last three are shown in Figure 4-26.

There are also names for the ways bricks are cut. Figure 4-27 shows those.

Figure 4-28 shows the more common bonding patterns: *American bond, English bond, Flemish bond, running bond,* and the *stack bond.* You may also use the *soldier stack bond,* the *header stack bond,* 1/3 or *Roman bond,* the *Dutch cross bond,* and any of the others illustrated in the figure.

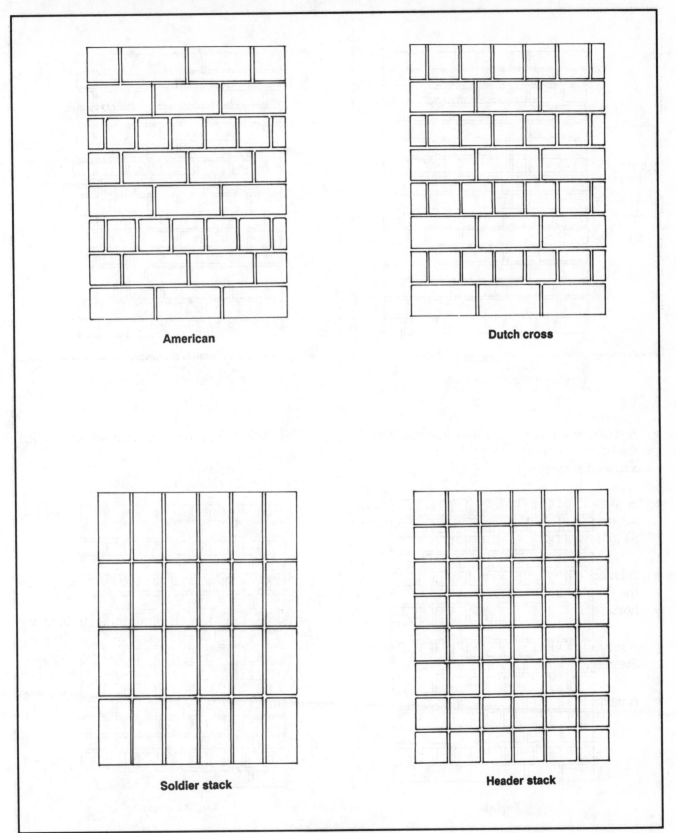

American

Dutch cross

Soldier stack

Header stack

Figure 4-28
Bonding patterns

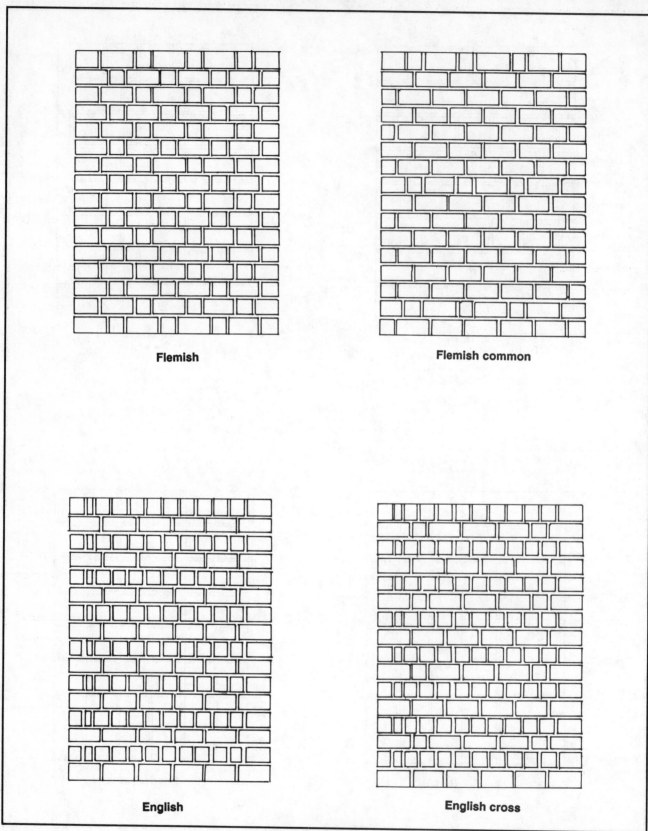

Flemish

Flemish common

English

English cross

**Figure 4-28 (cont'd)
Bonding patterns**

"FHHA" stack

"HH" stack

"FHH" stack

"FH" stack

Figure 4-28 (cont'd)
Bonding patterns

1/3 bond

Coursed ashlar

Running

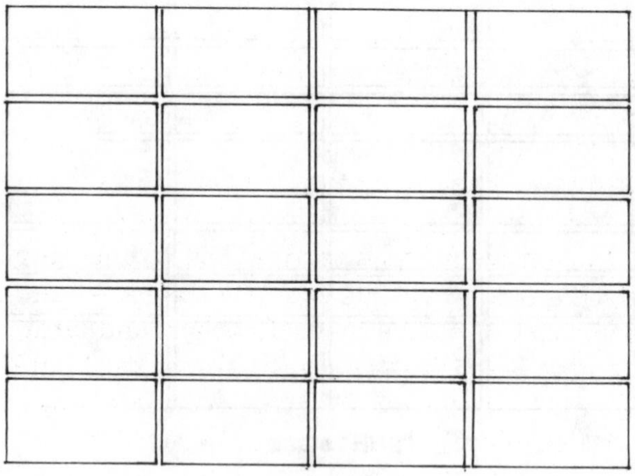

"F" stack

**Figure 4-28 (cont'd)
Bonding patterns**

five

Chain Link and Wire Fences

C hain link fences don't win many prizes for beauty and design. But chain link fabric is both versatile and practical when used as fence material. You see chain link fences everywhere. Homeowners use them to keep intruders out and their pets and children in. They keep kids from using swimming pools without supervision. Businesses use chain link fencing to secure tools, vehicles and inventory, and to partition large areas. Public agencies use thousands of miles of fencing along highways. That keeps pedestrians — and falling rocks — off the roads. Ranchers and farmers corral their livestock with chain link, wire mesh and barbed wire. And they feed cattle from bins made of chain link fabric.

In this chapter you'll learn how to put up chain link and wire fences for all these applications, and others besides. I'll cover the materials you'll use, the construction techniques, and the safety precautions you're wise to take. There's also some information about chain link and wire fences in the chapters on design, fence maintenance, and gates and entries.

Chain link fences are made from posts, fabric and mounting hardware. Let's start with the posts.

Posts

1) The *end post* is the primary anchor post, so it needs to be taller, thicker, and heavier than the line posts. The *terminal post* is the end post where you finish pulling the fence fabric. This might also be a *corner post*, where the fence changes direction.

2) *Gate* and *latch posts* also need to be sturdier than line posts, since they must withstand extra stress caused by opening and closing the gate. You can save money by using end posts as gate or latch posts, but I don't recommend that because of the extra stress. Also, if you have to replace a gate post that doubles as a terminal post, you have to remove the fabric and rails. That's a lot of extra work just to save a few dollars.

3) *Line posts* are the intermediate posts that support the top rail and the weight of the fence fabric. They carry a vertical load. Unlike gate, end and latch posts, line posts don't anchor, stretch or *tension* the fabric.

They only support the fence. So they can be smaller diameter and slightly shorter than the other posts. Another difference is that top rails rest on top of line posts.

You'll need a couple of other components to attach the top rail to the posts.

♦ *Loop caps* hold the top rail in position on top of the line posts. These are sometimes called *eye tops* or *eye caps*. They fit snugly over the top of the line post, but loosely around the top rail. That allows the top rail to expand and contract when the temperature changes.

♦ *Rail ends* attach the top rail to the end post. You use a *brace band* with a nut and bolt to secure the rail end to the end post. The top rail fits inside the rail end where it's allowed to slip. Don't push the top rail into the rail end too tightly. Leave about a 3/8-inch expansion space at both ends of the top rail. Figure 5-1 shows the junction of the top rail and the rail end.

Top Rails

Top rails are pipe that comes in 21 foot lengths with diameters ranging from 1-1/8 to 1-5/8 inches. The most common is 1-3/8 inches. You can get the pipe either straight or *swaged*, which means one end has been drawn through a die that makes it smaller in diameter than the other end. With swaged pipe, the smaller end fits inside the non-swaged end, so you'll have a continuous top rail with flush joints.

If you don't use swaged top rails, you have to use *sleeve connectors* to join the sections. They're about 4 inches long and fit over the top rail's diameter. Sleeve connectors make a strong joint, but they're more visible than a swaged connection. You can see a sleeve connector in Figure 5-2.

Tension Bars and Bands

A *tension bar* is a flat metal bar 3/4 inch wide and 1/8 inch thick. You thread it through the first (or last) diamond row in the fabric and then use it

Figure 5-1
Top rail and rail end connection

to fasten the fabric to the end post. If you try to stretch the fabric by fastening individual links, the fabric will loosen, pull out of shape, or break. The tension bar distributes the stretching force evenly along the fabric. Cut the tension bar 3 inches shorter than the fabric height. It needs to be long enough to grip every loop of the fabric without interfering with rail end connectors.

Figure 5-2
Sleeve connector for top rail

Figure 5-3
Tension bands connect tension bars to post

Figure 5-4
Aluminum ties secure the fabric to the post

You use *tension bands* to fasten the tension bar to the end post. Use enough bands so they're spaced not more than a foot apart on the end post. Even on low fences, less than 4 feet high, use at least four bands for each bar. Figure 5-3 shows tension bars and two styles of tension band.

Carriage Bolts

You'll need a nut and bolt for each tension band. The bolts you use are called *carriage bolts*. Unlike regular bolts, the shank end near the bolt head is square on a carriage bolt. The holes in the brace bands and tension bands are also square. This design lets you tighten the nuts without using two wrenches. Use 5/16 inch diameter by 1-1/4 inch long bolts for fencing. On gate hardware, use 3/8 by 1-3/4 inch bolts for the female hinges, and 3/8 by 3 inches for the male hinges.

Another characteristic of carriage bolts is that their heads are shaped like a flattened half moon so you can't grip them with a wrench or screw driver. You can only turn the nut. Since you often use fencing to secure an area, put the nuts on the inside, or protected side of the fence, with the bolt heads on the outside. Otherwise, anyone with a speed wrench can get inside in seconds. You can see a carriage bolt on Figure 5-3 also.

Use cadmium or zinc plated hardware for chain link fences. Posts and fabric should be vinyl or zinc plated. Even plated materials will rust eventually, but uncoated iron or steel will start to rust even before you're finished installing it.

If durability is a major consideration, you can use stainless steel or aluminum materials, but they're both scarce and expensive. If you can find them at all, they cost at least three times what coated materials cost. The exception is aluminum *fabric ties* that you use to tie the fabric to the line posts and top rails. You can buy these 6-inch lengths of 14 gauge aluminum wire in packages of 100. Use one tie for every linear foot of top rail, and three or more ties to secure the fabric to the line post. Loop the tie first around the fabric mesh, then around the post, and then again to the fabric mesh on the other side of the post. You can see how this is done on a line post in Figure 5-4.

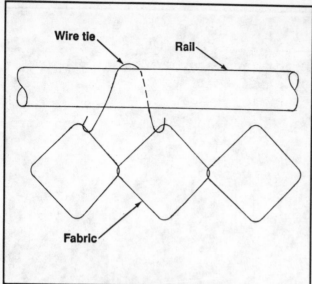

Figure 5-5
Wire fabric to top rail of fence

Figure 5-6
Acorn cap

Use a pair of pliers or heavy duty needle-nose pliers to bend the wire ties. Figure 5-5 shows how to wire the fabric to the top rail.

Post Caps

You use loop caps on line posts to secure the top rail. But loop caps aren't suitable for end posts. You want to dress those off with something that looks finished and attractive. An *acorn cap* is the type most commonly used for this purpose. It not only finishes off the post, but also keeps dirt and rain out so the inside won't rust as quickly. Many contractors go to the extra expense of filling the end post with grout to prevent rust and add strength to the post. Figure 5-6 shows a post with an acorn cap.

Now we know what goes into a chain link fence, so let's build one. Here's a typical job situation, and the steps you'd follow to complete it.

A Typical Job

Mr. Homeowner needs a fence to keep his child's pet rabbit from running away. He also has a swimming pool in his back yard, and the county and his insurance company have told him he must put a fence around it. His wife's garden grows in a back corner of the yard. The rear yard faces an alley where the sanitation engineers pick up the trash. Mr. Homeowner owns a recreational vehicle that he wants to store safely, out of the way. His children are two and nine years old, and he has a dog.

For this example, we'll assume that all the fencing will be chain link. In a real situation, an owner might prefer wood or block for the perimeter and RV storage, with chain link around the pool. Figure 5-7 shows you the dimensions of Mr. H's property. Here's how to measure the fencing for his job:

1) Measure the perimeter of the yard behind the house:

$$\begin{array}{r} 75 \\ 75 \\ 50 \\ +50 \\ \hline 250 \end{array}$$

2) Subtract the width of the house, 50 - 12 - 5:

$$\begin{array}{r} -33 \\ \hline 217 \end{array}$$

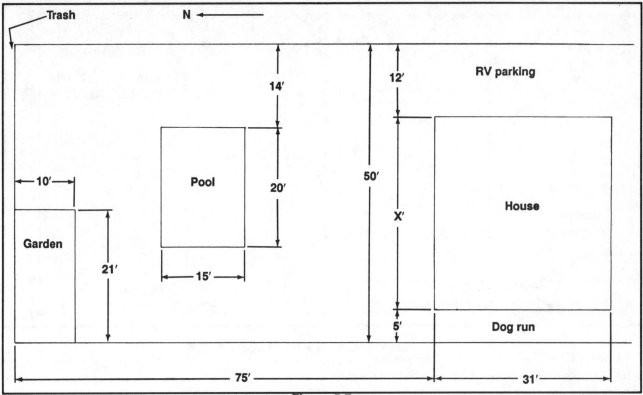

Figure 5-7
Plan view of Mr. Homeowner's yard

3) Deduct for a 3-foot access gate to the alley (to take out the trash), a 3-foot gate at the smaller side yard, and a 12-foot gate on the other side of the house. A wide gate lets Mr. H bring his RV into the yard and allows vehicle access to the pool. 3 + 3 + 12:

$$\frac{-18}{199}$$

4) But wait. Mr. Homeowner wants to secure that RV. Build him a fence down the side of the lot from the rear of the house to the front. Sell him one on the other side of the house too, for a dog run. (Note: You'll be adding two more gates, one each of 3 and 12 feet.)

$$\frac{+62}{261}$$

5) Even though the yard is fenced, Mr. H still needs a fence around the pool. The pool has to be kept locked so it's not accessible to his two children. Allow enough space around the pool for walking, sitting, landscaping, and access to the diving board. Walkways should be at least 5 feet wide. Leave at least 6 feet of clear area behind a diving board. Mr. H decided to extend the pool area 5 feet to the north, 8 feet to the south, 5 feet to the west, and to the original fence line on the east side, 39 + 39 + 28 = 106, less 3 feet for a gate:

$$\frac{+103}{364}$$

6) The garden fence shares the north and west border fences, so you only need to supply fencing for the other two sides, less a gate, 10 + 21 - 3:

$$\frac{+28}{392}$$

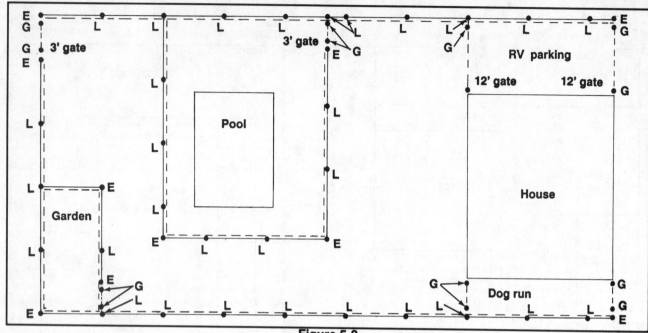

Figure 5-8
Mr. Homeowner's fence plan

How Much Fabric for the Job?

Chain link fence fabric is sold in 50 foot rolls. You'll need eight rolls of fabric if you buy pre-hung gates that already have fabric on them. If you're going to build your own gates, you'd have to add back all the gate deductions.

More Design Considerations

Here's a word of caution about those 12-foot gates. In our example, they set the fence line on the east side of the house, so be sure they don't extend past Mr. Homeowner's property line. You could wind up building a custom gate or two if 12 feet is too much.

Know your local building codes and restrictions. Be sure Mr. H can legally park his RV in the spot he's chosen and that it doesn't have to be hidden from street view. It's worth your taking the time to check this out, even if Mr. H says it's OK. If you build the fence and it turns out it's *not* OK after all, Mr. H sometimes forgets that he *told* you to put it there. See if trash containment areas have to be recessed into the resident's yard.

What about the dog and that rabbit? If the dog's not a digger and won't bite the neighbor kids, our design is OK so far. If he's a digger, you should bury the perimeter fence 18 inches into the ground so he can't dig under it. It's not good for your reputation to be outsmarted by a mutt.

The rabbit is definitely a digger, and even the buried perimeter fence won't contain it. Suggest a cage, or make a pen for it with fence fabric buried beneath the entire area bordered by the pen.

My purpose here is to show you some of the potential problems. There's a lot to think about any time you're building fences. It's not just a matter of where to dig the post holes. You have to satisfy each customer's special needs, and plan ahead to avoid future problems.

To simplify our task, I'm going to assume that the rabbit has his own cage and the dog is a good mutt.

Materials List

Now you can begin listing materials. You already know how much fabric and how many gates you'll need. The next step is to decide how many posts to order.

Figure 5-8 is a plan view of Mr. Homeowner's yard. You can see there are four "real" right angle corners, four "T" intersections, and six ends. So here's what we have so far:

Material List			
Item	Description	Quantity	Est. Cost
Fabric	6' x 50'	8 rolls	$192.00
Gate	3' walkway	4 each	$144.00
Gate	12' drive	2 each	$168.00
End post	8'	10 each	$48.00
Top rail	21'	20 each	$96.00

The job requires nearly 400 linear feet of fabric, so you'll also need about 400 feet of top rail. Remember, top rails come in 21 foot lengths, so you'll need a minimum of 19 pieces. Order 20 to be safe.

Pre-hung gates usually come with posts, but if they don't, you'll need two posts per gate. Assume in this example that posts are supplied.

Figure the line posts so the spacing between end posts and line posts is equal to the distance between line posts. Figure 5-9 shows the post-to-post distance and the number of posts required for various straight-line lengths of fence. To figure how many posts you'll need *without* the chart, do this:

1) Divide the fence length by 10.

2) If the answer doesn't come out even, round up to the next highest number, then add 1 for the last end post.

You can make exceptions, of course. For example, if your fence is 22 feet long, this formula gives you 4 posts, spaced at 7 feet 4 inches. You could also get away with 3 posts spaced 11 feet apart

On the east side of the lot, the fence length is 106 feet. The chart tells you 12 posts are required. They'll be spaced a bit over 9 feet 7 inches apart. (There are only 11 spaces, but you need 12 posts, one at each end.) If you look again at Figure 5-8, you see there are two end posts on that length of fence, so that means you need 10 line posts.

As you see in the diagram, you have to adjust the spacing to accommodate the places where two fences intersect. Study the rest of the diagram and you can see the following additions to the materials list:

Item	Description	Quantity	Est. Cost
Line post	8'	30 each	$144.00

Remember, the gates come with posts.

Chain Link Fence Post Spacing					
Number of posts	Fence length	Post spacing	Number of posts	Fence length	Post spacing
2	10'	10'	6	46'	9'2-1/2"
3	20'	10'	6	47'	9'5"
4	30'	10'	6	48'	9'7-1/4"
5	31'	7'9"	6	49'	9'9-1/2"
5	32'	8'	6	50'	10'
5	33'	8'3"	7	51'	8'6"
5	34'	8'6"	7	52'	8'8"
5	35'	8'9"	7	53'	8'10"
5	36'	9'	7	54'	9'
5	37'	9'3"	7	55'	9'2"
5	38'	9'6"	7	56'	9'4"
5	39'	9'9"	7	57'	9'6"
5	40'	10'	7	58'	9'8"
6	41'	8'2-1/2"	7	59'	9'10"
6	42'	8'5"	7	60'	10'
6	43'	8'7-1/4"	8	61'	8'8"
6	44'	8'9-1/2"	8	62'	8'10"
6	45'	9'	12	106'	9'7-1/2"

Figure 5-9
Chain link fence post spacing

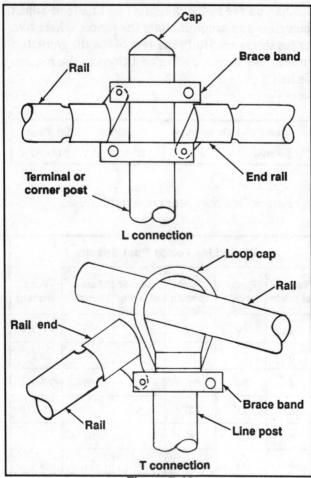

Cap

Brace band

Rail

Terminal or
corner post

End rail

L connection

Loop cap

Rail

Rail end

Brace band

Rail

Line post

T connection

Figure 5-10
Attach rail ends to posts

Each line post requires a loop cap, and each end post requires an acorn cap, so add those to the materials list:

Item	Description	Quantity	Est. Cost
Loop caps	1-5/8 x1-3/8"	30 each	$36.00
Acorn caps	2.5" diameter	10 each	$12.00

The four true corners require two tension bars each, and the ends and intersections require one tension bar each, for a total of 16.

The tension bars need to be 6 feet each, so we need a total of 96 linear feet of tension bar. Be careful how you order this. Many wholesalers sell tension bar by the linear foot. But if you order 96

linear feet and buy ten 10-foot lengths, you'll have 100 feet, but you won't have enough to do the job. You'll only have ten 6-foot lengths, and the other ten will only be 4 feet long. Be sure you order lengths that are multiples of the size you need. In this case, you need eight 12-foot lengths.

Add to the materials list:

Item	Description	Quantity	Est. Cost
Tension bars	6 foot	16 each	$19.00

Now, figure all the assorted hardware. You'll need a rail end and brace band for each end post and intersection, and two of each for each corner. Figure 5-10 shows you how to assemble these. You'll need four tension bands for each tension bar. All the brace bands and tension bands require a carriage bolt and nut. And you'll need about a half bag of concrete to anchor each post, including the gate posts. Add these items to the materials list:

Item	Description	Quantity	Est. Cost
Rail ends	1-3/8"	16 each	$10.00
Brace bands		16 each	$10.00
Tension bands		64 each	$53.00
Carriage bolts	5/16"x1-1/4"	80 each	$16.00
Nuts	5/16"	80 each	$6.00
Concrete	94 lb	22 sacks	$90.00

Equipment Rentals

Digging 43 fence posts by hand can be tedious work. If you don't own a power post hole digger, plan to rent one. The cost will be about $48 a day. Also consider renting a cement mixer if you don't already own one. The cost will be about another $48 a day. A fence stretcher costs about $18 a day. If you're working alone, count on a minimum of two days rental for these items. Now, put these on your materials list.

Item	Description	Quantity	Est. Cost
Rental	Digger	2 days	$96.00
Rental	Mixer	2 days	$96.00
Rental	Stretcher	2 days	$36.00
Misc.	Ties & cord		$12.00

The completed materials list is in Figure 5-11.

Material List			
Item	Description	Quantity	Est. Cost
Fabric	6' x 50'	8 rolls	$192.00
Gate w/2 post	3' walkway	4 each	$144.00
Gate w/2 post	12' drive	2 each	$168.00
End post	8'	10 each	$48.00
Line post	8'	30 each	$144.00
Top rail	21'	20 each	$96.00
Loop caps	1-5/8 x 1-3/8"	30 each	$36.00
Acorn caps	2.5" diameter	10 each	$12.00
Tension bars	6'	16 each	$19.00
Rail ends		16 each	$10.00
Brace bands		16 each	$10.00
Tension bands		64 each	$53.00
Carriage bolts	5/16 x 1-1/4"	80 each	$16.00
Nuts	5/16"	80 each	$6.00
Concrete	94 lb.	22 sacks	$90.00
Rental	Digger	2 days	$96.00
Rental	Mixer	2 days	$96.00
Rental	Stretcher	2 days	$36.00
Misc.	Ties & cord		$12.00
			$1,284.00

Figure 5-11
Materials list

How Much Should You Charge?

If you follow the rule of thumb that materials account for 40 percent of the job, then this job should sell for $3,210, allowing $1,926 for your labor. If your labor rate is $35 per hour, you'll have to finish the job in 55 hours to make that much. If you're working alone, I doubt that you could do it. If you figure on an hour per post, it would take you almost that long just to dig the holes, mix the concrete, set and level the posts and double-check your work.

Let's look at this again. Figure on spending a day selling and estimating the job, including the materials and labor planning. The site layout can take another day. Count on a third day to prepare and submit drawings, apply for permits, get the contract signed and collect your deposit.

Give yourself two full days to dig the post holes, and two full days to set the posts. Now you can go do something else for a few days while the concrete sets up properly.

Once you're back on the job, you'll spend two days to stretch and secure the fabric, and one day to hang the gates, make final adjustments and collect your money. That's 10 working days, or 80 hours at $35 an hour, for a total of $2,800. Add the materials, and the job total comes to $4,084. Let's round that off to $4,100 for good measure.

Have you still thought of everything? How about sales tax on the materials? What if you hit a big rock 5 inches underground at one of the corner posts and have to spend two hours digging it out? What if Mr. H's kids break open three sacks of concrete just as it starts to rain? Better add another hundred to the price to cover the inevitable contingencies.

Construction Techniques

I'm going to describe two typical chain link fence installations — one on fairly level ground, and the other on a hillside. Even so-called level ground usually isn't. It has high and low spots, but they won't cause you much trouble if they're not too extreme.

Your first job is to walk the fence line and determine the lay of the land. Find both ends of the fence, and drive a 24-inch stake into the ground at both points. Tie a string between the stakes and hang a line level on the string. Adjust the line on one or both stakes until the string is level. Walk the string line with a tape measure and measure from various points on the string to the ground. All measurements should be within 3 inches of each other, that is plus-or-minus 1-1/2 inches from the height of the string on the stake. This will work for runs up to about 50 or 60 feet. Beyond that, I suggest you use a transit.

If there are high spots, dig them out and set the dirt aside for now. Don't fill the low spots yet. An alternative is to set the fence on the high spots and fill in the low spots later. The problem with this is that you have to have a source for fill dirt.

Dig your corner post holes and set the posts to the proper height. Remember, the fabric will be about an inch below the top of the end post. The table in Figure 5-12 shows the height of the end post from the ground if the fabric is to touch the ground. Add an allowance if the bottom of the fabric will be above ground. The last column shows the cut size of the end posts if they're buried 18 inches, the minimum recommended depth for all locations.

Fabric size	End post height	18" deep end post
36"	37"	55"
42"	43"	61"
48"	49"	67"
60"	61"	79"
72"	73"	91"
84"	85"	103"
96"	97"	115"
108"	109"	127"
120"	121"	139"
132"	133"	151"
144"	143"	161"

Figure 5-12
End post height vs. fabric size

Digging Post Holes

Dig your terminal post holes with a 10-inch diameter at the top and a 12-inch diameter at the bottom. Line post holes should be 8 inches at the top, 10 inches at the bottom. Use the proper-sized

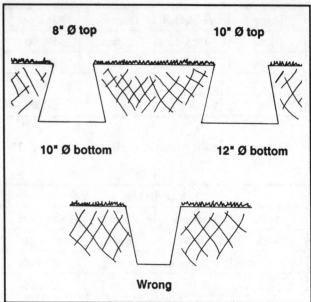

Figure 5-13
Proper shape for post holes

auger for the holes, and then dig out the *key* at the bottom by hand. The reason for the larger diameter key is to hold the concrete, and thus the post, so it resists lifting out vertically. The drawing in Figure 5-13 illustrates the fine art of post hole digging.

Dig the holes 2 or 3 inches deeper than you need for the concrete, to allow for drainage and leveling. Fill the bottom of the hole with coarse sand or wet grout to a depth of 4 inches. Put the post in the hole and set it level and plumb. Brace the post into position and pour in the concrete a few inches at a time. Recheck for level and plumb several times. Overfill the hole so the concrete extends about 3 inches above ground level. Trowel this so it slopes away from the post, to provide a path for water to drain.

Double-check each terminal post for height, plumb, and position. Wait several days for the concrete to cure before you go on.

Locate Your Fabric Line

Now string a line from one end of each straight run of fencing to the other. Put the line on the outside of the posts (the side where the fabric will go) and 3-1/2 inches from their tops. Put another

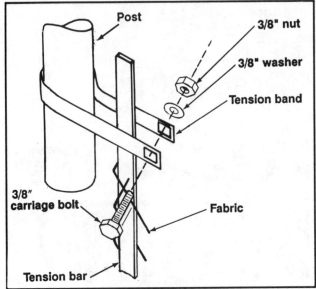

Figure 5-14
Tension band installation

string at the bottom of the posts, at ground level. Measure along the bottom string from the end, terminal, or corner post to the position of the first line post. The line post should be at least 7 feet, but not more than 10 feet from the end post. Mark the position of the first line post with chalk or a stake.

Measure all the line post positions the same way, marking each as you go. Double-check to be sure the positions came out the way you expected. You want to make any necessary changes *before* you start digging. Now set your line posts the same way you did the end posts, double-checking as you go. Then let the concrete cure for a couple more days.

You may have already dug the holes for the line posts when you dug for the terminal posts. It's acceptable to do it that way, but you'll get more accurate positioning and spacing if you install the end posts before you dig for the line posts.

Assemble the Fence

Once the concrete has cured, it's time to start assembling the fence. Slide the required number of tension bands onto the end post. Be sure the flat side of the band is to the outside, the fabric side of the post. See Figure 5-14. Now fasten a rail end to the end post using a brace band and a carriage

bolt. Position the rail end so it's angled upward. It should be 1 inch from the top of the end post.

Next, slide a few loop caps onto a length of top rail. Set the top rail in place on the line post with the swaged end away from the end post. Put the non-swaged end of the top rail into the rail end until it bottoms, then slide it back out 3/8 of an inch. Continue down the fence line, adding top rails with the required number of loop caps until you get to the end. You'll usually have to cut the last piece to fit. The piece you cut off will have the swaged end, so you can use it later in another section of fence.

To install the last piece of top rail, first slide enough tension bands onto the end post so they'll be evenly spaced about a foot apart between the top and bottom of the post. Remember to mount them with the flat side out. Slip the rail end onto the top rail and put a brace band onto the end post. Match the brace band to the rail end, and connect the two with a carriage bolt. If you did everything right, the top rail will be level along its entire length. Now, tighten all the carriage bolts.

Install the Fabric

When you look at the roll of fabric, you'll notice a difference between the way wire ends are tied on the two edges of the roll. On one end of the roll, the mesh is looped together so the edge is smooth. On the other end, the wire is cut and twisted together and forms barbs. Figures 5-15 and 5-16 show the difference. Which edge do you want at the top of the fence? Put the barbed edge on top for security fences, the smooth edge up for residential or low divider fences where people or animals might get cut by barbs on the fence top.

Beginning at the first post, roll the fabric out on the outside of the fence line, and 8 to 10 feet beyond the last post. Go back to the first post and thread a tension bar through the first set of loops in the fabric. Raise the fabric into position and secure the tension bar to the post with the tension bands, using carriage bolts. Remember, the heads of the carriage bolts go outside the fence, the nuts on the inside.

Figure 5-15
Chain link smooth edge

Figure 5-16
Chain link barbed edge

Now, lift the fabric and tie it loosely to the top rail with aluminum ties every few feet. The fabric should extend about 1/2 inch above the top rail.

Stretch the Fabric

Once you've attached the fabric to the full length of the fence, it's time to stretch it. A ratchet-type stretcher is best. The stretcher has a bar with hooks every few inches that grab the fabric. Attach the bar to the fabric at the last post and begin stretching it.

If you attach the stretcher to the terminal post, grab the fabric loops about 1-1/2 feet into the fabric and let the excess hang down. When it's stretched, fasten the loops closest to the pole with a tension bar and tension bands. Cut off the excess fabric and remove the stretcher. Or you can attach the stretcher to a temporary pole in line with the fabric direction and 1 to 2 feet beyond the end post.

Properly stretched, fence fabric won't sag or hang. It should give just slightly and then snap back when pushed.

Find the fabric links that come closest to the last end post. Insert a tension bar, and attach it to the post with tension bands, as you did at the beginning. Remove the stretcher and check the

tension again. If it's too loose, move the tension bar to the next set of diamonds away from the end post. If it's too tight, move the tension bar to the row in the opposite direction.

Cut the fabric with a bolt cutter or heavy-duty wire cutter. Make the cuts between the tension bar links and the end post. Be careful you don't cut the links being held by the tension bar.

Now, all you have to do is snap the acorn caps onto the end posts and fill any low spots under the fence. You can use the dirt you removed from the high spots at the beginning of the project. Go back and add aluminum ties along the top rail at 12 to 18 inch intervals, and tie the fabric to the line posts also. Use at least four evenly spaced ties on the line posts.

Make a final pass to tighten all the carriage bolts, and then go collect your money. Take a picture of the fence if the owner doesn't mind — you can use those pictures when you're selling other jobs.

In Chapter 9 I explain how to splice two sections of chain link fabric together. That's necessary if you want to make a continuous run of over 50 feet.

Figure 5-17
A mid-rail adds extra strength

Some Variations

Here are some alternatives to the installation method I've described above:

1) You can stretch a wire along the bottom edge of the fence and tie the fabric to the wire. This stabilizes the fence during high winds and keeps people from trying to squeeze under the fence.

2) You can use a bottom or mid-height rail, the same size as the top rail, as shown in Figure 5-17. I recommend a bottom rail for retaining wall applications, to prevent damage and push-out.

Fabric Fences on Hillsides

In the example above, I described how to level the fence path by cutting the high spots and filling the shallows. There's no rule that says a fence has to be level. You might install fences on hillsides, across valleys, or over large bumps, following the contour of the land. You can use chain link "on the bias," as much as 30 degrees off level.

When you install a fence that's not level, try to keep the change in elevation constant from post to post. On very uneven ground, that won't be possible. Then you'll have to terrace the fence, making each post-to-post section level, but stepping up or down at posts whenever needed.

If there are radical changes in the slope along the fence line, you may have to install end posts and tension rods at intermediate points along the line. You'd tension each section independently. Figure 5-18 illustrates this. You'd have to remove

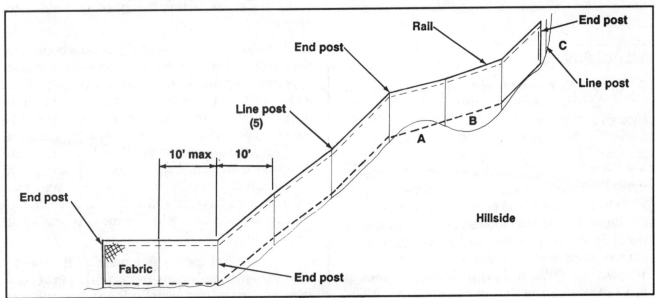

Figure 5-18
Hillside fencing

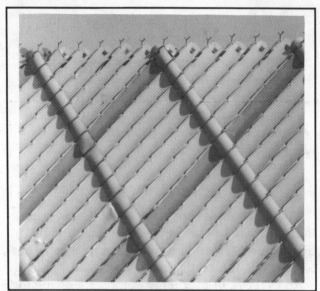

Figure 5-19
Plastic strips give visual privacy to chain link fencing

Figure 5-20
"Keepers" prevent plastic slats from sliding out

the mound at point A in the drawing. At point B, you can do two things. Either fill in the depression, or install a bottom rail on the fence and hang extra fabric from it. Anchor the fabric to the ground with heavy metal stakes.

You may have to add extra line posts at point C to fill the gap. Place them no more than 6 to 8 inches (oc) apart.

Visual Privacy

Chain link fence has one major advantage. It won't blow over, even in strong winds. There isn't enough surface area to provide much wind resistance. But that advantage is also a disadvantage. Standard chain link fencing doesn't provide much privacy. But you can insert wood, metal or plastic strips in the wire to create a sight screen. Figure 5-19 shows fence fabric with plastic strips woven through it. Figure 5-20 shows a detail of the *keepers* that stop the strips from sliding out. These inexpensive strips come in a variety of sizes and colors. You can weave them diagonally like the ones in these pictures, or vertically using wood lath like the fence in Figure 5-28 near the end of this chapter.

Wire Fences and Barbed Wire

Woven wire fences have horizontal strands of wire called *fillers* and vertical strands called *stays*. The fillers are interwoven between the stay wires which are held in place by heavier gauge top and bottom strands. Stay wires are usually spaced 6 or 12 inches apart. The intersections of filler and stay wires are either factory wrapped or welded to keep everything in position.

The filler wires are spaced from the bottom to the top of the mesh in preset increments. The first wire from the bottom is 3 inches up, the next 3-1/2, in 1/2 inch increments up to 32 inches in mesh height. Then the increments change to 1 inch difference. The difference in mesh spacing makes it hard for little animals to get their heads through the mesh. If an animal can get its head through an opening, it can usually get its body through, too. Baby animals have small heads and live close to the ground, so that's why the mesh is smaller at the bottom.

Why not just use the fine mesh all the way to the top? Fine mesh costs more, and animal containment fences are usually long. A small cost savings per linear foot can add up fast if you're building miles of fence.

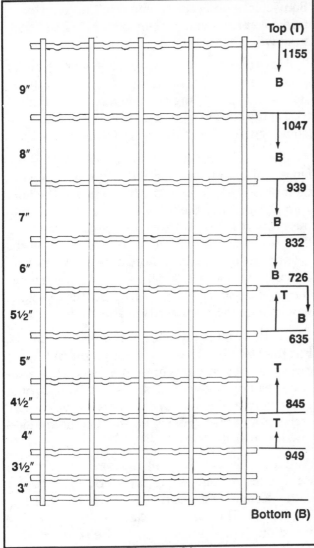

Figure 5-21
Spacing of wire mesh fencing

Code number	Number of strands	Height in inches
635	6	35
726	7	26
832	8	32
845	8	45
939	9	39
949	9	49
1047	10	47
1155	11	55
1948	19	48
2048	20	48
2158	21	58
2360	23	60
2672	26	72

Figure 5-22
Woven wire mesh fence code numbers

You buy woven wire mesh in rolls of 20 or 40 *rods*. That translates to 110 or 220 yards, or 330 or 660 feet. You order it by code number that tells how many filler strands there are and the height.

Chicken wire has six-sided mesh rather than rectangular mesh. *Hardware cloth* is the name for woven wire material with 1/4 or 1/2 inch squares.

Here's how wire fencing is rated:

Quality	Top and bottom strands	Filler strands
Very heavy duty	9 gauge	9 gauge
Heavy duty	9 gauge	11 gauge
Regular duty	10 gauge	12.5 gauge
Light duty	11 gauge	14.5 gauge

"Gauge" represents the wire thickness — the higher the gauge, the thinner the wire. Here are common wire sizes you'll use in chain link and wire fencing:

Figure 5-21 shows the standard spacing for various mesh designs. For example, design #949 starts at the point shown, with 4 inches between the first two fillers, and extends to the top of the chart for a total height of 49 inches. Design #1047 has 8 inches between the top two strands, and extends to the bottom of the chart. It's 46-1/2 inches high and contains 10 fillers. Design codes starting with #1948 and up are poultry fencing and spacing is different, usually 1 or 2 inches between strands and stays. Figure 5-22 is a chart of wire fencing specifications.

#6	.1920 inches
#9	.1483 inches
#11	.1205 inches
#13	.0915 inches

You can get wire with protective zinc (galvanized) or aluminum coatings. The galvanized coatings come in three classes. Class #3 has twice the protective zinc that class #1 has, so a fence made of class #3 material will last longer. Aluminum coating is best, but it's also the most expensive.

You can also get wire fencing with green vinyl or white painted coatings. These are generally used only for home garden mesh fences, the ones with a "loop" top. See Figure 5-23.

Wire Fencing Applications

Woven wire fences are often used to contain animals. Sometimes you'll have to combine wire fence with barbed wire either on the fence top or bottom. If you're containing chickens, ducks, or other birds, you'll need mesh that's a constant size all the way to the top and over the enclosed area.

Figure 5-23
Loop top garden fencing

(Baby chicks don't fly, so you don't need an overhead cover for them. A 12-inch high, 1/2 to 1-inch mesh will contain them.)

Hogs don't fly, but they root or try to dig under a fence. You can hold them in a fence 26 to 39 inches high, providing you put a strand of barbed wire at the bottom of the fence to discourage them from digging when they bump into it.

Sheep don't fly or root, so a 26- or 32-inch-high fence will keep them in. But it might not keep out their predators. To keep the sheep in and the wild animals out, bury the fence 18 or more inches into the ground so dogs, foxes and coyotes can't dig their way in. A 2 to 3 foot apron of mesh on the ground just outside the fenced area will work also. To keep predator animals from jumping over sheep fence, string barbed wire from the top of the woven wire mesh upwards to about 6 feet.

Cattle don't fly, root, or have many predators. But they tend to think the grass is greener in the next field. When they come to a fence, they'll always lean on or over it. Use a 47- to 55-inch-high fence with a single strand of barbed wire a few inches above the top of the mesh. That discourages grazing over the fence.

Horses, like cattle, think life is better in the next field. Use the same setup for work horses as for cattle. Eliminate the barbed wire for show or racing horses. The barbs can cause cuts that lead to infection. Use a single strand of electrified wire along the top of the fence instead. Horses aren't very smart, but they learn very quickly not to lean against electrified wire.

Use hardware cloth cages to contain small chewing animals like rodents and rabbits. They must be restrained from above, below and all the way around.

Don't even try to keep fur-bearing animals such as mink or muskrat inside wire fencing. They can chew their way through any wire fence made. Use a solid steel cage instead.

For dogs, use a fence 47 to 55 inches high without barbed wire on top. If the dog is a digger, either run a strand or two of barbed wire at the bottom or bury wire mesh to discourage him. Sometimes you'll have to install wire mesh on top of a wood fence to keep a dog from jumping over.

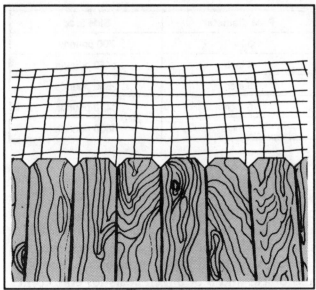

Figure 5-24
Add extra height to a wood fence with wire mesh

One pet owner I know uses the setup in Figure 5-24.

Don't bother trying to fence in a cat. They go anywhere they please.

Sometimes, you'll need to keep animals out, not in. Deer are a real problem in some rural areas. They have great appetites, and their favorite food is in your new garden. Their second favorite is fruit hanging on trees. You'll need a fairly high fence, 55 to 72 inches, to keep them out. They can jump a 6-foot fence when frightened and reach food more than 7 feet high without leaving the ground.

To protect bushes and trees from animals, just bury a ring of fencing about a foot into the ground, 12 to 18 inches out from what you want to protect. No posts are needed.

Posts

You can use wood, concrete, or metal posts for woven or barbed wire fences. If you're using wood or concrete, you still have to dig post holes. Metal posts are a different story. You only need to set the end or anchor posts in concrete. You can drive the line posts into the ground with a sledge hammer.

In places where wood fence posts are common, you can probably rent a motorized post driver to set the posts. With one of those, you can drive an 8-inch wood line post directly into the ground with a few blows. Set uncemented line posts 30 inches deep, anchor posts to 42 inches. Wood posts may topple during the rainy seasons, but that's less likely if the posts are set deep enough.

Be sure to set the posts extra deep where needed. Posts for rural fences are usually set at greater intervals. That means each has to support more weight. A long fence will usually have to support tremendous side loads from wind — and probably a few 800-pound cows.

Won't wood posts driven directly into the ground rot? Yes, they will, but not as quickly as they will if you anchor them in concrete. That may surprise you after our earlier discussion in the chapter on wood fences. Here's the reasoning: Rural fences are often made from unmilled, undried lumber, even logs. If you set them in concrete, they'll eventually shrink away from the foundation and leave a gap. Water and bugs get into the gap and cause dry rot and wood fiber destruction. Pretty soon, no more post.

Freezing weather tends to fracture concrete. If water gets into cracks in a concrete post hole and freezes, the water expands and breaks the concrete. Once the concrete is weakened, the post no longer supports the fence. It's true that a wood post planted directly in the ground *is* subject to dry rot, but usually only twice a year, in spring and fall. Winter bacteria goes dormant in the summer. Heat and dryness kills it. If water freezes around a post in the ground in winter, the water in the ground expands and may actually tighten its grip on the post.

There another reason why it's not necessary to set rural fence posts in concrete. Most residential fences are privacy fences and have a large surface area exposed to the wind. Rural fences are usually open wire and offer very little resistance. So they aren't as likely to be damaged by wind, even if anchored in the soil.

Post Materials

In the chapter on wood fences, I described the species of lumber used to build fences. In rural areas, fences are often built from whatever materials are readily available. For example, posts and boards might be cut locally from species that aren't harvested commercially. Posts in rural areas are usually *peeler logs* that have been pressure treated. Figure 5-25 shows how long untreated posts cut from various kinds of trees can be expected to last.

Wood	Life expectancy
Cottonwood	1 to 3 years
Aspen	1 to 3 years
Ponderosa pine	2 to 4 years
Lodge pole pine	2 to 4 years
Western hemlock	3 to 6 years
Douglas fir	3 to 6 years
Western red cedar	12 to 15 years
Oak, hickory	15 to 20 years
Black locust	20 to 22 years
Western juniper	20 to 22 years
Osage orange	25 to 30 years

Figure 5-25
Life expectancy of untreated wood fences

If you pressure-treat any of these woods, you can expect them to last from 15 to 20 years longer. Remember that the heartwood in any species is the insect and dry rot-resistant wood. The sapwood is not. If you use it, always have it pressure treated. You can treat these woods yourself by immersing them in preservatives (see Chapter 3), which will add from 5 to 15 years useful life. The estimates in Figure 5-25 are average ranges. Local weather conditions will influence post life expectancy.

Posts come in diameters from 3 to 8 inches and in lengths from 5-1/2 feet to 8 feet. The thicker the post, the more side load it can handle. Typical side loads a post can withstand before it snaps are as follows:

Post diameter	Side load
3 inch	700 pounds
4 inch	1450 pounds
5 inch	2650 pounds
6 inch	3450 pounds
7 inch	3800 pounds

These are average figures for solid timber that's fairly dense. To be on the safe side, use the next higher-rated material from the ones shown above. In other words, if you expect a maximum side load of 400 pounds, use the 4 inch post, not the 3 inch. I generally use 4 inch posts for line posts and braces and 5 or 6 inch posts for end, corner, and gate posts.

Anchor Corner, Gate and End Posts

Not every rural wood post can be set directly in the ground. Wooden corner, gate, and end (terminal) posts *should* be set in concrete. Do this not so much to anchor them as to form a *footing*. A footing distributes forces transferred from the post to a wider area.

Make the post hole a minimum of three times the post diameter and wider at the bottom than at the top. Use treated wood for these posts. Dig your hole 6 inches deeper than the post will be set. Fill that 6 inches with gravel. Place your post on the gravel and pack concrete around it, building it up slightly around the post above ground level. This creates a drainage path for water. Figure 5-26 shows how this is done, and how to anchor the line posts with dirt and rocks.

After about six months, check the cemented post bases for cracks. If you find any, fill them with hot tar or silicon caulking sealer.

Metal Posts

Metal posts are easy to install. Pound them into the ground with a sledge hammer or post driver. Metal posts have several advantages:

- They'll ground lightning strikes to some extent. For best protection, add regular ground

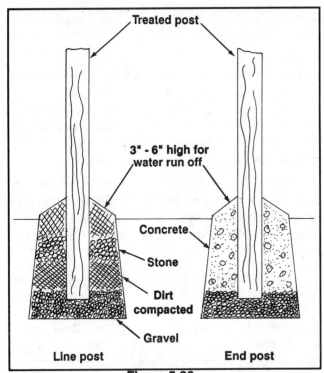

Figure 5-26
Line and end post

Figure 5-27
T-shaped metal post supports barbed wire

rods for every 150 feet of fence. See the discussion at the end of this chapter.

- They're insect and rot proof.

- They won't burn.

- They're cheap, lightweight and easy to handle.

- They're strong.

The disadvantages are that they rust if not painted, and they're not especially attractive.

Metal posts have studs that work like a yardstick. You can count them to see how far the post has been driven into the ground, and to keep the strands of wire even. The studs help hold the wire mesh in place, and keep the mesh and ties from sliding down the posts. Figure 5-27 shows barbed wire on a T-shaped metal post.

Metal posts come in lengths of from 5 to 8 feet, in 6 inch increments. There's usually an anchor plate attached which helps keep them upright and stable against side loading.

Cement metal posts into the ground if they're terminal or corner posts. Dig a hole 18 x 18 inches at the top, 20 x 20 inches at the bottom, and at least 30 inches deep. Fill the hole with concrete, compact it, and then insert the post. You'll need about 6.25 cubic feet of concrete for each post. This foundation pier transfers side force on the post to the ground, keeping the post from tipping or pulling out.

It's also a good idea to brace the post diagonally in the direction of the side force. Set the braces in 12 x 12 x 12 inch concrete piers. (Each pier will take 1 cubic foot of concrete.)

Notice that metal posts for wire fence require larger foundations than posts for chain link fence. That's because chain link fencing has a top rail. This top rail supports the weight of the fabric vertically so the loading force is downward. Wire mesh fences have no top rail, so the weight of the mesh and any force against it is transferred directly to the posts.

Stretching Wire Fences

There's another difference between installing chain link and wire mesh fencing. You stretch chain link to within a few inches of the terminal

Figure 5-28
Barbed wire adds security to a chain link fence

post and then attach it. You check the tension by pulling and pushing on the fabric.

When you install wire mesh or barbed wire, you must stretch the mesh *beyond* the terminal post. This means you have to install a temporary post several feet past the end of the fence. Then fasten the stretcher to the dummy post so the wire is under tension right up to the terminal post. Also, wire mesh has what are called *tension loops*. These are bends in the horizontal filler wires between each vertical (stay) wire. When you stretch a mesh or wire fence, you remove about 30 to 50 percent of the bend in those loops. *Do not* tension the material so you remove the loops completely. Leave 50 to 70 percent of each loop, so the fence stays tight over the years.

The tension loops act like a spring to maintain overall tension. But extended exposure to heat and cold will cause them to relax over time. Eventually it will be necessary to re-tension the fence.

Barbed Wire

Barbed wire is used mainly on farms, but it does have applications on business and residential properties. You can combine it with other fences to discourage climbing. Figure 5-28 shows barbed

wire on top of a chain link fence that also provides visual security with wood slats.

Barbed wire is dangerous to work with. The barbs are sharp. Wear heavy leather gloves, jeans, and a leather jacket. And most important, protect your eyes when you're working with barbed wire. The stuff is curled like a spring and it'll lash out at your eyes the moment you pull on it. I wear a motorcycle helmet with a full face shield.

Roll barbed wire off the end of the spool, not the side. If it comes off the side of the spool, you'll have a tangled, dangerous mess on your hands. Keep the wire under tension while you're unrolling it.

Don't try to stretch barbed wire by pulling on it with your truck. Use a ratchet-type tensioner or a block and tackle. Tension until it vibrates or oscillates when you pluck it. If you pull it too tight, it will break and recoil at high speed and with great force. Anyone in the way is going to be cut.

Here's a suggestion for vertical spacing of a barbed wire fence:

Total wires	Ground to first strand	Distance between strands
3	16 inches	16 inches
4	16 inches	10 inches
5	12 inches	10 inches
6	12 inches	8 inches

Suggested post-to-post spacing is 20 feet. You can put the posts farther apart if it's necessary to cross a stream or other obstruction. If you do space posts farther apart than 20 feet, install wire stays between posts, or at least every 15 feet. Twist the stays around each line wire to hold them in place. If you do this, you can space your posts as much as 100 feet or more apart.

♦ Attach barbed wire to the end post by wrapping it around the post and then twisting it on itself. Twist the wire at least six times. See Figure 5-29.

♦ Fasten barbed wire to concrete or metal line posts with wire ties.

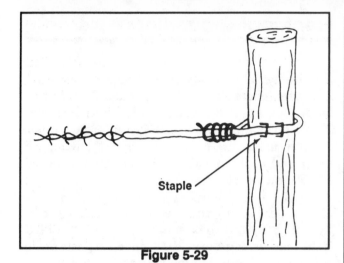

Figure 5-29
Post connection

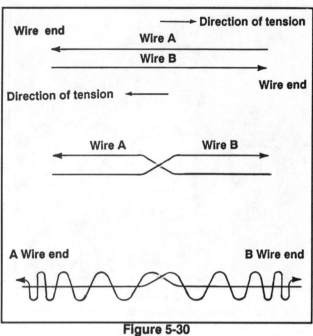

Figure 5-30
Splice wire

◆ Use U-shaped metal staples on wood line posts.

When you use staples, drive them in at a diagonal to the wire path. Angle them down slightly. Don't pound them tight against the wire, leave some space. If you hammer the staples tightly into the wire, you may nick the wire, causing a weak spot that will eventually break.

There's another reason to leave some slack in the staples on the line posts. Wire is stretched from terminal post to terminal post. The line posts just keep the wire in proper position. If you pound the staples tight at the line posts, you won't be able to retighten the wire without removing or loosening the line post staples. Also, you need to allow for expansion and contraction of the wire as the temperature changes.

Don't Splice Wire

I don't recommend that you splice woven mesh or barbed wire. Try to make your terminations before the roll ends. Barbed wire is sold in 80 rod rolls, 1,320 feet. Mesh comes in 20 and 40 rod rolls, 330 and 660 feet respectively.

If you must splice wire, then note how I've done it in Figure 5-30. You can also splice mesh by crimping, as in Figure 5-31. Insert the wires into a metal sleeve and then crush the sleeve around the wire with a crimping tool. If one splice comes apart, the other wires will still hold the mesh together. Don't crimp barbed wire, since all the tension is on each strand. Splice it instead.

You can also buy aluminum strip wire (sometimes called *razor wire*) for maximum protection against intrusion. It's installed in coils on top of the fence. I don't recommend it for containing animals. It does too much damage to anything that gets tangled in it. Aluminum strip wire is used on top of the wood fence in Figure 5-32.

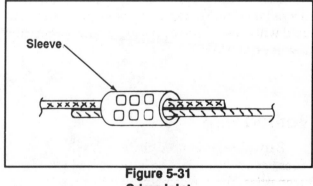

Figure 5-31
Crimp joint

Figure 5-32
Coiled aluminum strip wire

Electrical Grounding

Finally, a word about grounding. All metal and wire fences should be grounded. You do this by driving a 6- to 8-foot copper rod into the earth. Then you clamp one end of a #12 or larger copper or aluminum wire to the copper rod. Attach the other end to the metal fence wire. Do this every 150 feet on long fences. The purpose is to bleed off electricity from lightning strikes. Any person or animal near an ungrounded wire that's struck by lightning is going to be seriously injured or killed if the fence isn't grounded. Metal fence posts make good ground rods, but they have to extend at least 8 feet into the ground to be effective.

In the next chapter, I'll tell you about some of the more unusual types of metal fence materials.

six

Metal Fences

Factory-made metal railings are widely used in residential, commercial and industrial buildings. They're sturdy and effective, and they don't detract from the appearance of a building because they're nearly transparent. When you combine them with block walls and shrubs, they can make an area both inviting and attractive. Figure 6-1 shows one way metal railings are used in residential buildings.

Metal fencing isn't limited to factory manufactured units. Look at the attention getter in Figure 6-2. It's a metal fence the owner welded together out of scrap metal, tools, wagon wheels and horseshoes. There's even a gate (Figure 6-3). All you need is imagination to make an attractive, interesting fence.

Look again at Figure 6-1. The metal railings shown there are factory-made. You can buy them in 20 foot lengths and assemble them on site. The top rails are 1-1/2 by 3/4 inches, bottom rails 3/8 x 1, vertical bars are a half inch square, and the vertical posts are 1-1/2 inches square. These railings are made of painted steel tubing that's been *arc welded* together. I'll cover this in more detail later in the chapter.

You bolt the railing sections to the underlying structure, then *gas weld* the sections together. In gas welding, the heat for the weld is created by burning a mixture of acetylene and oxygen. You heat the metal to just below its melting point, then touch a *filler rod* of like material to the heated area.

Figure 6-1
Metal railings for safety

Figure 6-2
An unusual metal fence

heat the metal to just below its melting point, then touch a *filler rod* of like material to the heated area. The filler rod melts and forms the joint. I'll also describe that in detail. Figure 6-4 shows the weld joints where two sections are connected.

This picture illustrates a common welding mistake. The joint should have been ground smooth before it was painted. Look at Figure 6-5. It shows a corner joint that's been finished properly. There's no bead of filler material, called a *fillet*, where the top rails are joined at the corner.

Look for manufactured fencing that has the vertical bars welded to the top and bottom rails on all sides. If there are gaps in the weld, moisture can get inside the tubing and cause it to rust. Then the rust stains the fence itself, and the surface under it.

Figure 6-3
Old tools make a gate

Figure 6-4
A sloppy weld

Figure 6-5
Properly welded and finished joint

Figure 6-6
A nice prefab fence installation

Figure 6-7
The mounting system

There's one major disadvantage to fully welded metal fencing. You can't bend the material to fit the angle of a stairway, so you have to order or custom-build stair railings. That takes extra time and money.

You can use prefab railings that have flat metal strips for the vertical bars. The strips are twisted for added strength, but are flat where they're attached to the top and bottom rails. By holding the bottom rail steady and pushing laterally on the top railing, you can make these railings fit a stairway of any angle.

You can buy these railings at building centers in 4-, 8-, and sometimes 12-foot lengths. They come factory finished, usually in white or black. They also come with the necessary nuts and bolts, L-brackets, and post caps. You choose suitable anchors to fasten the railing into concrete, soil, or wood. Gates and associated hardware are also available.

Figure 6-6 shows a nicely installed prefab metal fence. Figure 6-7 shows a close-up of the mounting system. You fasten the L-bracket to the block with an expansion bolt. First, drill the block to accept the bolt and its sleeve. Then insert the sleeve into the hole. When you drive the bolt into the sleeve, the sleeve expands and locks in place. You can still remove and reinstall the bolt at any time.

You'll need a 1/2 HP variable-speed drill and carbide-tipped drill bits for this job. Depending on the size and weight of the fence, use 1/4-, 3/8-, or 1/2-inch bolts to secure it. The catalog or package label for the expansion bolt specifies the size drill to use.

The railings in Figure 6-8 are cemented into the ground next to the concrete steps. If it's necessary to remove them, it can be done without destroying the steps.

Figure 6-9 shows a different type of metal stair railing. It's used in front of a bank and adds a feeling of strength and security to both the bank and the railing. The top rail is cut from *sheet* steel that's notched, formed and welded.

Sheet steel is usually sold in 4 x 8- and 4 x 10-foot sheets. You need a *shear*, a cutter capable of cutting the sheets into strips. Then you use a power *brake* to bend the steel into the shape you

Figure 6-8
Railings cemented into the ground, not the steps

Figure 6-9
Rails cut from sheet metal

Figure 6-10
Round pipe used as vertical bars

need. Both these tools produce several tons of force and should be used only by operators who know how to handle them properly. I recommend farming this kind of work out to a fully-equipped metal fabricator.

The vertical posts in Figure 6-9 were cemented to the steps. This makes it hard to remove them if that's necessary. A better way to install these would be to drill holes in the concrete slightly larger than the posts. Then insert the posts in the holes and pour quickset hydraulic cement or an epoxy in the hole around the post. Hydraulic cement expands as it cures. If you mount the posts this way they'll hold tight, but they can be removed without breaking the concrete.

Figure 6-10 shows a metal fence with vertical bars of round pipe and horizontal rails of rectangular tubing. The rails are drilled to accept the pipe sections. The top rail is drilled all the way through, and the bottom rail is drilled only through one surface. The pipe was inserted and then *tack welded* in place. A tack weld is a small spot weld.

Metal expands and contracts when the temperature changes. If you don't include expansion joints, long sections of fence may warp and buckle. Figure 6-11 shows an expansion joint in the fence in Figure 6-10. To make a joint like this one, weld a tube to the post that's smaller than the horizontal rail. Cut a slot in the tube along its length. Slip the horizontal rail over the tube and bolt it in place through the slot. But don't tighten the bolt entirely.

That way, the horizontal rail can slip back and forth a little on the tube that's welded to the post. The top rail is installed the same way.

Figure 6-12 is a security fence that's designed to discourage climbers. Would you try to climb over those spikes? The bend is toward the outside of the fence. The points are *swaged*, welded, and ground to shape. You swage the metal by placing it into a form, then pressing or hammering it to the shape of the form.

Figure 6-11
Expansion joint

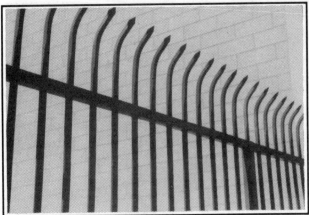
**Figure 6-12
Security fence**

**Figure 6-13
Highway railing**

Figure 6-13 shows a familiar highway railing. It's made of sheet steel with a galvanized coating to prevent rust. As you can see from the gaps around the bolt heads, the joint is fairly loose. There's another metal plate behind this joint that's bolted tightly to the wooden post. The rail sections *float* over the stationary plate when the metal expands and contracts.

In Figure 6-14 you see a corral made of welded pipe. The fence might be factory-made or built on the site. Either way, it's effective. And the horses won't hurt themselves on the smooth, round pipe.

The fence in Figure 6-15 borders an equestrian trail. The top rail is mounted on posts that are bent to prevent horses and riders from hitting the posts if they get too close. There are two ways to furnish the bent posts. You can heat a length of straight pipe to just below the melting point, then bend it in a form. You'd need a kiln and heavy-duty bending equipment to do that, so it's probably not a practical operation for the average fence contractor. Instead, use the method shown here. Buy factory-bent elbows and weld them to the vertical posts. You can see the weld on the first post from the right at the bottom of the picture.

Build Your Own or Use Prefab Fencing?

The prefab metal fencing business looks easy enough. If you're only going to install it, and if it's designed to go together without welding, you

don't need much more than hand tools. A wrench, hacksaw, hammer and some drills should be enough. But if you want to make metal fencing your specialty, you'll have to learn about welding and metal working.

Square or rectangular tubing is easy to work with and available in a wide range of sizes and weights. Price varies from 15 cents to several dollars a foot depending on the size and material. To work it, you'll need a table saw or a radial arm saw and welding equipment. You'll also need a bench grinder and a half-inch variable-speed power drill, some cleaning chemicals, and painting materials and tools. You can set yourself up with enough to get started for under $1,000.

**Figure 6-14
Corral fence**

Figure 6-15
A welded, bent-rail fence

Round tubing is a little harder to work with. To weld a circular rail and post together, you have to grind the end of the rail to a curve so its shape conforms to the shape of the post.

Working with sheet stock is the most difficult, and the most expensive. You need high-powered shears and brakes that cost $30,000 or more apiece. Unless you plan to make it your primary field, you're better off farming that work out to a shop that's equipped for it.

No matter what kind of metal fencing you build, you'll need welding equipment, and people who know how to use it. You won't have a lot of competition in this end of the business because of the specialized equipment, knowledge, and skills required.

Welding Safety

Welding is dangerous to both property and people. Here are some essential safety rules:

1) Always protect your eyes against ultraviolet radiation. U/V rays damage the retina of the eye, causing blindness.

2) Keep the welding area clear of all combustible materials.

3) Have a fire extinguisher nearby.

4) Welding fumes can kill. Use a respirator, preferably one that contains its own air supply.

Careless welders cause millions of dollars in property damage each year. Always follow strict safety practices so you're not the one to start a fire.

Some Welding Basics

There are several types of welds, and blueprint symbols for all of them. Figure 6-16A is the basic arrow symbol that drafters use to show where a weld is required. They add other symbols to the arrow to indicate the type of weld you're to perform, and how to finish it. In Figure 6-16B the arrow shows where a seam weld will join two pieces of flat iron.

In Figure 6-17, the inverted V under the arrow specifies a V-groove continuous weld at the seam where the arrow points. Because the V is on the bottom of the arrow, it means you only weld on

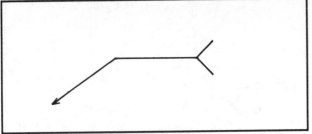

Figure 6-16A
Weld symbol

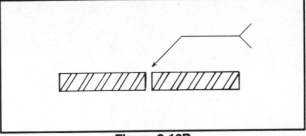

Figure 6-16B
Weld here only

one side of the two pieces of metal, the side the arrow points to. To indicate a weld on both sides, you'll see a mirror image of the welding symbol on the top of the arrow. Figure 6-18 illustrates this. Certain welds *can't* be double-sided welds. Plug, slot, spot and seam welds are all one-sided welds. I'll explain more about those later in the chapter.

You make a V weld by first grinding a bevel on the edges of both pieces of metal where they're going to butt together. You heat the groove with the welding torch, and touch the *filler* to the groove. If you clean and grind the metal properly, use the right filler and *flux*, and heat the metal to the right temperature, your finished weld looks like part A of Figure 6-19.

If you don't thoroughly clean the metal, or if you use the wrong flux, your weld joint will fail. In Figure 6-19 B, the dark areas between the metal and the weld represent dirt, oil, oxides and flux. The metal is *not* securely welded together.

Grind or wire brush all metal before you attempt to weld it. Use a degreaser to remove oil. If the metal is rusted, *pickle* it. That means to clean it in a solution of nitric acid or other commercially-available rust remover.

Flux

Welding flux can be separate from, or incorporated into, the filler rod. When heated, it forms an inert gas barrier around the weld joint that prevents airborne oxygen from entering the weld and combining with the heated metal to form oxides. Oxides are salts, and salts inhibit good welds because they prevent the heated metals from flowing together. Flux also acts as a cleaner, but it's not a substitute for thoroughly cleaning the metal before you weld it.

Filler

The filler rod provides the metal to replace the material you grind off to make the weld seam. Always use a filler of the same material as the metal you're welding, or you won't get a strong weld joint.

The diameter of the welding rod is also a factor in making a good weld. If the rod is too thin, you won't get enough filler into the joint. A rod that's too thick may not melt, and will probably give you a sloppy looking joint. As a rule of thumb, begin

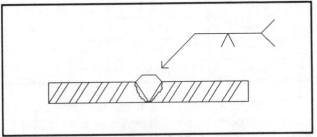

Figure 6-17
End view of V-groove weld

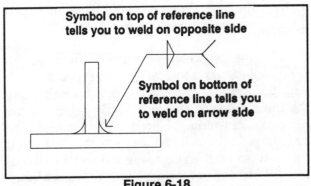

Symbol on top of reference line tells you to weld on opposite side

Symbol on bottom of reference line tells you to weld on arrow side

Figure 6-18
Two-sided weld

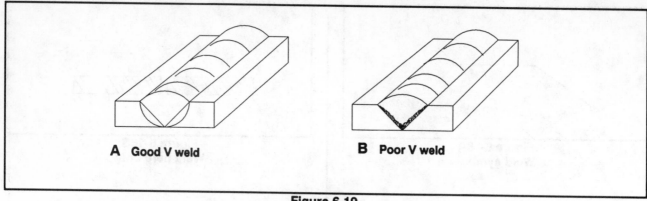

Figure 6-19
Weld examples

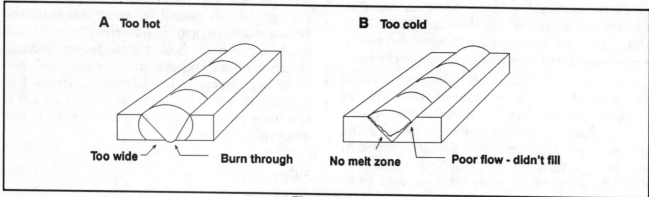

Figure 6-20
Improper welding temperature

with 1/8-inch diameter welding rod. If the weld doesn't fill the void properly, select a larger size. If the weld mounds excessively, use a smaller diameter rod.

The wrong welding tip or heat range affects the quality of your weld joint. If the heat is too low, the welding rod doesn't properly melt into the surface. Too much heat, and your weld may burn through, as shown in part A of Figure 6-20.

With the correct temperature, the metal you're welding just starts to liquify. When you touch it with the welding rod, the rod melts. *Don't* apply the torch flame to the rod. Apply it only to the metal you're welding. Here's why: If you heat the rod, the rod will melt and drip into the joint. But if the joint isn't hot enough, the rod metal will cool too quickly and not form a bond. This *lack of penetration* produces a *cold weld*. Figure 6-20 B illustrates this.

Here's a chart that shows the melting point for several commonly-used metals.

	Fahrenheit	Centigrade
Tin	450	232
Lead	621	327
Zinc	786	419
Aluminum	1220	660
Silver	1762	961
Copper	1981	1083
Nickel	2647	1453
Iron	2795	1535

The angle at which you grind the two pieces of metal is important. Keep it between 15 and 22-1/2 degrees, so the full angle formed by the two pieces is between 30 and 45 degrees. If the V is too steep, you won't get enough heat into the bottom of the

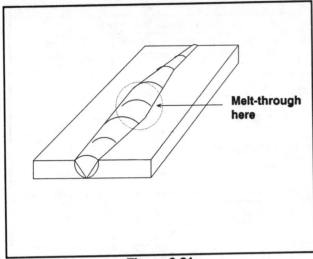

Figure 6-21
Uneven grinding

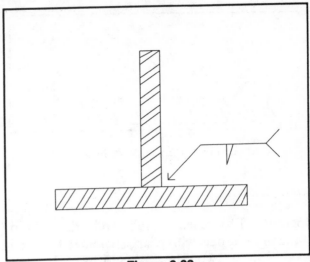

Figure 6-22
Symbol for fillet weld

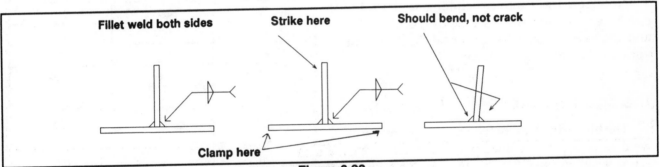

Figure 6-23
Test of good weld joint

weld. The filler rod won't melt all the way into the joint, allowing air pockets to form. That makes weak welds.

A groove that's too shallow is just as bad. Your material will melt properly, but you'll use much more welding rod. That also contributes to a weak joint, because the weld is never as strong as the base material. Ideally, you'll replace as little of the metal as possible with welding rod.

If the grind isn't straight along its full length you get *melt-through* wherever the mating pieces don't match. You'll have twice as much finishing work to do (you have to finish both sides) and the weld will be weak besides. Figure 6-21 shows the results of uneven grinding.

Test Your Welding Skill with a Fillet Weld

Cut two pieces of 12 gauge sheet metal 2 inches wide and 6 inches long. Weld the two pieces together into a T, using a fillet weld. The blueprint symbol for a fillet weld is a right triangle suspended from the arrow with the right angle on the left, the slant to the right. See Figure 6-22.

You can buy triangular fillet rods for this, but they're hard to find, and round rods are easier to use. Your weld should form triangles about 1/8-inch high and wide on each side of the T. See Figure 6-23. The fillet symbol on both sides of the arrow indicates that you weld both sides of the joint.

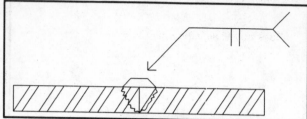

Figure 6-24
End view of square groove butt weld

When you've finished the weld, clamp the upside-down T to something solid and strike the top of the upright part with a large hammer. Give it a good blow or two. The T should bend, but not snap off. You shouldn't see any hairline cracks on either side of the weld.

Now, saw the T into 1-inch-long sections. Inspect the cut weld joints for flux, dirt, cold welds, and cracks. Keep practicing. Repeat this test until your welds are clean and secure.

The Square Groove Weld

The blueprint symbol for a square groove butt weld is two parallel lines perpendicular to the arrow, as in Figure 6-24. This weld isn't as simple as it looks. It's hard to heat the seam adequately to get good penetration. You can use it on 16 gauge metal or thinner, but I don't recommend it for thicker welds.

By the way, sheet metal thickness is measured in gauge number. The higher the number, the thinner the metal. Figure 6-25 is a chart that translates gauge to thickness. It's hard to weld thinner metals, because they melt too easily. Never try to weld anything thinner than 24 gauge. Use glue, solder, brazing, or mechanical fasteners instead. I'll cover these later in this chapter.

Use a *backer* plate when you weld thin metal. Use copper at least a half inch thick, a 12 gauge sheet of stainless steel, or a specially-formulated backer plate from your welding supply source. The backing plate prevents melt-through, as illustrated in Figure 6-26. Remember that metal liquifies at welding temperatures. The backing plate keeps the hot metal from dripping all over the place until it cools and becomes solid again.

Sheet metal thickness		
Gauge number	Weight per SF (pounds)	Thickness, approximate (Inches)
7	7.5	3/16
8	6.9	11/64
9	6.25	5/32
10	5.6	9/64
11	5.0	1/8
12	4.4	7/64
13	3.75	3/32
14	3.12	5/64
15	2.8	9/128
16	2.5	1/16
17	2.25	9/16
18	2.0	1/2
19	1.75	7/16
20	1.5	3/8
21	1.4	11/32
22	1.25	1/32
23	1.12	9/32
24	1.0	1/4
25	.87	7/32
26	.75	3/16
27	.68	11/64
28	.62	5/32
29	.56	9/64
30	.50	1/8

Figure 6-25
Sheet metal thickness

Because thin metals warp easily when heated, clamp them to a solid non-combustible surface when you weld them. Clamps are a must for welding tubing if you want to keep it straight. When you heat tubing to welding temperatures, it may warp for several feet if it's not clamped in place.

Slot Welds and Plug Welds

Slot and plug welds help prevent melt-through and warping because you're only heating

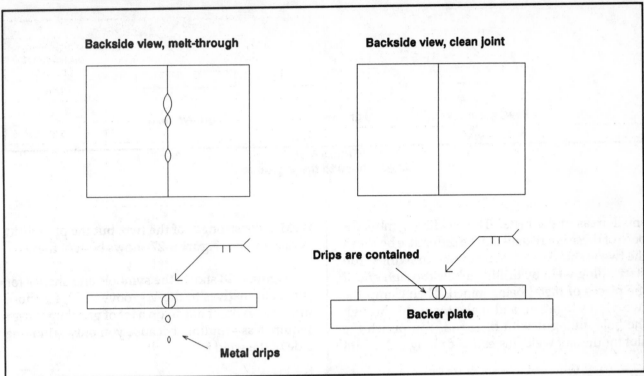

Figure 6-26
Use a backer plate to prevent melt-through

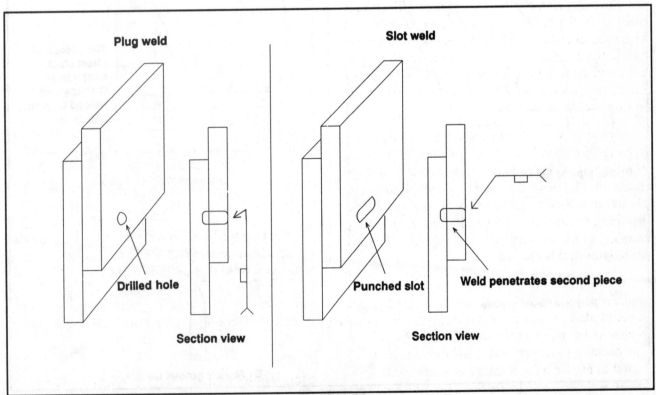

Figure 6-27
Plug and slot welds

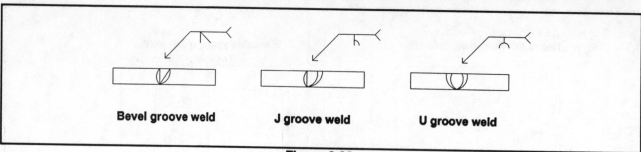

Figure 6-28
Alternatives to the V groove

small areas of the metal. The welding symbol for both of these is a rectangle. The difference between the two is shown on the fabrication drawings. You start a plug weld by drilling a hole through one of the pieces of metal being joined. Then clamp the two pieces together, and make the weld through the hole, filling it with filler rod. You punch the slot for the slot weld, instead of drilling it. The slot

weld is the stronger of the two, but the plug weld is easier to do. Figure 6-27 shows both of these.

Figure 6-28 shows the symbols and shapes for some alternatives to the V groove weld, for those of you who don't like to do a lot of grinding. These require less grinding, because you only grind one side of the weld joint.

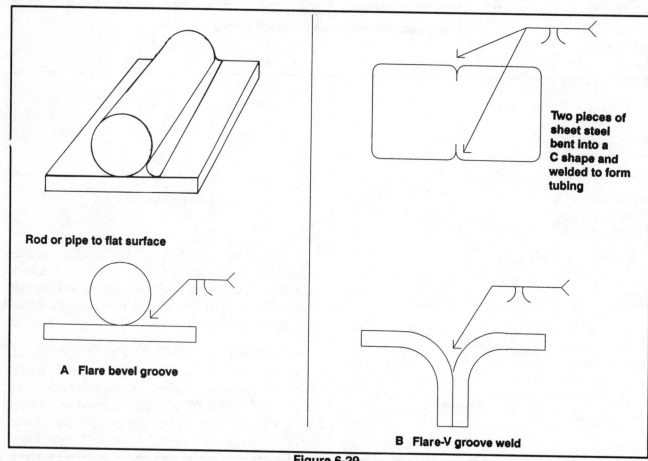

Figure 6-29
Flare groove welds

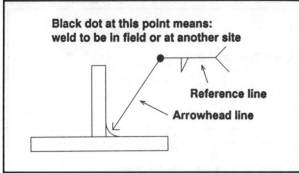

Figure 6-30
On-site weld symbol

Notice that you *do* have to grind both sides of the U groove if you start with square-edged material. But if the cut was made with a cutting torch, the result is a rounded edge that doesn't require grinding.

Figure 6-29 shows two kinds of flare groove welds. You can use the flare bevel when you add ornamentation to an otherwise dull-looking fence or railing. Use the flare-V to make tubing from flat sheet metal. Notice in Figure 6-29 B that you're allowed to extend two arrows from the same reference line on your drawings.

The symbol for welds that you make on the job site is a solid dot at the intersection of the reference line and the arrowhead line of the arrow symbol. You can see this in Figure 6-30.

If you're welding pipe or tubing to a flat surface and want the weld to go all around, show a circle at the junction of the reference line and the arrowhead line, like the one in Figure 6-31.

When You Want Melt-Through

You can prevent melt-through with a backer plate, but sometimes you want it to melt through. It makes a stronger joint, and it hides the seam on the back side of the two pieces of metal you're welding together. You do the primary weld on one side, then do a smaller weld on the opposite side. The symbol is an open half-moon. If you only make the primary weld and just let the welding material fill to the opposite side, the symbol is a filled half moon. Both of these are demonstrated on Figure 6-32.

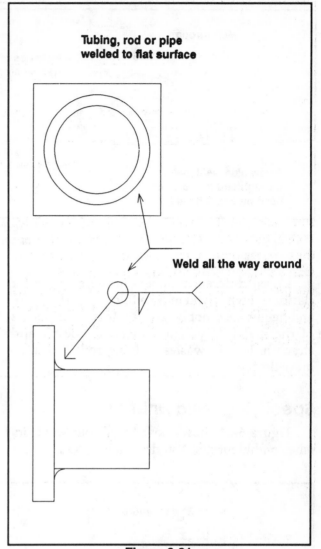

Figure 6-31
Weld all the way around

Figure 6-33 shows how the thickness of the back or melt-through welds is indicated. You can use either fractions or decimals, but be sure you're consistent in your use of one or the other. Most contractors prefer fractions.

This figure also shows how to describe weld sizes and distances. The illustration is of the test T joint we discussed earlier. The symbols call for fillet welds 1 inch long, 3 inches apart on center, and 1/8 inch high. Notice the positioning of the numbers. The width is first, then the height, both on the left side of the welding symbol. The weld length and center-to-center spacing, or *pitch*, appear on the right side of the symbol.

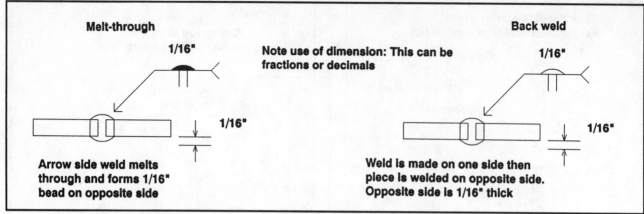

Figure 6-32
Welds on both sides

I used different numbers in the example for clarity, but when you make a fillet weld, the width and height need not be greater than the thickness of the metal. If you use more, it doesn't add strength. It only wastes welding rod, and takes more time.

Specifying Weld Finishes

Figure 6-34 shows how to call out weld finishes on blueprints. You draw a line, and put the appropriate letter next to or under the weld type symbol. G stands for grinding, M calls for machining, and C means chipping. Grinding is most commonly used for fence or field work.

Grinding is done with an abrasive wheel, while machining is done on a lath or flat-bed milling machine with cutting tools. Chipping is to remove excess material with a chipper, or by hand with a hammer and chisel.

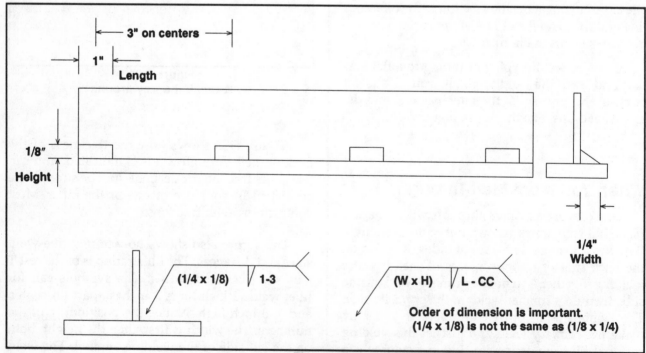

Figure 6-33
How to specify weld size and spacing

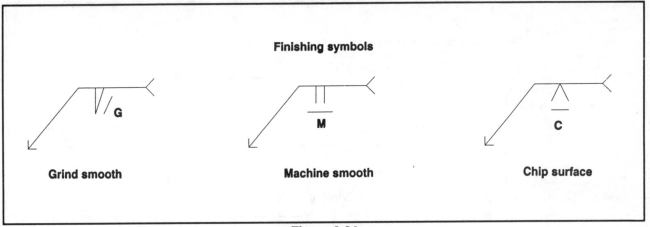

Figure 6-34
Weld finish callouts

Special Welding Types

The joints and symbols we've discussed so far apply to gas and arc welding. There's also spot or projection, resistance, and seam welding. You need a GTAW welding unit for spot welding. GTAW stands for Gas Tungsten Arc Welder. Those cost from $2,500 to $10,000 or more, depending on the features. These electrically-powered welders are usually used in the factory, though some can be driven by a gasoline-driven electrical generator on the job site. They make a very quick, clean weld joint that requires minimum, if any, finishing.

GTAW welders operate in either contact or arc mode. In contact mode, you tightly clamp the two pieces of metal to be joined, and press the tungsten rod tip against the metal where you want the weld. Spray the weld area with nitrogen, helium, or argon to prevent oxidation, and turn on the switch. Presto — a spot weld. The symbol is a circle, with the letters "GTAW" placed as shown at the back of the arrow in Figure 6-35.

Use a GTAW welder in the arc mode for seam welding. That means you hold the tungsten tip about 1/4 inch away from the weld surface. The arc generated by the tip melts the metal, and it flows together to create the seam joint. Figure 6-36 shows how to draw plans for a seam weld.

In the factory, seam joints are created differently. An electrical current passes through a wheel that contacts the metal as shown in Figure 6-37. This is called *resistance welding*. It's the method used to manufacture most square and rectangular tubing.

When you use a GTAW in contact mode, you don't use a filler rod. But it may be necessary in arc mode when the heat of the arc dissipates some of the base metal, leaving a void.

Gas Welding

You're not likely to do much arc or resistance welding as a fence contractor. But you will use a gas welding technique known as the *oxyacetylene* method. Here's the equipment you'll need:

- Two gas tanks, one filled with oxygen and the other filled with a highly flammable gas, acetylene. The oxygen tank is either orange or green, the acetylene tank, red.

- Two regulator valves each with two gauges. One is the high pressure gauge and shows you the gas pressure remaining in the tank. The second is a low pressure gauge and shows you the gas pressure entering the hoses.

- A dual-section hose, about 15 feet long with one side green and one side red.

- A handle or tip holder that contains two small adjustable valves. These valves regulate the amount of gases reaching the tip.

- A couple of welding tips, a brazing tip and a cutting tip. The welding tips are cone-shaped

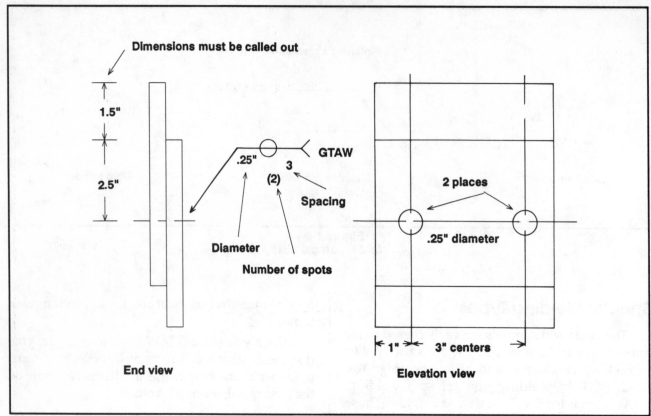

**Figure 6-35
Spot welds**

and have one outlet. The brazing tip is similar but its outlet is larger. The cutting tip has three or four outlets.

- A pair of heat-resistant gloves

- A face shield and a U/V dark-glass eye shield

- A flint sparker

- Wrenches for tightening the valve fittings

The cost for this equipment starts at around $550.

Before you begin welding, secure the tanks so they can't be knocked over. Use a specially-designed cart, chain them to a wall or post, or place them in some type of stationary enclosure. That's important for two reasons. First, the valve and gauge assemblies are expensive. But more important, if you knock over a tank and the main valve breaks, you'll have an unguided missile on your hands. These tanks are pressurized to several

thousand pounds and will take off like a rocket, destroying anything, or anyone, in their path.

Once the tanks are secure, screw on the regulator valve assemblies and tighten them with a wrench. Now screw on the hose assembly and tighten. These should all be tight enough so they don't leak, but be careful you don't strip the threads. Connect the green hose to the oxygen, and the red or orange hose to the acetylene. You probably can't reverse those. Most have clockwise threads on the oxygen, counter-clockwise threads on the gas. Now screw on the tip handle assembly and tighten it. Select a tip and fasten it to this assembly.

Before you fire up your welding outfit, be sure there are no combustible materials within 10 feet of the work area. That means no dry grass or leaves, no paper, wood, or trash. Wet the area down with a water hose if you have to.

The materials you're going to weld should be all ready. That means they're ground to the proper

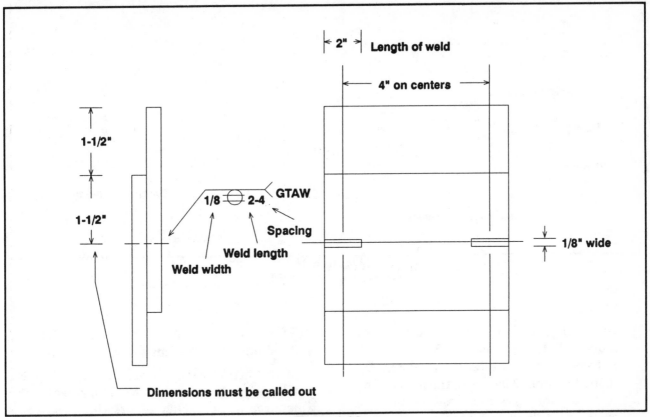

Figure 6-36
Seam weld

angle, degreased, and wire brushed free of all rust and scale.

They should also be free of paint. Paint burns at welding temperatures. Most paint gives off toxic fumes when it burns. Some are deadly.

Put on your welding mask and gloves, and get your sparker (igniter) out. You can work with your gloves on, if they're pliable enough. Follow these steps:

1) Turn off the small valves on the welding tip holder.

2) Turn on the main valves to the two tanks. You should be getting 2,000 to 3,000 PSI (pounds per square inch) pressure readings on one gauge of each tank.

3) Turn on the tank regulator valves, on the gauge packs. Set the pressures for 20 PSI. (There must be pressure to the valves and meters before you can adjust them.)

4) Turn on the small valve on the tip holder for the acetylene gas. *Do not turn the oxygen on yet.*

5) Open the gas valve about 1/4 to 1/2 turn.

6) Strike a spark with the igniter about 3 inches from the tip nozzle. The gas should ignite and burn with an orange flame. You'll see some black smoke. Use the small valve to set the flame to about 6 to 8 inches.

7) Very slowly turn on the small valve for the oxygen. The flame should start to get shorter in length and turn from orange to red to blue. You'll start to hear a hissing sound: this is normal.

If you get a loud pop, don't panic, just turn off the small valves and start again. The pop is caused by adding too much oxygen too fast.

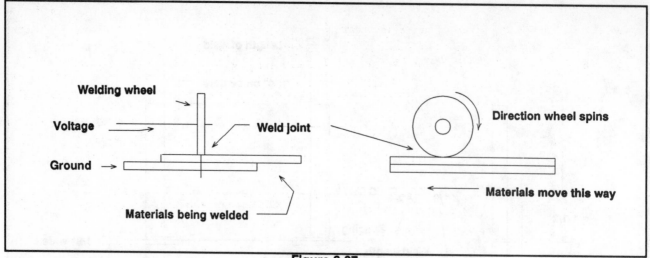

Figure 6-37
Resistance seam welding

8) Once you get it right, you'll have a blue or blue-white flame about 2 to 3 inches long. Put your eye protection on and bring the flame to within 2 inches of the items being welded. Don't get too close as this will smother the flame and it will go out.

9) Heat the materials evenly where you're going to make the weld. The metal should start to glow cherry red and then start to become liquid. When the metal liquifies, apply your welding rod to the joint. The rod should start to melt and puddle. There will be some smoke from the flux. There may be sparks flying. This is normal.

10) Work the heat and the welding rod along the seam you're welding. You should have a series of overlapping puddles as shown in Figure 6-38.

If you have bubbles, or breaks in the weld seam, it's probably because the metal wasn't cleaned properly. Turn everything off and try again.

Once you've completed the welding and everything has cooled off, it's time to finish the job. Use a wire brush to remove excess carbon and flux from the weld area.

Now use a grinder or power drill with a sanding wheel attached. Begin with #80 grit to grind off the excess weld material. Change to #100, #120,

#150, and finally, #180 grit. Your weld will be flat and unnoticeable. It's time to prime and paint.

Now here's some practical advice. Suppose you have two U channels to weld together to form a handrail or post. They're 6 feet long, so you'll have to weld two seams for a total of 12 feet. A good welder can do 1/2 to 1 inch of seam weld per minute. That means almost 2-1/2 hours of welding, and another hour to grind. Is there a faster way? Yes, there is.

You really don't need full strength the full length of the seam. You can do a series of 1 inch welds every 6 inches. Now you only have 26 one-inch welds, about a half hour's work, and another 10 minutes of grinding. That's quite a saving in labor. But maybe you're not satisfied with the way the job *looks*.

You can fill the voids between the welds on the seam. Solder melts at about 860 degrees. It flows like water and leaves an almost finished surface that requires a minimum of grinding. You can apply solder quickly, since you don't have to heat the base metal to its liquid state. You should be able to solder with your welding torch at a rate of about a foot a minute. Use a solder with a paste soldering flux. Clean-up is with water.

Brazing is another process you can use. It's faster than welding, but slower than soldering. The temperature you must reach, and the strength of the finished product is also between the two

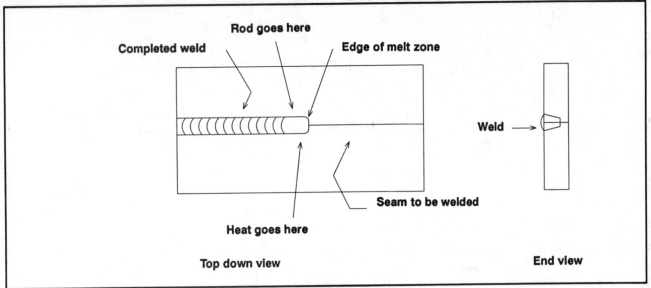

Figure 6-38
Forming a quality weld joint

other methods. The procedure is the same. You heat the metal so when you touch the joint with the brazing rod, the rod melts and flows into the joint. The difference is that a brazing rod is made from an alloy of copper, brass, and bronze, not the same material as the metal you're welding.

Welding melts the material being welded. The material merges and keeps its original characteristics. Brazing and soldering don't combine with the host material. The strength of a welded joint is as good as the metal itself. The strength of a brazed or soldered joint relies on the strength of the brazing alloy or solder. That's why brazing and soldering are used more as a filler than for structural reasons.

Figure 6-39 illustrates five kinds of weld joints. Learn to do top-quality welds on each of them, and you'll be able to handle anything that comes your way in the metal fencing business.

Some General Information

1) Your work will probably be limited to steel and iron. Don't even attempt to weld stainless steel or aluminum, unless you're already an expert. These metals take a lot of skill and special techniques. Pass these jobs along to a subcontractor, but check them

out first. Lots of people claim they can weld stainless and aluminum, but when it comes down to doing a quality job, they can *not*.

2) For degreaser, try Gunk™, available at auto parts stores. It does a good job and cleans up with water.

3) For filling a long seam, try Bondo™, an auto body filler.

4) For joining seams that have a hidden return bend, such as two C channels, try Super Glue™ in its gel form (Figure 6-40). You can also get industrial acrylic two-part metal glues that hold like iron. You just paint them on the pieces you want to join, then clamp the parts together for a minute or two.

5) Use a drill-mounted wire brush to prepare metal for welding.

If you plan to manufacture metal fences, you'll need an arc welder, ($3,000), a cut-off saw, ($400), a belt sander, ($250), and an alignment jig. You need the cut-off saw to cut pipe and tubing accurately, either square or at a specific angle. You use a sander to finish the edges of the cut tubing before you weld it. The alignment jig holds everything in place while you're working on it. When metal is

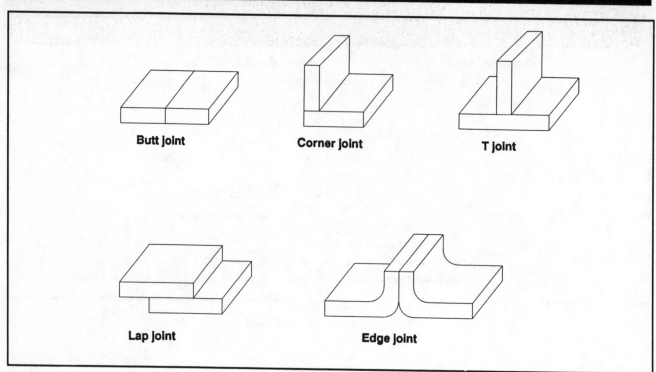

Figure 6-39
Five basic welding joints

heated for welding, it warps and bends very easily.

You'll also need an exhausted cleaning tank which is approved by federal, state, and local authorities. Raw steel sheets, pipe, and tubing are dirty. They're covered with oil, dirt, grease, and scale. You have to remove all these before you weld or paint the material. You can clean steel in a dip tank filled with nitric acid or other acid. But this is dangerous. Unless you're experienced, leave it to the experts.

You'll need an *electrostatic spray booth* to paint fences in your shop. Electrostatic attraction draws paint evenly around the fence or rail, leaving a smooth, even paint job. You spray the powder onto the fence and then sweep up and reuse any excess that doesn't stick to the metal surface. Next you bake the coated fence section in a large oven until the paint powder melts into a liquid. Electrostatic spray equipment costs about $15,000, including the explosion-proof paint booth. The expense of all this equipment keeps most fence contractors from getting into the prefab metal fence business.

If you want to learn more about welding, many trade schools offer courses. Try your public school system first. Commercial welding schools also offer classes, but the cost will be much higher.

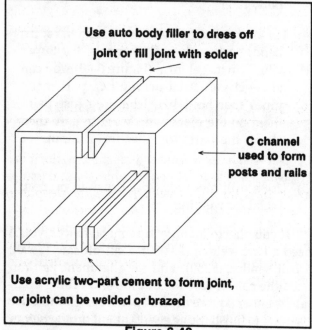

Use auto body filler to dress off joint or fill joint with solder

C channel used to form posts and rails

Use acrylic two-part cement to form joint, or joint can be welded or brazed

Figure 6-40
Alternate methods of joining and finishing

seven

Gates and Entries

A fence or wall isn't much good if you can't get through it to go in or out. So you build a gate — the gateway to your world. Gates are symbolic of possession to some people. They go to great lengths to secure their gates with alarms and locks. Others design gates just for decoration. Regardless, they're an essential part of most fences.

In this chapter, I'm going to tell you how to select and build gates. I'll show you what can go wrong with gates, how to design them to prevent early failure, and what materials to use.

Figure 7-1 shows a gate that's warped in both directions. It doesn't fit snugly any more. The builder used unseasoned or wet lumber for both the rails and the face lumber. Don't make that mistake. Always use kiln-dried lumber for your gates. Redwood and cedar are the best choices, followed by pine or fir. Use structural grades, because there's a lot of stress on the supporting members of a gate.

Use short rail sections. Two 6-foot sections are better than one 12-foot section. The shorter the lumber, the less it warps and twists. Secure the post and rails with nuts and bolts or metal sup-

ports. Nails and screws pull out. Use heavy duty hardware and hinges. After all, your customers expect their gate to last for years.

The sturdy gate in Figure 7-2 is about 15 years old, and still doing fine. Notice the heavy-duty hinge, nuts and bolts. The cutout at the bottom helps prevent rotting due to collected moisture.

Gate Design and Location

For a gate to do what it's designed to do, it has to be big enough to let people, animals, and equipment pass through easily. A gate for people to walk through should be at least 36 inches wide — 40 inches is better. A vehicle entry gate should be a minimum of 7 feet wide. Trucks and RVs require an opening of 8 to 10 feet. Farm equipment and mobile homes require 10 to 15 feet.

When you pick a location for a gate, think about the route people would take if there were no fence at all. I've seen some pretty thoughtless arrangements. In one, the fence began beside the

Figure 7-1
Warped gates don't work

Figure 7-2
A gate that's built to last

driveway but the gate was in the middle of the yard. When you drove up, you had to walk an extra 30 feet from the driveway to the gate. It's usually better to curve the sidewalk from the drive to the main entry, putting the entry gate near the garage or carport. Another solution would be to install two gates, one at the front of the house, the other on the driveway side.

Determine which direction the gate will open before you install the hardware. Most gates open toward the enclosed area, but this isn't always practical. There may be plants or buildings in the gate's swing path. Or you might want the gate to swing back against a wall or an adjoining fence. If there aren't any physical limitations, follow the owner's preference. Find out whether the owner is right- or left-handed, and whether they're more likely to be carrying things when they go in or out. Right-handed people usually carry things in their left hand, with their right hand free to open a latch or turn a knob.

Leave a space under a gate if you can — 3 to 6 inches is best. That allows you to sweep or hose under the gate without opening it. It also permits a little sagging or warping before the gate binds. That isn't practical if you use the enclosed area to contain animals or children. If they can get their heads through the gap, they can get their bodies through, too.

Every gate is different. These are guidelines, but you'll have to design each gate you build to suit the particular situation.

Plan Your Gate on Paper First

Here's a way to design a wooden gate. Use 2 x 4s and 1 x 8 KD fir face boards. First, find out how wide to make the opening in the fence to accommodate the gate.

Use finished (S4S) lumber for the gate posts. They'll be 1-1/2 inches thick. You have to allow some space between the posts and the gate for expansion of the lumber, and the *swing arch*. The swing arch is the amount of clearance you need between the edge of the gate and the post when the gate swings on its hinges. Guidelines here are 1/4 inch on the hinge side, and 5/8 inch on the latch side. Figure 7-3 illustrates the swing arch allowance on the latch side.

Plan to use five face boards. Their finished width is 7-1/2 inches each. Allow 1/8 inch between face boards for expansion. Add these all together:

Posts   1-1/2" x 2 = 3"

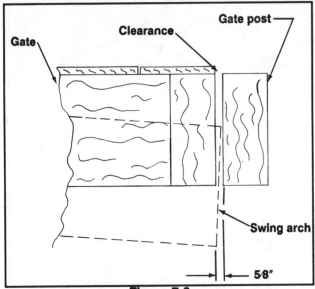

Figure 7-3
Allow for the gate to swing

Hinge post clearance   1/4"

Latch post clearance   5/8"

Face boards   7-1/2" x 5 = 37-1/2"

Clearance between boards   1/8 x 4 = 4/8"

Change all the fractions to eighths so you can add them more easily.

$$3-0/8$$
$$2/8$$
$$5/8$$
$$37-4/8$$
$$\underline{4/8}$$

Total: 3 + 37 = 40, + 15/8, (or 1-7/8) = 41-7/8

Allow for a total opening of 41-7/8 inches. You can round that off to 42 inches if you want to.

This measurement, 42 inches, is the opening between the two end fence posts. You'll bolt the gate posts to the fence posts. I don't recommend using fence posts as gate posts. They aren't heavy enough. Gate posts get a lot more stress. Eventually you'll need to replace them. It's easier to replace a bolted-on gate post than a fence post that's buried or cemented 2 feet into the ground. If you do decide to use the fence posts for gate posts, deduct 3 inches for the extra 2 x 4s. Your opening will now be 39 inches.

Height of Your Gate

For a wooden fence, cut your gate posts 1 inch shorter than the fence posts. Nail or bolt the two together, beginning at the top, with the two posts flush with each other. The gate posts will end 1 inch above ground level.

If you're bolting a gate post to a block wall like the one in Figure 7-4, set the gate post to the height of the gate. This drawing also shows typical spacing for gate components.

How high should the gate be? If you want adults to see over it, make it no higher than 60 inches. Otherwise, make the top of the gate even with, or just slightly lower than, the height of the fence.

If the fence is over 8 feet high, make the gate not more than 84 inches high. Fill the space above the gate with a header like the space over a doorway. Put the header at least 84 inches above the ground.

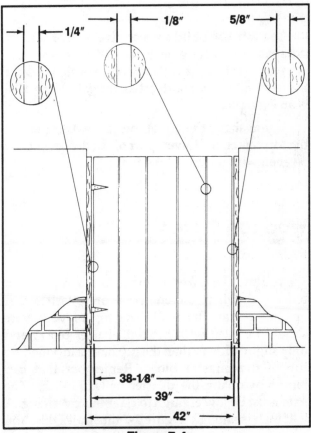

Figure 7-4
Plan your gate dimensions carefully

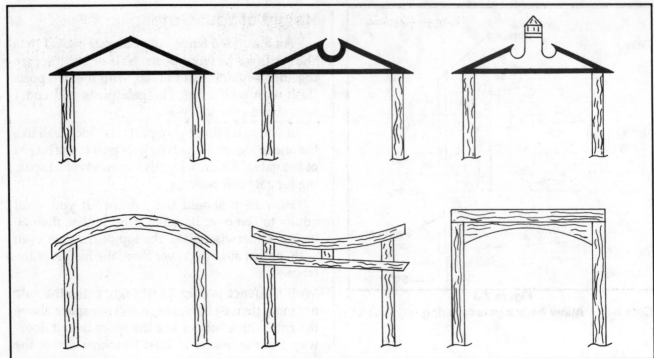

Figure 7-5
Gate headers or top patterns

You can also build a decorative arch or filler in the space above the gate. Figure 7-5 shows several attractive arch designs. Adapt these designs where the fence or wall is shorter than the gate. Figure 7-6 is an example.

If you shape the top of the gate with a peak at the top center, the lowest part of the design should be even with the top of the fence.

Wooden Gates

You may be asked to install a wood gate in a block wall where the end posts are pilasters that are taller than the wall. The top of your gate should be even with the top pilaster block, and only slightly lower than the cap blocks installed on top of the pilaster block. Remember that cap blocks overhang the pilaster or wall blocks. The gate must be low enough to clear this overhang. A half inch is enough. Figure 7-7 illustrates this. You can also offset the cap blocks like the ones in Figure 7-8.

To make a sturdy gate, use a diagonal cross support in a Z design for the main structural members. Cut the top rail of the box or Z to accommodate the face boards and the spaces between them. In the earlier example, you'd cut the 2 x 4s 38 inches long. Your rails will be just slightly nar-

Figure 7-6
Gate with header that's taller than the fence

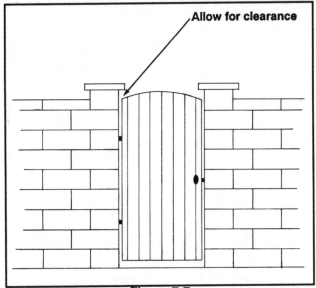

Figure 7-7
Gate must swing clear of overhanging cap blocks

Figure 7-8
Offset cap blocks allow for gate

rower than the finished width of the gate. Let the face boards overhang the frame by 1/16th of an inch on each side. Figure 7-9 shows the steps to cut and assemble a Z-frame gate.

Next, decide how far apart to place the top and bottom rails, and cut the vertical boards for the frame. Attach them to the rails using any of the

methods shown in Figure 7-10. If the fence is a wood rail fence, line up the gate rails with the fence rails. The result will be a clean-looking gate and fence combination like the one in Figure 7-11.

When you're building a gate with a patterned top, put the top rail at least 2 inches below the lowest part of the design. Make the top and bot-

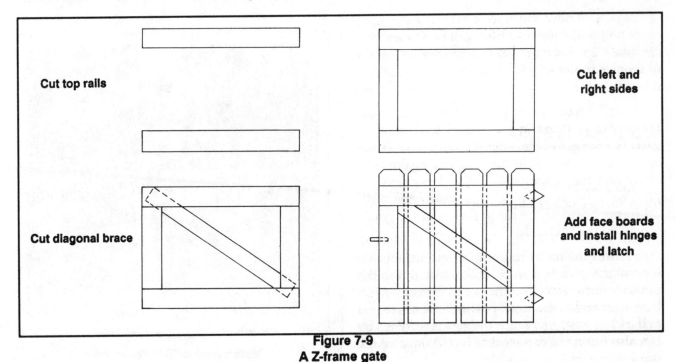

Figure 7-9
A Z-frame gate

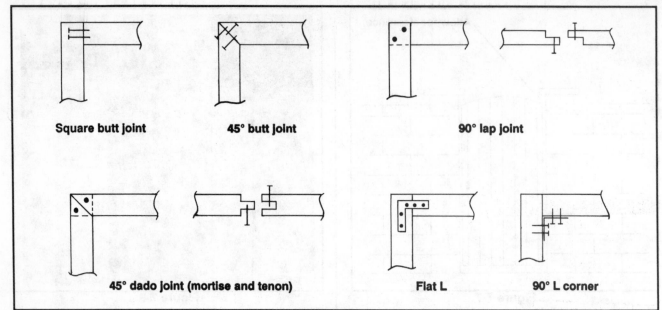

Square butt joint   45° butt joint   90° lap joint

45° dado joint (mortise and tenon)   Flat L   90° L corner

Figure 7-10
Gate frame joints

tom rails correspond to the hinge locations. That way you'll have something solid to screw the hinges into.

Bracing the Gate

Be careful how you brace a gate. The diagonal brace on a wood gate can be one of two types. You can use a 2 x 4, or a metal rod or wire. There's a difference in the way these work, and you install them differently.

Install a wood brace with its lower end at the hinge post. The top end goes at the latch side of the gate. The weight of the outer edge of the gate rests on the brace, which in turn pushes against the hinge and the hinge post. Cut and position the diagonal brace so the miter cuts contact the vertical frame board at the hinge side, and the gate's top rail at the latch side.

A threaded metal rod or wire and turnbuckle is an alternative to a wood brace. Install it in the opposite direction from the wood brace — with the upper end at the hinge post and the lower end at the latch post. Any sag in the gate is stiffened by tension of the rod or wire which pulls against the upper hinge and hinge post.

Use threaded eye bolts to secure wire braces to the gate frame. Pass the wire through the eye, wrap it back around itself, then crimp it in place with a sleeve and crimping tool or a pair of pliers.

Use L brackets to hold threaded rod in place. Predrill the brackets to accept the rod, then use

Figure 7-11
Match gate rails to fence rails

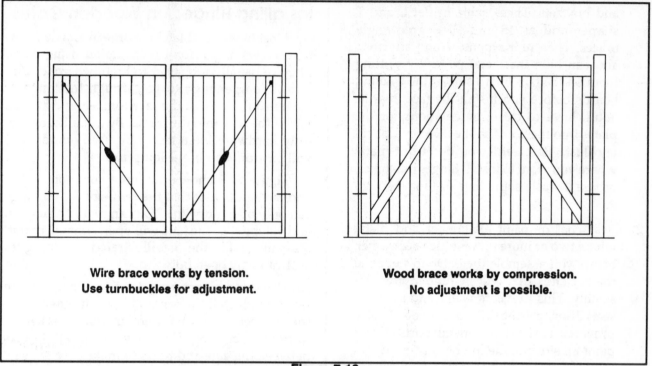

Wire brace works by tension.
Use turnbuckles for adjustment.

Wood brace works by compression.
No adjustment is possible.

Figure 7-12
You attach wooden and metal braces differently

nuts and washers to fasten the rod on both sides of the brackets.

None of these braces will work if they're installed backward, however. Figure 7-12 illustrates braces attached in the right direction.

The wire or rod brace is the easiest to install. Many hardware stores carry kits that include eye bolts, turnbuckle, wire, and wire clamps. Some carry truss rod kits. If you can't find a kit for your gate, a sharp salesperson can probably make one up for you from items they have on the shelf.

There are special bracing kits for metal frame gates of all sizes and shapes. The difference is in the way the wire or truss rod attaches to the gate. The typical kit contains corner gussets that you weld into place. Then you fasten the wire or rod to the gussets.

It's cheaper to use wood braces, but they're a little trickier to install. They have to be cut very precisely. If you're off by as little as 1/8 inch, the brace won't work. Also, unlike the metal braces, there's no way to adjust a wooden brace after you've installed it.

Here's how to cut the angles on the braces:

1) Build the box frame and square it.

2) Lay the lumber for the brace *under* the frame. Position it so the miter cut will contact the top rail and the hinge post. Mark the intersection angles on the cross brace.

3) Make your cuts outside of your marks, that is, toward the ends of the boards.

4) Fit the brace in place and make any fine adjustments with a wood rasp or power sander.

5) When you're sure you have a proper fit, fasten the brace in place with flat head wood screws and reinforcing plates.

Build Gates to Last

I'm going to suggest a few things that will make *your* gates last years longer than the average.

1) Reinforce the joints where the rails and diagonals or verticals meet with metal plates

and brackets. These come in flat L and T shapes and as 45 and 90 degree angle braces. They're inexpensive and effective. You can hide the metal plates by putting them on the face board side of the framing boards before you install the face boards. You'll have to chisel indentations for the plates into the 2 x 4s so the face boards will lay flush. Be careful you don't put metal where you want to install hinges or latches, or you'll waste some time drilling through it.

2) Clear coat or paint all lumber and metal where two or more pieces touch each other, before you assemble them. Do this even to the cut ends that will be hidden after assembly. This prevents water and most insects from getting into the wood. It also prevents rust on the metal parts. Don't paint all sides of the lumber just now. You need to leave some bare wood for moisture to escape if your lumber isn't entirely dry.

3) In addition to the fasteners, use construction glue to join pieces of lumber together.

4) Use bolts or screws instead of nails.

5) Check the frame for squareness often during the construction process.

6) Use screws to attach the face boards to the frame. Phillips head wood screws work best. Use brass screws if the face lumber is redwood or cedar. Predrill the holes using a drill size just slightly smaller than the screw shaft size. Use two screws for each place the face board touches the frame. Put screws every 6 to 8 inches in the boards on the outside edge of the gate if you use a box frame.

7) Run a bead of exterior paintable silicon caulk along the top joint where the face boards contact the rails. This will prevent water from getting in between the face boards and the rails and rotting the lumber. Don't caulk the bottom joints. Leave these open to let moisture escape. You can get clear, colored, or paintable silicon caulk at most lumber, paint, and hardware stores.

Installing Hinges on Wooden Gates

Most hinges and latches come in kits that contain screws. But I don't recommend using them. They're usually too short to be much good. Buy screws long enough to go through the hinge or latch metal, through the face lumber, and at least 1/3 of the way into the frame. Buy quality, heavy-duty hardware intended to be used outdoors. It will pay for itself in the long run.

Figure 7-13 shows the more common hinges and latches. Notice that the semi-concealed hinge can only open outward. You can mount plane pin and H hinges so the gate will open either in or out. Strap hinges like the ones illustrated later in Figure 7-21 can only open outward.

Use three hinges on gates that are 6 or more feet high. Install the top and bottom hinges first, then the center hinge. Careful alignment is a must to prevent binding. Use a level or insert spacers between the gate and posts to make sure the gate is plumb and not sagging when you position the hinges. Check the swing before you install the center hinge.

When you're ready to install hinges, put a spacer board under the gate to support it at the height you want it, and level everything. You should already have checked the gate posts to be sure they're plumb. Use screws or bolts to install the hinges. Leave about 1/4 inch clearance between the gate and the hinge post. When you close the gate, there should be 5/8 inch clearance between the gate and the latch post. Install your latch and lock, if you're using one.

You may have to install a stop to keep the gate from swinging past the closed position. That's because most hinges can swing in an arc of about 270 degrees, or 3/4 of a circle. Close the gate and set the latch side flush with the front of the gate post. On the latch post, mark a line where the back of the gate meets the post. Nail a full length stop to the latch post. The stop can be finished trim lumber, quarter-round, or a 1 x 2. The stop prevents the gate from swinging too far and tearing the hinges off.

You might also need a stop for the open position. You can use a pipe, a 2 x 4, a block or brick in the ground behind the gate. Or you can use a spring or door closer.

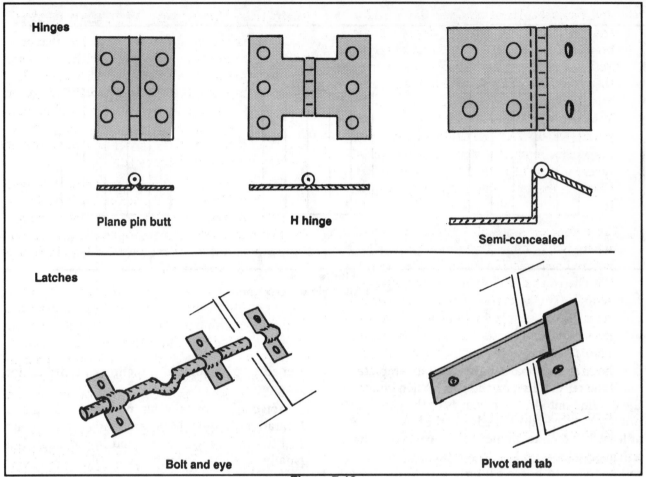

Figure 7-13
Common hinge and latch designs

Don't be in too much of a hurry to finish a gate. Sometimes, you'll be under pressure to finish the job quickly, but try to allow some extra time for everything to settle and dry out. Wood is an unstable building material. It shrinks. It expands. It does other things that can mess up an otherwise good job. Wait a few days, a week if you can, before you install the latch, or paint your new gate.

If you install the latch when the hinges are brand new, there's a better than average chance that the gate will sag slightly and the latch won't fasten properly after a few days. If you wait a week, the hinges have a chance to wear in and loosen a bit. As they do so, the gate will sag, and the latch position on the gate post will change. It's best to wait till it does before putting on the latch.

Decorative Top Patterns

Now's the time to cut the top pattern in your gate. You might think it would be better to cut the pattern while the gate is on the ground, and it probably is easier that way. But things do go wrong. Once the gate is hung, you can draw and cut the top pattern so it *looks* right, even if the gate sags a bit, or isn't perfectly symmetrical.

Most designs are cut so each half is a mirror image of the other half. Use a piece of thin cardboard the width of your gate for a pattern. Fold the cardboard in half and draw one half of the design on it. Then cut the cardboard according to your drawing and unfold it. That way you're sure both halves of the design are identical.

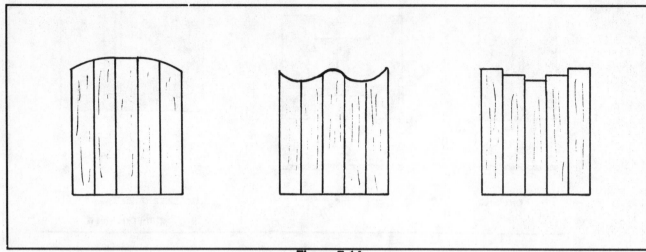

Figure 7-14
Add a little style to your gate

Use the cardboard pattern as a template to mark the cutting line on the gate. When you trace the cut line onto the face boards of the gate, don't put it too close to the top edge of the boards. Leave at least 1/2 inch to an inch. That way, you'll have a firm base for your saw to rest on. Be sure the top rail of the gate doesn't interfere with the lowest point in your pattern. Make your adjustments on the cardboard. You can do it easily then. Once you start cutting the wood, it becomes a problem. Figure 7-14 suggests some common gate designs.

After you cut your design, lightly sand the cut edge to remove splinters. Then paint or clear coat the cut edge. Check the operation of the hardware and put a few drops of oil on the hinges and latch parts. Your wood gate is finished.

Metal Gates, Latches and Hinges

Fence contractors often buy factory-manufactured metal gates. Making these gates requires processes most of us aren't equipped to handle. Factory-built metal gates are usually square,

primed or painted, and sometimes predrilled for hanging.

You can buy metal gates in a range of sizes and decorative designs. Most are made from square steel tubing, sometimes formed into designs but usually straight. Security gates may have wire mesh welded on one side, and an extra large plate at the latch position. Figure 7-15 is a typical security gate.

Figure 7-15
Wire mesh security gate

Figure 7-16
Metal plates help secure entry lock

Figure 7-17
A hook and eye hinge

If you're using an entry lock like the one in Figure 7-16, weld two plates to the gate, one on each side. There should be 1-3/8 inches of space between the plates. You may have to add spacers, but that's not likely because most manufactured gates accept a standard lock. Predrill each plate to accept the lock set. There should be a template and full instructions for drilling and installation enclosed with the lock.

Note that the plate on the outside extends past the gate and over the post, covering the strike plate and latch bolt. This keeps someone from slipping a credit card or metal strip in to push the latch bolt open. The inside plate is flush with the gate.

Notice that the gate in this picture is installed on a block wall. The metal gate post is attached to the block. You can do this several ways.

1) Buy posts with studs on one side. When you lay the block, cement the studs into place along with the block. This makes a strong, sturdy connection, but it's hard to replace the post if that becomes necessary.

2) Use *hook and eye* hinges. These come in 6 inch, 8 inch, and 10 inch sizes. The gate in Figure 7-17 is attached to a hook that was cemented into the mortar joint during con-

struction. The hooks come with a flat tang, but if there's room inside the wall cavity, you can bend the tang downward to make it harder to pull out. You weld the tube to the gate in position so it rests on the hook.

3) Use a hook and eye T-strap hinge like the one installed in the wooden gate in Figure 7-18. You assemble the two parts as you install the hinge. First, attach the hooks with bolts or lag screws. Then position the gate and install the eyelet straps.

4) You can also get hook and eye hinges where the hook anchor is a coarsely-threaded screw. Some people use these in block and brick, but they'll eventually pull out. They're more suitable for wood posts.

My main objection to hook and eye hinges is that anyone can lift the gate off the hinge to get inside. Prevent this by swaging the top of the hook after the gate is installed. Use a large bolt cutter. Put just enough pressure on the cutter to deform the hook above the eye. Now you can't remove the gate without filing the hook smooth again.

A second and better way is to position the hooks so the bottom one faces up and the top one

Figure 7-18
A hook and eye T-strap hinge

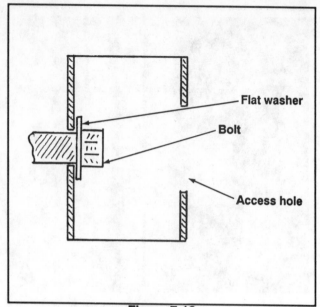

Figure 7-19
Bolt installed through metal post

faces down. Brace the gate in place, and install the eyelets. This way, no one can lift the gate off the hooks. They'd have to remove the eyelets — something most intruders would rather pass up.

5) You can bolt the gate post directly into the block after the cement is cured. To do this, drill a hole into the block and insert a Rawl-Bolt™. This is an expansion bolt that consists of a threaded bolt inside a metal sleeve. When you torque the bolt down, it expands the sleeve and causes it to lock into place. Rawl-Bolts come in sizes from 3/8 x 2-1/4 to 3/4 x 8-1/4 inches.

You have to drill tubular metal posts properly to accept this type of anchor. If you put the bolt through both sides of the tubing, it may protrude from the tubing enough to keep the gate from closing. Install the bolt only through the side of the tubing that's adjacent to the wall. Drill a hole in the gate side of the tubing that's large enough to accept a socket wrench and the Rawl-Bolt washer. See Figure 7-19.

You can use Rawl-Bolts to anchor wood posts to brick and block also. Countersink the bolt head into the wood, leaving enough clearance for a socket wrench. Figure 7-20 illustrates this.

Follow the manufacturer's directions for using these bolts. Use a torque wrench and torque to their specifications. Overtightening can damage the bolt, expansion sleeve, and block. If you undertighten, the anchor sleeve won't expand and

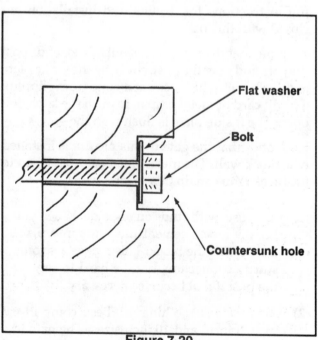

Figure 7-20
Bolt installed through wood post

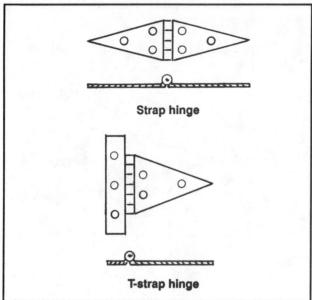
Figure 7-21
Strap hinges

Figure 7-22
Pneumatic closers work on all swinging gates

grip properly. It's a good idea to clean any cement dust out of the hole after you drill into the block.

You can use strap hinges to mount a gate flush with the gate post. Attach them with bolts or screws. Figure 7-21 shows two kinds of strap hinges. The T-strap requires less space and will fit on the narrow side of a 2 x 4 gate post. The conventional strap requires a post at least 3 to 4 inches wide.

If you're installing a gate on a block wall that you didn't build, be sure the block has been filled with grout. If it's hollow, your anchor or bolt has nothing to grip. This also happens when you cut a new opening in a block wall. Remove the cap block and pour grout into the wall cavity. The post will stay in place, and the entire block, post and gate area will be stronger.

You can secure hinges to metal gates with bolts, screws, or by welding them in place. I prefer welding since a would-be intruder can't just unbolt the hinge and get in. The post side of the hinge is usually protected from tampering by the gate itself, so you can use bolts or screws on that side. If the gate is damaged or needs replacing, you can remove it when it's open.

Always buy the metal gate *before* building the wall or cutting the gate opening in an existing wall. You can easily cut and modify a wood gate to fit an opening. It's not so easy with a metal gate. Buy the gate first and build the wall opening around the physical dimensions of the gate.

A pneumatic closer can be installed on any kind of gate. You can install them on wood, metal, or block. Figure 7-22 shows a typical installation.

Chain Link Fabric Gates

You can use chain link gates anywhere, but they're most common on chain link fences or block walls. The frame is welded galvanized pipe. Then the chain link fabric is fastened to the pipe frame. Use tension bars and bands on gates, the same as you do for chain link fences.

Materials for chain link gates are made from *galvanized* materials. That means the fabric and pipes are protected against rust by a zinc coating. If you damage the coating, touch it up or replace it. You can fix small nicks in the coating with clear enamel or even clear fingernail polish. Those repairs will last several years. For bigger jobs, buy some aerosol paint that contains zinc. It's available in a color very similar to the original coating.

Today, many chain link gates and posts are made of aluminum which doesn't rust and is self-

Figure 7-23
Chain link fence and gate posts

Figure 7-24
Hook and eye hinge for chain link

healing. Scratches oxidize so quickly the metal is protected. The main drawback to aluminum gates is that they don't stand up as well to abuse. Steel gates are much stronger.

You can buy chain link gates in a variety of sizes that are ready to hang. You can also find gates in kit form that have a welded frame, but you have to assemble the fabric and hardware. I recommend you buy fully manufactured gates. The difference in cost isn't enough to offset what you save in labor.

If you must make a gate to fit a pre-built opening, assemble it from parts. Buy tubular L corners and cut your pipe to the proper size to fit between them. The corners are slightly larger than the pipe so the pipe fits inside them. Fasten the pipes and corners together with small bolts or screws. Then apply the fabric, just as with a kit. These gates built "in the field" aren't quite as strong as factory-built gates, but they're entirely satisfactory.

To refresh your memory about chain link fabrication methods, Figure 7-23 shows a chain link gate and fence post. The fence is on the left, and you can see that the fence post is larger in diameter than the gate frame. The fence post has to be stronger because it supports the gate and also anchors the end of the fence.

Use tension bars to stretch fabric on the gate. Fasten bars to the frame with tension bands. In Figure 7-24 you see a hook and eye hinge. The hook is secured to the post, and the eye to the gate. Notice that the installer put the bolt on the gate backwards — the nut should be inside.

Chain link walkway gates come in standard sizes of 32-3/4 and 38-3/4 inches wide. The openings between gate posts are 36 or 42 inches wide. For driveways, gates come in pairs to fit openings of 10 and 12 feet. They're either 57-1/4 or 69-1/4 inches wide.

Center-opening double gates need hardware to fasten the two sections together when they're closed. Use a *fork latch*, or a *butterfly latch*, and an *L bar* for this. The latches wrap around the posts to lock them together. The L bar slides into a pipe buried in the ground where the two closed sections meet. You operate fork latches by hand. The butterfly latch is hinged so it drops onto the post by itself.

Here are some guidelines for chain link gates:

1) Cut the tension bars about 2 inches shorter than the fabric height. When they're installed, there should be about 1 inch of mesh above and below the tension bar.

Figure 7-25
A gate that skates

Figure 7-26
A gate that rides on a track

2) Install tension bands every 10 to 12 inches along the tension bars. Use three for gates that are 3 to 4 feet high, four for gates that are 5 feet high, and five for gates that are 6 feet high.

3) Be sure you use the correctly sized tension bands, post latches and hinges. These are sold by their inside diameter (ID). Match them to the post's outside diameter (OD). Remember, the hook section of your hinge must fit the fence post, while the eye section fits the gate frame.

Alternatives to Hinges

Some gates don't have hinges at all. Chain link gates can glide on wheels mounted on a rigid axle so they can only travel in a straight line. Figure 7-25 shows this. Install a grate under the gate's path to provide a smooth rolling surface, and to catch loose dirt and water.

The gate in Figure 7-26 is a 14-foot-wide sliding auto entry gate installed at an apartment complex. This type of gate is often chain-driven and operated by an electric motor that's triggered by a switch or security key.

The bottom of the gate has rollers along its length that ride on a V track. Figure 7-27 shows the parts of this system. This type of installation requires the wall or fence next to the gate to be at least as long as the gate so the gate can clear its

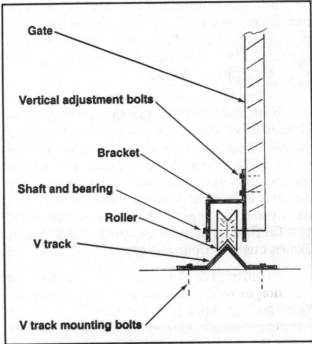

Figure 7-27
Details of a sliding gate mechanism

Figure 7-28
Rollers keep a sliding gate on track

Figure 7-29
Top guide for sliding gate

opening. Weld a stop to the track to keep the gate from passing the full open position.

Install rollers like the ones in Figure 7-28 at the top of the gate to keep it on track and hold it upright. The post at the open end of the gate has a pair of rounded brackets at the top to guide it and hold it in place. You can see these in Figure 7-29. Install a bumper on the gate to cushion it and the post as the gate closes. This will also prevent damage to a vehicle that happens to stop in the way while the gate is operating.

The motor control system contains a feedback circuit and clutch that reverses the gate if an obstacle gets in its way. You can adapt a garage door opener to operate a small gate of this type for under $100. Follow the manufacturer's instructions for installing the garage door opener, but mount it in line with your gate. Follow local electrical codes, and protect the motor in a weatherproof enclosure. Mount the gate on a track system like Figures 7-25 through 7-27.

Gates of All Kinds

In Figure 7-30 you see a gate that blends so well into its fence that it's almost impossible to find. The only telltale sign is the string that's attached to the inside latch. I prefer gates that are more noticeable and distinctive. Use material different than in the fence, install a fancy latch, or shape the gate different from the fence. That makes the gate more obvious.

The gate in Figure 7-31 guards an entry to a housing project in Lake Tahoe. The combination of

Figure 7-30
An "invisible" gate

Figure 7-31
Wood, metal, and stone blend well

Figure 7-32
A simple but effective gate

stone, wood, and metal blends with the natural surroundings and looks elegant and substantial. The gate itself is steel-plated wood with iron bars. You can probably play music on this harp.

The chain in Figure 7-32 is hardly a gate, but it serves the same purpose. This is a picture of a factory loading dock. The chain signals the truckers where the entry to the dock is, and it helps keep people from walking off the edge and falling 5 feet.

Figure 7-33 shows two kinds of gateways that admit people but bar large animals. You could build this type of fence out of any fence material. The openings are 28 to 32 inches wide, large enough for a person to pass through. But that's too small for horses, cattle, or other large animals. They can't bend their way around the opening.

Dutch door gates (Figure 7-34) were popular for homes many years ago. You can open the top section alone, or both sections together. A *talking*

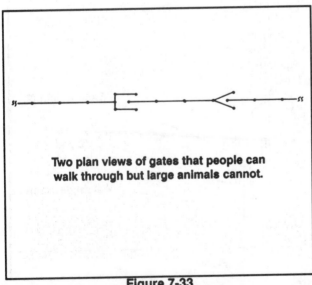

Two plan views of gates that people can walk through but large animals cannot.

Figure 7-33
Animal proof pedestrian gate

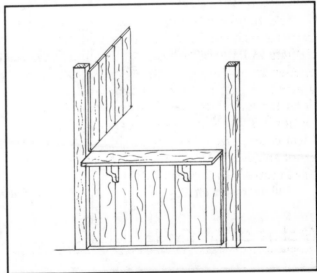

Figure 7-34
A friendly gate for visiting

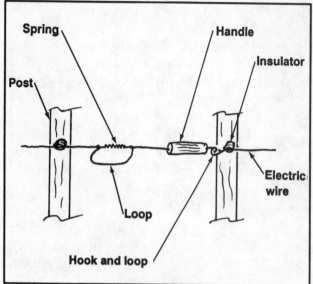

Figure 7-35
Electric fence gate

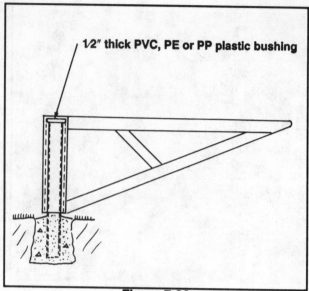

Figure 7-36
"Pipe in a pipe" gate

shelf is usually installed on top of the bottom section. The owner could lean on the shelf and visit with neighbors on the other side of the fence all day long.

Figure 7-35 shows a gate for an electric fence. The handle insulates the operator from shock. The

spring keeps the wire under tension so the latch stays engaged.

Figure 7-36 is a gate where the post is the hinge. This is a popular park entry gate.

The gate in Figure 7-37 is ideal where there's plenty of vertical clearance, but no swing or stack

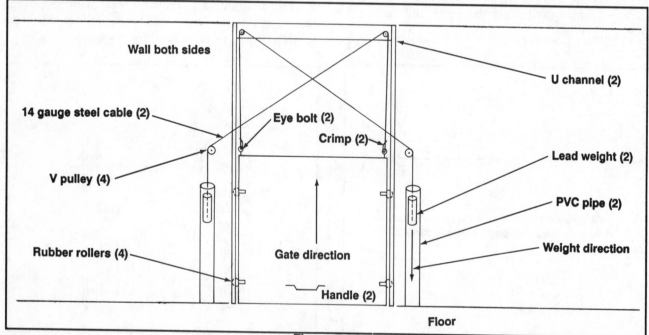

Figure 7-37
Lift gate

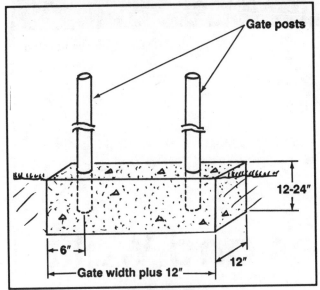

Figure 7-38
A solid gate foundation

space. The crossed cables keep the gate square in the U-channel frame, and the lead weights counterbalance the gate itself. Use ball bearing V rollers for the cable guides, and ball bearing rubber rollers at the sides of the gate.

The point I'm making here is that you can design gates made from many kinds of materials. I've seen one made from old tools, and another trimmed with horseshoes. Consider first the purpose of the gate and how strong it has to be. Then plan its best location and appearance. The last thing to worry about is the cost. You want your gate to last for years, so use the best materials you can afford. Of course, cost is a factor when you're competing for a job. But emphasize the superior quality of your gates over other, cheaper ones, that might not be built as well.

Once you've built a sturdy, quality frame, you can face it with whatever you want. Use wood, bamboo, wire mesh, tile, or old organ pipes! Use your imagination.

You can add openers, closers, lights, locks, windows, alarms, planters, or shelves to your gate. You can leave it unfinished or paint it any color of the rainbow. Make it tall or short, almost any size at all. The design can be plain or fancy, rustic or elegant, antique or space-age. The tips in this chapter should help. The rest is up to you.

One final word about making your gate sturdy: If you build where there's heavy rain, freezing weather, or shifting soil, here's a tip to keep your gates standing level and plumb. Build a solid foundation to support both gate posts. Figure 7-38 illustrates this. Posts installed this way will always stay in precise relationship to each other because the entire foundation moves as a monolithic block. It costs more to build a gate this way, but you'll never have to worry about it binding because one or the other of the posts has moved.

eight

Finishing Fences and Walls

I'm going to use the term *coating* instead of *paint* in this chapter to describe the finish you'll use on fences and walls. That's because many of the coatings you'll use aren't paints at all. They're chemical compounds formulated to do much more than just change the color of the fence.

The way you build your wall or fence has a lot to do with how durable the coating will be — and how soon re-coating is needed. If you don't do it right, your customer will have a fence coating that peels, flakes, or even changes color.

This chapter will cover the things you need to do to prevent premature coating failure. It also covers the various coatings you'll use, and the best ways to apply them. I'll give you tips on how to do the job faster and easier.

Painting is a good off-season occupation for fence contractors where weather makes working outdoors impossible for part of the year. You'll already have most of the equipment you need, so you might as well use it. If you want more information on painting in general, order a copy of *Painter's Handbook* from Craftsman Book Com-pany. There's an order card in the back of this book.

Protective Coatings Defined

The main reason for coating any surface is to protect it. The second purpose is to make it look better. Select coatings for their protective qualities. If the best protective coating only comes in black and costs $100 per gallon, use it. If the best protective coating is available for $8 and comes in a rainbow of colors, *then* pick the color you like.

Here are the things you need from a good protective coating:

- It must stand up to everything it's exposed to.

- Its cost to buy and apply must be reasonable, and it must last long enough to justify its cost.

- You have to be able to remove it or apply additional coatings over it.

- It must be flexible enough to expand and contract with the material under it.

◆ It must penetrate and adhere to the surface it's applied to.

◆ It must be hard enough to not scratch off, but soft enough to dent and not loosen, chip or peel off.

◆ It must prevent water penetration into the surface under it, yet breathe enough to let water vapor pass through it.

◆ It must spread easily and form a mark-free coating.

◆ It must dry fast enough to prevent dirt and insect entrapment, but not so fast that it won't spread easily and penetrate the surface.

◆ It should be washable with soap and water.

◆ It should be resistant to most airborne chemicals.

◆ It should resist the effects of ultraviolet radiation, fading and discoloration.

◆ Some type of solvent should work to clean hands and tools.

Fortunately, most of today's commercially available coatings do most of these things, but not all of them do everything. Some may do one thing very well, and others poorly. Others might do everything on the list, but none of them well. Take time to talk to your local paint store — they generally know what's available and what will hold up to local conditions.

Since coating formulas vary, different coatings are needed for different applications. And, the more you're willing to pay, the better product you'll probably get. Paints and coatings are chemical blends of various elements and compounds. The type and quantity of the ingredients determine the characteristics and cost of the coating. But don't discount local non-brand products. Even though they don't have big names, they may be formulated specifically for your area and less expensive in the bargain.

Notice that I said less expensive, not *cheap*. Cheap coatings are generally just that — cheap. Many aren't formulated to have the properties you're looking for. You have to find out if the coating will do what you expect. Read the labels and product literature to select the finish that's best for each job. I'll explain what to look for.

The coatings you'll be using for fences and walls are classified as *exterior* coatings. Interior coatings, the ones you'd use inside, aren't made to stand up to extremes of weather, rain, wind and U/V radiation.

Tools and application methods depend on the surface you're coating. You'll use different coating materials for foundations, posts, block, brick, redwood, cedar, other lumber. You may use several different types on the same fence or wall.

You can apply coatings with a brush, a pad, a glove, a roller, or a spray outfit. Using the right tools makes the job easier and final result better.

The coating base, called the *vehicle* or *carrier*, is the liquid part of the coating that evaporates as the coating dries and cures. That can be oil/alkyd, water/latex, alcohol or petroleum. Some coatings come in dry form, and you add the base. Cement paint is an example of this.

Composition of Coatings

◆ Clear coatings let you see the grain and other natural characteristics of the material you're coating. They include shellac, urethane, varnish, poly, and epoxy.

◆ Semi-opaque coatings let some of the material show through, but still add color. Stains and tinted clear coatings fit this description.

◆ Opaque coatings completely hide the coated material. Paint and petroleum or tar-based products are opaque.

◆ Chemical formulations and silicon products can make the coatings water and insect repellant. You can buy insect repellants for about $2 to $4 an ounce and add them to most coatings. Just pour in one ounce of repellant for each gallon of coating. Generally the water repellant is applied after the final color coat, but I've had luck putting it on a few weeks *before* the paint.

Quality	Inert Pigment or Additive
Abrasion resistance, strength	Clay, mica and talc
Algae and barnacle control	Tributyltin and copper compounds
Bacteria control	Teflon
Bleaching, waterproofing	Pentachlorophenol
Durability, weathering	Clay, calcium carbonate, mica, magnesium silicate and talc
Fire resistance	Nitrogen compounds
Heat resistance	Aluminum and bronze powders
Insect control	Cinerin, dieldrin, Paris green, and chlorpyrifos
Rapid drying time	Cobalt or manganese salts
Rust resistance	Red lead and zinc chromate
U/V protection	Carbon black

Figure 8-1
Paint additives and what they do

Coatings are composed of the vehicle and *pigments*. There are two types of pigments, *active* or *prime*, and *inert*. Prime pigments are the ones that give coatings their color. Most of today's prime pigments are manmade. Years ago they were natural, derived from plants, clays and mineral ores.

Inert pigments are added to give coatings some qualities besides color. They're not dissolved in the vehicle, they're suspended in it. Some inert pigments, like ground walnut shells or sea shells, give body or thickness to the coating. Minerals, metals and synthetic compounds can provide some special characteristics.

Additives are another group of pigments, generally liquid, that dissolve in the vehicle. Figure 8-1 is a list of coating characteristics and the additives that produce them.

Most of these pigments add some color to the coating, but not all of them. The pigments are added to the vehicle as a percentage of weight of the vehicle. Since inert pigments are in suspension and don't chemically combine with the vehicle, they can settle. When you buy the coating, you must put these pigments back into suspension. You do that by mixing, shaking, or *boxing* the coating. Boxing is pouring the coating from can to can several times.

If you have two cans of a particular material, I recommend boxing so all your material is a uniform color. Use a third can and pour half of each full can into it, then pour the remaining half of one can into the remaining half of the other. Repeat this six to ten times. If pigment sticks to the bottom of a can, use one of the wooden paddles the paint store gives you to loosen the pigment.

Special additives can be used to condition the surface to be coated by removing oxidation and contamination. These additives are usually acids.

Catalysts make up another group of additives. They start a chemical reaction that develops the heat needed to cure and solidify the coating. Epoxies, polyesters and fiberglass are compounds that require catalysts to harden them. Without a catalyst, these plastic materials won't cure. You can also add cobalt to control hardening time.

Make Your Coatings Stick

Coatings stick to surfaces for two reasons:

1) Electrostatic attraction makes paint stick the same way your socks stick to your shirts when they come out of the dryer. According to laws of physics, opposite forces attract. Negatively charged coatings are attracted to a positively charged surface. One carries a negative charge and the other positive.

2) Surface roughness is another reason coatings stick. The coating gets into all the nooks and crannies. When the coating hardens, the pigments wrap around all the little bumps and hang on. Even a smooth surface like glass isn't really smooth if you look at it under a microscope. Most fence materials are very rough, and will provide a good gripping surface.

Even under the best of conditions, take some precautions before you start to paint.

♦ Clean the surface of all loose dirt, sawdust, oil and grease. Remove efflorescence if the surface is concrete.

♦ Let the surface "age."

♦ Prepare and prime the surface.

In most cases, cleaning with soap and water and rinsing with clear water is enough. For difficult cleaning jobs you may need acids or chemical cleaners. Stains on new lumber are usually inks and waxes used by the mill or lumberyard to mark

the material. If they're not removed, they'll bleed through the top coating. Remove them by sanding or chemical cleaning.

Older walls and fences will have dirt splashed on them, stains from chemical leaching, oxidation and rust. Figure 8-2 is a list of stain removers and their applications.

Most of the chemicals are inexpensive and widely available at paint and hardware stores. *They're all somewhat hazardous to use, so wear rubber gloves and eye protection. Don't breathe the fumes.*

The gas and fume stains in Figure 8-2 don't come from the gas you put in your car. These are chemical stains from airborne gases that industrial plants, and sometimes sewers, put out. These fumes make paint turn dark, brown, or metallic gray.

Tannic acid is a natural stain found in cedar and redwood. It reacts with many metals and coatings, forming dark brown to black stains below the metal. You need to use coatings specially formulated for cedar and redwood. Isolate metal from the lumber in these cases with rubber strips, caulk, or paint.

Don't omit the neutralizing step where it's recommended. Acids and bleaches get rid of stains but leave a residue that can attack and discolor or destroy many coatings. The residual effect lasts for months, even years. The neutralizer rinse turns the acids to a water-soluble salt that rinses off easily.

Avoid Problems with Coatings

Figure 8-3 shows extensive efflorescence on a block wall. A coating won't adhere to this powdery surface, so you have to remove the powder before you coat it. And if you don't find and correct the source of the moisture that causes the efflorescence, it will come back and take the new paint off. In this illustration, the water got in through the uncapped blocks.

Dry rot is a fungus that consumes wood as it grows. Dry rot keeps coatings from sticking to wood fences. You'll find dry rot most commonly in areas where there's little direct sunlight and lots of moisture. You'll see it on the north side of

Stain	Remover and Process
Ink, crayon, wax	Use trichloroethylene, or xylene, or a solution of half alcohol and half water. Follow with a solution of half water and half household bleach if stain persists. Use Type A neutralizer (see next page).
Dirt, mud, clay	Wash with household detergent and water, rinse with clear water.
Dry rot	Use household bleach, applied with a hand sprayer or spray bottle.
Grease, oil, tar	Use xylene or toluene or mineral spirits. If there's a heavy accumulation, try one cup of lye crystals dissolved in a gallon of water. Follow with clear water rinse.
Rust	Mix four ounces of oxalic acid crystals in one gallon of water. Brush on, allow to sit for three to four days and rinse with clear water.
Efflorescence	Wash with muriatic acid, followed by its neutralizer (see next page) and a clear water rinse. For mild stains, use one cup of acid to one gallon of water. Use a 50 percent solution for heavier stains. Use the acid full strength for very heavy stains.
Efflorescence on cultured stone	One part white household vinegar to five parts clear water.
Gas stains	Use 3 percent hydrogen peroxide (right out of the bottle), or 1 part bleach to 9 parts water, or 1 part muriatic acid to 19 parts water. Finish with a clear water rinse.
Fume stains	Add one pint household bleach to one gallon of water. Brush on, allow several hours to work, and then neutralize with Type A or B neutralizer. Rinse with clear water.
Welding flux remover	Six ounces of sodium carbonate (washing soda) or six ounces of sodium bicarbonate (baking soda)and one gallon of clear water.
Whitewash remover	Use a mixture of half hot water and half vinegar, or use 10 percent hydrochloric acid in place of the vinegar. Rinse with clear water and apply new whitewash while surface is still damp.
To make:	**Use:**
Glass cleaner	Mix one pint non-sudsing ammonia and one quart clear water.
To clean:	**Use:**
Aluminum siding	Two tablespoons of T.S.P. dissolved in one gallon of water. Hose siding first and wash from bottom to top. Finish with clear water rinse. T.S.P. is trisodium phosphate (sodium carbonate & sesquicarbonate)

Figure 8-2
Stain removers and their appications

Galvanized metal (and stainless steel)	Mix 1/4 cup household detergent with one gallon of water. Rinse with clear water and dry. Rub down with mineral spirits.
Rusted metal	Brush or sand off as much as possible then coat with phosphoric acid (Naval Jelly). Rinse well with clear water, towel dry, and immediately apply prime coat.
Plastic and Plexiglas	Use mild soap and water. Use no abrasives or powder-type cleaners. Kerosene or naphtha will work on heavy dirt and stains.
Stucco	One cup household laundry detergent to one gallon of water. Finish with clear water rinse. Allow to dry two to three days before coating.
Painted surfaces	Wipe with liquid sanding solution, available at most paint stores.
Ceramic tile	Sandblast lightly or use hydrofluoric acid to etch surface.

Neutralizers

Bleach neutralizer (Type A)	One cup white vinegar and one quart of clear water.
Bleach neutralizer (Type B)	One cup borax and one quart clear water.
Muriatic acid neutralizer	Mix 1 part ammonia with 9 parts water, or 1 part potassium hydroxide (lye) and 9 parts water. Follow with clear water rinse.
Tannic acid neutralizer	One quart denatured alcohol and one quart water.

Figure 8-2 (cont'd)
Stain removers and their applications

Figure 8-3
Efflorescence on a block wall

homes, the shaded sides of fences, and where posts, rails and face boards join each other. If you discover it when you're coating a fence, correct the source of the problem to keep it from coming back.

Replace any damaged lumber. You can use wood fillers to repair small areas of contaminated wood. Dig out the damaged material. Then spray the void with bleach and let it dry for an hour or two. Next, rinse with Type B bleach neutralizer followed by clear water, then let it dry. Apply the wood filler, and coat.

Figure 8-4 shows a common problem. Paint was applied to a board with sharp corners. The paint is always thinnest at the corners, so that's the place where the coating fails first. To avoid this problem, use lumber that's been milled with flat or

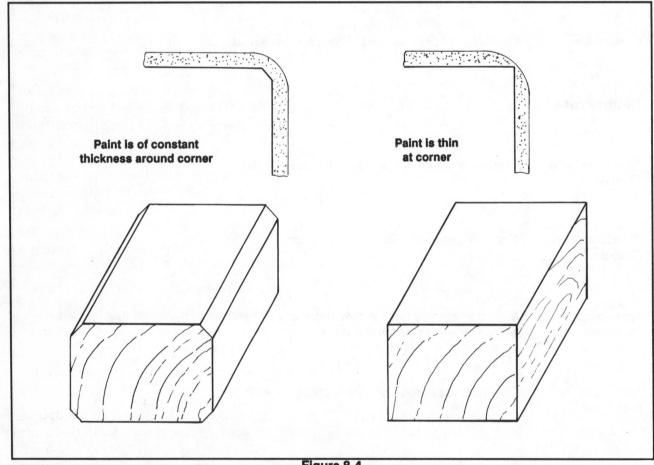

Paint is of constant
thickness around corner

Paint is thin
at corner

Figure 8-4
Paint thins at sharp corners

Figure 8-5
Oxidation on a steel rail

rounded corner surfaces. Coatings will stick better, and water will evaporate faster.

In Figure 8-5 you can see another problem with painted surfaces — oxidation. Notice the whitish marks on the top steel rail. This railing was factory coated. Oxidation is a natural process where atoms of oxygen combine with other substances. Some materials oxidize very quickly. Aluminum, for instance, begins to oxidize in seconds. Other materials oxidize very slowly, taking thousands of years. But all materials oxidize eventually.

Oxides are inert substances, and very much like salts. Inert substances don't combine readily with other substances. If you try to paint over an oxide, the paint won't stick. It will peel off. You have to sand the oxides off before you can coat the surface successfully.

Oxidation isn't always a problem. Since oxides are inert and don't combine with other elements, they're good protective coatings themselves. Once the surface of the material has oxidized, no further damage will occur. Many bridges and buildings are built of steel that's formulated to oxidize, or rust, which is a form of oxidation. Many aluminum structures are uncoated. The aluminum oxide protects them. In fact, aluminum is self-healing, since it oxidizes within seconds.

Pay attention to the weld joints on metal railings. These railings are hollow. Factory-finished metal railings are completely assembled and welded before they're painted, so the welds aren't easy to see. An incomplete weld joint lets water into the tubing so it can rust from the inside. Rust dissolves in water, so the rusty water will eventually leak out through the defective weld joint. When the water evaporates, the rust remains to stain the railing and the surface under it.

If you discover poor welds, you can use auto body epoxy or body filler to patch them before you paint or repaint metal railings. Let the patch harden for a day or two before you paint.

Don't Paint Too Soon

Newly-built fences and walls are too young to paint or coat. They need to age and weather before they'll accept coating materials. That presents a problem for you, the fence contractor. Time is money, and you want to complete your jobs as quickly as you can. But you might get into trouble by doing so.

The trees that produce the lumber drink a lot of water in their lives. The salts and minerals in the water are trapped within the lumber, and leach out of the lumber with age. If you paint newly-cut lumber, the salts and minerals will attack your paint from the inside out. Lumber also contains oils that prevent the new paint from adhering properly.

So, how do you prevent the problems that come up when you paint raw wood? There are three ways:

1) Buy your materials in advance and store them outdoors for several months.

2) Build your fence, and then wait several months before you paint it.

3) Buy unseasoned lumber and age it artificially.

The best solution, from a painting standpoint, is the first one. But for a contractor, that's not always practical. And nobody wants a job left unfinished for several months, especially your customer. So consider the third alternative. Natural aging or weathering lets the pores of the lum-

Material	Natural weathering time	Artificial aging time
Wood siding	90 days	15 days
Treated lumber	90 days	15 days
Trim lumber	90 days	15 days
Wood shingles	180 days	90 days
Cedar lumber	90 days	30 days
Redwood lumber	90 days	30 days
Plywood	90 days	30 days
Stucco	30 days	30 days
Cement	360 days	90 days
Cement block	30 days	15 days
Masonry	30 days	15 days
Brick	360 days	90 days
Galvanized metal	30 days	immediately
White rust metals	180 days	same

Figure 8-6
Weathering times

ber open so the oils and water can evaporate. Rain and morning dew help wash away the salts and minerals and open up the pores. You can speed up the process by mist-spraying the lumber with a hose several times a day for a week or two. Allow the lumber to dry between wettings for this process to be effective.

You should also age brick, block and concrete before you coat them. Manufacturers use a mold release to make the blocks come out of the molds more easily. If it stays on the masonry, it can keep the coating from adhering. It may even react chemically with the coating, causing color changes and premature failure. Most clay and concrete also contains traces of salts and minerals, which must be removed. Again, the best thing is to let the material age for a year or so before you coat it. Once again, you can speed this up by hosing it down several times a day. Allow the surface to dry between each wetting.

For galvanized metals, use the cleaning process from Figure 8-2 to remove the oils used in the manufacturing process.

If you're able to age your materials, Figure 8-6 shows the recommended times required.

As you can see, the weathering times are quite long. That's why most fences are left unfinished.

The alternative to weathering block or brick is to select materials that are already the finished color you want. That way, no further coating is needed.

You can buy metal fencing that's already cleaned and coated. Factory coatings use harsher chemicals and more durable materials. Most factory coatings are baked on, and will last much longer than air-dried coatings.

When you're ready to paint, scuff sand wood and metal surfaces. Sandblast concrete, cement, brick, block, stucco, ceramic and metals. *Do not* sand plastics or galvanized metal. The process will scratch plastic and destroy the protective qualities of the galvanized coating on metal. Don't sand stainless steel or anodized metals, either.

Protect Against Ultraviolet Radiation

When ultraviolet radiation penetrates the surface of materials, its energy is dissipated or transferred to the material. At the atomic level where the coating bonds to the surface, the transfer of energy can break the coating bonds. For this reason, the manufacturers of paints and coatings for exterior use add U/V inhibitors. These additives slow down the energy transfer to a point where no damage to the bond occurs. Carbon black (soot) is a good U/V inhibitor. Most clear coatings for exterior use have iron oxide, another U/V inhibitor. It causes a slight amber color. Opaque coatings are generally immune to severe U/V damage because the pigments in the coating absorb the U/V rays. Clear coatings are most vulnerable to damage from radiation if they're not especially formulated for exterior use. They'll turn white, flake, peel, and powder if they don't contain a U/V inhibitor.

Remember, there are four things that affect the life and service of coatings: water, oxidation, contamination, and ultraviolet radiation. As a professional, you have to take all these into account and deal with them. Don't take shortcuts, or your jobs and your reputation will suffer.

Coatings and Their Uses

Here's an alphabetical list of coating materials and their applications.

Asphalt (or tar) is one of the prime coatings used to protect fence posts and foundations. It's a petroleum product that's black, thick, toxic and flammable. Roll or brush it on the back side of retaining walls, on both sides of foundations, and on the bottoms of both metal and wooden posts. It protects surfaces from water penetration at a reasonably low cost.

Asphaltum is a thin version of asphalt. It's an effective coating for posts above ground, rails and boards. You can brush, roll, or spray it. When heated, it thins out even more and penetrates deeper into the surface. Asphaltum is a preferred coating for fences used on horse ranches. It sinks in to protect the wood, and it tastes bad enough to discourage the horses from chewing the fence.

Creosote is derived from coal-tar and is similar to asphalt. It protects wood from rot and insects. But it's banned in many areas because it's toxic when burned.

Cement paints are water-based paints with pigment added. They're actually portland cement, and may also contain calcium chloride, aluminum stearate, hydrated lime, zinc sulfide or titanium dioxide, and up to 50 percent fine sand as a filler. Some brands use epoxy instead of water/latex as a carrier, which makes the paint very water resistant. The sand filler makes it fill large spaces and voids. It's a good cement block filler. You apply it with a trowel or special spray equipment. Cement paint is usually applied to a thickness of 1/8 to 1/4 inch. You buy it in powder form ready to be mixed with water and specially formulated colorants.

Cement paint works well on iron that's exposed to water for long periods of time. The paint prevents rusting because it's a *base* (chemically). You'll have to think back to your days in high-school chemistry for this. Both acids and bases will attack most other materials, etching wood, plastics, glass and metals. So both acid or base paint will etch and adhere to metal. But since cement paint is thick, it lasts longer and protects from rust better.

Enamel paints are available with carriers of varnish, polyurethane, acrylic, and oil/alkyd resin. Enamel dries to a hard glossy film that's weather resistant and sticks well to most surfaces. Enamel isn't my first choice for exterior work because it won't let water vapor flow through it. When water is trapped in a fence or wall, it makes the enamel blister or peel. Oil-based enamels are being discontinued by most manufacturers because they're too toxic. The newer latex (water-base) enamels are taking their place. Unfortunately, water-base enamels still aren't quite up to the quality of the oil-based ones.

Latex paints are the most popular paints today. They're inexpensive, easy to apply, and clean up with soap and water. The latex in latex paints is actually a synthetic, polyvinyl acetate. You can get latex paints in flat, semi-gloss, or full-gloss enamel finishes. Use flat for block and cement walls, semi-gloss for board fencing. Coverage and durability are very good. Touch-up is easy, even weeks after the initial application. I like latex for concrete and stucco work, because it breathes and lets moisture vapor pass through. It lets the underlying surface dry out, so it doesn't peel or blister.

Masonry paints are liquid paints in the latex family, made from polyvinyl acetate. They aren't cement based, but they do resist the alkali of the cements they're applied to. Masonry paints are applied the same as any paint, with brush, roller or spray. They're an effective water seal.

Plastic coatings dry to a hard, tough, shiny finish. They resist water, alcohol, chemicals, heat, abrasion, and household cleaners. The most common type is polyurethane. Its only drawback is that the drying time is long, several days between coats. It takes several coats to give an "under glass" look. Specify a U/V inhibitor in plastic coatings for use outdoors. You'll probably never have to finish a fence like this, but the owner may want a high-gloss finish on a railing around a patio or balcony.

Some of the newer urethanes set up tack-free in one to four hours, so you can re-coat within that time, or wait 48 hours. You just can't re-coat between four and 48 hours or you'll end up with wrinkles or maybe even cracks.

Stains are dyes made from plants and mineral ores mixed into a carrier. Stains do a better job of coating lumber than paints do. They sink in deeper and surround the wood fibers. Paint remains on the surface. Stains fade, but very seldom peel or flake. Stain is available in dozens of natural wood colors, as well as decorative shades like red and blue. It comes either transparent or opaque. Opaque stains mar easily, so I don't recommend them for anything that people will sit or walk on like decks or benches. Use the semi-transparent stains for these, instead.

Varnish is the generic name for coatings that dry to a hard, lustrous finish. Most varnish is clear, but you can tint it. The best varnish for fencing applications is *spar varnish*, the kind used to protect boats and exterior railings. Apply it with a brush or spray outfit.

Wood green is replacing creosote for most applications. It protects against rot and insects when it's applied correctly. To be effective, it must be applied by injection, not brushing. This is a factory treatment. Chemicals are applied under great pressure.

Wood preservative paints are made from a variety of ingredients. The most common ones are oil with creosote, cuprite, Paris green, or pentachlorophenol. Some are made from petroleum hydrocarbons, such as asphalt and bitumen. Some contain balsam, an oil resin from plants. All do a fine job protecting fences and fence posts.

When to Apply Coatings

Once your project has weathered properly and you've cleaned it thoroughly, you're ready to apply the coating.

You can apply asphalts and tar-based products almost any time of day. The hotter the better. In warm weather the coating sinks into the surface and grips better. In cold weather, use a *hot pot*, a temperature-controlled kettle, to heat the coating material. *Do not heat over an open flame.* The vapors and the materials are flammable and can explode.

Wait until after any dew has evaporated to apply stains and paints. Surface and air temperature should be from 60 to 80 degrees F. Lower temperatures will slow drying, make application more difficult, and possibly trap moisture. Higher temperatures will speed drying to the point where application becomes very difficult and the coating won't be absorbed enough to adhere properly.

If you must work in very warm weather, schedule your painting for the morning hours or follow the sun. Keep working in shady areas as the sun moves across the sky during the day.

Avoid painting in the late afternoon or early evening hours. Night air is very moist and will keep the paint from drying properly. Also, in many areas the temperature drops very rapidly when the sun goes down. This rapid drop in temperature is a shock to the coating. It tries to contract too quickly and cracks. That's bad for new paint.

Painting Tools of the Trade

The best painting tool is no tool at all. If you can get away with it, try to avoid having to coat fencing material. Bricks come in several colors that don't require coating. Block comes in colors also. You can buy metal railing fences coated at the factory. Most aluminum, steel, or vinyl siding materials are precoated. Use wire mesh with a vinyl rubber or urethane coating. Stainless steel, brass, chrome, aluminum, rocks, cedar and redwood don't have to be coated.

But if you must apply a coating, you have a wide choice of tools. Among them are brushes, rollers, paint pads, paint gloves, canister sprayers, airless sprayers, and pump sprayers. Each is good if used properly and for the intended application.

For instance, you wouldn't try to paint a chain link fence with an airless spray outfit. This equipment can spray up to a gallon of paint in 45 seconds. On a chain link fence, about 98 percent of the paint sprayed would be lost in the air. On a block or stucco wall, about 99.5 percent should land on the wall and stick to the surface.

You can use a brush to coat a metal railing or pipe fence very effectively. But you can do the same job with a paint glove in about a tenth of the time. A paint glove is a rubber glove that's coated with fabric similar to a paint roller. You dip your hand into the paint and rub the paint onto the surface. It's very fast and easy. You can buy paint gloves for about $4.00, less than most brushes cost.

Here's a list of the common fence painting jobs and the best tool to use for each:

Chain link fences: Use a medium to long nap roller. Make one pass down one side of the fence and a second pass down the other side. Do touch-ups with the roller or with a brush.

Wire mesh fences: Same as chain link.

Pipe fences: Use a paint glove or a brush.

Siding fences: You can paint wood, metal, or vinyl with a brush, roller, or airless spray. The airless sprayer is the best, with a roller second best.

Block, brick, and concrete walls: If they're very smooth, use a roller. If they're rough, use an airless spray. If you use a roller, use the serrated foam rubber type designed specifically for rough surfaces. Most nap-type rollers will catch and pull on these surfaces. The roller won't last long, and the nap will stick to the surface you're painting. You can't use the serrated rubber rollers if there are lots of sharp or jagged edges, such as on a stucco wall.

Use a trowel to apply very thick coatings like tar or filler paints to brick, block and concrete walls. These coatings go on from 1/8 to 1/4 inch thick, compared to six to 40 thousandths of an inch thick for most paints. Some can be applied with a brush or special spray outfit.

Wood, smooth: Use a brush, roller, or airless spray, depending on how the lumber is spaced. For instance, use a brush or roller for a picket fence because you'd lose too much paint if you use a sprayer. Use a sprayer for a board fence — a brush would take too long. You can do either one with a roller or paint pad.

Wood, rough: Use a spray or a brush, depending on the spacing of the lumber. Rollers and pads

don't work well because the nap catches on the rough surface.

Wood, alternate method: The best and fastest way to coat wood stock is to do it before you build the fence. This method uses more paint but gives a better, deeper-penetrating coating in much less time. It's a trade-off between cost of time or cost of paint. This is the preferred method for applying a wood preservative. Use a paint bin filled just deep enough to coat one side of the lumber. Soak the boards for at least a few seconds and up to a minute or so. Then turn the boards over. To test for penetration, cut a piece off a board and look at the cut edge. A penetration of 1/8 to 1/4 inch is considered very good.

Glass and plastic panel fences: These aren't usually painted, but sometimes you'll need to coat them to control the sun or block the view. For best results, use a conventional spray gun. The coatings for these materials are thin. An airless sprayer won't handle them as well as a conventional spray gun will.

Be very careful of runs and drips. You can use a roller or a brush. But it's hard to get good coverage and a smooth finish that way. For small areas, use a canned aerosol spray. The disadvantage with canned aerosols is their high cost. An aerosol can will only cover about 40 square feet of surface area. Four aerosol cans, which will cost about the same as a gallon of paint, will cover 160 square feet. A gallon of paint covers 350 to 450 square feet. So aerosols cost more than double.

How much do painting tools cost?

♦ A paint brush can cost from $1.00 to $30.00, depending on the kind of bristles, size, and quality. Most brushes are synthetic bristle brushes you can use for stains, polys, lacquers, enamels, and latex paints. Natural bristle brushes are preferred by many painters. They're great for doing quality interior work using oil-based paints. Don't use natural bristle brushes for latex or water-based paints. The bristles soak up the water and swell, ruining the brush in the process.

Polyester or nylon/polyester brushes are best for fence work. Natural bristles will abrade and don't hold up to the surface roughness of most wood fences and block walls. Nylon softens from the sun's heat and won't apply an even, controlled coating when hot.

♦ Rollers come in lamb's wool or synthetic materials. Professional painters prefer lamb's wool for quality interior work, but the synthetics are fine for fences. They cost from $2.50 to $4.00 for a 9-inch roller cover. So you can afford to use them once and throw them away. Cleaning usually takes too long, especially if you try to get them completely clean. A long-napped roller is best for most fences.

♦ Paint pads and paint gloves fall into the throw-away category, also. They cost less than $5.00, so they're not worth the bother of cleaning.

Here's a tip for keeping brushes, pads and rollers in good condition between uses or during a break: Don't wash them, just cover them with aluminum foil or plastic wrap. You can keep your tools this way for up to a day or so. After that, throw the pads and rollers out. You can keep a brush in good condition for up to a year if you soak it in the proper cleaning solution, wrap it in foil, and keep it in the refrigerator.

♦ Power rollers use a small compressor to pump paint into the roller or pad as you use it. The covers cost about $7.00 to $12.00 each. You save time by not having to dip the roller in the paint tray, but the additional cost of the rollers might not be worth the extra convenience.

♦ Conventional spray units cost from $100 to $500 or more. They're great for spraying fine work with light-body paints and stains. I don't recommend you spend that much money for fence work. The materials you'll use are medium- to heavy-bodied and won't spray well with a conventional sprayer.

♦ An airless spray outfit is almost essential today. An airless can spray paints as thick as tar. With enough horsepower and the correct spray tip, you can spray stucco. For outside work, I recommend a three to five horsepower gasoline-driven unit. A used one may cost from $200 to $500. A rebuilt one costs between $500 and $1,200. A new one can cost from $1,200 to $3,500. You can rent airless units in many places for about $45 a day.

Don't fall for one of the very cheap airless units on the market. They're designed for the homeowner who'll do one paint job every five years, not every day or week.

Color

Everything you paint will both absorb and reflect light. It's this reflected light that we see as color. But color can be tricky. It's only what people perceive it to be. Some people see red as pink, others see it as violet, still others see it as gray. You need to help your customer select the right color for the job. Sometimes it's helpful to make a little sketch of the wall or fence you're building and color it in. It helps you and the customer see how well it will blend with nearby structures and landscaping.

Here are some other things to look out for:

1) Make sure the color looks the same when it's applied as it does on the sample or in the can.

2) Use a color that's suitable for the neighborhood. Many neighborhoods have owners' associations that have the right to approve exterior color schemes for the community. You paint a fence bright green in a neighborhood where all the other fences are tan, and you'll get a reputation for being a troublemaker.

3) Color changes with viewing direction, the kind and level of light, and surface smoothness. Coat a sample spot before you plunge in and paint an entire wall or fence. Allow the sample to dry completely. Some paints change color as they dry. Look at the color from several different directions and under different light conditions, morning, noon, and evening. If both you and your customer are satisfied, then finish the job.

4) Avoid bright or dark colors. The pigments will fade very quickly in the sun. Use tans, grays, and whites and you shouldn't have

any fading problems. Bright colors turn whitish very quickly. Brown is one exception. Dark brown fades to light brown that's still acceptable to most people. There's one situation where dark colors work best, however. In areas with a lot of moisture and little sunlight, dark colors help to absorb the heat and dry out the excess moisture. It's also a good idea to add chemicals to the coating to kill mold and mildew.

5) Consider the effect of the color on the plants in the area. A large flat white wall or fence reflects a lot of sunlight and heat. It can raise the temperature to over a hundred degrees up to 3 feet away from the wall. That's hot enough to kill many plants. In areas with a lot of bright sun, use darker colors to absorb the heat.

Some colors are traditionally used for certain applications. If you build a lot of picket fences, then stock up on lots of white paint. Ornamental iron fences are often black. Wood fences are usually shades of brown, from tan to dark. Block walls are mostly white or tan or pink pastel colors.

Certain fences *should* be painted a bright color. Snow fences, for instance, are usually painted bright red where they mark the boundaries of fields, driveways and roads. You want them to be very visible to the guy driving the snow plow.

If you work for the government, check Federal Specification 595a. It lists the colors you must use for various applications. You can get a copy from

Federal Supply Service
Standardization Division
Specifications and Standards Branch
Washington, DC 20402

What happens if you don't paint the newly-installed fence or wall? Most woods will turn to a silver-gray color. Metals will turn rusty red.

Aluminum turns gray-white. Brick and block usually don't change color unless they contain a concentration of minerals such as vanadium or molybdenum. Then they may take on a greenish color. Redwood turns brown unless there's metal touching it, in which case it turns black from the tannic acid reaction.

Keeping the Coating on the Fence

Here are a few tips to help you make sure that the coating you apply stays where it belongs. First, consider whether the material to be coated is smooth or rough. I call wood smooth if I can run my hand over it without losing skin or picking up splinters. Of course, glass, plastic and metal are smooth. Most masonry is rough.

Why does the surface texture matter? Because materials expand and contract with heat and cold. The coating also has to expand and contract at the same rate, or it will crack and peel off. Here's the rule of thumb:

On *smooth* surfaces, apply a coating that's as thin as possible while still coloring and protecting the surface. Thin coatings expand and contract much more easily than thick coatings.

On *rough* surfaces, apply a fairly thick coating to counter the effects of weather and contaminants. The roughness of the surface will hold the coating in place.

Besides the texture of the surface, consider the weather conditions. Where there are wide temperature extremes, use rough surfaces and thick coatings. They'll hold up better. And in areas with little rain — or acid rain — advise the homeowner to wash down the fence or wall every few months. That will remove the dirt, acids and other contaminants that will attack the coating. In areas with heavy rains, apply a water seal product at least once a year. Finally, consider a mildewcide and an insecticide in areas threatened by termites, ants and other boring insects.

nine

Troubleshooting and Repairs

*F*ences are like everything else in the world — they break, they wear out, and they need care. Sun and rain make them dry out, discolor, or rot. Wind blows them down. Water seeps into metal fences, block and brick walls, causing deterioration. Trees and plants grow in, over, and under fences and walls. As that happens, the fence may be undermined and eventually destroyed.

If you're building a new fence, this chapter will help you avoid the more common problems that shorten the useful life of a fence. If you're repairing an existing fence, let this chapter be your guide to making the right repair at the right time.

Throughout this chapter I'm going to make my point by examining actual fence problems — fences that have deteriorated long before the end of their normal life expectancy. I hope that seeing the errors of others will help you avoid the same mistakes.

You can make a good business out of just maintaining fences. It's an inexpensive way for a beginning contractor to start out. All you need is skill, knowledge and a few hand tools. Then sell your services to homeowners, businesses, and local government. Many homeowners don't have the time, energy, or talent to make their own fence repairs. They're just too busy doing what they do best. They'll be more than willing to pay a knowledgeable professional $20 or more an hour to fix their fences.

Maintenance Contracts

You can do repairs "on call" or as part of a maintenance agreement. Sign your customers up for *preventive maintenance* contracts. Agree to inspect their fences and do routine upkeep jobs like oil hinges and tighten screws and bolts. A fee of $120 a year is reasonable for this service. Charge your regular rate for any major repairs at the beginning of the contract, then you have an easy time the rest of the year.

Suppose you make eight maintenance calls a day on each of the 21 working days each month. That would give you 168 active contracts for an income of $20,160 a year. You should be able to make those eight visits in three to five hours, which leaves you three to five hours for other work.

Using an average of four hours per day at $35 per hour, your regular work would bring in another $35,280 (4 hours x $35 x 21 days x 12 months). Add that to your maintenance income, and you have a total of $55,440.

The best thing about maintenance contracts is that they get your foot in the door. Do a good job on the contract work and you're in a good position to sell the fence owner larger construction jobs. Figure 9-1 is an example of a preventive maintenance contract.

Is It Worth Fixing?

When it comes to repairs, remember three things:

1) The item being repaired worked and was in good shape once.

2) Something has happened to make it not work correctly.

3) It can be fixed.

But is it *worth* fixing? Here's the rule of thumb I use: If fixing costs more than 40 percent of the replacement cost, then replace it. As a fence maintenance contractor, you know how much it will cost to replace a fence or wall. Keep your repair cost between 15 and 40 percent of that cost. At less than 15 percent, you'll probably lose money on the job unless the repair is minor and very inexpensive. If you quote more than 40 percent, you probably won't get the work. Either someone else will underbid you, or the fence isn't worth spending that much on because all the components are weathered and worn.

The older a fence gets, the more problems you'll find. Some fences fall apart during the first three years because of faulty design, materials or construction. Once they're over ten years old, they fail just from exposure and lack of maintenance. In my neighborhood, about 90 percent of the fences and walls need some kind of repair. Most of them are over ten years old.

Here are some design problems that cause fences to fail before their time:

♦ Foundation not deep enough to support a wall

♦ Not enough support for line and corner posts

♦ Posts set too far apart

♦ No internal support (rebar) in block walls

♦ Wood in contact with the earth

♦ Poorly designed rail-to-post connections

♦ Fence or wall located too close to trees and root systems

♦ Lack of proper caps and water drainage devices

These are material problems:

♦ Wrong kind of fasteners and nails

♦ Wrong lumber used, especially for posts

♦ Incorrect concrete, cement, or mortar used

♦ Incorrect or inferior sealer or paint used

♦ Uncoated steel used for latches and hinges

Here are poor construction techniques that can lead to failure:

♦ Lack of expansion joints or improperly-spaced expansion joints

♦ Improperly finished joints on block or brick walls

♦ Sloppy workmanship

♦ Use of mortar that's too dry or mixed more than two hours before use

♦ Unfinished weld joints on metal fences

Preventive Maintenance Contract

Scope: To service and maintain in good condition the fences, walls and gates located at_____, in the city of _____ state of _____.

Includes: Service shall include a monthly inspection on the _____day of each month or within _____ days of that date.

Service: The service includes, but is not limited to, nailing of loose lumber, oiling of gate latches and hinges, tuckpointing of loose mortar, minor bracing and repairs.

Service: The service does not include painting, rebuilding, alterations, or major damage repairs. Said repairs are to be quoted at the prevailing wages and materials cost.

Warranty: All materials and workmanship provided under terms of this contract shall carry a _____ day warranty.

Cost: This contract is $_____ and will continue in force from this date _____ and for a period of_____ months.

Cancellation: Contract ☐ may ☐ may not be cancelled by either party. If cancelled, the funds remaining will be refunded on a _____ month prorated basis.

Payments: Customer will pay for contract in full upon acceptance, or may elect to pay $_____ per month for _____ months.

Customer: _____

Address:_____ Phone: _____

Contractor: _____

Address: _____ Phone _____

Acceptance: Customer signature _____Date _____

Contractor signature_____Date _____

Paid $_____ by ☐ cash ☐ check # _____or

Bank card _____ **number**_____

Figure 9-1
Preventive maintenance contract

Figure 9-2
Badly designed and maintained fence

- Improper stretching of fabric on wire mesh fences

- Over-tightening of screws and fasteners

These maintenance jobs are often neglected:

- Oil hinges regularly

- Seal or paint when needed

- Fix small problems as they develop

- Cut back trees, vines, and other plants from fence

- Keep drainage holes and pipes clean

And then there's normal abuse that all fences have to stand up to:

- Climbing people (small and large) and animals

- Vehicles that run into them

- Graffiti artists

- Water from sprinklers

- Pets that dig and chew

- Vandalism

And then there are effects from the weather:

- Severe wind storms

- Ultraviolet destruction of sealers and paints

- Snow loads that topple the fence

- Rain and ice

- Expansion and contraction caused by changes in temperature

- Shifting ground moving posts out of line

All these things will create a demand for your fence repair services. Let's get on with the kinds of failures you'll run across, and what to do about them. I'll begin with wood fences.

Maintaining Wood Fences

Wood fences are among the easiest and cheapest to build. They also need the most care. Figure 9-2 is a prime example of one that wasn't designed well in the first place, and has been neglected besides. This short fence was built between two block walls. It was made of redwood and the slats touched the ground. The rail rotted out where it touched the cement block. Water was trapped at the point of contact and seeped into the lumber. The end cuts absorb water much faster than the surface cuts will. Those end cuts should have been sealed with tar when the fence was built.

Fencing lumber absorbs water in three places: the top cut, the bottom cut, and where it contacts the rails. In this situation, the rail should have been sealed before the face lumber was attached.

You'd have to rebuild this fence entirely. Use treated lumber for the rails. Mount the lumber so it's 6 inches above ground if you can. If that's not practical, leave at least 1 inch.

Remember that redwood isn't entirely rot-proof. Heartwood resists rot, but the white wood isn't much better than pine or fir. Most redwood sold for fencing has a lot of white wood. Treat it if it's going to be exposed to wet conditions.

When a fence starts to lean over like the one in Figure 9-3, the first thing to look for is rotted posts. We found them here. Of course they rotted — they were set in dirt when the fence was built. The only

Figure 9-3
Rotted posts cause fence to lean

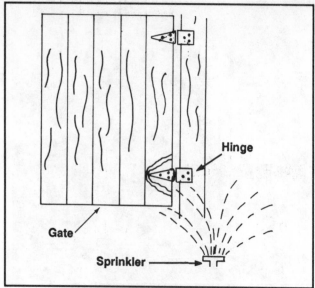

Figure 9-4
Sprinklers are hard on fences

solution was to rebuild the fence, but we were able to salvage some of the face lumber. This time we set treated posts in concrete and left a gap under the fence for drainage. You saw details of how to do that in Chapter 3, on wood fences.

I once ran into a situation where a gate hinge broke off and the supporting wood rotted away. There wasn't an obvious reason for the problem until the sprinklers came on and I discovered the gate was being watered every day. I installed a new face board on the gate, replaced the hinge, and repainted the gate. Then I had the owner get a different sprinkler head that watered the lawn and not the gate. Figure 9-4 shows what led to this repair job.

You'll often need to replace loose face boards. Several things can cause this problem.

1) Nails that are too short, and not rustproof.

2) Unseasoned lumber that dries out and pulls away from the nails.

3) Plants that encroach on the fence and push it apart.

One fence I was called on to repair had all three of these problems. The plants in question were bamboo — a very invasive plant — and the fence was double-sided. The bamboo grew between the two faces of the fence and pushed them outward.

To keep the same thing from happening again, I convinced the owner to cut the bamboo and apply a weed killer to the area. I renailed the fence with hot dipped galvanized nails, placing the nails 1/2 inch from the original nail holes.

The fence section in Figure 9-5 has pulled loose from its anchor rod in the block wall. Notice the slant of the top edge of the fence. When this fence was built, the face boards were attached with only

Figure 9-5
Several problems caused this failure

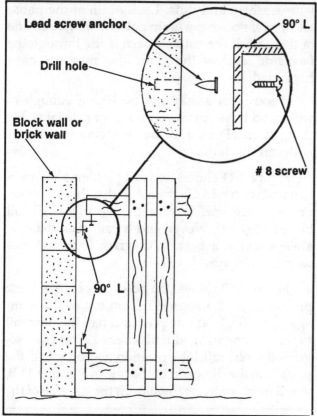

Figure 9-6
Attach a wood fence to a block wall with L brackets and screw anchors

one nail each. When the end of the fence came loose, the face boards pivoted on their nails.

There were more problems here. The foundation of the block wall had shifted, allowing the wall to tilt away from the wood fence. Also, the connection between the fence and the wall wasn't secure. The builder had drilled a hole in the end of the rail and shoved the rail onto the piece of exposed rebar you see at the right in the picture.

First, I had to level the block wall (as I'll explain later), and then use 4-inch L brackets to fasten the wood rails to the block. Then I drilled holes in the block, installed lead anchors, and used #8 screws as shown in Figure 9-6. I also renailed the face boards.

Don't fasten a fence to a stucco wall like the one in Figure 9-7. Stucco is a finishing material, not a structural material. In this case, the stucco began to dissolve where it was exposed to water trapped behind the post. Water also damaged the rail-to-post attachment. When the wind blew hard

enough, the fence pulled away from the wall. A closed-board fence like this gets the full force of the wind.

The solution here was to cut the fence back 6 inches and install a new post next to the wall. This time I anchored it in the ground with concrete and nailed another rail to the original, damaged one. The stucco had to be scraped away and replaced where it had crumbled.

Don't nail a fence to brick, either. Brick fractures easily and turns to powder. Instead, use L brackets with screws and lead anchors.

Figure 9-8 shows a peeler log rail fence that's been eaten by termites or ants. Peeler logs are untreated logs that have had their bark peeled off. The first step in solving this problem was to probe the rest of the fence with a screwdriver to find if there was any more damage. Solid lumber won't give way when you poke it; insect-ridden lumber will disintegrate. Remove the infested logs and spray the area with insecticide. Then replace the damaged logs with new, treated lumber.

If you look back at Figure 2-1 in Chapter 2, you'll see a split rail fence where the post has split and a section has fallen out. Figure 9-9 shows you how to fix this. Cut a block of matching lumber that's slightly narrower than the cut for the rail. Drill through the post and the block and insert long carriage bolts or threaded rod and fasten it

Figure 9-7
Don't attach a fence to stucco

Figure 9-8
Insects ate this fence

with washers and nuts. Look again at the photo and you'll notice the grain pattern on the cut side of the post. If the cut had been made through the face side, against the grain, this may not have happened.

Wood screws may not be strong enough to withstand the stresses you put on a gate latch. Fix the gate in Figure 9-10 by replacing the screws with carriage bolts.

Figure 9-11 shows two rail problems common to wood fences. In diagram A, either the rail broke, or the fence was built with two pieces of rail butted together. Never end a rail in mid-air — always end at a post. In diagram B, the rail has warped with age.

Figure 9-12 shows you how to fix both of these problems. Add a second rail on top of the damaged one. Begin at one post and nail the new rail to the old one with 8d nails every 12 inches or so. Push the old rail into position as you go. If the warp is in the direction of the one in Figure 9-11 B, you'll need someone to push on the slat side of the

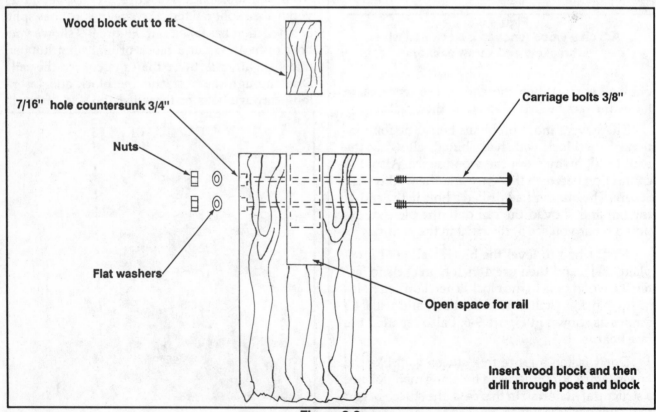

Wood block cut to fit

7/16" hole countersunk 3/4"

Nuts

Carriage bolts 3/8"

Flat washers

Open space for rail

Insert wood block and then
drill through post and block

Figure 9-9
Repairing a split rail fence post

Figure 9-10
Replace screws with carriage bolts

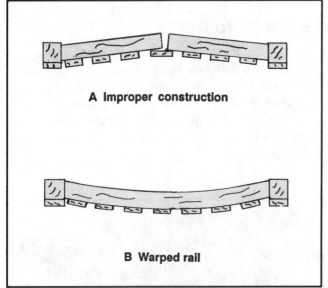

A Improper construction

B Warped rail

Figure 9-11
Fence rail problems

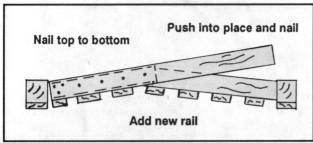

Nail top to bottom

Push into place and nail

Add new rail

Figure 9-12
A fence rail solution

fence while you work on the rail side. Or you could remove the face boards while you fix the rail, and then replace them.

I once had a problem like the one in Figure 9-13. Where I live, in southern California, the land sometimes shifts around by itself, and takes along with it things that are standing on it. In this case, post D shifted out of line with A and B, and post C loosened and tilted backward. The solution here was to take the fence apart between posts A and B, dig a new post hole in line with them, then rebuild the fence.

The detail in Figure 9-13 shows how I shored up post C. I drilled through both posts and used 1/2-inch bolts to attach a new post to the old one. Quick-set post concrete kept the base of the new post in place. I also tapered the top of the new post. It looks better and lets water drain off.

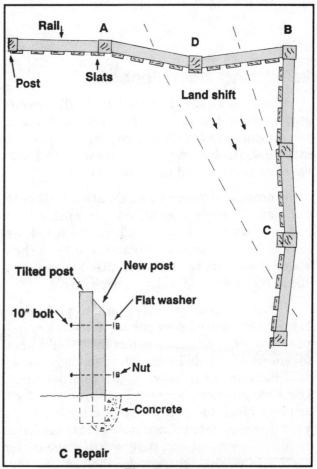

Figure 9-13
A fence that moved

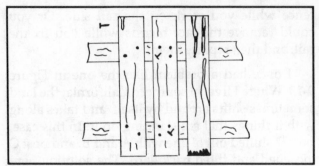

Figure 9-14
Board fence problems

Figure 9-14 shows a board fence with three problems. The first board has cracked near the top edge. You can probably fill a small crack with wood glue and small (2d or 4d) finishing nails. Replace the popped nails in the second board with hot dipped galvanized nails. Replace the third board entirely. It's rotted at the bottom, and the splits are too big to fix.

Refinishing Wood Fences

Many fences aren't painted. But if the weathered look isn't what an owner wants, you can recommend a wide variety of coatings. I explained in the last chapter how to paint a new fence. Here, we're more interested in follow-up care.

Fences should be recoated about every three to four years — more often if the fence starts to look bad or if water no longer beads on the wood. As long as the water beads, the coating is intact. When water doesn't bead, it means that the wood is absorbing water and will soon begin to rot.

When the coating really starts to peel, as in Figure 9-15, suspect poor preparation work or improper coating selection. In this case, you'd have to remove all the old loose coating and lightly *scuff sand* the remainder before you recoat the fence. Use #100 grit sandpaper wrapped around a 2 x 4 sanding block to keep the splinters away from your fingers. Better yet, waterblast the entire fence right to bare wood and start over. If some of the coating is peeling, chances are the rest will too. When it does, your new coating will peel off with the old.

Figure 9-15
Sand thoroughly or waterblast before recoating

Fence "Surprises"

Before I leave the subject of wood fence repairs, here's a funny story about a not-so-funny repair job. Hinges take a lot of strain, too. The one in Figure 9-16 ripped out from the weight of the gate the owner built for his storage shed. I expected to remove and reinstall the hinge — about a 10-minute job.

Figure 9-16
This turned into a two-day job

Figure 9-17
You can straighten this tilted wall

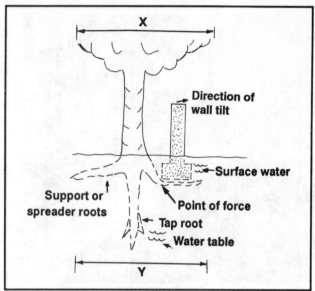

Figure 9-18
How a tree can displace a wall

We all know about "surprises" when you're doing repair or remodeling work in a house. But those are nothing compared to the surprises you can find when you do outdoor work. In this case, the owner had built the gate by nailing 1 x 2 redwood boards to a sheet of 1/4-inch plywood. Unfortunately, he had used interior plywood, and it was splitting apart. And he had nailed and clinched the hinges to the wood, so when the hinges ripped out, the lumber was torn up, too. I couldn't find replacement boards for the broken and missing ones, so I wound up making a new gate from 1 x 3 redwood mounted on a 1 x 6 frame. I prepared to finish the job with new hinges and long screws. But it wasn't that easy.

Now I discovered the gate post and adjacent fence were loose, so I had to brace and renail those. The whole area was overgrown with ivy that had to be cut back and poisoned. When I was doing that, I ran across a nest of black widow spiders — my very favorite.

I built the gate on the ground and cut it square, but when I installed it, it didn't look right. The roof of the shed sloped, and that made it look like the gate was sagging. I had to trim the gate to match the roof line to make it look "straight." By then it was time to go home.

It rained during the night, so the gate I so carefully fitted the day before didn't open. The lumber was swollen. A little more effort with a wood rasp and plane finally finished the job.

Here's the point of this long story: *Don't take anything for granted.* Know what you're getting into before you start, and double-check everything. When you quote a repair job, allow something extra for situations like this one.

Maintaining Walls

Figure 9-17 wasn't printed crooked. The block wall is tilted, the fence was cut to match, and so was the white gate on the right. The owner "fixed" the fences in this case. The cause of all this was a tree that grew under the wall. The freestanding wall was on a concrete foundation. But as the tree grew, its roots tilted the wall more than 6 inches out of plumb.

Figure 9-18 shows the root system of a typical tree. The tap root usually doesn't create a problem because it grows straight down. The spreader roots near the surface are the ones that can give you trouble. As you see in the drawing, the X and Y dimensions are usually about the same. You can

Figure 9-19
Straightening the wall with bracing . . .

Figure 9-20
. . . and a hydraulic jack

tell by the spread of the tree how far the roots extend underground.

One solution is to remove the tree. If you can't do that, cut or saw the roots off about 3 feet away from the wall on both sides of the wall. That shouldn't damage an established tree.

Figure 9-21
Pour new cement to hold it in place

Here's how to straighten the wall:

Dig to near the base of the foundation on both sides and flood the area to soften things up. (Notice I had to remove some brick pavers, too.) Use braces and a hydraulic two-ton automobile jack to over-plumb the wall by about 1/4 inch. See Figures 9-19 and 9-20. You may have to drive stakes into the ground behind the jack to keep it from sliding backward.

Dig under the foundation about 6 inches on the side the wall was leaning toward. Pour new concrete under the foundation and up the side of it (Figure 9-21). Let the concrete cure for at least several days, then release the jack and let the wall settle back to plumb. Now, even up the fence and gate boards. By the way, the pipe in Figure 9-21 is an old sprinkler line, not part of the repair job.

That tree cost this owner a lot of money. Damage from plants and tree roots is a common problem you'll probably have to deal with eventually.

In this case, it wasn't practical to rebuild the wall, because there wasn't access for a backhoe and bulldozer to tear out the old wall and foundation. Anyway, the repair was much cheaper than replacement, as you can see in Figure 9-22.

This wall was only 12 feet long, but you can do the same thing with a long wall if you use several jacks.

	Repair	Replace	Remarks
Tree removal	$350	$ 350	
8 hours digging	280	0	
Dozer rental	0	400	Remove old wall
Concrete	30	180	New foundation
4 hours mix and pour	140	280	
Blocks and mortar	0	100	New wall
8 hours mason's labor	0	280	
Removal of old material	0	140	
2 hours cleanup	70	70	
Total	$870	$1800	

Figure 9-22
Repair and replacement chart

Figure 9-23
This column had tilted

Another common problem is how to replace old fence and wall components that aren't manufactured any more. Suppose your customer knocks the cap off a pilaster and breaks it. Twenty years ago, when his fence was built, cap blocks were 1 inch thick. Today the standard thickness is 1-1/2 inches. A new cap would look out of place with the old ones.

One alternative would be to replace them all. A better one is to use a product called *Fix All™*. It's a cement/plaster for outdoor use and is available at most paint and hardware stores. Use it to fix block, brick, or even lumber. I've used *Fix All™* to cement the pieces of cap block back together. Where there were pieces missing, I used the cement to fill in the gaps.

In Figure 9-23 the column the gate is mounted on has tilted about half an inch. I couldn't shore up the foundation this time because the foundation is the driveway slab. The cure here is to break the column away from the foundation and then wedge it into plumb. You use *pickle bars* to do this. Pickle bars are wedges like the one in Figure 9-24. You can buy them for about $15 at auto supply stores. They come in sizes from 12 to 20 inches long. They're intended for cars — to break apart stuck ball joints. But I use them in my fence work. I use a good, sturdy sledge hammer to bang them

into place under the wall. In this case, it only took one bar to raise the column half an inch.

Once the column is plumb, squeeze a layer of Type II mortar under it. I used a mason's trowel and a few short pieces of wood to squeeze the mortar in tight. Let it set up for a few days, then remove the wedges and fill the remaining space with fresh mortar.

Figure 9-25 shows a typical problem with a brick wall. Bricks are loose and missing. This almost always happens on top or top end bricks. You have to chip off the old mortar and replace the brick, using new mortar.

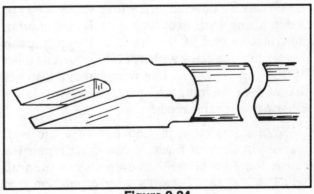

Figure 9-24
Pickle bar

Figure 9-25
Loose and missing bricks

Figure 9-26
Efflorescence on a block wall

I have a theory about the cause of this problem. By the time the person laying the brick gets to the top row, the mortar is drying out. Dry mortar doesn't penetrate the brick well, so the bond isn't secure. *Always use newly-mixed mortar on the top layers of block or brick walls.* In hot or dry weather, wet the bricks before you install them to prevent over-absorption of water from the mortar. Over-absorption leads to a dry, powdery bond layer.

Mortar that's too dry can also cause cracks in block walls — but they're more likely to be caused by the foundation settling or part of the foundation being raised by tree roots. In either case, repair the cracks before moisture gets in and damages the wall.

The technique you use to repair cracks is called *tuck pointing.* Chip out as much of the old mortar as you can. Remove all dust with a strong spray of water. Using hydrated Type II or Type S mortar, start at one end of the crack and tightly push mortar into the crack with a pointed trowel. Finish by striking off with a tool whose shape matches that of the remaining wall joints. *Repointing* is another name for this repair.

While you're at it, find out why the wall cracked in the first place. If you don't repair the cause, there's a better-than-even chance the wall will crack again. Then it's your reputation that gets cracked along with the wall. Look for tree roots or inadequate footings. Another possible cause of the problem is a footing that isn't heavy enough.

Figure 9-26 shows *efflorescence* on a block wall. Efflorescence is a white scale that forms on the face of concrete masonry. It comes from mineral salts leaching out of the concrete surface. That usually happens when water seeps into the block. Apply a cap block to keep the water out or waterproof the back side of the wall.

Once the cause of the problem is identified and solved, remove efflorescence with *muriatic acid.* You can buy a 10 percent solution from a paint or hardware store for about $3.00 a gallon. Always protect your eyes and use a respirator and rubber gloves when you use muriatic acid.

Apply muriatic acid with a plastic pump sprayer. They're available at home and garden centers for about $25.00. Dilute the acid at a rate of one gallon of 10 percent muriatic to each gallon of water. Use a stiff scrub brush to remove heavy concentrations of efflorescence. When the efflorescence is gone, use a neutralizing solution of 10 percent ammonia or potassium hydroxide (lye) and 90 percent water. Use a water spray for the final rinse.

Graffiti is a very common problem in urban areas. It's very hard to remove the "handwriting on the wall." And when you have, the wall probably has to be repainted to get the proper color

Figure 9-27
Use lye to remove these stains

Figure 9-28
Install a bumper after you repair this

match. Here are answers to graffiti problems on a block wall:

1) Muriatic acid in a 10 to 18 percent solution straight from the bottle removes mineral-base stains.

2) Acetone removes fingernail polish and some acrylic spray paints. Use it full strength.

3) Use lacquer thinner full strength for lacquer or lacquer sprays.

4) Dissolve two teaspoons of lye crystals in a cup of water to remove oil-base paint. This solution won't affect latex paints.

5) Full strength methyl chloride (commercial paint remover) removes most paints, including latex.

6) Denatured alcohol (100 percent) takes shellac off.

7) Household bleach mixed with an equal part of water gets rid of many inks. Use a neutralizing rinse of one cup vinegar in one quart of water.

You can buy commercial coatings that resist vandalism, but they work most effectively on smooth surfaces. Block and brick are porous, and therefore harder to protect.

If chemicals don't work, you can use a waterblaster or sandblaster. These are motor driven machines that spray water or sand at very high pressure. The particles easily cut through paint and rust. But be careful with both water and sandblasters. They produce pressures in excess of 2,000 PSI. Don't use the spray tip too close to the wall — you can eat a hole through stucco, brick, block and wood in seconds. *Never* check for pressure by putting your hand in front of the spray tip, and *never* point the spray tip at anyone.

You can rent a waterblaster for about $65 to $75 a day at most rental yards. New ones cost about $3,500.

In Figure 9-27 the stain is a natural one that's caused by the vanadium and molybdenum compounds contained in the clays the bricks are made from. You can remove this green-tinted stain by washing the brick with a solution of one cup sodium hydroxide (lye) mixed in ten cups of water. Rinse with clear water when the green color disappears.

Do not use muriatic acid on this type of stain. It'll turn the stain from green to brown and set it permanently. Whenever you clean bricks with muriatic acid, always test a small spot first. Most bricks will clean up and brighten in color. Some won't, and others will stain.

Figure 9-28 shows a prime example of poor design. The knob on this security gate has

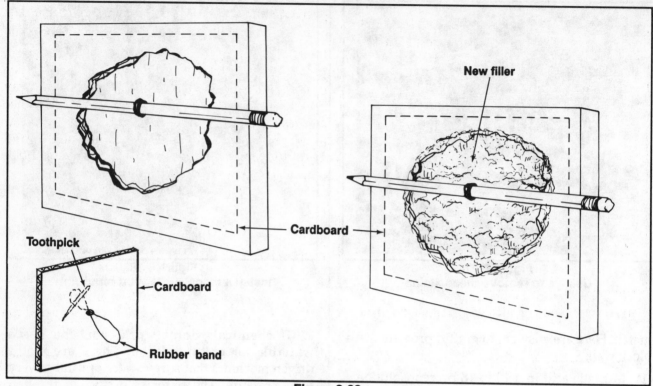

Figure 9-29
Repair a hole in plaster or stucco

punched a hole through the stucco wall. The solution is to repair the wall and then install bumpers.

To repair a hole in a frame wall that's covered with plaster or stucco, cut a piece of heavy cardboard that extends about an inch all around the hole. Punch a hole through the center of the cardboard, and pass a short rubber band through the hole. Use a toothpick on the back of the cardboard to hold the rubber band in place. Poke the cardboard through the hole, and slip a pencil through the rubber band. Use the pencil to twist the rubber band until the cardboard rests snugly against the back of the hole. Figure 9-29 illustrates this.

Use plaster, wood filler, auto body filler, or *Fix All*™ to fill the hole to just below the level of the finish coat. Let it dry until it's very firm. Then clip off the rubber band with scissors, and apply and texture the finish coat to make the patch even with the existing surface.

An alternate solution would be to cover the hole with a painted metal plate. You could use a 4 x 4 electrical box plate, and secure it with toggle bolts. Or have a sheet metal shop make you a stainless steel plate. Then you wouldn't have to worry about painting *or* rust.

Repairing Chain Link

If there's an outdoor movie theater near you, you've probably had calls to repair chain link that's been cut. Sometimes you can just tie-wire the cut section together. If the cut is large, or some of the fabric is missing, you have to splice a new section of fabric into place.

You can remove the vertical strands from chain link quite easily. Just pull and twist the strand upward and out. Butt a new piece of fabric next to the old one and reinstall the vertical strand by twisting it back in. See Figure 9-30.

If the damaged section is very large, I recommend you install tension bars and loops on the sections of fabric on both sides of the damaged section and attach them to the line posts. Replace

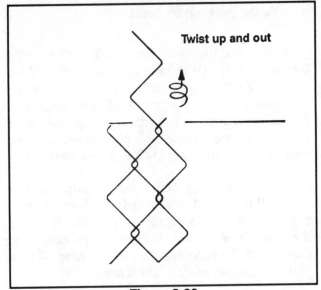

Figure 9-30
Removing a vertical strand of a chain link fence

the damaged section with new fabric and attach it to the posts with bars and loops. See Figure 9-31.

Galvanized chain link fencing shouldn't rust. If it does, it's because the coating has been cut or abraded, exposing the steel. Clean the rust away with a rust remover such as *Naval Jelly* and rinse with clear water, towel dry, and then apply a clear enamel or lacquer. You can also use galvanized spray paints to seal abraded spots. They're available in hardware and auto supply stores.

Removing Chain Link Fences

When you have to remove a chain link fence, you can often salvage the fabric and reuse it. Cut the tie wires and unbolt the tension loops and the

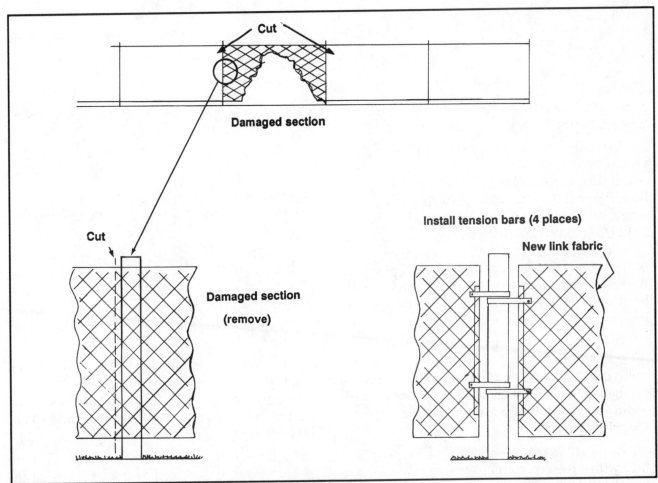

Figure 9-31

fencing will drop. If the posts are anchored in concrete, there are several ways to remove them:

1) Use a backhoe or a bulldozer to dig the posts out.

2) Cut the posts off at ground level with a hacksaw or a welder's cutting torch.

3) Twist the pole out of the foundation concrete. To do that, remove the cap and fill the pole with chipped ice. That should make the post contract away from the concrete. Now, grab the base of the pole with a 36-inch plumber's pipe wrench. You may have to add a 6-foot length of pipe to the wrench handle to get more leverage.

4) Dig the post out by hand.

If you use the torch, be sure there's nothing that will burn in the area around the cut. Also, remember that you're cutting pipe that's coated with zinc and lead. The fumes are very dangerous. Proper ventilation is essential. This is also true if you're welding galvanized pipe together. Wear protective clothing and U/V eye protection.

Remember, any fence can require maintenance. But neglect will nearly always be more expensive than making timely repairs. Of course, the best solution is to anticipate the problems I've mentioned. Fortunately, it's not too hard — once you understand what cause fences to fail.

ten

Wiring and Plumbing

Most fence contractors aren't electricians or plumbers, so you might wonder why I'm including this chapter in a book on fences and retaining walls. It's because fence contractors need to know a little about both of these trades. Many times I've had to move sprinkler lines out of the way or install a hose bib. And sometimes I got the job by offering to install lighting fixtures on posts or hang an electric gate. To your customers, it makes sense to hire a fence contractor who can handle little plumbing and electrical jobs like this. It saves your customers time and money. It should also put some extra money in your pocket.

If you want to sell the add-ons with your fence jobs, here's a good way to do it: Find a good supplier for exterior light fixtures and gate security devices. Bring along product literature, samples and pictures when you make sales calls. For lighting, place a temporary lamp or two where you propose to install lighting. Connect the lights to a power source with an extension cord. Leave them overnight. I call this *puppy dog* selling. Leave a puppy with someone for a day or two and they'll

want to keep it. The same thing will happen with your temporary lights. Your customers will appreciate the beautiful lamp fixture near their gate or entry. They'll appreciate the extra protection and visibility exterior lighting offers. And they'll want to keep it.

You may need to install electrically controlled gates, or "hot" fences. In some cases, you'll be asked to include plumbing for a waterfall in a wall, and many fence jobs require changes in sprinkler systems or spigots.

True, you may subcontract this work out to plumbers, electricians, or security experts. But even then, you need to know something about their trade to supervise and approve their work.

The first step is to get a copy of the National Electrical Code (NEC) from a local bookstore. Descriptions of several electrical reference books are at the back of this book. To get you started, here's a fence contractor's primer on electricity and plumbing.

Some Basic Definitions

The flow of electricity is called *current*. In electrical formulas and specifications, current is represented by the letter I. Current is measured in *amperes*, or *amps*. Think of amps as the volume of flow. The greater the amperage, the more current will flow. Electrical force is called *voltage* or *volts* and is represented by the letter E. You can think of voltage as the pressure behind the flow of current.

When you install a pressure regulator in a water line, the flow decreases. There's *resistance* to the flow. When electricity flows through wires, motors, and light bulbs, those things produce resistance to current flowing through them. Electrical resistance is represented by the letter R and is measured in *ohms*. The symbol for ohm is the Greek letter omega, Ω.

There's a direct relationship between current, voltage, and resistance. If voltage stays the same and resistance changes, then the current will change. The relationship is called *Ohm's Law*, after the man who discovered it. The formula for Ohm's Law is E = IR (voltage equals current times resistance). In formulas like this, if two values, or constants, appear together without a mathematical sign between them, you multiply them together. As with any three-value formula, if you know any two of the values, you can find the third by turning the formula around.

For example, find the current if the voltage is 100 and the resistance is 100 ohms: Divide the voltage (E) by the resistance (R). The formula is:

$$E/R = I$$

The answer in this case is one amp of current. (100/100 = 1)

The unit of energy or *power* that's produced by the flow of current through a resistor is represented by P, or W, which stands for *watt*. Watt is the name of the man who discovered the relationship that gives us another formula, and the name for the unit of power. Watt's formula is P = IE, which means that power equals current times voltage.

If you substitute the values from the example above, you find that one amp of current times 100 volts equals 100 watts of power.

You can express Ohm's Law and Watt's formula in several ways to solve for any of the values. Here's a summary:

Ohm's Law:

E = IR, or I = E/R, or R = E/I

The Watt formula:

P = IE, or I = P/E, or E = P/I

You can also substitute values between the formulas:

Since P = IE, you can also say that P = I times IR, because E = IR. You can also write the last formula as $P = I^2R$ which means you multiply I by itself, and then multiply by R. (I^2 is the same as saying "I squared," or "I multiplied by itself.")

$P = E^2/R$ is another variation of the power formula. You get this formula if you substitute E/R for I.

Safety Features

Electrical devices are designed to operate under specific conditions. They're rated by those limits. The ratings tell you how much current, voltage, or power the device or appliance can handle safely.

But sometimes things go wrong. The power company may have a brown-out or power surge. Installers may hook something up wrong, or connect it to the wrong power source. Or maybe the device is defective or wears out. In any case, you need to protect electrical systems from shock or fire. You do that with *fuses* or *circuit breakers*.

Fuses and circuit breakers *blow* or *trip* when there's an overload of either voltage or current. Breakers and fuses are rated by the voltage they can handle, and the maximum current that can pass through them before they interrupt the flow. Too much current or voltage on a circuit with a fuse or breaker and the circuit opens. No current can flow. If the device is a fuse, you replace it. If it's a circuit breaker, you reset it.

Let's back up a minute and clarify a few terms. A *brown out* occurs when the voltage from the power company falls below the standard required. In the United States, residential lighting fixtures and receptacles provide 120/240 volts AC. The minimum is 110/220 volts AC, and the maximum is 127/254 volts AC. When output voltage falls below 120/240 volts AC, it's considered a brown out.

During brown outs, lights will dim, operating motors and compressors will stall, overheat and possibly burn out. Poorly-designed timers and security systems will either not work or will require resetting.

A *circuit* is completed when power flows from the source, to the device being powered, and back to the source. If the circuit is not complete, it's called an *open* circuit. A circuit that shows zero resistance, not infinite, (when measured with an ohm meter) is a *short* circuit. The supply and return lines are connected without a load resistance in between.

Short circuits blow fuses, trip circuit breakers, and sometimes burn up wiring or components. The danger in short circuits is that they can set fire to the structure that contains the short. For this reason the electrical code requires fuses or circuit breakers be sized to protect the wiring contained within a structure. Separate fuses or circuit breakers, installed where power enters an electrical device, protect the equipment.

Most electrical devices have at least several parts. If one of those parts shorts out, the circuit will still be complete, and there will still be some resistance. That's called a *partial short*, or an *overload*. You'll usually notice this first from the smell — the shorted device overheats and sometimes burns. If you design the circuit properly, a breaker will open to prevent further damage. This is important when you're installing an electrically operated gate, for example. If a car hits the gate, the gate motor may stall, overheat and burn out. A fuse or circuit breaker should protect the motor.

Here's an important safety note: AC and DC voltages below 48 volts are not considered harmful to humans. AC and DC voltages above 48 volts *are* harmful.

Electric Power and How It Travels

The power supplied by the power company is AC power. AC stands for *alternating current*. DC or *direct current* is generated by batteries or converted from alternating current. The electrons in AC power flow in waves that vary in frequency (changes of directions) and amplitude (power). Frequency is measured in cycles per second. The name for cycles per second is *Hertz*, which is abbreviated Hz. Each cycle has a positive and a negative pulse. In the U.S., power is delivered at 60 Hz.

In many other parts of the world power is supplied at 50 Hz. Equipment containing timers won't keep correct time if they're operated at the wrong frequency. Television monitors and cameras designed to work on 50 Hz will not function properly on 60 Hz. Motors, fans and heaters must also be run on the proper frequency.

DC power doesn't pulse, but travels in a constant flow from the source to the thing it's applied to — its *load*.

Think of wire as the pipe through which electricity flows. Water flows through the middle of the pipe. Electricity flows along the surface skin of a wire, not through the center. That's why wire comes in various diameters. The larger the diameter, the more surface area, so more current can flow.

Wire size is measured by *gauge*. The higher the gauge number, the smaller the diameter of the wire, and the less current it can handle. Most wire is covered by an insulating jacket of rubber or plastic that keeps current from jumping to other *conductors*.

A conductor is anything (such as wire) that lets electricity flow through it. You, yourself are a conductor. So is water and most metals. An *insulator* is anything that won't conduct electricity very well. Glass, wood, plastic, and rubber are all good insulators.

Converting AC to DC

Lights and motors operate better on AC than on DC. Control circuits operate better on DC. When you design a control circuit, you have to convert the AC line voltage to DC with a *power supply*. This is usually a *transformer*, a *diode bridge*, and a *filter network*. Most of the gate opener circuits

Figure 10-1
Key lock gate entry

and alarm circuits you install will include a power supply.

A transformer converts AC voltage from one level to another. A *step down* transformer converts from high to lower voltage, for example, from 110 volts AC to 12 volts AC. A *step up* transformer converts the input voltage to a higher output voltage. An *isolation transformer* produces output voltage the same as the input voltage, though it limits the current that flows to the load side of the transformer.

You use a diode to control the flow of current, since diodes only let current flow in one direction. You use four diodes in what's called a *diode bridge* in a power supply to convert AC input to DC output. But the DC output that results will have spikes and ripples that can damage sensitive components. You use a filter network to clean up the DC.

The filter network probably has a *capacitor*, a storage device that passes AC but blocks DC flow. When you apply voltage, the capacitor charges to the maximum voltage. If you disconnect the current, the capacitor will hold its charge for a long time. This makes it very dangerous to work on capacitor circuits. You can get a shock from a charged capacitor even when it's disconnected.

It's good practice to discharge capacitors before you begin working on any device that includes a capacitor. Create a resistance path for the current to escape. Discharge time depends on the amount of resistance you switch in.

Switches

The most common switch is the wall-mounted light switch. It's made of two terminals and a moveable metal conductor strip. When the switch is in the "off" position, the conductor only touches one of the terminals, so the circuit is broken. When you turn the switch "on," both terminals are contacted and the circuit is complete. Switches control all kinds of electrical equipment.

Relays are electromagnetic switches. An electrically charged magnet moves the conductor to and from the terminals. Relays can be designed so they're either open or closed when no power is applied.

Use Sensors to Operate Switches

Both alarm and gate circuits need to sense the presence of people or vehicles. Alarm circuits are often triggered by *light emitting diodes* (LED's). They produce infrared light that's detected by a sensor that doesn't respond to ordinary light. As long as the infrared beam isn't broken between the diode and the sensor, nothing happens. Once an intruder breaks the beam, the alarm goes off. You could also use this kind of sensor to keep an electric gate from closing if something is blocking its path.

You can also buy inexpensive detectors that use sound waves to turn switching circuits on and off. All these have two things in common, a signal transmitter and a receiver that drives an output switch to turn something on and off.

These are all *non-contact* systems. Direct contact systems require some kind of physical contact by the user. Figure 10-1 shows a key lock gate entry system. When you turn the key, the circuit closes to release the gate. Some security systems respond to a number code. You enter the code on a keypad like the one in Figure 10-2. Or, you use the keypad

Figure 10-2
Security telephone keypad

to telephone someone inside the building who releases the lock.

Pressure-activated switches use a special cable that's embedded in the ground or pavement. The cable has two conductors separated by an air gap. When the cable is compressed, the two conductors touch each other, and the circuit is complete.

Invisible Fences

Electronic fences are becoming more common. They're usually used to keep animals in. These aren't the same as *electric* fences, which are charged with enough voltage to shock a person or animal that touches it. An electronic fence transmits a radio signal that either annoys an animal into withdrawing, or triggers a receiver on the animal's collar that sets a switch to deliver a mild shock. The animal learns to avoid the source of the shock — the invisible fence. In each case, you bury a wire in the ground and connect a radio transmitter to it. These systems are available through stores that sell pet and farm animal supplies and equipment.

An Electrician's Primer

Some fence contractors don't handle work that requires any understanding of electricity. I think that's a mistake. Remember this: an important function of most fences is to improve security. A fence or wall by itself is great for keeping *honest* people out. It's the dishonest ones you need to stop with lighting, an alarm, or a security system. Offer these, and you'll be a full step ahead of your competition.

You can do this two ways. Either hire an electrician, or learn to do the work yourself and charge for the service accordingly. Licensing rules vary widely for this. Some states require an electrician's license, others cover these activities under their licensing requirements for fence contractors. In some places you only need a building permit, but no license, and in others, you don't even need a permit if the dollar amount is small. Most jurisdictions *don't* require a license for low voltage systems requiring less than 49 volts.

A security system built as part of a fence is nearly always better than a security system added later. It's easier to conceal and protect from damage by intruders.

Figure 10-3 shows some of the common electrical symbols. In Figure 10-4 you see several of these symbols used in the schematic drawing for an alarm system. Figure 10-5 is my list of materials needed for the alarm system in Figure 10-4.

You don't have to know the purpose of each component in a circuit to install an alarm system or gate operator. You *will* need to know where and how to install each part of the circuit. You also have to know something about your local electrical and building codes, and how to identify and select the appropriate components.

Color Codes

A little electrical knowledge can take you a long way. Here's something you can learn in a minute and may use many, many times: *Biloxi booze rots our young guts but vodka goes willingly.* Remembering that sentence helps me identify

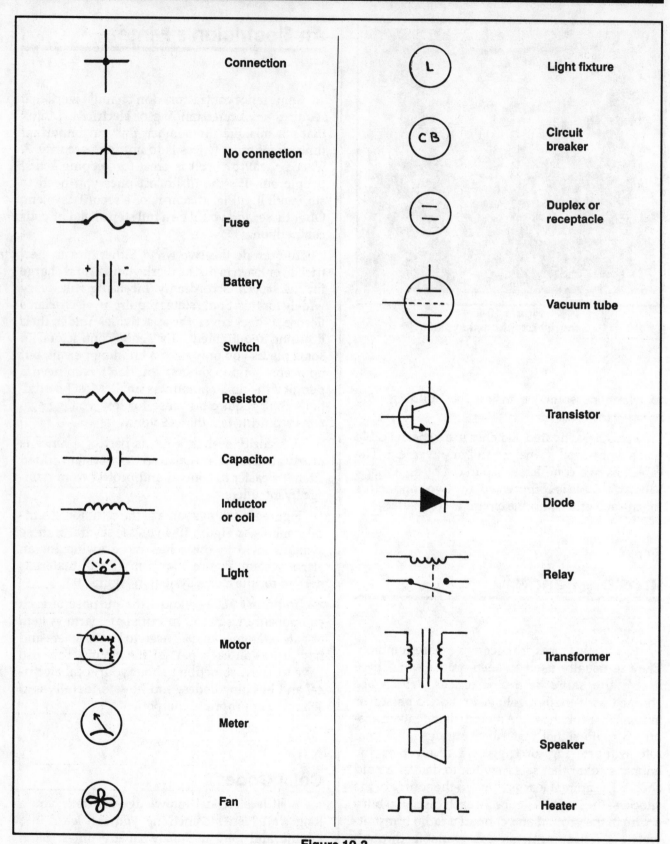

Figure 10-3
Symbols for schematic drawings

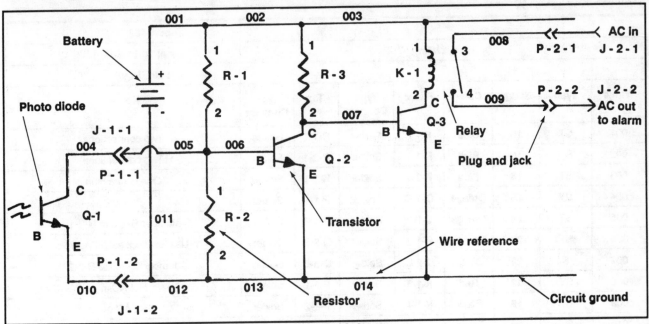

Figure 10-4
Alarm system schematic

	Material Take-Off				Job: A-452
					Date: 10-22-89
					By: McElroy
Item	Description	Quantity	Mfg	P/N	Notes
Bty	Battery 9VDC	1	EV	9N32	Screw terminals
P-1/P-2	Plug 2 pin	2	Plugco	2F	
J-1/J-2	Jack 2 pin	2	Plugco	2M	
Q-1	Photo transistor	1	Tranco	2NPT01	
Q-2/Q-3	Transistor	2	Tranco	2N2200	
K-1	Relay SPST 9V	1	BP	9VSP120	Contacts rated at 250 VAC
R-1	Resistor 22K 1/2W	1	Risco	223.5	5%
R-2	Resistor 10K 1/2W	1	Risco	213.5	5%
R-3	Resistor 2.2K 1/2W	1	Risco	203.5	5%
-	Wire 16G blue	A/R	YCO		
-	Wire 28G orange	A/R	YCO		
-	Wire 22G brown	A/R	YCO		

Figure 10-5
Material take-off

Wire Listing								Job: A-452
								Date: 10-21-89
								By: McElroy
Wire #	Type	Gauge	Color	From:	Type Connect	To:	Type Connect	Notes:
001	ST	16	Blue	Bty +	Screw	R-1-1	Solder	Two connections
002	ST	16	Blue	R-1-1	Solder	R-3-1	Solder	Two connections
003	ST	16	Blue	R-3-1	Solder	K-1-1	Solder	One connection
004	ST	28	Orange	Q-1-C	Solder	P-1-1	Solder	
005	ST	28	Orange	J-1-1	Solder	R-1-2	Solder	Jumper R-1-2 to R-2-1
006	ST	28	Orange	R-1-2	Solder	Q-2-B	Solder	Use low heat soldering iron
007	S	22	Red	Q-2-C	Solder	Q-3-B	Solder	Jumper Q-2-C to R-3-2
008	ST	12	Red	K-1-3	Screw	P-2-1	Solder	Hot AC in
009	ST	12	Black	K-1-4	Screw	P-2-2	Solder	Hot AC out
010	ST	28	Brown	Q-1-E	Solder	P-1-2	Solder	
011	ST	22	Brown	J-1-2	Solder	Bty -	Screw	Two connection
012	ST	22	Brown	Bty -	Screw	R-2-2	Solder	Two connection

Figure 10-6
Wire listing

electronic color codes. The first letter of each word in the sentence stands for a color. Each color has a corresponding number. Here's a chart:

0	Black		5	Green
1	Brown		6	Blue
2	Red		7	Violet
3	Orange		8	Gray
4	Yellow		9	White

You'll see these colors on resistors, capacitors, and wires. Resistors are marked with colored bands. The band nearest the end is the first number of the resistor value. The next band is the second number, the third band is the number of zeros to add, the fourth band is the tolerance. For example, a resistor with bands of red, yellow, and green, in that order, is a 2,400,000 ohm resistor. The red band is the first number, 2. The yellow is the second number, 4. The green band means add five

zeros. The fourth band will be brown or silver or gold, representing 10, 5, and 1 percent tolerance respectively.

Sometimes wire colors are listed on schematics by codes: #9 is white, #0 is black. You may also see #4/#0, which means yellow with a black tracer or strip. Wire gauge may also be shown by number, from #000 through #32. A *wire listing* associated with a schematic lists each wire, its gauge and color, and both ends of its termination. Figure 10-6 is a wire listing drawn from the schematic in Figure 10-4.

Some Simple Schematics

Figure 10-7 is a schematic of a simple switch and lamp. Notice the wire color codes. The *hot* lead is always black on 110 volt AC circuits. The neutral or AC return lead is white. The switch is a SPST (single pole single throw) switch. The black wire from the line (plug) goes to the gold terminal. Figure 10-8 shows the same circuit using a DPST

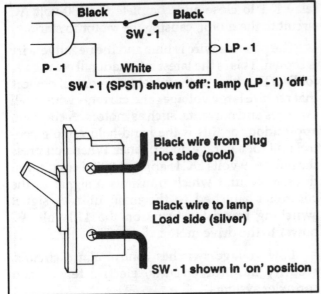

Figure 10-7
Switch and lamp/switch schematic

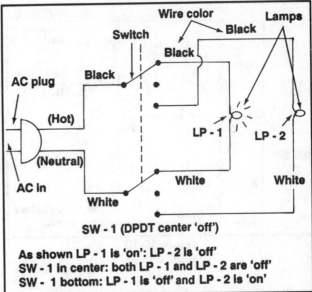

Figure 10-8
Lamp circuit with double pole switch

(double pole single throw) switch. The black wire goes to the gold terminal and the white wire goes to the silver terminal. Be careful, though. While this is the standard for AC switches and switching circuits, some might be wired wrong, or require that the hot lead goes to the silver terminal. Always turn the power off or check the terminals with a volt meter before you work on any switching circuit.

In Figure 10-9 you see two separate switches controlling a single lamp. This is a three-way

switch circuit. The switched wire is orange to show that it may or may not be hot. Blue and red are also used as switched wires. A circuit like this allows you to turn a light on or off from either switch location. For instance, you could turn a light on at the gate, and off at the garage or inside the house.

Figure 10-10 shows a DC circuit, a switch, relay, and a battery. When switch SW-1 is closed, a positive DC charge is applied to the base of the transistor Q-1. (A transistor is a three-terminal

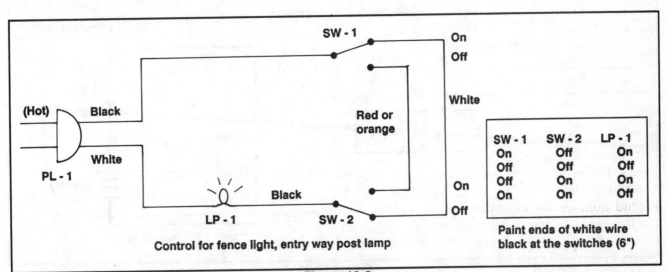

Figure 10-9
Two switches control one lamp

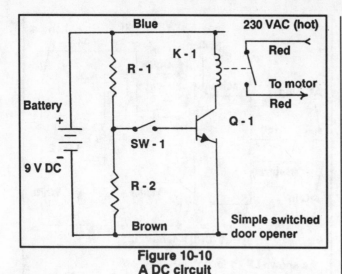

Figure 10-10
A DC circuit

semiconducting device that switches or amplifies low voltage signals. Most garage door openers and alarm systems contain transistors.) This DC charge on the base of the transistor causes the

relay K-1 to close and complete the 230-volt AC circuit to the motor, causing the motor to start.

The positive wire is blue and the negative wire is brown. This is the latest international color code for DC. This type of circuit lets you control devices that require large voltages and currents with small switches and currents, such as motors. A common application for this is the hand-held remote control unit for a garage door opener. When you press the button, 9 volts DC is applied to the circuitry in the remote unit which transmits a signal to the controller attached to the main unit. A signal switching transistor turns on the 110 volt AC power to the drive motor.

Low voltage switches control alarm circuits, security monitor circuits, electric fences and sprinkler systems.

Figure 10-11 is a magnetic switch system. When the gate is closed, a magnet on the gate opens a switch on the gate post. If someone opens the gate, the magnetic field is broken and the switch on the gate post closes, completing the

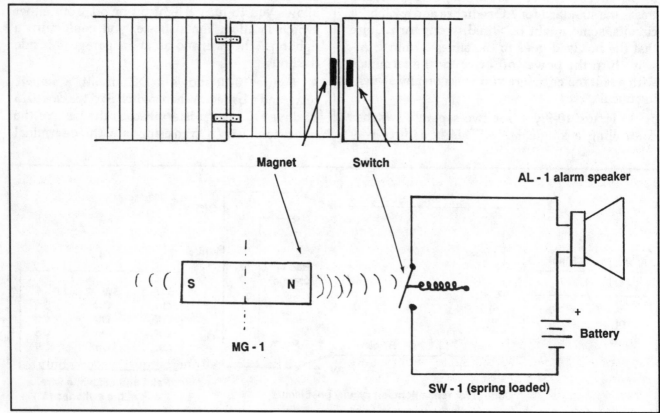

Figure 10-11
Magnetic switch system

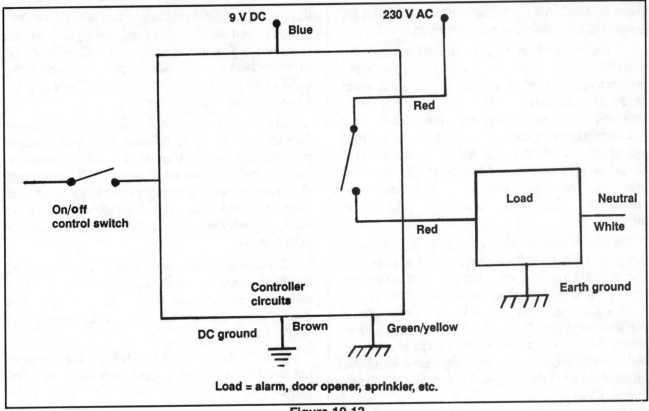

Figure 10-12
A black box diagram drawing

alarm circuit. The switch in Figure 10-11 is a magnetic reed switch. You can buy these as a two-piece plastic-encapsulated set at most electronic hobby stores. One piece contains the magnet (MG-1), the other the reed switch (SW-1). Power comes from a 9-, 12-, or 24-volt DC battery. The speaker (AL-1) is a special speaker designed to work on DC current.

This low voltage system is not recommended for voltages above 48 volts. You only need one wire or conductor per circuit. An 18 gauge wire will do. It loops from the battery to the switch, from the switch to the speaker and back to the battery.

Each switch requires a separate circuit, but they can all connect to the same battery and speaker. For instance, you can install one circuit and switch for the rear yard gate, one for the front yard gate and one for the driveway gate. This system has a very low voltage and current drain, so the battery can be several hundred feet away.

You can substitute a low voltage lamp for the speaker. Just be sure it matches the battery voltage. You can also add a toggle switch at the battery to turn the system off when it's not required.

Figure 10-12 shows a black box diagram of a circuit. The load can be an alarm system, a sprinkler system, a fire detector or a garage door opener. The term *black box* refers to a self-contained manufactured unit. A drawing that includes a black box is called a block diagram drawing. It doesn't show any of the circuitry in the box — it only shows you how to connect it to external switches, controls and devices. That way, the manufacturer doesn't have to give away any of their trade secrets.

This type of drawing is much easier to read than a fully detailed one, because it shows only the hookup points and external devices.

Notice the color code for the *earth ground* wire. Green with a yellow stripe is the international color code for ground wires. In the U.S., plain green is used. All electronic equipment must be grounded to protect the operator from shock.

If there's a short in the equipment and the short is to the chassis, the earth will absorb the electricity. All conduit run to, in, or from your fence or wall must have a bare copper wire clamped to it. This *ground wire* then clamps to a 1/2-inch diameter copper rod buried vertically 6 feet or more in the ground. All power meters and circuit breaker boxes must also be earth grounded this way. The wire clamping must be metal-to-metal, with all dirt, oil, paint, and insulators removed.

Sand the surface where you're going to attach the ground strap with some 120 grit sandpaper. Use 10 or 12 gauge bare copper wire from the equipment chassis to the ground rod. Most chassis have a green grounding screw where you attach the ground wire. If there isn't one, then either attach the wire to a case screw on the chassis, or drill a hole and use a self-tapping screw. Bend the ground wire into a hook shape and attach it as in Figure 10-13 F.

Building supply centers carry 1/2-inch by 6 or 8 foot ground rods and wire clamps.

Use AC outlets with GFCI (ground-fault circuit interrupter) protection. You can buy those for about $15, and install them in place of unprotected outlets. These outlets contain a breaker that prevents the user of an electrical device from getting a shock if something shorts out. You can also get GFCI circuit breakers to replace existing ones in the main electrical panel.

Under most codes, all wet area and outdoor AC outlets must be GFCI protected. Wet areas are baths, kitchens, laundry rooms and pool or spa areas. Circuit breakers are easy to change. Most of them just snap into the panelboard. Turn the main power off at the meter to be on the safe side.

Conduit

Conduit is metal or plastic pipe used to protect electrical wires. If the electrical code doesn't allow the use of unprotected cable, you'll have to install conduit and then pull electric conductors through that conduit. Metal conduit is available in several weights: *thin wall*, *intermediate* and *rigid*. You can bend thin wall conduit with a conduit bender so it turns corners and fits odd angles. You can't bend rigid conduit. It has to be cut and threaded for elbow fittings to turn corners.

Check with your local building inspector before you install conduit. Some cities and counties prohibit the use of thin wall conduit outdoors. Plastic conduit is available as gray PVC (polyvinyl chloride) pipe. It's designed just for electrical work. Don't confuse it with the white PVC or black polyethylene pipe which is only suitable for water lines.

Conduit comes in sizes from 1/2 inch up to 12 inches in diameter. You'll use either 1/2, 3/4 or 1 inch conduit for most work. The size you need depends on the number, size, and type of wire you're installing.

Refer to Table 3A of the NEC for a complete list. But here's a short guide to minimum requirements.

Wire gauge	1/2" conduit	3/4" conduit	1" conduit
#8	1 wire	3 wires	5 wires
#10	4 wires	6 wires	11 wires
#12	4 wires	8 wires	13 wires
#14	6 wires	10 wires	16 wires

NEC is *National Electrical Code* published by the National Fire Protection Association. The NEC is the bible for all electrical work.

Planning a Wiring Job

How do you know how many wires you'll need, and their sizes? Your circuit diagram, the schematic, will give you your wire count. The size is determined by the *load* the wire must carry. Load is the total current the wire must carry from all sources. The lamp on the driveway wall in Figure 10-14 will use a 110 volt AC, 100 watt bulb. Remember, current equals power divided by voltage. So the load current will be one amp (100 watts divided by 110 volts AC). A #14 wire, rated at 15 amps, will handle this load with no problem. Now suppose you had ten of these lamps all hooked to

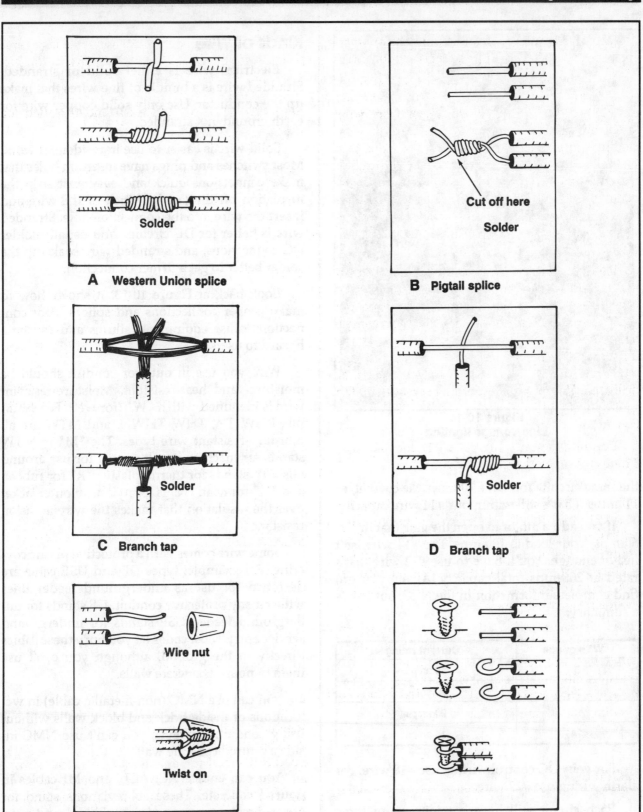

A   Western Union splice

B   Pigtail splice

Cut off here

Solder

C   Branch tap

D   Branch tap

Solder

Wire nut

Twist on

E   Wire nut

F   'J' hook

Figure 10-13
Proper wire connections

Figure 10-14
Line voltage lighting

Kinds of Wire

Electrical wire is either solid or stranded. Stranded wire is a bundle of fine wires that make up the conductor. Use only solid copper wire for earth ground, not stranded.

Solid wire is easier to use in residential work. Most switches and plugs have insertion holes that make connections quick and easy. Just strip the insulation off the last half inch of the wire and insert the wire into the connection hole. Stranded wire is better for DC circuits. You usually solder DC connections, and stranded wire soaks up the solder better to get a firmer connection.

Look back at Figure 10-13. It shows how to make proper connections and splices. Poor connections cause equipment failures and can be a hazard to users.

Wire you use in outdoor conduit should be moisture- and heat-resistant. Moisture-resistant wire is identified with a "W" (for wet). For example, RHW, TW, THW, THWN, and MTW are all moisture-resistant wire types. The "M" in MTW stands for machine use. It's rated for use around oils. "T" stands for thermoplastic, "R" for rubber, and "H" for heat. "N" is for nylon, an outer jacket over the insulation that makes the wire abrasion resistant.

Some wire comes with a protective plastic covering. For example, types UF and USE cable are designed for use as underground feeder lines without any protective conduit. UF stands for underground feeder, USE stands for underground service entry. Most codes let you bury these cables directly in the ground, although you can't use them in poured concrete walls.

You can use NMC (non-metallic cable) in wet locations or inside brick and block walls without using conduit. However, you can't use NMC inside a poured concrete wall.

You can encase AC, ACL, and MI cables in poured concrete. These abbreviations stand for *armored cable*, *armored cable lead shielded*, and *metal shielded*, respectively. AC, ACL, and MI cable are designed for use in concrete. They stand up under heat during curing and corrosion from alkali and minerals in the mix.

the same circuit. You have 10 times the current, or 11 amps. That's still within our #14 wire capacity.

If you add a motor to open the gate that draws 6 amps, your load is 16 amps. The #14 wire isn't heavy enough. You'll have to use #12 wire that's rated at 20 amps total capacity. Again, you can find complete information in the NEC, but here's a summary:

Wire gauge	Current rating
8	40 amps
10	30 amps
12	20 amps
14	15 amps

For your DC control wiring, use #18 wire. For alarm wiring use #22 wire.

Each circuit will have a minimum of three wires: hot, neutral, and ground. If you use metal conduit, that can serve as the earth ground. If you're using plastic conduit, you'll need a fourth wire, bare copper with no insulation.

It's usually cheaper to bury cable than it is to run wire in conduit. But buried cable has a disadvantage. If wire in conduit has to be replaced, it's usually easy to pull the old wire out and install new. Burying new cable can be a major project. I recommend you use conduit for all buried and embedded applications. The wire is cheaper, replacement is easier, and you'll meet code requirements without any question.

Use plastic-coated cables outdoors for low-voltage lighting (less than 49 volts AC). Malibu lights and similar systems use 12 or 24 volt circuits, so plastic cable is acceptable. For fixtures that use regular 110 volt AC power, use AC or MI cable.

...Before You Dig

Be careful when you're digging footings and foundations for fences and walls. There might already be underground wiring (or plumbing) in place. Telephone and electrical service lines should be in conduit, but you may find some that aren't. If you suspect that electrical, phone, water or gas lines exist where you're going to dig, check with the utility companies. They usually mark the location of their lines. Look for a yellow caution tape buried over the lines, about 18 inches under ground. There should also be a piece of 2 x 10 lumber buried about 12 inches above the lines, but don't count on that.

Pulling Wire Through Conduit

Conduit is installed without any wire in it. Once it's installed, you *pull* the wire through it. The method depends on the type of conduit you're using. With flexible conduit, you snake a flexible wire (sometimes called a *fish line*) through the conduit, attach conductors to the line, then pull the line back out until the conductors are pulled all the way through. Pulling wire is easier if bends in flexible conduit have a minimum radius of 14 inches. It also helps to use talc or commercially-available pulling lubricant on the wires. NEC Article 346-10 specifies code requirements for bends.

If you're using rigid conduit, install *junction boxes* at each turn. You pull the wire from junction box to junction box. Don't cut the wire at the inter-mediate boxes unless you're branching to a second or third location.

You may need a helper at each box to help guide and feed the wire so it doesn't get tangled.

Support for Conduit

When you install conduit above ground, suspended below a fence rail for instance, be sure to secure it adequately. NEC Articles 346-12 and 347-8 give the maximum distances between supports. I suggest no more than 36 inches for all types of conduit. At terminal locations for motors, lamps, or switches, put a cable support within 12 inches of the box or fixture.

Buried Cable

When installing longer runs of buried cable, I use a small gas-powered trencher with digging blades on a revolving wheel. A trencher makes short work of digging a 6-inch-wide, 2-foot-deep trench for cable. It will cut through most soils and many tree roots. Rental costs about $120 per day. You can cut a 50-foot-long cable trench in less than an hour. Depending on what you pay for labor, it doesn't make sense to hand dig a trench that's much more than 10 feet long.

Use watertight conduit outside. That means you can't use thin wall electrical conduit and fittings, or rigid conduit, both of which are restricted to indoor use, *unless* they have watertight fittings. Flexible BX type conduit isn't permitted in wet areas with one exception, that of connecting a motor to a junction or cut-out safety switch box. PVC Schedule 80 conduit is permissible. PVC conduit uses solvent welded (glued) fittings. Metal conduit should be connected with fittings that have a rubber O-ring compression seal.

Junction Boxes

The NEC requires that you leave 6 inches of unshielded wire inside any junction box where you connect to the load. That means if you're using shielded cable, you have to strip the shield and leave 6 inches of unshielded wire inside the box. That allows some slack in case you have to cut the end off the wire to replace or repair the load device. You'll still have enough wire to splice into. Otherwise, you might have to pull a new length of cable to the box.

Junction boxes are covered by code, also. There must be a required amount of free air space inside them for working and cooling purposes. As a rule of thumb, use a 2" x 4" box to connect a single load device to the line. Use a 4" x 4" box for up to three devices. Article 370 of the NEC lists box sizes and the wires they'll accommodate. Allow 3 cubic inches of space inside the box for each wire. For example, a 4" x 4" by 2-1/8" box contains 30.3 cubic inches. That's enough space for 15 #14 wires, 12 #10 wires, or 10 #8 wires.

When you buy junction boxes, they don't have any holes for the wires, only *knockouts* (circular indentations) on all sides. Each indentation can be removed with the tap of a pointed tool. Remove only the knockouts you need. Most boxes have knockouts of several sizes. Knock out only as much as you need for the size conduit or cable you're using. Don't knock out any holes you won't use. The electrical inspector will reject the job if your junction boxes have unused holes.

Electrical junction boxes come in several sizes and types. Select those designed for wet areas or outside use. Some codes allow plastic boxes, some don't. I prefer molded plastic boxes since they don't rust or corrode. Covers and fittings for junction boxes are sold separately. Be sure to buy watertight covers and fittings for outside use.

Concealing Cable and Conduit

How do you run conduit up a wood post without it being noticeable? It's buried underground along the fence line, but what about where you want to install a lamp fixture on the post? First, make a 90 degree bend to the post. Then there are a couple of things you can do.

1) *Dado* a channel on the post for the cable, staple your cable into it, nail a face board over it, then paint everything to match.

To dado a channel, you need either a router with a straight bit or a radial arm saw with a set of dado blades. They're small chipper blades sandwiched between two outer cutting blades. You can buy the blade sets for about $60 at most builder's hardware stores. Dado blades let you cut grooves from 1/4 to 1 inch wide with one pass of the saw.

Use electrical staples which are about 5/8-inch wide and have an insulated flat top on them to secure the cable.

2) Make your post from four separate pieces of lumber nailed together to form a square raceway. Your wire goes inside.

Figure 10-15 shows how to hide the wiring.

Choose the Right Fixtures

Remember that post lamp fixtures vary in the way you mount them. Some bolt down onto a solid wood surface, while others slip over the post. The ones that fit over posts come with bases of different shapes and sizes to fit round or square posts, rough or finished lumber. The job is easy with the right fixture, and very hard with the wrong one.

Place Fixtures Carefully

What is your lighting intended to do? Light a walkway? Provide security? Create a mood? Let's start with a mood.

Mood lighting should be low voltage lamps with colored lenses. Place them so they shine on trees, plants, or walls. Lights along a wall should be about 10 feet apart.

You can also use low voltage systems for walkway lighting. Place the lamps about 18 inches high, again, about 10 feet apart. The fixtures should direct light down onto the walk. If you place walkway lighting on posts, be careful to direct lights down at the walk, not at eye level. A good height for walkway lighting is 48 to 52 inches, and 24 to 30 inches for driveways.

Don't put driveway lighting too close to the drive where it's easy to hit with a car. Pay careful attention to the height, also. If lights are too low,

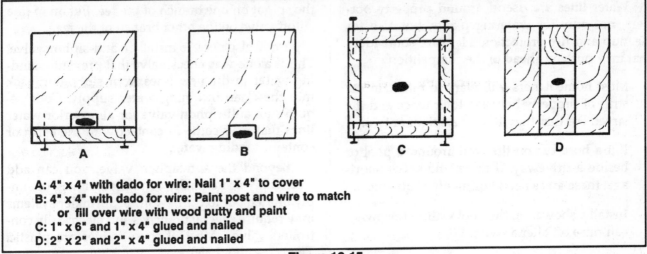

A: 4" x 4" with dado for wire: Nail 1" x 4" to cover
B: 4" x 4" with dado for wire: Paint post and wire to match
     or fill over wire with wood putty and paint
C: 1" x 6" and 1" x 4" glued and nailed
D: 2" x 2" and 2" x 4" glued and nailed

Figure 10-15
Hide wiring in fence posts

the driver can't see them, too high and they shine in the driver's eyes. Experiment and find the height your customer is most comfortable with.

Use flood lamps for security lighting. Wire these so they're switched on only when there's a suspected intrusion. (They consume a lot of electricity, so they're expensive to operate.) Position them so they flood the entire area with light, including corners and walls. Because these lights are very bright, they can be disturbing to motorists and neighbors — that's why they're rigged to come on only when necessary.

You can now buy inexpensive floodlight units that contain motion sensors. They turn on for a preset time whenever movement occurs within a certain range in front of them. This is handy for driveway or entry lighting. Check these out for the features you need. Some models don't have a sensitivity adjustment, so they may come on every time a person or vehicle passes the building. Also, get one with a daylight sensor, so they won't come on during the day.

You can also use low wattage perimeter lights that stay on all night. Forty to 60 watt lamps usually aren't disturbing unless they shine directly into someone's room.

Use timers or photocells to activate outdoor lamps. Mount photocells so they're not triggered by headlights or street lighting.

Make a plan view drawing of the property before you install security lights and alarms. Mark the sensitive areas such as walks, driveways, entries, and corners. Walkway lamps will light an area about 5 feet in diameter. A lamp placed on a post will light a 10 to 20 foot circle. Flood lamps shed light in a V pattern for 30 to 40 feet.

Sketch in the light coverage on your plan. Once it's the way you want it, decide on the best paths for the cable runs. You may need several — one for low voltage lamps, one for line voltage lamps, one for the front yard, another for the back, and separate lines for entries and driveways. Include a fuse or circuit breaker in each line, a disconnect switch, and a timer or sensor. You'll want a disconnect switch so you can maintain the system without turning power off at the main.

Make the cable runs as short as you can to cut costs and increase performance. Then prepare your materials list from the plan drawing.

Plumbing

A plumbing code is enforced in your community just like the electrical code is enforced. I strongly suggest you follow the code. The order form at the back of this volume lists several helpful books on the subject.

Water lines are useful around property borders, not only for watering plants, but also for cleanup and fire protection. Here are some ideas that may put you ahead of the competition:

◆ Most homeowners will want to maintain the strip of property between their fence and the street. For this, they'll need a spigot or two.

◆ Put a hose bib on the wall around a pool or beside a driveway. If there's no water shortage, these areas need hosing off frequently.

◆ Install a shower on the pool wall so the owner can rinse off after a swim.

◆ Mount a large wash basin with both hot and cold water in the side or back yard for washing off tools, pets, kids, and dad, when he's through working on the car.

◆ Build a fountain at the back corner of the yard or beside the patio.

◆ Install drip irrigation along the fence line so sprinklers don't water the fence. Include some hose outlets to use in case of fire, when it might not be possible to get close to the building.

◆ If you enclose an area for trash containers, put a sprinkler head on the fence. It could prevent a disaster, and may lower fire insurance costs.

Plan Your Layout

First, determine where the nearest water source is, and where you'll hook into the existing system. Now, use graph paper to draw a plan to scale. Locate all your connections and label them. Decide what kind of materials you'll use, and what size. And you'll need to know whether the lines will go above ground, underground, or inside a wall.

The best place to connect to the existing water line is often at the main inlet turnoff valve, the one where the pressure regulator is. There's usually a spigot there, too. The next best location is at an existing spigot that's close to where you want the new line.

Turn off the water at the main valve, and remove the existing spigot. Add a tee and reinstall the spigot on one branch of the tee. Put an in-line cutoff valve on the other branch of the tee.

You'll also need to install an anti-siphon valve. This is a one-way check valve that prevents standing water in the new lines from siphoning back into the clean incoming water supply. Code requires an anti-siphon valve for all exterior water lines that may come in contact with the earth or contain standing water.

Beyond the anti-siphon valve, you can add electrically or manually controlled valves, or simply branch out to the new lines. Sprinkler systems may require several branches and electrically controlled valves. Most of these valves are plastic. They cost about $30.

PVC pipe for outdoor installations costs about $1.25 per 10-foot length. Install it so it's protected from physical damage and freezing. In most places, it's acceptable to bury the pipe in the ground, 12 inches below the frost line.

Use 3/4-inch pipe for the main runs and 1/2-inch pipe for the branch runs. If you need more branches off the 1/2-inch pipe, use 3/8-inch flexible PVC tubing for the branches. You'll need bends, ells, and tees. These cost about 50 cents each.

Connecting PVC Pipe

First, sand the mating surfaces to remove the manufacturing glaze from the plastic. Then condition the connections with "purple primer" and wait a minute or more for the primer to set up.

Follow with PVC cement as follows: Apply a liberal application of the cement to one or both surfaces. Hold the pieces you're joining so that one of them is a quarter turn away from its finished position. Quickly push the two pieces together and twist them a quarter turn back to the way you want them. Twisting the pieces together helps spread the cement and prevents voids that can result in leaks. You can handle the pieces within minutes, but I suggest you don't pressure or water test them for at least 24 hours, after everything has had a chance to set properly.

If you're connecting a fountain, sink, or fire sprinkler to the line, put a cutoff valve near the fixture to make servicing easier. When you install irrigation sprinklers, you'll need cutoff risers.

These are short lengths of pipe, threaded at both ends. One end screws into a threaded coupler, and the sprinkler head screws into the other end.

Install a tee or an elbow at each sprinkler head location along the water line. Install the threaded couplers on the tees or ells. Insert the risers into the coupler, then attach the sprinkler heads.

Use pop-up sprinkler heads if they're to be installed at ground level. Water pressure makes these pop up, but they retract into the ground when the water is turned off. This makes it easy to rake or mow. Make sure that when they're up, they're up enough. I've seen some that weren't.

Outdoor Sinks

Use a sturdy mounting for an outdoor sink. They take a lot of abuse from home mechanics and dog-washing kids. If you're installing hot water as well as cold, you'll need a separate line. You'll also need a heater, if it's not practical to connect to the owner's main hot water supply. You're also required to install an anti-siphon valve and a cutoff. Insulate the hot water lines if you can.

Your building department may require that you use copper or brass for these lines, but CPVC or PB may be acceptable. CPVC is chlorinated polyvinyl chloride. It is gray/brown in color and is rated for hot water use. It's about 3 to 5 times more expensive than PVC, and requires different primer and cement.

PB is polybutylene, a heat-resistant flexible thermoplastic. You can get information about PB from Genova Products™, Davison, Michigan. PB isn't acceptable everywhere, so check your local code.

If you must use copper lines, I suggest you use flexible copper tubing. First, install 1-inch diameter PVC pipe with bends made to a radius of 12 to 18 inches or more. Then feed the flexible copper lines through the PVC pipe. There are two advantages to doing this. The copper won't corrode where it contacts the earth or concrete, and it's easier to make repairs. Copper tubing requires copper fittings.

Drain water from an outdoor sink is considered *gray water*. This means that it's not contaminated with human waste. Some localities will allow you to drain this water directly into the ground, while others require you to connect to the sewer line or provide a dry well.

Some codes may consider water supplied to an outdoor sink to be non-potable, that is, not safe to drink. If that's the case, you'll probably have to post a sign to that effect.

Fountains and Waterfalls

In most places, garden fountains are required to be recirculating — the same water is used over and over. You'll need a pump, and your customer will probably want lights as well. Be sure to provide electrical outlets for both of these.

Put a screen or filter on the recirculating drain or pump inlet to keep debris out of the pump.

Install a spigot near the base of the fountain or waterfall, and include a small spillway to the pool so it's simple to replenish evaporated water. That way the owner can overfill the pool once in a while to flush away floating dirt and leaves.

Fire Sprinklers

Sprinklers are rated according to their type of use, and the temperature that will set them off. Some will reset themselves after the fire is out, but others have to be reset manually. Install an in-line cutoff valve just ahead of the sprinkler line. Install this valve in a secure location, or outfit it with a lock to prevent unauthorized or accidental shut-off.

If you're installing sprinklers over a trash collection area, your local code might specify the height to install the sprinkler heads above the trash bins. Most codes require the water feed line be protected against fire damage and freezing. You can probably meet this requirement by embedding the water line in concrete or large diameter steel pipe.

And, speaking of fire, Figure 10-16 shows key access for an electronically operated gate. The police and fire departments have keys to open these. This type of lock may be required in some cities for

Figure 10-16
Emergency access to secured gate

areas that are secured by electronic code or phone systems.

Maintaining Electrical and Plumbing Systems

Lights, receptacles, alarms, and electric gates need periodic maintenance. So do spigots, automatic sprinklers, waterfalls, and fountains. Light bulbs burn out, sockets rust and corrode, switches and sensors fail or wear out, and motors need service. Sprinklers get clogged, valves leak, pipes freeze, and pumps burn out.

Even if you don't choose to install these things yourself, you should know something about them. I've been called on many times to do some trouble-shooting and make minor repairs.

So what's so hard about changing a light bulb? Usually nothing. Usually. Except for outdoor lamp fixtures. They're often flimsy, made from steel with a brass or painted coating. They rust quickly. And they're usually mounted on a 6- or 7-foot post. If you didn't install the fixture, just getting *to* the bulb might take a Houdini. And, if the fixture isn't grounded properly, you may be in for a shock.

Here's my suggestion: Turn off the switch, or better yet, cut off the electricity at the circuit breaker box. Especially if the fixture is controlled by more than one switch. Three- and four-way circuits can still be dangerous, even when the light is off.

Look for knurled nuts on the top or sides of the fixture. Those usually let you gain entry. In some cases, when you loosen the nuts, the rails that hold the glass in place loosen also. If it looks like that's the case, wrap some masking tape around the fixture. That may help keep things in place. If the glass falls out and breaks when you're changing the bulb, guess who gets to buy new glass — if it's still available.

Removing a Stubborn Light Bulb

Too often, when you start to unscrew the burned-out bulb, one of two things happens. Either it won't come loose, or the whole socket or lamp base moves. What's happened is that the socket has bonded to the fixture by *galvanic action*. Metal molecules from one material have migrated to the adjacent piece of metal.

Now what? First, turn off the power, then slip a small plastic bag over the bulb. Put on some thick leather gloves and grab the bulb as close to the base as you can. Then turn. You may have to hold the socket base at the same time to keep it from moving. Most of the time, the bulb will come out in one piece. If it does break, the gloves should protect your hands and the plastic bag should contain the glass fragments.

When this happens, you're left with the base of the bulb stuck in the socket. Be sure the power is *off*. Slip one tong of a pair of needle-nose pliers between the socket and the base of the bulb. Tighten your grip on the pliers. Turn the pliers through 90 degrees. This should bend the bulb base away from the socket without damage to the socket. Do this several times around the bulb base until it comes loose.

When you install the new bulb, coat the threads with *non-conductive* electrical heat sink grease. You can buy it from electronic hobby stores for about $1.50 a tube. It keeps the new bulb from sticking the next time it needs changing. Put some more of this grease on the threads of the bolts that hold the fixture together. That makes the next bulb change *much* easier.

By the way, most outdoor fixtures are rated for bulbs only up to a certain size. Look for the maximum wattage stamped on the fixture somewhere. Don't put in a larger bulb. It may melt the fixture, or cause a fire.

Repairing Outlets or Sockets

Use an *outlet tester* or a *VOM* to check outlets. You can get the outlet tester at most electronic stores for about $6. It looks like a two-to-three-prong adapter plug with three LEDs on the face. The LEDs (light emitting diodes) glow to show if the circuit is live or not, whether the ground is connected, and if the hot side of the plug is wired correctly. As you look at a three-prong electrical plug with the U-shaped opening down, the right socket should be the hot, or voltage, side. The left side is the neutral, or return, side. The U is the ground. If the tester shows that this is not so, *turn off the electricity* and replace the socket.

To remove a socket or duplex receptacle, remove the screw in the center of the cover and then the two screws on the ears of the socket. Pull the socket straight out about 5 to 6 inches. Using a pair of dikes, clip the wires as close to the socket as you can. Strip the insulation from the wires with a wire stripper. Don't nick or cut into the copper wire. Strip about 1/2 inch of insulation from the end. There's a gauge on the back of the new socket to show you how much to strip.

Hold the socket in position with the U down and facing you. Tip the socket forward and insert the white wire in the top round hole to the left on the back of the socket. The black wire goes in the hole on the right. Bend the green wire (or the bare wire) into a U and attach it to the green hex-head screw terminal on the side of the socket. Push the socket into the box, and screw it into place.

For outdoor fixtures, the socket should have a water-resistant socket cover. The cover has a rubber gasket. Put a thin layer of silicon grease or caulk on the gasket and then install the cover. Turn on the electricity and test the socket with your outlet tester.

Your maintenance kit should also include the VOM I mentioned above. The letters stand for volt-ohm meter. Buy one with a 3- to 4-inch-wide meter. They cost about $60. I can recommend both Simpson™ and Triplett™ meters. VOMs are sold for as little as $5, but you get what you pay for. A better meter will have a longer life bouncing around in the back of your truck.

Here's how to use a VOM to check an outlet:

1) Set the range scale to 250 volts AC.

2) Insert one probe into the U, and the other into the left socket hole. You should get a voltage reading of zero.

3) Now insert the probes into the U and the right socket hole. The reading should be from 105 to 120 volts AC.

If the voltage is under 105 volts AC, suspect a bad connection, a bad switch, or a bad circuit breaker. If the voltage is over 120 volts AC, but far less than 230 volts AC, look for a problem in the wiring. If the reading is zero, the ground connection has failed. Rewire it.

To check a lamp socket, set the VOM on the 250 volts AC scale. (Checking 220 volt power on a lower scale could damage the meter.) Put one probe on the bare metal of the outside of the socket. Touch the other probe to a water pipe or a copper rod pushed into the ground. The reading should be zero. If the meter shows any deflection at all, lower the range scale to 100 volts AC. The reading should be zero. Keep lowering the range until you get a reading. If this reading is above 10 volts AC, suspect a faulty ground connection. This is a dangerous situation. Correct it. Check the lamp base for a bare or green wire. Make sure this wire is attached to a water pipe, metal conduit, or ground rod.

Where there are several lamps around a property, test for *line loss*. This happens when wire is corroded, too small for the load, nicked or damaged. To check for line loss, first measure the voltage at the circuit breaker. Record this reading, then go to the most distant light or outlet socket. Measure this voltage and record it. The drop or difference between the readings should be from zero to a maximum of 2 or 3 volts AC. If the drop is from 3 to 8 volts AC, there's a potential problem. If the drop is over 8 volts AC, the problem already exists. Find it and correct it.

Use the *half way* method to isolate the problem. Repeat the check on a fixture or outlet half way between the circuit breaker and the last device you checked. If the reading is normal there, you know the problem is between that point and the end of the line. Otherwise, it's between that point and the breaker. You can continue to check midpoints within sections until you isolate the problem.

When you locate the problem, use the ohm meter part of the VOM to identify the cause. Turn the power off at the circuit breaker. Now, re-test the voltage with the voltage meter. It's important to re-test. You may have turned off the wrong circuit, or there may be a cross connection between two circuits. If you test a live circuit with your ohm meter, you'll have to buy a new meter.

On the voltage scale, *zero* means there is no voltage. On the ohm scale, it means there *is* a connection. If the meter registers infinity (∞), it indicates a lack of a connection. Anywhere in between means there is a connection with a resistance. If you check both ends of a wire, or across a closed switch, or from a neutral to a ground, you should get a reading of zero or near zero. If the reading is several ohms or more, then there's a problem of high resistance. High resistance will cause the voltage to be lower on one side of the component than on the other side. If the reading is infinite, try moving your probes. You may not be making a good connection.

If the reading is infinite after you try several test points, the item you're testing is *open* and won't conduct a current. Check switches in both the off and on positions. Replace the bad component with a new one. Switches and AC sockets are inexpensive, so keep a few in your tool box. They only cost a dollar or so, but you can charge from $5 to $35 to replace one.

Maintaining Gates and Security Systems

Whether or not you install them, you may be required to service automatic gates. They're relatively maintenance-free if they're tuned up regularly. Motors and chains should be oiled at least every few months. Clean trash and dirt from motors, chains and tracks. Oil rollers and wheels. Check for proper operation of rollers, motors and electrical circuits. Check for proper tension on the drive belt or chain.

Alarm systems require maintenance, too. First, make sure they're armed and respond when they're supposed to. Test key and button controllers. Lubricate keyholes, especially after wet weather. Use the DC volt meter on your VOM or the ohm meter to check sensors that don't work.

To maintain electrical fences, check for loose, broken, cracked, or missing insulators. You should be able to locate the manufacturer's name and part number on one of the remaining good insulators on the fence line. Most insulators simply thread out or unbolt from the post they're installed on. Insulators are available from agricultural suppliers or feed and grain stores. Cut back any bushes, grass, or tree branches that may contact the fence. Turn the power off before you do any of this, of course.

Make sure that all wire mesh and chain link fences are properly grounded. Metal fences both attract and conduct lightning strikes. Make sure there's a 1/2-inch copper rod driven at least 6 feet into the ground for every 150 linear feet of fence. Be sure the clamps that tie the fence to the ground rod are secure. (Fence posts can themselves serve as a ground rod, if at least 6 feet of their length is buried.)

Plumbing Repairs

Turn spigots on at least once a month, so they don't "freeze" in the closed position. Noisy spigots are usually the result of dirt that's lodged in the valve. Leaky ones probably need a new washer. Remove the spigot and give it a good cleaning. Replace washers if necessary.

Sprinkler heads become clogged so they don't spray where they're supposed to. Sometimes turning them on high will clear them. Otherwise, unscrew the head from the pipe and clean out any dirt, bugs, and little snails that may have moved in.

Water pumps are self-lubricating, but the motor that drives the pump usually is not. Oil motor bearings at least once every six months.

When you're called out for a repair, or if you're doing routine maintenance, look for physical damage, deterioration, blocked drainage and weep holes. Repair small things and do minor cleanups at no charge, as a gesture of good will that your customers will remember. Report any major problems you find, and write an estimate to repair them.

This chapter gave you some very basic information about plumbing and electrical work as it applies to fence and wall contracting. If you decide to offer these services, do your homework. Check out the local codes, and learn the latest tricks and techniques of each trade. Read about these subjects — the order card in the back of this manual is a good source for books.

Visit electrical and plumbing suppliers, talk to the people there, and pick up the free flyers. You can have some fun, and you'll learn things that will make money for you.

eleven

Retaining Walls and Rock Walls

Y ou build fences and ordinary walls to keep people, animals or things in or out of an area. You build retaining walls to keep land or water out of areas where people, animals or things need protection from them. Just as the purpose for retaining walls is different, the way you build them is different, too.

The earth we live on lets us use it in many different ways. We can build on it, dig it up and move it, burrow into it, level it off, and pile it up. The problem with earth is that sometimes it moves by itself. Hillsides come tumbling down during heavy rains and earthquakes. Mountains of rock fall down in the spring.

Water also takes its toll. Rivers, lakes, and oceans rise and fall when it rains, or when the moon's gravity pulls them. Sometimes they flow right through our homes and businesses.

People build retaining walls and dikes to help control this movement of earth and water. Most fence contractors can build small retaining walls and dikes and make money on them. Leave the big ones to heavy equipment operators and engineers.

Natural Earth Barriers

Some slopes have their retaining walls built in. You often see those in residential developments where the lots are filled on hilly ground. The front yard is level, but the lot slopes down to street level. Grass is planted on the level section, with ivy or other ground cover planted on the slope to hold the earth in place when it rains. I'm sure lots like the one in Figure 11-1 are familiar to you.

On steeper slopes, you can grade to create a series of steps, or *terraces*. The level parts break the force of flowing water. You can protect the terracing either with plants, or by reinforcing it with retaining walls. Figure 11-2 shows a terraced hillside.

Figure 11-1
A sloped lot with an ivy retainer

Figure 11-2
Terraces held by rocks

Reinforced Earth Barriers

Sometimes you'll have to face a bank with asphalt or concrete to protect it from erosion or undercutting by water flowing along its base. Use at least 4 inches of paving material for this pur-

pose. If you have a project like this with plenty of time to complete it, and you work near a concrete plant, you might be able to make a deal with the plant owner. He needs a place to clean out his trucks and dump excess concrete at the end of the day. You need the concrete, so you could probably work out a good trade.

Retaining Walls

Figure 11-3 shows a typical hillside residential lot where your talent for building retaining walls will be in great demand. The home builder has to contain the dirt at both the back and the front of the lot.

In Figure 11-4, you can see an inexpensive yet functional retaining wall. You can use this type of wall to a height of about 3 feet. This picture shows pressure-treated lumber, but used railroad ties work almost as well. You interlock the timbers at the corners and spike them together. Here I used number 60 spikes fitted through predrilled holes. You can buy drill bits made for telephone linemen to drill holes up to 14 inches deep. Then drive the spikes in from the top of each piece of lumber as you stack them. For extra security, you can spike the end pieces to the side pieces they butt up to.

You can use the same materials for higher retaining walls, but you fasten them together differently. First you have to dig and pour a foundation

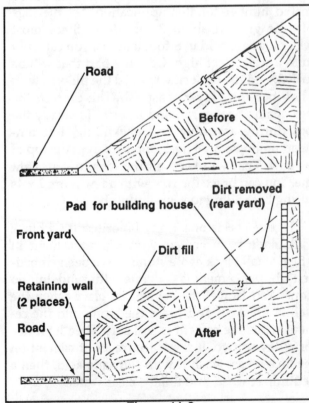

Figure 11-3
Residential lot retainers

Figure 11-4
Lumber retaining wall

Figure 11-5
Peeler logs shore up a planting bed

just like you would for a block wall. Then you insert rebar into the foundation every few feet, but never more than 3 feet apart. Check your local building code for the spacing required in your area. Remember, you can't put in too much rebar, but you can put in too little. Here's the rule of thumb I use: The distance between rebar shouldn't exceed three times the thickness of the wall. So for a 6-inch wall, I'd space the rebar 18 inches apart — *unless the building code calls for them to be closer.* Drill the timbers and set them down over the rebar. You can build a retaining wall up to 8 or 10 feet high this way.

Here's an important word of caution: Always check with your local building department when you build retaining walls over 3 feet high. And I recommend that you get help from a qualified engineering firm before you build a wall over 8 feet high.

You should have a copy of the code adopted in your area, but it's still a good idea to check with the inspector. What you need is his *interpretation* of the code. Reading and understanding the Uniform Building Code, or any of the other model codes, is a nightmare. I have nine years of college and years of experience in building engineering and construction, and I still have trouble interpreting the code. If you have the same problem, there's a book that explains the code in plain English. It's called *Contractor's Guide to the Building Code*, and you can

order it using the order form bound into the back of this manual.

You can build low retaining walls out of peeler logs. Figure 11-5 shows one. They don't have to be treated lumber for this application. Set the logs into the ground about 3 feet deep. Since most peeler logs are sold in 8-foot lengths, you can only build a wall 5 feet high. Coat the part that will be buried, and the back side toward the fill dirt, with a 1/4-inch-thick layer of asphalt. This protects the logs against water, rot, and insects. To steady the logs during assembly and backfilling, I recommend nailing a 2 x 4 horizontally across the top of the row. That will keep all the logs in a straight line. You can brace the row with a few more 2 x 4s during backfilling to keep it plumb.

Figure 11-6 is one of my favorites. It's a block wall that's been coated with topper cement in which small black agate stones have been embedded. Topper cement is concrete with sand, but no stone. You trowel the cement in place when the wall is finished, and press the stone into the cement while the cement is still soft. Then let it dry for a day or two. If there are traces of cement on the face areas, wash it with muriatic acid, then a neutralizer rinse, and finally, clear water.

Figure 11-7 shows another good idea. Here the block wall was coated with stucco. This picture

Figure 11-6
A block wall faced with stone

Figure 11-7
Coat a block wall with stucco

was taken in a small restaurant park area, but the idea would work well in an otherwise dull back yard.

You can cement angle brackets for the benches in place during construction, or add them later. Use two brackets for each 4 linear feet of bench. Secure the brackets in solid grout, or extend them completely through both sides of the block.

You can fill the area behind the bench with dirt, or leave it at grade. If there's a tree behind the wall like there is in the picture, don't backfill dirt against the tree trunk. You'll kill it. If necessary, build a second, smaller wall around the tree and then fill the area between the inner and outer walls with dirt.

In Figure 11-8, the combination planter and retaining wall is made from poured-in-place concrete. The vertical lines can be part of the mold or sawed into the concrete after the molds are released. A circular saw fitted with a masonry blade works well for cutting these grooves. Be sure to wear eye protection and a dust mask while cutting. The sloped front adds some character and style, as does the beveled top edge and inset bottom edge. You'd use both horizontal and vertical rebar in this, just as you would for building a foundation.

You can use piled rock to retain hillsides. Figure 11-9 shows rock retaining a slope on the western shore of Lake Tahoe in California. A poured concrete barrier holds the rock in place and the weight of the rock holds the hillside in place.

Figure 11-8
A poured concrete retaining wall

Figure 11-9
Loose rock retaining wall

Figure 11-10
A wall to prevent water erosion

Figure 11-11
View of a storm channel retainer

How do you build a retaining wall like the one in Figure 11-10? One way is to dig a trench about 15 to 20 feet away from the water's edge. The trench should extend down below the water line by whatever depth you desire the final water depth to be at the wall. For example, if the water will be 10 feet deep at the completed wall and the land elevation is currently 6 feet above the water line, dig your trench 18 feet deep. That's 10 feet for the water depth, 6 feet for the land elevation, and a minimum of 2 feet for the foundation. Now you can build your retaining wall in relatively dry earth. After it's cured for several weeks, backfill the land side and use a backhoe to dig out the water side.

More Retaining Walls

The retaining wall in Figure 11-11 defines a storm channel. The small stream in the background is fed by many other mountain streams and sometimes floods the area with terrific force. The farmer who owns the nearby fields likes the water for irrigation, but not when it washes his crops away. The two rows of steel posts were set into the ground and filled with concrete. Wire mesh was attached to the posts and the area inside the mesh filled with field stone and riverbed stone. Note the retaining rods between the rows of posts to keep the weight of the stones from pushing out the sides. When a flood comes roaring through, the stones deflect most of the force back into the

stream, and some of the water leaks through to irrigate the fields.

Figures 11-12 and 11-13 show a four-part retaining wall. The first part is the rock fill you see on the left of Figure 11-13. The second is the 2 x 12 rough-sawn pressure-treated lumber that holds the rock and dirt in place. Third, there are poured concrete pillars that hold the rock, dirt, timber, and guard rail in place. Fourth is the guard rail to keep vehicles from crashing into the retaining wall. You can see the guard rail bracket on the bottom right of Figure 11-13. That's a snow pole sticking up at an angle on the left side of Figure 11-12. It marks the location of the roadway in winter, for the snowplows.

You can also build retaining walls with chain link fencing and wire mesh. Those are often used on mountain roads where the amount of mud and rock that falls is minimal, but can still be a hazard to people and vehicles. A 2- to 3-foot-high chain link fence at the base of the hill catches the rocks. Chicken wire or hardware cloth, attached to the chain link, catches smaller pebbles and mud. The chain link fabric supports the finer mesh wire.

Another easy-to-build retaining wall is made of old tires. The wall keeps the land in place, of course. It also uses a few of the millions of discarded tires that are piling up in landfills throughout the country. Tires don't rot readily. Stack the tires in staggered layers and fill each layer with soil as you go.

Figure 11-12
A complete retaining wall

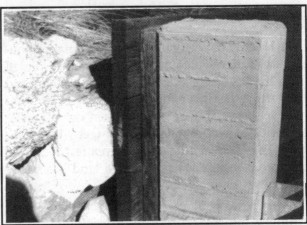

Figure 11-13
Detail shows rock fill, lumber
fence and concrete pillars

You can use old tires for *breakwater barriers* as well. A breakwater is a retaining wall that smooths out wave action. Tie the tires together in a staggered pile and sink them. Use #12 solid core copper or aluminum electrical wire for your tie wire. Avoid steel wire because it will rust eventually. Once they're tied, the tires will sink of their own weight. Keep building this pile until it extends 2 to 3 feet above the highest water line. Waves will break against the tires, protecting the area between the breakwater and the shore.

You can also use *well tiles* to build a retaining wall. Well tiles are circular concrete cylinders used to line the interior of dug wells. They're about 3 feet in diameter and from 2 to 3 feet high. Stagger stack the cylinders upright against the hillside and fill them with dirt. The visual effect is especially interesting if you slope them up the hillside by offsetting each tile about 50 percent of the one below it. Then you can plant ground cover in the exposed earth in each row of well tiles.

Temporary Retaining Walls

Before building a retaining wall near water, you have to get standing water out of the area. You do this with a temporary retaining wall, called a *cofferdam*. Cofferdams are effective down to about 90 feet.

You build a cofferdam by driving large, narrow sheets of steel into the bottom of the body of water. Use sheets long enough to embed 3 feet into the bottom and still extend above the highest water line. The thickness depends on the water depth. Use 12 gauge for water up to 6 feet deep, 3/8 inch to 15 feet deep, and 1/2 inch or more for water over 15 feet deep. Since you can usually only buy sheet metal in lengths up to 12 feet, you're limited to water 9 feet deep unless you weld sheets together.

Place the sheets in two or more parallel rows, at least 18 inches apart, 10 to 15 feet outward from where you want to build the wall. You'll need cross-bracing and lots of bolts to hold it all together. Fill the core between the sheets with dirt to stop water leakage and hold the cofferdam in place. Pump the water out of the work area, and you're ready to begin construction. Once the retaining wall is finished, you remove the cofferdam.

If that all sounds dangerous, it is. I'm not suggesting that you buy some sheet steel and start doing deep water projects. You'd probably drown. I just want you to know that there are ways to accomplish almost any job. There are firms that specialize in building cofferdams, and I highly recommend using one if the need ever arises.

If you need to divert water from a river or stream, dig another stream bed around the area where you have to work. Then dam the section you want to work in. Once you're finished, open the dam and refill the temporary channel with dirt.

Dikes

In the delta region of California, many thousands of square miles of land have been reclaimed from the Sacramento River. The flood plains and portions of the river bottom were isolated from the river by *dikes*. These are mounds of dirt about 20 feet wide at the top and 40 to 50 feet wide at the base. They can be anywhere from a few feet to 40 or more feet high. The reclaimed land is actually below the water level.

Where do you get the dirt? A lot of it you can bulldoze into place from the surrounding land. You can probably take some from the water side with a steam shovel. But most of it will have to be hauled in. And you'll have to cover the completed dike with grass or ground cover to prevent erosion. If the water side is exposed to running water, you may have to cover it with rock or concrete.

Designing Retaining Walls

Earth compacts and it expands. It moves both vertically (down) and laterally (sideways). It's composed of various types of soil, each of which acts differently from the others. It may be very dry, or saturated with water to form underground rivers. Your job is to determine soil type and build a retaining wall that will hold it in place.

Friction and Landslides

Try this. Rub your hand across your kitchen counter. Now wet a section of the counter and rub your hand across it again. Feel the difference? Your hand didn't move across the dry section as easily as it did over the wet section. *Friction* is the reason. The same thing happens with the ground. During a dry spell, a hillside remains in place due to friction between the dirt granules.

During a rain storm, friction is reduced. That creates both lateral and vertical pressure. When you dig into a hillside, you open a space for the compacted dirt to flow. As the ground becomes saturated with water, the ground may begin to move laterally. This happens most often to layers of sand or clay. If these layers are near the bottom

of the hillside cut, they flow out and leave the layers above unsupported. These upper layers collapse from their own weight. You have a landslide.

Old tires and well tiles help retain the soil because they increase surface friction, which resists lateral movement.

Gravel and rock layers offer more friction than sand or clay when moist or saturated. They resist lateral movement, so they need less lateral support. That's why retaining walls made of piled rock work so well. The highly irregular shape of most rock helps to lock it together.

Ice

Ice can also cause landslides. Water seeps into the soil and rocks, freezes, and expands. The force of this expansion is capable of cracking solid granite. When the ice thaws, a fracture is left in the rock. If the fracture is deep enough, some rock may be chipped off. Usually only the top 18 inches or so of the soil is affected. That's why retaining walls built to hold rock slides are only a few feet high. They're tall enough to catch the relatively small chunks of rock that break off and slide during the spring thaw.

You build rock slide walls 3 to 5 feet away from the base of the hill. All you need is a small catch area. Falling rock hits the ground in the catch space before it hits the wall. The ground absorbs most of the force, and the wall isn't damaged. The wall can be prefabricated concrete, wood, or even wire or chain link. You'd usually set these walls in place on the ground or bolt them into place in rock. That way, it's easy to remove sections to clean out the catch area in case of a slide. For a hillside homeowner, a wall like this can keep not only rocks but also mud and water from filling the back yard. You can build in benches or planters to make them more attractive.

Building Retaining Walls

Figure 11-14 shows a typical retaining wall. First, you'd trench the earth perpendicular to the wall's surface (the area within the broken line). As you build the wall, install steel rods called *dead*

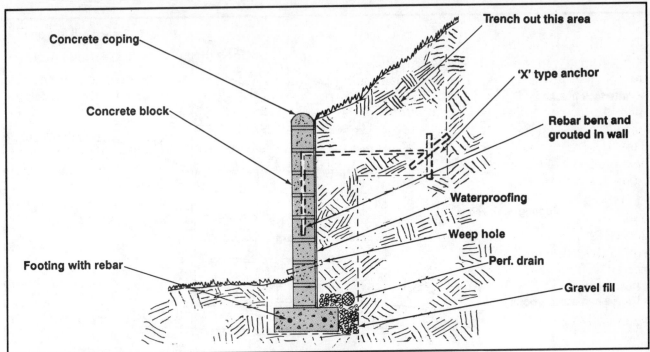

Figure 11-14
Typical retaining wall

man anchors. They're L-shaped within the wall and X- or dish-shaped at the other end. Use 1/2-inch rebar for the L shape and make the X section at least 18 inches long. The anchors should be at least 8 to 10 feet long, spaced on 4-foot vertical and 8-foot horizontal centers. So a wall 6 feet high and 30 feet long needs at least four anchors. If the same wall were 10 feet high, you'd need eight anchors, two rows of four. The distance from the top or side of the wall to the anchor should be more than 12 inches but less than 36 inches.

When the wall is completed, backfill the trench, burying the anchor rods. That helps the wall resist lateral or outward push of the earth. Backfill between the wall and the anchor also helps anchor the wall.

Figure 11-15 shows another way to stabilize a block retaining wall. Dig trenches perpendicular to the wall and build walls in these trenches. The perpendicular wall sections help resist lateral forces. You can use the same principle to anchor poured concrete, concrete block and timber walls. Interlock the walls together where they join. Use rebar bent into an L shape to make the connection in poured concrete or block walls. For block walls,

also interweave the blocks from the retaining wall and the perpendicular wall at the corner.

The distance between the perpendicular walls isn't critical, since most of the loading is downward instead of outward. For retaining walls up to 12 feet long, I recommend one perpendicular wall in the center. For walls over 12 feet long, use one every 8 to 16 feet.

Figure 11-16 shows a reverse solution. Here the perpendicular walls extend out from the face of the retaining wall to form braces. Although I show the brace extending the full height of the retaining wall, it's not necessary to make it that high. A brace wall will be effective as long as it's at least 70 percent as high as the retaining wall. These braces reduce the usable area in front of the wall. But that may not be a disadvantage if the piers separate parking spaces, for example.

The coping shown in Figure 11-16 is poured concrete. You make a form with two 2 x 10s held in place against the block with braces, concrete nails or large C clamps. Make one of the 2 x 10s about 1/8 inch lower than the other to create a slight slope for water drainage. Then pour the thick concrete and trowel it smooth. Or you can nail ply-

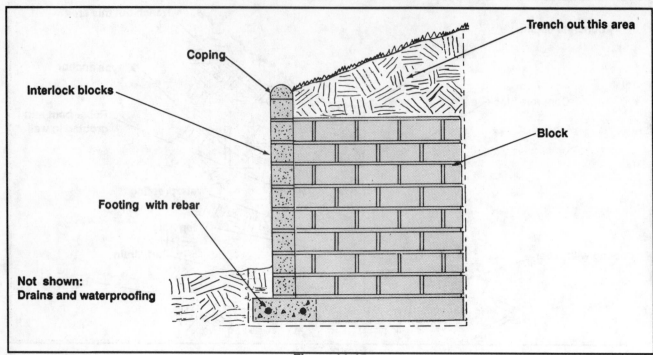

Figure 11-15
A perpendicular wall to stabilize a retaining wall

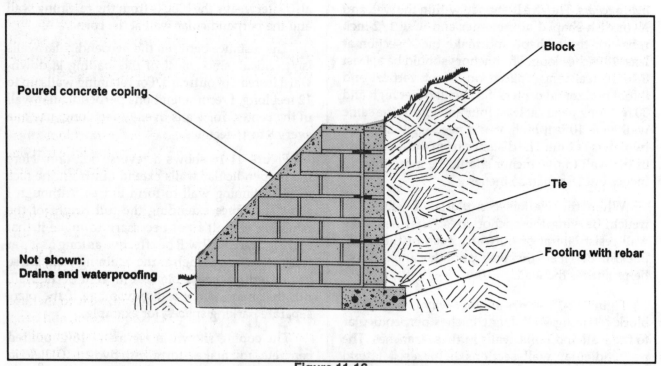

Figure 11-16
Supporting wall outside retainer

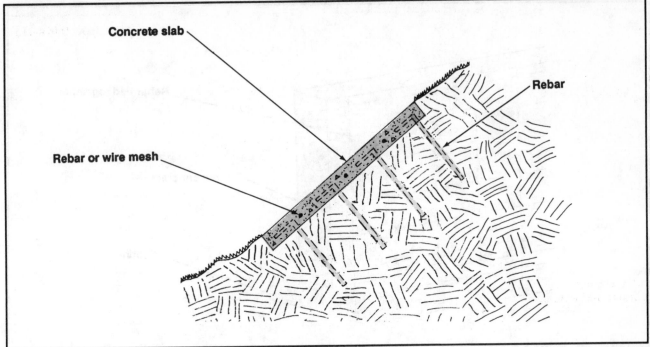

Figure 11-17
Concrete slab to retain a slope

wood across the form boards to form a tunnel, and fill it with concrete. That forms a smooth top, so you don't have to trowel. If you want a rounded top on the coping, you can trowel the partially set concrete or use a forming tool. That's simply a 2 x 10 in the shape you want the coping to be. Use it to scrape and pound the partly dry concrete into shape. Then pour small sections (1 to 2 feet) on sloped walls. For flat sections of wall, you can pour the whole section at once.

All three of these methods to stabilize a retaining wall work well, although each relies on a different physical principle. The dead man anchor holds the wall by tension — a pulling force. To tip over, the wall would have to pull out the anchor and all the dirt in front of the anchor.

The "in the hillside" perpendicular wall works on friction. To move, the retaining wall would have to pull out the brace wall *and* all the dirt exerting pressure on it. The "outside the hillside" brace wall also works on friction, but it's only the friction of the brace wall and the earth under it. It's not as effective against horizontal movement, but it's better at keeping the retaining wall from toppling over.

The dead man anchor and the "in the hillside" brace wall require trenching, so they're usually more difficult and expensive to build. And if neighbors are close, you may not be able to excavate into the hillside to build the brace wall.

No matter which kind you build, be sure to provide water drainage through the walls. Water buildup behind the wall exerts tremendous pressure and softens the dirt. Wet dirt has little friction, or holding power. You can use weep holes, a bed of gravel, or drainage pipes.

Figure 11-17 shows a hillside covered with concrete. Pour the slab in sections that are 3-1/2 to 6 inches deep. To help you plan, remember that a 5-yard load from a ready-mix truck will cover 405 square feet to a depth of 4 inches. Pound rebar 6 to 10 feet into the ground, perpendicular to the face of the slope. Leave about 2 feet exposed, and bend that at a right angle so it follows the contour of the slope and extends 2 to 4 inches above it. That way, the rebar will be embedded in the concrete. Space the rebar on 4 foot centers in all directions. Put wire mesh in the slab to prevent cracking. This wire mesh, designed just for embedment in cement, is available at most professional building

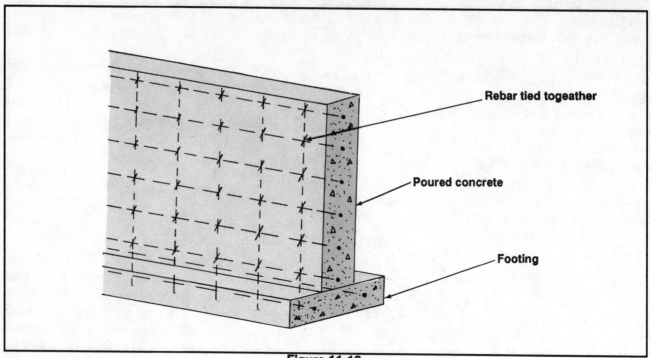

Figure 11-18
A poured concrete wall

supply centers. Check your local building code for specifics. You can use this method for slopes up to 45 degrees.

Here are a couple of tips to make pouring easier: First, start your pour from the top and work down, pushing the concrete downhill instead of uphill. Second, keep each section to a workable size. I recommend sections 8 to 10 feet wide and not more than 30 feet long. To cover a very large area, form sections in a checkerboard design and pour into alternate sections. After they've cured for a few days, go back and fill in the other spaces. It might seem easier to pour a 30 by 40 foot area all in one shot — but you'd probably have cracked concrete in a few months.

To minimize cracking, incorporate expansion joints into the slab. You can buy the tool to do it for about $4.00. It looks like a trowel with a V shape in the middle. You just lay a 2 x 4 across the partly-set concrete as a guide, then use the jointer to cut a V every 4 to 8 feet in each direction. That way, if the earth settles, the concrete will crack through the expansion joints where the cracks aren't apparent.

You should also consider "true" expansion joints. They're either plastic strips or redwood lumber strips separating each section. They provide space for the concrete to expand without buckling and cracking.

Pour a Concrete Retaining Wall

Figure 11-18 shows a poured concrete retaining wall. Use rebar in the footing, and insert rebar into the foundation every 12 to 16 inches. When the foundation is cured, tie horizontal rebar to the uprights, again at 12 to 16 inch intervals. Now put metal, fiberglass, or plywood forms in place. Most forms are built to "pin" together. The sections butt together, and pins inserted through eye loops hold them together. The front and back sections are held together with pinned metal tie braces which are left in the concrete after it dries. To remove the outside forms, just pull the pins and cut off the exposed ends of the embedded tie braces. Pour the concrete to a maximum depth of 20 inches. Wait a day or two for the concrete to form up, then make your second pour. Keep pouring layers until the forms are completely filled.

Once the entire wall is cured, waterproof the back side of the wall. Then backfill behind the wall. Use small stones or gravel, from 12 to 24 inches deep, for the bottom part of the backfill.

When you pour a concrete retaining wall, make the base wider than the top. Figure 11-19 shows several possible designs. These designs are all similar to those used to build dams, and they work for retaining walls, too. They all give added resistance to lateral force at the base.

Drawing A in Figure 11-19 could also be half of a *restraining* wall like the barrier you see in the center of divided highways. Those are designed to let an out-of-control vehicle ride up the side, rather than impact directly.

Water Pressure

Water weighs 62.4 pounds a cubic foot. That means if you make a container one foot square and a foot high and fill it with water, it will weigh 62.4 pounds plus the weight of the container. Now, if you make the container 4 feet high, the water weighs 249.6 pounds. The deeper the water, the higher the pressure at the bottom.

The bottom of a 1-foot-square by 4-foot-high container is 144 square inches (12 x 12), so to find the pressure of the water per square inch, divide the weight of the water by 144.

249.6 +144 = 1.73 PSI (pounds per square inch)

When a liquid, including water, tries to seek its own level, it exerts force in all directions. The PSI is the same to the side as it is downward. That's why, if the 1 by 1 by 4 foot container of water is made of concrete block, it will leak, because concrete block lets water flow through it at pressures above 1.7 PSI.

At higher points on the wall of the container, the pressure decreases until it reaches zero at the top. That's why dams are built with narrow tops, and very thick bottoms.

You need to be aware of all this when you're building retaining walls, or you might just be building a big strainer.

Here's an example. Suppose the water behind a dam is 150 feet high: 150 feet times 62.4 pounds is 9,360 pounds. Divide by 144, and you get 65 PSI at the bottom. That doesn't sound like too much until you consider that the dam is 100 feet long.

Now you have 100 times 9,360 or 936,000 pounds of force trying to push the bottom of the dam outward. That's just at the bottom. If you add up the pressures at each point up the wall, you see that it's into the millions of pounds.

What does this mean to you when you're building a retaining wall? Let's think about a typical hillside residential lot again. The builder had to dig into the hillside to make the foundation pad. The vertical cut is 24 feet deep. The soil layers are, top to bottom, topsoil and dirt, compacted earth, clay, gravel, compacted earth, and sand. Let's say each layer is 4 feet deep. The gravel layer is, therefore, 12 to 16 feet down from the top of the hill.

Now let's assume that there's a lake on the opposite side of the hill. See Figure 11-20. The elevation of the water in the lake is 20 feet higher than the elevation of the top of the gravel vein. Gravel layers between compacted soil and rock are good conductors of water. In fact, a gravel layer can become a flowing stream.

Lake water will try to reach the lowest level possible. The bottom of the gravel layer is 24 feet lower than the top of the lake (20 feet plus 4 feet of gravel). We know that water exerts force in all directions including sideways. We know that force is 62.4 pounds a square foot times the height of the water. Thus 62.4 times 24 is 1,497.6 pounds per square foot. In PSI it's 1,497.6 divided by 144, or 10.40 PSI. That's the water pressure at the bottom of that gravel layer. If the hillside cut is 50 feet wide, there's a problem. A fair-size river will be flowing into that lot.

Use these calculations to help you decide on the material to use for this retaining wall. If you use concrete block, it will leak. A water pressure of 10.40 PSI will push water right through the block. You could use several blocks to build up the thickness. How many blocks would it take? Divide 10.40 by 1.70. The answer is 6.11. You should use block stacked 7 rows deep. The average block is about 8 inches thick, so you would have 7 times 8, or 56 inches of thickness. That's not very practical.

Block leaks because it's porous. If you fill the block with compressed grout or concrete, it becomes quite resistant to the flow of water. You could possibly build this retaining wall with one row of 12-inch-wide, rebar-reinforced, compressed grout-filled, concrete block. You could

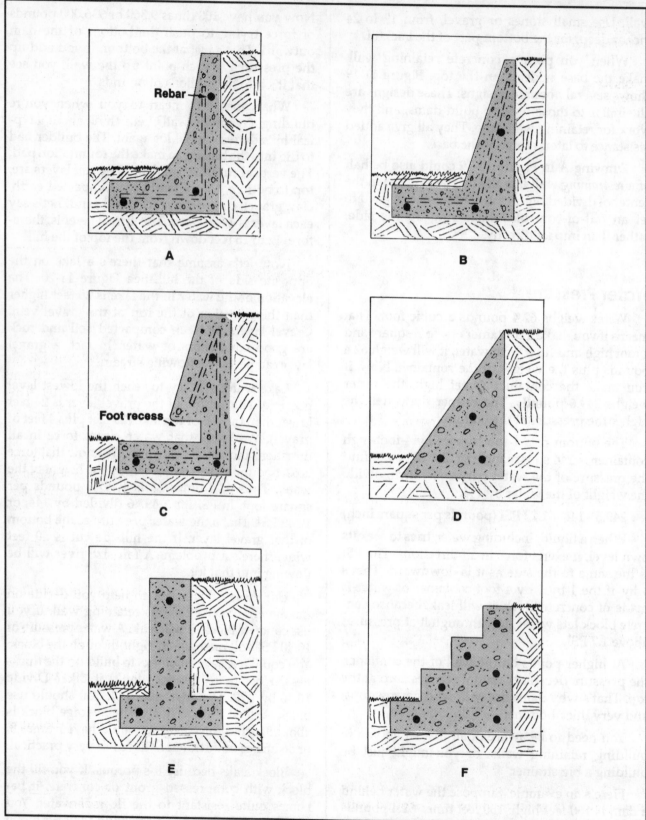

Figure 11-19
Wall shapes to resist lateral force at the base

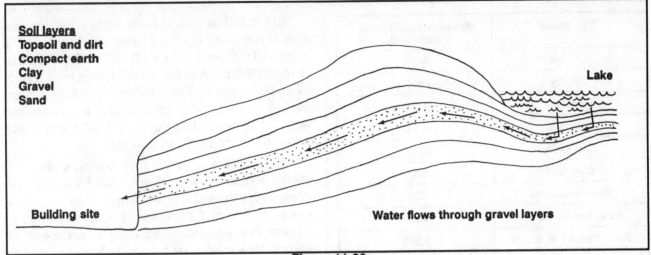

Figure 11-20
Plan for water pressure on the retaining wall

build it from rebar-reinforced poured concrete about 12 inches thick. Both of these should work. Grout and concrete can withstand pressures of from 1,500 to over 3,000 PSI.

I wouldn't recommend timbers here, even though they would hold the soil in place. It's too hard to hold back the water.

That was an extreme case, with the lake directly above the building lot. But a layer of gravel can cover hundreds of square miles. The building lot could be 25 miles away and still get the force of the water from the lake. To put it simply, if you hit a band of gravel, design for water pressure from the highest water source around.

House foundations dug below grade are a form of retaining wall. Most areas have what is known as a *water table*, the level to which water will rise in an open pit. This is the level of ground water below the surface, usually in a gravel layer. In the summer and fall, the water table drops by several feet. In the spring and winter, it rises several feet. If you build a foundation or wall in the summer, the water table may be higher six months later.

Leaky basements are common in many areas in late winter and throughout the spring. Be sure to provide adequate drainage lines around your wall. Coat the ground side of the wall with water-proofing asphalt. Coat the inside of the wall with a waterproofing cement.

Soil Properties

I've shown some examples of retaining walls and suggested how to design and protect them. Let's look at the soil under them for a bit. This information is important for foundations of all types.

There are many different soil types, with different properties. Gravel lets water flow through easily. Clay doesn't. Rocks and gravel tend to stay where you put them. Sand and clay don't. You need to know the *compression strength* of the soil you're working on so your walls don't crack and collapse.

Compression strength refers to the amount of weight a square foot of soil can support before it moves or compresses to the point of becoming a liquid. Figure 11-21 is a table that lists the maximum *bearing load* for various kinds of soil. The bearing load is the weight of the structure being built.

Here are weights for some common building materials in pounds per cubic foot:

Concrete, dry mix	130 PCF
Concrete, cured	150 PCF
Sand	105 PCF
Rock	105 PCF

Type of soil	Maximum bearing load permitted
Silt, wet	None
Silt, dry	500
Adobe	1,000
Clay, soft	1,000
Clay, sandy	2,000
Clay, hard	3,000
Sand, loose, fine	500
Sand, compacted, fine	1,000
Sand, compacted, coarse	1,500
Rock, and gravel	5,000*
Rock, base rock, solid	40,000
* or 20% of the PSF it takes to crush it.	

Figure 11-21
Type of soil and maximum bearing load permitted (pounds/ft^2)

Suppose you're building a concrete retaining wall 40 feet long, 8 feet high, and 1 foot wide. The foundation is 1.5 feet high and 1.5 feet wide. Can you build it on soft clay?

First, figure out how many cubic feet of material there are in the wall. Then multiply the answer by the weight of the material per cubic foot. The foundation is 1.5 x 1.5 x 40. Multiplying, we get 90 cubic feet. Multiply that by 150 pounds per cubic foot for the material. The answer is 13,500 pounds for the foundation.

Add to that the weight of the wall, (1 x 8 x 40 x 150 = 48,000), and the total weight for wall and foundation is 61,500 pounds.

The wall's footing is 60 square feet (1.5 x 40). You can see in Figure 11-21 that the maximum bearing load for soft clay is 1,000 pounds. The maximum weight then, for a structure that's supported on 60 square feet of ground, is 60,000 pounds. This wall is too heavy. The soil will compact under the weight and the wall may crack. You'll either have to lower the height of the wall, decrease its thickness, make the foundation wider to distribute the weight over a larger area, or change the soil.

My solution would be to widen the foundation. If you make the foundation 2 feet wide, it will weigh 18,000 pounds (1.5 x 2 x 40 x 150). Add that to the 48,000 pounds for the wall, for a total weight of 66,000 pounds. But now the foundation occupies 80 square feet of ground (2 x 40), which can support up to 80,000 pounds. That's more than enough for the 66,000 pound wall.

In some areas, you'll find *expansive soil* — it swells when it's wet. If you build on this soil, chances are the soil will swell under your wall and crack it. You can have a soil analysis done, or simply ask your local building department. Of course, they might just tell you to have an analysis done, but they *may* know what kind of soil you're dealing with.

There are two ways to handle expansive soil:

1) Dig below the expansive soil to build your foundation.

2) Remove the expansive soil and fill the trench with compacted coarse sand. Build your foundation on the sand, but below the frost line.

The Uniform Building Code requires footings to be a minimum of 12 inches below the frost line. Frost lines vary with climate. In south Texas it's only one inch. But allow 72 inches in northern Maine. Your building department will know the accepted depth for footings in your area.

Soil Weight

We've discussed how water pressure extends in all directions. But what about pressures in soil? A cubic foot of common dirt weighs about 100 pounds. This weight is distributed straight down. So a column of earth 1 foot wide by 1 foot long and 8 feet high exerts a force of 800 pounds on the bottom of the column. The spread, or horizontal force, is minimal, unlike water. If you cut a hillside straight up and down, and if there's no water in the soil, and if the bottom layer of soil can support the load of the layers above, the bank should stay in place by itself. That's a lot of *ifs*.

Chances are the cut won't be straight up and down and some diagonal force will be involved. Chances are the soil will be moist or wet during a

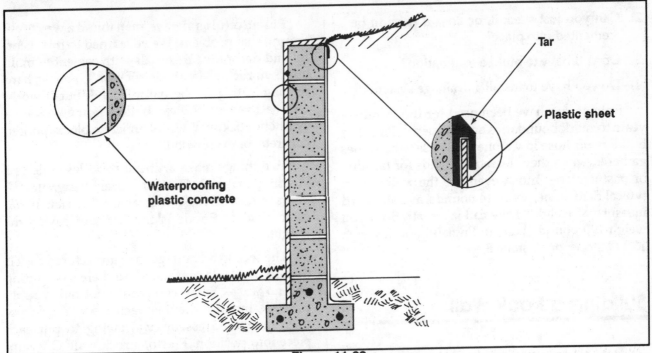

Figure 11-22
Waterproof a block retaining wall

rain. Chances are some of the soil layers are unstable. Chances are good the hillside *won't* stay in place by itself.

For the most part, you can protect a straight up and down, reasonably dry, compact soil bank with a retaining wall made from standard 8 x 16 inch concrete block. Use a foundation and footing, put in rebar every 16 inches or less, waterproof the backside, and fill hollows containing rebar with grout. Finish with a coping that has a rounded top, made from wood or concrete. It seals the hollow block from dirt and water.

Figure 11-22 shows how to make a block retaining wall waterproof. The plastic sheet is 12 mil black polyethylene. You can use any hot or cold application asphalt waterproofing emulsion for the tar. And there are dozens of commercial waterproofing coatings to choose from for the plastic concrete.

If you don't want to build a retaining wall at all, cut the slope at less than 1 foot vertical for each 2 feet of horizontal excavation. That's a 2:1 slope or a maximum of 22.5 degrees. Most building codes don't require a retaining wall for a slope like that.

Summary of Retaining Wall Specifications

For retaining walls under 5 feet high, you can use timber, lumber, rock, block, brick, wire mesh, and concrete as construction material. For retaining walls 5 to 20 feet high, you can use block or concrete. For retaining walls over 20 feet high, poured concrete is usually the only material that will do the job economically.

Walls under 5 feet high generally don't require professional engineering or inspection. Most walls over 5 feet high *will* require inspection. You'll usually need a professional civil engineer to design walls over 20 feet high.

Designing Rock Walls

Here are some things to consider when you plan to build a wall out of rock:

1) How available is the material?

2) Can you just stack it, or does it have to be cemented into place?

3) Do you have to build a foundation?

4) Do you have to install a drainage system?

Field stones have been used for thousands of years to mark boundaries and property lines. The builders of those low stone walls used the stones gathered when they cleared the fields for farming or pasture. The British even use the weight of a typical field stone, about 14 pounds, as a standard measure of weight. They call it a *stone*. So if you weigh 190 pounds here, in England you'll weigh 13-1/2 stone, or 13 stone 8.

Building a Rock Wall

Field stones usually have an irregular shape, so they stack and hold fairly well. Some field stones, and river rock, have been worn smooth by ice, friction, glaciers or water. You usually have to cement those together to keep them in place.

Since you can find field stone and river rock on or near the earth's surface, they're relatively inexpensive. A cubic yard of river rock can cost as little as $10.

Quarried Rock

Rock you have to mine or dig up is more expensive. *Quarried* rock, as this is called, includes slate, granite, marble, and volcanic rock. Even though these are often irregular in shape and stack well, you'll probably still want to cement them into place because of their value. The cost of a cubic yard can range from $20 to $200.

Slate and marble are cut from the earth in slabs or sheets. They can be cut to shape and are usually ground and polished. You'd use these as veneer over concrete block or poured concrete.

Artificial Rock

Even though rock is plentiful, it's not a renewable resource. It took millions of years to form. Once it's used up, there won't be any more.

Resourceful as always, man found a way to get around that problem. We've learned to mix colorful and decorative materials with cement to mold our own rocks. Manmade rock isn't quite as hard or long-lasting as the natural kind, but it works well as a veneer. You can build a framework for a synthetic rock wall out of concrete block, poured concrete, or even wood.

Two things make artificial rock desirable as a building material. First, it closely resembles all kinds of natural rock. You can get "Hawaiian volcanic rock" in Rhode Island, without paying the freight.

The second advantage to manufactured rock is that it's available preshaped, so there's no cutting and no waste. Some companies not only supply the rock, but also number each piece. You follow their numbered assembly drawing to put each piece into position. Presto, a rock wall! One supplier cuts grooves into their rock. You put metal clips into the grooves to hold the rocks in place while you grout them.

Check your phone book under "stone" for sources and information. You can also write to:

Stucco Stone Corporation
P.O. Box 270
Napa, CA 94559

Building Techniques for a Rock Wall

If you're building a rock wall that's less than 4 feet high, you can *dry stack* the rock. That means you just pile the rocks on top of each other. Friction and their irregular shapes hold them together. If the wall is higher than 4 feet, you need to cement the rocks together. That's called a *wet stack* wall.

If you use dry stacking, you don't need a foundation. Just dig a trench about 6 inches deep and 4 inches wide, and begin stacking the rocks. In freeze zones, the wall will rise and fall with the expansion and contraction of the earth it sits on.

Don't attempt to build a dry wall with river rock. It won't hold together. If you must use it in a

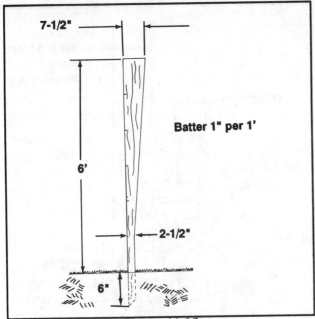

7-1/2"

Batter 1" per 1'

6'

2-1/2"

6"

Figure 11-23
Make a batterboard

dry stack wall, cut or break the rock into irregular shapes first.

To cut stone, use a mallet and a chisel. If you look carefully at the rock, you should see some sort of grain line. Using your chisel, follow the grain line and apply short, sharp mallet blows. The rock should crack into two pieces. Wear eye protection when you do this. Slivers of rock fly off like shrapnel.

You must lay a foundation for a wet stack wall. Dig down to or below the frost line and start your wall there. A wet wall is a *monolithic* wall. That means the combination of concrete and stone forms a single unit. It weighs too much to just rise and fall with the earth without cracking itself apart.

Batter Your Wall

Batter means to slope the wall faces inward from the bottom to the top of the wall. This keeps the higher stones from falling. Their weight is fully supported by the stones under them.

If the wall is a freestanding divider wall, not retaining anything, it can be either a dry or a wet wall. If it's under 2 feet high, its faces can be

straight up and down. If it's over 2 feet high, you'll have to batter it. A dry wall requires a batter of 2 inches for each 1 foot of vertical wall height. The wet wall requires a batter of 1 inch for each foot of wall height.

Here's how to form a batter with a string line, for a freestanding, wet wall that's 5 feet high:

1) Cut four 1 x 8 boards 6-1/2 feet long.

2) Call one end of the boards the *top* and measure 5 feet from that end of one board. At that point, measure in 5 inches from the edge of the board.

3) Cut a diagonal from that point back to the top corner of the board that's on the side you measured the 5 inches from.

4) Make a straight cut from the bottom of the board to the point where the diagonal cut begins. The remaining part of the bottom of the board will be 2-1/2 inches wide.

5) Cut a point on the bottom end of the board. Then cut the other boards to match.

Figure 11-23 illustrates a batterboard.

Drive two of these boards into the ground at each end of your wall's path. Sink them up to the point where the diagonal cut begins. You'll place the boards opposite each other, with the diagonal cuts facing each other. Make the distance between the boards where they enter the ground the width of your wall at the base.

Now string lines between the boards, one at ground level, the other at the top. You'll place the rocks within these string lines.

If you're building a rock retaining wall, put the batter on the exposed surface only. The side of the wall toward the landfill is straight up and down.

Wall Base Width

The width of your wall at the base is determined by the size of the rock you're using. The top layer of your wall should be a minimum of two rocks wide. Decrease the size of the rocks as you build, with each layer made of rocks smaller than those below.

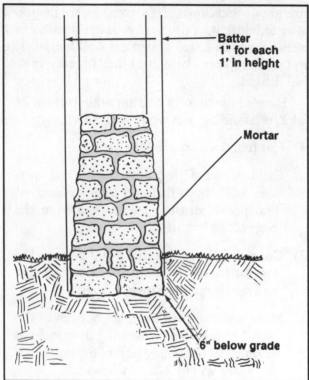

Figure 11-24
Wet stack freestanding rock wall

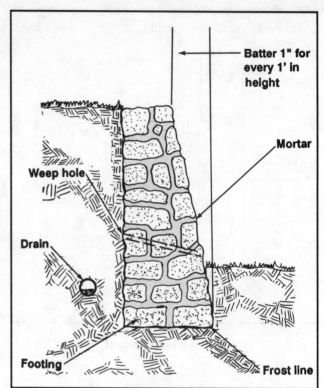

Figure 11-25
Wet stack rock retaining wall

Here's an example. Suppose your load of stone has rocks ranging from 5 to 10 inches in diameter. If you put two 5-inch rocks side by side on the top layer, that's 10 inches. If you're building a wet wall, allow another inch for the cement.

You're going to build a freestanding wet wall 5 feet high, so you'll batter it 5 inches on each side, for a total of 10 inches at the base. Allow another 2 inches for cement. Then add the 11-inch width of the wall at the top. The total base width is 23 inches. You can make than an even 2 feet.

If you're building the wall in a freeze area where the frost line is at 36 inches, you'll have to batter it another 6 inches, 3 on each side. The foundation trench needs to be 30 inches wide by 36 inches deep. You'll make the foundation of the same material as the wall — rocks and cement. Be sure to order enough material for this. You can figure the cubic yardage you'll need, or take the plans to your supplier and let him calculate the quantity. After all, it's his product, so he's the expert on how much is needed. He can also advise you on the rock size to order. If you order 6-inch

rock, for example, there will be some 4-inch and some 8-inch rock included, but the average size will be 6 inches. Figure 11-24 shows a cross section of a wet stack rock wall.

Rock Walls Illustrated

Figures 11-25 and 11-26 show how to build wet and dry retaining walls. Notice the differences between these and freestanding walls. The batter is straight on the side of the wall facing the dirt on the retaining walls. The retaining walls have a perforated drain pipe running their full length. Note that the drain pipe location is different for wet and dry walls. On a wet wall, you need to relieve water pressure behind the solid mass of the wall. Install *weep holes* every few feet along its length by inserting lengths of 1-inch polyethylene or PVC pipe through the wall. You can space them at 2, 3 or 4 feet, depending on the amount of rainfall expected.

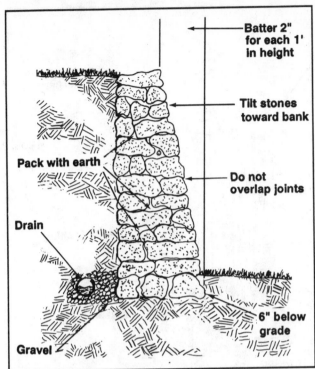

Figure 11-26
Dry stack rock retaining wall

Figure 11-27
Rock veneer over concrete block

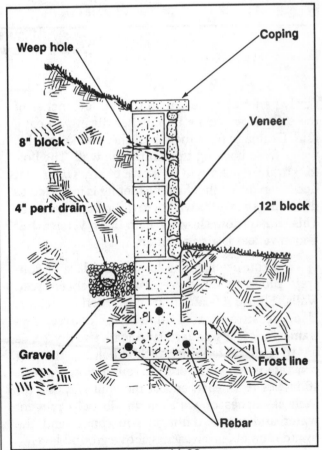

Figure 11-28
Veneer-faced retaining wall

On the dry wall, you've got water seeping through from the front *and* the back. In both cases, the idea is to keep water from building up behind the wall and saturating the ground under it, undermining the base. The drain pipe should slope at least 1/8 inch for each 10 feet of length and empty into a dry well or other open area.

Figure 11-27 is a freestanding veneer wall. It has a structural core of concrete block. It also has straight walls, no batter. It does have a foundation of poured concrete. The foundation has a step built into it, just below ground level. This step helps support the weight of the veneer stone. You use *wall ties* to keep the veneer from falling forward off of the block. These are small metal strips embedded in the block's mortar. They're available at most block and brick suppliers. Buy ones that are long enough to extend through the block and embed into the rock veneer mortar. The cap stones give the wall a finished look and seal out water.

Figure 11-28 shows you how to build a veneer-faced retaining wall. Notice that the weep holes are high on the wall. That's because rain water

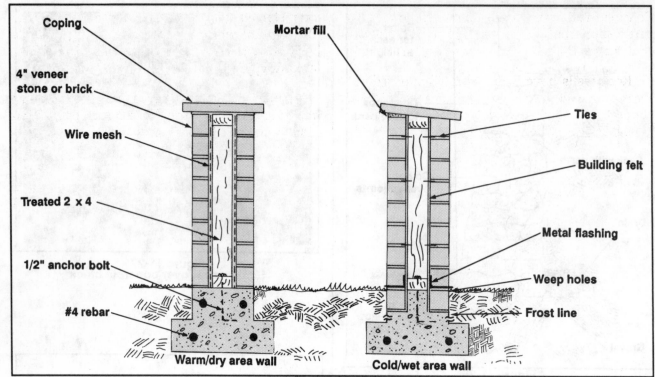

Figure 11-29
Veneer walls with lumber core

rarely penetrates more than the top few inches of the soil — perhaps 6 to 8 inches during a heavy rain. Drainage near the top of the wall keeps this water from backing up behind the wall. The bottom drain system will take care of any water that does seep down that far. The footing is included to distribute the wall's weight to the ground below it. This illustration shows 2-inch-thick veneer, but 4-inch veneer is also common.

You can use framing lumber in place of concrete block to build freestanding veneer-faced walls. Figure 11-29 shows construction details. Use pressure-treated lumber, of course. The framework is a standard stud wall, usually 2 x 4s on 16 inch centers. Set anchor bolts in the wet concrete when you pour the foundation. Put one 18 inches from each end of the wall and one for each 48 inches of wall length. To help prevent water and insect damage, you can extend the foundation at least 6 inches above ground level.

The building felt shown in the cold or wet area wall goes over the top of the top 2 x 4 and over the top edge of the metal L flashing. The weep holes

are just areas with no mortar between every fifth or sixth brick of the first course of bricks. Staple or nail diamond mesh wire screening to the lumber to hold the mortar in place. Finally, rake the mortar joints and use a commercial water sealer to protect the wall from moisture damage.

Figure 11-30 is a rock rubble retaining wall. It's about 3 feet high and has stood for about 30 years.

Figure 11-30
Rock rubble retaining wall

Considering that the road behind it is fill dirt that's partly supported by the interlocking rocks of the wall, I'd say this was built to last, wouldn't you?

Rock walls have been used for hundreds of years and may still be a good choice for some applications. They give an appearance of solidness, beauty and distinction to a property. There aren't too many wall and fence contractors who do this type of work, so this could be a profitable specialty for you. Do a quality job and charge accordingly.

In the next chapter, I'll tell you how to organize the business end of your fence contracting operation.

twelve

Get Your Business Started Right

*I*n the previous chapters, I've described how to build all kinds of fences and walls. But this business is much more than building walls and fences. If you're just getting started in fence contracting, let me offer some advice. No matter how good you are, knowledge and skill in the trade are never enough. I've known some very good tradesmen who got in way over their heads as fence contractors. There's a big difference between being good at *wall or fence building* and being a good *wall or fence contractor*. That's the purpose of this chapter: to explain the part of fence contracting you've never seen if you've never run a contracting business.

I'm going to start with the basics. Here's why. I've seen construction companies come and go. Plenty of them. And when I see a company fail, it's usually because someone wasn't paying attention to the most basic, most elementary parts of the business. Don't make that mistake. If you haven't run a successful contracting company before, I

suggest you keep reading. The recommendations I make here may be some of most valuable advice you're likely to get.

Before I get into the business of fence contracting, let's explore some of the reasons why you might want to be a wall and fence contractor.

If you dream of short hours and big income, forget it. Running a business is demanding work. And sometimes there won't be enough money in the account to pay tradesmen and suppliers, not to mention your own salary. That's especially true in the beginning.

Do you dream of being totally independent of others? Forget that, too. You have to depend on others, whether family, suppliers, employees, lenders or customers. You have to depend on them to do right by you.

So why are *you* willing to risk your reputation, bank account and future? Here are the reasons some people give:

♦ I don't like my boss. I can do better than he can.

♦ I want to be independent, set my own hours.

♦ I want to keep what I earn, not give it to someone else

♦ I can't get along with others. I'd rather work alone.

♦ I want to leave something for my family.

♦ I think I can do it. It's a challenge.

♦ I'm out of work and no one will hire me.

♦ I'm the best and I can prove it.

These are good reasons, and they might enter into your decision to start your own business. But be careful. Many of these reasons deal with feelings, not facts. Here are some of the things that inspire the *successful* business owner:

♦ I want a successful career most of all.

♦ I have the training.

♦ I have the money and the time.

♦ I know my friends and family are behind me.

♦ I know I can do better than the competition.

♦ I know I can earn a good, if not better, living than I do now.

♦ I enjoy being the boss.

♦ I know there's a real need for my services.

Now, that's more positive. Be honest. If you agree with all *those* statements, you're more than ready to go on.

Your Business Specialty

What kind of business are you going into? Yes, I know, it's wall and fence contracting. But that's a broad field. I gave you lots of options in Chapter 1. Now's the time to pick the specialty you prefer. I'll give you a clue about how to do this.

Take a pencil and a piece of paper and begin by making a list of your strengths and the things that you most enjoy doing. In a column next to that list, put down your weak points and dislikes. Don't worry about order — you can assign priorities later. List at least ten reasons why you want to go into the fencing and retaining wall business. Put any obstacles to those reasons in the second col-

umn. Then list ten reasons why the location where you live now is a good place for your business. Again, list any disadvantages in the second column.

List the parts of your education that will help you in business, and in the opposite column, put things you need to learn more about. Evaluate your talents, financial position and personal characteristics.

Now copy the lists over into three categories: business, personal and financial. Assign a priority value to each entry on both sides of the lists. One means "very important to me or the success of my business," down to 10 for those things you don't care about, or won't make much difference. You can use the same number for more than one item on the list.

Copy each list again, this time with all the 1's at the top, the 2's next, and so on. You can refine the lists further if you want, but by now you'll have a pretty good picture of your strengths and weaknesses, likes and dislikes. If you prefer working in rural areas, then specialize in the kinds of fencing farmers and ranchers use. If you like working alone, then concentrate on small jobs you can do yourself, not big projects that require lots of manpower. If design isn't your long suit, then stick to chain link fences or ordinary block walls. Don't go into bricklaying if you know nothing about laying brick, especially if you're a great carpenter.

And, if you can't solve or work around the obstacles or disadvantages that rank in the 1-to-3 range, then you'd better think twice about going out on your own at all.

If you're like many new business people, your weak points may be sales, accounting, and business management. Most people who open their own businesses are good at their trade but lack education and experience in management. That's why 95 out of every 100 new businesses fail within the first year.

Of the five remaining, only one will survive five years. Here are some reasons:

♦ Poor management

♦ Not enough money to get the business going

♦ Business was started for the wrong reasons

♦ Customers didn't need your services

- Costs were higher than expected
- Product or service was overpriced
- Not enough advertising
- Poor location
- Owner got sick and couldn't work
- No systems or paperwork control
- Owner didn't know the business

There are probably a few dozen more reasons, but these are the most common. They all stem from the first item: poor business management and planning.

You don't need a graduate degree in business administration to run a small business, but you do need to know more than how to use a hammer or trowel. How much do you want to learn about being in business? Spend some time with this book and you'll learn a lot. But can you put this information to good use? Only you can answer that question.

The Owner Makes a Business Successful

The owner has the ultimate responsibility for the success of any business. They have the most at stake, and have to be willing to spend the time and effort to make it work. The owner has to be able to solve problems and be willing to take chances now and then. The owner may have to live for the business, learning to do everything the business has to get done.

A business owner raises the business like a parent raises a child. And a new business is like a child. It has to grow, it gets hurt once in a while, it needs patience and discipline, has growing pains, but eventually may mature into something well worth the effort.

Your Business Structure

What kind of legal setup will your company have? Is your business going to be a sole proprietorship, partnership, limited partnership, closed corporation or open corporation? Let's discuss the differences between these and the advantages and disadvantages of each.

Sole proprietorships are is the easiest and fastest to set up. You own everything, including all the risk. All you need to get started is a few dollars for a business license. In some states, you'll have to prove that you have a contractor's license. More on that later.

Most proprietorships and partnerships also need a "DBA." That stands for "doing business as." You need one if your business name is something other than your own name. For example, "George's Fences & Retaining Walls" would have to be a DBA. You register your DBA with your city or county government, and you have to publish a notice for several weeks in a newspaper that's authorized to publish legal notices. It will cost you about $70, and it's usually good for several years.

The advantage to a sole proprietorship is that it's easy and doesn't cost much to set up. The major disadvantages are that you have to come up with all the money, and you're personally liable for all losses.

Partnerships are almost as easy to start as the sole proprietorship. Two or more people own the business and run it under a partnership agreement. You have more talent and more startup money available. The main disadvantage of a partnership is potential conflicts between the partners. Also, partnerships are dissolved at the death of a partner.

A written partnership agreement is a must. This agreement spells out in detail the responsibilities of each partner. It details who is liable for what and who earns what. It defines what happens in the event of an unsettled dispute. Get your lawyer involved right at the beginning. In many states you'll have to file your *Articles of Partnership* when you apply for a business license. You also need a DBA. And, if your state requires it, at least one partner must have a valid contractor's license.

Limited partnerships are less common in the United States than in Europe. It's the same as a general partnership, with one major exception. The partners are only liable for the amount they put into the company. In the event of a lawsuit or bankruptcy, the partners' personal property and bank accounts can't be reached by creditors. In a sole proprietorship or partnership, creditors can use your personal assets to satisfy a claim. A limited partnership is more complicated to set up, and you'll need a lawyer.

Proprietorships and partnerships don't pay any special income tax. Income to the proprietorship is reported on Schedule C of your Form 1040. Partnerships file an information return only, disclosing income and how it's distributed among partners. Each partner then pays tax on the appropriate share of the income.

Corporations are treated just like a person under state law. The corporation has the right to enter contracts, sue and be sued, and pays taxes at special corporate rates. The corporation has its own credit, bank accounts, assets, and liabilities. If more money is needed or more people are needed to run the company, more shareholders can be brought in or more shares can be issued.

Closely-held corporations are usually owned by a few family members. They can sell or give stock to a limited number of other people. That's a big advantage. The corporation continues even if a shareholder dies. Since company records are private in a closely-held corporation, outsiders can't easily learn the corporation's secrets.

The disadvantage of incorporating is the cost. Corporations are formed under state law. That can cost several hundred, or even thousands of dollars. Since the corporation is a separate taxpayer, you'll have the extra cost of filing an extra set of tax returns.

A major advantage of incorporating is limited liability. Creditors have no claim against stockholder assets beyond the investment of each investor. Unfortunately, that makes it hard to borrow money in the early years. Banks and suppliers probably won't extend credit without the personal guarantee of several owners. If you guarantee a corporation loan, your personal assets are liable for payment on that loan.

Publicly-held corporations are like closely-held corporations with one very major difference. The stock of most publicly-held corporations can be traded on the open market. Because the buying public has the right to be informed about the company, key records are open to public scrutiny.

The main advantage of a publicly-held corporation is that it can raise money through the sale of stock — if willing investors can be found. The disadvantage is cost. Qualifying for a public stock offering can cost several hundred thousand dollars in legal fees alone.

Figure 12-1 summarizes the advantages and disadvantages of the different types of business organizations.

Even under the best of circumstances, it's rare for a bank to loan money to a new business. Remember, 95 out of 100 fail the first year. So where does the money come from?

You Supply Startup Money

Where do you get the money to start a new business?

♦ Your own savings

♦ You contribute property to the business

♦ You borrow against your life insurance

♦ You borrow from family and friends

♦ You continue to work while setting up your business

♦ You have a mate with a good job

♦ You mortgage your home

♦ You inherit money

There are many places to get seed money. Some are better than others. I strongly suggest that you plan to have enough before you get started. Plan very carefully how much you'll need. And then allow a little extra. And leave some money in your bank account to meet normal household expenses. If your circumstances are anything like mine were, most of the other options aren't open to you.

Now we have you in some sort of fence and retaining wall contracting business, and you've got some startup money, so what's next?

ADVANTAGES

DISADVANTAGES

Sole Proprietorship

- ☞ cheaper and easier to start
- ☞ owner has total control
- ☞ all profits go to owner

- ☞ owner liable for all damages
- ☞ profits taxed as personal income

General Partnership

- ☞ legal and financial responsibilities shared
- ☞ combines talent of two or more people

- ☞ partners must agree on decisions
- ☞ history of failure due to personal conflicts
- ☞ profits taxed as personal income

Limited Partnership

- ☞ investments made by several people
- ☞ liability of limited partners can't exceed their investment
- ☞ general business partner maintains control of business

- ☞ general partner has all responsibilities and liabilities but must share profits
- ☞ profits taxed as personal income

Corporation

- ☞ investments come from many people
- ☞ disputes settled by voting shares
- ☞ shareholders are not liable for corporation debts

- ☞ loss of personal control
- ☞ shareholders may sell out
- ☞ most difficult and expensive type of business to set up

Figure 12-1
Types of business organizations

Find a Customer or Two

Customers have to know that you're in business. If they don't, then you aren't. It's customers who keep the money flowing in.

Here's a thought to guide you in bringing in customers: Remember, you're someone else's customer. How do you want to be treated? What attracts you to a company's store or business? Why do you keep going back to them? Your answers to those questions will give you some clues about how to advertise effectively. It's half the secret of good advertising. The other half is technique.

Effective Advertising

What is advertising? Advertising is getting your message to other people. A message that's appealing and persuades them to use your product or service. "I build fences and retaining walls" is advertising — or is it? First, who is "I"? Second, what kind of fences and retaining walls? Third, where do I find "I"? Try this instead:

I Build GREAT FENCES & RETAINING WALLS

All types, all sizes, in Anytown, USA

Call Bill at

BILL'S FENCES & RETAINING WALLS

123-4567

Open 8 am to 8 pm M-S

That's information a customer can use. It tells what, where, when, who and how. You'd be surprised at the number of ads that omit a clear description of what's being sold. Or omit the address or phone number. It happens because the ad writer is too close to the product and assumes or overlooks the obvious. Make a checklist when you write an ad. Be sure to include:

- Company name

- Your product or service

- Your phone number, and if you wish, your address

- Days and hours of operation

- Who to contact

- Any special information

By the way, when you decide on your DBA, think about this: Most advertising is billed by the word. A typical weekly paper will charge from $1.25 to $9.50 per word. You'll spend too much if you pick a DBA of "William's Quality Stone and Brick Fences of America, Inc." instead of "Bill's Masonry Fences." Three words versus nine. Also, Bill comes before William alphabetically, so Bill's ad will appear first in the phone book.

Make your DBA memorable. Test it before you apply for it. Try it out on a few friends. Mention it and then go and do something else for an hour. Then see if they remember the name. Then check the phone book to make sure someone isn't already using your DBA or something confusingly similar.

Where Do You Advertise?

That's easy. Where everyone else in your business advertises. After all, your competition isn't spending good money without getting results. Check your local newspapers, TV and radio programs. Chances are you'll find your competitor's ads in one of those places.

Where You _Must_ Advertise

You _must_ advertise in the Yellow Pages of your local phone book. That's where people look for the services they need. To many of them, if you're not in the Yellow Pages, you're not in business. Take out the biggest ad you can afford. Just remember that the fee for this ad will be on your phone bill every month.

If you use your home phone number for your business, you continue to pay for the ad even if you go out of business. If the ad is in the current directory, and you're still using the phone number, you pay.

If you have a separate business phone and you shut down, you won't have to continue paying for the ad, but if you reopen a similar business and want to advertise again within a year, you'll have to pay all back Yellow Pages billings.

Follow the checklist above when you write your ad for the Yellow Pages. Look at the other ads and copy their style, especially if they've been in business for a few years. If you can afford a display ad with pictures or graphics, then go for it. Pictures catch the reader's eye. If there isn't too much color on the page where your ad will appear, buy color. But if there's over 30 percent color on the page, don't bother. It won't be effective.

Remember that the Yellow Pages are only published once a year. If you miss the deadline for the next issue, it will be another year before your ad will appear. So call your Yellow Pages representative *right now* and find out when the next issue closes. Write that date down here:

_____.

Newspaper Advertising

Ads in a large metropolitan newspaper might not be effective. Those papers have so many lavish display ads that people won't notice your little ad. Your message stands a better chance of being seen in a small, local paper. The major problem with newspapers is that people scan through them, then put them in the bottom of the bird cage. You must keep your name in front of people at all times. They're not going to be in the market for fencing every day, but you want them to find you when they need you.

It's expensive to advertise in the newspaper constantly. But a newspaper ad is excellent when you want to advertise a special. That's when you'll catch the marginal customer — the one who needs a new fence, but is holding out for a sale. Run a nice big display ad, and be sure to include enough in your bids to cover the cost of the ad.

Weekly Freebies

Many communities have weekly "shopper" newspapers that have nothing but local ads. Circulation covers all homes in a relatively small area. These can be a good advertising buy. People usually read them cover to cover, looking for a bargain or some special item. Most carry advertisements for local contractors. Where there are two or more weeklies, contractors will often all advertise in the same one. That's the one you want to use. Plan on running your ad in the same position every week. Potential customers know where to find your ad and will look there when they need a bid on a fence.

Flyers

Get a few extra prospects during a slow period by distributing flyers door-to-door. A one-page flyer shouldn't cost much more than $40 a thousand at your local print shop. Make your flyer as informative as possible. You have a lot of space on an 8-1/2 x 11 inch sheet of paper. Hire school kids to hang them on front doors in targeted neighborhoods.

If your delivery crew puts flyers on cars in parking lots, some sheets will probably end up littering the streets. This is a poor way to advertise. Be specific with your delivery instructions. And don't expect a flood of orders the day after your flyers go out. It just doesn't happen. Flyers help make your name known. They don't sell jobs right away. Some people will file them for future reference. Put a discount coupon on your flyer. People keep and use those. Don't forget the expiration date.

Posters

I've run some very effective startup campaigns using posters tacked to utility poles. It's easy to put posters up all over town. People are creatures of habit. They use the same routes every day, and they see your ads over and over.

The problem with posters is that they can get you into trouble with local authorities and utility companies. The authorities object because posters may violate sign ordinances. Utilities don't like them because the staples or nails left in their poles are a hazard to workers. If you use posters, be careful where you put them.

You can have a printer produce a hundred 11 x 17 inch posters for about $40. Have them use clay-coated stock and waterproof rubber ink. Black ink is best. Don't use red. Most red inks will fade within a few days if left outdoors. Make the lettering 2 to 3 inches high. Keep the design simple and clean. You want people to read your message quickly as they drive past.

Business Cards

You can't afford not to have these. They're inexpensive, about $30 per thousand, so you can pass them out wherever you go. Your printer can help you design an attractive, informative card. Many printers have catalogs of sample designs. They also have *clip art*, professionally-drawn pictures you can use in your ads. Keep a good supply of business cards on hand. It's your cheapest advertising. People keep business cards and refer to them when they're needed.

Radio and TV

I've never seen a specialty contractor make money on either radio or TV ads. The cost isn't necessarily too high. Some spots cost only a few dollars. The problem is that most radio and TV ads are *image* advertising. They help you project an image of being the biggest and the best. That's not much help to a specialty contractor. You need prospects, people calling asking for bids. Engraving your company's name in the minds of potential customers isn't your top priority. In the early stages of your business, *getting* customers is.

Signs

When you do get a job putting up a fence or wall for someone, be sure to post signs on the job site. Those signs will tell passersby and neighbors that you're doing the work. This is very effective. Where a new fence is needed or an old one needs repairs, there are likely to be others. Of course, you need your customer's permission to put up a sign. A few will object — they're paying you to do a job, not advertise at their expense. But most will let you do it. Many people will even let you put a small permanent sign on the completed wall or fence.

The job signs you use should be portable but large enough that they can be read from the street. Most silk-screen shops will make signs for you. Small ones for attaching to completed jobs will run around three dollars each in quantities of 100.

Large job site signs will cost about $100. Be sure your phone number is on the sign.

Put a note on the bottom of the large sign that says, "Please phone . . . don't disturb our workers." Your customer won't appreciate crew members answering neighbor's questions when they should be working.

Vehicle Signs

Make your truck a traveling billboard. Most contractors do. You can buy magnetic stick-on signs for less than $100, or decals for about the same. Or you can have a professional sign painter paint one on for a few hundred dollars or less. People all over town will see your name. Be sure your truck or van projects a good image. Keep it clean and neat.

More Signs

Put your company name and logo on your work shirts and caps. People notice you at the lumberyard, building material store, at the bank, and when you're working. This, too, is advertising.

Word of Mouth

This is the cheapest and the best advertising you can get. Do a good professional job for someone and they'll recommend you to others. It's hard to find experienced professional contractors who are anxious to give quotations, will do good work and finish on time for the price quoted. Be a contractor who does and the word will get around. Take the time to do a little extra. Clean up when the job is done, be fair and pay attention to your customer's needs. Settle disputes fast and to your customer's satisfaction. If you do all that, you've got the best advertising program ever developed.

My last job brought in five referrals. That's five new customers I didn't have to spend hard-earned dollars to get. Ask your satisfied customers to refer you to others. Yes, ask them. People like to talk about their doctor, dentist, lawyer and contractor. If you did a good job and ask for referrals, you'll probably get them.

Advertising In General

Advertising can be a waste or a money maker. Try to get by without it and you'll probably be bidding too few jobs. Do a lot of good advertising and keep track of the effectiveness of your ads. Track what they cost, how many jobs they produced, how fast customers responded. Keep a notebook with samples of all your ads. Note the results for each. When things get slow, and they will, you'll have a record of which ads worked. Adapt the best ads for use again.

By the way, the money you spend setting up or running your business is tax deductible. That includes your business license, DBA, office supplies, phone calls, letters you've written, and all your advertising. Keep accurate records of these items. I'll show you how in the next chapter.

Advertising and Your License

If your state requires a contractor's license, be sure you read the rules. You may be required to display your license number in all your advertising. In some states, an unlicensed contractor may be subject to large fines if their advertisements state a price.

OK, now you're in business, have some startup money, and an advertising strategy. What's next?

The Necessary Evils

When a small business goes belly up, it's usually because the owner lost control. The owner doesn't know where the company is going, where it's been, or where it is now. The owner doesn't see problems developing. The company just stumbles along until a crisis puts an end to all operations.

Control requires a good paperwork system. I've seen million-dollar companies go bankrupt because they didn't have good records. Paperwork is a nuisance. Don't do any more than you have to. But you need some records to stay out of trouble. In the next chapter, I'll explain a record keeping system that will work for a small fence and retaining wall contractor. For now, I'll offer a few basic principles every contractor should follow to stay out of trouble. I'll start with taxes.

Taxes, Taxes, and More Taxes

As a small businessman you'll have a partner — the I.R.S. They're going to be looking over your shoulder every step of the way. They have the right to review your business records periodically to see what you've spent and what you've earned. And they're going to require regular deposits of withheld employee taxes and estimated company (or personal) income taxes.

In 1989, here's how the typical business taxes stacked up:

Federal income tax	12 to 38 percent of net earnings
State income tax	1 to 10 percent of net earnings
Social Security tax	7.51 percent of taxable wages
Federal unemployment tax	6.2 percent of first $7,000 earned
State unemployment tax	5.4 percent of the Federal Tax (FUTA)
Disability insurance	1.2 percent of first $21,900

If that's not enough, you may also have to contend with these:

◆ Personal property tax

◆ Local income tax

◆ Inventory tax

◆ Transportation tax

◆ County or city tax

◆ Federal excise tax

◆ State sales tax

◆ Bond issue tax

◆ Value added tax

◆ Use tax

There are more, but this gives you an idea. Of course, state and local tax rates depend on where you live and work. It's your responsibility to know about these taxes and pay them when due.

Here's a suggestion: Contact your local I.R.S. office and request a copy of their forms and publications list. The list and the publications are free. These will be useful to you, the business person:

# 17	Your Federal Income Tax
#334	Tax Guide for Small Business
#505	Tax Withholding and Estimated Tax
#508	Educational Expenses
#533	Self Employment Tax
#552	Record Keeping for Individuals
#583	Information for Business Taxpayers
#587	Business Use of Your Home
#590	Individual Retirement Arrangements
#917	Business Use of Your Car
#912	Tax Reform Act of 1986 for Business

You should also request a copy of these forms:

Schedule C	Profit or loss from a business
Schedule SE	Self employment taxes
Form 1040-ES	Estimated tax due
#2106	Employee business expenses
#4136	Credit for tax on fuels
#4562	Depreciation and amortization
#4797	Sale or exchange of business property
#8606	Nontaxable I.R.A. distributions

If you can't reach the I.R.S. on the phone, write to whichever of the following is closest to you:

Forms Publication Center
P.O. Box 12626
Fresno, CA 93778

Forms Publication Center
P.O. Box 9903
Bloomington, IL 61799

Forms Publication Center
P.O. Box 25866
Richmond, VA 23260

Write to your state and local taxing agencies as well. Ask them to recommend the forms and publications that apply to a new contracting business. Contact your local city hall or county assessor's office for information on property and local taxes. Take the time to "get legal" right from the start. Know the bad news right from the beginning. It may save you a lot of time and trouble.

What Are Wages?

For tax purposes, wages are all pay for work done. That includes money, bonuses, commissions, vacations, and so on. For the employer these items are tax deductible as a business expense. For the employee they are taxable as income.

Insurance

Most people have some type of insurance. A life and health policy, renter's or homeowner's policy, and vehicle coverage are a good start, but when you're in business, that's not enough. I'll give you a brief description of the basic business coverage. You can probably combine most of them under a one-premium package. Shop around, talk to several different agents. Premium rates can vary by up to 100 percent or more. An independent insurance agent is your best bet. They know how to shop for the best deals. Make sure the agent you pick understands your business and the risks.

Business Liability Insurance

This is usually called *public liability insurance*. It protects you if you're sued by someone claiming an injury you caused. What if you dig too close to a house foundation, causing the walls to collapse? Or suppose a worker leaves a shovel laying in your customer's yard and someone trips over it and breaks an arm. The insurance agrees to provide the legal defense to the claim and pay any damages awarded by a court.

This type of insurance usually carries a deductible — the amount you pay before the insurance takes over. The more you're willing to pay as a deductible, the lower your premiums.

Loss of Income (Disability) Insurance

This coverage pays you a wage if you can't work because of a major health problem. You're covered if you break a leg, or suffer a serious illness like a heart attack. Remember, self-employed people don't qualify for unemployment benefits. That's another advantage to incorporating your business. As an officer of a corporation, you *do* pay into the unemployment fund and can collect benefits.

Casualty Insurance

This insurance reimburses you for loss to property. It will pay for repairs to your building in case of a catastrophe, and covers the replacement cost of stolen tools and equipment. These policies usually have a high deductible. Damage from earthquake and flood are usually excluded from the basic policy. You add them as an extra cost rider.

Business Vehicle Insurance

You probably already have insurance on your car or truck. That's great. But look closely at your policy. Most do *not* cover business use. There are two reasons for this. Insurance covering personal use of a vehicle is based on the cost to replace the vehicle, the area the vehicle is driven in, and the driver's record. You usually put more miles on a vehicle you use in business. And you may drive it over a wider area. The biggest problem, from the insurance company's standpoint, is that the vehicle may be driven by several people — drivers the company knows nothing about. That's why a business vehicle will have a higher rate than a personal vehicle.

Umbrella Coverage

This policy covers claims that exceed the limits on any of your policies. Million-dollar awards are common in most states. This policy provides coverage to higher-than-normal limits.

Personal Life Insurance

You may already have a life insurance policy on yourself. But as the value of your business grows, your life coverage should grow. If you die, will there be enough money available to pay taxes and continue the business? Can your survivors afford to hire or train someone to take over the business? For affordable insurance, consider a term life policy. Term life is pure insurance without built-in extras or saving accounts. It pays face value when you die. Term life is the least expensive life insurance you can buy. Depending on your age when you buy it, a $50,000 policy can cost as little as $20 per month. The younger you are, the less it costs.

Personal Health Insurance

Here's where you find out how expensive insurance is. Major medical coverage will cost several hundred dollars per month. If you're working for someone else now, and covered by group insurance, you may be given the option of continuing that coverage even though you're no longer a member of the insured group. That's an advantage, because it's hard to buy new coverage for a small company. Also, a new policy wouldn't cover any pre-existing condition.

Employee Health Insurance

Employers aren't required to offer health coverage to employees. But good health insurance can help you keep good employees. Offer to share the cost with your employees if you can't afford to pay the whole cost yourself.

You should also consider life insurance on key employees. Buy it for any employee whose death would severely jeopardize your business. Cover your business against the loss, and also make part of the benefits payable to the employee's survivors.

Workers' Compensation Insurance

This is mandatory if you hire employees. *Homeowners, beware.* If you hire someone to work for you, even the neighbor's kid, you're required to have workers' comp for that worker. Some states now require minimum coverage for casual employees to be included in homeowners' policies automatically. See your insurance agent for complete rules and requirements.

Social Security for Employees

Employers must match employee contributions to Social Security (FICA). In 1988 that amounted to 7.51 percent of the first $45,000 of employee wages during the calendar year, and in 1989, the rate applied to the first $48,000 of earnings. The I.R.S. Circular E, Employer's Tax Guide, gives you the details about collecting and paying Social Security and withheld income tax. You use I.R.S. Form 941, which you file quarterly.

Social Security for You

Self-employed people pay FICA taxes when they file their personal income tax return. In 1988, the rate was 13.2 percent of business income. If your company is a corporation and pays wages, the employee's FICA tax is withheld from wages. The company also pays an equal amount in FICA tax.

Employer Identification Number

Once you hire employees, you have to file for a federal employer's identification number. Get I.R.S. Form SS-4 from the post office, the I.R.S. or any Social Security office. You may also need a tax ID number from your state. Check with your state employment or income tax office.

Business Paperwork

Like it or not, paperwork is part of doing business. Earlier, I listed a pack of forms for you to read and fill out. Where do you get the information to put on these forms? Your daily, weekly, monthly, quarterly, and yearly company and employee records. These records are part of your business history.

Payroll records are only one type of record your company must keep. Together, your business records should show how sick or healthy your business is. They help you make the decisions that should keep your company profitable.

What forms should you keep? I'd keep estimates, bids and contracts for five years. Your accountant or bookkeeper needs ledgers and spreadsheets, financial statements, job logs, inventory and tax forms. Again, I'd keep these for at least five years. You're *required* to keep records that support I.R.S. returns for at least four years from filing date or tax payment date, whichever is later.

I've included sample blank forms in this manual. Make a few copies of them on a copy machine. As you use them, modify them to fit your needs and the way you work. Then, after you're satisfied that you have a set of workable forms, get them printed in quantity. Copies will cost only a few cents each.

Here's a quick review of the records you'll need for your fence and retaining wall contracting business. In the next chapter I'll look at each of these and explain how each is used.

Bid Forms

These are *non-binding* sales contracts. You use them when you quote a job for doing some work. In some states, a bid is binding when you submit it to a government agency. The reason most bids are non-binding is that they haven't been agreed to by both parties. You generally use them to start the negotiation that leads to a sales contract.

Make your bids as accurate as you can. Avoid *lowball* bids. Some contractors use them to get their foot in the door, hoping to raise the price later during negotiation or when the customer makes changes. That can only lead to bad feelings. Do good work and charge a fair price for that work.

Sales Contracts

This may be your most important job document. It details your agreement with your customer about what you're going to do and how much they're going to pay. To be legally binding, be sure all parties sign and date the contracts. Each should receive a copy of the completed and signed contract. You can get sales contract forms from many stationery stores. Figure 12-2 is a sample sales contract form used in California.

Proposal and Contract

For Residential Building Construction and Alteration

Date_____19____

To _____

Dear Sir:

We propose to furnish all material and perform all labor necessary to complete the following:

_____

_____

_____

_____

_____

Job Location:

All of the above work to be completed in a substantial and workmanlike manner according to the drawings, job specifications, and terms and conditions for the sum of

Dollars ($_____)

Payments to be made as the work progresses as follows:_____

_____

_____

the entire amount of the contract to be paid within_____days after substantial completion and acceptance by the owner. The price quoted is for immediate acceptance only. Delay in acceptance will require a verification of prevailing labor and material costs. This offer becomes a contract upon acceptance by contractor but shall be null and void if not executed within 5 days from the date above.

By_____

"YOU, THE BUYER, MAY CANCEL THIS TRANSACTION AT ANY TIME PRIOR TO MIDNIGHT OF THE THIRD BUSINESS DAY AFTER THE DATE OF THIS TRANSACTION. SEE THE ATTACHED NOTICE OF CANCELLATION FORM FOR AN EXPLANATION OF THIS RIGHT."

You are hereby authorized to furnish all materials and labor required to complete the work according to the drawings, job specifications, and terms and conditions on the back of this proposal, for which we agree to pay the amounts itemized above

Owner _____

Owner _____ Date_____

Accepted by Contractor_____ Date_____

Figure 12-2
Sample proposal and contract

Right of Rescission

This form must be a part of every contract. Federal law gives the owner the right to cancel the sale any time within three working days. That cooling-off period protects consumers from high-pressure salesmen. There's a sample rescission form in Chapter 14 (Figure 14-2).

Ledgers and Journals

These are forms used to record all your business transactions. You list all income and expenses. From those figures, you can find your problem areas, budgets, forecasts, and taxes. You fill out some of these daily. The daily records are consolidated into weekly sheets, the weeklies to monthlies, and so on. The balance sheet and profit and loss statement show company finances at a particular time. Figure 12-3 is a sample spreadsheet. You'll see how to use it in Chapter 13.

Inventory Control Forms

Inventory falls into three categories: capital equipment, expendable items, and inventory for sale. Inventory is like money — and poor inventory control is money wasted. These control sheets help you keep track of what you own and how much it's worth. You'll need these forms when figuring the value for property tax purposes and depreciation for income tax purposes. Chapter 13 gives examples.

Financial Statements

Some day you're going to want to borrow money at the bank. You'll march down to the bank and say, "I want to borrow some money." The banker will smile at you and say, "Sure, let's see your P&L." You've read this manual, so you can say, "Sure, here it is." That puts you ahead of the game and more likely to get your loan.

Figure 12-4 is a blank financial statement form similar to forms used by many lenders. Page 1 of the form is a balance sheet, showing net worth. The top of page 2 covers the information you usually find on a profit and loss statement (P&L). The rest of the form is supporting information.

Make copies of this form and fill one out. Do this before you start your business, even if you're not applying for a loan. Make it part of your business plan. It gives you an idea of how much you're worth.

For more details on preparing P&Ls and other forms essential to your business, order a copy of *Contractor's Growth & Profit Guide*. There's an order form for it, and other construction manuals, at the back of this book.

Stationery and Envelopes

These present the only image of your company that many will ever see. When you first start your business, you'll type your name and address on your correspondence. As you grow and start earning, you can have these printed.

You'll need a logo or unique symbol that identifies your business. Visit your local print shop. They can probably suggest several logos that might be appropriate.

Personnel Forms

Once you have people working for you, you'll need employment applications. Then you'll need I.R.S. Form W-4 to certify withholding rates. You may use an employment contract, or a non-disclosure form to prevent an employee from telling others about your business. You'll need formats to discipline, review and inform employees. You'll have to keep track of wages and deductions, taxpayer's ID numbers, mailing addresses and emergency contacts. You'll need records of hours worked, vacations, holidays, and compensatory time.

In recent years, there's been an increase in lawsuits brought by employees against their employers. Smart employers keep very accurate records of what their employees are doing, and what agreements they've made.

Job Logs

This is your job history. It shows what you sold, how much you sold it for, what your costs were, and how much profit you made. You'll use these to analyze growth and pricing and respond to slow periods and new competition. There are more details in Chapter 13.

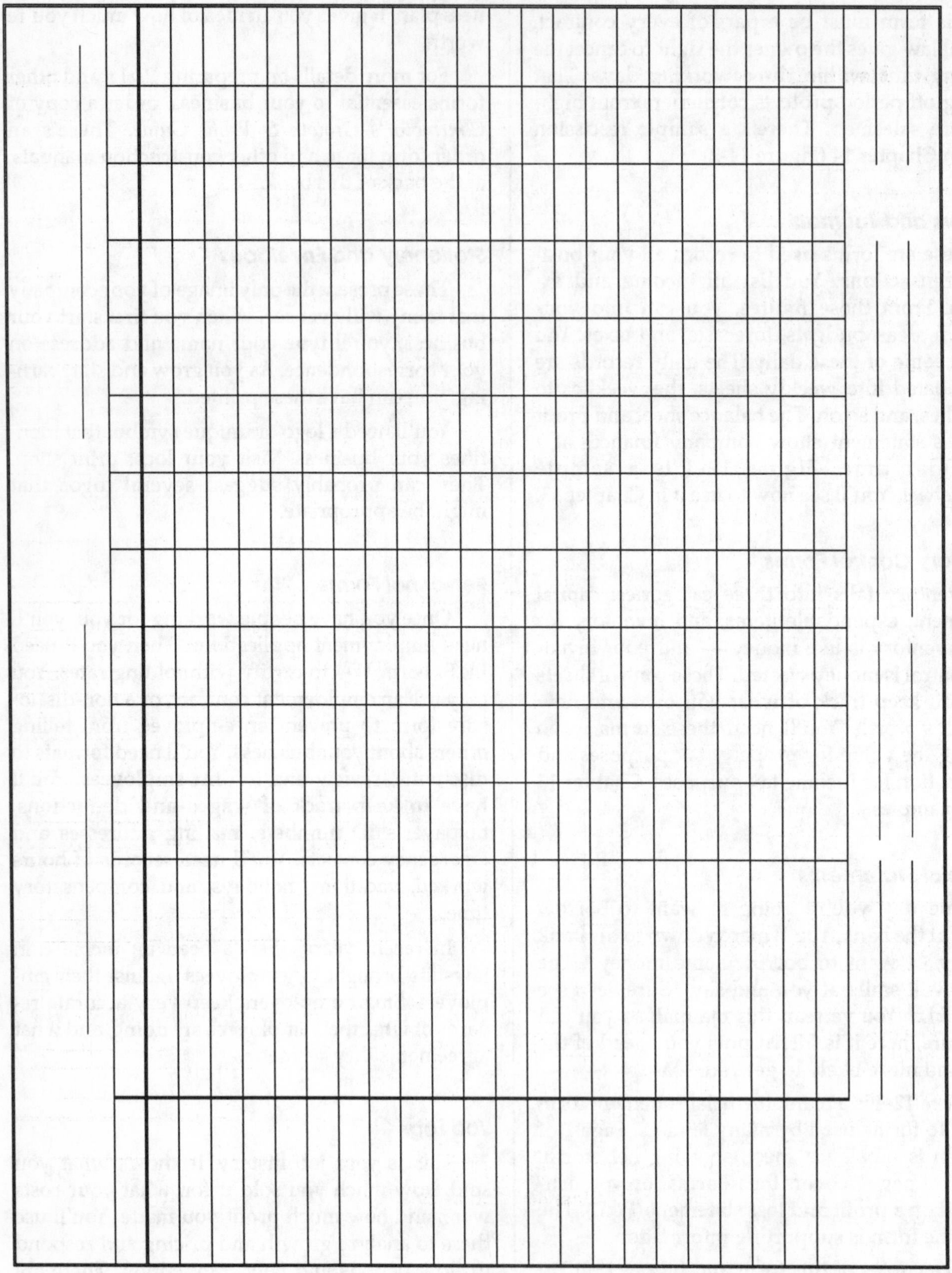

Figure 12-3
Spreadsheet format

Financial Statement - Sole Proprietor

(Individual who is sole proprietor of a business)

_____Office

Name_____

Address_____ Business_____

FINANCIAL CONDITION AT CLOSE OF BUSINESS...................................., 19.......

ASSETS				LIABILITIES			
Cash on Hand and in Bank - - - - - -				Accounts Payable—Not Due - - - - - -			
Accounts Rec. Customers—Current $_____				Accounts Payable—Past Due - - - - - -			
Accts. Rec. Customers—Past Due $_____				Notes Payable This Bank - - - - - - -			
Total Accounts Receivable - $_____				Notes Payable Other Banks - - - - - -			
Less: Reserve Doubtful Accts. $_____				Notes or Trade Acceptances Payable for Mdse.			
Notes Receivable—Customers - $_____				Other Notes Payable - - - - - - - -			
Less: Reserve Doubtful Notes $_____				Portion of Equipment Contracts and Chattel Mortgages Due Within One Year - - - -			
Trade Acceptances Receivable - - - - - -				Income Taxes Payable - - - - - - - -			
Merchandise—Finished - - - - - - -				Other Taxes Payable - - - - - - - -			
Merchandise—In Process - - - - - - -				Accrued Liabilities - - - - - - - - :			
Merchandise—Raw Materials - - - - - -				Other Current Debt (describe):			
Readily Marketable Securities (Schedule 2) - - -							
Net Cash Surrender Value Life Insurance (Sched. 1)				Portion of Long Term Debt Due within One Year			
TOTAL CURRENT ASSETS - - - - -				TOTAL CURRENT LIABILITIES - - -			
Real Estate and Bldgs. (Sched. 3) $_____				Real Estate Encumbrances (Schedule 4) - - -			
Less: Reserve for Depreciation $_____							
Machy., Equip., Fixtures - - - $_____				Non-Current Portion of Equipment Contracts and Chattel Mortgages - - - - - - -			
Less: Reserve for Depreciation $_____				Other Non-Current Debt (describe):			
Automobiles and Trucks - - - $_____							
Less: Reserve for Depreciation $_____							
Interests in Controlled or Affiliated Cos. (describe):				TOTAL LIABILITIES - - - - - -			
Other Securities Owned (Schedule 2) - - - - -				Other Reserves (describe):			
Mortgages Receivable (Schedule 5) - - - - -							
Other Non-Current Receivables (Schedule 5):							
Deferred and Prepaid Items - - - - - - -				NET WORTH - - - - - - - - - -			
TOTAL - - - - - - - - -				TOTAL - - - - - - - - -			

Figure 12-4
Financial statement

OPERATING RECORD FROM_____ 19___ **TO**_____ 19___ :

If profit and loss statement does not fit your operations, please attach a statement on your own form.

Net Sales for Period - - - - $_____

Cost of Goods Sold - - - - $_____

  Gross Profit - - - - - - - $_____

Selling Expense - - - - - - $_____

Administrative Expense - - - $_____

General Expense - - - - - $_____

  Total Operating Expense - - - - - - - $_____

Operating Profit - - - - - - - - $_____

Other Income - - - - - - - - - $_____

  Total - - - - - - - - - $_____

Federal & State Income Taxes $_____

Other Deductions - - - - - $_____

  Total Deductions - - - - - - - - $_____

Net Income - - - - - - - - - $_____

Total Depreciation and Amortization included above $_____

Deductions for Bad Accounts included above - - $_____

Do above expenses include salary to yourself?_____

  If so, how much? - - - - - - - - $_____

Reconciliation of Net Worth:

Net Worth at beginning of Period - - - - $_____

Net Income - - - - - - - - - $_____

*Other Additions - - - - - - - $_____

Total - - - - - - - - - - - $_____

Personal Withdrawals - - - $_____

*Other Deductions - - - - $_____ $_____

Net Worth as of this statement date - - - - $_____

*If Other Additions and Deductions involve important transactions please give details below:

_____

_____

_____

_____

_____

MONTHLY SALES

Please enter here your approximate sales by months during the past fiscal period:

Jan_____ Apr_____ Jul_____ Oct_____
Feb_____ May_____ Aug_____ Nov_____
Mar_____ Jun_____ Sept_____ Dec_____

Do the above figures include all of your income (both from your business and otherwise)?_____or do they relate to your business only?_____

Please describe here any unusual factors influencing your volume or earnings during the past fiscal period_____

_____

_____

OPERATING RECORD FOR PAST FIVE YEARS IF NOT PREVIOUSLY FURNISHED

Year	19	19	19	19	19
Sales or Gross Income					
Net Income					
Personal Withdrawals					

STATEMENT: By whom was this statement prepared?_____

Fiscal year ends on_____Regular time of taking inventory_____Regular time of balancing books_____

Are your books audited by an independent accountant?_____If so, by whom?_____

As of what date was his last audit made?_____Was a separate signed report prepared by the accountant?_____

Does this statement include all of your assets and liabilities as an individual (i.e. personal non-business assets and liabilities as well as those relating to your business)?_____If not, please also file a personal statement with us or describe here the extent and nature of your outside personal assets and liabilities_____

_____

_____Have your personal income taxes for last year been paid?_____

Are you married?_____If so, does this statement include any separate property of your wife (husband)?_____Explain_____

Have you made a will?_____Who is named executor of estate?_____

LEGAL STATUS: Do you do business under any style other than your own name?_____If so, what?_____

_____Has a certificate of fictitious trade style been filed and published?_____

Have you ever gone through bankruptcy or compromised a debt?_____If so, please give details_____

OTHER BANKS USED:

Name   City   Do you borrow there?   Maximum Debt Past Year

_____ _____ $_____

Figure 12-4 (cont'd)
Financial statement

SALES AND RECEIVABLES: About what portion of your sales are for cash?_____ Are a substantial part of your sales to any one customer?_____ If so, approximately what portion?_____ What are your usual selling terms on credit sales?_____ Is any material part of sales customarily on longer terms?_____ If so, please explain _____

About what amount of customers accounts receivable was past due on statement date?_____ On what portion of credit sales do customers take discounts?_____ Does any part of receivables represent merchandise out on consignment?_____ Approximate amount $_____

PURCHASES AND PAYABLES: What are your usual buying terms?_____ Are a material portion of your purchases customarily on other terms?_____ If so, explain_____

Are you taking all available discounts?_____ Please list principal suppliers on Schedule 6.

MERCHANDISE: Is this statement based on actual or estimated inventory?_____ If actual, by whom taken?_____

If estimated, on what basis?_____

How is merchandise valued? (Specify clearly whether at original cost, replacement market, the lower of the two, or on what other basis)_____

Is any portion of inventory consigned to customers?_____ Approximate amount $_____ Is any material part of the inventory excessive, slow moving or obsolete?_____ If so, explain_____

SEASONAL INFLUENCES: Are your sales seasonal?_____ If so, when are they highest?_____ Are your purchases seasonal?_____ If so, when are they highest?_____ Are your collections seasonal?_____ If so, when are receivables at their low point?_____ Does inventory fluctuate seasonally?_____ If so, when is it highest?_____ When lowest?_____ Please do not omit the monthly sales figures requested above.

RENTAL: Does business rent?_____ Present monthly rental paid $_____ Date of expiration of lease_____

SCHEDULE 1—INSURANCE

Has your present coverage been reviewed and approved by an insurance broker or adviser?_____

Fire insurance:		Liability Insurance:	
On Merchandise - - - - - - - - - - - - -	$_____	Public Liability on Owned Autos - - - - - - -	$_____
On Mach'y, Equipt. and Fixtures - - - - - -	$_____	Property Damage on Owned Autos - - - - - -	$_____
On Buildings - - - - - - - - - - - - - - -	$_____	P.L. and P.D. on Non-owned Autos - - - - - -	$_____
		Building & Elevator Pub. Liab. - - - - - - -	$_____

Please check those of following which are carried:

___Explosion Ins.   ___Steam Boiler   ___Auto Fire, Theft   ___Business Interruption   ___Products Liability

___Riot and Strike   ___Auto Collision   ___Workmen's Compensation   ___Robbery or Burglary   ___Machinery Breakdown

Is the extended coverage endorsement attached to fire policies?_____ Do any policies contain a coinsurance clause?_____ Basis___ %

Is any insurance on a monthly reporting basis?_____ Are employees having custody or control of property adequately bonded?_____

Insurance on my life:

Beneficiary	Amt. of Policy	Cash Value	Amt. of Loans	Net Cash Value
_____	$_____	$_____	$_____	$_____
_____	$_____	$_____	$_____	$_____
_____	$_____	$_____	$_____	$_____

SCHEDULE 2—SECURITIES OWNED—Please attach separate schedule if needed.

Stock-Shares, Bond-Amounts	Description	Value at Which Carried on this Statement	Current Mkt. on Listed		Estimated Value on Unlisted		
			@	Amount	@	Amount	Yrly. Div.

In what name are the above securities carried?_____

If in the name of yourself and co-owner are they joint tenancy?_____

Figure 12-4 (cont'd)
Financial statement

SCHEDULE 3—REAL ESTATE AND BUILDINGS—Please give details of encumbrances on Schedule 4 opposite proper Parcel No.

	Location and Description Include Nature of Improvements	Title in Name of	Monthly Income	Valuation		Amount of Encumbrance (Details Below)	Assessed Valuation
				Land	Improvements		
Parcel # 1							
Parcel # 2							
Parcel # 3							
Parcel # 4							
Parcel # 5							

Are any properties in joint tenancy?_____If so, which Parcel Nos.?_____Has a homestead been filed?_____

If so, on which Parcel No.?_____Are taxes or assessments delinquent on any of your properties?_____If so, please give amount and details _____

SCHEDULE 4—REAL ESTATE ENCUMBRANCES

	Amount Owing per Sched. 4	Nature of Encumbrance and To Whom Payable	Int. Rate	Due Date	How Payable	Are Int.* and Prin. Current?
On Parcel #1 Above						
On Parcel #2 Above						
On Parcel #3 Above						
On Parcel #4 Above						
On Parcel #5 Above						

*If any payments of principal or interest are delinquent, please give details _____

Has foreclosure been instituted?_____Details_____

SCHEDULE 5—MORTGAGES, AND OTHER NON-CUSTOMER RECEIVABLES

Name of Debtor	Amount Due	How Payable	Remarks (include description and value of any security)

SCHEDULE 6—PRINCIPAL SUPPLIERS—Please list concerns from which you buy large quantities and approximate amount due them on statement date.

Name and City	Amount Owed	Name and City	Amount Owed
	$		$
	$		$
	$		$

GENERAL REMARKS—Please explain here or in a supplementary letter any important differences between carrying values and actual values, any unusual receivables or payables of importance, or any other factors which have a bearing on interpretation of your financial statement.

For the purpose of procuring credit, from time to time, from the bank addressed, I furnish the foregoing as a true and accurate statement of my affairs on the date indicated. I have answered the questions on page two of this exhibit and certify that I have no liabilities except as reported therein and elsewhere in this exhibit. I agree to notify the said bank immediately, in writing, of any unfavorable change in my financial condition. I have carefully read the financial statement and supporting information on the four pages of this exhibit, both printed and written, and I solemnly declare and certify that this is a true and correct account of my financial condition on the date stated.

FOR BANK USE
BRANCH CERTIFICATION: This is a copy of the original statement, properly signed, in the credit files of this Branch.

Date_____ _____
Manager

_____
(Date Signed)

_____
Signature

Figure 12-4 (cont'd)
Financial statement

Estimating Sheets

These worksheets will help you calculate material requirements, manhour requirements, and costs. Develop a reliable estimating system and update it regularly. There's more information about this in Chapter 16.

Let's recap all we've covered in this chapter. You've thought about why you want to start your own business. You've found a source for the money you need. You've applied for your business license and DBA, and decided what your legal setup will be. You've started advertising and lined up a few customers. You know where to get more information about taxes and insurance, and you have an inkling of what you'll need to run your office.

All of this will cost you about $800 for a sole proprietorship, and up to several thousand for a corporation. Of course, these costs don't include materials or tools or any office equipment.

In the next chapter I'll show how to set up an accounting system and use the forms I mentioned in this chapter.

thirteen

The Books You Keep

Your company is nearly three years old now and business is great! You've got two fence crews busy most of the time and your bank account is swelling. You've established trade credit with several suppliers and can get good discounts on most materials. You have two trucks and the equipment you need to handle almost any job that comes your way. You've set up a small office in a spare bedroom at home. Your ads are in two local newspapers every week. Things are going so well you're thinking of adding a third crew. It's a great feeling.

Then the wheels start to fall off:

1) You're in a dispute with a major supplier over some old credits. They claim you took return credits for materials that were never actually returned. You can't find the paperwork but remember sending nearly a full load of posts back.

2) Your accountant needs a current equipment list so he can develop a depreciation schedule. You can't find any paperwork that shows what you paid for the company mixers.

3) The state made a "routine audit" of your second year's state tax return. No problem, except that you were paying some employees in cash during part of that year. The auditor found those payments. Now the state has sent a demand for the money due.

4) You're bidding two small jobs for the county and need bid and performance bonds for both. The bonding company won't issue the bonds until you bring in a current balance sheet and P&L for the year. These jobs are important to you. They could open up a whole new (and profitable) market for your company. But without those financial records, you're sunk.

5) Your credit line at the bank is due for renewal. But the bank is getting nervous about the state tax deficiency. They won't even talk about the credit line until you bring in current financials.

I think you're in trouble.

These are the types of things that happen when you don't keep adequate business records. Unfortunately, problems like these are all too common. A good, profitable, growing business gets into serious trouble because the owner is better at building than he is at office procedures. Some specialty contractors can recover from problems like these. Others never do.

You don't have to fit the typical mold. You can be the contractor with enough business smarts to avoid problems like these. Keep business records that comply with state and federal tax laws. It's not hard. Then, when the I.R.S. comes to audit you — and eventually they will — you'll be prepared.

The Chart of Accounts

The most basic document in every record-keeping system is the chart of accounts. It's a list that shows assets, liability, sales and expense categories by name and reference number. Each account has an assigned number because computers love numbers. Your numbering system should group similar items together and leave gaps in the numbers so you can add sub-accounts for more detailed classification.

Figure 13-1 is the chart of accounts I use. It probably has more detail than you'll need. But too much detail is better than too little. Use my numbering system or get your bookkeeper or accountant to recommend a system that's better for your company. The important thing is to have convenient categories for each type of income and expense, asset and liability.

Notice how many expense categories I've created. One reasons so many businesses fail in the first year is that they don't anticipate all their expenses.

The next step is to set up a filing system. If you've got the spare cash, buy a four-drawer steel filing cabinet. A cardboard file box works almost as well and costs lots less. But don't skimp on file folders, file hangers, and file markers. Get plenty.

If you're short on cash, just buy some heavy 9-1/2 x 12 envelopes. Label one for each account number on your chart of accounts. Put the following information in the upper left corner of each envelope:

Date file started ___/___/___

Account number _____

Account name_____

Closing date ___/___/___

Use these envelopes to store your receipts and notes on each account. File the envelopes by account number in a desk drawer, file cabinet, bookshelf or cardboard box. Of course, a file cabinet is most convenient, if you've got one.

Next, buy a loose-leaf binder and make 100 copies of Figure 12-3 from the last chapter. Punch holes in each sheet and put them in the binder. These forms are your business spreadsheets. If you have a computer and a spreadsheet program, use it instead.

You can choose from dozens of spreadsheet programs at computer software stores. Lotus 1-2-3 and Eight-in-One are two of the more popular programs. Eight-in-One also includes a word processing program — the one I used to write this book.

The Spreadsheet

Use spreadsheets to summarize your business transactions. You'll need three sets of spreadsheets. Use the first set to record each day's activity. The second set is a monthly summary, and the third set is a consolidated report by year. Here's how it works:

First, make a spreadsheet for each major account classification. Page 1 is for income. That's what you get paid for fence and retaining wall work. Page 2 is for expenses, the cost of completing your jobs and running your office. List the account names and numbers across the top of the form. List the days of the month down the left column. Now put the total of each day's activity for each account in the box corresponding to the account and date. A check you receive from a customer on the 2nd of the month, for example, would go under *Gross Receipts*, in the row labeled "2." If you pay the rent on the 10th, put the amount of the check in the *Rent* column in row 10.

10000		**ASSETS**	**40000**		**INCOME**
10100		Current assets	40100		Production income
	10110	Cash in bank		40110	Sales of labor
	10120	Petty cash		40120	Sales of materials
	10130	Accounts receivable		40130	Travel costs billed to customers
10200		Fixed assets	40200		Consultant services sold
	10210	Vehicles	40300		Equipment rentals
		10215 Depreciation reserve	40400		Interest received
	10220	Construction equipment	40500		Income from company owned investments
		10225 Depreciation reserve			
	10230	Office equipment			
		10235 Depreciation reserve	**50000**		**COST OF SALES**
10300		Prepaid assets	50100		Beginning inventory
	10310	Prepaid insurance	50200		Purchases for resale
	10320	Prepaid rent		50210	Freight in
				50220	Sales tax paid
20000		**LIABILITIES**	50300		Direct labor
			50400		Subcontract labor
20100		Current liabilities	50500		Materials and supplies
	20110	Accounts payable	50600		Other direct costs
	20120	Sales tax payable		50610	Permits, fees
	20130	Payroll tax payable		50620	Surveys
20200		Long term liabilities	50900		Ending inventory
	20210	Loans payable			
	20220	Auto loan	**60000**		**EXPENSES**
	20230	Truck loan			
	20240	Equipment loan	60100		Advertising
				60110	Yellow pages
30000		**EQUITY**		60120	Newspaper ads
				60130	Signs
30100		Owner's draw		60140	Business cards
30200		Retained earnings		60150	Promotional gifts
30300		Profit (loss)	60200		Bad debts
30400		Non-deductible expense	60300		Bank charges
				60310	Checking account charges

Figure 13-1
Chart of accounts

60320	Visa, MasterCard fees		61200	Office expenses
			61210	Office equipment under $100
			61220	Stationery
60400	**Car and truck**		61230	Computer supplies
60410	Gas and oil		61240	Printing
60420	Tires		61290	Coffee and donuts
60430	Repairs		61300	Rent on business property
60440	Maintenance		61400	Repairs on building and equipment
60500	Commissions		61500	Supplies
60600	Depreciation expense		61510	Tools under $100
60700	Dues and publications		61520	Shop towels, paper products
60800	Employee benefits		61530	Maintenance equipment
60810	Pension and profit sharing		61540	Safety equipment
60820	Medical, dental insurance		61541	Fire extinguishers
60830	Parties		61542	Medical kits
60840	Bonuses		61600	Taxes
60900	Insurance		61610	FICA - Employer's share
60910	Liability		61620	Unemployment tax
60920	Property		61630	Property tax
60930	Blanket umbrella		61700	Travel, meals, entertainment
60990	Paid deductibles		61800	Utilities, telephone
61000	Interest		61900	Wages (indirect labor)
61010	Auto loan		61910	Vacation Pay
61020	Truck loan		61920	Sick Leave
61030	Equipment loan		62000	Miscellaneous expenses
61100	Legal and professional services		62010	Business license
61110	Accountant		62020	DBA recording
61120	Lawyer			
61130	Consultant		**70000**	**INCOME TAX PROVISION**

Figure 13-1 (cont'd)
Chart of accounts

December Expense Log

DATE	ROW TOTAL	RENT	PHONE	UTIL	INSUR	VEHICLE	ADVERT	PAYROLL	TAXES	MATERIAL
2	1438.12	83.33			125.01		166.67	625.25	187.51	250.35
3	50.85									50.85
4	16.67		16.67							
5	0.00									
6	0.00									
9	1051.50						200.54			850.96
10	854.43			41.67				625.25	187.51	
11	25.33									25.33
12	12.54									12.54
13	0.00									
16	1250.64									1250.64
17	812.76							625.25	187.51	
18	0.00									
19	198.54						198.54			
20	300.89									300.89
23	0.00									
24	1161.87					333.33		625.25	187.51	15.78
25	0.00									
26	0.00									
27	72.45									72.45
30	185.25									185.25
31	65.85									65.85
Total	7497.69	83.33	16.67	41.67	125.01	333.33	565.75	2501.00	750.04	3080.89

Figure 13-2
Daily expense spreadsheet

At the end of the month, total each column and enter that figure at the bottom of each column. If you're using a computer, the program will do this automatically.

Next, transfer totals at the foot of each column to the monthly spreadsheet. The monthly spreadsheet is nearly the same as the daily sheet. I call it the *monthly consolidation*. The top line shows the same column headings as the daily sheets. List the months of the year in the left column instead of the days of the month.

At the end of the year, total the columns on the monthly consolidation and transfer the numbers to the annual spreadsheet. Label this the *yearly consolidation* and put the year in the left column. This gives you running totals for all income and expense accounts. You can use this record to ana-lyze your performance, identify your strong and weak points, plan, and make changes. You'll also have a tax record that will satisfy the I.R.S.

These sheets show exactly where every penny is spent. You'll know how much you earned. You'll have the information a lender needs when it's time to renew a credit line. You'll have answers for your accountant, banker, tax attorney and shareholders.

Figure 13-2 is the detailed spreadsheet you'd fill out after each day's business. Figure 13-3 is the monthly consolidation and Figure 13-4 is the yearly consolidation.

It's easier to see your company's business trends if you graph these numbers. The simplest graph is the *line graph*. Just connect the dots and you see what's happening. Each dot represents a

DATE	ROW TOTAL	RENT	PHONE	UTIL	INSUR	VEHICLE	ADVERT	PAYROLL	TAXES	MATERIAL
Jan	5,461.65	83.33	22.35	41.67	125.01	32.56	550.25	2,100.00	650.25	1,856.23
Feb	5,737.11	83.33	21.46	38.52	125.01	158.41	525.55	2,100.00	650.25	2,034.58
Mar	7,319.64	83.33	15.25	34.98	125.01	1,675.23	650.35	2,100.00	650.25	1,985.24
Apr	7,913.45	83.33	17.89	32.54	125.01	333.33	600.45	2,200.00	675.25	3,845.65
May	8,275.54	83.33	14.75	28.46	125.01	333.33	525.85	2,200.00	675.25	4,289.56
Jun	8,796.25	83.33	16.78	25.78	125.01	333.33	500.65	2,200.00	675.25	4,836.12
Jul	8,813.07	83.33	22.51	32.56	125.01	333.33	450.25	2,300.00	700.85	4,765.23
Aug	8,491.71	83.33	18.32	42.91	125.01	333.33	400.75	2,300.00	700.85	4,487.21
Sep	8,848.19	83.33	16.45	48.12	125.01	333.33	475.85	2,300.00	700.85	4,765.25
Oct	7,577.12	83.33	15.85	43.15	125.01	333.33	525.65	2,400.00	725.35	3,325.45
Nov	6,930.85	83.33	17.12	40.85	125.01	333.33	550.95	2,400.00	725.35	2,654.91
Dec	7,497.69	83.33	16.67	41.67	125.01	333.33	565.75	2,501.00	750.04	3,080.89
TOTAL	91,662.27	999.96	215.40	451.21	1,500.12	4,866.17	6,322.30	27,101.00	8,279.79	41,926.32

Figure 13-3
Monthly consolidation spreadsheet

YEAR	ROW TOTAL	RENT	PHONE	UTIL	INSUR	VEHICLE	ADVERT	PAYROLL	TAXES	MATERIAL
1986	66,687.81	450.25	350.12	212.65	550.25	1,125.45	2,850.65	22,355.00	6,145.32	32,648.12
1987	78,182.17	850.55	285.95	322.45	675.25	1,652.45	4,500.00	25,000.00	7,436.54	37,458.98
1988	91,662.27	999.96	215.40	451.21	1,500.12	4,866.17	6,322.30	27,101.00	8,279.79	41,926.32
TOTAL	236,532.25	2,300.76	851.47	986.31	2,725.62	7,644.07	13,672.95	74,456.00	21,861.65	112,033.42

Figure 13-4
Yearly consolidation spreadsheet

number from your spreadsheet. If you're using a computer spreadsheet program, it can probably make the charts and graphs for you. Figure 13-5 shows a line graph, a bar graph, and a pie chart.

The line graph in Figure 13-5 compares advertising expense for the previous three years, but you could also use it to show a relationship between certain kinds of income and expense. For instance, you could show advertising for the year with one line, and income for the same period with another. Then you can see how sales relate to advertising expense.

The bar graph is a good way to compare several items of income or expense against the same items during a previous period.

Pie charts let you see at a glance what percentage of income or expense is represented by various categories.

Asset Records

Keeping track of expenses and income isn't enough. You also need to follow changes in company *assets*. Assets are the things your company owns: tools, materials in inventory, cash in the bank, accounts receivable, and office equipment. There are several good reasons to keep a list of your assets:

1) If you decide to sell your company, your potential buyer will want to know what they're getting.

2) A lender will want a list of your assets as collateral for a loan.

3) When equipment is lost or destroyed, your insurance company will want to know what they're replacing.

4) Many states have property taxes on the value of equipment and office furnishings. You have to describe fixtures and equipment and list the cost on the assessor's form.

5) When your company buys a truck (or any expensive equipment or building), the purchase price isn't an expense in the year of purchase. Instead, tax law requires that you take a portion of the cost as expense each year over the expected life of the asset. This is called depreciation or "cost recovery." It's a complex subject best left to the person or firm that prepares your tax returns. But no matter who prepares your return, they'll need an accurate list of what you own, when you bought it, and how much it cost.

Figure 13-6 shows some of the assets on my current equipment schedule. Keep a list like this for all your company assets.

Please notice the numbering system. The first number is the classification. The last three digits are the item number. You can put up to 999 items in each file, more than enough for most small businesses.

Notice also that I've got separate classifications for items over and under $100. Generally your accountant will want to expense in the current year anything that costs less than a certain amount. You have to depreciate more expensive items over several years. Let your accountant suggest what should be expensed and what has to be depreciated.

By the way, use an engraver to mark your company name on tools and equipment. You may be able to borrow an engraver from your local police station. Use a special code name or number so if your property is stolen and recovered, you'll be able to identify and claim it.

Inventory

I generally have some inventory of materials on hand. Eventually I'll either use it, sell it, or return it for credit. There are three types of inventory to keep track of:

1) *Expendable inventory* includes items like computer paper, work gloves, nails, miscellaneous hardware, etc. You probably don't need to keep track of small value items like these. But watch out for "shrinkage." If you're buying far more computer paper than you're using, some paper is probably disappearing out the door before it's used.

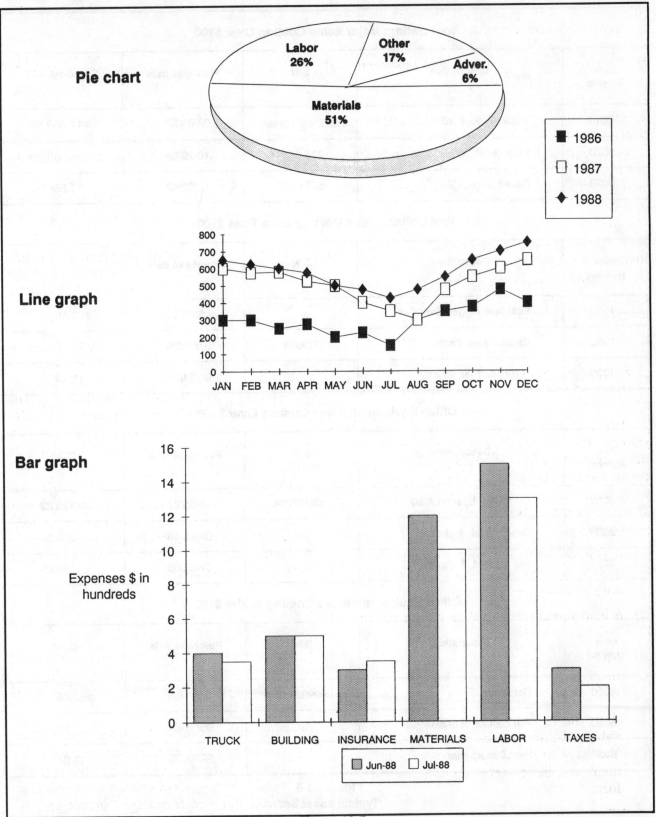

Figure 13-5
Use graphs to show business trends

Tool Listing: Major Items Costing Over $100

Item number	Description	S/N	Purchase date	Cost
0010	Truck, 2 ton, Ford	1N237656378954	08/01/87	$11,560.00
0020	Chain saw, 18", Beaver	236-56444	10/29/86	285.00
0030	Power auger, Clint	568742	12/22/87	1,268.00

Tool Listing: Items Costing Less Than $100

Item number	Description	S/N	Purchase date	Cost
1010	Post hole digger, SandCat		06/25/86	$33.50
1020	Circular saw, Craft	21/3654	07/12/86	72.50
1030	Claw hammer, 22 oz.		06/14/86	15.23

Office Equipment: Items Costing Over $100

Item Number	Description	S/N	Purchase date	Cost
2010	Computer, Epson LX-80	12P57264	10/25/87	$2,125.32
2020	Desk, metal, 4 drawer		09/25/86	250.54
2030	File cabinet, 4 drawer		07/02/86	185.65

Office Equipment: Items Costing Under $100

Item number	Description	S/N	Purchase date	Cost
3010	Calculator, Brant	999521	06/11/86	$62.85
3020	File cabinet, 2 drawer		06/11/86	92.31
3030	Pencil sharpener		07/12/86	18.64

Figure 13-6
Typical asset list

2) *Usable* or *current* inventory is material you'll probably need in the next few weeks for a job. Say you have 1,000 board feet of redwood 2 x 4s. When you deliver this inventory to a job, subtract the amount delivered from your inventory record. When you reach a specified low point, it's time to re-order.

3) *Obsolete* inventory is material you've had on hand for a long time. Most unsold inventory that's over two years old is probably obsolete. Obsolete inventory ties up your cash. It's idle money not being used to make more money. Better to sell it at a loss than have it take up valuable space. Some money is better than no money at all. Give it away if you have to.

Inventory in storage loses value every day. Would you take a $100 bill out of your pocket and leave it out in your yard? Let it get rained on, snowed on, dried out, weathered and rotted? Allow it to sit there for six months or more? That's what happens to a pile of redwood lumber. The odds are better if you put that $100 into the lottery than if you leave $100 in materials idle in storage.

It's called a *turn* when you move inventory into your yard and then out to your customer, collecting its cost and your profit as you do. Track your inventory to see how many turns it makes in a year. If your inventory value is $10,000 and inventory purchases totaled $100,000 for the year, you turned inventory ten times that year. In the fence and retaining wall business, inventory should turn from four to twelve times a year. The best way to improve your inventory turn is to keep little or no inventory at all.

You might say, "I don't care if that lumber sits there for a year, I'll use it eventually." That's probably true, but look at it this way:

Let's say you invest $1,000 in redwood 2 x 4s. They sit there for a year unsold. If you'd had that $1,000 in the bank during the year, it might have earned interest of $55. That's not a lot, but it's $55 ahead of what your lumber pile did.

Now, let's say you bought redwood 1 x 3s instead and sold them the first month and made a $55 profit on the sale. Now you reinvest the origi-nal $1,000 and do the same thing again. Each month you continue to sell out and make a profit of $55.

In the first case you made nothing from your investment. In the second case you made $55. But in the third case, you made $660. That's not too shabby. Your inventory turn made the difference. This is called *ROI* or Return On Investment. The ROI in the first case is zero, the second, 5.5 percent, and the third, 66 percent. Which do you prefer?

How do you end up with too much inventory?

1) You don't want to spend hours each week at the lumber or masonry supply yard, so you buy in quantity.

2) You want to increase your margin, so you buy larger quantities to get a better discount.

3) You accumulate leftovers when you over-order for a job.

4) You buy materials in anticipation of jobs that are canceled.

5) You buy materials by mistake

It doesn't matter *why* you have inventory. What matters is keeping track of it. Keep inventory records like this:

Current Inventory on Hand					
Item Num	Description	QTY	Pur. Date	Cost	U/M
10010	Redwood, 1 x 3 x 6'	550	01/12/89	$ 1.05	each
10020	Fir 2 x 4 x 8'	25	1/12/88	1.90	each
10030	Pine 1 x 4 x 6'	45	2/15/87	.79	each
20010	Block, stretchers	120	3/24/87	1.65	each
30010	Cement, 94 lb sacks	10	4/01/87	6.00	bag

Do the same thing for expendable and obsolete inventory. Add an "extension" column showing the quantity times the price per unit. That way you can see the total investment. And you might want to add columns to show product type, size, grade, storage location, minimum order quantities, selling price, source and buying history.

I include the size and grade in the description column. If you have separate columns for these, and later convert to computer, you'll have an advantage. Computers can sort and select very quickly with software like the programs I mentioned. I can tell the computer to sort and list all the 1 x 3s I have in stock, or all the tan block. I have the list in seconds.

There's one other list you may find helpful. List things you've bought in the past but don't keep on hand regularly. The list will identify usage and cost for your non-stock items. If you start using more of an item, you might want to add it to your regular inventory. And the list is a reminder of where you got seldom-used items and where they were cheapest.

Vendor File

The companies you buy from are your *vendors*. Keep a list of all of them. Include the vendor's name, address, phone number, hours of operation, credit terms, and person to contact. You may also want to add items like delivery policy, product quality, products handled, billing date, payment dates, and your purchase history. Keep this list on computer, in a log book, or in a card file.

You'll probably find credit terms on your vendor's invoices. They look something like, "2% 10, net 30." This means you can deduct 2 percent from the invoice total if you pay it within ten days. The full amount is due within 30 days, after which time the vendor may add a service charge. Vendors offer the additional discount as an incentive for customers to pay their bills promptly. It worked with me.

Markups and Overhead

Markup is the factor you add to the cost of an item to cover your expenses and make a profit. Markup includes your *overhead*.

Cost + overhead + profit = selling price

Your markup is the factor you multiply by your cost to find the selling price. Figure 13-7 is a table of markups from one to 99. As you can see, the SPF (selling price factor) begins to jump rapidly once the markup percentage reaches about 70 percent. That's the point where the SPF times your cost gives a price that's probably more than your buyers are willing to pay.

Most retailers use an SPF of 1.66 to 2.5. Wholesalers use an SPF of 1.11 to 1.47, while manufacturers generally use 2.5 to 3.33. For contractors, an SPF of from 1.98 to 3.33 is about right. That means you'd sell an item that cost you $100 for from $198 to $333 to cover your profit and overhead.

Overhead is office expense, all costs except direct job costs such as labor, materials, equipment, supervision, and permits. When you sell a wall or fence, you buy the materials to build it. You know how much those materials cost because you have a bill from the vendor. You also know how much profit you want to make on the job. But how much should you charge for overhead?

There are two kinds of overhead expenses, *fixed* and *variable*. Fixed expenses tend to stay the same, even when the amount of business you're doing goes up or down. Rent, mortgage, loan payments, your salary, and utility bills are examples of fixed expenses. Variable expenses change with your business volume. For example, if you have more work, you may have to hire some part-time temporary employees or rent another truck. Sales commissions, some insurance, taxes, and the amount you spend on office supplies will vary with your sales volume.

If your fixed expenses are $2,500 the first month you're in business, you can expect to spend $30,000 the first year. If you work 40 hours a week for 52 weeks a year, that totals 2,080 hours. If you divide $30,000 by 2,080 hours, that means you'll have to make $14.42 per hour just to cover your fixed expenses.

Now, let's add another $30,000 per year for your pay. That makes the hourly rate $28.84. But you won't actually be producing fences and retaining walls the whole time you're working at your business. According to the national average, 15 percent of labor hours are *loss time*. This is the time you're not working at paying jobs because of

Markup Table

Markup %	SPF	Markup %	SPF	Markup %	SPF	Markup %	SPF	Markup %	SPF
0	1.000	20	1.250	40	1.666	60	2.500	80	5.000
1	1.010	21	1.265	41	1.694	61	2.564	81	5.263
2	1.020	22	1.282	42	1.724	62	2.631	82	5.555
3	1.030	23	1.298	43	1.754	63	2.702	83	5.882
4	1.041	24	1.315	44	1.785	64	2.777	84	6.250
5	1.052	25	1.333	45	1.818	65	2.857	85	6.666
6	1.063	26	1.351	46	1.851	66	2.941	86	7.142
7	1.075	27	1.369	47	1.886	67	3.030	87	7.692
8	1.086	28	1.388	48	1.923	68	3.125	88	8.333
9	1.098	29	1.408	49	1.960	69	3.225	89	9.090
10	1.111	30	1.428	50	2.000	70	3.333	90	10.000
11	1.123	31	1.449	51	2.040	71	3.448	91	11.110
12	1.136	32	1.470	52	2.083	72	3.571	92	12.500
13	1.149	33	1.492	53	2.127	73	3.703	93	14.285
14	1.162	34	1.515	54	2.173	74	3.846	94	16.666
15	1.176	35	1.538	55	2.222	75	4.000	95	20.000
16	1.190	36	1.562	56	2.272	76	4.166	96	25.000
17	1.204	37	1.587	57	2.325	77	4.347	97	33.333
18	1.219	38	1.612	58	2.380	78	4.545	98	50.000
19	1.234	39	1.639	59	2.439	79	4.761	99	100.000

Figure 13-7
Markup table

sickness, accidents, bad weather, equipment breakdowns, pulling permits, or any other reason. And I haven't even mentioned time spent correcting mistakes.

So now you have to meet fixed expenses and your salary with only 1,768 productive hours per year (2,080 hours less 15 percent.) So your hourly rate is $33.94. That means that for every eight-hour day you work, you have to charge $271.52, plus materials, *plus profit*.

Suppose you have a job that's going to take three working days. Material cost will be $1,000.

Materials	$1,000.00
Labor & overhead	814.56 (3 times $271.52)
	$1,814.56

Now you have to add profit. Let's use 9 percent. After all, why should you be in business if you can't make some money? You've risked your money, time and reputation, so you should get back *at least* what your money would have earned if you'd put it in the bank. Multiply $1,814.56 by 1.09 (your principal plus 9 percent interest) and you have $1,977.87. That's what you have to charge your customer.

You can convert this to a markup factor by dividing the selling price by your cost for materials:

$$1,977.87 \div 1,000 = 1.98$$

Now you can apply the markup factor to the material cost to find your selling price. If your next job requires $200 worth of materials, your selling price would be $396.

$$\$200 \times 1.98 = \$396$$

At this price, you should cover all your bills and expenses, earn a good wage for your time, and make a profit. And don't forget to include sales tax on your customer's bill, if you're required to collect it.

How Much Do You Want to Make?

I gave you a gross yearly salary of $30,000. After taxes you may keep about $21,000. I gave you a gross profit of 9 percent, but that may only be 2 percent net, depending on your tax bracket, other income, and deductions. Remember, these figures were based on a 40-hour work week, less some time for non-productive activities. I didn't include the time it will take you to do paperwork or the hundred and one other things you can't bill directly to your customers.

In most small businesses, the owner works 50 to 70 hours a week. If you work 60 hours, your hourly pay will be $9.62. (Sixty hours a week is 3,120 hours per year. $30,000 divided by 3,120 is $9.62.) If you apply this formula to an 80-hour week, your pay will only be $7.21 per hour. You can earn more than that working for someone else, and not have the risk or headaches. So let's go back and set a more realistic salary for you, the business owner.

You've seen how to set up a chart of accounts for your business. Now, do one for yourself. List all your personal expenses for a year. Include the rent, phone, lights, food, clothes, miscellaneous costs. Give yourself a "profit," a bank account for future growth, vacations, kids' education, and retirement.

Begin by filling out a form like the one in Figure 13-8. Fill in the blanks based on your past spending history. Be sure to give yourself a reserve for income and Social Security taxes, about 32 percent of the total. If you want a new car or home, show the new payment amounts under future expenses. It all adds up, doesn't it! You can use the table in Figure 13-9 to convert annual income to monthly, weekly or hourly rates. Finally, plug your hourly rate into the above examples, and recalculate those jobs.

Now I'm going to sling some mud into the picture. Most new businesses don't start producing a living for the owner for the first six to 18 months. That's a fact, and you better count on it. Do you have at least a six-month reserve in your bank account? You'll need that much, plus what it will cost to set up your business and keep it running for a few months. In 1989 it took about $45,000 cash to start a new business with a good chance for success. Maybe you can do it for less, but your chances aren't good.

I don't want to discourage you from starting your own company. I've started my own business from scratch. It's made me a good living. Maybe I was lucky. Most businesses that start with no capital don't survive very long. The odds are better if you hold off starting a business until you're ready. Hop in with your eyes closed and you'll lose more than a lot of sleep.

Since you're still reading, I'll assume you're determined to start your own business. How did you come out with your salary projection? My guess is, you probably want to make about $50,000 a year before taxes. I'll also guess that you'll want to be earning about 18 percent profit on your business before taxes. If you went back and plugged in the figures, you probably came up with a markup of about 2.3 times material cost. My experience tells me you're still too low. I suggest a minimum markup of 2.5. On small jobs, under $200, use a 3.3 markup. If you manufacture prefab fencing, use 2.7. The material cost is higher and the labor cost is lower.

The markup figures I've given you work out to between $35 and $45 per hour. I suggest you bill a minimum of four hours on any job. Even on a little repair job, it takes you that long to make the sale,

	Current expenses Per year	Anticipated expenses Per year
HOUSING		
Rent or mortgage	$_____	$_____
Taxes, property	_____	_____
Gas and electric	_____	_____
Telephone	_____	_____
Insurance	_____	_____
Maintenance*	_____	_____
Improvements	_____	_____

*Maintenance should include lawn care, appliance repairs, repainting, cleaning, and all other expected and emergency repairs

VEHICLE #1		
Cost or depreciation	$_____	$_____
Loan repayments	_____	_____
Taxes, road	_____	_____
Registration fees	_____	_____
Insurance	_____	_____
Maintenance	_____	_____
Emergency repairs	_____	_____
Gas and oil	_____	_____
VEHICLE #2		
Cost or depreciation	$_____	$_____
Loan repayments	_____	_____
Taxes, road	_____	_____
Registration fees	_____	_____
Insurance	_____	_____
Maintenance	_____	_____
Emergency repairs	_____	_____
Gas and oil	_____	_____
FOOD	$_____	$_____
ENTERTAINMENT	_____	_____
TRAVEL	_____	_____
CLOTHING	_____	_____
EDUCATIONAL, SELF OR MATE	_____	_____
SAVINGS	_____	_____
TAXES		
Income, Federal & State	$_____	$_____
FICA	_____	_____
SDI	_____	_____
Other	_____	_____
CHILDREN		
Education, general	$_____	$_____
Education, special & reserve	_____	_____
Insurance, special or sports	_____	_____
Toys and other goodies	_____	_____
INSURANCE		
Life, self or family	$_____	$_____
Health, self or family	_____	_____
TOTALS	$_____	$_____

Figure 13-8
Personal expenses

| \multicolumn{5}{c}{Pay Rate Conversion Chart} |

Hourly	Daily	Weekly	Monthly	Yearly
4.25	34.00	170.00	736.66	8,840
4.50	36.00	180.00	780.00	9,360
4.75	38.00	190.00	823.33	9,880
5.00	40.00	200.00	866.66	10,400
5.25	42.00	210.00	910.00	10,920
5.50	44.00	220.00	953.33	11,440
5.75	46.00	230.00	996.66	11,960
6.00	48.00	240.00	1,040.00	12,480
6.25	50.00	250.00	1,083.00	13,000
6.50	52.00	260.00	1,126.66	13,520
6.75	54.00	270.00	1,170.00	14,040
7.00	56.00	280.00	1,213.33	14,560
7.25	58.00	290.00	1,256.66	15,080
7.50	60.00	300.00	1,300.00	15,600
7.75	62.00	310.00	1,343.33	16,120
8.00	64.00	320.00	1,386.66	16,640
8.25	66.00	330.00	1,430.00	17,160
8.50	68.00	340.00	1,473.33	17,680
8.75	70.00	350.00	1,516.66	18,200
9.00	72.00	360.00	1,560.00	18,720
9.25	74.00	370.00	1,603.33	19,240
9.50	76.00	380.00	1,646.66	19,760
9.75	78.00	390.00	1,690.00	20,280
10.00	80.00	400.00	1,733.33	20,800
10.25	82.00	410.00	1,776.66	21,320
10.50	84.00	420.00	1,820.00	21,840
10.75	86.00	430.00	1,863.33	22,360
11.00	88.00	440.00	1,906.66	22,880
11.25	90.00	450.00	1,950.00	23,400
11.50	92.00	460.00	1,993.33	23,920
11.75	94.00	470.00	2,036.66	24,440
12.00	96.00	480.00	2,080.00	24,960
12.25	98.00	490.00	2,123.33	24,480
12.50	100.00	500.00	2,166.66	26,000
12.75	102.00	510.00	2,210.00	26,520
13.00	104.00	520.00	2,253.33	27,040
13.25	106.00	530.00	2,296.66	27,560

| \multicolumn{5}{c}{Pay Rate Conversion Chart} |

Hourly	Daily	Weekly	Monthly	Yearly
13.50	108.00	540.00	2,340.00	28,080
13.75	110.00	550.00	2,383.33	28,600
14.00	112.00	560.00	2,426.66	29,120
14.25	114.00	570.00	2,470.00	29,640
14.50	116.00	580.00	2,513.33	30,160
14.75	118.00	590.00	2,556.66	30,680
15.00	120.00	600.00	2,600.00	31,200
15.25	122.00	610.00	2,643.33	31,720
15.50	124.00	620.00	2,686.66	32,240
15.75	126.00	630.00	2,730.00	32,760
16.00	128.00	640.00	2,773.33	33,280
16.25	130.00	650.00	2,816.66	33,800
16.50	132.00	660.00	2,860.00	34,320
16.75	134.00	670.00	2,903.33	34,840
17.00	136.00	680.00	2,946.66	35,360
17.25	138.00	690.00	2,990.00	35,880
17.50	140.00	700.00	3,033.33	36,400
17.75	142.00	710.00	3,076.66	36,920
18.00	144.00	720.00	3,120.00	37,440
18.25	146.00	730.00	3,163.33	37,960
18.50	148.00	740.00	3,206.66	38,480
18.75	150.00	750.00	3,250.00	39,000
19.00	152.00	760.00	3,293.33	39,520
19.25	154.00	770.00	3,336.66	40,040
19.50	156.00	780.00	3,380.00	40,560
19.75	158.00	790.00	3,423.33	41,080
20.00	160.00	800.00	3,466.66	41,600
20.25	162.00	810.00	3,510.00	42,120
20.50	164.00	820.00	3,553.33	42,640
20.75	166.00	830.00	3,596.66	43,160
21.00	168.00	840.00	3,640.00	43,680
21.25	170.00	850.00	3,683.33	44,200
21.50	172.00	860.00	3,726.66.	44,720
21.75	174.00	870.00	3,770.00	45,240
22.00	176.00	880.00	3,813.33	45,760
22.25	178.00	890.00	3,856.66	46,280
22.50	180.00	900.00	3,900.00	46,800

Figure 13-9
Conversion chart

get the materials, drive to the job site, do the work, drive back, unload your truck, and do the billing and other paperwork.

When you're starting out, it's tempting to put off the paperwork and get on with the "more important things." *Don't do it*. Your business records are essential to your success.

Budgeting Business Expenses

Let's say you've set up your chart of accounts and copied some spreadsheet forms. Let's see how these can help you. If you have a computer and suitable software, then you can use them to play *"what if"* number games. What if I increase my earnings by 10 percent? What if I cut my advertising by 2 percent? In a blink of the eye you can see the results of any changes you plan to make.

I'll assume you don't have a computer for now, and I'll show you how to do some *ratio analysis* instead. We use ratios to find out how one thing relates to another. How does income relate to expenses? How does advertising relate to the number of jobs sold?

If you can, compare your ratios with other fence and retaining wall contractors. See how your company stacks up. You'll probably see very quickly where your company is weak and needs improvement.

Your banker uses balance sheets and expense ratios to figure how much credit he can extend. The I.R.S. uses ratios to select companies for audit. Ratios are a powerful tool when used correctly. Let me show you how to put them to work in your business.

Any whole item contains 100 *percent*. You can express any part of that whole as a *percentage* of that item. You can find out what percentage of an item is represented by any part of that item. And you can find out what percentage of one whole item is represented by another whole item. This lets you build some comparisons, or *ratios*, to show you how your business is doing.

You can use your total income or expense figures and find out what percentage of those totals each expense category represents. Let's play with some numbers. Here are some figures from my business the way it was a few years ago.

Income	$100,000
Material Expenses	30,000
Advertising Expense	2,000

The ratio of material expenses to income is 30,000:100,000. You can eliminate the same number of zeros from each and get a ratio of 3:10. Now you can figure a percentage by dividing 3 by 10 and multiplying by 100 to get 30 percent. Material expense is 30 percent of income.

Use the same procedure to find out what percentage of either income or expenses this company spent on advertising:

2,000:100,000 = 2:100

2 ÷ 100 = 0.02 x 100 = 2 percent

Advertising is 2 percent of total income.

2,000:30,000 = 2:30

2 ÷ 30 = 0.066 x 100 = 6.7 percent

Advertising is 6.7 percent of material expenses.

You can do this for every item on your chart of accounts. If you do it correctly, the total of all the individual items will be 100 percent. Figure 13-10 is an example of expenses compared to total income for a small fence contracting business.

Now, let's use these percentages to make a *budget*. In Figure 13-11, let's multiply each percentage by $100,000. That tells you how much of your total income you expect to spend for each expense item.

As you see, the total is $100,000. But as you look this preliminary budget over, you'll see it's not realistic. You need to make some adjustments.

1) Office expense seems too high, and insurance too low. Reverse them.

2) The phone item seems too high, since the business only makes local calls. But it includes charges of $25 per month for the Yellow Pages ad. That's $300 a year, or 0.3 percent of total income. Move those charges to advertising, but don't change the amount of the advertising budget.

Expense item	Percent of total income
Rent	9.0
Phones	.5
Utilities	4.5
Postage	.5
Vehicle	7.0
Office	2.0
Insurance	1.0
Salary	33.0
Materials	22.0
Other	.5
Taxes	12.0
Advertising	8.0
Total	100.0

Figure 13-10
Typical expense percentages

Expense item	Budgeted amount
Rent	9,000
Phones	500
Utilities	4,500
Postage	500
Vehicle	7,000
Office	2,000
Insurance	1,000
Salary	33,000
Materials	22,000
Other	500
Taxes	12,000
Advertising	8,000
Total	$100,000

Figure 13-11
Typical expense costs

3) *Where's the profit?* Profit is the difference between income and expenses. You want your profit (after you pay yourself) to be at least 9 percent. So you have to add an item to the list of ways to split up income. But where's the money going to come from?

4) Unfortunately, in a case like this, the first place it comes from is the owner's draw. Reduce your salary from $33,000 to $30,000.

5) Your materials estimate is too low. In order to gross $100,000 with an SPF of 2.7, you'll have to turn $37,000 in materials. ($37,000 x 2.7 = $99,900.) You still have some adjusting to do.

6) Give up the office and work from home for a while. That will cut your rent and utilities costs. Cut down vehicle expense — it's a little out of line — and pare some from advertising, insurance, and profit.

Now, the revised budget looks like Figure 13-12.

Expense Item	Annual budgeted amount	Monthly budgeted amount
Rent	1,000	83.33
Phones	200	16.67
Utilities	500	41.67
Postage	500	41.67
Vehicle	4,000	333.33
Office	1,000	83.33
Insurance	1,500	125.00
Salary	30,000	2,500.00
Materials	37,000	3,083.33
Other	500	41.67
Taxes	9,000	750.00
Advertising	6,800	566.67
Profit	8,000	666.67
Total	$100,000	8,333.34

Figure 13-12
Revised budget

This sample budget is in line and everything balances. Remember, your figures might be far different from these. Just make sure that they're realistic. Also, some items, like rent, can't be changed easily.

You can break this down further by dividing again by 21 (there are 21 working days in an average month), to see what your daily billings have to be to reach the projected income level.

Compare Expenses to Your Budget

Now, when you fill out your monthly spreadsheets, you can test the totals against your budget percentages. Use the monthly income and expense figures. If you find an item that's out of line, do something about it. Let's say that in January your phone expense is way over budget. Maybe your budget is too low and you have to take some money from another category. Or is someone using your phone for personal business? Has the phone company made a mistake? In either case, you should do something about it.

Compare your actual expenses to your budgets regularly. Just a 1 percent overrun on several of your larger expenses could cost you $1,000 a year. Even if you have someone else doing your books, *you need to pay close attention to them yourself.* It's your business and your responsibility. Your bookkeeper or accountant may be very good at bookkeeping or accounting. But they probably don't understand fence and retaining wall contracting. Only *you* can identify the problems, see the opportunities, do more of what's working and fix what's broken.

Don't Forget the Tax Man

Here's one way to get in the hole quickly. Employers have to file I.R.S. Form 941 quarterly. We discussed that already. But if you're self-employed and have no employees, you still have to file an estimated tax return and pay the amount due each January, April, July and October. Be sure to put money aside from every job for this.

You can postpone *almost* any bill without creating a major problem. Creditors may give you a hard time, but they'll usually wait a month or so before they turn you over to a collection agency. Collection agencies will hassle you for a few months before they turn you over to a lawyer. The courts will delay payment a few months more. Eventually they'll issue a judgment or give you a payment schedule and plan. As a last resort, you can declare bankruptcy. Then you may keep your business and agree to a schedule of payments, or lose your business but keep most of your personal possessions. The important thing to notice is that all this takes time, maybe months or years.

But there's one creditor who operates a little differently. That's the I.R.S. They're really ruthless. When they send you a bill, you have 30 days to pay. *Period.* If they think you're not going to pay them, they'll just come and get it. They'll attach bank accounts, personal property, business assets, vehicles, accounts receivable, everything. Don't mess with the I.R.S. Borrow the money if you have to, but pay them.

A little more about the I.R.S. They will quite likely audit you eventually. New businesses in their second full year seem to get audited regularly. Maybe the I.R.S. knows from experience that this is a key period in the life of many companies.

If you keep your paperwork in order, you shouldn't have any problems. You'll be able to produce an explanation for why you spent $105 on peanut brittle or whatever. Without your paperwork, they'll *estimate* your income and expenses for you — and tax you accordingly. That could get expensive, as the I.R.S. often seems to see things differently from the way you or I do. Not only will you have to pay what they think you owe them, but also penalties. Penalties generally start at 10 percent of what you owe and climb at a rate of 1.5 percent per month for each month your payment is late.

You could be audited in the first year, or even several years in a row. That happens because the I.R.S. computers are set up to flag anything that's out of the ordinary. In the example above, let's say the advertising budget was 18 percent rather than 8 percent. Eight percent is considered normal for most businesses: 18 percent is not. If you claim a deduction of 18 percent for advertising, you'll be flagged for audit. The I.R.S. flags personal tax returns the same way.

More Paperwork Controls

We've covered income and expenses, inventory and equipment logs. But there are several other things you need to keep track of. Keep a quote log and a job history file. Record your vehicle mileage and maintenance costs. You need to know how much money you owe, and who owes you. You need to schedule your time. If you have employees, you need a record of their pay rates, the hours they worked, and how much you owe and have withheld in payroll taxes. You can set all these logs up manually now, and convert them to computer later, if you decide to go the computer route.

Keep Track of Bids

The *quote log* is a list of sales calls and quotes offered. Record the customer's name, assign a customer number, and show the customer's address, the date of the estimate or quote, the type of work or job quoted on, and the amount you quoted. Leave space to show any follow-up information, including whether or not you made the sale.

You can keep the customer's name, address, and phone on 3 x 5 cards in a customer file. Number each card, and put the number on your log sheet to make cross referencing easy.

Here's a format for a quote log:

Customer number	Quote date	Quote amount	Follow-up	Results
CN00010	10/22/86	$2,550.00	10/25/86	None
CN00020	10/23/86	1,250.00	None	Sold
CN00030	10/24/86	185.00	None	Sold

Here's what the 3 x 5 card would look like for the first entry on the log:

CN00010	Mr. J. J. Jones 2525 Beechnut St, Anytown, KS, 55555 Phone: 555-9999 after 8 p.m. except Sat.

CN00020 is the next customer, and so on. Extend the log to include travel time and mileage, the time it took to prepare the bid, the cost of gifts or premiums you gave the customer, and any other costs incidental to the quote.

The Job Log

Your job log is the same as the quote log, but with more detail. You add columns for labor, materials, permits, deliveries, sales taxes, and travel. The job log is a detailed journal of each job where you record all costs, and what the customer paid. You refer back to this information when you want to update your estimating resources.

Back up the job log with numbered copies of your customer invoices. Keep them in a separate binder, or file. Now you have a complete record of what you did on every job. Have your customers sign your copy of the invoice to show that the work was completed to their satisfaction.

Include a picture if a job was especially outstanding or required unusual or difficult construction techniques.

Here's a sample job log:

Customer number	Date started	Date complete	Hours	Material	Tax	Travel time
CN00020	11/05/88	11/10/88	15	700.23	42.03	2
CN00030	11/24/88	11/11/88	3	18.23	1.10	1

How Well Are You Selling?

The information for these logs comes from your quote or estimate and your sales contract. You can use the logs to see how well you're doing in your sales efforts. For example, suppose you spent 22 hours quoting ten jobs last month. You sold six of the jobs for a total of $15,000. You can use ratios again to get valuable information.

You sold six of ten jobs, or 60 percent. That's very good. My average is 35 percent. There are 173.33 working hours available during an average month, and you spent 22 of them selling. That's more than 12 percent of your productive time ($22 + 173.33 = 0.1269 \times 100 = 12.69$). Estimates don't come cheap. Let's figure out how much the estimates on last month's jobs cost the company.

The six jobs averaged $2,500 ($15,000 + 6). If your hourly billing rate is $45 and you spent 22 hours selling, you can figure exactly how much it cost you to make each sale.

$$\$45 \times 22 = \$990 + 6 = \$165 \text{ per sale}$$

You can also divide your selling cost per sale by the income from the sale to see what percentage of your sales income you spend to sell the jobs:

$$\$165 + \$2,500 = 0.066 \times 100 = 6.6 \text{ percent of income}$$

Now you can track your performance month by month. If your gross income per job starts to drop, you can either raise prices or be more selective in your bids. If the time you spend selling goes up, or your conversion rate drops, it may indicate a tighter market or a new competitor. You may have to sharpen your selling skills. If leads drop off and you're quoting fewer jobs, you may have to increase advertising expense.

You can use the totals from your job log to give you even more information. First, here are some accounting terms you should know:

♦ Gross income (or gross revenue): The total of all sales.

♦ Gross profit: The sale amount less costs of materials, job-site labor, equipment rental, and supervision.

♦ Net operating profit: The gross profit less expenses and overhead.

♦ Net profit: Net operating profit, less taxes.

In the above example, materials, labor, expenses and overhead cost a total of $12,000, which averages $2,000 for each of the six jobs. The net operating profit for each of the jobs is $500 ($2,500 - $2,000). That's not bad. Using ratio analysis again, that's 20 percent:

$$\$500 + \$2,500 = 0.2 \times 100 = 20 \text{ percent}$$

If you're in a 30 percent income tax bracket, your income tax on each job would be $150:

$$\$500 \times 0.30 = \$150$$

The net profit (after all costs and taxes) is $500 - $150 = $350. The after-tax profit ratio is:

$$\$350 + \$2500 = 0.14 \times 100 = 14 \text{ percent}$$

If your profit drops a point or two the following month, you can suspect you're either quoting too low, or the cost of materials, labor, or both, went up. You need to make some adjustments.

After the adjustments, the next month's figures show a rise in income per sale, but the conversion ratio dropped to 30 percent. (Remember, that was 60 percent two months earlier.) That might mean you over-adjusted and are pricing yourself out of the market, so you have to lower prices again.

You'll have to make these kinds of adjustments for several months when you start a new business. Eventually, the ratios will stabilize at a comfortable level. I suggest you try to convert 30 to 40 percent of your quotes into sales and make 18 to 22 percent profit before taxes.

Your conversion rate shouldn't drop below 25 percent — one sale for every four quotes. Your profit before taxes should be at least 14 percent. Anything below this indicates a major problem somewhere.

Watch Your Equipment

Keep a *vehicle log*, a history of vehicle use, performance, and service. Write down the beginning and ending mileage for each trip you take. When you fill the tank, put down the number of gallons and the cost. Make a note of what each trip was for. If you use the vehicle for both business and personal travel, you *must* keep these records to satisfy the I.R.S. They won't let you deduct your vehicle as a business expense if you can't break down the usage.

Keep track of *miles per gallon* (MPG) also. That can be an early indicator that you need a tuneup, your tires are low, or that a major problem is developing. Flag the vehicle log at certain mileage intervals for preventive maintenance. Have the oil and filter changed every 5,000 miles. Get a lube job and safety check at 15,000 miles. See if you need tires after every 30,000 miles. Check your owner's manual for specific requirements.

Why is this important? Suppose your gas mileage drops from 18 MPG one month to 12 MPG the next, but you're not keeping a log, so you don't notice. You drive 2,500 miles per month, and don't discover the drop in MPG for four months.

10,000 miles at 12 MPG = 833.33 gallons

10,000 miles at 18 MPG = 555.55 gallons

If gas is running about a dollar a gallon, you've wasted $277.78 in just four months. That's a pretty high price to pay for running on low tires or not checking your plugs and points.

The Office in Your Home

Many contractors use part of their home for an office. This is a tax deductible expense, providing you keep accurate records. First, determine the total square footage of your home. Then find the square footage of the office area. Figure what percent of your home the office occupies.

Suppose your home is 2,000 square feet, and your office is 8 x 10 (80 square feet).

80 ÷ 2,000 = 0.04 x 100 = 4 percent

You can deduct 4 percent of your utilities and rent or mortgage as a business expense if you meet I.R.S. requirements. Follow your tax advisor's advice. No doubt, your advisor will recommend that you keep very accurate records. The I.R.S. is very touchy about home-office deductions.

If you do keep your office in your home, consider renting a post office box, or a box in a commercial mailbox center for your business mail. This has an added advantage of keeping customers and salesmen from dropping in on you at odd hours of the day and night. This is a deductible business expense.

Your Business Phone

You can use your home phone for business and deduct those charges also. But you *must* keep an accurate log of both your personal and business calls. The I.R.S. won't allow the deduction if you don't. I recommend you have a separate line installed for your business. It keeps the records straight. You can also put an answering machine on the business line and keep your personal line free. Use the business phone in your ads. Who wants 40 calls a day on their private line? And worse, who wants to lose a lead because your teenager kept the phone tied up for 45 minutes?

Congratulations! If you're doing what I suggest in this chapter, you've passed *Accounting 101 for Fence & Retaining Wall Contractors*. The next chapter covers contractor's law and much more information on improving sales.

fourteen

Sales and Contractor's Law

This chapter should be essential reading for every specialty contractor. I'm going to explain how to build a good business while staying out of trouble with state, federal and local government agencies. You've spent a considerable amount of money setting up your business, buying equipment and tools, and advertising. But none of that does much good if you can't sell your services to a customer.

Advertising can raise potential customers' interest in your product or service — but advertising doesn't sell. Your competition advertises the same services and products. What makes the customer buy from you instead of the competitor? The answer is *salesmanship*.

Why Do *You* Shop Where You Do?

- Do you buy from a particular store because it's the only one with the product or service you want? I doubt it. Competition is intense in nearly every business.

- Do they have the lowest prices in town? Probably not. Prices change from place to place every day. Someone's always having a sale.

- Is it the store hours? Not really. Most stores, banks and companies that serve the public are open long hours.

- Is it because they have a big ad in the phone book? Certainly not. There are plenty of big ads in the phone book.

- Is it because they treat you with courtesy and give good value for your dollar? Almost certainly.

Of course, there's no single reason why people buy from most merchants. But everyone likes to buy where they feel welcome — where the customer is always right. That's how your customers have to feel when they come to you. Listen to their problems and be concerned. Help them the way you'd like to be helped. Too many salespeople today forget who really pays their salary. It's not their boss or the company. It's the customers.

Most of us aren't born knowing how to sell. We have to learn. Anyone willing to invest some time and effort can master the basics of selling. Let me show you some tricks of the trade.

Sell Yourself

Although *we* know better, many people think most contractors are cheats. Some may be. But most aren't. Most contractors are hard-working people with valuable skills. But public perception of construction contractors puts you at a disadvantage when you're talking with prospective customers. You have to sell not only your product or service, but yourself.

A new prospect will evaluate your appearance first. Wear dirty, worn-out clothes and a three-day growth of beard and you've just about killed the sale. You don't have to dress like a banker in a three-piece suit. But you *do* have to look presentable. Dress casually in slacks and a sport shirt. You want to make your customer feel comfortable.

The Presentation Booklet

One effective way to spark your customer's trust and confidence is to make up a presentation booklet. Design an informative and attractive handout that tells about you and your company. Don't go overboard; a few pages will do. Here's what to put in your booklet.

1) A copy of your business license.

2) A copy of your contractor's license.

3) An outline of the major features of your standard contract and warranty.

4) A list of your credit terms.

5) Copies of references from past customers.

6) Membership certificates from the Chamber of Commerce or Better Business Bureau.

7) A picture of your building or vehicle if they're attractive and distinctive.

In my opinion, you shouldn't include pictures of past jobs. *You* might like a fence you built, but your customer might not.

An attractive presentation booklet will put you a step ahead of your competition. *They* probably won't offer one.

Be Prepared

Have a good supply of blank contracts, estimate forms, pencils, pens, and note paper with you when making sales calls. Carry a heavy-duty tape measure and a battery-operated calculator. If you have to borrow supplies from your customer, you'll probably lose the sale. After all, if you can't prepare for a simple sales call, can you be trusted to build a decent fence or wall?

Notice I didn't say to bring a ton of samples with you. I have mixed opinions about bringing samples to a customer. Most customers have either seen your samples or already know what they want. You'll just make them nervous if you confuse them with too many choices.

On the other hand, a *few* choices can help clinch a sale. A prospect might find 3-inch-wide cedar more attractive than 2-inch-wide redwood. It's up to you to judge whether to carry samples to the sales meeting. Here's my suggestion: Bring all the samples you can, but leave them in your truck. If your customer is undecided during the sales pitch, then bring in a few samples. By that time, you'll have a pretty good idea of what they want.

Sell Security and Confidence

One reason customers call you is that they're afraid to do the job themselves. They don't know the construction techniques, problems, or laws that apply to building a fence or wall. You have to show them that you're the expert, that you're confident about what you can do, that you know your trade. That's the key to making sales.

For example, make suggestions that show your experience and professionalism: "Mr. Jones, I know you'll want to get several bids on this job. When the bids are in, be sure you're comparing apples to apples. My quote includes both the building permit and the survey."

Win Trust to Win the Job

Don't talk price with customers until they're sold on you, your service, and your product. Customers want to feel confident in the company they hire for a job. If you inspire confidence you'll probably get the job, even if your price isn't the lowest.

Know Your Business

The most important thing is to know your services and products thoroughly. That sounds so basic it's almost silly, doesn't it? But how often have you met salespeople who couldn't explain how their product works, or what it's made of, or how to take care of it? Think about it.

Do this: Sit down with a mate or friend. Have them ask you questions a customer would ask if they were about to accept your bid to build a two thousand dollar fence. If you can't answer every legitimate question, then you don't know your business. Make a list of any questions you couldn't answer and develop good answers. Then do it again. When you can answer all the questions that may come your way, you're ready to make the sale.

Listen and Ask Questions

Learn to listen. You won't make the sale until you've answered every question the prospect has and overcome every objection. To find out what's holding up the sale, you have to listen. Listen with both your ears *and your eyes*. The ears hear words, the eyes hear body language.

A person sitting there with crossed arms is objecting. They feel defensive and are protecting themselves. A person whose eyes are wandering is probably distracted or disinterested.

Next, learn to answer questions with questions. Question their question or statement. This puts you in control. Picture this:

Joe Homeowner: "Can you build this fence within 30 days?"

Contractor: "Sure, I can do that"

Joe: "Can you do it in the next three weeks?"

Contractor: "Well, I think so."

Joe: "How about this week?"

Contractor: "Sorry, I can't do that."

You probably just lost the sale, and guess who was in control? Here's how you should have steered that conversation:

Joe: "Can I get this fence built within the next 30 days?"

You: "Mr. Homeowner, if I can finish the fence in 30 days, do I have the order?"

Find the Prime Objection

Joe can't play games with you any more. He has to give you an answer, either "Yes" or "No." If he says "Yes," hand him the contract (and a pen). If he says "No," then you know that having the fence built within 30 days wasn't his prime objection. Now you have to find out what that was. Do so by asking another question:

"Mr. Jones, quick completion isn't so important to you. What is the most important consideration?" Once again the ball is in his court. Now he has to think of an answer. You've confirmed that time wasn't the key. And you're about to find out how to make the sale. This is called *selling the objection back to the customer*.

Know When to Be Quiet

Are you a talker? If so, that's one habit you'll have to overcome to be a good salesperson. There are times to talk, and there are times to keep quiet. When your customer asks for a direct answer to a question, then talk. Give them a direct and complete answer. When you ask your customer a question, then *shut up*.

Don't say another word until after the response is complete. When you ask a question, the person you're talking to has to come up with an answer. If you get impatient and start talking, the opportunity to get the answer is lost. They're off the hook.

Why is this important? The answer is a clue to the remaining objections. Until this last objection is passed over, you're not going to make the sale. Until you get the answer, silence is golden. It can put money in your pocket. Even if you have to sit dead silent for two minutes, do it. Let your customer have time to think and answer. This is especially true whenever you ask *the* major question, "Mr. Jones, when do you want me to get started?" It's hard to keep from talking during a long silence. But do it — if you want the sale.

Ask for the Order

You'd be surprised at the number of salespeople who don't do this. You'll get very little in life if you don't learn to ask. You'll reach a point in the negotiations when you think your customer is ready to buy. They'll be out of questions. Ask for the sale and then *wait for the response*. Chances are good you'll close the sale. Asking doesn't always have to be verbal. Many times all you'll have to do is put the bid form and a pen in front of your customer.

Remember, customers come to you. They take the time to call you, meet you, and listen to you. That means they're serious about buying. Otherwise they wouldn't waste the time. True, most say, "I'm just getting estimates now." But don't leave it at that.

Look at it this way: Didn't you just take the time to meet with the prospect? Didn't you just spend an hour with them educating them about fences? Didn't you just thoroughly prepare an estimate, complete with drawings and sketches? Then why just hand that estimate over to the prospect so they can take it to your competitor? That competition will use your estimate to cut you out of the job. While you're there with your customer, sell, *sell*, **sell**.

Be Fair to Your Competition

I just said that the competition will use your estimate to cut you down. Don't stoop to those tactics yourself. Don't badmouth your competition. It doesn't speak highly of you, and may cost you the sale. But you can point out that you give better service or quality than the others. Say, "Mr. Jones, I think that after you review our conversation and my estimate, you'll agree that I'm the best-qualified fencing contractor in town." Or,

"Mr. Jones, do your other estimates include sales tax and any permits we'll need?"

Special Selling Situations

The Multiple Buyer

You'll face one problem selling fences that usually doesn't crop up in other kinds of contracting. Until now, I've assumed that you'd be making a sale to a single customer. But fences often divide land and sit on the property line. Many times you'll have to deal with two or more adjacent property owners. One wants a redwood picket fence, the other, a block wall. One wants to spend $500, the other is willing to spend $1,000.

You have three choices.

1) Stay and battle with both of them, trying to iron out their differences and close the sale. Your success is highly doubtful.

2) Make your presentation, then leave them to fight out the decision by themselves. You may or may not get the job, depending on whether you sold the stronger or weaker of the two.

3) Suggest two fences back to back, each within their respective properties. You may get one or both or none.

I've been caught in this position myself, but I can't give you a pat answer to this problem. The best solution is probably to give both parties an estimate for a joint fence, and leave it to them to iron out their differences.

I once lost a job for a joint fence to another contractor. Later, one of the parties called me. She was very unhappy with the fence, *and* with her neighbor. I'm rather happy that I didn't get that job.

When to Say No

Sometimes you'll run up against someone you just don't want to do business with. You'll develop a sixth sense for recognizing the troublemakers. They're the ones you can't satisfy, no matter what you do. They'll pick on your every word and action, and drive you nuts. Here's one trick I use to avoid working for this kind of person. I tell them I'd love to do the work for them, but the first date I have open is six weeks from now. That's usually enough to send them off to a competitor. Let some other contractor have the problems.

Don't Try "Bait and Switch"

A major complaint heard by consumer agencies is the bait and switch. That's where a seller advertises a product at a *very* reasonable price, then delivers something else, usually inferior, or higher priced, or both. That's against the law, and unprofessional. You have a responsibility to your customers and your industry to avoid illegal and unethical behavior.

When Your Bid's Too Low

Sometimes you'll make a mistake and bid a job too low. What do you do? One option is to say nothing and substitute cheaper, lower-quality materials. Or you can leave the job half done. But you can lose your contractor's license for trying either of those choices — and in my opinion, you deserve to. But in either case, your reputation will suffer when your customer spreads the news all over town. And you may have to redo the job at your own expense anyway. That's worse than taking the loss for your mistake.

There's one alternative. You can go back to the customer and tell them flat out that you made a mistake. If they're reasonable people they'll understand and may let you re-bid the job. But if they're out to find a bargain, they just got one. Take your licking with a smile and do the job professionally. We all make mistakes and we all get to pay for them. Maybe they'll be shamed and ask you to bid on another job. And this time you'll be more careful.

The solution to this problem is prevention. Know what you're doing in the first place. If you need a day or two to properly research and prepare your estimate, then take it. Don't guess. Don't rush the bid. Put everything in writing. Be specific about what you'll do, what materials you'll use, and any extras you'll include. Here's a checklist:

1) Description of the work
2) Full materials description
3) Transportation or delivery charges
4) Rental charges for special tools or equipment
5) Subcontractor charges
6) Sales taxes
7) Permit and fee charges
8) The date you'll start work
9) Estimated completion date
10) Payment schedule

This checklist does two things for you. First, it makes you think about the job and all the costs involved. Second, it forces you to tell the customers exactly what you're doing for them. If the customers comes back later and say they want more, or that you're not doing what you contracted for, you have your agreement in black and white.

As a point of law, some states *require* that you include the items listed above in your contract. Public Works projects will require those items on your *bid* also.

There's a third advantage to a detailed quote. If you didn't close the sale during the first sales call, the customer is probably going after another estimate. Now they'll have your written estimate when they go to your competition. Most prospects won't show your estimate to your competitor, but they'll compare it with other estimates.

Maybe the competition's price is lower. But they may not be as well organized as you are. If their estimate isn't as detailed as yours, it raises questions. The customer will wonder why your competition's bid didn't include certain items, or whether materials are the same quality as in your bid. Your prospect will question whether the competition really knows what they're doing.

As a precaution, I suggest you include this paragraph at the bottom of your estimate form:

This is an estimate of the materials, labor and services I will provide. Please read it fully, and compare it on the same basis with any other estimates you may receive. I trust that you'll keep this estimate in confidence. If you have any questions or want to change your original specifications, please call me right away at (your phone number).

With any luck at all, the customer will call you back and you'll have another chance to sell the job.

The "No Sale"

The *get lost* or *no sale* person is a tough bird to counter. But there are ways to sell these guys, too. Review the rules of salesmanship: Know your product, overcome the objection, ask for the sale, then shut up. A *no sale* is a clue you did something wrong. Either you didn't overcome the customer's objection, or you talked yourself out of the job.

A method sometimes used by the pros is to *give up* and walk out. Just pack up your things and leave. Be very quiet, as though you were upset. This person you've been trying so hard to sell for the last hour has beaten you. When you get to the door, thank them for their time and for listening to you. Then ask a question, or I should say, *the* question. "Mr. Jones, what did I do wrong? What did I do to offend you?"

Now you're no longer a threat, the sales call is over. Mr. Jones will let his guard down. You're disappointed. The natural instinct is to be sympathetic. People don't want to insult someone who's been beaten. Mr. Jones will probably come out and tell you now why he didn't buy from you:

"No, I don't dislike you, I think you're a fine fellow. I just didn't like the idea of you trying to sell me plain concrete block. I would have preferred something fancier." Now you're back in the selling business, assuming you can offer fancy block. You answer, "Mr. Jones, is that all that's keeping us apart?" Now you can put together a better offer.

Here's another solution to the no sale. If the customers are going to build their own fence, offer to rent them the tools they'll need. Or offer to split the work with the customer. Or offer yourself as a consultant for an hourly fee.

If your customer takes you up on one or all of these offers, you still might turn it into a sale. If they want to rent tools from you, you explain what each tool is used for, the techniques for using them, and the dangers of using each tool. I wouldn't suggest renting out your best tools, of course. Rent only what you can afford to lose. And of course, don't rent out the ones you use yourself.

If the customer agrees to split the work, then describe in detail what each of you will do. Be sure to throw in a few comments to suggest how hard the job may be. If they want to use you as a consultant, go into great detail about every part of the job.

See where this is leading? The more information you provide, the more your customer is going to wonder if they can do the work. Do they really understand everything that's involved? Can they really use those tools safely? Do they really want to get their hands dirty, to work *that* hard? Chances are you'll wind up doing the whole job, and at your price.

Be honest with them. They may indeed decide to do it themselves. If you've misled them and the job turns into a mess, they'll tell everyone they meet about your lousy advice. But if you give true, factual information and the job is a success, they'll recommend you to others.

Add-Ons

Here are some ideas to increase your sales by offering things your customers didn't even know they wanted, until you told them.

1) Don't just sell a wall or fence. Sell a maintenance contract along with it. This keeps you in contact with your customer so you're around for referrals.

2) If you're equipped to do everything required, sell a whole package that includes painting, plumbing, electrical work and anything else that goes with a job.

3) If an old fence or wall has to come down, contract for the removal. Many times you can use the salvaged materials on the same or other jobs. I have a friend in Michigan who removes old concrete and block. He breaks the concrete up, mixes it with new concrete as a filler in place of gravel, and sells it back to his customer as a new wall, walk, or driveway. He cuts his material cost by over 50 percent. Used lumber and brick

are in demand in communities where a weathered look is popular. You can sell used wire as scrap for 5 to 20 cents a pound.

4) Sell *fancy*. Suggest ways to make the wall or fence look better or more personalized.

5) Sell at group rates. This is where you tell your customer that if they can get several of their neighbors to buy from you at the same time, you will discount the jobs by 10 percent. I know some roofers who do this regularly.

Money Talk

Quote your estimates in whole dollars, *don't* use cents. Better yet, quote a round number and give yourself a plus or minus percentage:

Total cost: $1,500 plus or minus $75 (or plus or minus 5 percent.)

If you quote an exact amount, i.e., $1,503.45, that's what you're stuck with. This is a point of law, and the courts will make you accept the figure you gave if you quoted to the penny.

You may have noticed that I used a lump sum estimate. I could have broken it down this way:

Materials	$ 500
Labor	$1,000
Total	$1,500

If you do that, the first question your customer will ask is, "How many hours do you think this will take?" If you tell them it will take 40 hours, you'll probably lose the job. They'll do the calculation: $1,000 divided by 40 is $25 an hour. That may seem like a lot of money to your customer. Most customers don't understand that you have business expenses to cover. They think you're putting that $25 in your pocket.

You could say the job will take 100 hours, in which case the charge would only be $10 per hour. But I'll bet your customer will be watching their clock while you work. They'll want a rebate when they find out you only worked 40 hours.

Some fence contractors charge on a time-and-materials basis. If you do that, include a maximum and minimum charge for the job. You might say, "Mr. Jones, I charge $10 an hour for labor. I don't mark up the material cost and you'll receive copies of invoices for all materials I use. I estimate that the least I can do this job for is $550. To be fair to both of us I'll put a maximum cap on the job. Does $600 sound fair?"

As I said before, sell the job, then the price. If you've sold the job, the price usually won't be an obstacle. Notice I said *usually*. You'll come across all sorts of people. Some will balk at the price. Some always want just a little bit better deal, no matter what you do. Some will ask for credit. Part of being a good salesman is knowing how to counter the customer's objections to price. Here are some suggestions:

A customer who balks at price still wants the job done, but they want to see if they can get it done cheaper. Tell them, "Yes, I can do it cheaper. I can use #3 common pine instead of redwood, iron nails instead of galvanized nails, and space the boards 1/2 inch apart instead of 1/4 inch. But the fence will probably only last 10 or 12 years instead of 15 or 20. I fully understand that you have a budget and appreciate your wanting to stick within that budget. Maybe I can offer you some alternatives."

What did you just do to this person? First, notice the compliment about their efforts to stick to a budget. That's a point in your favor. But, you sold them insecurity as well. They really don't want an inferior fence. They may just sign the contract as it stands, or they'll ask for the alternatives. What are the alternatives you're prepared to offer?

If you're smart, you already have about $50 extra built into the total price. You could offer a $50 discount without hurting yourself. The next alternative is to offer to share the work with them. "Gee, Mr. Jones, we could cut $75 out of this estimate if you want to do the painting and cleanup after I install this fence." You just offered to be the customer's partner and save him some money. Mr. Jones will wonder if $75 is worth his time and effort. Probably not.

If he does accept your offer, don't worry about it. Just change the contract to reflect that he is doing that portion of the job. Don't worry about it? No, because the $75 you knocked off is only about half of what you figure it would have cost you. You still make a profit.

Now, how should you handle the person who's looking for something for nothing? Have something available, but don't give it to them until they ask. I have to admit that I like to get a little something extra once in a while. Most of us do when we spend a lot of money at one place. It gives us a small sense of being on top of things; we've made a good deal. Have a few under-$5 gifts available like pen sets or pocket calculators. Print or engrave your ad or logo on the item. Then, when you've made the sale and the contract is signed, give the customer your gift as a goodwill gesture.

I had one guy who really wanted to beat me out of something extra. I was on a sales call for a large company. He'd already made up his mind to buy from me. But he wanted to feel like a winner. He sat with the contract in front of him for more than an hour. He finally complimented me on my $5 battery-operated calculator. All I had to do was slide it over to his side of the table and say, "It's yours." He signed the contract within 10 seconds.

Financing

Once in a while you're going to meet a customer with less than fifty bucks in their checking account. They want the fence but want to pay for it in easy installments. There's a difference between *progressive* payments and *time* payments. Progressive payments are standard in the contracting business. The customer makes a down payment, then pays you at various stages of the work, according to your written agreement. I'll get into this in more detail later in this chapter.

Time payments probably don't begin until the job is finished. Do you offer credit? If you don't, I suggest you look into doing so. Having credit available to your customers can be a key selling point. Many people can't afford an expensive fence or wall. Others just don't want to take the money from their bank account.

Ask your local bank for a Business Credit Account. If you've got a storefront office, or you're a good bank customer, you'll probably get it, either MasterCard, Visa, or some other popular card. They'll supply you with a *crash printer*, the little machine that prints the customer's credit card information on the sales slip. You'll also get a supply of sales and credit blanks. For all this good stuff, the bank will charge a small annual fee and from 4 to 6 percent of every dollar your customer charges with you. The typical percentage is 5 percent. But if your average sale is large, $500 or more, you should be able to negotiate a lower rate. Even then, 1.5 percent is about the best you'll do.

The advantage of charge card sales is that you should have no collection problems. The bank or card company assumes the responsibility for the debt. You get paid in full when you deposit the sales slip into your bank account. The bank's fee is tax deductible as a business expense. But you can't charge this fee back to your customers. Build it into your selling price as part of your overhead. As a sales tool, you *can* offer a discount to your cash customers.

Now, let's move on to some of the laws governing contractual sales. As a contractor, licensed or not, you have certain obligations under the law. Your customer also has obligations to you. Of course, laws vary from state to state. All I can do is flag the issues you might want to explore. In any case, the law of the state where the work will be done will apply.

Contractor's Law

Where a contractor's license is required, an unlicensed person can't quote a price for any job where the cost of labor and materials exceeds some threshold amount, usually a few hundred dollars. To operate legally as a contractor, you must have a valid license. You'll probably have to show your license number on any advertising, including signs, and on your contract form.

Licenses Are Trade Specific

Licensed contractors can only advertise for work in the field in which they hold a valid license. Thus, a painting contractor can't advertise as a fencing contractor. If you hold a painter's license, you can't use "Will's Painting and Fencing" as your DBA unless you're also a licensed fencing contractor.

Home Improvement Sales

The term *home improvement* means any remodeling, addition, alteration, repair, modernization, or addition of value to a residence or residential property.

A home improvement salesperson may solicit, negotiate, and sell home improvement contracts. Salespeople employed by a licensed contractor don't need a license. If they work as an independent contractor, they need a license in the field they're selling. In some states, contractors must register the names of their salespeople with the Contractor's Board.

There's a misconception that home improvement salespeople must be paid in full before any other worker involved in the execution of the contract is paid. This isn't true. The salesperson might be paid last.

Payment Schedules

Some states limit the down payment you can require when the contract is signed. In California it's 10 percent of the job, or $1,000, whichever is less. The total of the down payment and progressive payments may not exceed 100 percent of the contracted price for the job. The customer doesn't have to agree to give you a down payment, and you're not required to accept the contract if they don't.

During progressive payments, the customer may hold back 10 percent of the total contract amount to be sure the work fully complies with the contract.

Contract Forms

Contracts may be written or oral. Beware the latter. The contract may be between a contractor and a tenant, a contractor and an owner's repre-

sentative, or a contractor and the owner. An authorized salesperson can represent a contractor. A contract the salesperson negotiates is fully binding on the contractor.

Your contract must contain a full description of the work to be done. It must also contain an estimated beginning and ending date for the job. There must be a statement that further defines when the work will substantially begin. For example, "Work will be considered started upon delivery of the first truckload of brick to the job site." If there are progressive payments, the contract must specify the schedule of payments.

Your full name, address, and contractor's license number must appear on any written contract. Figure 14-1 is a sample proposal and contract form that complies with California law. This, and the other sample forms in this chapter, are produced by *Wolcotts, Inc.*, P.O. Box 467, Paramount, California, 90723. They're available at most stationery and office supply stores. If you're buying forms in package quantities, you can order them direct from *Wolcotts*.

The Rescission Notice

If your customer signs a contract which can create a lien on their home, you have to include a notice of the customer's right of rescission, or cancellation notice. Figure 14-2 is a sample of this federally-required format. It gives the customer the right to cancel the contract up to midnight of the third business day after they sign it. You have to return all the money they gave you as a deposit, if they cancel.

Customers Who Don't Speak English

If you negotiate a sale in a language other than English, the contract and rescission notice must be in the language of the negotiation. If you make your sales pitch in Spanish, then the contract must be in Spanish, also. You can include an English copy if it's identical in content, but the Spanish copy will be the legally binding one.

PROPOSAL AND CONTRACT FOR HOME IMPROVEMENT*

Date: _____, 19____ TO _____

_____
_____, (hereinafter "Owner"), Telephone no. (_____)_____

_____ (hereinafter "Contractor")

propose(s) to furnish all materials and perform all labor necessary to complete the following: [Insert a description of the work to be done and a description of the materials to be used and the equipment to be used or installed, and state the address of the job site.]

_____
_____
_____

All of the above work is to be completed in a substantial and workmanlike manner according to standard practices for the sum of _____

_____ Dollars ($ _____).

Progress payments to be made as follows and in accordance with the terms and conditions of paragraph 1 on the reverse side:

Amount of Work or Services to be Performed or Description of any Materials or Equipment to be Supplied	Amount of Payment (Must be shown as a sum in dollars and cents)

The remaining balance of the contract is to be paid within _____ days after completion.

This proposal is valid until _____, and if accepted on or before that date, work will commence approximately on _____

and will be substantially completed approximately on _____, subject to delays caused by acts of God, stormy weather, uncontrollable labor trouble, or unforeseen contingencies.

The following constitutes substantial commencement of work pursuant to this proposal and contract: [Specify]

> **FAILURE BY CONTRACTOR WITHOUT LAWFUL EXCUSE TO SUBSTANTIALLY COMMENCE WORK WITHIN TWENTY (20) DAYS FROM THE APPROXIMATE DATE SPECIFIED IN THIS PROPOSAL AND CONTRACT WHEN WORK WILL BEGIN IS A VIOLATION OF THE CONTRACTORS LICENSE LAW.**

Any alteration or deviation from the above specifications, including but not limited to any such alteration or deviation involving additional material and/or labor costs, will be executed only upon a written order for same, signed by Owner and Contractor, and if there is any charge for such alteration or deviation, the additional charge will be added to the contract price of this contract.

If any payment is not made when due, Contractor may suspend work on the job until such time as all payments due have been made. A failure to make payment for a period in excess of _____ days from the due date of the payment shall be deemed a material breach of this contract.

Respectfully submitted,

> **NOTICE TO OWNER OR TENANT: You have the right to require Contractor to have a performance and payment bond.**

Name and Registration No. of any Salesperson who solicited or negotiated this contract:

Name: _____ No. _____

By _____
Name of Contractor

_____
Signature

_____
Street Address

_____ _____ _____ (___)_____
City   State   Zip   Telephone No

_____
Contractor s State License No

ACCEPTANCE

You are hereby authorized to furnish all materials and labor required to complete the work mentioned in this Proposal, for which I/we agree to pay the contract price mentioned in this Proposal, and according to the terms thereof. I/we acknowledge that before entering into this contract, I/we received a copy of the Notice to Owner which appears on the reverse side hereof. I/we have read and agree to the provisions contained on the front and reverse sides hereof, and in any attachments hereto, which are made a part hereof and are described as _____

_____

ACCEPTED: _____
(Owner s Signature)   (Date)

_____
Owner's Name

_____
Street Address

_____ _____ _____
City   State   Zip

_____
Business Address

(___)_____
Business Phone No.

> **Contractors are required by law to be licensed and regulated by the Contractors' State License Board. Any questions concerning a contractor may be referred to the Registrar, Contractors' State License Board, P.O. Box 26000, Sacramento, California 95826.**

If either the proposal and/or the acceptance of this Proposal and Contract is made at other than the premises at which Contractor or Owner normally carries on a business, then you, the Buyer, may cancel this transaction at any time prior to midnight of the third business day after the date of this transaction. See the attached Notice of Cancellation form (Wolcotts Form 570) for an explanation of this right.

The provision that Owner may cancel this transaction within three business days shall not apply to a contract in which Owner has initiated the Contract and which is executed in connection with the making of emergency repairs or services which are necessary for the immediate protection of persons or real or personal property, provided that Owner furnishes Contractor with a separate dated and signed personal statement describing the situation requiring immediate remedy and expressly acknowledging and waiving the right to cancel the sale within three business days (Wolcotts Form 570). **IMPORTANT: SEE REVERSE SIDE FOR IMPORTANT INFORMATION** © 1984 WOLCOTTS, INC.

WOLCOTTS FORM 564—PROPOSAL AND CONTRACT FOR HOME IMPROVEMENT (padded)—Rev. 12-84   *See Form 564NHI for a Proposal and Contract NOT for Home Improvement (padded)
(Price class 4-2P)   (This form also available as a quad set - order Wolcotts Form 564Q)   or Form 564NHIQ for a Proposal and Contract NOT for Home Improvement (quad set)
Before you use this form, read it, fill in all blanks, and make whatever changes are appropriate and necessary to your particular transaction. Consult a lawyer if you doubt the form's
fitness for your purpose and use. Wolcotts makes no representation or warranty, express or implied, with respect to the merchantability or fitness of this form for an intended use or purpose.

Courtesy: Wolcotts, Inc.

Figure 14-1
Proposal and Contract for Home Improvement

NOTICE OF CANCELLATION/AVISO DE CANCELACION
(Home Solicitation Contract/Contrato de Solicitación de Casa)

Job/Contract No:
Nu. Destajo/Contrato: _____

Transaction Date: _____
Fecha de Transacción: _____

Under section 1689.7 of the California Civil Code, you may cancel this transaction, without penalty or obligation, within three business days from the above date.

If you cancel, any property traded in, any payments made by you under the contract or sale, and any negotiable instrument executed by you will be returned within 10 days following receipt by the seller of your cancellation notice, and any security interest arising out of the transaction will be cancelled.

If you cancel, you must make available to the seller at your residence, in substantially as good condition as when received, any goods delivered to you under this contract or sale, or you may, if you wish, comply with the instructions of the seller regarding the return shipment of the goods at the seller's expense and risk.

If you do make the goods available to the seller and the seller does not pick them up within 20 days of the date of your notice of cancellation, you may retain or dispose of the goods without any further obligation. If you fail to make the goods available to the seller, or if you agree to return the goods to the seller and fail to do so, then you remain liable for performance of all obligations under the contract.

To cancel this transaction, mail or deliver a signed and dated copy of this cancellation notice, or any other written notice, or send a telegram to

Bajo la sección 1689.7 del Código Civil de California, usted puede cancelar esta transacción (negociación) dentro de tres días negociables a partir de la fecha indicada arriba, sin castigo o compromiso.

Si usted cancela, cualquier propiedad dada en cambio, cualquier pago hecho por usted bajo el contrato o venta, y cualquier instrumento negociable ejecutado por usted será regresado dentro de 10 días después de haber recibido, el vendedor, su aviso de cancelación, y cualquier interés de garantía provisto por la negociación será cancelado.

Si usted cancela, tendrá que hacer accesible (disponible), en condición sustancialmente buena, cualquier efectos (enseres) entregados a usted bajo este contrato de venta, o. podrá, si usted desea, cumplir con las instrucciones del vendedor concerniente al envío (regreso) y gasto del vendedor.

Si usted pone los efectos (enseres) a disposición del vendedor y el vendedor no los recoge dentro de 20 días, a partir de la fecha de aviso de cancelación, usted podrá retener o disponer de los enseres sin ningún otro compromiso. Si usted falta en hacer disponibles los enseres al vendedor, o si usted concuerda de regresar los enseres al vendedor y no lo hace, entonces usted permanece responsable del cumplimiento de todos los compromisos bajo contrato.

Para cancelar esta negociación, envíe por correo o entregue una copia firmada y fechada de este aviso de cancelación, o cualquier otro aviso por escrito, o envíe un telegrama a _____

_____
(Name of Seller)

_____
(Nombre de Vendedor)

at _____
(Seller's Business Address)

en _____
(Dirección del Negocio (Oficina) del Vendedor)

no later than midnight of (Date) _____

no más tarde de la medianoche de (Fecha)
_____

Name _____

Address _____

City _____ Zip _____

Nombre _____

Dirección _____

Ciudad _____ Zona _____

I hereby cancel this transaction.

Por medio de esto cancelo esta negociación.

Date _____

_____
(Buyer's Signature)

Fecha _____

_____
(Firma del Comprador)

In the event of emergency the right to cancel may be waived. (See Wolcotts Form 570.)

En el caso de emergencia el derecho de cancelar puede ser renunciado. (Vea Wolcotts Form 570S.)

WOLCOTTS FORM 560 – NOTICE OF CANCELLATION (Home Solicitation Contract) (Spanish Language) – Rev. 9-84   © 1984 WOLCOTTS, INC.

Courtesy: Wolcotts, Inc.

Figure 14-2
Notice of Cancellation

Recovering Your Property

Once you complete a job, you have 10 days in which to demand and recover anything you've left at the customer's property. After 10 days, the customer may keep your belongings free of charge.

Substitutions, Price Changes

You can't vary from the contracted price or materials without getting prior written approval from your customer. If you find you're losing money on a job, you may try to renegotiate the contract. If the customer doesn't agree to renegotiate, you're legally compelled to fulfill the contract under the stated terms.

Bonds, Liens and Permits

In some states, if you bid and accept a job for more than a few hundred dollars, you must file notice of the contract with your county recorder. You must also show that you have any license bond required by state law. You must also notify your customer that you're operating under the current lien laws, and give your customer a summary of the lien law provisions.

It's probably your responsibility to get the necessary city and county permits and plan approvals. Unlicensed contractors aren't exempt from this. Before you start building fences and walls, find out what rules and restrictions apply. You can be fined or lose your license if you don't comply with them.

As a property owner, you don't need a contractor's license to build your own fence, wall or building. You may even hire someone to help you. But you still have to get the building permit required by law.

Holdbacks

Your customer can withhold money from you in certain cases. If you subcontract part of the job, and you haven't yet paid the subcontractor, the owner can hold back a total that doesn't exceed what you owe the subcontractors.

Contractors' Claims

In most states a contractor who isn't paid what's due can place a lien on the property. When the property is sold, the new buyer will probably demand that the lien be cleared before title passes. An unlicensed contractor can't file a mechanic's lien on the customer's property.

Figure 14-3 shows a mechanic's lien form. The contractor is the *claimant* in the lien, and the customer is the *defendant*. The lien claim must include the following information:

1) A description of all the services, labor, materials, etc., the contractor will use to perform the contract.

2) The customer's name, the contractor's name, and the names of any subcontractors or tenants involved.

3) The amount of the claim after deducting any prior payments.

4) A legal description of the parcel of property that received the improvements, and its legal owner's name.

Another avenue of claim by a licensed contractor is the *stop notice*. A stop notice is a lien on funds, not property. It's used where a third party supplies construction financing, or where a construction trust is set up by the customer to pay the contractor. Figure 14-4 shows a stop notice.

The information on the stop notice is the same as that on the mechanic's lien. You have to deliver a copy of the stop notice to the customer and to the agency holding the funds. You also have to supply a bond equal to 1-1/4 times the amount of the claim. If the claim goes to court and you lose, this bond covers your liability.

If the agency holding the funds has paid subcontractors or returned money to the customer, that agency is liable for your payment if you win the suit. If the customer is a public authority, such as a city or utility district, the stop notice is your only method of claim. You can't place a mechanic's lien on public property.

When you receive payment or release of payment, you have to file a release of mechanic's lien. See Figure 14-5.

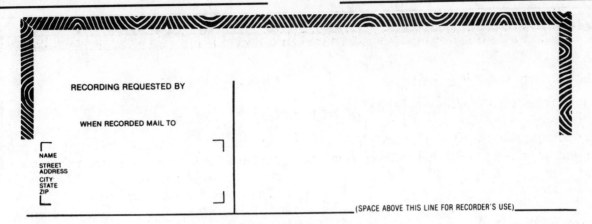

(SPACE ABOVE THIS LINE FOR RECORDER'S USE)

MECHANIC'S LIEN
(Claim of Lien)

The undersigned, _____, referred to
(Full name of person or firm claiming mechanic's lien)

in this Claim of Lien as the Claimant, claims a mechanic's lien for the labor, services, equipment and/or materials described below, furnished for a work of

improvement upon that certain real property located in the County of _____, State of California,

and described as follows: _____
(Description of property where the work and/or materials were furnished.
Although the street address is sufficient, it is advisable to give both the street address and the legal description.)

_____

After deducting all just credits and offsets, the sum of $_____, together with interest thereon at the rate of
(Amount of claim due and unpaid)

_____ percent per annum from _____, 19____, is due Claimant
(See note on reverse side)   (Date when amount of claim became due).

for the following labor, services, equipment and/or materials furnished by Claimant: _____
(General description of the work and/or materials furnished)

_____

The name of the person or company by whom Claimant was employed, or to whom Claimant furnished the labor, services, equipment and/or materials is

_____
(Usually name of person or firm who ordered from, or contracted with Claimant for the work and/or materials)

The name(s) and address(es) of the owner(s) or reputed owner(s) of the real property is/are: _____

_____
(This information can be obtained from the County Assessor's office where the real property is located)

**SEE REVERSE SIDE FOR
ADDITIONAL INSTRUCTIONS**

Name of Claimant _____
(See instructions on reverse side for proper signing)

By: _____
(Signature of Claimant or authorized agent and title)

VERIFICATION

I, the undersigned, declare: I am the _____ of _____, the Claimant
(Title)   (Name of Claimant)

named in the foregoing claim of mechanic's lien; I am authorized to make this verification for the Claimant; I have read the foregoing claim of mechanic's lien and
know the contents thereof, and the same is true of my own knowledge.

I declare under penalty of perjury under the laws of the State of California that the foregoing is true and correct.

_____, 19____   _____
(Date of signature)   (Signature of the individual who verifies that the contents of the claim of mechanic's lien are true)

Courtesy: Wolcotts, Inc.

**Figure 14-3
Mechanic's Lien**

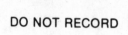

DO NOT RECORD

INFORMATION ABOUT MECHANICS' LIENS

A claimant who contracted directly with the owner must record his claim of mechanic's lien after he has completed his contract and within 90 days after completion of the work of improvement as a whole, unless the owner records a notice of completion or notice of cessation, in which case the claim of mechanic's lien must be recorded within 60 days after recordation of the notice of completion or notice of cessation. A claimant who did not contract directly with the owner must record his claim of mechanic's lien after he has ceased furnishing labor, services, equipment and/or materials, and within 90 days after completion of the work of improvement, unless the owner records a notice of completion or notice of cessation, in which case the claim of mechanic's lien must be recorded within 30 days after recordation of the notice of completion or notice of cessation.

This summary covers only some of the basic time periods applicable to mechanics' liens under California law, and does not purport to give a comprehensive review of this highly technical subject. Therefore, if you have any questions as to procedure, consult a lawyer.

RECORDING INFORMATION

The claim of mechanic's lien must be recorded in the county where the work of improvement is located. Check with the office of the county recorder where the claim of lien will be recorded for the correct fee. The recorder will not record a document unless it is accompanied by the correct fee.

INTEREST RATES

To establish the proper interest rate to be charged on the unpaid amount of the claim, refer to the applicable contract provisions. If the contract does not specify a rate, or if the contract is oral, interest may not be charged in excess of the legal rate of 7% per annum.

INSTRUCTIONS FOR SIGNING AND VERIFYING THIS FORM

Signature: If the claimant is a corporation, an officer or authorized agent should sign. If the claimant is a partnership, a partner or authorized agent should sign. If the claimant is a sole proprietorship, whether or not doing business under a fictitious business name, the owner of the business or an authorized agent should sign. Refer to the following examples:

CORPORATION

Name of Claimant _Johnson Electrical Co., Inc._

By _Sid Johnson, Pres._

PARTNERSHIP

Name of Claimant _Johnson Electrical Co._

By _Sid Johnson, Partner_

SOLE PROPRIETORSHIP (Fictitious Business Name)

Name of Claimant _Speedy Electrical Co._

By _Sid Johnson, Owner_

SOLE PROPRIETORSHIP (Own Name)

Name of Claimant _Sid Johnson Electric Co._

By _Sid Johnson, Owner_

Verification: This is a declaration under penalty of perjury under the laws of the State of California. It does not have to be notarized. However, to be valid, the verification must contain the date it is signed and the signature.

This standard form is intended for the typical situations encountered in the field indicated. However, before you sign, read it, fill in all blanks, and make whatever changes are appropriate and necessary to your particular transaction. Consult a lawyer if you doubt the form's fitness for your purpose and use.

WOLCOTTS FORM 1024—MECHANIC'S LIEN (Claim of Lien)—Rev. 5-82
(price class 3)

© 1982 WOLCOTTS, INC.

Courtesy: Wolcotts, Inc.

Figure 14-3 (cont'd)
Mechanic's Lien

STOP NOTICE

NOTICE TO WITHHOLD TO HOLDER OF FUNDS

TO:_____
(Name of owner, construction lender or public officer)

_____, HOLDER OF FUNDS.
(Address of owner or construction lender)

YOU ARE HEREBY NOTIFIED THAT the undersigned claimant,

_____
(Name and address)

has furnished or has agreed to furnish_____,
(labor, services, equipment, materials)

of the following kind_____,
(general description of labor, services, equipment or materials)

to or for_____, for the work improvement, located at, or known as:
(name of person to or for whom furnished)

_____.
(address, legal description, description of site or project identification)

The amount in value of the whole agreed to be done or furnished by claimant is $_____

The amount in value of that already done or furnished by claimant is $_____

Claimant has been paid the sum of $_____, and there remains due and unpaid the sum of $_____

plus interest thereon at the rate of_____per cent per annum from_____, 19_____

YOU ARE HEREBY NOTIFIED TO WITHHOLD SUFFICIENT FUNDS TO SATISFY THIS CLAIM WITH INTEREST.

Dated:_____   _____
Name of Claimant

_____
Address of Claimant

STATE OF CALIFORNIA
COUNTY OF_____ } ss.

_____, being duly sworn, deposes
and says: That ___he is the person(s) who signed the foregoing Stop Notice; that ___he has read the same and knows the contents thereof
to be true of h___ own knowledge, except as to any matters or things that may therein be stated on h___ information and belief and
as to those matters and things ___he believes them to be true.

_____

Subscribed and sworn to before me

this_____day of_____, 19_____

_____
Notary Public and in and for said State

This standard form covers most usual problems in the field indicated. Before you sign, read it, fill in all blanks,
and make changes proper to your transaction. Consult a lawyer if you doubt the form's fitness for your purpose.

STOP NOTICE
WOLCOTTS FORM 894—REV. 2-73   (price class 3)

Courtesy: Wolcotts, Inc.

Figure 14-4
Stop Notice

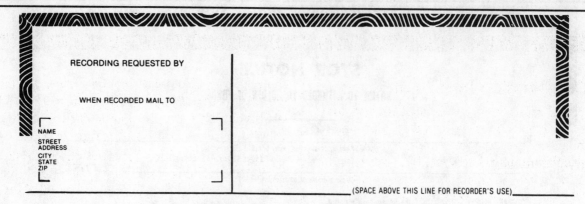

RECORDING REQUESTED BY

WHEN RECORDED MAIL TO

NAME
STREET
ADDRESS
CITY
STATE
ZIP

(SPACE ABOVE THIS LINE FOR RECORDER'S USE)

RELEASE OF MECHANIC'S LIEN

——◄►——

That that certain notice of lien executed by the undersigned against _____,

and claiming a lien upon the following described real property situated in the _____

_____ County of _____, State of California, to-wit:

dated the _____ day of _____, 19___, and recorded in

the office of the County Recorder of _____ County on the _____

day of _____, 19___, in Book _____ of _____

page _____ as Instrument No. _____, is hereby released, the claim thereunder having been fully paid and satisfied.

WITNESS my hand this _____ day of _____, 19___.

_____

_____

_____

STATE OF CALIFORNIA

COUNTY OF _____ } ss.

On this _____ day of _____, 19___, before me, the undersigned, a Notary Public in and for said State, personally appeared _____

_____,

personally known to me (or proved to me on the basis of satisfactory evidence) to be the person__ whose name__ _____ subscribed to the within instrument, and acknowledged to me that __he__ executed it.

Witness my hand and official seal.

_____
Notary Public in and for said State.

STATE OF CALIFORNIA

COUNTY OF _____ } ss.

On this _____ day of _____, 19___, before me, the undersigned, a Notary Public in and for said State, personally appeared _____

_____ and _____

_____, personally known to me (or proved to me on the basis of satisfactory evidence) to be the persons who executed the within instrument as President and Secretary, respectively, of the Corporation therein named, and acknowledged to me that the Corporation executed it pursuant to its by-laws or a resolution of its board of directors.

WITNESS my hand and official seal.

_____
Notary Public in and for said State.

Title Order No. _____

Escrow or Loan No. _____

MECHANIC'S LIEN—RELEASE OF
WOLCOTTS FORM 1018—Rev. 9-82

(price class 3)

This standard form is intended for the typical situations encountered in the field indicated. However, before you sign, read it, fill in all blanks, and make whatever changes are appropriate and necessary to your particular transaction. Consult a lawyer if you doubt the form's fitness for your purpose and use.
©WOLCOTTS, INC. 1982

Courtesy: Wolcotts, Inc.

Figure 14-5
Release of Mechanic's Lien

The Construction Trust Fund

Earlier I mentioned a *construction trust fund*. This is also called an *express trust*. It's an agreement between the customer and the contractor and any subcontractors or workers. It's money set aside in trust by the customer for payments due under the contract. It's somewhat like a compliance bond. Money is only released as specified parts of the job are finished. An express trust has the effect of both a stop notice and a mechanic's lien. A lien can be placed against the funds being held. But any claim in excess of the fund can become a claim against the property.

Customer's Recourse

Completion of a construction job may be delayed for various reasons. When that happens, the customer has a couple of choices. The first choice is always to put up with the delay. The customer can hire another contractor to finish the job *after waiting* 30 days from the last time any work was done. Next, the owner files a *notice of cessation* like the one in Figure 14-6. The notice has to show the legal description of the property and the owner's name and address. It also has to give the contractor's name, and the last date any work was done. Once this happens, the owner can legally withhold any further funds and hire another contractor to finish the job.

Unauthorized Work

If you own property and your tenant contracts to have work done on that property, you're legally responsible for payment to the contractor. You can protect yourself in this situation with a notice of non-responsibility like the one in Figure 14-7.

File the notice with your county recorder and post a copy of it in plain sight on the property being improved. You have to do this within 10 days of discovering that work is being done without your authorization.

Protect Yourself

As a contractor, you have to protect your business from these claims. If you filed a notice of

contract, then you must also file a *notice of completion* like the one in Figure 14-8 when you finish the job. If you don't, and the customer files a notice of cessation, you could lose your right to collect.

You file the notice of completion within 10 days after finishing the project. Then you have 30 days (if you're a subcontractor) or 60 days (if you're the prime contractor) to file a mechanic's lien.

Here's the sequence of events:

1) Your customer signs a contract and you begin work.

2) Within 30 days of starting work or delivering materials to the job site, give your customer a copy of the preliminary notice form (Figure 14-9). It tells the customer that you'll file a mechanic's lien if they don't pay you.

3) After completion of the job, file the notice of completion.

4) If you haven't been paid within 30 days after the notice of completion, file the claim of lien.

5) Within 90 days of claim of lien, file for *lien foreclosure action*. Also file a *Lis Pendens* and deliver your stop notices. A Lis Pendens is a notice that a lawsuit is pending. It tells all concerned parties that you are suing.

6) Near the end of the 90 days you must foreclose on the property. The only way to prevent foreclosure is to give a credit for payment to your customer. This extends the foreclosure an additional 90 days. You can do this for up to one year, then you must complete the foreclosure or lose your claim.

The Last Resort

In case of a major dispute, the last recourse for all concerned is the court system. If the claim is small, go to small claims court. The cost to file is low, usually less than $20, and both parties meet face to face with the judge. Attorneys aren't usually permitted. The customer can also use the small claims court to file a suit to comply or do the work against you.

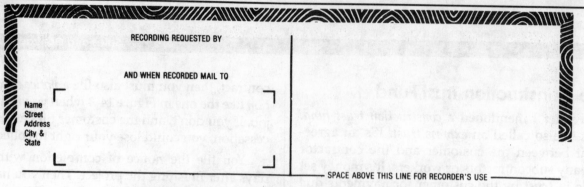

NOTICE OF CESSATION OF LABOR

I, _____
name   address

_____

hereby certify that:

I am now and was upon the _____ day of _____, 19____,
the owner of that certain real property situated in the City of _____
County of _____, State of California and formerly described as _____
street address

_____
if no street address give location or directions

in the City of_____, of said County and State, and which premises are
particularly described as follows, to-wit:

as per may recorded in Book _____ page _____ of _____
in the office of the County Recorder of said County.

The interest or estate of owner is that of _____
fee simple, lessee, vender, etc.

As such owner of said land, I, about the _____ day of _____, 19____,
entered into a contract with _____
name   address

as per permit (if any) No. _____ dated _____, 19____, for the
erection and construction, or work of improvement, upon the land above described, of a certain building____, or work of
improvement, to-wit:

Said building has been partially constructed or improved, but for a period of more than thirty days prior to the date hereof,
to-wit, on the _____ day of _____, 19____, there has been a cessation of labor upon the said
work; said cessation of labor has continued and is continuing to the date of recording of this Notice.

The original contractor for said erection and construction and work of improvement as a whole (if any) was _____
name

_____
address

The names and addresses of the other joint tenants or co-tenants (if any) are as follows: _____

_____

_____

This Notice is given in pursuance of the provisions of Section 3092 Civil Code of the State of California.

STATE OF CALIFORNIA } ss.   _____

COUNTY OF

I, _____ declare
that I am the owner of the property described in the foregoing notice; that I have read the same and know the contents
thereof, and that the same is true of my own knowledge.

I certify (or declare) under penalty of perjury that the foregoing is true and correct.

Executed on _____, 19____, at _____, California.

_____
(Owner)

NOTE:
Must be filed for record in the office of the County Recorder of the County in which property is situated.

WOLCOTTS FORM 1112—Rev. 8-81   ©1981 WOLCOTTS, INC.   This standard form covers most usual problems in the field indicated. Before you sign, read it, fill in all blanks, and make changes proper to your transaction. Consult a lawyer if you doubt the form's fitness for your purpose.

Courtesy: Wolcotts, Inc.

Figure 14-6
Notice of Cessation of Labor

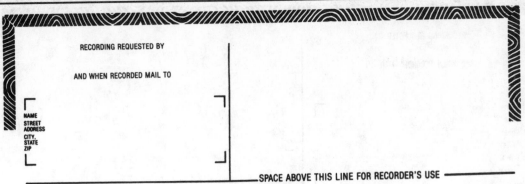

SPACE ABOVE THIS LINE FOR RECORDER'S USE

NOTICE

NON-RESPONSIBILITY (C. C. Sec. 3094, 3128 & 3129)

TO ALL WHOM IT MAY CONCERN: NOTICE IS HEREBY GIVEN

(1) That _____, to wit, _____
　　　　(I—we)　　　　　　　　　　　　(Insert name or names)

_____ (am—are)

the _____
　　　　　　(Insert herein the nature of title or interest)

_____

of certain property located in the City of _____

County of _____, State of California, and more particularly described as:

Lot _____, in Block _____, of Tract No. _____

_____, as

per map____ recorded in Book _____, Page _____ of _____

Records of _____ County, State of California.

(2) That _____, have obtained knowledge that _____
　　　　　　(I—we)　　　　　　　　　　　(Insert brief description of improvement, alteration or repair)

_____ (is—are)

_____ on said property.
　　　　　(in the course of construction—are being made)

(3) That ten (10) days have not elapsed since _____ obtained this knowledge.
　　　　　　　　　　　　　　　　　　　　　　　(I—we)

(4) That _____ will not be responsible for the_____
　　　　　(I—we)　　　　　　　　　　　　　　(erection, alteration or repair)

_____ of said _____,
　　　　　　　　　　　　　　　　　　　　(building—improvement)

or for the material or labor used or to be used thereon, or which has been performed, furnished or used in any manner or

way upon said land, or upon the _____ thereon, or addition thereto, or which
　　　　　　　　　　　　　　(building—improvement)

may hereafter be performed, furnished, or used upon said land or upon the_____
　　　　　　　　　　　　　　　　　　　　　　　　　(building—improvement)

thereon, or addition thereto, or for the services of any architect.

(5) That _____ (is—are)
　　　　　　　　(Insert name or names)

the purchaser____ of said property under a contract of purchase, or that _____
　　　　　　　　　　　　　　　　　　　　　　　　　(Insert name or names)

_____ (is—are)

the lessee____ of said property.

(6) That the street address of said property is_____,

City of _____, California.

Dated _____

STATE OF CALIFORNIA　　　　　　　} ss.

COUNTY OF _____

_____, being first duly sworn, deposes and says: That the above and within notice is a true

and correct copy of a notice posted in a conspicuous place on Lot _____, in Block _____, of Tract No. _____,

in the City of_____, County of _____, State of California,

on the _____ day of _____ 19____, by _____

and that the facts therein are true of h____ own knowledge, and that ____he is making this affidavit for and on behalf of the person____ for whose

protection said notice was given.

Subscribed and sworn to before me

this _____ day of _____, 19____.

_____
　　　　　Notary Public in and for said County and State.

Title Order No. _____

Escrow or Loan No. _____

NOTICE—Non-Responsibility (Recording Version)
WOLCOTTS FORM 1186—Rev. 3-81　　(price class 3)

Courtesy: Wolcotts, Inc.

Figure 14-7
Notice of Non-Responsibility

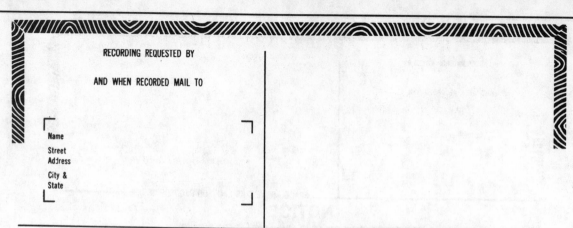

RECORDING REQUESTED BY

AND WHEN RECORDED MAIL TO

Name
Street
Address
City &
State

SPACE ABOVE THIS LINE FOR RECORDER'S USE

NOTICE OF COMPLETION

Notice pursuant to Civil Code Section 3093, must be filed within 10 days after completion. (See reverse side for Complete requirements.)

Notice is hereby given that:

1. The undersigned is owner or corporate officer of the owner of the interest or estate stated below in the property hereinafter described:

2. The full name of the owner is _____

3. The full address of the owner is _____

_____

4. The nature of the interest or estate of the owner is; In fee.

_____

(If other than fee, strike "In fee" and insert, for example, "purchaser under contract of purchase," or "lessee")

5. The full names and full addresses of all persons, if any, who hold title with the undersigned as joint tenants or as tenants in common are:

NAMES   ADDRESSES

_____

_____

6. A work of improvement on the property hereinafter described was completed on _____ . The work done was:

_____

7. The name of the contractor, if any, for such work of improvement was _____

_____

(If no contractor for work of improvement as a whole, insert "none".)   (Date of Contract)

8. The property on which said work of improvement was completed is in the city of _____ ,

County of _____ , State of California, and is described as follows: _____

_____

_____

9. The street address of said property is _____

(If no street address has been officially assigned, insert "none".)

Dated: _____

Verification for Individual Owner

_____
Signature of owner or corporate officer of owner
named in paragraph 2 or his agent

VERIFICATION

I, the undersigned, say: I am the _____ the declarant of the foregoing

("President of", "Manager of", "A partner of", "Owner of", etc.)

notice of completion; I have read said notice of completion and know the contents thereof; the same is true of my own knowledge.

I declare under penalty of perjury that the foregoing is true and correct.

Executed on _____ , 19____ , at _____ , California.

(Date of signature.)   (City where signed.)

_____

(Personal signature of the individual who is swearing that the contents of
the notice of completion are true.)

NOTICE OF COMPLETION—WOLCOTTS FORM 1114—REV. 6-74 (price class 3)   8 pt. type or larger

Courtesy: Wolcotts, Inc.

Figure 14-8
Notice of Completion

CALIFORNIA PRELIMINARY 20-DAY NOTICE
(PUBLIC AND PRIVATE WORK)
IN ACCORDANCE WITH SECTION 3097 AND 3098, CALIFORNIA CIVIL CODE

YOU ARE HEREBY NOTIFIED THAT...

L
E
N
D
E
R
'
S

C
O
P
Y

CONSTRUCTION LENDER or
Reputed Construction Lender, if any

_____
(name and address of person or firm—sender)
_____

has furnished or will furnish labor, services, equipment or materials of the following general description:

_____
(general description of the labor, services, equipment or materials furnished or to be furnished)

for the building, structure or other work of improvement located at:

_____
(address or description of job site sufficient for identification)
_____

———— FOLD HERE ————

The name of the person or firm who contracted for the purchase of such labor, services, equipment or materials:

_____

OWNER   or   PUBLIC AGENCY
or Reputed Owner   (on public work)
(on private work)

NOTICE TO PROPERTY OWNER

If bills are not paid in full for the labor, services, equipment, or materials furnished or to be furnished, a mechanic's lien leading to the loss, through court foreclosure proceedings, of all or part of your property being so improved may be placed against the property even though you have paid your contractor in full. You may wish to protect yourself against this consequence by (1) requiring your contractor to furnish a signed release by the person or firm giving you this notice before making payment to your contractor or (2) any other method or device which is appropriate under the circumstances.

The person or firm giving this notice is required, pursuant to a collective bargaining agreement, to pay supplemental fringe benefits into an express trust fund (described in Civil Code §3111), said fund is identified as follows: (strike if inapplicable)

_____
(name)
_____
(address)
_____
(name)
_____
(address)
_____
(name)
_____
(address)

———— FOLD HERE ————

ORIGINAL CONTRACTOR or
Reputed Contractor

Mailed this date: _____

_____
(signature)   (title)

An estimate of the total price of the labor, services, equipment or materials furnished or to be furnished is:

$ _____

DECLARATION OF SERVICE OF CALIFORNIA PRELIMINARY 20-DAY NOTICE
In Accordance With §3097.1(c) and 3098, California Civil Code

I,_____, declare:

On the _____ day of _____, 19____, at _____ ____.m., Declarant served the CALIFORNIA PRELIMINARY 20-DAY NOTICE on the interested parties as follows: (Check applicable box.)

☐ By placing a true copy thereof enclosed in a sealed envelope with first-class registered or certified postage prepaid in the United States mail at _____, addressed as follows:

☐ By delivering a true copy thereof to the parties listed below:

☐ By leaving a true copy thereof at the address or place of business with some person in charge, of the parties whose names and addresses delivered are listed below: (not to be used on public works)

I declare under penalty of perjury that the foregoing is true and correct. Executed on _____, 19____,

at _____, _____.

                              Declarant

WOLCOTTS FORM 15100 (Quadruplicate), Rev. 7-81b (price class 13D)   ©1981 WOLCOTTS, INC.   (PLEASE NOTE REVERSE SIDE)

Courtesy: Wolcotts, Inc.

Figure 14-9
California Preliminary 20-Day Notice

§ 3097. Preliminary 20-day notice (private work). "Preliminary 20-day notice (private work)" means a written notice from a claimant that is given prior to the recording of a mechanic's lien and prior to the filing of a stop notice, and is required to be given under the following circumstances:

(a) Written preliminary notice; parties. Except one under direct contract with the owner or one performing actual labor for wages, or an express trust fund described in Section 3111, every person who furnishes labor, service, equipment, or material for which a lien otherwise can be claimed under this title, or for which a notice to withhold can otherwise be given under this title, must, as a necessary prerequisite to the validity of any claim of lien, and of a notice to withhold, cause to be given to the owner or reputed owner, to the original contractor, or reputed contractor, and to the construction lender, if any, or to the reputed construction lender, if any, a written preliminary notice as prescribed by this section.

(b) Construction lender. Except the contractor, or one performing actual labor for wages, or an express trust fund described in Section 3111, all persons who have a direct contract with the owner and who furnish labor, service, equipment, or material for which a lien otherwise can be claimed under this title, or for which a notice to withhold can otherwise be given under this title, must, as a necessary prerequisite to the validity of any claim of lien, and of a notice to withhold, cause to be given to the construction lender, if any, or to the reputed construction lender, if any, a written preliminary notice as prescribed by this section.

(c) Time; content; architect, engineer or surveyor. The preliminary notice referred to in subdivisions (a) and (b) shall be given not later than 20 days after the claimant has first furnished labor, service, equipment, or materials to the jobsite, and shall contain the following information:

(1) A general description of the labor, service, equipment, or materials furnished, or to be furnished, and if there is a construction lender, he shall be furnished with an estimate of the total price thereof in addition to the foregoing.

(2) The name and address of such person furnishing such labor, service, equipment, or materials.

(3) The name of the person who contracted for purchase of such labor, service, equipment, or materials.

(4) A description of the jobsite sufficient for identification.

(5) The following statement in boldface type:

NOTICE TO PROPERTY OWNER

If bills are not paid in full for the labor, services, equipment, or materials furnished or to be furnished, a mechanic's lien leading to the loss, through court foreclosure proceedings, of all or part of your property being so improved may be placed against the property even though you have paid your contractor in full. You may wish to protect yourself against this consequence by (1) requiring your contractor to furnish a signed release by the person or firm giving you this notice before making payment to your contractor or (2) any other method or device which is appropriate under the circumstances.

(6) If such notice is given by a subcontractor who is required pursuant to a collective-bargaining agreement to pay supplemental fringe benefits into an express trust fund described in Section 3111, such notice shall also contain the identity and address of such trust fund or funds.

If an invoice for such materials contains the information required by this section, a copy of such invoice, transmitted in the manner prescribed by this section shall be sufficient notice.

A certificated architect, registered engineer, or licensed land surveyor who has furnished services for the design of the work of improvement and who gives a preliminary notice as provided in this section not later than 20 days after the work of improvement has commenced shall be deemed to have complied with subdivisions (a) and (b) with respect to architectural, engineering, or surveying services furnished, or to be furnished.

(d) Election not to give preliminary notice; subsequent rights. If labor, service, equipment, or materials have been furnished to a jobsite by a person who elected not to give a preliminary notice as provided in subdivision (a) or (b), such person shall not be precluded from giving a preliminary notice not later than 20 days after furnishing other labor, service, equipment, or materials to the same jobsite. Such person shall, however, be entitled to claim a lien and a notice to withhold only for such labor, service, equipment, or material furnished within 20 days prior to the service of such notice, and at any time thereafter.

(e) Waiver. Any agreement made or entered into by an owner, whereby the owner agrees to waive the rights or privileges conferred upon him by this section shall be void and of no effect.

(f) Service. The notice required under this section may be served as follows:

(1) If the person to be notified resides in this state, by delivering the notice personally, or by leaving it at his address of residence or place of business with some person in charge, or by first-class registered or certified mail, postage prepaid, addressed to the person to whom notice is to be given at his residence or place of business address or at the address shown by the building permit on file with the authority issuing a building permit for the work, or at an address recorded pursuant to subdivision (j) of this section.

(2) If the person to be notified does not reside in this state, by any method enumerated in paragraph (1) of this subdivision. If such person cannot be served by any of such methods, then notice may be given by first-class certified or registered mail, addressed to the construction lender or to the original contractor.

(3) When service is made by first-class certified or registered mail, service is complete at the time of the deposit of such registered or certified mail.

(g) Single notice; additional material, service, labor or equipment. A person required by this section to give notice to the owner and to an original contractor, and to a person to whom a notice to withhold may be given, need give only one such notice to owner, and to the original contractor and to the person to whom a notice to withhold may be given with respect to all materials, service, labor, or equipment he furnishes for a work of improvement, which means the entire structure or scheme of improvements as a whole, unless the same is furnished under contracts with more than one subcontractor, in which event, the notice requirements must be met with respect to materials, services, labor, or equipment furnished to each such contractor.

If a notice contains a general description required by subdivision (a) or (b) of the materials, services, labor, or equipment furnished to the date of notice, it is not defective because, after such date, the person giving notice furnishes materials, services, labor, or equipment not within the scope of such general description.

(h) Disciplinary action against contractors and subcontractors. Where the contract price to be paid to any subcontractor on a particular work of improvement exceeds four hundred dollars ($400), the failure of that contractor, licensed under Chapter 9 (commencing with Section 7000) of Division 3 of the Business and Professions Code, to give the notice provided for in this section, constitutes grounds for disciplinary action by the Registrar of Contractors.

Where such notice is required to contain the information set forth in paragraph (6) of subdivision (c), a failure to give such notice, including such information, that results in the filing of a lien or the delivery of a stop notice by the express trust fund to which such obligation is owing constitutes grounds for the disciplinary action by the Registrar of Contractors against the subcontractor if the amount due such trust fund is not paid.

(i) Construction lender; designation or permit application. Every city, county, city and county, or other governmental authority issuing building permits shall, in its application form for a building permit, provide space and a designation for the applicant to enter the name, branch, designation, if any, and address of the construction lender and shall keep the information on file open for public inspection during the regular business hours of the authority.

If there is no known construction lender, that fact shall be noted in such designated space. Any failure to indicate the name and address of the construction lender on such application, however, shall not relieve any person from the obligation to give to the construction lender the notice required by this section.

(j) Designation of mortgage, deed of trust or other instrument securing loan. A mortgage, deed of trust, or other instrument securing a loan, any of the proceeds of which may be used for the purpose of constructing improvements on real property, shall bear the designation "Construction Trust Deed" prominently on its face and shall state all of the following: (1) the name and address of the lender, and the name and address of the owner of the real property described in the instrument, and (2) a legal description of the real property which secures the loan and, if known, the street address of the property. The failure to be so designated or to state any of the information required by this subdivision shall not affect the validity of any such mortgage, deed of trust, or other instrument.

Failure to provide such information on such an instrument when recorded shall not relieve persons required to give preliminary notice under this section from such duty.

The county recorder of the county in which such instrument is recorded shall indicate in the general index of the official records of the county that such instrument secures a construction loan.

(k) Trust fund and lender; supplementary fringe benefits. Every contractor and subcontractor who is required pursuant to a collective-bargaining agreement to pay supplementary fringe benefits into an express trust fund described in Section 3111, and who has failed to do so shall cause to be given to such fund and to the construction lender, if any, or to the reputed construction lender, if any, not later than the date such payment due to such fund became delinquent, a written notice containing:

(1) The name of the owner and the contractor.

(2) A description of the jobsite sufficient for identification.

(3) The identity and address of the express trust fund.

(4) The total number of straight time and overtime hours on each such job, payment for which the contractor or subcontractor is delinquent to the express trust.

(5) The amount then past due and owing.

Failure to give such notice shall constitute grounds for disciplinary action by the Registrar of Contractors.

(l) Contract; name and address of owner; information to person seeking to serve notice. Every written contract entered into between a property owner and an original contractor shall provide space for the owner to enter his name and address of residence; and place of business if any. The original contractor shall make available the name and address of residence of the owner to any person seeking to serve notice required by this section.

§3097.1 Proof of service of preliminary 20-day notice, proof of service affidavit; receipt. Proof that the preliminary 20-day notice required by Section 3097 was served in accordance with subdivision (f) of Section 3097 shall be made as follows:

(a) If served by mail, by the proof of service affidavit described in subdivision (c) of this section accompanied either by the return receipt of certified or registered mail, or by a photocopy of the record of delivery and receipt maintained by the post office, showing the date of delivery and to whom delivered, or, in the event of nondelivery, by the returned envelope itself.

(b) If served by personally delivering the notice to the person to be notified, or by leaving it at his address or place of business with some person in charge, by the proof of service affidavit described in subdivision (c).

(c) A "proof of service affidavit" is an affidavit of the person making the service, showing the time, place and manner of service and facts showing that such service was made in accordance with Section 3097. Such affidavit shall show the name and address of the person upon whom a copy of the preliminary 20-day notice was served, and, if appropriate, the title or capacity in which he was served.

§3098. Preliminary 20-day notice (public work), stop notice; service; disciplinary action; exemption for express trust fund. "Preliminary 20-day notice (public work), stop notice" means a written notice from a claimant that was given prior to the filing of a stop notice on public work, and is required to be given under the following circumstances:

(a) In any case in which the law of this state affords a right to a person furnishing labor or materials for a public work who has not been paid therefor to file a stop notice with the public agency concerned, and thereby cause the withholding of payment from the contractor for the public work, any such person having no direct contractual relationship with the contractor, other than a person who performed actual labor for wages or an express trust fund described in Section 3111, may file such a notice, but no payment shall be withheld from any such contractor, pursuant to any such notice, unless such person has caused written notice to be given to such contractor, and the public agency concerned, not later than 20 days after the claimant has first furnished labor, services, equipment, or materials to the jobsite, stating with substantial accuracy a general description of labor, service, equipment, or materials furnished or to be furnished, and the name of the party to whom the same was furnished. Such notice shall be served by mailing the same by first-class mail, registered mail, or certified mail, postage prepaid, in an envelope addressed to the contractor at any place he maintains an office or conducts his business, or his residence, or by personal service. In case of any public works constructed by the Department of Public Works or the Department of General Services of the state, such notice shall be served by mailing in the same manner as above, addressed to the office of the disbursing officer of the department constructing the work, or by personal service upon such officer. When service is by registered or certified mail, service is complete at the time of the deposit of the registered or certified mail.

(b) Where the contract price to be paid to any subcontractor on a particular work of improvement exceeds four hundred dollars ($400), the failure of that contractor, licensed under Chapter 9 (commencing with Section 7000) of Division 3 of the Business and Professions Code, to give the notice provided for in this section, constitutes grounds for disciplinary action by the Registrar of Contractors.

(c) The notice requirements of this section shall not apply to an express trust fund described in Section 3111.

Courtesy: Wolcotts, Inc.

Figure 14-9 (cont'd)
California Preliminary 20-Day Notice

If the amount is more than $1,500, you'll have to go to a higher court. You'll probably need an attorney. The cost will probably be thousands of dollars. There can also be a significant delay before your case goes to trial.

Remember, laws vary from state to state and change every year. Check with your local authorities and consult an attorney if you have any doubts.

I'll end this chapter with one last appeal: Get it in writing! It's much easier to make claims under a written contract than a spoken one. And, even though there are many legal ways to resolve a dispute, it's always better to avoid one in the first place.

fifteen

Safety on the Job

In this chapter, I'll point out some of the dangers every fence and retaining wall contractor faces. I'll also give you some tips on how to prevent the most common types of accidents.

The first part of the chapter covers the law. In the last 20 years both state and federal governments have jumped into the safety business. They've passed laws intended to make illegal everything that's likely to be dangerous. No matter whether you think these laws are foolish or wise, they're the law. Let this chapter be your guide to what federal and state laws require.

In the second half of the chapter I'll suggest some things you can do to work safer, no matter what the law requires.

If this sounds boring and you're tempted to skip over this chapter, fine. Skip on to the next chapter. But there will come a time when you need a good reference on job-site safety. Have this book handy.

Here are three reasons why I think safety is important:

First, safety pays — and maybe saves you lots of money.

Second, the contractor's license exams emphasize safety. You have to be familiar with basic safety principles to pass the exam.

Third, your own personal welfare may be at stake. Just once in your professional career spend 20 minutes thinking about job-site safety. That 20 minutes could save your life or keep you out of the hospital. The time you spend reading this chapter may be well rewarded. After all, there's not a lot of point taking on a job if you're going to get injured doing it.

Fence or wall building isn't always done under ideal conditions. I've built walls and fences on the edges of cliffs, below water, and in dense underbrush. Every fence builder uses equipment and tools that can inflict severe injury when used improperly. Bulldozers, backhoes, axes, picks, and fence stretchers are just some of the more dangerous tools you'll use.

You'll be building fences and walls outdoors, an area populated by snakes, bugs, wild animals and hazardous plants. Retaining walls are often built on high and unstable hillsides — that's why a retaining wall is needed. There's some danger in most fence jobs. And it's all too easy to get engrossed in what you're doing and ignore the danger. In every case, good judgment and common sense are your best protection. This chapter should help you spot potential problems so your common sense can eliminate them.

Safety Is Everyone's Job

Who's responsible for safety? There's only one answer: *you* are. No matter who *you* are. Whether you're a homeowner, contractor, subcontractor, employer, or employee, safety comes first.

The best defense against a potential loss is understanding the dangers. It's knowing the dangers of the job and job site and taking proper precautions. It's being prepared to handle the inevitable emergency. It's using care and common sense. It's training yourself and your workers how to use proper tools and techniques. It's also the *law*.

Safety precautions are required by various authorities. Some you may impose yourself in the form of company safety regulations. The building inspector, your insurance company, and state and federal agencies also have safety requirements. Inspectors can close you down if they find your work or methods unsafe. Insurance companies will refuse claims or cancel policies. If you're convicted of negligence, state and federal health and safety agencies and contractor's licensing boards can fine you or revoke your license. Some violations carry criminal penalties.

The prime rule-setting body is *OSHA*, the Occupational Safety and Health Administration. They can inspect your work place whether or not you're a licensed contractor, and they can do so without advance notice. Their main purpose is to control, inspect, and instruct employers and employees on safe operating procedures at the work place. For the most part they do a good job. But, like so many government agencies, they're understaffed and so they only spot check or respond to complaints. They do require that all serious job-related injuries be reported to them immediately by phone. Employers are also required to file a written report with their state's division of labor statistics, and their insurance carrier.

Many states have their own OSHA department. State OSHA departments usually report to the state's Department of Industrial Relations. Contact them for more information and a copy of their official rules and regulations. The rules that follow may or may not apply in your state. State laws vary. And new laws are passed every year. Get specific information from your state OSHA office.

General Safety Regulations

◆ Every employer must display the state-issued safety posters at their place of business.

◆ Employers are required to see that all employees use safety equipment provided for them or required for the job.

◆ Prior to the start of work at a job site, the employer is to inspect the job site. Then the employer is to describe all unsafe conditions and give safe operating instructions to employees.

◆ If a chemical is involved, such as a wood preservative, the employer must inform the employees of the dangers of the chemical. The employer may be required to do this in writing.

◆ Make special note of any eye hazards. Furnish protection in the form of glasses, screens or shields.

◆ Employers must provide a first aid kit on the job site, housed in a waterproof container. The kit should include items to treat any injuries that may be expected at that job site. For example, include a snake bite kit if the job site is in an area where there are known poisonous snakes.

◆ Employers must furnish *potable* water at the job site. Potable means drinkable without a health risk. Water containers should have a fountain or faucet and be labeled "potable drinking water." Users shouldn't have to dip water from the container. Either provide each employee with a cup or use disposable cups.

Clearly label any non-potable water on the job site. Non-potable water is water that may not be safe to drink or wash in, like water stored for use in toilets or for fire fighting, or taken from streams, ponds, lakes or rivers.

♦ Employers must supply toilets at the job site. There must be one for each 20 employees. You can substitute urinals, as long as there are at least half of the number of toilets required. If you had 100 employees, for example, you could have three toilets and two urinals. If sewers and water are available, you can use standard flush toilets. If not, use chemical, combustion, or recirculating types. Maintain the facilities at all times. They need to have an adequate supply of toilet paper, be clean, and work properly. On-site facilities aren't required for a mobile crew that has transportation to a nearby toilet facility.

Polluted Air

On job sites where workers will be exposed to gases, vapors, fumes, dust, or other airborne contamination, you're required to provide an approved respirator unless you have exhaust ventilation sufficient to provide a minimum of 100 cubic feet per minute air velocity. And the employee is required to use it. If you have this amount of ventilation, then the use of a respirator may be optional.

But if you're welding or working with beryllium, zinc, lead, mercury, cadmium, fluorides, or chromium, you *have* to supply an air respirator no matter what ventilation system you have. Even if you're working in the open air, you have to use a respirator. The fumes from these metals can kill you.

Excavation

OSHA's rules for excavation are brief:

1) If employees will work in an excavation 5 or more feet deep, the hole must be shored or sloped to prevent a cave-in. You may need a permit.

2) Inspect excavations of less than 5 feet for safety and possible ground movement. In excavations of 4 feet or more, provide a safe way to enter or exit every 25 lateral feet. You can usually meet this requirement with a sloped side trench.

3) Adequate bracing of an excavation is required. If the soil is unstable, use trench bracing.

4) Store bracing materials safely. If bracing materials will be handled manually, you can't pile them more than 16 feet high. If you use a crane or forklift, piles can be 20 feet high. This applies to any stacked materials.

Removing Obstacles

Many fences are built over, around or through obstacles like trees, rocks or hills. On some jobs you may have to clear these obstacles by blasting with explosives. This is dangerous work. Most states require a special license for blasting work.

You're required to provide safe storage for any explosives. Store explosives in a bunker or magazine located at least 100 feet away from high voltage electrical lines (250 volts AC or more), and at least 25 feet from low voltage lines. Store caps separately from explosive materials. There must be at least 25 feet clearance to the nearest power distribution circuit or light. Prohibit smoking, flame or ignition sources within 50 feet. Place signs to clearly mark the boundary of the storage safety perimeter.

Hauling

Most fence and retaining wall contractors have to do some hauling of materials or soil. Here's a summary of typical regulations that apply to hauling operations.

1) Trucks have to be equipped with lights, brakes, fenders, and applicable safety equipment. There's one exception: You don't need fenders on a vehicle that can't exceed 15 miles per hour.

2) If you use a crane, hoist, power shovel, loader, or other heavy equipment to load the vehicle, the hauling vehicle must have a protected cab. This shield must be strong enough to protect the vehicle's operator from injury in the event a load is accidentally dumped on the cab.

3) All construction hauling vehicles of 2-1/2 cubic yards or more capacity must be equipped with an automatic backup sounding device, a horn, bell or beeper. You must be able to hear this sound clearly for a distance of 200 feet. It must activate immediately when the vehicle backs up.

4) Inspect all haulage vehicles once each shift, preferably at the beginning of the shift. Check brakes, steering, and other control devices. The operator can make this inspection. Keep an inspection log and fill it out daily.

5) If there's danger to other personnel, traffic controls are required at the job site. These controls can be signs, flags, flaggers, or barriers.

6) Cranes, cableways, or derricks can only be run by licensed operators. If the equipment is capable of lifting three tons or more, the operator must be tested and licensed by the U.S. Department of Labor. A licensed civil, mechanical, or structural engineer may give this annual exam. The equipment itself must also be certified. Keep a 5-pound type B:C fire extinguisher near cranes.

Fire Extinguishers

You're required to have a fully-charged 5-pound type B:C fire extinguisher within 75 feet of any construction area. Also keep extinguishers in or near any heavy equipment you're using. Make sure everyone on the job knows where the extinguisher is and knows how to use it. You're not permitted to use carbon tetrachloride extinguishers.

Damaged Tools

Don't try to save money by using damaged or worn out tools. Repair or replace them — you'll save money in the long run. Don't use axes and picks with handles that are rotted, split, or loose. Dull saws and drills slow the work and do a sloppy job. Worse, they can slip or break suddenly.

"I'm not going up whether you hold it or not!!"

Ladders and Scaffolds

You'll need these if you build balconies or second story railings. OSHA has strict rules for ladders and scaffolds. Nearly all ladder and scaffold manufacturers build products that comply with the law. But you still have to use the equipment correctly:

1) Maintain all ladders in good working condition. Remove any ladder from the job site if it has broken, weak or missing rungs.

2) Use all ladders within their rated load capacity.

3) Brace ladders so they won't slip or tip. Step ladders don't have to be braced.

4) Ladders you use as a platform for getting onto a landing must extend 3 feet above the landing. By the way, if you use a landing as a loading area, it must be at least 4 square feet and a minimum of 20 inches wide.

5) The rungs on ladders must be spaced no more than 12 inches apart, must be equally spaced give or take 1/4 inch, and be at least 11-1/2 inches wide.

Here are some safety tips for using ladders. They're just common sense rules, but they're worth repeating.

♦ When you use a ladder, don't put it where it's going to be hit by people or equipment.

♦ Don't set up your ladder in a passageway, doorway, traffic lane, or driveway.

♦ Don't set up a metal ladder within 4 feet of a power line.

♦ Don't stand on the top rung of a ladder.

♦ Don't place scaffold planks on the top rungs of step ladders.

♦ Don't tie or lash two or more ladders together to gain more height.

♦ Keep the ladder within reach of the work you're doing. Don't lean or stretch.

♦ Always place the ladder on a firm surface.

♦ Don't use a ladder that has broken or split rails or rungs.

If you build your ladder on the job, you must adhere to certain specifications.

1) For ladders up to 12 feet in length, the inside width of the base rung must be at least 16 inches. The minimum width is 1/4 inch less for each successive rung up the ladder.

2) The rungs must be of 1 x 3 or heavier lumber. The rails must be of 2 x 3 or heavier lumber.

3) For ladders over 12 feet and less than 20 feet in length, the bottom rung must be at least 18 inches wide, the rungs 1 x 3 or better, and the rails 2 x 4 or better.

4) Between 20 and 26 feet, the base rung must be a least 19 inches wide, the rungs of 1 x 4 minimum, and the rails 2 x 6 minimum.

5) Don't use double-headed nails on ladders. Use at least 8 penny nails. Safety specs require that rungs be nailed to the rail with three nails on each side.

6) You can support rungs one of two ways. Either cut a maximum 1/2-inch-deep slot into a 2 x 4 rail for each rung. Or use blocking or straps to support the rungs.

Extension Ladders

Extension ladders can't exceed 44 feet in height, including the lap section. Two-section ladders of up to 33 feet must have a minimum 3-foot lap. Two-section ladders of 33 to 44 feet must have a minimum 4-foot lap. Three-section ladders must have a 4-foot lap at each lap.

Scaffolds

Where a ladder isn't safe, you can use a scaffold. Scaffolds shouldn't be made of piles of rock, block, brick, lumber, or other building material. They should be platforms designed for safe working.

Scaffold platforms must be a minimum of 14 inches wide. If the platform is made of lumber, the lumber has to be structural grade. Use dressed 2 x 10 or 2 x 12's nailed or cleated together. (*Dressed* means milled lumber, not rough cut.) The platform can't be wider than 36 inches. Maximum spans are easy to remember: 2 x 10 is 10 feet, 2 x 12 is 12 feet.

I don't recommend you build your own scaffolds. There are few places where you can't rent code-approved scaffold sections when you need them. You can get them for as little as $25 per week.

If a wood pole scaffold is over 60 feet high, it must be designed and built under the supervision of a licensed civil engineer. All scaffolds of any material that are more than 125 feet high must be designed by a licensed civil engineer.

Rope

At times, you'll use rope to pull, haul, or lift materials, or as a safety line for workers on hillsides or scaffolds. Use 5/8 inch, 4,400 pound breaking strength manila rope. If the rope is old or worn the maximum safe load is 600 pounds.

You can use sisal rope if you downgrade the breaking strength. Sisal rope has 80 percent of the strength of manila rope. Sisal is a white fiber material, primarily grown in Mexico.

Power Tools

Although it's not required, it's better to use power tools with key locks to prevent unauthorized use. Always disconnect the power before you change blades or other moving parts. By disconnect, I mean *pull the plug*! You don't want any surprises when you start to pull the old blade out.

OSHA has a number of rules for power tools. Here are some highlights.

Airless Sprayers

Chances are you'll be painting a fence or two during your career as a fence contractor. The fastest way to do this is with an airless spray rig. An airless can pump a lot of paint very fast since it uses pressures in excess of 200 PSI (pounds per square inch). This makes it a dangerous tool. OSHA requires an automatic or visible manual safety on the gun to prevent accidental discharge of the paint. A tip guard is required to keep the tip from coming in contact with the operator.

Beware. Pressures are high enough that it's dangerous even if you don't touch the tip. *Never* try to check spray pressure by putting your hand in front of the tip and spraying; you'll inject paint into your skin. If you have a gun that doesn't have a safety, install a diffuser nut. This prevents high pressure discharge during tip replacement.

For more information on airless painting, order a copy of *Painter's Handbook*. It has a good section on airless spraying. There's an order form in the back of this manual.

Air Compressors

You'll use many air-powered tools. Drills, nailers, troweling machines, saws, and painting outfits are all available air powered. If you use air-powered equipment, you'll need an air compressor. Your compressor should be portable, and powered by a gas motor.

Manufacturers of compressors and compressed fluid tanks design to meet OSHA and other codes. Be sure your equipment has safety blow-off valves and drain valves. OSHA recommends that you drain the compressed air tank of liquid once a day, and pop the safety valve at least once each week. If there's a belt or fan, it should be covered so that no one can touch it while it's running. Block the unit, or lock its wheels to prevent it from rolling during operation.

Nailers

Most fence contractors prefer nailers over hammers. A nailer can make your work go faster with less effort. You can get electric- or pneumatic-powered drivers for nails or staples. But don't use nailers within 10 feet of other people. Disconnect the unit when you're not using it.

Table Saws

If you use a table saw, be sure it has a hood or guard that covers the blade's teeth at all cutting depths. This guard should adjust itself automatically to the thickness of the material being cut. You can use a manually-adjusted guard if you adjust it to within 1/2 inch of the material you're cutting. The blade must also be covered on the underside of the table platform.

If you use the saw for rip cuts, install an anti-kickback device. This prevents the blade from throwing or kicking the material out of the saw.

Use a push stick to feed material into the saw if pushing by hand is dangerous to the operator. It keeps the operator's hand clear of the blade area.

Everyone who operates power tools should be trained and qualified to use them. In my company, I issue operator's cards when an operator has been qualified to operate the tool.

Portable Circular Saws

The portable circular saw should have a blade guard that automatically adjusts to the thickness of the material you're cutting. Be sure a shield is in place that permanently seals the upper part of the blade from possible contact.

Radial Saws

These must have a guard that covers the arbors and upper half of the blade. The blade must be designed so that it can't be pulled past the front edge of the table. Use an anti-kickback device during rip cut operations.

Sealing Materials

There will be times when you'll have to use hot tar and pitch for sealing foundations, waterproofing pilings, preventing dry rot in posts, and waterproofing the backsides of retaining walls. You may want to subcontract this work. If you don't, you'll need to know the rules for handling heated kettles, tankers, and carry buckets.

1) Keep a class B:C fire extinguisher near each heated kettle. The larger the kettle, the larger the extinguisher should be. Up to 150 gallons, use an 8-pound extinguisher. Over 150 to 350 gallons, use a 16-pound extinguisher. Have a 20-pound extinguisher for anything larger.

2) Buckets used to carry the hot tar have to be at least 24 gauge steel. The maximum size is six gallons.

3) You can't fill carry buckets any closer than 4 inches from the top. Anything else used for carrying hot tar or pitch can't be filled more than 75 percent full.

4) Don't take filled carry buckets up ladders.

5) Heated kettles or tankers shouldn't be filled closer than 5 inches from the top surface when moved over a public street.

6) When the kettle is in use, someone has to be within 100 feet at all times.

7) The LPG (liquefied petroleum gas) used for heating must be kept far enough away from the flame and heat to prevent a temperature rise of more than 10 degrees Fahrenheit to the cylinder. You measure the temperature rise over a one-hour period with the burner at full blast.

Compressed Gas Storage

Gas cylinders that hold LPG, oxygen or acetylene are pressurized to several thousand PSI. If you drop one and the valve breaks, the cylinder will take off like a rocket. I've seen a cylinder go through three walls before it stopped. When you transport gas cylinders, take off the gauges and install safety caps tightly.

If you use gas cylinders regularly, build a cylinder rack on your truck. Lock cylinders securely in the rack before transporting them. Never use a rope or chain sling for lifting a gas cylinder. Use nets, boxes, or hoists designed for cylinders.

Don't store gas cylinders where they can contact electricity or electrical circuits. Keep oxygen separate from flammable gases. The distance from oxygen to a flammable gas in storage should be at least 20 feet. If this isn't possible, having a one-half hour, 5-foot high wall between the materials will usually meet code.

Oxygen tanks are usually painted green or orange. Acetylene and other flammables are usually red. The hoses should also correspond to this color coding. You can't connect hoses with fittings that will allow them to be pulled straight out. The fastener should be a twist-off type you loosen with a wrench. The valves used to dispense the gases should be designed and marked for the type of gas being used.

Welding Equipment

Rules for arc welding equipment are simple:

1) Keep cables in good repair and use holders designed for the welder and rod being used.

2) Cables may not contain any splices closer than 10 feet to the electrode holders on arc welding equipment.

3) Keep a 6:BC fire extinguisher in the work area and remove any items that may catch fire.

4) Use eye protection screens between the welders and other personnel. This prevents eye damage from ultraviolet rays to those who aren't wearing a welder's mask.

Now you know about OSHA rules, and many of the things that might be covered on a contractor's license exam. In the rest of this chapter, we'll discuss basic common sense safety tips. You may not read anything here you don't already know. But reviewing the basics may prevent an accident.

Risks, Hazards, and Accident Prevention

Work Shoes

Sneakers (athletic shoes) are fun to wear. They're comfortable, lightweight, washable, and cheap. They're also dangerous for anyone who's building anything. There's no protection against anything dropped on your foot. If you step on a nail, it will penetrate right to the bone. If you kick something, you'll feel it, and maybe get a broken toe. Wear good-quality boots or shoes made of heavy leather with steel inserts in the toes. They cost about $85, but they can save you hundreds in doctor bills and lost work.

Shirts and Pants

A tee shirt and a pair of shorts are great for lounging around the house. But they have no place on a fence job. Wear full-length heavy canvas or denim pants to prevent scratches, scrapes, sunburn, and bug bites. A long-sleeved flannel shirt or canvas jacket will do the same for your upper body.

Beware of ticks. They carry diseases, some of them very dangerous to humans. If you're working in areas where ticks are a problem, put rubber bands around your sleeves and pants cuffs to help prevent the ticks from reaching bare skin. Use insect repellent, and check for bites at the end of the day.

Safety Helmet

A safety helmet is a blessing when something falls on your head. I know it's hot, gets in the way, and 99 percent of the time you don't need it. But that 1 percent can kill or cripple you for life. If you're thinking of working on government contracts, then you better get used to wearing a safety helmet. It's almost always required.

Safety Glasses

As a fence contractor, you'll be swinging a pick, hammering nails, and doing a dozen other things hazardous to your eyes. Your eyes are your window to the world. Wear safety glasses or goggles when you do any work that can send things flying.

Safety Belt

When you're working on a steep hillside, use a rope or safety belt. Falls are the most common accidents on a construction site. They often end with broken bones.

Ear Protection

The power tools you'll use on the job generate intense noise. If you listen to that noise day in and day out, you'll eventually suffer hearing loss. Loud sounds over long periods of time can also result in brain damage and loss of balance. Some OSHA regulations require ear protection if noise levels exceed 90 decibels.

Open Fields — Farms and Ranches

When you're working in open fields, especially in the Northeast, wear bright orange clothing. Hunting season for groundhogs is all summer long. *You* may not think you look like a groundhog, but eager hunters don't always look that carefully.

Vehicle Traffic

Working adjacent to busy highways can be dangerous. *Never* assume that that oncoming car or truck knows you're there. Wear a bright orange or yellow vest and hat when you're working near roads and highways. Post signs warning that a work crew is present. Instruct your crew members to stay off the highway and shoulder whenever possible.

Slips, Falls and Broken Bones

As I said, falls are the most common cause of injury on a construction site. Wear shoes that give you a firm grip and plenty of support. Wet surfaces are especially dangerous.

Fire

Whether you're working in town, or in a rural area, always be careful that you don't start a fire.

♦ If you're a smoker, *field strip* your cigarettes when you put them out. That means tear the burning section off the filter or nonburning section.

♦ If you're welding, be sure there's at least a 5-foot clear space around your work area.

♦ When you use motor-driven machinery, be sure it has an approved spark arrester. Keep mufflers away from dry grasses or bushes.

You may have never seen or been in a brush or forest fire. I have, and I know they travel fast and destroy everything in their path. Don't *you* be responsible for starting one. Always carry a fire extinguisher with you. Many localities have passed laws making anyone who starts a fire, by accident or not, responsible for all costs involved. It can cost hundreds of thousands of dollars to bring a fire under control. Your company can't afford that.

Shock

If someone is injured on the job, they may go into shock. Get the injured person to lay down with their feet elevated higher than their head. Cover them to keep them warm. Within a few minutes their head will clear, the facial sweat will start to go away, and the blood pressure will return to normal. If you suspect injury to the back or spine, *don't* move them. Bring medical help to the injured person.

Stretching Wire

When you string wire mesh or barbed wire, you use a stretcher to tension the wire properly. The stretcher is a ratchet-type tool which exerts great pulling power on the wire. *Don't* overtension the wire. It can break. When it does, it recoils with great force.

Most wire fencing manufactured today has *tension loops*. These are "U" or "S" shaped bends along the wire. Pull these only to about one-half

their full extension. Don't pull them completely straight. *Never* use a tractor or other vehicle in place of the ratchet stretcher. It's too easy to overtension and break the wire.

Chemically-Treated Lumber

The primary chemical used to treat lumber for resistance to decay, dry rot, termites and other insects is chromated copper arsenate (CCA). Casual contact with the treated lumber poses no health problem. Continual contact may. Wear gloves when you work with treated lumber. Here are some other safety tips on treated lumber:

1) Don't use scraps for firewood. The smoke will release the chemicals into the air and coat everything it touches. Arsenate (arsenic) can be absorbed into your body through your skin and even reach lethal concentrations.

2) Don't use wood shavings or sawdust for animal litter or bedding. Don't use treated lumber for dog houses, pet runs, beehives, or other animal containment where there's a chance of the lumber being chewed on.

3) Don't use treated lumber where it will come into contact with human or animal food, or potable water.

4) Wash thoroughly after working with treated lumber, especially before you eat or smoke. Wash work clothes separately from other clothing.

5) Wear a dust mask when you cut treated lumber so you don't breath the sawdust.

6) Dispose of treated lumber in approved trash disposal areas. Your local sanitation department will have some recommendations.

Now that you know how to take care of yourself in the field, let's get back to the office. In the next chapter, I'll tell you about estimating.

sixteen

Estimating

*E*stimating is hard to master. How long will this job take? What materials do I need, and how much do they cost? What problems will I run into?

This chapter will send you on your way to becoming a skillful estimator. You'll learn to foresee all the alternatives you have to consider when you plan and price a job. Every job you do will be different from all the rest, but I'll show you how to approach each one, and tell you what to watch out for. These are guidelines that I and thousands of other contractors have learned the hard way — with our pocketbooks.

The Rules of Good Estimating

1) Understand your product. If you've read this book from the beginning, you already have a good start.

2) Know how much money you need to earn, and what it will take to make it. Chapters 12 through 14 should help you there.

3) Plan each job carefully and thoroughly, right down to the last nut and bolt. Don't take shortcuts when you lay out a job.

4) Know what things cost *now*. Keep your cost records and price lists up to date.

5) Account for all your time.

6) Don't overlook the indirect costs of doing business. Every job must cover licenses, insurance, your buildings and equipment, credit costs and taxes.

7) Remember, you're in business to make a profit and earn a good living.

Follow these rules, and estimating won't be a problem for you. The last rule is the most important one, so let's start with that.

Know Why You're in Business

Most rich people didn't get that way by accident. Even the ones who inherit their wealth won't keep it long if they don't plan carefully, and use their resources wisely. That's what construction estimating is all about. You have to plan every job so you make the most efficient use of your time, your materials, and your employees. You have to know which materials are best for the job, and where to get them at the lowest price. If you run your business so you just barely squeak by, you won't be inspired to do your best, and your customers will recognize that.

Base everything you do on the idea that yours is a classy and profitable operation, and it will be.

Know Your Product and Its Value

Do your homework. Find out what your competition charges for the same kind of work you do. If you don't, one of two things will happen. You'll underprice your work so you don't make enough profit. Or your estimates will be too high, and you won't get the jobs.

If you're getting one out of every three jobs you bid on, your prices are probably competitive. Less than one in three, and your prices may be out of line. If you get every job you go for, it's almost certain you're not charging enough, unless you've found a magic way to squeeze more profit out of your jobs than any of your competitors.

Do some research and keep up with the latest design trends, materials and equipment. Send for catalogs. Read building trade magazines. Use your library, and look for books on design and construction information at your builder's supply stores.

Here are some sources for publications about wood fences you can send for:

Outdoor Wood
The Koppers Company
436 Seventh Avenue
Pittsburgh, PA 15219

Western Wood Products Association
Yeon Building
Portland, OR 97204

For chain link fences, brick and block walls, contact:

American Society for Testing and Materials
(ASTM)
1916 Race Street
Philadelphia, PA 19103

How Much Do You Need to Earn?

If you haven't already done it, go back to Chapter 13 and do the budget projections for yourself and your business. Make sure they're realistic, and don't leave anything out. Those projections will tell you how much to mark up your prices so that you make a profit and earn a good living.

Cover costs to run your office, pay the utilities, telephone, insurance, and taxes. You also have to figure the cost of expendable tools, and incidental materials that are consumed during construction. It's easy to overlook things like saw blades, drill bits, screw anchors, and the small tools that get lost or broken, like screw drivers and tape measures. They don't cost a lot individually, but they can add up to a bundle over time.

Plan Your Jobs Carefully

Refer back to Chapter 2 for details about how to lay out your project. Mentally go through the steps you'll take to complete the job, and be sure you've accounted for every item of material and every operation you'll need to do. Don't forget rental costs for any special equipment you may need such as a backhoe, airless sprayer, or post hole digger. And don't forget to include sales tax if you have to pay it on materials or rentals, or if you're required to collect it from your customer.

To provide some guide to the readers of this book, I investigated the average purchase and daily rental costs for equipment you're likely to need to build fences and retaining walls. I surveyed prices in New York and Los Angeles. Figure 16-1 shows my findings, averaged out. Of course, rentals in your area won't be exactly the same, but these figures will give you a ball-park estimate. And if you rent by the week, you'll usually pay much less.

Equipment Cost and Rental Charges

Item	Cost	Daily rental		Item	Cost	Daily rental		Item	Cost	Daily rental
Airless, electric	2,850	48		Drill bit, masonry	8	4		Saw blades	11	5
Airless, gas	3,200	55		Drill bit, wood	3	1		Scaffold, 4 x 10 x 5	750	13
Aluminum brake, 10'	1,200	25		Fork lift, 2 ton	10,800	90		Stapler, elect.	260	7
Auger, gas, 8"	1,700	42		Form, concrete, 8'	240	24		Stapler, pneumatic	260	7
Backhoe, only	10,750	175		Grader	89,500	895		Stretcher, barb	150	7
with operator		375		Hand tool, asst.	600	10		Stretcher, chain	180	8
Bender, rebar	450	11		Hot tar pot, 25 gallon	1,200	25		Stud gun	380	18
Bin, trash	650	12		Ladder, 6'	85	3		Table saw	625	15
Brush chipper	5,700	95		Ladder, 8'	120	3		Tamper, gas	880	38
Brush hog	5,400	90		Ladder, 10'	140	4		Transit	640	22
Bull float	85	7		Ladder, 20'	185	5		Trailer, 3 ton	2,200	50
Bulldozer	47,500	475		Level, 2'	25	1		Trencher, 2' x 6"	9,650	120
Cable puller	330	15		Level, 6'	55	2		Trowels, masonry	425	10
Cement mixer, elect.	425	19		Log splitter	2,650	45		Truck, 1 ton	17,500	95
Cement mixer, gas	685	34		Masonry saw	2,450	40		Truck, 1.5 ton	22,500	125
Chain hoist, 3 ton	310	15		Metal detector	425	19		Truck, 2 ton	28,500	145
Chain saw, 20"	420	38		Mortar mixer	680	38		Vibrator, concrete	575	30
Circular saw	135	8		Mortar pan	45	3		Welder, 220v, 200A	1,450	25
Compressor, 6 cfm	425	26		Mortar tub	85	7		Welder, gas, 140A	2,480	40
Compressor, gas	625	34		Mower, tractor	16,500	175		Welder, gas, 200A	2,850	46
Compressor, diesel	3,800	100		Nailer, elect.	360	20		Welder, A/O gas	550	12
Concrete buggy	465	11		Nailer, pneumatic	360	20		gas and rod	150	8
Concrete chute, 10'	485	12		Pile driver, gas	18,750	325		Wheelbarrow	85	7
Concrete vibrator	575	30		Pipe vise, 2" elect.	900	35				
Cutter, rebar	240	8		Post hole digger	1,700	42		Average rental costs, N.Y. and L.A.		
Drill, 1/2"	185	9		Pumper, concrete	2,250	50		Costs will vary depending on location		
Drill, 6" diamond	3,400	60		Radial arm saw	625	15		and specifications.		

Figure 16-1
Equipment costs for purchase and rental

Even if you own your equipment, consider using rental charges in your bids. After all, you paid good money for the equipment, and you'll have to replace it when it wears out. If you charge rental rates for equipment, you can build a replacement fund for the time when you need it.

Scheduling

An important part of estimating is scheduling, because once you land the contract, you have to work it into your existing workload. And you have to be flexible enough to make use of spare hours that become available. If your transit-mix cement truck is going to be three hours late, and you know about it, you could spend the time on another nearby job.

Even if the truck arrives on time, you'll still have to wait several days for the concrete to cure before you can get on with the job. You need to have another project in the works during that time. This is where precise scheduling means the difference between break-even and profit.

Use a form like the milestone chart in Figure 16-2 to plan your jobs. This is your master schedule for each job. It's a quick reference calendar that shows when each step of the job must take place. You only include weekends and holidays as part of the project if they fall during waiting periods, such as curing time. Later in this chapter, in Figure 16-15, you can see how I've used this form.

Inspections can throw a monkey-wrench into your plans. They can delay you anywhere from a few hours to several days. Be sure to allow for them in your schedules.

Inspections generally occur after these events:

1) Excavation

2) Installation of the foundation rebar

3) Pouring of the footings or foundation

4) Completion of a wall or fence

5) Backfilling

Additional inspections may be required if you install electrical wiring, fixtures or plumbing. Each inspection will probably require at least an hour of your time, and inspectors rarely show up exactly when you expect them. There can be a delay of several days before you can proceed with your work.

Then there's always that rotten day when something doesn't pass inspection, and you have to rework it or do it over.

Always call the building inspector's office two or three days in advance to schedule inspections. And then be sure you have the work done on time.

Know What Things Cost

I'm not going to give you a price list for all the materials you might expect to use in your fence contracting business. There are a couple reasons for that. First, by the time you read this, prices printed here could be several years old. (Where I *have* shown examples, they reflect 1988 prices.)

Second, prices vary greatly from place to place. For instance, lumber is generally five to 20 percent cheaper in the New York area than it is in Los Angeles, while equipment rentals are 25 percent less in L.A. than on the east coast. The only prices that would be of any value to you are the ones in your location. You have to get those yourself. Talk to your local suppliers, get their current prices, find out about their credit and delivery terms.

Use a variation of the spreadsheet back in Chapter 12, Figure 12-3, to compare prices from different suppliers. List the items you're pricing in the left column and the suppliers across the top row. Then you can see at a glance where you'll get the best deal for any given item.

Update your price list continually to adjust for inflation, fluctuations in supply and demand, and manufacturers' or suppliers' price changes. Keep a file of new products and their prices. Pick up information from suppliers, decorating centers, lumberyards and home improvement magazines. I fill out the reader's service cards in the magazines and send for anything that will help me do a better job or save money. If you have a business license, you can request suggested retail price lists from the manufacturers.

Whenever I buy materials for jobs, I update my price logs. On items I use often, I keep running listings so I can anticipate price increases. For example: If an 8-foot S4S Douglas fir 2 x 4 costs $.90 in January, $.95 in March, $1.00 in June, I can expect it to cost about $1.05 in September, if there

Job or bid number	Estimate date							Customer									
Prepared by	Reviewed by							Address									
Calendar date																	

Daily Milestone Planning Chart

OPERATION	1	2	3	4	5	6	7	8	9	10	11	12	13	14	15	16	17	18

Figure 16-2
Chart your jobs

haven't been drastic changes in general economic trends.

Materials

Once you've finished your take-off sheet for materials and added the prices, add 5 percent to cover waste, damaged goods, defective goods, and mistakes. You could also include a place on your take-off form to list charges for special orders and deliveries.

Try to use materials that are commonly available in your area. You won't have to wait for delivery, and they'll be cheaper. If everyone in town is using cypress instead of redwood, concrete block instead of brick, chain link instead of wrought iron, there's probably a good reason.

Practically all areas in the U.S. have some frost. The code requires you to dig your post holes and footings at least 12 inches below the published frost level in your area. In southern California the frost level is about 3 inches in most areas, so your excavation has to be at least 15 inches deep. Suppliers of fence posts stock 8-foot posts. That allows for fence heights up to 6 feet 9 inches.

But what if you contract for a job in the mountains where the frost level is 36 inches? Now you have to sink your 8-foot post 4 feet into the ground — which only leaves you 4 feet above ground. If you want to build a 6-foot fence, you'll need to order 10-foot posts. That might require a special order, at a premium price. It will also cost you more for excavation. And it increases the chance that you'll hit some kind of underground obstacle, like a water, gas, sewer or underground phone line, or maybe water. I mention all this just so you'll be aware that you have to think about all possible consequences when you prepare your estimates.

You won't usually have problems with the quality of metal, brick or block. But lumber is something else again. You have to know what you're buying. Expect the cost of lumber to double for each increase in grade.

You'll be tempted by flyers in the mail advertising, "Special, 4 x 4 redwood posts 8 feet long, only $3.95." Watch out. They're probably not worth a dime when it comes to straightness, smoothness, and structural strength. Use that stuff if you want, but I'll bet you get complaints from your customers.

A word about variations in quality. On the west coast, even #1 structural lumber isn't always that great looking. East coast lumber of the same grade is generally of better quality and appearance. Also, if you want to use KD lumber, expect to pay the price. It runs about four times the cost of S-GRN, if you can get it at all. Inexpensive redwood 2 x 4s may be cut from the white wood or outer portions of the redwood tree. Don't use this lumber where it will contact the ground. Pay the extra price for heartwood to get the full benefits of redwood.

Visit your local lumberyard, or several lumberyards, and ask for a quote on about $2,000 worth of lumber. Ask for prices on a variety of items you expect to use. Most yards aren't anxious to prepare a list of prices for you unless they think you're going to buy from them, so make your request look like a real job. Use this list to start your own price book.

Will you cut materials on site, or order them cut by the mill or supplier? Most yards will cut your materials to size for a nominal fee if you give them enough time. The cost is usually from $.50 to $1.00 per cut, or free if you're a good repeat customer. That per-cut cost may sound like a lot, but consider this: Do you have saws that can cut a 4 x 4 in one cut? Most circular saws can't. You have to make at least two cuts and you rarely get a straight edge. At $35.00 an hour, a minute of your time is worth $.58. So why fool with poorly cut, poor fitting lumber? Let the yard cut it.

Stone suppliers will cut stone to order. Some will even number the pieces and give you a layout drawing showing which piece goes where. Some suppliers of stone veneer will score the edges so you can use metal hangers. Yes, this all costs extra, but the time and sweat you save in the field might be worth it. In any case, don't forget to include special cutting or handling charges in your estimate.

Hardware

When you build fences or walls, you'll need various kinds of hardware — hinges, latches, lock sets, closers, screws, bolts, nails, and so on. If you're just starting out in your business, then I suggest you buy just what you need for each job. Cash is short at this stage of the game.

As you get established, you'll find yourself with a collection of hardware left over from earlier jobs when you had to buy more than you needed. Try keeping them in plastic bags that zip shut, and put a note in the bag telling what it is and what you paid for it. If you have a computer you can even keep an up-to-date list of all these odds and ends. Sooner or later you'll find a use for them.

At the same time you may find that you're using some items more than others. Consider buying these in bulk. For example, if you do a lot of redwood fence work, you'll be using a lot of aluminum nails, aluminum decking screws and brass screws. They're expensive, about two to four times as much as the same things in steel. Let's say you plan to buy a box of 100 aluminum decking screws for $8.95. When you check with the supplier, you find you can get boxes of 500 for $35.80, or $7.16 per hundred. That's a nice $1.79 per hundred in your pocket. The larger the package, the less it should cost you. But don't go overboard. If you don't expect to use those 500 decking screws within a month or two, don't buy in bulk. Your money can be earning 8 to 10 percent elsewhere.

Here's a little trick. If you buy 25 pounds of nails in bulk, you may get the bulk price less 15 percent. Now say you have a job that requires $3,000 in materials, including 25 pounds of nails. If you expect to need them soon, order an extra 25 pounds of nails. On an order this large, you should be able to get a discount of up to 22 percent. So you can save 7 percent on those extra nails you'll need soon anyway.

But first, consider the cost of storage and possible losses when buying in bulk. Do you have a place to store them? Leave 25 pounds of steel nails sitting out in the rain and you'll have 25 pounds of rust. Do you have employees? Leave a box of 3-inch brass hinges sitting around and you may find you're short a few. It's a shame, but companies lose countless millions to "honest" employees who feel that pilferage is justified as part of their compensation for working.

Markup on hardware is about 32 to 44 percent at the local lumberyard. If you're a good customer, you should already be getting 10 to 15 percent discount. If you're not, arm yourself with past purchase receipts so you can show the manager what a good customer you really are. Ask for the discount you deserve. After all, they're not about to voluntarily give you part of their profits.

Ask about minimum price break schedules. Ask about purchasing in bulk. Ask about substitute items that may be as good or better, but less expensive than what you're currently buying. Find out about terms. Paying in 30 days instead of today gives you 30 days to earn interest on that money. That's like getting an extra discount.

Foundations and Mortar

Here again, if you can use it and if you have the storage space, buy in bulk. Bagged concrete weighs 94 pounds a bag. If you have a half-ton pickup truck, you can only carry eleven bags at a time. Most contractors have concrete delivered, at a charge ranging from $10 to $35. Most yards can deliver 54 bags at a time — so why pay for four extra deliveries if you don't have to?

I assume that you're using bagged concrete a little at a time. If you're pouring a 5-yard foundation, it doesn't make sense to mix your own. At about $1.65 per bag of concrete, it will take 202 bags ($332) plus some 40 hours of mixing and pouring time. You can buy the same 5 yards as ready-mix for about $275 and pour it in less than an hour. Here's my rule of thumb: For setting fence posts, use bagged concrete. For foundations or concrete retaining walls, use ready-mix.

Throughout this book I've shown several foundations that were poured into forms. Formed foundations look better and use less concrete, but you might consider just pouring into a open trench. That saves labor since you don't have to make forms. It saves material since you don't need form lumber. You can reuse form lumber many times as forms, but I wouldn't try to use it for anything else. The release oils and concrete prevent paint from sticking to the wood.

You'll have to use forms if you're pouring walls or a trench that's two or more times wider than the needed foundation. For most foundation work, however, I just pour concrete into the trench, filling it wall to wall. It may take up to 50 percent more concrete, but I eliminate several hours of extra labor.

Finishing

Paint and stain present some variables that complicate estimating. Prices may vary from store to store for the same product made by the same manufacturer. Suppose the hardware store sells ABC brand stain for $12.95 a gallon, and the lumberyard has it for $16.98. That's a 31 percent difference in price. But you're already at the lumberyard getting the rest of your materials. Is it worth a trip to the hardware store?

If you only need one gallon, just pick it up at the lumberyard and save a trip. It'll cost you more than the $4.03 you'll save to go to the other store. If you're buying two or more gallons, the drive to the hardware store and wait in line will probably be worth your time. Go to the hardware store.

Labor Charges

When you estimate labor charges, you'll have variables also. Can you use a nail gun or stapler to build your fence? Or will you nail it together by hand? Will you have to use screws or bolts for certain procedures? If so, can you drive screws directly, or will you have to drill pilot holes? It takes twice as long to nail than to staple, and four to six times longer to install bolts and screws.

There are also variations in coating time. An eight-hour brush job will take four hours with a roller and one hour with a sprayer. Be sure your estimate reflects the time it will take for the operation you'll have to do.

You can set your own labor rate according to the projections you made at the beginning of the chapter, but what about the people you'll hire? I'll try to give you some guidelines on what to pay employees and subcontractors.

◆ Hang out where the contractors in your area gather to talk. Pick up as much as you can about local rates and hiring practices.

◆ Read your local newspaper want ads. Many of the employment ads list salaries. If they don't, call the advertisers and ask what they're paying.

◆ Supervisors earn 20 to 25 percent more than the most experienced person they supervise. So if you expect to earn $20.00 per hour, your supervisor should get $16.00, his most experienced worker $12.80, and his helper $10.24 an hour.

◆ Check with your local department of employment. They generally have lists of local wage rates. The U.S. Government also publishes wage rate tables for most jobs.

◆ Use common sense. If it takes $8.00 an hour in your area for someone to live, then pay $8.00 per hour. Sure, you can find desperate people who'll work for less, but if they can't live on the $4.95 you're paying them, how long will

they stay after you've spent time and money training them? Will they steal from you to supplement that pay? And will they be loyal to you and really do a full day's work? I doubt it.

◆ Hiring on a piecework basis may be your best bet. You hire people to do certain repetitive operations for a set price per operation or piece, like $.10 per brick laid in place. The key to success here is to specify up front just what you expect. How many per hour, what type of mortar, who mixes mortar, who carries bricks, what kind of rake joint, who rakes the joint, starting times, ending times, breaks, days off, who handles problems, who supplies materials, who cleans up, and what quality do you demand?

In the manhour tables at the end of this chapter, the chart on brick laying allows one hour to lay 174 bricks. If you charge one hour at $35.00 in your estimate and your bricklayer takes three hours at $18.00 per hour, it costs you $54.00. You lose $19.00 instead of making $17.00. But if you figure 174 bricks at $.10, or $17.40, and charge your customer $35.00, you make $17.60 on the labor.

Always try for the lowest rate for the most experienced worker you can find. That's just good business sense. But be fair. Put yourself in their shoes. Would you do the job for the wage you're offering? Would you like to work for you? Could you live on what you're paying?

Figure 16-3 is a list of trades you may need to hire, and typical wage rates. But don't try to use my figures in an estimate. Use the actual wage rates you'll pay for that particular job.

Subcontractors

You know *your* overhead and salary requirements. Assume that your subcontractors have similar costs. If you would charge your customer $35.00 per hour for a job, then expect your subcontractor to charge you $35.00 per hour for the same job. You add 18 to 22 percent to their charges to cover your time and profit.

Start out by asking the subs what they charge. Then negotiate. Find out what's the least they'll do the job for. Ask if they have lower long-term rates

Trade	Hourly pay range	Median
Carpenter	$8 - 16	12
Design/Engineer	10 - 24	18
Drafter	6 - 18	14
Equipment operator	8 - 20	16
Laborer	4 - 8	5
Mason	10 - 18	14
Metal worker	8 - 16	12
Welder	8 - 20	14

Labor rates vary according to workers' skill level and whether or not they are licensed. Geographical area, local economy and unemployment levels influence rates also. You may pay more or less for part time workers, or those you employ through a job shop. Supervisors' rates are at the top of each range. Add a factor for employee taxes and benefits, which can be 20 percent (or more) of wages.

Figure 16-3
Trade skills and wages

or multiple contract rates. Ask about their benefit costs, working hours, quality standards, schedules, and warrantees. Agree on penalties for non-performance, who supplies what, who is responsible for what, your payment schedule, and so on.

In the back of this book is an order card. I recommend you order a copy of *Construction Estimating Reference Data* and the *National Construction Estimator*. Both books supplement this chapter and give you lots of detailed estimating figures.

Legal, Administrative Costs

Be sure to include permit fees in your estimates. Fees in many areas have a minimum charge, plus an added $5.00 to $10.00 for each $1,000 of evaluation for the finished product. For example, if the basic fee in your town is $30.00 plus $10.00 per thousand, the fee for a $3,000 job would be $60.00.

If you're unlicensed, it's best to let your customer get the building permits. Many areas require a contractor to be licensed in order to get a permit, and may also require a performance bond which

could cost hundreds or even thousands of dollars. Homeowners doing work on their own property don't need these bonds.

Don't try to duck the permit requirements. You may unknowingly overlook some local restrictions on the kind of material or hardware you plan to use. This is especially true if you're installing electrical or plumbing fixtures on a wall or fence. If you do something that's not to code and it's discovered later, you could be in hot water.

Account for All Your Time

Build into your estimates all the time it takes for things that aren't actually part of the construction process. That includes time to design the job, prepare estimates, pull permits, order and pick up materials, and travel time to and from the job.

Designing, estimating, and selling even a small a job can each take from one to three hours. And you could stand in line for an hour or three at City Hall to get your permits, too. Include a minimum of five hours in your estimates for these functions.

Now, figure from one to eight hours to order materials and see that they get where they belong when they're needed. Counter people and warehouse workers or delivery drivers aren't very concerned about your schedule. You have to allow for the time it takes to receive the load, count it, and haul it to the job site. You should also allow some time to go after missing, damaged, or forgotten items. There's always something — no job planning or estimating system is entirely foolproof.

Figure 16-4 shows minimum and typical times for selling and planning a job. When I estimate, I like to keep track of these hours to help me budget my time. But for the final estimate I build the cost of these operations into my overhead figure and markup. You can account for these jobs separately or as an overhead item, whichever is easier for you.

Be aware there's a risk here, though. Your competition might not know it takes 18 hours to sell and plan a job, and they won't include the cost in their bid, so they might very well underbid you.

Sales Calls	Minimum time		Typical time	
	Hours	Mins	Hours	Mins
Take inquiry call	.2	12	.1	6
Travel time	.5	30	.5	30
Interview customer	.3	18	.2	12
Walk fence line, take notes	.8	48	.7	42
Travel time	- -	- -	.5	30
Draw plans	- -	- -	3.5	210
Write up estimate	1.5	90	1.5	90
Arrange sales appointment	- -	- -	.2	12
Travel time	- -	- -	.5	30
Make presentation	.5	30	.5	30
Close sale	.5	30	.5	30
Collect contract, deposit	.2	12	.2	12
Travel time	.5	30	.5	30
TOTALS	5.0	300	9.4	564

Job Planning				
Typical time includes extra trip for permits				
Review job notes	.2	12	.2	12
Review materials list	1.5	90	1.5	90
Review manhour requirements	1.2	72	1.2	72
Make up schedule	1.5	90	1.5	90
Order materials	2.5	150	2.5	150
Schedule outside help	.5	30	.5	30
Schedule inside help	.5	30	.5	30
Inform customer of start date	.1	6	.1	6
Draw formal plans	2.5	150	2.5	150
Pull permits	2.5	150	4.8	288
TOTALS	13.0	780	15.3	918

Figure 16-4
Times for sales calls and job planning

But it's better to lose a bid than to win one that will come in at a loss.

As you see, you can spend as much as 18 to 30 hours on a job before you even get started.

Expect the Unexpected

It's hard, when you first inspect a job site, to know what you might run into once the job gets going. Check for anything that might cause problems along the wall or fence line. Obstructions can be trees, brush, old walls, large rocks, streams, abandoned vehicles, or hills and valleys. Determine, and state in your contract, *who is responsible for removing or compensating for these things*. If you have to do it, allow for any special equipment you'll need. You'll need to estimate how long it will take, and how much to charge per hour.

Underground Obstructions

Underground obstructions are harder — you usually can't see them. There may be a stream, rocks, tree roots, buried construction materials (or even animals), phone lines, power lines, water or sprinkler lines, or gas lines. Figure you'll probably hit something, somewhere along the path. A metal detector can help detect most of these items, but if in doubt, call the utility companies. They can tell you where their lines are.

Tree Roots

You'll need some kind of tool to cut tree roots. You can use a branch trimmer, or nubbers, for small ones less than an inch in diameter. You can buy those at the hardware store or garden supply for about $15. You may need a chain saw for large roots. That could cost from $85 to $300, or you could rent one. For high grasses you'll need a tractor-mounted mower.

You can have the owner clear the land, or you could hire a local farmer as a subcontractor to do it. Or you can do it yourself and charge accordingly.

In areas where there's a high danger of fire, it's almost mandatory to cut fire breaks, especially along roads. Since you have to clear the land anyway, why not plow it? Use fire prevention as a selling point.

Trees

You can do one of two things with a tree. Either end the fence on one side of the tree and restart it again on the other (leave space for the tree to grow) or cut down the tree. In the first case, you'll need an extra fence post, and associated hardware.

You'll definitely need a chain saw to cut down a tree if it's any size at all. You'll also have to dispose of the tree. The owner may want to keep the larger pieces for firewood, but you'll probably have to rent a dumpster for the small stuff. That costs from $50 to $100 per week. If there aren't too many small branches, you can cut them and tie them into bundles for the local trash pickup.

Here's my rule. I cut and charge for small trees — under 4 inches in diameter. I'm just careful that I don't crash one through someone's window. I use the trunk for firewood. But I make larger trees the responsibility of the owner, and suggest they hire a professional tree removal service. Taking down a good-sized tree is no job for an amateur.

Rocks

If you have to remove large rocks, you'll probably need a bulldozer, and maybe even dynamite. That can cost from a few hundred to several thousand dollars. Also, you'll probably need to hire licensed operators.

Buried Concrete

When you expect to dig post holes near an existing slab or building, test the ground before you prepare your bid. Many times a slab or foundation footing extends several inches beyond what shows at ground level. It's really hard to dig when you hit concrete. Test for this by driving a metal rod into the ground where you plan to dig. Test at the perimeter of the planned hole or trench, not the center.

Plain Ol' Bad Days

There's a saying: "If anything can go *wqong*, it will, and at the worst possible moment."

Consider this: You had 36 bags of post hole cement delivered to a job site. The driver dropped the load on the customer's driveway, and four bags broke and spilled all over the place. Not only did you lose the cement, but you had a mess to clean up. You tested some of the cement in a small area of the job, and it was fine. Later, it turned out that some of it was mortar mix in a mislabeled bag that turned to dust the day after you poured it.

You had to spend several hours convincing the supplier to take the cement back. Then you had to attend to the pickup and replacement, and finally, test the new batch. In a case like this, you either have to eat the cost, sue the manufacturer, or allow some slack in your estimates for contingencies like this. It depends on how hungry you are.

Mother Nature

Weather delays can add considerably to a job. I'm not just talking about rain and snow. In southern California, like many other places around the country, it gets hot. A job that should take five days will sometimes take ten, because production really drops off in 105-degree heat. People just can't work as many hours each day. It's going to cost you extra travel time and expense, and also more time wasted while you set up and tear down each day.

... And Other Things

You or a crew member is sick on Friday. The bug is gone by Monday, but by then it's raining. Tuesday the water pump breaks on your truck. And Wednesday the nail gun self-destructs. And on it goes. Sometimes you'll get socked no matter how accurately you estimate a job.

New and Unusual Jobs

On a job you've never tackled before, you may be at a loss when it comes to estimating the cost. I recommend you dig through your files to see if you can find an old job that resembles the new one. For example, if the new job requires metal railings between brick pilasters, you can look up your most recent jobs for a metal railing and a brick wall. Use the two old jobs to give you some idea of the cost. Then add 20 percent for the unknown.

Until you have good job records to rely on, you can use my manhour tables at the end of this chapter. Each table includes a breakdown of the major steps required to do the job, and the total manhours the job will take.

Can You Assign Unit Costs?

The *unit price* is a set price for an entire job component, including the material, handling, value added, overhead, and in some cases, the labor cost. For example:

Fence rail, 8 foot, 2 x 4, S-DRY, S4S, DFT	
Material	$1.45
Handling	0.15
Overhead	2.46
Value added	1.50
Labor to install	7.00
Total	$12.56

For each rail you install on the fence line, you'll charge $12.56. The "value added" can be painting, notching or cutting — anything that adds value to that 2 x 4. For example, suppose you set up an assembly line at your shop where you notch and paint several dozen posts which you keep in inventory for future use. Your cost for the materials, labor, and profit for this operation is the value added to the posts.

You can establish unit prices for posts, face boards, bricks, or any other item you use to build fences or walls. It will take time to calculate the unit price for every item you use, then add in the labor and overhead. But once you have the unit costs, it's quick and easy to use them to estimate the job cost.

Even after you've figured your unit costs, you have to update them constantly to reflect changing material prices and labor rates. Only you can decide if the time and trouble is balanced by faster and more accurate estimating. If you want to give it a try, you'll have to use your own costs for materials, value added, overhead and labor. But I can help with the labor times. In the rest of this chapter you'll find manhour tables you can use as guidelines for the time each operation will take.

When You Lose a Bid

What do you do when you've made your best estimate, but you don't get the job? First, try to find out why you didn't get it. A phone call to the customer sometimes works, but don't count on it. If the customer won't tell you, try to figure out what your competition is doing. Are they using inferior materials? Cheaper labor? Are they taking shortcuts in workmanship? Or, do they have better trained workers? Better equipment? Lower overhead?

Why bother trying to find out? Because, you'll be bidding against that same company again. You should know why you lost to them last time. If the labor, materials, workmanship and overhead are comparable, maybe you made a mistake in your estimate. Track it down. Maybe you allowed too much for travel time, or could have charged 5 percent less for contingencies. Maybe you just added wrong. If there was a mistake, find the reason and adjust your estimating procedure so it doesn't happen again.

Of course, it could have been your competition who made the mistake, and they might have lost a bundle on the job. In any case, it pays to double-check your estimating system, especially if you begin to lose out on an increasing number of jobs.

Track your estimating performance — the number of jobs estimated compared to the number of jobs sold. See the section on the "quote log" in Chapter 13. You want to track the number of bids, the number that resulted in sales, the selling price of each job quoted, the type of work involved, who made the presentation, who prepared the estimate, problems you ran into if the job sold, and profit or loss on jobs you sold. Record the date you presented the bid, the dates you made any follow-up calls, who you spoke to, and what they said. Try to find out how much the job sold for even if you didn't get it.

Do you get a second chance to bid a job? Not often. But sometimes after the sale you'll have to reprice a job whether you want to or not. Of course, once the contract is signed, you're committed to do the job at the quoted price, even if the there was a mistake in the estimate that will cause you to lose money. If that happens, it sometimes works to go back to the customer with a revised estimate and a defeated look. Explain that you inadvertently omitted certain items. Resell the job, using the revised numbers. You may get a new contract — or you may get thrown out, or threatened with a lawsuit. All you can do is try.

There's one other situation when you might want to revise the original contract. That's when the customer signed the contract for a fair price, then wants you to do extra work, free. You can throw in a little extra in the name of good will and customer satisfaction. But don't let the customer take advantage of you. This is where a change order comes in. In fact, I recommend having a formal change order printed up. Figure 16-5 is the form I use. If the customer wants to change the contract, I just write out a change order and explain all the price changes.

Notice the charge for restocking the original material. Be sure to add that to the price change.

Remember that special orders may not be returnable. You must either agree to keep them yourself and refund the cost, or they become the customer's property under the terms of the original contract. In either case, you charge for the replacement on the change order. Figure 16-6 is a blank you can copy and use.

The Take-off Forms

Figures 16-7 through 16-18 show the estimating forms I use. They start with the customer contact form, then the contract requirements, estimated labor hours, and various information and specification sheets. You're welcome to use them as they are, or adapt them for your own situation. You won't need all of these for a simple job, but the more information you collect, the more accurate your estimate will be.

Figure 16-7 is the customer contact form. You fill this in during your initial contact with any potential customer. I never recommend quoting prices over the phone — instead use this first phone inquiry as an opportunity to make an appointment for a sales call.

The next four forms are general information and specification listings. You'll use the general information form (Figure 16-8) to gather information for all your jobs. It includes space for the site conditions and facilities, rental equipment you'll need, and a blank section for sketches and notes. Figure 16-9, general specifications, covers the size, construction details, gates, latches and coatings. Then you'll use Figure 16-10 or 16-11 for fence specifications and wall specifications. You could print Figures 16-8 and 16-9 back-to-back on the same sheet of paper, and do the same with Figures 16-10 and 16-11.

I use a sheet like the one in Figure 16-12 as a second page to any of the above forms, where I need more room for notes and sketches. You could have this form printed on graph paper to make scale drawings easier.

Figure 16-13, estimated labor hours, is a summary sheet for the manhours the job will take. The

Change Order

Contract number A-123	Job foreman BILL M	Customer name SMITH, J.P.
Reason for change CUSTOMER WANTS DF FACING LUMBER CHANGED TO WORMY CEDAR		Change written by JIM
		Customer signature

Price change	Materials change	Customer request	Company convenience
☑ Price change	☑ Materials change	☑ Customer request	☐ Company convenience
☐ Required by building dept.	☐ Required by engineering	☐ Required by lender	

Description of change

CANCEL ORDER FOR 1,500 1.5" X 6' DF TO
450 6" X 6' WORMY CEDAR

☐ Drawings attached	☐ Drawings required	☑ No drawings required

Effect of changes

MAY HAVE RESTOCKING / CANCEL CHARGE

Cost differential (+/-) $
1500 DF @ .75 = 1125
450 WK @ 3.50 = 1575
+ $450 + 27.00 TAX

Action required by
☑ Accounting	☑ Cost control	☑ Foreman	☑ Material control

Other action required: UPDATE RECORDS - ORDER MATERIALS

Change approved by	Approval date
☑ Customer	8-22-89
☐ Building department	
☐ Designer	
☐ Foreman	9-11-89
☑ Management	9-10-89
☑ Sales	

Material control
☐ Purchase new items	
☐ Return old items	
☐ Stock old items	
☐ Deliver old items to customer	
☐ Cancellation charge	$
10% Restocking charge	$ 112.50

Accounting
Effect on original contract
☐ Deduct	
☐ Add	589.50
☐ Refund	
☐ Bill	
New contract price	$4850.00

Figure 16-5
Change order form

Change Order

Contract number		Customer name	
Reason for change		Change written by	
		Customer signature	

☐ Price change ☐ Materials change ☐ Customer request ☐ Company convenience

☐ Required by building dept. ☐ Required by engineering ☐ Required by lender

Description of change

☐ Drawings attached ☐ Drawings required ☐ No drawings required

Effect of changes

Cost differential (+/-) $

Action required by

☐ Accounting ☐ Cost control ☐ Foreman ☐ Material control

Other action required:

Change approved by Approval date

☐ Customer

☐ Building department

☐ Designer

☐ Foreman

☐ Management

☐ Sales

Material control

☐ Purchase new items

☐ Return old items

☐ Stock old items

☐ Deliver old items to customer

☐ Cancellation charge $

☐ Restocking charge $

Accounting

Effect on original contract

☐ Deduct

☐ Add

☐ Refund

☐ Bill

New contract price $

Figure 16-6
Sample change order

Customer Contact

Call taken by	Date of call
Customer name	Customer number
Street address	
City	Zip
Home phone	Hours
Office phone	Hours

Wants
- [ ] Information
- [ ] Quote
- [ ] Meeting
- [ ] Complaint

- [ ] Maintenance contract
- [ ] To talk to _____
- [ ] To visit office
- [ ] Lunch date

Action required
- [ ] Sales call
- [ ] Manager call

- [ ] Schedule visit
- [ ] Mail catalog

Appointment date   Time _____ AM ___ PM ___
- [ ] Phone to confirm   Phone number _____
Meeting place

_____

- [ ] Meeting completed   - [ ] Postponed   - [ ] Canceled

Results of meeting
- [ ] Sale made   - [ ] No sale   - [ ] New meeting scheduled
- [ ] Follow up dates
- [ ] Contact logged   - [ ] Contract number _____

Figure 16-7
Record your customer inquiries

column headed "From Figure #" refers to my manhour tables at the end of the chapter. Just delete it if you use your own labor figures. If you're relying on my manhour tables, enter the figure number of the table you're using. For "Time each" enter the estimated time for each unit in the previous column. The "Extended time" column is the product of the previous two columns.

In Figure 16-14, I've filled out the labor estimate form for a typical job to show you how it works. The milestone planning chart for that job is Figure 16-15.

If you use the manhour tables, I recommend that you make copies and keep them with the estimate. Arrange them in the order the work will be done, and you have a step-by-step description of how to do the job. If there are any steps on the tables you don't need for your particular job, just delete them from the totals. And add any steps that aren't listed.

Use Figure 16-16 for your materials list. Finally, summarize all of your job costs on an estimate summary like the one I've filled out for you in Figure 16-17. This is where you bring together your costs for material, labor, equipment, subcontractors, miscellaneous charges, overhead and profit, and calculate the final bid price. There's a blank copy of this form at the end of the chapter, in Figure 16-36.

General Information

Contract number	Job foreman	Customer

Site terrain
- [ ] Level
- [ ] One slope
- [ ] Varied slopes
- [ ] Hilly
- [ ] Mountainous
- [ ] Swampy
- [ ] Under water
- [ ]

Ground cover
- [ ] Clear, some grass
- [ ] Tall grasses
- [ ] Brush
- [ ] Small trees
- [ ] Large trees
- [ ] Small rocks
- [ ] Large rocks
- [ ] Mixture

Soil type
- [ ] Clay
- [ ] Dirt
- [ ] Gravel
- [ ] Loam
- [ ] Rocky
- [ ] Rock
- [ ] Mixed
- [ ]

Excavation
- [ ] By hand
- [ ] Two-man auger
- [ ] Truck auger
- [ ] Backhoe
- [ ] Dozer
- [ ] Soil test required
- [ ] Sub out job
- [ ]

Clearing by
- [ ] Hand
- [ ] Power mower
- [ ] Chain saw
- [ ] Backhoe
- [ ] Dozer
- [ ] Dredge
- [ ] Owner
- [ ] Sub out

Rental equipment required:
- [ ] Yes
- [ ] No
- See listing

Obstructions
- [ ] Hill
- [ ] Tree
- [ ] Boulder
- [ ] Stream
- [ ] Building

Underground obstruction
- [ ] Concrete
- [ ] Electric line
- [ ] Gas line
- [ ] Phone line
- [ ] Rocks
- [ ] Wood & roots
- [ ] Detected, unknown

Removal required
- [ ] Fence
- [ ] Concrete wall
- [ ] Stone wall
- [ ] Block/brick wall
- [ ] All ground cover
- [ ] Trash
- [ ] Sub out job

Site drainage
- [ ] Very good
- [ ] Fair to good
- [ ] Fair
- [ ] Poor
- [ ] Very poor

Notes

Site type
- [ ] Residential
- [ ] Commercial
- [ ] Industrial
- [ ] Local government
- [ ] Federal government
- [ ] Association

Site facilities
- [ ] Electric
- [ ] Toilet
- [ ] Hose bib
- [ ] Storage
- [ ] Security
- [ ] Rental yard
- [ ] Suppliers

Landscaping
- [ ] Required
- [ ] Sub out
- [ ] Grasses
- [ ] Bushes
- [ ] Flowers
- [ ] Trees

Figure 16-8
General Information

General Specifications

Contract number ____   Job foreman ____   Customer name ____

Fence or wall

Physical
- Length ____
- Height ____
- Base width ____
- Top width ____
- Frost line ____
- ☐ No. of corners
- ☐ No. of gates

Post mounting
- ☐ Direct in dirt
- ☐ Dirt fill
- ☐ Concrete
- ☐ Metal holder
- ☐ To wood deck

Post to rail connection
- ☐ Butt joint
- ☐ Miter joint
- ☐ Mortised
- ☐ Slotted
- ☐ Lap joint
- ☐ Metal holder

Post size
- ☐ 4 x 4
- ☐ 3" diameter
- ☐ 4" diameter
- ☐ 5" diameter
- ☐ 6" diameter
- ☐ 8" diameter
- ☐ Metal

Sections are
- ☐ Built on site
- ☐ Built in shop
- ☐ Purchased
- ☐ Both, specify

Foundation is
- ☐ Rebar reinforced

Final coating
- ☐ Painted
- ☐ Transparent stain
- ☐ Solid stain
- ☐ Masonry paint
- ☐ Water shield
- ☐ Natural

Notes

Picket style
- ☐ Square
- ☐ Rounded
- ☐ Bevel
- ☐ Gothic
- ☐ Mod. Gothic
- ☐ Fr. Gothic
- ☐ Pointed
- ☐ Dog ear
- ☐ Twin point
- ☐ Bent point

Gates
- ☐ Entry, 3' wood
- ☐ Entry, 3' metal
- ☐ Drive, 8' wood
- ☐ Drive, 8' metal
- ☐ Drive, 16' wood
- ☐ Drive, 16' metal
- ☐ Entry, chain link
- ☐ Drive, chain link
- ☐ Security
- ☐ Electric
- ☐ Self-closing

Gate top design
- ☐ Square
- ☐ Concave
- ☐ Convex
- ☐ Scroll
- ☐ Picket

Joint finish
- ☐ Concave
- ☐ Flush
- ☐ Bead
- ☐ Weather
- ☐ Raked
- ☐ Squeezed

Gate hinges
- ☐ Steel
- ☐ Brass
- ☐ Aluminum
- ☐ Wrought iron
- ☐ Strap
- ☐ Tee
- ☐ Concealed
- ☐ Butt

Other
- ☐ Entry arch
- ☐ Ground rods
- ☐ Spigots
- ☐ Lights
- ☐ Outlets
- ☐ Planters
- ☐ Security system

Lock type
- ☐ Standard
- ☐ Security

Latch type
- ☐ Hook & eye
- ☐ Bar & slot

Figure 16-9
General specifications

Fence Specifications

Contract number

Job foreman

Customer name

Fence style

Wood fence
- ☐ Basketweave
- ☐ Board
- ☐ Panel
- ☐ Picket
- ☐ Rail
- ☐ Virginia rail
- ☐ Alternating board
- ☐ Horiz. louver
- ☐ Vertical louver

Chain link
- ☐ Residential
- ☐ Commercial
- ☐ Tennis court
- ☐ Security
- ☐ Rental
- ☐ With barbs
- ☐ Privacy

Wire mesh
- ☐ Poultry
- ☐ Garden
- ☐ Pets
- ☐ Livestock
- ☐ Electric
- ☐

Barbed wire
- ☐ 1 strand
- ☐ 2 strand
- ☐ _____ Strands
- ☐ Razor wire
- ☐ Loose coil
- ☐ Electric
- ☐

Metal fence
- ☐ Guardrail
- ☐ Tubular
- ☐ Pipe
- ☐ Wrought iron
- ☐ Security
- ☐ Livestock
- ☐ Railing

Other
- ☐ Chain
- ☐ Rope
- ☐ Glass
- ☐ Fiberglass
- ☐ Logs
- ☐ Other
- _____

Materials

Surfaced
- ☐ Surfaced
- ☐ Rough
- ☐ Douglas fir
- ☐ Pine
- ☐ Redwood
- ☐ Cedar
- ☐ Wormy cedar
- ☐ Lattice
- ☐ Plywood
- ☐ Siding
- ☐ Site select
- ☐ Treated
- ☐ Other

Light duty
- ☐ Light duty
- ☐ Heavy duty
- ☐ Zinc coated
- ☐ Plastic coated
- ☐ Aluminum

Style number
- ☐ Zinc coated
- ☐ Plastic
- ☐ Other

Posts
- ☐ Wood
- ☐ Metal

Wire number
- ☐ 2 pt. barb
- ☐ 4 pt. barb
- ☐ Other

Posts
- ☐ Wood
- ☐ Metal

Painted
- ☐ Painted
- ☐ Zinc coated
- ☐ Aluminum
- ☐ Wrought iron
- ☐ Cast

Posts
- ☐ Metal
- ☐ Wood
- ☐ Pilaster
- ☐ Concrete

Selected
- _____
- _____
- _____
- _____
- _____

Figure 16-10
Fence specifications

Wall Specifications

Contract number

Job foreman

Customer name

Wall style

Block

- [ ] American bond
- [ ] Dutch cross bond
- [ ] Flemish bond
- [ ] Roman bond
- [ ] Running bond
- [ ] Stack bond
- [ ] Stack header
- [ ] Stack soldier
- [ ] Ashlar, coursed
- [ ] Ashlar, random
- [ ] Retaining

- [ ] 2 core
- [ ] 3 core
- [ ] Solid
- [ ] Split face
- [ ] Slumped
- [ ] Screen
- [ ] Offset
- [ ] Scored face

Mortar type _____

Brick

- [ ] American bond
- [ ] Dutch cross bond
- [ ] Flemish bond
- [ ] Roman bond
- [ ] Running bond
- [ ] Stack bond
- [ ] Stack header
- [ ] Stack soldier
- [ ] Ashlar, coursed
- [ ] Ashlar, random
- [ ] Veneer

- [ ] Smooth face
- [ ] Stipple
- [ ] Sand texture
- [ ] Scored face
- [ ] Water marked
- [ ] Fire brick
- [ ] Split face
- [ ] Used

Mortar type _____

Stone

- [ ] Rubble, stacked
- [ ] Split face
- [ ] Veneer
- [ ] Ashlar, coursed
- [ ] Ashlar, random
- [ ] Seawall
- [ ] Land clearing
- [ ] Dry set
- [ ] Wet set (mortar)
- [ ] Retaining

- [ ] Fieldstone
- [ ] Split face
- [ ] Sandstone
- [ ] Bluestone
- [ ] Hawaiian
- [ ] Volcanic
- [ ] Limestone
- [ ] Concrete

Mortar type _____

Poured concrete

- [ ] Retaining
- [ ] Seawall
- [ ] Base of other material
- [ ] Prefab sections
- [ ] Rebar reinforced
- [ ] Sculptured/free form
- [ ] Erosion control
- [ ] Traffic control

	Type	Size
[ ] Concrete	___	___
[ ] Rebar		
[ ] Forms		

Notes

Figure 16-11
Wall specifications

Sketches and Notes

Contract number	Job foreman	Customer name

Figure 16-12
Sketches and notes

Estimated Labor Hours

Job or bid number	Date of estimate	Customer name
Prepared by	Reviewed by	

General specifications

Sketch attached ☐

From Figure #	Operation required	Units installed	Time each	Extended time

Notes

Working hours subtotal _____

Times lost time factor ☐

Equals _____

Times experience factor ☐

Times terrain factor ☐

Plus additional hours for: _____

Total billable hours _____

☐ Working days   ☐ Calendar days

Figure 16-13
Estimated labor hours

Estimated Labor Hours

Job or bid number A-123	Date of estimate	Customer name SMITH, J.P.
Prepared by JIM	Reviewed by	

General specifications

200 LINEAR FEET OF DOUGLAS FIR FENCING.
8' OC POSTS, 2 RAILS, 1X6 FACE LUMBER, TWO 3' GATES.
DOWN SLOPE 5-6 DEGREES

Sketch attached ☐

From Figure #	Operation required	Units installed	Time each	Extended time
16-4	*SALES CALL ON CUSTOMER	1	5.0	5.0
16-4	*JOB PLANNING	1	13.0	13.0
16-21	*SITE LAYOUT	1	5.8	5.8
16-23	DIG POST HOLES	29	.2	5.8
16-24	INSTALL POSTS (WITH HELPER)	29	.21	6.0 + 6.0
16-25	INSTALL RAILS (PAINTED)	48	.2	9.6
16-25	ADD FACE BOARDS	367	.04	14.7
16-27	BUILD GATES	2	1.4	2.8
16-27	INSTALL GATES	2	.25	.5

Working hours subtotal		69.2
Times lost time factor	20%	13.84
Equals		83.04
Times experience factor	×1.1	91.34
Times terrain factor	×1.2	109.60
Plus additional hours for: TRAVEL		
	TRAVEL	6.00
Total billable hours		115.60

15 Working days   20 Calendar days

Notes

*INCLUDES TRAVEL TIME.

*IF SALES AND PLANNING ARE
INCLUDED IN OVERHEAD THEN
DEDUCT 23.8 HOURS FROM TOTAL.

ALLOW 2 DAYS NON-WORKING TIME
FOR CONCRETE TO CURE BEFORE
YOU ATTACH RAILS.

FINAL PAINTING SHOULD BE ON
SEPARATE CONTRACT SINCE LUMBER
SHOULD WEATHER FOR 90 DAYS.

Figure 16-14
Sample labor estimate

Job or bid number B-456	Estimate date 1/7		Customer JOE OWNER
Prepared by MAC	Reviewed by ✓		Address 234 MAIN ST
Calendar date	1/17 18 19 22 23 24 25 26 29 30 31 2/1		

Daily Milestone Planning Chart

OPERATION	1	2	3	4	5	6	7	8	9	10	11	12	13	14	15	16	17	18
SALES CALL	▨																	
SIGN CONTRACT	▨																	
COLLECT DEPOSIT	▨																	
PLAN JOB		▨																
ORDER MATERIAL			▨															
SCHEDULE HELP			▨															
SITE LAYOUT				▨														
RENT AUGER					▨													
DIG HOLES					▨													
COLLECT 20%					▨													
RETURN AUGER						▨												
RECEIVE CONCRETE						▨												
HELPER ON JOB						▨												
INSTALL POSTS						▨												
CURE TIME							▨											
COLLECT 20% ON CONCRETE COMP									▨									
INSTALL RAILS									▨									
INSTALL FACE BOARDS										▨	▨							
INSTALL GATES												▨						
CLEANUP												▨						
COLLECT BALANCE												▨						

Figure 16-15
Visual planning chart

Notice that the estimate summary contains information about your costs and markup rates that you'll want to keep confidential. It should be an internal company form, not disclosed to your customer or subcontractors, and perhaps not even to your superintendent.

When these forms are filled out, you have all the information you need for your salespeople, accountant, estimator, foreman, buyer, customer and any government agencies involved. Not bad for just checking off a few boxes.

Use a form like Figure 16-18 as an index to keep track of all the sketches, drawings, and blueprints you make for the job.

Figure 16-19 is the contract requirement form. You won't need all this information just to build a simple fence, but the form is complete enough to cover the most complex job. Use it as a checklist to be sure your final contract contains everything you want covered, and that you've followed through on all the closing details once the job is complete.

Materials Listing

Contract number | Job foreman | Customer name

Item number	Description	Used for	Quantity	Unit cost	Extended cost	Supplier	Date ordered	Date received

Sheet _____ of _____

Total cost: _____

Figure 16-16
Materials listing

Estimate Summary Sheet

Job number	A-250	Customer name	R. SMITH
Prepared by	MAC	Date	02/06/90

Materials Cost: $ 950.00 x 1.22 M/U = $ 1159.00

  Sales tax on material x 6.5 % = $ 75.34

Equipment rental charges = $ 45.00

  Sales tax on equipment rental x 6.0 % = $ 2.70

Subcontractor Cost: $ 450.00 x 1.18 M/U = $ 531.00

Subcontractor Cost: $ — x — M/U = $ —

Legal fees and permits = $ 85.00

Travel Miles 52 @ .40 /mile = $ 20.80

Additional expenses Cost: $ 15.00 x 1.10 M/U = $ 16.50

Materials total **Subtotal A** = $ | 1935.34 |

Labor

  Trade _____ Hours 22 x 8.50 Rate = $ 187.00

  Trade _____ Hours 30 x 11.50 Rate = $ 345.00

  Trade _____ Hours — x — Rate = $ —

Labor charges **Subtotal B** 532.00

  Times labor rate multiplier x 2.2

Labor total **Subtotal C** = $ | 1170.40 |

Estimate total Subtotal A + Subtotal C = $ | 3105.74 |

  Estimate range Less 2 % Plus 5 %

  Estimate $ 3044 to $ 3260

Estimate good for 30 days Estimate end date is 03/06/90

Page 1 of 8 pages On computer ☐ Yes ☑ No

Figure 16-17
Sample estimate summary

Master Drawing List

Contract number			Job foreman	Customer name				
Drawing number	Drawing size	Description		Date drawn	Drawn by	Checked by	Rev.

Sheet _____ of _____

File in master ☐   This is copy ☐   Keep for _____ months

Figure 16-18
Master drawing list

Contract Requirements

Contract type
- [ ] Time and material
- [ ] Fixed rate
- [ ] Cost plus
- [ ] Maintenance
- [ ] _____

Contract copies
- [ ] Office file
- [ ] Customer
- [ ] Foreman
- [ ] Sales
- [ ] Government

Drawings required
- [ ] Site layout
- [ ] Elevation
- [ ] Detailed
- [ ] Artist's concept
- [ ] Sketch only
- [ ] None required

Engineering
- [ ] Civil
- [ ] Design
- [ ] Firm name

Docs required
- [ ] Permit
- [ ] Bond
- [ ] Lien
- [ ] _____
- [ ] _____

Language
- [ ] Sales talk
- [ ] Sales contract
- [ ] Additional
- [ ] Both to customer

Drawings sets required
- [ ] Office file
- [ ] Foreman
- [ ] Fabrication shop
- [ ] Subcontractor
- [ ] Suppliers
- [ ] Building department
- [ ] Loan office
- [ ] Customer
- [ ] Homeowner's ass'n.
- [ ] Government

Contract information
- Date signed _____
- Start date _____
- Comp. date _____
- Contract price _____
- Master file no. _____

Contract end checklist
- Work comp. date _____
- Completion notice _____
- Bond returned _____
- Lien canceled _____
- Full payment rec'd. _____

Subcontractors
- [ ] Equipment operators
- [ ] Metal shop
- [ ] Carpentry shop
- [ ] Landscaper
- [ ] Tree removal
- [ ] Demolition
- [ ] Divers
- [ ] Blaster
- [ ] Hot tar application
- [ ] Painter
- [ ] Concrete

Customer information
- Name _____
- Address _____
- City _____ Zip _____
- Phone _____ Work _____
- Hours to contact _____

Payments
- Deposit _____
- Payment _____
- Payment _____
- Payment _____
- Payment _____
- Total paid _____

Staff required Name(s)
- [ ] Carpenter _____
- [ ] Drafter _____
- [ ] Driver _____
- [ ] Engineer _____
- [ ] Laborer _____
- [ ] Mason _____
- [ ] Metal worker _____
- [ ] Security _____
- [ ] Welder _____
- [ ] Job foreman _____

Figure 16-19
Contract Requirements

Notice the blank in the second column for "Language." That's to remind you that if you make your sales presentation in a language other than English, you must also give your customer a signed copy of the contract in that language.

Manhour Tables

Take time now to browse through my manhour tables. Get comfortable with their organization and layout. At the beginning of the tables there's a chart (Figure 16-20) for converting fractional hours to minutes (or minutes to seconds). Most of the tables have a column for hours, and the equivalent in minutes, but the conversion chart is there if you need it.

I've arranged the tables in chronological order (more or less), beginning with site layout and land clearing. Then there are tables for post holes and posts, wood fences, metal fences, gates, foundations and masonry fences and walls. Finally you'll find my charts for the factors to apply to the times in the manhour tables to adjust for terrain conditions and the experience of the workers. There are lines on the labor estimating chart for applying these factors.

Before you add the actual labor hours for construction to your estimate, pad it by 10 to 20 percent to account for lunches, breaks, talking to your customer, and those days when you don't feel top-notch and can't produce as much as you'd like to. That should be enough of a cushion. (If you and your crews aren't producing for at least 6-1/2 hours of each 8-hour workday, someone should be fired.)

Divide these total hours by the number of hours in your normal work day. This will give you the number of work days it will take to complete this job. And don't forget that's *work* days, not calendar days. You have to consider weekends, holidays, sick days, vacation days, and curing days. What are curing days? The two to five days when the concrete you poured is setting up. You have to factor them into your completion date. But find something else to do during that time.

Now for each day, add your travel time to and from the job. Also add 40 cents per mile per day to cover the cost of operating your vehicle. Not all contractors add this travel time and mileage. They figure they'd have to drive to work at their expense if they worked for someone else, so why charge their customers? I'll admit they have a point. But I'll charge for travel whenever I can do so and still remain competitive. Whenever I leave my office or home for a job, I'm on the *customer's* time.

It takes away from production time to set up and tear down each day. That's the time when you pull out your tools in the morning, and put them back again at night. That can take anywhere from 10 minutes to an hour each day. And you have to allow for cleanup at the end of the job. That can amount to several hours, depending on how messy you are.

You can also count on spending some time waiting around for others to do their jobs. Earlier in the chapter I mentioned the problem of the late transit-mix truck. Suppose you order a load of concrete for Monday morning at 8:00. Your crew finished digging the trench and placing the rebar on Friday. Now it's 10:15 Monday, and there you sit. Finally the truck pulls in and sets up, and you work your fanny off for an hour until the pour is complete. But you've lost 2-1/2 hours when you could have been working on another job.

You can't hope to anticipate *all* the things that might throw your schedule off. But your past experience will help. Keep accurate records of things that cause delays, and correct the problems or allow for them on future jobs. It would be nice if you could pad your jobs to cover all potential problems, but you'd probably price yourself out of the market if you did that. Try to cover yourself, but be realistic.

Let's look at a few of the manhour tables. Figure 16-23 gives you an idea of the time it takes dig post holes, considering the soil type and method of excavation. Say you need to dig 20 holes in gravelly soil with a two-man gas a (one man if he's big and strong). It takes 0.2 per hole, or 4 hours (20 x 0.2 = 4). That's 8 hours if there are two men on the auger.

When the holes are dug, use Figure 16-24 to estimate how much concrete you'll need for the foundation, and how long it will take to set the posts. To plant those 20 posts, figure 0.21 hours each times 20, or 4.2 hours. That's 4 hours and 12 minutes. (See the time conversion chart, Figure 16-20, where 0.2 hours equals 12 minutes.) If you have a helper mixing concrete, add him in at 4.2 hours also.

Ready for the rails? Look at Figure 16-25. Paint all rail and post lumber wherever they come in contact. My manhour estimates include time for this painting. There's also a factor to multiply by if you're using metal rail hangers or if you're making miter or other cuts in the post or rail. Look back to the chapter on wood fencing for more information on attaching rails to posts.

By now you may be wondering why I don't just give you a total job time for each fence or wall instead of breaking it down into tasks. There are two reasons. First, I want you to understand what it takes to do a job. Second, there's no way to give you a manhour estimate for a chain link fence, for example. There are just too many variables. No two jobs are exactly alike. Of course I could give you labor estimates like that, but I can just about guarantee that they wouldn't apply to the job you're doing. With my tables, you can use the times for each step that your job includes, and

customize them further with the terrain and experience factors.

I suggest you keep accurate job records and compare your actual times to the ones in my tables. Then change the tables to reflect your experience. Here's a list of the tables you'll find on the following pages:

Figure 16-20: Time conversion chart

Figure 16-21: Site layout - minimum and typical times

Figure 16-22: Land clearing

Figure 16-23: Excavation

Figure 16-24: Posts

Figure 16-25: Wood fences

Figure 16-26: Chain link, wire, and metal fences

Figure 16-27: Gates

Figure 16-28: Reinforced concrete foundations

Figure 16-29: Masonry

Figure 16-30: Concrete and veneer

Figure 16-31: Pilasters

Figure 16-32: Mixing mortar or concrete

Figure 16-33: Install ground rod

Figure 16-34: Terrain difficulty factor

Figure 16-35: Experience factor

Figure 16-36: Estimate summary sheet

Hours to minutes or Minutes to seconds	
.010	0.6
.015	0.9
.020	1.2
.030	1.8
.040	2.4
.050	3.0
.100	6.0
.200	12.0
.300	18.0
.400	24.0
.500	30.0
.600	36.0
.700	42.0
.800	48.0
.900	54.0
1.000	60.0

Figure 16-20
Time conversion

Site layout Operation	Minimum time		Typical time	
	Hours	Mins	Hours	Mins
Travel time	.6	36	.6	36
Walk fence line	.2	12	.2	12
Review plans	.2	12	.2	12
Mark fence line	1.5	90	1.5	90
Mark post positions	2.5	150	2.5	150
Discuss changes	- -	- -	.5	30
Write change order	- -	- -	.2	12
Confirm customer's approval	.2	12	.5	30
Travel time	.6	36	.6	36
Adjust labor & material	- -	- -	.8	48
TOTALS	5.8	348	7.6	456

Figure 16-21
Times for site layout

Land clearing

Per 100 feet of fence line, 6 feet wide, average

Operation	Equipment	Hours	
Remove high grass, small shrubs	Mower	1.0	
Remove medium to dense brush	Hand cut	4.0	
Remove soil, hillside, per cubic yard	Dozer	0.1	
Remove small boulders, less than 3' dia.	Dozer	1.0	
Remove large boulders, over 3' dia.	Dynamite	2.0	each
Remove small trees, less than 4" dia.	Chain saw	0.5	each
Remove large trees, over 4" dia.	Chain saw	3.5	each

Figure 16-22
Land clearing

Post hole excavation

Time in hours for 8" diameter, 18" deep hole

Operation	Loam	Gravel	Rocky	Solid
Dig by hand	0.4	0.6	1.0	n/a
Dig with power auger	0.2	0.2	0.3	n/a
Dig with truck auger	0.1	0.1	0.2	n/a
Drill, 2.5" diameter diamond drill	n/a	n/a	n/a	2.4

Foundation trench excavation

Time in hours for 12" wide, 18" deep trench, 10 linear feet

Operation	Loam	Gravel	Rocky	Solid
Dig by hand	4.0	5.0	8.0	n/a
Backhoe	0.3	0.3	0.5	n/a
Trencher	0.8	1.0	n/a	n/a

Figure 16-23
Excavation

Post planting

Operation	Hours	Mins
Lay in gravel drainage	.01	0.6
Set post in place	.01	0.6
Check alignment with other posts	.01	0.6
Plumb and brace	.12	7.2
Pour concrete or dirt fill	.03	1.8
Tamp	.01	0.6
Trowel drainage crown	.01	0.6
Inspect	.01	0.6
TOTALS	.21	12.6

Add for digging holes and mixing concrete. Double the time if you're using a helper.

Figure 16-24
Post planting

Concrete required for posts

8" diameter, 18" deep hole	Bags	Cubic Inches
Metal post	.60	710
2.5" diameter pipe post	.41	487
4 x 4 wood post	.36	422

A 94 lb bag is 2/3 cubic foot = 1152 cubic inches.
Examples: 10 each 4 x 4 posts require .36 x 10 or 3.6 bags. A 2' x 2' x 18" pilaster foundation requires 10,36 cubic inches divided by 1152 equals 9 bags.

Figure 16-24 (cont'd)
Post planting

Wood rail installation

Operation	Hours	Mins
Measure post opening	.01	.6
Measure and cut each rail	.01	.6
Measure rail position on post	.01	.6
Nail one end in place	.01	.6
Position other end	.01	.6
Check for level	.01	.6
Nail second end in place	.01	.6
Recheck level	.01	.6
Adjust if necessary	.01	.6
Paint cut edges, post connections, and side toward facing lumber	.11	6.6
TOTALS	.20	12.0
Add for each metal rail hanger	.01	.6
Add for miter or cut joints	.10	6.0

Typical time for 2 rails, painted, 24 minutes
Typical time for 2 rails, not painted, 12 minutes

Face board installation

Operation	Hours	Mins
Measure and cut each board	.01	.6
Nail each board to top rail	.01	.6
Plumb with level	.01	.6
Nail each board to bottom rail	.01	.6
TOTALS	.04	2.4

Typical time for nailing, 25 face boards per hour, 40-70 boards with labor savers. Typical time for stapling, 50 face boards per hour, 65-100 boards with labor savers. Add 36 seconds per board for painting contact side

Labor savers:
Nail all boards with bottom even, cut all tops at once. Use a spacer as a jig for spacing boards evenly. Plumb only every few feet. Have a helper supply boards to nailer as needed. Soak-paint all boards before installation

Cutting picket patterns

Operation	Hours	Mins
Make pattern	.50	30.0
Make template	.10	6.0
Mark pattern on picket	.01	.6
Cut pattern	.02	1.2

Typical time to mark and cut 100 pickets, 3 hours
Labor savers:
Trace pattern from an existing fence.
Cut several pickets at once with a band saw.

Figure 16-25
Wood fences

Chain link installation

Operation	Hours	Mins
Roll fabric length of line	.10	6.0
Place tension bands on end post	.01	.6
Lift fabric and install tension bar	.02	1.2
Install rail end on end post	.02	1.2
Install loop cap on each line post	.01	.6
Slip each top rail section in place	.02	1.2
Cut last top rail to fit	.10	6.0
Install rail end on rail and end post	.02	1.2
Lift fabric and tie to each top rail	.02	1.2
Secure puller to end post	.04	2.4
Lift fabric onto puller	.01	.6
Stretch fabric	.05	3.0
Install tension bar and bands to end post	.04	2.4
Cut fabric	.05	3.0
Tie fabric to each line post	.01	.6

Typical time for 50 foot fence line with 6 posts, 54 minutes
Typical time for 100 foot fence line with 11 posts, 78 minutes

Welding metal tubing

Operation	Hours	Mins
Measure and cut tubing to length	.02	1.2
Grind end surface	.01	.6
Wire brush and clean	.01	.6
Heat to temperature	.01	.6
Apply welding rod	.01	.6
Cool to touch	.02	1.2
Wire brush and clean	.01	.6
Grind smooth	.02	1.2
Paint	.01	.6
TOTALS	.12	7.2

This is the average time to weld 4" of seam joint, for example, a 1 inch square tube to another surface.

Figure 16-26
Chain link, wire, and metal fences

Form metal rail from sheet metal

Sheet metal cut, bent, welded into two "C" channels. 28 to 12 gauge CRS

Operation	Hours	Mins
Shear (cutter) setup - one time	.200	12.0
Brake (bender) setup - one time	.200	12.0
Shear up to 10' length, per cut	.005	.3
Brake each piece, up to 10', per bend	.005	.3
Remove grease and scale at weld area	.100	6.0
Clamp to table and second piece	.050	3.0
Weld, per linear inch	.020	1.2
Let each weld cool to touch	.020	1.2
Remove flux, wire brush, per unit	..020	1.2
Grind surface smooth, per unit	.500	30.0
Degrease entire assembly, per unit	.050	3.0
Paint entire assembly, per unit	.050	3.0

Typical time for 10' rail, 2 pieces less setup, 3.33 hours.
Typical time for two 10' rails with end caps, full seam welded, 7.6 hours.

Mount metal railing on a deck

Operation	Hours	Mins
Install first post holder	.10	6.0
Install each post	.01	.6
Fit railing and mark location for second post	.02	1.2
Install second post holder	.02	1.2
Install second post	.01	.6
Insert railing "L" brackets and tighten all fasteners	.04	2.4
Additional operations:		
Cut railing section to fit	.05	3.0
Install prefab gate and latch	.20	12.0
Bend 2 railings to fit stairs	.20	12.0
Touch up paint edges	.20	12.0
Install in concrete, per section	.20	12.0

Total time for section installed on wood, 12 minutes
Typical times for a 3 sided deck, 12' x 24', with stairs and gate:
  4 foot sections, 3.25 hours
  6 foot sections, 2.45 hours
  8 foot sections, 2.4 hours

Figure 16-26 (cont'd)
Chain link, wire, and metal fences

String barbed wire, posts 20' OC

Operation	Hours	Mins
Attach wire to first post	.10	6.0
Loose attach wire to each line post	.01	.6
Attach stretcher to wire	.02	1.2
Stretch wire	.04	2.4
Attach wire to end post	.05	3.0

Typical time per strand per 100 feet, 15.6 minutes

String wire mesh fence, posts 10' OC

Operation	Hours	Mins
Attach wire to first post	.10	6.0
Roll out wire and attach to each line post	.02	1.2
Install stretcher on wire	.02	1.2
Stretch wire	.04	2.4
Attach wire to end post	.10	6.0
Cut excess wire	.01	.6

Typical time for 100 foot fence, 30 minutes

Figure 16-26 (cont'd)
Chain link, wire, and metal fences

Build a wooden gate

Operation	Hours	Mins
Layout and design	.50	30.0
Measure and cut frame lumber	.10	6.0
Nail frame together	.10	6.0
Square up and measure cross brace	.05	3.0
Cut cross brace and nail in place	.05	3.0
Square up and add metal brackets	.10	6.0
Paint framing and face boards with roller	.10	6.0
Nail on 7 face boards	.07	4.2
Make top pattern	.11	6.6
Mark top pattern on gate	.02	1.2
Cut top pattern	.20	12.0
TOTALS	1.40	84.0

Typical time for 3 foot wide gate, 1.4 hours
Typical time for 8 foot wide gate, 1.6 hours

Build a tube steel gate, 39" wide, bars 5" OC

Operation	Hours	Mins
Measure and cut frame, 45 degree cut	.15	9.0
Measure and cut 6 vertical bars	.10	6.0
Clean weld areas	.10	6.0
Weld frame	.15	9.0
Weld in bars	.40	24.0
Weld on two hinges	.10	6.0
Weld on latch assembly	.10	6.0
Remove flux and grind smooth	.15	9.0
Degrease assembly	.10	6.0
Spray paint assembly	.10	6.0
TOTALS	1.45	87.0

Build a chain link gate, single section, any size

Operation	Hours	Mins
Layout and design	.50	30.0
Measure and cut framing members	.20	12.0
Slip on tension bands	.01	.6
Slip on hinges and latch sections	.01	.6
Fit framing to corner gussets	.05	3.0
Bolt on gussets	.10	6.0
Cut fabric to fit opening	.05	3.0
Install first side tension bar	.05	3.0
Stretch fabric	.05	3.0
Install second side tension bar	.05	3.0
Trim excess fabric	.05	3.0
Install cross brace	.10	6.0
Install top decoration	.10	6.0
TOTALS	1.32	79.20

Figure 16-27
Gates

Install a site-manufactured gate

Operation	Hours	Mins
Place into position	.05	3.0
Install top hinge	.06	3.6
Plumb and mark bottom hinge location	.01	.6
Install bottom hinge	.06	3.6
Install latch	.06	3.6
Check operation and oil hinges	.01	.6
TOTALS	.25	15.0

Times are for assembling with screws, using a power screw driver. Add 5-10 minutes for drilling and bolting together, or using a hand screw driver.

Install a purchased 3' gate with hinges attached

Operation	Hours	Mins
Lift gate into position	.01	.6
Install top hinge	.05	3.0
Install bottom hinge	.05	3.0
Check for plumb	.01	.6
Install latch assembly	.05	3.0
TOTALS	.17	10.2

Time is less for a purchased gate, since most come predrilled, and some with hinges already attached. For a double gate, add 30 minutes for center latch.

Figure 16-27 (cont'd)
Gates

Build 2x wood forms

Operation	Hours	Mins
Measure and cut lumber, per cut	.02	1.2
Nail on wood stakes, each	.01	.6
Place into position	.02	1.2
Nail on each cross brace	.01	.6
Level and square	.02	1.2
Apply release agent, oil	.02	1.2

Typical time to install a 10 foot, two sided, 2 x 8 form is 28 minutes.

Install rebar in foundation

Operation	Hours	Mins
Make each wire cradle	.01	.6
Place each cradle in trench	.01	.6
Cut rebar to length, per cut	.02	1.2
Bend rebar for corners, per bend	.03	1.8
Lay in each horizontal rebar	.01	.6
Set each vertical rebar	.01	.6
Tie each connecting joint	.01	.6

Typical time to install rebar into a 10 foot section of foundation is 48 minutes.

Pour concrete, per cubic yard (12" x 18" x 18 feet)

Operation	Hours	Mins
Pour	.10	6.0
Tamp or vibrate	.10	6.0
Trowel semi-smooth	.10	6.0
Cover or wet down	.10	6.0
Remove forms	.10	6.0

Allow for curing time.
Add 6 minutes for getting into position to begin pour.
Typical time for ready-mix straight from a truck chute is 30 minutes per cubic yard, 18 minutes for a 12" x 18" x 10 foot section of foundation.

Figure 16-28
Reinforced concrete foundations

Build 10 foot stone wall, 36" high x 22" wide

Operation	Hours	Mins
Butter foundation as you proceed	.50	30.0
Lay 425 - 6" diameter stones, with mortar	4.25	255.0
Rake joints	.50	30.0
Acid wash and clear water rinse	1.00	60.0
TOTAL	6.25	375.0

Allow 2 - 4 days curing time
Add 10 - 15 percent to total for selecting stones
Add 1.2 minutes per cut for cutting stone

Typical time for wet set wall, 8 hours, for dry set, 4 hours.

Brick wall, common bond, single thickness, 3' x 10'
Operation

An experienced mason can butter a brick, place it into position, tap it level and plumb and butter the brick end in about 20 seconds, or about 174 bricks per hour. That's enough for a 3 x 10 foot common bond wall, one brick thick.

A hollow-core, double sided, reinforced wall 3 x 10 feet will take about 2.5 hours, including grouting. See Figure 16-28 for time required to install rebar.

Add about 1 minute per cut for cutting.
Add 30 to 50 percent to these rates for other bond patterns.

Times are for mason only. Allow the same amount of time (at a different rate) for a helper to mix mortar, rake joints, and supply bricks.

Concrete block wall, single thickness, 32" x 10 feet long
Operation

The time to butter, lay in, level and plumb the 30 standard blocks required for a block wall is only slightly less than that for a brick wall of the same size. This is due to the size and weight of the block. Use the same time estimates, 1 hour for a single, 2.5 hours for a double-sided wall with a grout-filled core.

Figure 16-29
Masonry

Poured concrete wall

Operation	Hours	Mins
Clean foundation concrete	.10	6.0
Install pre-built form, one side	.20	12.0
Apply oil or release fluid	.10	6.0
Install horizontal rebar	.15	9.0
Apply oil or release to second form	.10	6.0
Install second form	.20	12.0
Pour or pump in concrete, 42" deep	.50	30.0
Vibrate concrete	.50	30.0
(Allow curing time, 2 to 5 days)	- -	- -
Clean top of existing concrete	.10	6.0
Pour or pump remainder	.70	42.0
Vibrate concrete	.70	42.0
(Allow curing time, 1 day)	- -	- -
Remove and clean forms	1.00	60.0
(Cover and allow curing time, 2 to 5 days)	- -	- -
Remove cover, install cap	1.10	66.0
TOTALS	5.45	327

Allow for extra travel time because of job interruptions for curing.

Apply veneer to an existing wall, per 6 x 10 foot section

Operation	Hours	Mins
Lay out veneer on ground along wall line	.70	42.0
Apply 1/2" thick mortar to a 2 x 2 foot wall area	.02	1.2
Press veneer into mortar	.02	1.2
(Repeat for each 2' x 2' area)		
Press mortar into all joints	.50	30.0
Wall with brush and clear water	.50	30.0
Rake joints	.50	30.0
Acid wash and clear water rinse	1.00	60.0

Allow for curing time and extra travel time.
Allow time for mixing mortar, or for a helper.

Typical time for a 6 x 10 foot wall, 3.8 hours.

Figure 16-30
Concrete and veneer

Pilaster made from brick, 22" x 22" x 6 feet

Operation	Hours	Mins
Butter foundation	.01	.6
Lay 240 bricks	1.33	79.8
Cut and insert 4 rebar	.10	6.0
Mix and pour 18 bags grout	.60	36.0
Install cap block	.02	1.2
TOTALS	2.06	123.6

Allow for helper to mix mortar, rake joints
Typical time with grout, 2 hours
Typical time without grout, 1.3 hours

Pilaster made from pilaster block, 9 blocks, 6' high

Operation	Hours	Mins
Butter foundation	.01	0.6
Lay in each alternate block	.02	1.2
Lay in each pilaster block	.02	1.2
Cut and insert 4 rebar	.10	6.0
Mix and pour 12 bags grout	.40	24.0
Install cap block	.02	1.2

Typical time with grout, 42 minutes
Typical time without grout, 18 minutes

Mount a rail between pilasters

Operation	Hours	Mins
Measure and cut railing	.10	6.0
Insert "L" brackets in rail ends	.01	.6
Mark holes in pilaster	.05	3.0
Drill holes	.10	6.0
Insert expansion bolt sleeves	.01	.6
Place railing in position	.01	.6
Insert bolts and tighten	.05	3.0
TOTAL	.33	19.80

Figure 16-31
Pilasters

Mixing mortar or concrete

Operation	Hours	Mins
Pour mix into wheelbarrow or tray	.02	1.2
Dry stir	.02	1.2
Measure water	.01	.6
Add half of water and mix	.02	1.2
Add water until mix feels right	.06	3.6
Complete mixing	.02	1.2
TOTAL	.15	9.0

Typical time to mix 1 bag by hand, 10 minutes
Typical time to mix 2 to 4 bags by machine, 15 minutes

Figure 16-32
Mortar

Install ground rod, minimum 5 feet into ground

Operation	Hours	Mins
Pound 8' x 1/2" copper rod into ground	.10	6.0
Attach 1/2" cable clamp	.02	1.2
Clean fence metal or wire to bare metal	.02	1.2
Attach 12 gauge wire and clamp	.01	0.6
Attach wire to ground rod	.01	0.6
TOTAL	.16	9.6

Typical time to install one rod, 10 minutes. Ground rod required every 150 feet on metal or wire fencing.

Figure 16-33
Ground rod installation

Terrain difficulty factors (add to total job)

Terrain type	Multiply hours by
Level, clear	1.0
Level, with obstructions	Add for clearing
Slope in one direction, clear	1.2
Multiple slopes, some obstructions	1.4
Very rough, hilly	1.6
Very rough, mountainous	2.0

Apply this factor to total job hours to allow for added difficulty in bringing materials and equipment to the job site, and working on uneven terrain.
See also: Figure 16-22, Land clearing

Figure 16-34
Terrain difficulty

Experience factor

Experience	Multiply time by
Fully qualified	1.0
Qualified, but hasn't done job before	1.1
General understanding of job	1.2
Limited experience in construction	1.4
Trainee, no experience	1.6
Homeowner, working part time	2.0

Apply different factors to parts of multiple tasks, depending on who is doing the work. Allow plenty of time for jobs the homeowner elects to do. Customers often lack experience, they won't be working under supervision, and are unlikely to devote the entire workday to the job so they'll spend extra time on setup and cleanup.

Figure 16-35
Experience factor

Estimate Summary Sheet

Job number _____   Customer name _____

Prepared by _____   Date _____

Materials   Cost: $ _____ x _____ M/U   = $ _____

    Sales tax on material   _____ x _____ %   = $ _____

Equipment rental charges   = $ _____

    Sales tax on equipment rental   x _____ %   = $ _____

Subcontractor   Cost: $ _____ x _____ M/U   = $ _____

Subcontractor   Cost: $ _____ x _____ M/U   = $ _____

Legal fees and permits   _____   = $ _____

Travel   Miles _____ @ _____ /mile   = $ _____

Additional expenses   Cost: $ _____ x _____ M/U   = $ _____

Materials total   **Subtotal A**   = $ [_____]

Labor

    Trade _____ Hours _____ x _____ Rate   = $ _____

    Trade _____ Hours _____ x _____ Rate   = $ _____

    Trade _____ Hours _____ x _____ Rate   = $ _____

Labor charges   Subtotal B   _____

    Times labor rate multiplier   x _____

Labor total   **Subtotal C**   = $ [_____]

Estimate total   Subtotal A + Subtotal C   = $ [_____]

    Estimate range   Less _____ %   Plus _____ %

    Estimate $ _____   to $ _____

Estimate good for _____ days   Estimate end date is _____

Page _____ of _____ pages   On computer ☐ Yes ☐ No

Figure 16-36
Estimate summary for your use

seventeen

Contractor's Math

Like it or not, every contractor has to know some mathematics. There's no way around it. You have to measure distances, find square footage, measure angles, order materials and estimate contracts. That's in addition to your accounting jobs. If your state requires that fence contractors be licensed, the license exam will include a section on mathematics.

But don't panic, even if math wasn't your best subject in high school. There's nothing very complex in this chapter. And I'm going to take it slow and easy. When you've worked your way through this chapter you'll know enough math to estimate nearly any job.

First, I'll define some terms for you and provide formulas needed to solve most fence problems. In the formulas, I'll use letters to represent numbers. Just replace my letters with your numbers, the actual numbers from your jobs. You'll have it made! Now, let's get started.

A Glossary of Mathematical Terms

Here are the math terms you'll need to understand.

Acute angle: An angle of less than 90 degrees.

Angle: The intersection of two straight lines, measured in degrees.

Apex: The peak of a triangle.

Arc: Part of the circumference of a circle.

Area: The amount of space in a flat surface. Measured in square inches, feet, yards, centimeters, etc.

Chord: A line between two points on the circumference of a circle that does not pass through the center of the circle.

Circle: A plane surface in which the boundary line is a closed curve with every point upon it the same distance from the center.

Circumference: The distance around a circle. Also, the boundary of a circle.

Cube: A box with all sides of equal size.

Cubic measurement: The volume inside a three dimensional object, measured in cubic inches, feet, centimeters, etc. A cubic foot is the volume inside a box that's a foot high, a foot long, and a foot wide.

Degree: A unit of measurement representing one 360th of a circle. Angles and arcs of a circle are measured in degrees.

Diameter: The distance across a circle at its center.

Ellipse: A closed, regularly shaped curve that is *not* a circle.

Exponent: A number written to the right and slightly above a value that tells how many times to multiply the value by itself.

Hypotenuse: The side of a right triangle that's opposite the right angle.

Line: Designates location and direction and has no width or depth. A line has length only.

Linear measurement: Distance between two points.

Minute: One 60th of a degree.

Obtuse angle: An angle between 90 and 180 degrees.

Parallel: Describes two straight lines that are the same distance apart along their entire length. They will never meet.

Parallelogram: A four-sided figure with opposite sides equal and parallel but without right angles.

Perimeter: The lines that define the outline of a plane surface.

Perpendicular: Describes two lines that cross each other at a right angle.

Pi: Greek letter representing the relationship between a circle's diameter and its circumference. The circumference of a circle is 3.1416 times the diameter.

Plane surface: A flat surface defined by only two dimensions, length and width (or height).

Point: A geometric location and has no length, width, or depth, (breadth or thickness).

Radius: The distance from the center of a circle to its circumference.

Rectangle: A plane surface with four sides and square corners. Opposite sides are parallel and equal in length.

Reflex angle: An angle over 180 degrees.

Right angle: An angle of 90 degrees, the same as the corner of a perfect square.

Right triangle: A triangle that contains a right (90 degree) angle.

Round off: To shorten a decimal number to a specific number of decimal places.

Second: One 60th of a minute.

Sector: Part of a circle defined by the circumference and any two radii.

Segment: Part of a circle defined by the circumference and a chord.

Solid object: A geometric shape that has three dimensions, length, width and depth.

Square root: A number that, when multiplied by itself, returns the given number. Example: The square root of 9 is 3 (3 times 3 equals 9).

Square: A plane surface with four equal sides and four equal (90 degree) angles.

Tangent: A straight line that touches the circumference of a circle at only one point.

Trapezoid: A flat surface with four sides, only two of which are parallel to each other.

Triangle: A plane surface with three sides and three angles. The sum of the angles of a triangle is 180 degrees.

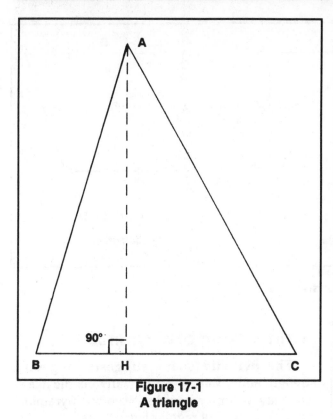

Figure 17-1
A triangle

Value: A mathematical expression that's written as a number, symbol, or formula.

Vertex: The point where two straight lines intersect.

Volume: The amount of space in a three-dimensional object, such as a globe or a cube. Measured in cubic inches, feet, etc.

Areas of Flat Surfaces

You'll have to calculate the area of flat surfaces over and over again. How else will you estimate how many boards you'll need to face a fence, or how much paint it will take?

Area of a Triangle

When would you need to find the area of a triangle? Let's assume you're building a wall around a piece of property and the owner decides he wants you to put in a concrete pad for a patio.

The patio runs on a diagonal between two walls, forming a triangle. Of course you're a wall builder, not a patio builder — but you have the equipment and manpower you need right there. Are you going to turn down a quick profit? Of course not. So you have to find the area of that triangle and give the homeowner a quick estimate.

Formula: Area = One half the (H)eight times the (B)ase, where the base is the side the triangle rests on, and the height is the length of a line perpendicular to the base that intersects the apex. In a right triangle, the height and base are the two lines that form the right angle.

Example: The area of a triangle with a base of 18 feet and a height of 21 feet is 189 feet (18 times 21 divided by 2). See Figure 17-1, where the line BC is the base, and AH is the height. The triangles AHC and AHB are right triangles.

Area of Rectangular Surfaces

This formula applies to squares, rectangles, parallelograms. See Figure 17-2. Most of your jobs will have rectangular surfaces.

Formula: Area = (L)ength times (W)idth (or (H)eight)

Example: The area of a fence 6 feet high by 40 feet long is 240 square feet (6 times 40 equals 240).

Area of a Flat Surface with More Than Four Sides

They aren't as common as squares and rectangles, but sooner or later you'll need to know these formulas. Perhaps you'll have to estimate the area of decorative lumber inserts in a block wall. Or maybe you just need this information to pass the contractor's license exam.

Pentagons, hexagons, and octagons have five, six, and eight sides respectively. In each case, all the sides are the same length. To find the perimeter of each of these, you measure one side and multiply by the number of sides.

Here are formulas for their areas: ([L]ength is the length of one side.)

Area of a pentagon equals (L)ength^2 times 1.720

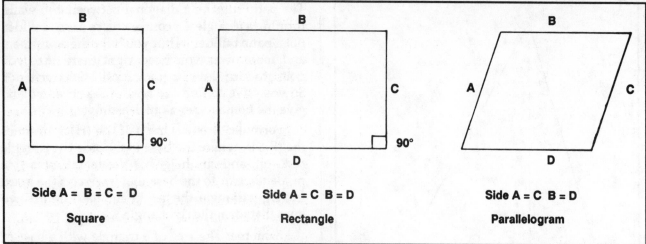

Figure 17-2
Rectangular surfaces

Area of a hexagon equals L^2 times 2.598

Area of an octagon equals L^2 times 4.828

Example: The area of a pentagon with sides five feet long equals 5^2 times 1.720, or 43 square feet.

Area of a Trapezoid

Many of the lots you'll be asked to fence won't be rectangles. Developers like to add interest to their housing projects with curving streets and cul-de-sacs. Many of those odd-shaped lots are trapezoids.

Formula: (H)eight times the sum of the lengths of the two parallel sides divided by two = H(a + b)/2, where a and b are the parallel sides. The height is the distance between the two parallel sides, measured along a line perpendicular to them.

Example: You want to know the area of a lot on a cul-de-sac. The property line on the street side is 50 feet long (side A). Side B at the back of the lot is 75 feet long. The distance between them is 100 feet. See Figure 17-3.

Area = 100 times (50 + 75)/2

When a part of a formula is enclosed in parentheses, you calculate that part first, before you continue to figure the formula. The answer is 100 times 125 divided by 2, or 6250 square feet.

Surface Area of a Pyramid

The pyramid shape suggests longevity, strength and mystery — and many people like it. Someday you may be asked to build pyramidal columns instead of regular fence posts.

The sides of a pyramid are triangles. The base of a pyramid can have any number of sides, begin-

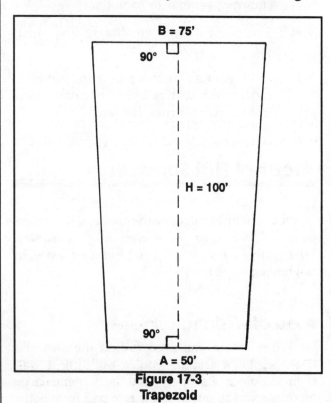

Figure 17-3
Trapezoid

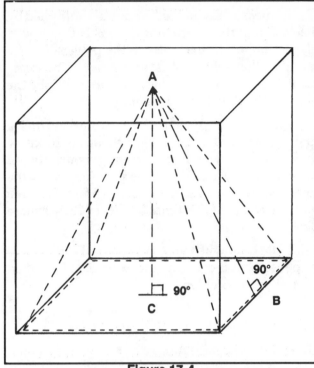

Figure 17-4
A pyramid with a rectangular base

ning with three. You saw how to find the areas of flat surfaces in the last section. Use those formulas to find the area of the base of a pyramid. Then add the area of the base to the lateral area of a pyramid to get the total surface area.

Formula: Lateral surface area of a regular pyramid (where all sides of the base are the same length) equals ½([H]eight (the distance from the base perimeter to the apex of the triangular side) x

(L)ength of one side of the base x (N)umber of sides of the base) = HLN/2.

Example: The lateral area of a pyramid with a square base that's 3 inches on a side and sides that measure 5 inches from base to peak is 30 inches (5 x 3 x 4) / 2 = 30. The area of the base is 9 (3 x 3), so the total surface area of the pyramid is 39 inches. In Figure 17-4, line AB is the height of one face.

The formula for the total surface area of a pyramid on a rectangular base is LH + WH' + LW, where L is the length of the rectangular base, W is the width of the base, H is the height of the triangles with base L, and H' is the height of the triangles with base W.

Measuring Curved Shapes

When you want to build an arch, or a circular wall, or a wall with a rounded corner, you'll have to know how to calculate circles, and parts of circles. Figure 17-5 illustrates the names that define parts of a circle.

If you know the radius of a circle, you can find the diameter by multiplying the radius by two. If you can measure the diameter of a circle, you can find the radius by dividing the diameter by two.

Here are the formulas you'll use with circles:

(D)iameter = (R)adius times 2 = 2R

(R)adius = (D)iameter divided by 2 = D/2

(C)ircumference = (D)iameter times 3.14159265+

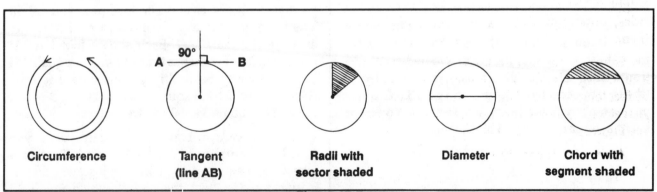

| Circumference | Tangent (line AB) | Radii with sector shaded | Diameter | Chord with segment shaded |

Figure 17-5
Names used with circles

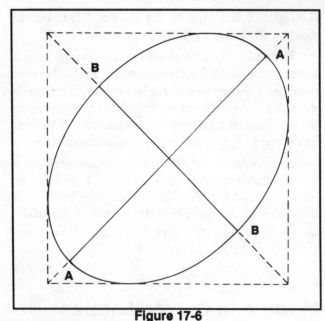

Figure 17-6
An ellipse with major axis AA and minor axis BB

Let's stop a minute and look at that awkward little number, 3.14159. That's a "constant" you'll use often when you calculate circles and other curved objects. It's represented by the Greek letter "pi." Pi is written π. You use π as a shorthand symbol for the number, which you can round off to 3.1416 (or even 3.14) for all practical purposes. Thus you can also write the formula for the circumference of a circle as πD. Since the diameter is twice the radius, you can also write 2πR.

Example: Your customer wants to make a circular tree well 10 feet in diameter with a low wall around it. You'll build the wall from standard 16-inch block, two layers high. How many blocks do you need?

The circumference of a circle 10 feet in diameter is 10 times pi, or 31.416 feet. You're using 16-inch block, so convert the answer to inches: 31.416 times 12 equals 376.992 inches. Divide that by 16 (the length of each block) and you get 23.562. Since you can't buy half a block, figure on 24 blocks for each layer of the wall, 48 blocks total.

The Area of a Circle

Formula: Area of a circle = πR^2.

R^2 means "R squared," or radius multiplied by itself. Computer shorthand for this is R^2 where the ^ symbol means "raise to the power of." The number that follows it is an *exponent*. The exponent tells you how many times to multiply the value preceding the exponent by itself.

Example: Suppose your customer wants a patio instead of a tree well, and needs to know how many square feet of paving stones they'll need to fill the area inside the wall. You know the diameter is 10 feet, so the radius is 5 feet. The area of the circle is 5^2 (25) times 3.1416, or 78.54 square feet.

Note than when you solve formulas that have exponents, you calculate the exponents first, then complete the problem.

Area of an Ellipse

Formula: πAB/4, where A is the longest distance between opposite sides (major axis) and B is the shortest (minor axis). See Figure 17-6.

Example: Area of an ellipse with a major axis of 6.5 and a minor axis of 4.25 is 21.6966 (6.5 x 4.25 x 3.1416/4 = 21.6966).

Convert Area Units of Measurement

You can convert from one unit of measurement to another very easily. For instance, you might want the answer to a formula in square inches instead of square feet. Each square foot has 144 square inches (12 inches times 12 inches equals 144 square inches.) So multiply each square foot by 144 to find the total square inches: 240 square feet times 144 equals 34,560 square inches.

If you want to convert to square yards, you divide the number of square feet by 9. That's because each square yard contains 9 square feet. A square yard is 3 feet times 3 feet, which equals 9.

Figure 17-7 is a conversion chart for area measurements.

To convert	to	you	by this
Square inches	Square feet	Divide	144.00
Square inches	Square yards	Divide	1,296.00
Square feet	Square inches	Multiply	144.00
Square feet	Square yards	Divide	9.00
Square feet	Square rods	Divide	272.25
Square yards	Square inches	Multiply	1,296.00
Square yards	Square feet	Multiply	9.00
Square yards	Square rods	Divide	30.25
Square rods	Square yards	Multiply	30.25
Square rods	Square feet	Multiply	272.25

Figure 17-7
Conversion chart for area measurements

Convert Linear Units of Measurement

Suppose you need to know how many 1 x 3 boards you need for a 40-foot-long fence. First you need to convert the fence length to inches, then divide that by 3:

40 feet times 12 inches equals 480 inches.

480 inches divided by 3 (inches per board) equals 160. It will take 160 1 x 3 boards to cover the fence.

You could also convert the 3-inch boards to fractions of a foot:

$\frac{3}{12}$ of a foot is $\frac{1}{4}$ or 0.25 feet.

Divide 40 feet by 0.25 (feet per board) and you still get 160. If the length of the fence is an odd amount, and you wind up with a fraction in your answer, just add one board to the whole number in your answer.

Figure 17-8 is a conversion table for point-to-point measurements.

Volume of Solid Objects Bounded by Planes

Applies to any three-dimensional linear object.

Formula: Volume = (L)ength times (W)idth times (H)eight

Example: The volume of a trench 3 feet deep (high) by 2 feet wide by 40 feet long is 240 cubic feet.

Convert Volume Measurements

Since you buy ready-mix concrete by the cubic yard, you need to convert the trench measurement from cubic feet to cubic yards. Each cubic yard contains 27 cubic feet (3 feet long times 3 feet wide times 3 feet high equals 27 cubic feet). You'll need 9 cubic yards of concrete for a 2 x 3 x 40 foot trench (240 divided by 27 equals 8.8888 cubic yards). If you know that a cubic yard of concrete costs $50, you can multiply 50 times 9 to find that it will cost you $450 to fill the trench. Figure 17-9 is a conversion table for volume measurements.

Armed with the above formulas and conversion charts, you can figure out most of your fence and wall problems. The measurement examples that follow aren't as common, but they're just as simple. You may find some of this on your contractor's exam, and you may have occasion to use it in the field.

Volume of a Cylinder

Formula: (V)olume = π times (R)adius squared times (H)eight = $\pi R^2 H$. (A cylinder is any object that's shaped like a soda can, with straight sides and a curved top and bottom.)

Example: Let's go back to the tree well. How much dirt will it take to fill the well to the top of the blocks? First, figure the exponent, R^2 = 5 times 5 = 25 feet. Multiply 25 times 3.1416 times the height of the wall.

To convert	to	you	by this
Inches	Feet	Divide	12.00
Inches	Yards	Divide	36.00
Inches	Rods	Divide	198.00
Feet	Inches	Multiply	12.00
Feet	Yards	Divide	3.00
Feet	Rods	Divide	16.50
Feet	Miles	Divide	5,280.00
Yards	Feet	Multiply	3.00
Yards	Rods	Divide	5.50
Yards	Miles	Divide	1,760.00
Rods	Feet	Multiply	16.50
Rods	Yards	Multiply	5.50
Rods	Miles	Divide	320.00
Miles	Feet	Multiply	5,280.00
Miles	Yards	Multiply	1,760.00
Miles	Rods	Multiply	320.00

Figure 17-8
Conversion chart for point-to-point measurements

The wall is two blocks high, and each block is 8 inches high, so the total height of the wall is 16 inches. You have to convert inches to feet, since the formula won't work if you don't use the same unit of measurement for each part of the formula. Divide 16 inches by 12 (inches per foot) to get 1.333 feet. Now you can finish the calculation:

25 times 3.1416 times 1.333 equals 104.69 cubic feet of dirt. Divide by 27 to convert to cubic yards: 104.69 divided by 27 equals 3.88 cubic yards.

You could have also converted all the measurements to inches. Five feet equals 60 inches, so 60^2 times 3.1416 times 16 equals 180,956.16 inches.

Divide by 1728 (cubic inches per cubic foot) to get 104.72 cubic feet. Then divide by 27 to get 3.88 cubic yards.

To find the volume of a cylinder wall where the inside of the cylinder is empty, the formula is: $V = \pi(D^2 - D'^2)H/4$, where D is the diameter of the outside wall and D' is the diameter of the inside wall. Remember to clear the exponents first, then do the operation inside the parentheses before you solve the rest of the problem.

Example: Suppose you want to build a circular planter out of poured concrete like the one in Figure 17-10. The outside diameter of the planter is 24

To convert	to	you	by this
Cubic inches	Cubic feet	Divide	1,728
Cubic inches	Cubic yards	Divide	46,656
Cubic feet	Cubic inches	Multiply	1,728
Cubic feet	Cubic yards	Divide	27
Cubic yards	Cubic inches	Multiply	46,656
Cubic yards	Cubic feet	Multiply	27

Figure 17-9
Conversion chart for volume measurements

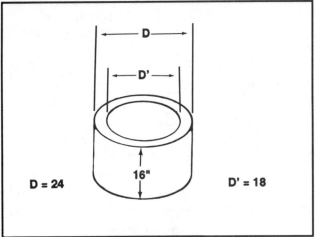

Figure 17-10
A hollow cylinder

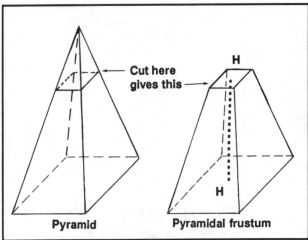

Figure 17-11
A pier block

inches, the inside cavity is 18 inches, and the planter is 16 inches high. The problem looks like this:

$\pi \times (24^2 - 18^2) \times 16 / 4 =$

$\pi \times (576 - 324) \times 16 / 4 =$

$\pi \times 252 \times 16 / 4 = 3166.7328 = 1.83$ cubic feet of concrete.

Volume of a Pyramid

Formula: V = ⅓ the area of the base times the altitude. It occupies ⅓ the space inside an upright figure that will contain it. Look back at Figure 17-4. The altitude is the length of the line AC from the apex of the pyramid to its base, perpendicular to the base. Notice, this isn't the same as the height of the side of a pyramid (line AB) that you use to find surface area.

Example: The volume of a pyramid with a 12 inch square base, 12 inches high at the tip equals 576 cubic inches. (12 x 12 x 12 / 3 = 576)

Volume of a Frustum

A frustum is what's left when you cut the top off a cone or pyramid, and make the cut parallel to the base. You use frustum shapes for pier blocks, and decorative columns and wall posts.

Formula for a conic frustum: V = π times ⅓ the (H)eight times (R^2 + RR' + R'^2) where R is the radius of the bottom circle, R' is the radius of the

top circle. Again, clear the exponents and the parentheses, then proceed.

Example: The volume of a conic frustum with a base radius of 8 inches, a top radius of 6 inches, and a height of 9 inches:

$\pi \times (9 / 3) \times (8^2 + (8 \times 6) + 6^2) =$

$\pi \times 3 \times (64 + 48 + 36) =$

$\pi \times 3 \times 148 = 1394.87$ cubic inches

You can also solve this using the diameter with the formula V = 0.2618 times (H)eight times (D^2 + DD' + D'^2), where D is the bottom diameter, and D' is the top.

You'll recognize the pyramidal frustum in Figure 17-11 as the familiar pier block you can buy at the lumberyard. Here's how to figure how much concrete you need to build one yourself.

Formula for a pyramidal frustum: V = ⅓ the (H)eight times A plus A' plus the square root of (A times A') = $H/3(A + A' + \sqrt{AA'})$ where A is the area of the base, and A' is the area of the top surface and H is the height of the frustum (the line HH in the illustration.)

Example: The volume of a pier block 12 inches square at the base, 8 inches square at the top, and 9 inches high equals:

$3 \times (144 + 64 + \text{the square root of } (144 \times 64)) =$

$3 \times (208 + \text{the square root of } 9216) =$

$3 \times (208 + 96) =$

$3 \times 304 = 912$ cubic inches = .5277 cubic feet

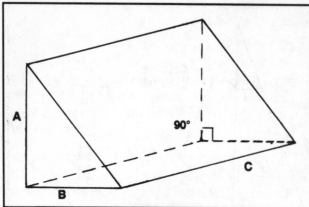

Figure 17-12
A right triangular prism

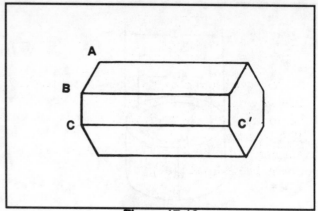

Figure 17-13
Hexagonal prism

Volume of a Prism

Formula: V = Area of the base times the altitude.

Example: The right triangular prism like the one in Figure 17-12 is a shape you might use for a seawall or retaining wall. The area of the base is (A x B)/2. Multiply that answer by C (the "altitude") to get the volume. If A = 5, B = 6, and C = 12, the volume is 180.

You can use a hexagonal prism like Figure 17-13 for piers and posts. To find the volume, use the formula for a hexagon to find the area of the base, and multiply that by the height of the prism. In the figure, all the sides are the same as AB, and CC' is the altitude.

Square Root

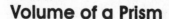

The easiest way to find the square root of a number is to look it up in a book of mathematical tables, or punch it in on your calculator. But if you don't have a book or calculator handy, here are a couple of other ways to do it:

First, you can use trial and error. Suppose you want to know the square root of 81. You know 10 x 10 is too much. That makes 100. Try 8 x 8 — but 64 isn't enough. How about 9 x 9? Sure enough,

that's it. But what if your number is 1056.25? You could experiment all day before you find the answer. Here's the second way:

Rewrite the number, separating the digits into pairs beginning at the decimal point, marking off pairs in both directions:

10 56.25

There will be one digit in the answer for each pair of digits in the original number, and for any single digit that remains at the far left or right of the decimal.

Begin with the first pair, and find the whole number that comes closest to the first pair, 10, when multiplied by itself, but without exceeding 10. That number is 3, because 3 x 3 = 9. The next number, 4, would be too much because 4 x 4 = 16. Write the 3 above the first 2 digit pair. It's the first digit in your answer.

Now, multiply 3 by itself, and write the answer, 9, below the 10. Subtract 9 from 10, and bring down the next two-digit pair.

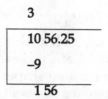

```
       3
     ┌──────────
     │ 10 56.25
     │ −9
     └──────────
        1 56
```

Now, multiply the first digit of your answer by 2, and write it to the left of the 156, and leave room for another digit.

```
          3
    ┌─────────────
  10│56.25
     -9
  6?      1 56
```

You want to replace the ? with a mystery digit that, when multiplied by 6? gives the closest number to 156 without exceeding it. Since 3 times 63 is 189, let's try 2. Multiply 2 by 62 and write the answer under the 156. Then subtract and bring down the next pair of digits:

```
          3 2.
    ┌─────────────
  10│56.25
     -9
  6?      1 56
  62      1 24
          32 25
```

The mystery digit was 2, the second digit of your answer.

Now, do the same thing again. Double the answer you have so far, leave room for another digit, and divide. You see that 5 times 645 equals exactly 3225, and 5, the mystery digit is the last number in your answer:

```
          3 2. 5
    ┌─────────────
  10│56.25
     -9 00.00
  6?      1 56
  62      1 24
  64?        32 25
  645        32 25
                 0
```

Bingo! If you multiply 32.5 by itself, you'll see the answer is 1056.25. You've found the square root of 1056.25.

Later in the chapter, under the discussion of right triangles, you'll see how this might come in handy.

Fractions and Decimals

Builders do most of their measuring with a tape that shows fractions of an inch down to $\frac{1}{16}$th. In fact, fractions smaller than that aren't practical when you're working with construction materials.

But working with fractions can sometimes be tricky.

Example: $\frac{1}{16} + \frac{1}{4} + \frac{1}{8}$

To add these as fractions, you first have to change them all to the *lowest common denominator* (LCD), the lowest number that can by divided evenly by all the denominators. In this case, 16.

$$\frac{1}{16} + \frac{4}{16} + \frac{2}{16} = \frac{7}{16}$$

Notice that you only add the numerators together. The denominator stays the same. The same is true of subtraction — you only operate on the top part of the fraction, once you've converted to the LCD.

Sometimes it's easier to solve equations with decimals than it is with fractions. You convert a fraction to a decimal by dividing the top number of the fraction (the *numerator*) by the bottom number of the fraction (the *denominator*).

Let's do it again, this time with decimals:

.0625
.2500
.1250
─────
.4375 (This is the same as $\frac{7}{16}$ths, as you'll see below in the section on converting decimals to fractions.)

Figure 17-14 is a conversion chart to change fractions to decimals.

1/16	= .0625	9/16	= .5625
1/8	= .1250	5/8	= .6250
3/16	= .1875	11/16	= .6875
1/4	= .2500	3/4	= .7500
5/16	= .3125	13/16	= .8125
3/8	= .3750	7/8	= .8750
7/16	= .4375	15/16	= .9375
1/2	= .50001	6/16	= 1.0000

Figure 17-14
Conversion chart from fractions to decimals

Reduce Fractions

Sometimes when you calculate fractions, your answer will be something like $\frac{8}{16}$, or $\frac{24}{32}$. Make these easier to read and understand by *reducing* them. You do that by finding a number that divides evenly into both parts of the fraction. You can start with 2 or 3, but sometimes it will be obvious that a larger number will work.

Example: Both parts of $\frac{8}{16}$ can be divided evenly by 8, so you can reduce the fraction to $\frac{1}{2}$. Try it with $\frac{24}{32}$, dividing each time by 2:

$$\frac{24}{32} = \frac{12}{16} = \frac{6}{8} = \frac{3}{4}$$

You can verify that all these are equal by converting them to a decimal. All of them equal 0.75.

Multiply Fractions

To multiply fractions, you multiply both the top and bottom numbers.

Example: $\frac{1}{4} \times \frac{1}{8} = \frac{1}{32}$, or, $\frac{3}{16} \times \frac{1}{2} = \frac{3}{32}$

Divide Fractions

In division, the number you're dividing is called the *dividend*, the number you're dividing by is called the *divisor*. To divide one fraction by another, *invert* the divisor, and multiply. Invert means to turn the fraction over. Thus $\frac{1}{2}$ becomes $\frac{2}{1}$

Example: $\frac{1}{4} \div \frac{1}{8} = \frac{1}{4} \times \frac{8}{1} = 2$ (There are 2 eighths in a quarter.)

Notice that in the original answer, the top of the fraction was larger than the bottom. When that happens, the fraction represents a number greater than one. To convert it to a whole number (plus a fraction, if one remains) you divide the top of the fraction by the bottom.

Example: $\frac{3}{2} = 1\frac{1}{2}$

Here's an application using fractions:

You're building a fence 18 feet long. You want to face it with alternating boards, $3\frac{1}{4}$ inches wide and $5\frac{5}{8}$ inches wide. How many of each size do you need?

First, add the sizes of the two boards to see how much space each pair will cover:

$$3\frac{1}{4}$$
$$+\ 5\frac{5}{8}$$

Remember, to add fractions, you have to convert them to the LCD, so change the top one, and add:

$$3\frac{2}{8}$$
$$+\ 5\frac{5}{8}$$
$$8\frac{7}{8}$$

Now, find how many $8\frac{7}{8}$-inch combinations you need to cover 18 feet. First, convert feet to inches:

$$18 \times 12 = 216$$

Then, convert $8\frac{7}{8}$ to a fraction. Start with the whole number, 8. A whole number is the same as a fraction with the whole number on top, and 1 on the bottom. Since the fractional part of the number is eighths, you convert the whole number to eighths, also.

$\frac{8}{1} = \frac{64}{8}$ (You multiply both parts of the fraction by 8.)

Now, add the fraction to the whole number: $\frac{64}{8} + \frac{7}{8} = 7\frac{1}{8}$

Divide 216 inches by $7\frac{1}{8}$ inches. (Remember, you invert the divisor and multiply):

$$\frac{216}{1} \times \frac{8}{71} = \frac{1728}{71} = 24\frac{24}{71}$$

Do it again, using decimals:

$8\frac{7}{8} = 8.875$ (You divide 7 by 8 to get 0.875)

$216 \div 8.875 = 24.34$

You'd order 25 of each size board (you can't buy 0.34 of a board) to cover the fence, if you intend to install the boards with no space between them.

Convert Decimals to Fractions

In the above problem, as in most of this kind, the answer didn't come out to an even whole number. When that happens, you may want to convert the number to something you can read on your tape measure. You do that by dividing 1 by the decimal. The *reciprocal* of the answer is the fraction you're looking for. (The reciprocal of a number [which may be a fraction] is the number or fraction you multiply the first number by to get 1.)

Example: To convert 0.169 inch to a fraction:

1 ÷ .169 = 5.917

The reciprocal of 5.917 is 1/5.917.

That's still not much help when you look at your tape measure. The next step is to *round* the answer.

Round Your Answer

Decimal fractions that go beyond two or three decimal places aren't very practical for a contractor. How often do you have to measure something down to a thousandth or a hundred-thousandth of an inch? And even in money calculations, only the first two decimal places are significant.

You round a number by adjusting it to be as accurate as possible for a given number of decimal places. Look at the number to the right of the number you want to keep. If it's four or less, just drop it, and the numbers that follow it. If it's five or more, drop it and the numbers that follow it, and add 1 to the number that came before it.

Example: Round 6.1745 to three places: 6.175

Round 6.1745 to two places : 6.17

Round 6.1745 to one place: 6.2

Round 6.1745 to a whole number: 6

Now, to return to the decimal conversion problem, you can change 1/5.917 to ⅙. When you convert ⅙ back to a decimal, you get 0.1667, only 0.0023 less than the 0.169 you started with — hardly enough to worry about unless you multiply the error by hundreds or more. In practice, it's better for overall accuracy to do your intermediate calculations to three or four decimals, and then round off the final answer.

One-sixth still isn't the best answer for working with a tape measure. Here's how to convert a decimal to a number you can work with: Multiply the decimal by the number you want for the denominator of the resulting fraction. The answer is the fraction's numerator.

Example: To convert 0.169 to 16ths of an inch, 0.169 x 16 = 2.704. Round the answer to the whole number 3, and the resulting fraction is 3/16. The error is 0.0185 of an inch. You could get closer by converting to 32nds: 0.169 x 32 = 5.408. When you round the answer, the resulting fraction is 5/32, or 0.156, an error of only 0.013.

Decimal/Fraction Equivalents

Figure 17-15 is a chart of decimals converted to the lowest common fraction and to 64ths of an inch.

Decimal	Fraction of inch	64ths of inch
.015625	1/32	2
.062500	1/16	4
.093750	3/32	6
.125000	1/8	8
.156250	5/32	10
.187500	3/16	12
.218750	7/32	14
.250000	1/4	16
.281250	9/32	18
.312500	5/16	20
.343750	11/32	22
.375000	3/8	24
.437500	7/16	28
.500000	1/2	32
.562500	9/16	36
.625000	5/8	40
.687500	11/16	44
.750000	3/4	48
.812500	13/16	52
.875000	7/8	56
.937500	15/16	60
1.000000	1.0	64

Figure 17-15
Decimal/fraction equivalents

Use Right Triangles to Calculate Measurements

Suppose you're bidding on a job to fence a lot like the one in Figure 17-16. You visited the site and measured sides A, B, and C, and then got distracted and drove back to the office before you measured side D.

If you draw a line from the intersection of A and D to side C, and perpendicular to side C, you'll divide the lot into two parts, a rectangle and a right triangle. Redraw the triangle like the one in Figure 17-16. There's a rule for right triangles that comes in very handy for this kind of a problem.

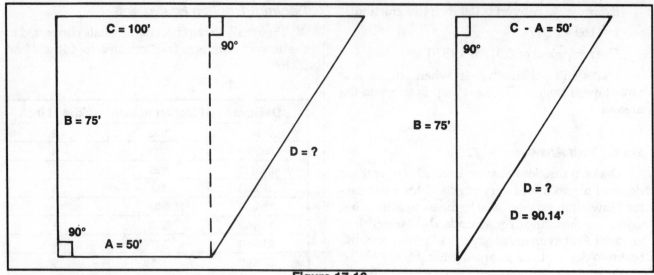

Figure 17-16
Find a missing dimension using a right triangle

The rule is:

For any right triangle, the sum of the squares of the sides equals the square of the hypotenuse.

The "sides" are the two sides of the triangle adjacent to the right angle; the hypotenuse is the side opposite.

Example: Find the hypotenuse of the right triangle in Figure 17-16, where side A is 50 feet and side B is 75 feet.

$$C^2 = 50^2 + 75^2$$
$$C^2 = 2500 + 5625$$
$$C^2 = 8125$$
$$C = \sqrt{8125} = 90.14 \text{ (rounded)}$$

Now you can calculate the length of the fence line for this odd-shaped lot:

$$50 + 75 + 100 + 90.14 = 315.14$$

Square a Corner

You can also use the special properties of a right triangle to be sure a corner is square. The "perfect" right triangle has sides that are multiples of 3, 4, and 5 like the one in Figure 17-17. After you lay out your fence lines for a rectangular fence, measure 3 feet down one line from the corner, and mark the spot. Then measure 4 feet down the other line from the same corner, and mark that as well. The distance across the angle between the two marks should be exactly 5 feet. If it's not, your corner isn't square. An error of only 1/16 of an inch here could put your fence line 6.2 inches off the mark a hundred feet away. Figure 17-18 illustrates this principle.

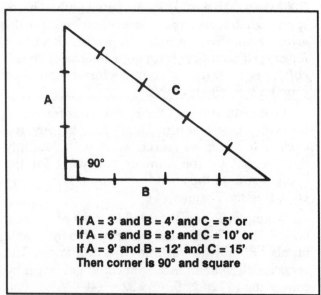

If A = 3' and B = 4' and C = 5' or
If A = 6' and B = 8' and C = 10' or
If A = 9' and B = 12' and C = 15'
Then corner is 90° and square

Figure 17-17
The "perfect" right triangle

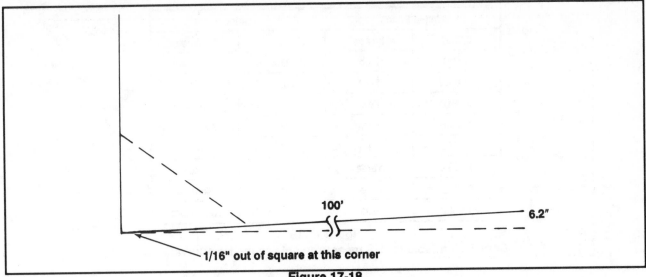

Figure 17-18
Use the right triangle rule to project accurate fence lines

You can make this process even more accurate if you use longer measurements. Use 6, 8, and 10 feet, or even 9, 12, and 15.

What if you need to find the length of a side of a triangle, and it's not a right triangle? Turn back for a moment to Figure 17-1. If you want to know the length of line AC, drop a line from angle A perpendicular to line BC. It's line AH in the figure. Now you have two *right* triangles to work with. The length of the line AC is the square root of the total of line AH^2 + line HC^2.

Calculate Degrees, Minutes and Seconds

Angles and circles are measured in degrees (°). Each degree contains 60 minutes ('), and each minute contains 60 seconds ("). When you work with angles and parts of a circle you may need to combine these by adding them together, or subtract one from another.

Example: Add 22° 45' 22" to 18° 10' 15".

22° 45' 22"

18° 10' 15"

40° 55' 37"

Now try this one:

22° 45' 22"

18° 21' 49"

40° 66' 71"

The answer is right, but not *correct*. When minutes and seconds are more than 60, you convert them to the next larger unit. Change 71 seconds to 1' 11", and add the minute to the 66 in the answer. Now the answer is:

40° 67' 11"

Now change 67 minutes to 1° 7' and add the degree to the 40. The final answer is 41° 7' 11".

When you subtract, you may have to "borrow" to make your answer come out right. Just remember, if you borrow a degree, you increase minutes by 60, and if you borrow a minute, you increase seconds by 60. You can use the same system to figure time cards, only you use hours instead of degrees.

Example: Your employee worked from 7:45 a.m. to 5:15 p.m., and you want to know how many hours to pay him for. Subtract 7 hours, 45 minutes (your employee's time in) from 17 hours, 15 minutes (their time out on a 24-hour clock.)

17 15

- 7 45

United States		Metric	
0.3937	Inches	1	Centimeter
1.000	Inch	2.54	Centimeters
1.000	Foot	30.48	Centimeters
3.2810	Feet	1	Meter
1.0936	Yard	1	Meter
1.0000	Yard	0.914	Meters
1,093.6	Yards	1	Kilometers
0.6214	Mile	1	Kilometer
1.0000	Mile	1.6093	Kilometers

Figure 17-19
Conversion table for US measurements to metric equivalents

First, borrow an hour from 17, and add its 60 minutes to 15:

16 75

- 7 45

Now you can figure your employee's time, 9 hours, 30 minutes.

Metric Conversion Table

The United States is just beginning to get in step with the rest of the world in the use of the metric system for measurements. The metric system is a base-ten system, where each unit of measurement is a multiple of 10 of each of the others.

Based on the meter, a centimeter is 1/100th of a meter, a millimeter is 1/1000th of a meter, a kilometer is a thousand meters.

Figure 17-19 is a conversion table for traditional U.S. measurements, and the metric equivalents.

You don't have to memorize all this if you're not taking the contractor's exam in California. But remember it's here if you need to refer to it later.

Glossary

A

Abutment Structure (natural or constructed) that supports a dam, bridge or arch.

Adobe Clay building material made from straw and sun-dried earth or Playa Clay.

Adze A tool used to shape wood. Looks somewhat like a pickax with a chisel-shaped head.

Anta Portion of a wall that is thicker than the rest, acts as a post.

Auger Large, coarse screw bit, typically 8 to 12 inches in diameter and driven by an electric or gas motor. Used for boring post holes.

Awl Hand tool with long sharp pointed tip. Used for making holes in wood or to make indent, starter hole, for a drill bit.

B

Backhoe Power machine used for excavation. Has digging bucket that is on the end of an articulating arm which is pulled toward the operator.

Balcony Platform surrounded by railing usually on upper stories of a building.

Bamboo Tall grass with a woody stalk, usually about 1/8 to 1 inch in diameter and 8 to 12 feet tall. Used for furniture and fences.

Band saw Power saw with a continuous steel blade, used for cutting irregular shapes.

Banister Railing used as a hand hold on stairways and landings.

Barbed wire Stranded wire with sharp-pointed ends twisted into it that protrude every 4 to 6 inches along its length.

Base The bottom or supporting structure of a column or pier or wall. Usually reinforced and wider than the object it supports.

Batten Joint sealer or reinforcement made from narrow strips of wood. Also the stakes used to hold the string that marks the boundary of a wall or foundation.

Block and tackle A device that decreases the amount of power needed to move a given load.

Boss Architectural term for portion of decorative ornamentation that protrudes outward.

Bow saw Used for cutting logs, a tensioned saw blade attached to an arched or bow-shaped handle.

Brace To reinforce a fence or wall so it does not collapse or fall over. Also a hand tool used to drill holes in wood.

Bracket Support for shelves or vertical loads, usually made of metal. Also used to reinforce angles.

Brad Thin small-headed nail.

Brick Clay formed and heat-cured into a basic building block.

Broach To open up a hole or square off the bottom of a hole.

Brownstone A reddish-brown sandstone building material.

C

Cantilever Beam supported on one end only.

Cap Top of wall, usually overhangs both sides of wall to deflect water away from wall.

Capillary action Liquid flow through an object.

Cast iron Molded iron manufactured from silicon, iron, and carbon. Used for decorative items.

Cattle gate Bars installed over a hole at ground level. Bar size and spacing allows people and vehicles to cross, but not cattle.

Cement Building material used to bond materials, blocks, bricks, together. Manufactured from finely pulverized ores, usually iron oxide, alumina, lime, silica, and magnesia.

Center bit A wood boring tool with a center screw that extends beyond two sharpened wings or spurs which shave the circumference of the hole.

Center punch A tool you strike with a hammer to make an indent used as a starter hole for drilling.

Chain saw Power saw used to cut timber, with a continuous revolving chain that has cutting teeth every few inches.

Chalk line Straight line marked on an object or surface. Also the device used to make the line, a roll of string enclosed in a box of powdered chalk.

Chamfer The edge of a bevel. Also a column with groves cut along its length, or the act of cutting groves along the length of a column.

Chisel A hand tool struck with a hammer or pushed by hand, used to cut groves or irregular shapes from the surface of wood. Special hardened chisels also cut or split block, brick, mortar, cement, or stone.

Chuck The portion of a drill that is used to hold the bit.

Clapboard Type of wood siding material. Wide at its top and narrower at its bottom.

Clasp To hold together. Also: an object designed to hold items together, such as a hook to keep a gate closed.

Clench To bend the protruding pointed end of a nail so it can't be pulled out.

Clinkerbuilt Overlapping of boards, such as siding.

Cofferdam Enclosure used to divert water from a construction area. A hollow, watertight structure lowered to the bottom of a water-filled area, and extending above water level which is then pumped out to expose the bottom surface.

Column Vertical post used as a support.

Concrete Building material used to form foundations and walls. Made from a mixture of cement, small rock, and water.

Console Ornamental bracket for holding up a shelf or overhead.

Coping The cap of a wall.

Coping saw Small hand-held bow saw with thin narrow blade, used for cutting decorative strolls in wood.

Corbel A support attached to the side of a wall. Usually scroll-cut wood that supports a shelf.

D

Dado A groove cut in any material. Also, the blade used to cut the groove, or the act of cutting the groove.

Dead-air space The enclosed space in blocks where there is no air movement. Acts as an insulator to heat and cold.

Dead load Weight on foundation from wall or structure above. A constant weight that doesn't include people, vehicles, snow, etc. See also *Live load*.

Die Device used for cutting threads on screws and pipes.

Dovetail Type of wood joint where each piece being joined is end-cut into sections that are wider at the ends than at the base.

Drawknife Also called *Drawshave*. A knife blade with handles on both ends. The knife is drawn or pulled in a shaving motion across the piece of wood being shaped.

Dry wall Rock wall construction in which no mortar is used. The roughness and weight of the stone hold the wall in place.

Duramen (Heartwood) The center portion of a log which is dense, hard, and usually dark in color.

Dutch door or gate Gate or door that is split horizontally. Both sections are independently hinged and locked. Allows one to open top half, to see out or talk to someone, while bottom half remains closed.

E

Eye bolt Bolt formed with a head that forms a closed circle.

F

Face The front portion of a wall or fence.

Filigree Fine design ornamental work.

Foot print Drafting term that refers to the horizontal area covered by an object being placed in that area. Also, the outline of wall or fence looking from the top downward.

Footing The enlarged base section of a foundation, used to distribute the weight of the structure being supported.

Frame Structural supporting structure of a wall or building.

G

Galvanize Apply a zinc coating to metal to prevent rust and deterioration.

Gate A passageway between two adjacent areas that are separated by a freestanding fence or wall.

Gate post Posts on either side of a gate. One holds the hinges, the other the latch.

Girder A structural component that extends horizontally and supports a vertical load.

Girth Measurement of distance around an object.

Gouge A narrow scoop-type chisel used for digging out wood.

Grade The slope or elevation of the land from flat (horizontal).

Grate Covering over an opening which consists of open mesh or bars. See *Cattle gate*.

Gravel Pebbles or sand and rock mixture. Rock size is generally less than an inch in diameter.

Ground plan Plan or layout of where a structure will rest on a plot of land.

Ground water Water beneath the surface of the ground, such as an underwater stream or pool.

H

Hacksaw Small bow saw used for cutting metals.

Half-timber A structure, wall, or fence with exposed wood separated by plaster, masonry or concrete.

Hardhat A reinforced safety helmet worn during construction to protect wearer from falling or airborne objects.

Hasp Two-component door or gate latch composed of a U-shaped fitting on one member which passes through a slot in the other. The parts are usually secured with a padlock.

Header Supporting structure placed above an opening, such as a doorway, window, gate.

Hedge Fence or barrier of low plants, bushes, or trees.

Hedgerow Hedge lined up in a row that acts as a fence.

Heelpost Hinged side of a gate post.

Hinge Two-component device. One section is fixed in place, the other is allowed to turn or swivel on the first.

Hoist A lifting device usually of block and tackle design used to lift heavy objects into place.

Hone Stone made of fine, hard-packed grit. Used for sharpening knives, axes, etc.

I

Impost Beginning of an arch. The portion of the wall or fence the arch rests on.

Incline A slope.

Inorganic Dirt and rock soil which is not the result of decomposed plants or animal matter.

Insoluble Not capable of being dissolved.

Insulator Material which restricts the flow of heat or cold.

K

Kerf A saw or knife cut.

Keystone Wedge-shaped stone which is the last to be placed into the center top of an arch and locks the arch together.

Kiln An oven used for drying clay, such as that used to manufacture brick. Also, an oven used to dry fresh cut (wet) lumber.

King post The center vertical post of a truss.

L

Levee Bank of earth used to contain water from a lake, stream, river, or ocean.

Line posts Posts between the anchor or terminal posts in a fence.

Lintel Beam above a window or doorway that supports the wall above.

Live load Load a structure is designed to support, including animals, people and equipment.

Louvers Slats arranged across an opening in such a way that air passes through, but view or rain is fully or partly blocked.

M

Mason One who builds with stone, brick, or block.

Matchboards Lumber that when put together forms a tight fit, such as tongue and groove.

Maul Hammer with a large heavy head. Used to drive stakes, wedges, etc.

Miter Joint formed by two or more pieces that have been cut at an angle and butted together.

Moldboard Forming lumber used when laying in concrete. Also: the angle plow or blade of a bulldozer.

Molding Finish lumber used to cover joints and cracks.

Mortar Mixture of cement and sand used to bond block and bricks together.

Mortarboard Hand held board, 18 inches square, used to hold mortar during the brick laying process.

N

Newel post Starting post of a railing located at the head or foot of a stairway, or the center post of a circular stairway.

Niche A recessed shelf area in a fence or wall.

P

Parcel A small plot of land, a lot.

Peavey A tool for manual handling of logs.

Pediment A decorative structure over a gate or entry way.

Percolate To pass through a material, as water passing through a wall.

Pilaster The terminal post of a block wall.

Pile driver Machine used to drive piles into the bottom silt of a body of water.

Pile Large diameter post sunk into the bottom of a body of water. Used to hold up piers.

Plan view A drawing showing a top down view of an object or property.

Plate rail Bottom horizontal railing of a fence which is fastened to a foundation.

Podium The wall that forms the base or foundation of a fence.

Portal An entrance.

Postern Refers to a private entry or gate which is not the front or main gate.

Protractor Drafting tool used to draw circles and arches. Measures angles in degrees.

Pull or pulley See *Block and tackle*.

Q

Quadrant A quarter section of an area.

Quarter section 160 acres of land bounded by a square of 1/2 mile on each side.

Quoin The keystone of an arch or corner stone of a wall. Usually larger and a different color than the wall.

R

Rail The horizontal beam of a fence. The face boards are secured to the rails.

Railing A low fence, under 4 feet high, used as a handrail on balconies.

Relief map (Topographic) A plan view map showing the elevations of a piece of property or area.

S

Scythe A blade for cutting tall grasses.

Seismic Pertaining to earthquakes. Metal holders that meet earthquake standards for construction.

Shot hole Hole drilled into solid rock or compacted earth in which a dynamite charge is placed.

Sluice Water channel or gate used to divert a stream around the work area.

Spandrel Decorative arch built into an otherwise square entry way.

Stay The vertical wires of a woven wire mesh. Also the vertical wire(s) used to space and hold two or more strands of barbed wire.

Stile A stairway or group of steps passing over a fence. Also, a vertical cut in a post in which a face board is inserted.

Stockade A type of wooden fence made up of 2 inch or 3 inch diameter poles or wide boards with rounded fronts.

Stull Timber support used to hold back earth when digging a mine or trench.

T

Tamp To compress and remove trapped air in earth or concrete using short sharp blows.

Tarp (Tarpaulin) Fabric (often canvas) or plastic protective covering.

Tensiometer A gauge used to determine the amount of pull or tension on a wire fence during installation.

Terne Alloy coating of 1 part tin to 4 parts lead. Applied as a protection to metal.

Toriia Japanese style gateway or entry. Two vertical posts with one or two inverted arches on top.

Tracery Ornamental wood or metal work of the Gothic period. Fine intersecting lines form a pattern.

Transit A surveying instrument for determining grades, elevations, and angles.

Trowel A hand held tool used for applying mortar to block or brick.

V

Vault A storage area built into a wall or fence to secure valuables. Also an arched ceiling or roof.

Veneer A non-structural, decorative facing of block or brick.

W

Wet wall A rock or stone wall constructed using cement or mortar as a bonding agent.

Wythe One horizontal row of brick in a brick wall. Also the vertical seam of mortar between bricks in a wall.

Index

Other Practical References

Electrical Blueprint Reading

Shows how to read and interpret electrical drawings, wiring diagrams and specifications for construction of electrical systems in buildings. Shows how a typical lighting plan and power layout would appear on the plans and explains what the contractor would do to execute this plan. Describes how to use a panelboard or heating schedule and includes typical electrical specifications. **128 pages, 8-1/2 x 11, $13.75**

National Construction Estimator

Current building costs in dollars and cents for residential, commercial and industrial construction. Prices for every commonly used building material, and the proper labor cost associated with installation of the material. Everything figured out to give you the "in place" cost in seconds. Many time-saving rules of thumb, waste and coverage factors and estimating tables are included. **544 pages, 8-1/2 x 11, $19.50. Revised annually**

Estimating Electrical Construction

A practical approach to estimating materials and labor for residential and commercial electrical construction. Written by the A.S.P.E. National Estimator of the Year, it explains how to use labor units, the plan take-off and the bid summary to establish an accurate estimate. Covers dealing with suppliers, pricing sheets, and how to modify labor units. Provides extensive labor unit tables, and blank forms for use in estimating your next electrical job. **272 pages, 8-1/2 x 11, $19.00**

Contractor's Guide to the Building Code Revised

This completely revised edition explains in plain English exactly what the Uniform Building Code requires and shows how to design and construct residential and light commercial buildings that will pass inspection the first time. Suggests how to work with the inspector to minimize construction costs, what common building shortcuts are likely to be cited, and where exceptions are granted. **544 pages, 5-1/2 x 8-1/2, $24.25**

Berger Building Cost File

Labor and material costs needed to estimate major projects: shopping centers and stores, hospitals, educational facilities, office complexes, industrial and institutional buildings, and housing projects. All cost estimates show both the manhours required and the typical crew needed so you can figure the price and schedule the work quickly and easily. **304 pages, 8-1/2 x 11, $30.00. Revised annually**

Building Cost Manual

Square foot costs for residential, commercial, industrial, and farm buildings. In a few minutes you work up a reliable budget estimate based on the actual materials and design features, area, shape, wall height, number of floors and support requirements. Most important, you include all the important variables that can make any building unique from a cost standpoint. **240 pages, 8-1/2 x 11, $14.00. Revised annually**

Cost Records for Construction Estimating

How to organize and use cost information from jobs just completed to make more accurate estimates in the future. Explains how to keep the cost records you need to reflect the time spent on each part of the job. Shows the best way to track costs for site work, footing, foundations, framing, interior finish, siding and trim, masonry, and subcontract expense. Provides sample forms. **208 pages, 11 x 8-1/2, $15.75**

Residential Wiring

Shows how to install and finish wiring in both new construction and alterations and additions. Complete instructions are included on troubleshooting and repairs. Every subject is referenced to the 1987 National Electrical Code, and over 24 pages of the most needed NEC tables are included to help you avoid errors so your wiring passes inspections - the first time. **352 pages, 5-1/2 x 8-1/2, $18.25**

Construction Estimating Reference Data

Collected in this single volume are the building estimator's 300 most useful estimating reference tables. Labor requirements for nearly every type of construction are included: site work, concrete work, masonry, steel, carpentry, thermal & moisture protection, doors and windows, finishes, mechanical and electrical. Each section explains in detail the work being estimated and gives the appropriate crew size and equipment needed. **368 pages, 11 x 8-1/2, $26.00**

Residential Electrician's Handbook

Simple, clear instructions for wiring homes and apartments: understanding plans and specs, following the NEC, making simple load calculations, sizing wire and service equipment, installing branch and feeder circuits, and running wire. Explains how to estimate the cost of residential electrical systems, speed and simplify your estimates using composite unit prices, and provides the forms and labor and material tables you need. **240 pages, 5-1/2 x 8-1/2, $16.75**

Carpentry Estimating

Simple, clear instructions show you how to take off quantities and figure costs for all rough and finish carpentry. Shows how much overhead and profit to include, how to convert piece prices to MBF prices or linear foot prices, and how to use the tables included to quickly estimate manhours. All carpentry is covered; floor joists, exterior and interior walls and finishes, ceiling joists and rafters, stairs, trim, windows, doors, and much more. Includes sample forms, checklists, and the author's factor worksheets to save you time and help prevent errors. **320 pages, 8-1/2 x 11, $25.50**

Rough Carpentry

All rough carpentry is covered in detail: sills, girders, columns, joists, sheathing, ceiling, roof and wall framing, roof trusses, dormers, bay windows, furring and grounds, stairs and insulation. Many of the 24 chapters explain practical code-approved methods for saving lumber and time without sacrificing quality. Chapters on columns, headers, rafters, joists and girders show how to use simple engineering principles to select the right lumber dimension for whatever species and grade you are using. **288 pages, 8-1/2 x 11, $17.00**

Estimating Tables for Home Building

Produce accurate estimates in minutes for nearly any home or multi-family dwelling. This handy manual has the tables you need to find the quantity of materials and labor for most residential construction. Includes overhead and profit, how to develop unit costs for labor and materials, and how to be sure you've considered every cost in the job. **336 pages, 8-1/2 x 11, $21.50**

Residential Electrical Design

Explains what every builder needs to know about designing electrical systems for residential construction. Shows how to draw up an electrical plan from the blueprints, including the service entrance, grounding, lighting requirements for kitchen, bedroom and bath and how to lay them out. Explains how to plan electrical heating systems and what equipment you'll need, how to plan outdoor lighting, and much more. If you are a builder who ever has to plan an electrical system, you should have this book. **194 pages, 8-1/2 x 11, $11.50**

Wood-Frame House Construction

From the layout of the outer walls, excavation and formwork, to finish carpentry, and painting, every step of construction is covered in detail with clear illustrations and explanations. Everything the builder needs to know about framing, roofing, siding, insulation and vapor barrier, interior finishing, floor coverings, and stairs — complete step-by-step "how to" information on what goes into building a frame house. **240 pages, 8-1/2 x 11, $14.25. Revised edition**

Remodeling Kitchens & Baths

This book is your guide to succeeding in a very lucrative area of the remodeling market: how to repair and replace damaged floors; how to redo walls, ceilings, and plumbing; and how to modernize the home wiring system to accommodate today's heavy electrical demands. Show how to install new sinks and countertops, ceramic tile, sunken tubs, whirlpool baths, luminous ceilings, skylights, and even special lighting effects. Completely illustrated, with manhour tables for figuring your labor costs. **384 pages, 8-1/2 x 11, $26.25**

Audio: Estimating Remodeling

Listen to the "hands-on" estimating instruction in this popular remodeling seminar. Make your own unit price estimate based on the prints enclosed. Then check your completed estimate with those prepared in the actual seminar. After listening to these tapes you will know how to establish an operating budget for your business, determine indirect costs and profit, and estimate remodeling with the unit cost method. **Includes seminar workbook, project survey and unit price estimating form, and six 20-minute cassettes, $65.00**

Carpentry Layout

Explains the easy way to figure: cuts for stair carriages, treads and risers; lengths for common, hip and jack rafters; spacing for joists, studs, rafters and pickets; layout for rake and bearing walls. Shows how to set foundation corner stakes, even for a complex home on a hillside. Practical examples show how to use a hand-held calculator as a powerful layout tool. Written in simple language any carpenter can understand. **240 pages, 5-1/2 x 8-1/2, $16.25**

Contractor's Growth and Profit Guide

Step-by-step instructions for planning growth and prosperity in a construction contracting or subcontracting company. Explains how to prepare a business plan: selecting reasonable goals, drafting a market expansion plan, making income forecasts and expense budgets, and projecting cash flow. Here you will learn everything required by most lenders and investors, as well as solid knowledge for better organizing your business. **336 pages, 5-1/2 x 8-1/2, $19.00**

Running Your Remodeling Business

Everything you need to know about operating a remodeling business, from making your first sale to ensuring your profits: how to advertise, write up a contract, estimate, schedule your jobs, arrange financing (for both you and your customers), and when and how to expand your business. Explains what you need to know about insurance, bonds, and liens, and how to collect the money you've earned. Includes sample business forms for your use. **272 pages, 8-1/2 x 11, $21.00**

Handbook of Construction Contracting

Volume 1: Everything you need to know to start and run your construction business: the pros and cons of each type of contracting, the records you'll need to keep, and how to read and understand house plans and specs to find any problems before the actual work begins. All aspects of construction are covered in detail, including all-weather wood foundations, practical math for the job site, and elementary surveying. **416 pages, 8-1/2 x 11, $24.75**

Volume 2: Everything you need to know to keep your construction business profitable: different methods of estimating, keeping and controlling costs; estimating excavation, concrete, masonry, rough carpentry, roof covering, insulation, doors and windows, exterior finish, specialty finishes; scheduling work flow; managing workers; advertising and sales; spec building and land development; and selecting the best legal structure for your business. **320 pages, 8-1/2 x 11, $24.75**

Carpentry for Residential Construction

How to do professional quality carpentry work in homes and apartments. Illustrated instructions show you everything from setting batterboards to framing floors and walls, installing floor, wall and roof sheathing, and applying roofing. Covers finish carpentry, also: how to install each type of cornice, frieze, lookout, ledger, fascia and soffit; how to hang windows and doors; how to install siding, drywall and trim. Each job description includes the tools and materials needed, the estimated manhours required, and a step-by-step guide to each part of the task. **400 pages, 5-1/2 x 8-1/2, $19.75**

Masonry Estimating

Step-by-step instructions for estimating nearly any type of masonry work. Shows how to prepare material take-offs, how to figure labor and material costs, add a realistic allowance for contingency, calculate overhead correctly, and build competitive profit into your bids. **352 pages, 8-1/2 x 11, $26.50**

Video: Stair Framing

Shows how to use a calculator to figure the rise and run of each step, the height of each riser, the number of treads, and the tread depths. Then watch how to take these measurements to construct an actual set of stairs. You'll see how to mark and cut your carriages, treads, and risers, and install a stairway that fits your calculations for the perfect set of stairs. **60 minutes, VHS, $24.75**

Builder's Office Manual Revised

Explains how to create routine ways of doing all the things that must be done in every construction office — in the minimum time, at the lowest cost, and with the least supervision possible: organizing the office space, establishing effective procedures and forms, setting priorities and goals, finding and keeping an effective staff, and getting the most from your record-keeping system (whether manual or computerized). Loaded with practical tips, charts and sample forms for your use. **192 pages, 8-1/2 x 11, $15.50**

Basic Plumbing with Illustrations

The journeyman's and apprentice's guide to installing plumbing, piping and fixtures in residential and light commercial buildings: how to select the right materials, lay out the job and do professional quality plumbing work. Explains the use of essential tools and materials, how to make repairs, maintain plumbing systems, install fixtures and add to existing systems. **320 pages, 8-1/2 x 11, $22.00**

Home Wiring: Improvement, Extension, Repairs

How to repair electrical wiring in older homes, extend or expand an existing electrical system in homes being remodeled, and bring the electrical system up to modern standards in any residence. Shows how to use the anticipated loads and demand factors to figure the amperage and number of new circuits needed, and how to size and install wiring, conduit, switches, and auxiliary panels and fixtures. Explains how to test and troubleshoot fixtures, circuit wiring, and switches, as well as how to service or replace low voltage systems. **224 pages, 5-1/2 x 8-1/2, $15.00**

Builder's Guide to Accounting Revised

Step-by-step, easy to follow guidelines for setting up and maintaining an efficient record-keeping system for your building business. Not a book of theory, this practical, newly-revised guide to all accounting methods shows how to meet state and federal accounting requirements, including new depreciation rules, and explains what the Tax Reform Act of 1986 can mean to your business. Full of charts, diagrams, blank forms, simple directions and examples. **304 pages, 8-1/2 x 11, $17.25**

Drywall Contracting

How to do professional quality drywall work, how to plan and estimate each job, and how to start and keep your drywall business thriving. Covers the eight essential steps in making any drywall estimate, how to achieve the six most commonly-used surface treatments, how to work with metal studs, and how to solve and prevent most common drywall problems. **288 pages, 5-1/2 x 8-1/2, $18.25**

Plumber's Handbook Revised

This new edition shows what will and what will not pass inspection in drainage, vent, and waste piping, septic tanks, water supply, fire protection, and gas piping systems. All tables, standards, and specifications are completely up-to-date with recent changes in the plumbing code. Covers common layouts for residential work, how to size piping, selecting and hanging fixtures, practical recommendations and trade tips. This book is the approved reference for the plumbing contractor's exam in many states. **240 pages, 8-1/2 x 11, $18.00**

Remodeling Contractor's Handbook

Everything you need to know to make a remodeling business grow: Identifying a market for your business, inexpensive sales and advertising techniques that work, and how to prepare accurate estimates. Also explains building a positive company image, training effective sales people, placing loans for customers, and bringing in profitable work to keep your company growing. **304 pages, 8-1/2 x 11, $18.25**

Roof Framing

Frame any type of roof in common use today, even if you've never framed a roof before. Shows how to use a pocket calculator to figure any common, hip, valley, and jack rafter length in seconds. Over 400 illustrations take you through every measurement and every cut on each type of roof: gable, hip, Dutch, Tudor, gambrel, shed, gazebo and more. **480 pages, 5-1/2 x 8-1/2, $22.00**

Blueprint Reading for the Building Trades

How to read and understand construction documents, blueprints, and schedules. Includes layouts of structural, mechanical and electrical drawings, how to interpret sectional views, how to follow diagrams (plumbing, HVAC and schematics) and common problems experienced in interpreting construction specifications. This book is your course for understanding and following construction documents. **192 pages, 5-1/2 x 8-1/2, $11.25**

Bookkeeping for Builders

This book will show you simple, practical instructions for setting up and keeping accurate records — with a minimum of effort and frustration. Shows how to set up the essentials of a record-keeping system: the payment journal, income journal, general journal, records for fixed assets, accounts receivable, payables and purchases, petty cash, and job costs. You'll be able to keep the records required by the I.R.S., as well as accurate and organized business records for your own use. **208 pages, 8-1/2 x 11, $19.75**

Builder's Comprehensive Dictionary

Never let a construction term stump you. Here you'll find almost 10,000 construction term definitions, over 1,000 detailed illustrations of tools, techniques and systems, and a separate section containing most often used legal, real estate, and management terms. **532 pages, 8-1/2 x 11, $24.95**

Building Layout

Shows how to use a transit to locate the building on the lot correctly, plan proper grades with minimum excavation, find utility lines and easements, establish correct elevations, lay out accurate foundations and set correct floor heights. Explains planning sewer connections, leveling a foundation out of level, using a story pole and batterboards, working on steep sites, and minimizing excavation costs. **240 pages, 5-1/2 x 8-1/2, $11.75**

Masonry & Concrete Construction

Every aspect of masonry construction is covered, from laying out the building with a transit to constructing chimneys and fireplaces. Explains footing construction, building foundations, laying out a block wall, reinforcing masonry, pouring slabs and sidewalks, coloring concrete, selecting and maintaining forms, using the Jahn Forming System and steel ply forms, and much more. Everything is clearly explained with dozens of photos, illustrations, charts and tables. **224 pages, 8-1/2 x 11, $17.25**

Spec Builder's Guide

Explains how to plan and build a home, control your construction costs, and then sell the house at a price that earns a decent return on the time and money you've invested. Includes professional tips to ensure success as a spec builder: how government statistics help you judge the housing market, cutting costs at every opportunity without sacrificing quality, and taking advantage of construction cycles. Every chapter includes checklists, diagrams, charts, figures, and estimating tables. **448 pages, 8-1/2 x 11, $27.00**

Pipe and Excavation Contracting

How to read plans and compute quantities for both trench and surface excavation, figure crew and equipment productivity rates, estimate unit costs, bid the work, and get the bonds you need. Explains what equipment will deliver maximum productivity for each job, how to lay all types of water and sewer pipe, and how to switch your business to excavation work when you don't have pipe contracts. Covers asphalt and rock removal, working on steep slopes or in high groundwater, and how to avoid the pitfalls that can wipe out your profit on any job. **400 pages, 5-1/2 x 8-1/2, $23.50**

Concrete Construction & Estimating

Explains how to estimate the quantity of labor and materials needed, plan the job, erect fiberglass, steel, or prefabricated forms, install shores and scaffolding, handle the concrete into place, set joints, finish and cure the concrete. Every builder who works with concrete should have the reference data, cost estimates, and examples in this practical reference. **571 pages, 5-1/2 x 8-1/2, $20.50**

Electrical Construction Estimator

If you estimate electrical jobs, this is your guide to current material costs, reliable manhour estimates per unit, and the total installed cost for all common electrical work: conduit, wire, boxes, fixtures, switches, outlets, loadcenters, panelboards, raceway, duct, signal systems, and more. Explains what every estimator should know before estimating each part of an electrical system. **416 pages, 8-1/2 x 11, $25.00. Revised annually**

Estimating Home Building Costs

Estimate every phase of residential construction from site costs to the profit margin you should include in your bid. Shows how to keep track of manhours and make accurate labor cost estimates for footings, foundations, framing and sheathing, finishes, electrical, plumbing and more. Explains the work being estimated and provides sample cost estimate worksheets with complete instructions for each job phase. **320 pages, 5-1/2 x 8-1/2, $17.00**

Paint Contractor's Manual

How to start and run a profitable paint contracting company: getting set up and organized to handle volume work, avoiding the mistakes most painters make, getting top production from your crews and the most value from your advertising dollar. Shows how to estimate all prep and painting. Loaded with manhour estimates, sample forms, contracts, charts, tables and examples you can use. **224 pages, 8-1/2 x 11, $19.25**

Painter's Handbook

Loaded with "how-to" information you'll use every day to get professional results on any job: the best way to prepare a surface for painting or repainting; selecting and using the right materials and tools (including airless spray); tips for repainting kitchens, bathrooms, cabinets, eaves and porches; how to match and blend colors; why coatings fail and what to do about it. Thirty profitable specialties that could be your gravy train in the painting business. Every professional painter needs this practical handbook. **320 pages, 8-1/2 x 11, $21.25**

Craftsman Book Company
6058 Corte del Cedro
P. O. Box 6500
Carlsbad, CA 92008
FAX # (619) 438-0398

☎

In a hurry?
We accept phone orders charged to your MasterCard, Visa or American Express Card
Call 1-800-829-8123

Mail Orders
We pay shipping when you use your charge card or when your check covers your order in full.

Name (Please print clearly)

Company

Address

City / State / Zip

Send check or money order

Total Enclosed _____
(In California add 6% tax)

If you prefer, use your ☐ Visa, ☐ MasterCard, or ☐ American Express

Card Number _____

Expiration date _____ Initials _____

These books are tax deductible when used to improve or maintain your professional skill.

10-Day Money Back GUARANTEE

- ☐ 65.00 Audio: Estimating Remodeling
- ☐ 22.00 Basic Plumbing with Illustrations
- ☐ 30.00 Berger Building Cost File
- ☐ 11.25 Blueprint Reading for Building Trades
- ☐ 19.75 Bookkeeping for Builders
- ☐ 24.95 Builder's Comprehensive Dictionary
- ☐ 17.25 Builder's Guide to Accounting Revised
- ☐ 15.50 Builder's Office Manual Revised
- ☐ 14.00 Building Cost Manual
- ☐ 11.75 Building Layout
- ☐ 25.50 Carpentry Estimating
- ☐ 19.75 Carpentry for Residential Construction
- ☐ 16.25 Carpentry Layout
- ☐ 20.50 Concrete Construction & Estimating
- ☐ 26.00 Construction Estimating Reference Data
- ☐ 19.00 Contractor's Growth & Profit Guide
- ☐ 24.25 Contractor's Guide Building Code Revised
- ☐ 15.75 Cost Records for Construction Estimating
- ☐ 18.25 Drywall Contracting
- ☐ 13.75 Electrical Blueprint Reading
- ☐ 25.00 Electrical Construction Estimator
- ☐ 19.00 Estimating Electrical Construction
- ☐ 17.00 Estimating Home Building Costs
- ☐ 21.50 Estimating Tables for Home Building
- ☐ 24.75 Handbook of Construction Contracting Vol. 1
- ☐ 24.75 Handbook of Construction Contracting Vol. 2
- ☐ 15.00 Home Wiring: Improvement, Extension, Repairs
- ☐ 17.25 Masonry & Concrete Const.
- ☐ 26.50 Masonry Estimating
- ☐ 19.50 National Construction Estimator
- ☐ 19.25 Paint Contractor's Manual
- ☐ 21.25 Painter's Handbook
- ☐ 23.50 Pipe & Excavation Contracting
- ☐ 18.00 Plumber's Handbook Revised
- ☐ 18.25 Remodeling Contractor's Handbook
- ☐ 26.25 Remodeling Kitchens & Baths
- ☐ 11.50 Residential Electrical Design
- ☐ 16.75 Residential Electrician's Handbook
- ☐ 18.25 Residential Wiring
- ☐ 22.00 Roof Framing
- ☐ 17.00 Rough Carpentry
- ☐ 21.00 Running Your Remodeling Business
- ☐ 27.00 Spec Builder's Guide
- ☐ 24.75 Video: Stair Framing
- ☐ 14.25 Wood-Frame House Construction
- ☐ 23.25 Fences and Retaining Walls

BUSINESS REPLY MAIL
FIRST CLASS MAIL   PERMIT NO.271   CARLSBAD, CA

POSTAGE WILL BE PAID BY ADDRESSEE

Craftsman Book Company
6058 Corte Del Cedro
P. O. Box 6500
Carlsbad, CA 92008-0992

BUSINESS REPLY MAIL
FIRST CLASS MAIL   PERMIT NO.271   CARLSBAD, CA

POSTAGE WILL BE PAID BY ADDRESSEE

Craftsman Book Company
6058 Corte Del Cedro
P. O. Box 6500
Carlsbad, CA 92008-0992

BUSINESS REPLY MAIL
FIRST CLASS MAIL   PERMIT NO.271   CARLSBAD, CA

POSTAGE WILL BE PAID BY ADDRESSEE

Craftsman Book Company
6058 Corte Del Cedro
P. O. Box 6500
Carlsbad, CA 92008-0992